Tax Planning 2010–11
International & Specialist

Tax Planning 2010–11
International & Specialist

a Wolters Kluwer business

Wolters Kluwer
145 London Road
Kingston-upon-Thames
Surrey
KT2 6SR
Telephone: (0) 844 561 8166
Facsimile: +44 (0) 208 547 2638
Email: cch@wolterskluwer.co.uk
Website: www.cch.co.uk

This publication is sold with the understanding that neither the publisher nor the authors, with regard to this publication, are engaged in rendering legal or professional services. The material contained in this publication neither purports, nor is intended to be, advice on any particular matter.

Although this publication incorporates a considerable degree of standardisation, subjective judgment by the user, based on individual circumstances, is indispensable. This publication is an aid and cannot be expected to replace such judgment.

Neither the publisher nor the authors can accept any responsibility or liability to any person, whether a purchaser of this publication or not, in respect of anything done or omitted to be done by any such person in reliance, whether sole or partial, upon the whole or any part of the contents of this publication.

Legislative and other material

While copyright in all statutory and other materials resides in the Crown or other relevant body, copyright in the remaining material in this publication is vested in the publisher.

The publisher advises that any statutory or other materials issued by the Crown or other relevant bodies and reproduced and quoted in this publication are not the authorised official versions of those statutory or other materials. In the preparation, however, the greatest care has been taken to ensure exact conformity with the law as enacted or other material as issued.

Crown copyright legislation is reproduced under the terms of Crown Copyright Policy Guidance issued by HMSO. Other Crown copyright material is reproduced with the permission of the controller of HMSO. European Communities Copyright material is reproduced with permission.

Telephone Helpline Disclaimer Notice

Where purchasers of this publication also have access to any Telephone Helpline Service operated by Wolters Kluwer (UK), then Wolters Kluwers total liability to contract, tort (including negligence, or breach of statutory duty) misrepresentation, restitution or otherwise with respect to any claim arising out of its acts or alleged omissions in the provision of the Helpline Service shall be limited to the yearly subscription fee paid by the Claimant.

© 2010 Wolters Kluwer (UK) Limited

ISBN 978-1-84798-291-9

All rights reserved. No part of this publication may be reproduced, stored in a retrieval system, or transmitted in any form or by any means, electronic, mechanical, photocopying, recording or otherwise, without the prior permission of Wolters Kluwer (UK) Limited or the original copyright holder.

No responsibility for loss occasioned to any person acting or refraining from action as a result of any material in this publication can be accepted by the author or publisher. Material is contained in this publication for which copyright is acknowledged. Permission to reproduce such material cannot be granted by the publisher and application must be made to the copyright holder.

British Library Cataloguing-in-Publication Data

A catalogue record for this book is available from the British Library.

Typeset in-house at Wolters Kluwer (UK) Ltd
Printed in the UK by Hobbs the Printers Ltd

About the authors

General editors

Ray Chidell (MA Cantab) trained as a Tax Inspector and then worked in the accounting profession for 14 years, including six as tax partner with Mazars (previously Neville Russell). Ray provides consultancy services through his company Claritax Ltd (*www.claritax.co.uk*) and writes extensively for CCH, especially in relation to the taxation of businesses and employees. Ray has a particular interest in capital allowances for businesses that buy, sell or refurbish property.

Keith Gordon is a barrister specialising in tax and chancery law. He practises from Atlas Chambers in Grays Inn (*www.atlaschambers.com*). Keith is also a fellow of both the Institute of Chartered Accountants in England and Wales and the Chartered Institute of Taxation. Keith worked at the Inland Revenue as part of the Tax Law Rewrite Project and subsequently reviewed the work of the Project as one of the two CIOT representatives on the Projects Consultative Committee. Keith is also a member of a number of the CIOTs technical sub-committees and served as the joint chairman of the CIOTs London Branch between 2006 and 2008. He was appointed to the CIOT Council in 2009. Keith lectures and writes on a wide range of tax-related topics. In 2006, Keith was a runner up in the tax-writer of the year category of the LexisNexis Taxation awards and in 2009 won the Chartered Tax Adviser of the Year category.

Sarah Laing is a Chartered Tax Adviser. She has been writing professionally since joining CCH Editions in 1998 as a Senior Technical Editor, contributing to a range of highly regarded publications including the British Tax Reporter, Taxes – The Weekly Tax News, the Red & Green legislation volumes, Hardman's, International Tax Agreements and many others. She became Publishing Manager for the tax and accounting portfolio in 2001 and later went on to help run CCH Seminars (including ABG Courses and Conferences). Sarah originally worked for the Inland Revenue in Newbury and Swindon Tax Offices, before moving out into practice in 1991. She has worked for both small and Big 5 firms. She now works as a freelance author providing technical writing services for the tax and accountancy profession. Sarah is a director and the news editor of TaxationWeb Limted (*www.taxationweb.co.uk*), which provides free information and resources on UK taxes to taxpayers and professionals.

Authors

Sarah Bradford BA (Hons), ACA CTA (Fellow) is the director of WriteTax Ltd, a company providing technical writing services on tax and National Insurance contributions.

Harriet Brown MA (Cantab) Barrister and Jersey Advocate was called to the Bar in 2005, before qualifying as a Jersey Advocate and English Barrister. She practises from Tax Chambers, 15 Old Square. She advises on all direct and indirect taxes and represents clients before all levels of Tribunal.

Bob Fraser is a Chartered and Certified Financial Planner, a Fellow of the Chartered Insurance Institute (Personal Financial Society) and a member of the Society of Trust and Estate Practitioners. He is a wealth adviser with Towry Law, one of the leading UK wealth management companies.

Nick Parkes read law at Leeds University and joined the Inland Revenue in 1970. Subsequent to leaving the Revenue he set up Parkes Tax Consultancy in 1985. He is the co-author of the British Tax Investigations Reporter and of the Tax Investigations Guide, both published by CCH Editions Ltd.

Howard Roberts is a solicitor with over 15 years of commercial experience, both in the UK and the Cayman Islands. He is also a qualified Insolvency Practitioner, an accredited Mediator and a member of the Cayman Islands Bar. He is a partner in Schofield Sweeney Solictors, Leeds.

Preface

The tax topics addressed in these volumes are those faced every day by businesses of all sizes. Such businesses, and their advisers, are under pressure to operate with ever greater efficiency, reducing costs wherever possible. Tax is high on the list of such costs, whether payable on trading profits, on one-off transactions, as part of the cost of employing staff or under any number of other guises. And individuals too, facing an ever-increasing tax burden, expect their professional advisers to reduce their exposure to taxation in all legitimate ways.

At one level, of course, tax planning has been seen as the preserve of the few, using expensive schemes that have been subjected to many layers of scrutiny by Counsel; such schemes have been the focus of particular government attention in recent years and the resulting disclosure requirements are discussed in depth in Chapter 63. The main focus of these volumes, however, is on the everyday opportunities that can be taken to reduce tax bills: ensuring (for example) that maximum capital allowances are claimed on property transactions, that share transactions are thought through to the best advantage of all concerned, that the many quirks of the employee benefits legislation are well used and that those with overseas tax considerations are kept abreast of developments in that fast-changing field.

Tax planning will move many practitioners out of the areas of taxation with which they are most comfortable. An additional feature that has been included throughout these volumes is therefore to give warnings of where dangers lie. The intention is that the director or professional adviser will thereby be made aware of topics that may merit further consideration or that may, in certain cases, make a particular form of tax planning unsuitable for the circumstances under review.

All chapters have been thoroughly reviewed for developments in the past year, including in particular those in the two Finance Acts and two Rewrite Acts of 2010, as well as any legal decisions and miscellaneous guidance issued by HM Revenue & Customs.

The first section in this volume, entitled Overseas matters, covers various international tax planning aspects. An increasing number of British citizens are now going overseas for substantial periods of time for either work or retirement purposes, and all the recent cases in this controversial area are covered in Chapter 59. Since tax is territorial there will inevitably be tax planning considerations and, as always, it is best to plan well in advance. It is also increasingly important that practitioners understand the tax rules governing both UK and overseas tax matters. Of particular importance are the changes to the remittance basis of taxation, which

Preface

took effect from April 2008, and are covered in Chapters 55 to 60. Chapter 60 looks at the use of offshore trusts.

The final section in the series is entitled Specialist, and is an attempt to cover areas that, whilst perhaps not dealt with on a day-to-day basis, throw up various tax planning issues and opportunities. Several of the chapters deal with the specific detail of various tax efficient investment vehicles currently on offer (the Enterprise Investment Scheme at Chapter 64 and Venture Capital Trusts at Chapter 77), whilst Chapter 75 provides an overview of tax efficient investments in general.

A series of tax planning books would not be complete without a chapter dedicated to the subject of pensions. With the pensions tax simplification legislation now well under way followed by pensions complication with anti-forestalling rules in this years Finance Act, anyone advising individuals interested in contributing to a pensions scheme should find the material in Chapter 76 particularly useful.

Finally, the General Editors would wish to recognise the contributions made to Chapters 58, 60 and 61 by Harriet Brown, Barrister and Jersey Advocate.

Ray Chidell, Keith Gordon and Sarah Laing
General Editors, Tax Planning
September 2010

Contents

About the authors   vii
Preface   ix
Abbreviations   xix

VOLUME 1 – BUSINESS

Section 1 – Business in General

1   General business income tax planning
2   Lifecycle of a business
3   Considerations on whether to incorporate (tax and other implications)
4   Arctic Systems and Income Shifting
5   Partnership planning
6   Cross-border trading
7   Plant and machinery allowances
8   Fixtures when buying and selling property
9   Capital allowance credits
10   Flat conversion allowances
11   Business premises renovation allowances
12   Intellectual property
13   Research and development capital allowances
14   Research and development reliefs and tax credits

Section 2 – Corporate

15   General corporation tax planning
16   Extracting profits from a family company
17   Family companies
18   Losses – companies
19   Capital gains – companies
20   Purchase by a company of its own shares

21 Share transactions in private limited companies
22 Group aspects of tax planning
23 Demergers
24 Company reorganisations and takeovers
25 Transfer pricing
26 Controlled foreign companies

VOLUME 2 – INDIVIDUALS

Section 3 – Individuals
27 Personal income tax planning
28 Major events for individuals
29 Income tax losses
30 School fees planning
31 Tax planning for retirement
32 Tax credits planning

Section 4 – Employment
33 Employed or self-employed
34 Benefits and expenses
35 Dispensations and PAYE settlement agreements
36 Salary sacrifice
37 Travel and subsistence
38 Relocation expenses
39 Tax-free benefits
40 Company cars and fuel
41 Company vans and other vehicles
42 Living accommodation
43 Employment-related loans
44 Compensation and termination payments
45 Tax relief for working from home
46 Enterprise management incentives

47   Employee share schemes

Section 5 – Capital Transactions

48   Capital gains tax planning

49   Entreprenuers' relief

50   Passing on the family business

51   Main residence relief

52   Inheritance tax planning

53   Pre-owned assets

54   Stamp Duty Land Tax (SDLT)

VOLUME 3 – INTERNATIONAL & SPECIALIST

Section 6 – Overseas Matters

6	Overseas Matters, What's New		3
55	**Working in the UK**		5
	55.1	Introduction	5
	55.2	Residence of individuals	5
	55.3	Employees	12
	55.4	PAYE	18
	55.5	Trades, professions and vocations: foreign income	22
	55.6	Non-residents trading through a branch or agency	26
56	**Working overseas**		29
	56.1	Working abroad	29
57	**Domicile and non-domicile**		35
	57.1	Relevance of domicile	35
	57.2	Domicile of origin	35
	57.3	Domicile of choice	36
	57.4	Residence	40
	57.5	Intention	41
	57.6	Abandonment of domicile of choice	42
	57.7	Married women	42
	57.8	Miscellaneous considerations	44
	57.9	Domicile of dependency	46
	57.10	Children	46
	57.11	Mentally incapacitated persons	47
	57.12	Domicile of corporations	47
	57.13	Domicile and inheritance tax	56
	57.14	Capital gains tax	60
	57.15	Remittance basis	65

xiii

	57.16	Remittance of money	70
58	**Double taxation relief**		**75**
	58.1	Introduction	75
	58.2	Forms of double tax relief	76
	58.3	Model treaty provisions as typically used in the UK	77
	58.4	Effect of exemptions under double tax treaties	86
	58.5	Calculation of double tax credit relief available	86
	58.6	Foreign tax as an expense	88
	58.7	Companies and double tax relief	88
	58.8	Unilateral relief	94
	58.9	Unrelieved foreign tax companies	98
	58.10	Capital gains tax	102
59	**Residence status of individuals**		**111**
	59.1	Introduction	111
	59.2	General principles	112
	59.3	Residence	112
	59.4	Ordinary residence	119
60	**Offshore tax planning through trusts**		**123**
	60.1	History of the taxation of offshore trusts	123
	60.2	Creation of offshore trust	124
	60.3	HMRC information powers	125
	60.4	Migrant settlements	127
	60.5	Export of UK trusts	127
	60.6	UK trusts exported on or after March 1991	129
	60.7	Beneficiaries of offshore trusts	135
	60.8	Disposal of settled interests	138
	60.9	The supplementary charge	143
	60.10	Matching capital payments with gains	146
	60.11	Liability of settlors of non-resident trusts	154
	60.12	Qualifying settlements	157

Section 7 – Specialist

7	**Specialist, What's New**		**169**
61	**A practical guide to trusts**		**171**
	61.1	Introduction	171
	61.2	What is a trust?	171
	61.3	The rules against perpetuities and the restriction of accumulation periods	174
	61.4	Management of the trust	176
	61.5	Types of trust	177
	61.6	The uses of trusts	185
	61.7	Tax aspects of trusts	186
	61.8	Some important legal considerations	187

	61.9	Tax planning opportunities with trusts	190
	61.10	Checklist of considerations on using trusts	191
62	**Construction Industry scheme**		**195**
	62.1	Introduction	195
	62.2	Background	196
	62.3	Employment status	197
	62.4	Contractors	197
	62.5	Non-resident contractors and subcontractors	204
	62.6	Subcontractors	206
	62.7	Payments to subcontractors	208
	62.8	Registration	214
	62.9	Compliance	216
63	**Disclosure of direct tax avoidance schemes**		**221**
	63.1	Introduction	221
	63.2	Notifiable arrangements	227
	63.3	Notifiable proposals	230
	63.4	A tax advantage must arise	230
	63.5	The tax advantage must be a main benefit	232
	63.6	Duties to disclose	233
	63.7	HMRC's response to a disclosure	249
	63.8	Duties with respect to reference numbers	250
	63.9	Parties' duties with respect to notifiable arrangements	252
	63.10	Legal professional privilege	255
	63.11	Penalties	257
	63.12	What schemes are prescribed?	259
64	**Enterprise investment scheme**		**273**
	64.1	Introduction and overview	273
	64.2	Income tax relief	277
	64.3	CGT reinvestment relief	297
	64.4	Tax-free sale of EIS shares	309
65	**Farming in the UK**		**313**
	65.1	Overview	313
	65.2	One trade	315
	65.3	Losses	316
	65.4	Stocks	319
	65.5	Herd basis	320
	65.6	Averaging of fluctuating profits	324
	65.7	Capital allowances	328
	65.8	Revenue receipts and payments	330
	65.9	Partnerships and joint ventures	333
	65.10	Capital gains tax	336
66	**HMRC enquiries**		**341**
	66.1	Introduction	341
	66.2	Selection for enquiry	352

	66.3	Opening the enquiry	369
	66.4	Information and inspection powers	382
	66.5	Records	393
	66.6	Interviews	409
	66.7	Business economics	411
	66.8	Re-opening earlier years	418
	66.9	Completion of enquiry	424
	66.10	Serious fraud investigations	446
	66.11	Money laundering	448
67	**Insolvencies**		**453**
	67.1	Introduction	453
	67.2	Measures to help businesses meet liabilities	458
	67.3	Crown's priority in insolvencies	459
	67.4	Penalties in insolvencies	460
	67.5	Companies in liquidation, administration or receivership	462
	67.6	Insolvency Act 1986 (prior to 15 September 2003): related problems	477
	67.7	Administration under post-14 September 2003 Insolvency Act 1986 procedures	489
	67.8	Administration – consequences for group relief	492
	67.9	Hive down – how a resurrection really feels	493
68	**Interest relief**		**509**
	68.1	Introduction	509
	68.2	Interest on loan to buy machinery or plant	511
	68.3	Interest on loan to invest in a close company	513
	68.4	Interest on loan to invest in a co-operative	518
	68.5	Interest on loan to invest in an employee-controlled company	519
	68.6	Interest on loan to invest in partnership	522
	68.7	Interest on loan to pay inheritance tax	526
	68.8	Interest on loan to purchase life annuity	527
	68.9	Interest and other costs of borrowing	529
	68.10	Finance lease rental payments	532
69	**Lloyd's underwriters**		**537**
	69.1	Introduction	537
	69.2	Syndicate accounts	537
	69.3	Taxation of Lloyd's underwriters	541
	69.4	Treatment of losses	544
	69.5	Chargeable gains	545
	69.6	Lloyd's estates	548
	69.7	Payment of tax	549
70	**Money laundering reporting**		**553**
	70.1	General	553
	70.2	Requirements	553

	70.3	Key concepts	555
	70.4	Offences	556
	70.5	Failure to disclose	558
	70.6	Internal reporting procedures	559
	70.7	The training requirement	563
71	**National Insurance Contributions**		**565**
	71.1	Introduction	565
	71.2	Liability to NICs	565
	71.3	Earnings	571
	71.4	Class 1 NICs	582
	71.5	Class 1A NICs	594
	71.6	Class 1B NICs	597
	71.7	Class 2 NICs	598
	71.8	Class 3 NICs	601
	71.9	Class 4 NICs	602
	71.10	Interaction of NIC classes and annual maxima	607
	71.11	Administration	609
72	**Property income**		**619**
	72.1	Introduction to property income	619
	72.2	Basic principles	620
	72.3	Chargeable income	626
	72.4	Deductible expenses	631
	72.5	Deductibility of interest	639
	72.6	Properties not let at a commercial rent	643
	72.7	Capital allowances	645
	72.8	Furnished lettings	649
	72.9	Furnished holiday lettings	653
	72.10	Rent-a-room relief	660
	72.11	International issues	665
	72.12	Compliance issues	667
73	**Raising business finance**		**669**
	73.1	Introduction	669
	73.2	Borrowing money	669
	73.3	Loans to individuals for business-related purposes	674
	73.4	Raising finance through issuing shares	681
	73.5	Expenses of raising finance	687
74	**Tax aspects of charities**		**691**
	74.1	Introduction	691
	74.2	Definitions and general principles	691
	74.3	Tax exemptions and reliefs	700
	74.4	The tax aspects of giving to charities	720
	74.5	The beneficiaries of charities	734
	74.6	Foreign aspects	736
75	**Tax-efficient investments**		**739**

Contents

	75.1	Introduction	739
	75.2	Enterprise investment scheme	740
	75.3	Venture capital trusts	751
	75.4	Individual savings account	754
	75.5	Friendly societies	757
	75.6	Child trust funds	758
	75.7	Life assurance (qualifying policies)	759
	75.8	Life assurance (single premium bonds)	760
	75.9	National Savings	762
	75.10	Purchased life annuities	763
	75.11	Investments with IHT relief	764
	75.12	Woodlands	766
	75.13	Tax-efficient investment checklist	769
76	**Pensions**		**771**
	76.1	Introduction	771
	76.2	Types of pension schemes	771
	76.3	Pension transfers	781
	76.4	Overview of 'pension simplification'	783
	76.5	Types of retirement income arrangements	797
	76.6	Overview of state retirement benefits	812
	76.7	Contracting-out of S2P	814
	76.8	Changes in personal circumstances	818
	76.9	Tax planning opportunities	821
77	**Venture capital trusts**		**831**
	77.1	Introduction and overview	831
	77.2	Income tax relief on investment	834
	77.3	Relief for dividends received	837
	77.4	Tax-free sale of VCT shares	837
	77.5	Approval of companies as VCTs	839

Case Table	**843**
Legislation Finding List	**849**
Index to Concessions and Statements	**863**
Index	**865**

Abbreviations

The following abbreviations are commonly used throughout this publication.

ACT	advance corporation tax
AEA 1925	Administration of Estates Act 1925
AIM	Alternative Investment Market
AIS	accrued income scheme
AL	aggregates levy
App.	appendix
APR	annual percentage rate
APRT	advance petroleum revenue tax
ARPA 2004	Age-Related Payments Act 2004
art.	article(s)
ATCSA 2001	Anti-Terrorism, Crime and Security Act 2001
BB	Customs and Excise Business Briefs
BEN	business economic note
BES	business expansion scheme
BN	Budget Notes
BSA 1986	Building Societies Act 1986
B(S)A 1985	Bankruptcy (Scotland) Act 1985
BTC	British Tax Cases, 1982–current (CCH)
CA 1985	Companies Act 1985
CA 2006	Companies Act 2006
CAA 1968	Capital Allowances Act 1968
CAA 1990	Capital Allowances Act 1990
CAA 2001	Capital Allowances Act 2001
CCH	CCH Information, a division of Wolters Kluwer (UK) Ltd
CCL	climate change levy
C & E Commrs	Commissioners of Customs and Excise
CED(GR)A 1979	Customs and Excise Duties (General Reliefs) Act 1979
CEMA 1979	Customs and Excise Management Act 1979
CFC	controlled foreign company
CGT	capital gains tax
CGTA 1979	Capital Gains Tax Act 1979
Ch.	Chapter(s) (of a statute/SI etc.)
CIC	close investment-holding company
CIOT	Chartered Institute of Taxation
CJPA 2001	Criminal Justice and Police Act 2001
cl.	clause(s)
col.	column(s)
Commr; Commrs	commissioner; commissioners
Conv.	convention
CPA 1947	Crown Proceedings Act 1947
CRCA 2005	Commissioners for Revenue and Customs Act 2005
CRT	composite rate tax
CSPSSA 2000	Child Support, Pensions and Social Security Act 2000
CT	corporation tax
CTD	certificates of tax deposits
CTFA 2004	Child Trust Funds Act 2004
CTT	capital transfer tax

Abbreviations

CTTA 1984	Capital Transfer Tax Act 1984
DDA(S)A 2002	Debt Arrangement and Attachment (Scotland) Act 2002
Dir.	EC directives
DLT	development land tax
DLTA 1976	Development Land Tax Act 1976
DPA 1998	Data Protection Act 1998
DSS	Department of Social Security
DTI	Department of Trade and Industry
EA 2002	Employment Act 2002
EA 2004	Energy Act 2004
EC	European Community/Communities
edn.	edition
EEC	European Economic Community
EEIG	European Economic Interest Grouping
e.g.	(exempli gratia) for example
EIS	enterprise investment scheme
EMPA 2003	Electricity (Miscellaneous Provisions) Act 2003
ERA 1996	Employee Rights Act 1996
ESC	extra-statutory concession
ESOP	employee stock ownership plan
ESOT	employee share ownership trust
etc.	(et cetera) and so on
et seq.	(et sequens) and the following
EU	European Union
FA	Finance Act
FA 2008	Finance Act 2008
FI 1985	Films Act 1985
FIA 2000	Freedom of Information Act 2000
FII	franked investment income
F(No. 2)A	Finance (No. 2) Act
FSMA 2000	Financial Services and Markets Act 2000
FYA	first-year allowance
GAAP	generally accepted accounting practice
Grp.	Group (VAT legislation)
HA 1988	Housing Act 1988
HM	Her Majesty
HMIT	Her Majesty's Inspector of Taxes
HMRC	HM Revenue & Customs
HMSO	Her Majesty's Stationery Office
HRA 1998	Human Rights Act 1998
IA	initial allowance
IA 1986	Insolvency Act 1986
ICAEW	Institute of Chartered Accountants in England and Wales
ICAS	Institute of Chartered Accountants of Scotland
ICTA 1970	Income and Corporation Taxes Act 1970
ICTA 1988	Income and Corporation Taxes Act 1988
i.e.	(id est) that is
IHT	inheritance tax
IHTA 1984	Inheritance Tax Act 1984
INA 1978	Interpretation Act 1978
IoT	Institute of Taxation
IPT	insurance premium tax
IR Commrs	Commissioners of Inland Revenue
IRDec.	Inland Revenue decision
IRInt.	Inland Revenue interpretation

Abbreviations

IRRA 1890	Inland Revenue Regulation Act 1890
IT	income tax
ITA 2007	Income Tax Act 2007
ITEPA 2003	Income Tax (Earnings and Pensions) Act 2003
ITTOIA 2005	Income Tax (Trading and Other Income) Act 2005
LAUTRO	Life Assurance and Unit Trust Regulatory Organisation
LFT	landfill tax
LIFFE	London International Financial Futures and Options Exchange
LLPA 2000	Limited Liability Partnerships Act 2000
LPA 1907	Limited Partnerships Act 1907
LPA 1925	Law of Property Act 1925
LRRA 2006	Legislative and Regulatory Reform Act 2006
LSG	Law Society Gazette
MCT	mainstream corporation tax
MIRAS	mortgage interest relief at source
Misc.	miscellaneous items (denoted by number)
NB	(nota bene) note well
NHA 1980	National Heritage Act 1980
NI	Northern Ireland
NIC	National Insurance contributions
NICA 2002	National Insurance Contributions Act 2002
NICA 2004	National Insurance Contributions and Statutory Payments Act 2004
NICA 2006	National Insurance Contributions Act 2006
NICA 2008	National Insurance Contributions Act 2008
NICSPA 2004	National Insurance Contributions and Statutory Payments Act 2004
NR	Customs and Excise News Releases
O.	Order(s)
OJ	Official Journal of the European Communities
OJ 'L' series	Official Journal of the European Communities, Legislation Series (cited by year, issue number and page, for example OJ 1989 L1/1 is the first page of the first issue of the legislation series of the Official Journal for 1989)
OPB	Occupational Pensions Board
Ors	others
OTA 1975	Oil Taxation Act 1975
OTA 1983	Oil Taxation Act 1983
p.; pp.	page; pages
PA 2004	Pensions Act 2004
PA 2007	Pensions Act 2007
p.a.	per annum (each year)
PACE 1994	Police and Criminal Evidence Act 1994
para.	paragraph(s)
PAYE	pay as you earn
PCA 2002	Proceeds of Crime Act 2002
PCTA 1968	Provisional Collection of Taxes Act 1968
PEP	personal equity plan
PET	potentially exempt transfer
PLDA 1808	Probate and Legacy Duties Act 1808
PN	Customs and Excise Press Notices
PPS	personal pension scheme
PR	press release(s)
PRP	profit-related pay

Abbreviations

PRT	petroleum revenue tax
PRTA 1980	Petroleum Revenue Tax Act 1980
PSA 1993	Pension Schemes Act 1993
PSO	Pensions Schemes Office
Pt.	Part(s)
QCB	qualifying corporate bond
r.	rule(s)
RA 1898	Revenue Act 1898 and similarly coded for appropriate subsequent years
RA 2005	Railways Act 2005
R&C Commrs	Revenue and Customs Commissioners
RDDA 1998	Regional Development Agencies Act 1998
reg.	regulations
reg.	regulations
Regulations	EC Regulations
RPI	retail prices index
RSC	Rules of the Supreme Court 1965
s.	section(s)
SA 1891	Stamp Act 1891
SAYE	save as you earn
SCA 1981	Supreme Court Act 1981
Sch.	Schedule(s)
SDMA 1891	Stamp Duty Management Act 1891
SDLT	stamp duty land tax
SDLTCN	Stamp Duty Land Tax Customer Newsletter
SDRT	stamp duty reserve tax
SD(TP)A 1992	Stamp Duty (Temporary Provisions) Act 1992
SERPS	state earnings-related pension scheme
SFO	Superannuation Funds Office
SI	statutory instrument
SMP	statutory maternity pay
SOCN	Stamp Office Customer Newsletter
SOCPA 2005	Serious Organised Crime and Police Act 2005
SP	Statement of practice
SPCA 2002	State Pension Credit Act 2002
SRO	self-regulating organisation
SR & O	statutory rules and orders
SSA 1975	Social Security Act 1975
SSA 1980	Social Security Act 1980
SSA 1986	Social Security Act 1986
SSA 1989	Social Security Act 1989
SSA 1998	Social Security Act 1998
SSAA 1992	Social Security Administration Act 1992
SSAP	Statement of Standard Accounting Practice
SSCBA 1992	Social Security Contributions and Benefits Act 1992
SS(CP)A 1992	Social Security (Consequential Provisions) Act 1992
SS(TF)A 1999	Social Security Contributions (Transfer of Functions, etc.) Act 1999
SSFA 2001	Social Security Fraud Act 2001
SSHBA 1982	Social Security Housing Benefits Act 1982
SS(MP)A 1977	Social Security (Miscellaneous Provisions) Act 1977
SSP	statutory sick pay
SSPA 1975	Social Security Pensions Act 1975
SSPA 1994	Statutory Sick Pay Act 1994
STA 1963	Stock Transfer Act 1963

STB	Stamp Taxes Bulletin
subcl.	subclause(s)
subpara.	subparagraph(s)
subs.	subsection(s)
TA 2000	Transport Act 2000
TAURUS	Transfer and Automated Registration of Uncertified Stock
TB	Tax Bulletin article
TBSE	Tax Bulletin special edition
TCA 2002	Tax Credits Act 2002
TCEA 2007	Tribunals, Courts and Enforcement Act 2007
TCGA 1992	Taxation of Chargeable Gains Act 1992
TERA 2000	Terrorism Act 2000
TESSA	tax-exempt special savings account
TMA 1970	Taxes Management Act 1970
TR	technical release
TSBA 1985	Trustee Savings Bank Act 1985
TULR(C)A 1992	Trade Union and Labour Relations (Consolidation) Act 1992
TWDV	tax written-down value
UCITS	Undertakings for Collective Investment in Transferable Securities
UK	United Kingdom
USM	Unlisted Securities Market
VAT	value added tax
VATA 1983	Value Added Tax Act 1983
VATA 1994	Value Added Tax Act 1994
VCT	Venture Capital Trust
vol.	volume(s)
WDA	writing down allowance
WDV	written-down value
WFT	windfall tax
WRPA 1999	Welfare Reform and Pensions Act 1999
¶	CCH paragraph

Section 6 – Overseas Matters

Section 6 – Overseas Business – What's New

- 55.6: Commentary on *Grainger & Son v Gough* included
- 57.13.2: Commentary on IHT aspects of non-UK domiciled persons
- 59.3.1.4: Update for *Grace* case (residence)
- 59.4.1: Update for *Genovese*, *Tuczka* and *Turberville* cases (ordinary residence)

55 Working in the UK

55.1 Introduction

This chapter examines the income tax position of foreign nationals working in the United Kingdom. It is assumed that the individuals are not domiciled in the UK and, in the case of employees, it is further assumed that they are employed by non-resident employers so that their earnings qualify as 'chargeable overseas earnings' under the provisions of ITEPA 2003, s. 23(2) for the purposes of ITEPA 2003, s. 10(2). The subject of domicile is dealt with in **Chapter 57**.

55.2 Residence of individuals

55.2.1 Introduction

It has become more and more common for individuals to travel and work around the world, and consequently, the subject of residence for tax purposes has become increasingly important. Practitioners are more likely to be required to deal with issues concerning residence than ever before. **Chapter 59** examines the subject of residence in detail. In this chapter we look specifically at issues surrounding individuals working in the UK.

The meaning of 'residence' for tax purposes is the same as its everyday English meaning. In The Oxford English Dictionary, the word 'reside' is defined as:

> 'To dwell permanently or for a considerable time, to have one's settled or usual abode, to live in or at a particular place.'

It is for the commissioners to decide whether a taxpayer is resident or not in any tax year and because this is a question of fact it is one with which the courts will not interfere unless no tribunal acting reasonably could have come to that decision on the evidence available. In practice, the matter will often be decided on the basis of a residence ruling by HM Revenue & Customs (HMRC).

To be resident, an individual must, generally, be physically present in the UK during some part of the year of assessment. Where a person is present for any period whereby he is regarded as resident for that time, he is strictly also regarded as resident for the whole of the tax year. There is no statutory provision for splitting a tax year in relation to residence (but there are HMRC concessions in this area).

A Commonwealth citizen (or citizen of the Republic of Ireland) who is ordinarily resident in the UK is regarded as resident in the UK where he has left the country for only occasional residence abroad. 'Occasional residence' is not defined, but a person who for a number of years spent the major part of each year living abroad in hotels was held to have left the UK for only occasional residence abroad.

HMRC booklet (HMRC 6) gives guidance on residence, ordinary residence and domicile and liability to UK tax.

Any question on the application of the rules to particular individual circumstances should be addressed to HM Revenue & Customs, Claims Branch (International).

In deciding if one is resident or not in the UK, the following factors should be considered. Where there is no standard pattern of working hours (35–40 being considered as a typical UK working week), HMRC will look to determine full-time employment in the cases below on the basis of the nature of the job and local conditions or practices; it might include several concurrent part-time jobs.

55.2.2 Physical presence in UK – the six-month rule

Generally, a person must be physically present in the UK during the tax year in order to be found resident. An individual who is in the UK for some temporary purpose only, and not with a view establishing his residence there, is only to be treated as resident if he spends at least 183 days (i.e. six months) in the UK in the relevant tax year.

Wilkie v IR Commrs (1951) 32 TC 495 established that six months means six calendar months and that periods of less than a whole day are to be calculated in hours. In that case the taxpayer's actual physical presence in the UK between the moments of arrival and departure amounted to 182 days and 20 hours. The Crown contended that fractions of a day should count as whole days and that the period of presence was thus 184 days. Donovan J rejected the Crown's contention and found the taxpayer not to be resident.

When counting the number of days that a taxpayer has been present in the UK during a tax year, all of the days spent in the UK at the end of the day (that is, midnight) are counted. It is the number of days counted in this way that is important, not the number of visits made to the UK. These rules apply from 6 April 2008.

The *Finance Act* 2008, s. 24 (amending ITA 2007, s. 831) specifies that from 6 April 2008, an individual should only be deemed to have spent a day in the UK if 'the individual is present in the United Kingdom at the end of the day'. However, a day of presence will be discounted where an individual is in transit between two places outside the UK, provided that:

- the individual departs from the UK on the next day; and
- during the time between arrival and departure the individual does not engage in activities that are to a substantial extent unrelated to the individual's passage through the UK.

The changes to the legislation introduced in the section are in respect of the 183-day test only. However, the Explanatory Notes to the Finance Bill 2008 stated that from 6 April 2008, all day-counting tests, such as the non-statutory 91-day test, will follow the same principle that any day where the individual is in the UK at the end of the day will be included as a day of residence. The same exception from the general rule will apply where the individual is a passenger in transit and their activities whilst in the UK are not substantially unrelated to that travel.

This will catch personal as well as business activities and the following examples set out in the Explanatory Notes to the Finance Bill indicate that HMRC will look to enforce this provision strictly.

> ### Example 55.1
>
> Peter works for the Jersey arm of HSBC and is travelling from Jersey to Frankfurt. He flies from Jersey to Gatwick and will catch his onward flight the next day to Frankfurt from London City airport. He travels from Gatwick to Canary Wharf for a meeting with several colleagues before staying overnight in a nearby hotel.
>
> The meeting with colleagues is not an activity substantially related to completing travel to a foreign destination. The transit passenger provisions will not apply.

> ### Example 55.2
>
> John works for the Jersey arm of HSBC and is travelling from Jersey to Frankfurt via Gatwick and London City airport. In the lobby of his hotel, he unexpectedly spots another colleague who has just arrived from Paris. They have a couple of drinks together and their conversation covers a number of business-related issues. John then travels to London City airport to catch his onward connection.
>
> This meeting was not planned and therefore it can be considered that John's activities in the UK substantially related to completing travel to a foreign destination. The transit passenger provisions will apply.

> ### Example 55.3
>
> Shirley lives in Guernsey and is travelling to New Zealand via Gatwick and Heathrow. She planned to spend most of the day with her daughter and grandchildren, who live in Crawley and will also spend the night there before travelling to Heathrow for her onward flight.
>
> Her visit is not an activity substantially related to completing travel to a foreign destination. The transit passenger provisions will not apply.

Further examples are set out in the Explanatory Notes to the Finance Bill 2008 at: http://services.parliament.uk/bills/2007-08/finance.html.

The period of 183 days must fall within a single tax year. Thus, an individual who is present for the first six months (183 days) of a tax year will be resident for that year. However, an individual who is present for (say) the final 182 days of a particular tax year followed by the first 182 days of the following tax year will have been present in the UK for a single continuous period of 364 days without being resident. This is because such an individual is not physically present in the UK for at least six months in either tax year. The corollary of this is that an individual who is absent from the UK for a period of 365 days, not corresponding exactly to a tax year, will remain both resident and ordinarily resident in the UK throughout his period of absence (provided he was so resident and ordinarily resident before the period of absence). However, the fact that such an individual may establish residence elsewhere during his period of absence will not preclude a finding that he is resident in the UK throughout the period in question. Where such dual residence is established, the individual may take the benefit of any double taxation agreement that exists.

In looking at the question of whether the visit is for a temporary purpose and without an intention to establish residence HMRC attach importance to whether the individual has spent an average of three months in the UK over a four-year period. Where this is a consideration they will disregard days spent in the UK because of exceptional circumstances such as illness, but each case is judged strictly on its own merits, and the practice does not apply in determining whether a period of six months in any year is exceeded. The practice was formalised in SP 2/91.

> **Planning point**
>
> A HMRC concession deals with the status of a spouse who accompanies his or her husband or wife who works full-time abroad. The concession enables the accompanying spouse to benefit, *inter alia*, from the concessionary treatment for the years of departure and return which is available to a person taking up full-time employment abroad.

Law: ITA 2007, s. 831, 832; ESC A78: *Residence in the UK: Accompanying spouse*; *Iveagh v IR Commrs* [1930] IR 386; *Wilkie v IR Commrs* (1951) 32 TC 495

55.2.3 The 'split-year' concession

Where a person is present for any period whereby he is regarded as resident for that period (i.e. 183 days or more), he will be regarded as being resident for the entire period of assessment in which the period of residence falls. There is no statutory provision enabling the tax year to be divided into periods of residence and non-residence. Thus, an individual who is present in the UK for the first six months of a tax year will be resident for the entire year even though he may be absent from the UK for the second half of the tax year in question. However, the harshness of this rule is mitigated by concession on the part of HMRC whereby they will allow division of the tax year into periods of residence and non-residence. The instances in which HMRC will allow such division of the tax year are to be found in ESC A11. These may be summarised as:

- where the individual satisfies HMRC that prior to his arrival, or departure (as the case may be) he was not ordinarily resident in the UK. The concession would not apply, for example, where an individual who had been ordinarily resident in the UK left for intended permanent residence abroad but returned to reside here before the end of the tax year following the tax year of departure;
- where an individual goes abroad for full-time service under a contract of employment and:
  - both his absence from the UK and the employment contract cover a complete tax year; and
  - any interim visits to the UK during the period do not amount to 183 days or more in any tax year; or an average of 91 days or more in a tax year (the average is taken over the period of absence up to a maximum of four years).

The Centre for Non-Residents (CNR) is responsible for dealing with the liability of the split year for individuals who leave the UK, becoming not resident and not ordinarily resident in the UK and who are liable to UK tax on sources of UK income arising after they leave. CNR does not, however, take responsibility for split year cases where an individual's main tax office is a Public Department District, Cardiff 1 (Seafarers) or Centre 1 (Foreign Unit).

Where split year treatment is due for the year in which an individual arrives in the UK, CNR will only deal with the liability for that year if the individual leaves the UK again later in the same year and becomes not resident and not ordinarily resident from the day after the date of departure to the following 5 April.

'Full time service'

HMRC published their interpretation of the term 'full-time service' in Tax Bulletin, February 1993. They point out that there is no statutory definition of 'full-time', nor any guidance from the Courts, thus it must be interpreted in accordance with its ordinary, non-technical meaning. Whether an individual is working 'full-time' in an employment will always depend upon the particular facts of the case. Where a job involves a standard pattern of hours and an individual is putting in what a layman would clearly recognise as a full working week (around 35 to 40 hours per week), they will accept it as full-time.

HMRC acknowledge that there are other, less structured, employments, for example, a mixture of round-the-clock working followed by a rest period, those without a fixed number of working days or, in the case of sportsmen, days of playing and training interspersed. In those cases they would take into account the nature of the job, and, where appropriate, local conditions and practices in that particular occupation. Someone who had several part-time jobs overseas concurrently might also be accepted as being in full-time employment. If, for example, they had several appointments with the same employer or group of companies, it might be reasonable to aggregate the total time spent on them for the purposes of the full-time test. This approach could also apply where an individual was simultaneously engaged in employment and self-employment abroad. However, where a person has a main employment abroad but also works in the UK in some unconnected occupation (for example, as director of a family company), HMRC would consider whether the extent of the UK activities might cast any doubt on the full-time nature of the main employment outside the UK.

The days of departure from, and arrival in, the UK are normally regarded as days of residence and ordinary residence.

55.2.4 UK visits and temporary residence

If an individual spends six months or more of any tax year in the UK he will be deemed to be resident there for tax purposes. If such an individual spends less than six months in the UK he may yet still be found to be resident dependent upon the frequency and duration of any visits made to the UK. Generally speaking, the more frequent the individual's visits to the UK are, the greater the likelihood that he will be found resident. This remains so notwithstanding the fact that the individual maintains no place of abode in the UK. It will be easier for HMRC to establish an individual as becoming resident by virtue of regular and substantial visits in the instance of a person who has previously been resident (and, if ordinarily resident, all the more so) in the UK, than in the case of an individual who has never previously been either resident or ordinarily resident in the UK. As Viscount Cave LC remarked in *Levene*:

> 'But probably the most difficult case is that of a wanderer who, having no home in any country, spends a part only of his time in hotels in the United Kingdom and the remaining and greater part of his time in hotels abroad. In such cases the question is one of fact and of degree, and must be determined on all the circumstances of the case ... If for instance such a man is a foreigner who has never resided in this country there may be great difficulty in holding that he is resident here.'

Law: TCGA 1992, s. 9(3); ITA 2007, s. 829(1), (2), 831, 832; *Levene v IR Commrs* [1928] AC 217; *Wilkie v IR Commrs* [1952] Ch 153; *Gaines-Cooper v R & C Commrs*(2006) Sp C 568

Other guidance: ESC A11, 'Residence in the United Kingdom: year of commencement or cessation of residence'; ESC A78, 'Residence in the United Kingdom: accompanying spouse'; SP 2/91, *Residence in the UK: visits extended because of exceptional circumstances*; Revenue Interpretation, *Tax Bulletin*, February 1993: *www.hmrc.gov.uk/bulletins/tb6.htm#anchor3136769*; HMRC6, *Residents and non-resident: Liability to tax in the United Kingdom*

55.2.5 Establishing ordinary residence

Like 'residence', 'ordinary residence' is not defined in the Taxes Acts. The expressions do not have the same meaning, since an individual may be resident in the UK without being ordinarily resident, or ordinarily resident without being resident. This latter would occur, for example, where an individual was absent from the UK for an entire tax year but had been ordinarily resident prior to his period of absence (see HMRC 6, Chapter 3). A person may be ordinarily resident in more than one place.

'Ordinarily resident' is broadly equivalent to habitually resident. It means the way in which a man's life is usually ordered, the qualifying adverb 'ordinarily' being used in its primary and natural sense of 'in conformity with rule or established custom' or 'practice'.

In 1981 HMRC issued a statement of practice (SP 3/81) concerning the ordinary residence status of an individual coming to the UK. This provided that an individual would be regarded as becoming UK ordinarily resident:

- from the date of his arrival if he has, or acquires during the year of arrival, accommodation for his use in the UK which he occupies on a basis that implies a stay of three years or more; or
- from the beginning of the tax year in which such 'permanent' accommodation becomes available; or
- from the beginning of the fourth year if he has no such accommodation available.

If 'permanent' accommodation is obtained but is disposed of and the individual leaves the UK within three years of arrival, he will be regarded as not ordinarily resident if that is to his advantage.

In a further statement of practice (SP 17/91), the Revenue explained how the ordinary residence of an individual who comes to the UK not intending to stay for three years or more is determined.

The statement indicates that ordinary residence will, in these circumstances, normally apply from the beginning of the tax year after the third anniversary of the person's arrival in this country. This has been the practice for some time for those taking up employment here. The treatment of others is now being brought into line with that of employees.

Law: Re Norris (1888) 4 TLR 452

55.3 Employees

55.3.1 Emoluments

Emoluments are calculated under the normal tax rules, including benefits in kind. Apart from the travelling expense rules already mentioned, expenses are deductible only according to the normal test of being wholly, exclusively and necessarily incurred in the performance of the duty of the employment. Pension contributions to an approved scheme are deductible, but the pension will be taxed when received, and, being UK source income, will remain permanently liable to UK income tax. Pensions paid on behalf of a foreign employer are not liable to UK tax.

Many international employers operate tax equalisation schemes, also known as tax protected pay or net pay. It is an arrangement that ensures that an employee has the same take-home pay wherever employed. Payments under these schemes are taxable. Golden handshakes are also taxable but, in addition to the general £30,000 allowance substantial foreign service may give a full or further partial exemption.

Stock options or share acquisition schemes may give rise to taxable income. Gains on the grant of an option escape tax if the individual is not resident and not ordinarily resident and his emoluments are foreign emoluments for duties wholly performed outside the UK. Gains on the exercise of an option will not necessarily escape if the individual is then non-resident. Gains arising in relation to share acquisition schemes are chargeable in the normal way, unless the employee is non-resident at the time the gain arises.

Corresponding payments will be permitted as deductions from foreign emoluments if they are paid out of them and there is insufficient overseas income not liable to UK tax to meet those obligations. Such a payment is one that would qualify for relief under UK tax rules if it were not paid under a foreign obligation (e.g. interest on a loan to buy a principal private residence, alimony and pension contributions). Pension contributions are deductible regardless of other income.

It is necessary to consider the status of an employee in a tax year to determine whether earnings are taxable in principle. If they are, they are actually taxed when received, even if the employment is not held then and regardless of the status of the individual at that date. There is a difference between received and remitted. An employee may receive the income proceeds into, say, a foreign bank account, but not remit the money to the UK.

55.3.2 Procedures

HM Revenue & Customs (HMRC) have introduced a number of administrative changes to the way in which the tax affairs of individuals coming to the UK for secondments or temporary employment are handled. The changes are designed to enable the residence status and domicile of such people to be dealt with more quickly.

Form DOM1 obtains information necessary to determine the individual's domicile.

Form P85 (form P85(S) in repayment cases) is for completion by employees when they subsequently leave the UK. Since self assessment, these forms are still required to be completed but in addition, any individual who receives a return form is required to complete the 'Non-residence' supplementary pages. It should be noted that HMRC no longer give residency rulings.

55.3.3 Tax treatment

General earnings for a tax year in which the employee is not resident in the UK are charged on the receipts basis if they are:

- general earnings in respect of duties performed in the UK; or
- general earnings from overseas Crown employment subject to UK tax, as defined in ITEPA 2003, s. 28.

This applies whether the earnings are for that year or for some other tax year, and whether or not the employment is held at the time when the earnings are received.

By implication, an employee who is not resident in the UK in a tax year is not subject to income tax on foreign earnings, i.e. general earnings which do not fall into either of the categories listed above. This holds true whether the employee is ordinarily resident in the UK or not, and whether the employee is domiciled in the UK or not.

Law: ITEPA 2003, s. 27

55.3.4 Travel costs and expenses: employee not domiciled in UK: duties performed in UK

Employee's travel

ITEPA 2003, s. 373 is, roughly, the mirror image of ITEPA 2003, s. 370. It gives a non-UK-domiciled employee a deduction from earnings charged on receipt from an employment for duties performed in the UK. The deduction is given for the amount included in respect of (a) the provision of travel facilities for a journey made by the employee or (b) the reimbursement of expenses incurred by the employee on such a journey. Two conditions must both be met.

The first condition is that the journey ends on, or during the period of five years beginning with, a date that is a 'qualifying arrival date' in relation to the employee.

The second condition is that the journey is made:

- from the country outside the UK in which the employee normally lives to a place in the UK in order to perform duties of the employment, or
- to that country from a place in the UK in order to return to that country after performing such duties.

If the journey has a dual purpose, the deduction is given for so much of the amount included in earnings as is properly attributable to the work purpose.

Law: ITEPA 2003, s. 373(3), (4)

Travel costs for family of employee not domiciled in UK: duties performed in UK

ITEPA 2003, s. 374 is, roughly, the mirror image of ITEPA 2003, s. 371. It gives a deduction from earnings which are charged on receipt from an employment for duties performed in the UK against an amount included in respect of (a) the provision of travel facilities for a journey made by the spouse or child of the non-UK domiciled employee or (b) the reimbursement of expenses incurred by the employee on such a journey. Three conditions must all be met.

Condition 1 – journey
The journey must:

- be made between the country outside the UK in which the employee normally lives and a place in the UK; and
- end on, or during the period of five years beginning with, a date that is a 'qualifying arrival date' in relation to the employee.

Condition 2 – employee's presence in the UK
The employee must be in the UK for a continuous period of at least 60 days for the purpose of performing the duties of one or more employments from which the employee receives earnings for duties performed in the UK.

Condition 3 – family members
The spouse, civil partner, or child must be:

- accompanying the employee at the beginning of the 60 day period;
- visiting the employee during that period; or
- returning to the country outside the UK in which the employee normally lives, after so accompanying or visiting the employee.

'Child' includes a stepchild and an illegitimate child but does not include any child who is aged 18 or over at the beginning of the outward journey.

In one way at least, the third condition is unfortunately worded. The journey by a member of the employee's immediate family must be between the country outside the UK in which the employee normally lives and the place of performance of his duties in the UK.

> **Planning point**
>
> The number of return journeys made by the same individual, for which a deduction can be given, is restricted to two per tax year.

If the journey has a dual purpose, the deduction is given for so much of the amount included in earnings as is properly attributable to the work purpose.

Law: ITEPA 2003, s. 374

> **Example 55.4**
>
> Henry, who is domiciled in New York, divorces his wife. She obtains custody of their children and takes them to live in her native Toronto. A journey made by the children to visit their father in the UK would not qualify under this provision if it was direct from Canada (not the taxpayer's usual place of abode). Equally a return journey could not qualify, as to do so it must follow a qualifying journey. The cost of travel from Canada to a point of departure in the USA would equally fail to come within the relief.

Qualifying arrival date

ITEPA 2003, s. 375 defines 'qualifying arrival date' in relation to a person as a date on which the person arrives in the UK to perform duties of an employment from which the person receives earnings for duties performed in the UK and which meets either of two conditions.

(1) The person has not been in the UK for any purpose during the period of two years ending with the day before the date.

(2) The person was not resident in the UK in either of the two tax years preceding the tax year in which the date falls. If this condition is met and there are two or more dates in the tax year on which the person arrives in the UK to perform duties of an employment from which the person receives earnings for duties performed in the UK, the qualifying arrival date is the earliest of them.

> **Example 55.5**
>
> Al, who is domiciled in New York, comes to the UK in June 2003 to work as a freelance journalist. He makes a home here, although he regularly returns to the US for about half the year. In March 2007, he is appointed US correspondent for a UK newspaper. He remains in the US during his tenure of that employment. He returns to the UK in May 2009 to take up another post with the same

Working in the UK

> newspaper. Throughout this period he maintains a house in the UK available for his use. He has a wife and family in the US.
>
> Al satisfies the conditions because:
>
> (1) he is non-resident in the two tax years before that in which he returns to the UK (being physically absent for the duration) and it does not matter that he might nevertheless be regarded as ordinarily resident;
>
> (2) he does not return to the UK at any time between May 2007 and May 2009.
>
> If he returns to the UK for any purpose in this latter period (e.g. for holiday or interview) then he fails condition (2).

Travel within a foreign country

Although travel may commence or end at any place in the UK, the travel to or from the country outside the UK in which the employee normally lives can, on a strict reading, only qualify if it is to or from the point of arrival or, as the case may be, departure in that country.

> **Example 55.6**
>
> Alan, who is domiciled in California and has lived for many years in Los Angeles, travels to take up a post with the London branch of an American bank. Rather than take a direct flight over the North Pole, he travels via New York, stopping over for one night between flights. His point of departure is New York. The flight from Los Angeles to New York is not from the country outside the UK in which Alan normally lives; rather it is within it.

However, the Revenue indicated that they will interpret the phrase 'usual place of abode' in the predecessor legislation pragmatically, so that bona fide cases will qualify for relief (notes of meetings held between the accountancy bodies and the Revenue in May and June 1986, published as TR 631 by the Institute of Chartered Accountants in England and Wales). Doubtless this practice will continue.

55.3.5 Foreign accommodation and subsistence costs and expenses (overseas employments)

Expenses incurred in providing board and lodging to enable an employee to perform the duties of his overseas employment are deductible if either the board and lodging outside the UK is provided directly by the employer, or the employee incurs the expense and is reimbursed by the employer and the following conditions are met:

- the duties of the employment are performed wholly outside the UK;
- the employee is resident and ordinarily resident in the UK; and

- in a case where the employer is a 'foreign employer', the employee is domiciled in the UK (apart from this, the employee's domicile is irrelevant).

Where the board and lodging is provided partly for the performance of the duties and partly for another purpose, only the expenses attributable to the former are allowable as a deduction.

> *Example 55.7*
>
> David is sent to Nice by his employer on business which takes one week to conclude. Whilst in Nice he decides to take a further fortnight's holiday. The hotel expenses of the three weeks are paid for by the employer.
>
> In these circumstances only the hotel expenses relating to the first week are allowable as a deduction.

Law: ITEPA 2003, s. 376

55.3.6 Double tax treaties

Many such treaties provide that a resident of a foreign country who can claim the protection of the treaty will not be liable to UK tax on emoluments for duties performed in the UK if:

- the individual is present in the UK for periods not exceeding in total 183 days in any tax year;
- the emoluments are paid by an employer who is not resident in the UK; and
- the cost of the emoluments is not borne by a permanent establishment or fixed base that the employer has in the UK.

Treaties often exclude public entertainers and sports people from the protection of such a provision, and their earnings are often paid under deduction of tax.

> *Planning points*
>
> The following points may be considered by a foreign national taking up employment in the UK.
>
> Relief under a double tax treaty or exemption from UK tax may be obtained if the visitor is considered non-UK-resident in any year and meets certain other treaty conditions.
>
> A claim for allowances on arrival in the UK may avoid the withholding of excessive PAYE deductions.
>
> The length of an employment arrangement is crucial in claiming non-ordinary residence status. A contract of employment or letter from a foreign employer specifying the intended length of assignment can greatly assist.

55.4 PAYE

55.4.1 Introduction

Any employer must withhold PAYE tax, even if both the employer and the employee are non-resident, provided the employer has a trading presence in the UK and the remuneration is liable to UK income tax. Class I National Insurance contributions must also be withheld.

55.4.2 Intermediate employers, etc.

With effect from 3 May 1994, primary legislation governs the PAYE liability of non-resident employers, and of those to whom employees are seconded in cases where the employer does not operate PAYE (ITEPA 2003, s. 689 and 691: see below).

Employee of overseas employer

Where:

- an employee works for a person (the 'relevant person') other than his employer; but
- is still paid by his employer or an intermediary of his employer (see above) or of the relevant person;
- PAYE regulations do not apply to the payer or, if he makes the payment as an intermediary of the employer or of the relevant person, the employer; and
- PAYE is not deducted or accounted for in accordance with the regulations by the payer or, if he makes the payment as an intermediary of the employer or of the relevant person, the employer,

then the relevant person is required to account for PAYE on payments to the employee, grossed-up if the payments are net of any income tax.

Where, under the 'notional payments' provisions (ITEPA 2003, s. 710), an employer would be treated for the purposes of the PAYE regulations as paying an amount to an employee, he is also treated for ITEPA 2003, s. 689 purposes as making a payment of that amount. Where this happens, the amount of assessable income which the employee is treated as receiving is regarded as a gross amount.

In determining whether a payment is made by an intermediary of the person for whom the employee works, the same approach is taken as in ITEPA 2003, s. 687(4).

Mobile UK workforce

Where employees of a UK employer ('the contractor') work for another person, but continue to be paid by or on behalf of the contractor, and it is likely that PAYE will not be accounted for even though all parties are based in the UK, the Board may give a direction that the person to whom the employees are seconded must deduct PAYE tax from any payments made by that person to the contractor in respect of the work done by the employees.

A direction must specify both the contractor and the person to whom the employees are seconded, must be given by notice to that person, and may be withdrawn at any time by notice to that person. The Board must take 'such steps as are reasonably necessary' to ensure that the contractor is given a copy of any such notice as relates to him.

Law: ITEPA 2003, s. 691

55.4.3 Payments to non-resident employees

The House of Lords decided in *IR Commrs v Herd* [1993] BTC 245, that there is no obligation on an employer to operate PAYE in respect of a payment only part of which is assessable under the charge on employment income provisions. This cast doubt on the validity of PAYE deductions in respect of payments to non-resident employees in circumstances where only part of their emoluments was liable to tax under the charge on employment income provisions (formerly Schedule E). In response, a provision was introduced with effect from 3 May 1994 which applies where an employee is not resident, or not ordinarily resident, in the UK, and works partly in the UK and partly overseas, so that while some of his income from employment is taxable under the charge on employment income provisions (formerly Schedule E Case II), an unascertainable proportion of it is not so assessable (ITEPA 2003, s. 690). In such cases, the employer, or a person designated by the employer, may apply for a direction that a particular proportion of any payment made to the employee in a tax year should be treated as liable to PAYE. If, however, there is no direction in force, the entirety of any payment made to the employee in the tax year will be liable to PAYE.

An application for a direction must give 'such information as is available and is relevant to the application' (ITEPA 2003, s. 690(4)). The application itself must be given by notice to the employer or the person designated by the employer, and must specify the employee and the tax year. The direction may be withdrawn by notice to the employer or designated person from a specified date, which must be no less than 30 days from the giving of the notice (ITEPA 2003, s. 690(6)).

Whether or not a direction is in force, the validity of any assessment of the employee's income, and any right to repayment of overpaid tax or obligation to pay tax underpaid, remain unaffected.

55.4.4 Relevant payments

PAYE is to be applied on the making of a 'relevant payment' (*Income Tax (Pay As You Earn) Regulations* 2003 (SI 2003/2682), reg. 21(1)). With certain exceptions (see below) the term 'relevant payment' is defined to mean a payment 'of, or on account of, net PAYE income'. 'Net PAYE income' is then defined as PAYE income, less allowable pension contributions and allowable donations to charity (as further defined in each case). To complete the circle, 'PAYE income' is defined in accordance with ITEPA 2003, s. 683 (i.e. encompassing employment income, pension income and social security income).

The following are excluded from the definition of 'relevant payment':

- PAYE social security income, but subject to the exceptions in Pt. 8 of the PAYE regulations;
- UK social security pensions;
- excluded relocation expenses;
- excluded business expenses;
- excluded pecuniary liabilities; and
- excluded notional payments.

An employer who provides an employee with assessable income in the form of 'readily convertible assets' is treated as making a payment to the employee of an amount liable to PAYE. The PAYE net is similarly extended to remuneration by way of non-cash vouchers, credit tokens and cash vouchers. Payments of assessable income deemed to have been made under these provisions are called 'notional payments', and there are particular rules for accounting for tax on such payments.

Apart from statute, there is no obligation on an employer to operate PAYE in respect of a payment only part of which is assessable under the charge on employment income provisions. In *IR Commrs v Herd*, the taxpayer acquired shares in the company of which he was director and after little more than three years sold them back to the original vendor at a considerable profit. It was agreed that on the disposal of the shares, the taxpayer was liable to income tax under former Schedule E on their increase in value since acquisition, and the question arose whether PAYE should have been deducted by the payer. The House of Lords held it should not, as only part of the sale proceeds (the amount representing the increase in value) was taxable under former Schedule E. Lord Mackay of Clashfern said at p. 251:

> 'Neither the empowering provisions of the [1988] Act nor the [PAYE] regulations themselves include an obligation on the payer to deduct tax from a payment only part of which is assessable to income tax under Sch[edule] E. Indeed, this is emphasised by the provision that the obligation to deduct arises on the making of any payment of, or on account of, any income assessable to income tax under Sch[edule] E. Where the provision is as detailed as that, if the intention had been to impose an obligation to make a deduction from a payment which was in part to be treated as income under Sch[edule] E. I would have expected this to have been expressly provided for and,

even more important, some machinery set up for distinguishing in the single payment between the amount to be subject to deduction and the balance.'

An exception to this rule is provided by ITEPA 2003, s. 690, which subjects to PAYE certain relevant payments to employees not resident, or not ordinarily resident, in the UK, who work partly overseas and partly in the UK.

The key issue is whether a relevant 'payment' has been 'made'. The passing of cash is clearly payment whereas the provision of certain benefits in kind (e.g. a car) does not involve payment to the employee, except insofar as they constitute 'notional payments'. *The Employer's Further Guide to PAYE and NICs* (CWG2)) gives the following non-exhaustive list of different kinds of payment which count as pay for PAYE purposes:

- '• Salaries, wages, fees, overtime, bonuses, pensions, commission, honoraria, perks
- Payments in the form of pensions
- Cash payments such as Christmas boxes
- Amounts voted to a director and credited to an account with the company that a director can draw on
- Payments used for subscribing for shares in a company
- Payments used to reduce a debt that an employee owes the employer unless tax has already been paid on the money when it was advanced to the employee
- Payments made in advance, on account or after an employee has left. These include drawings in advance or on account of a director's remuneration
- Pay in respect of sickness or other absence from work
- Statutory Sick Pay
- Statutory Maternity Pay
- Holiday Pay
- Tool and clothing allowances for employees in the building trade
- Vouchers that can be exchanged for cash including Premium Bonds
- Certain payments under the Employment Protection Act such as maternity pay or arrears of pay
- Payments for travelling between the employee's home and normal place of employment. In the case of agency workers this is the cost of travelling from home to the client's office
- Round sum allowances
- Payments for time spent in travelling
- Cash payments for meals at the normal place of work
- Payments instead of benefits in kind
- Certain lump sum payments made when an employee stops working for you
- Most lump sum payments made when you take on a new employee. These include payments made to the employee before he or she has left the old job
- Tips or service charges paid by you to the employee in addition to normal wage or salary. If tips are shared out by a troncmaster, PAYE should be operated separately on these payments by the troncmaster.
- Payments in the form of tradeable assets, or vouchers or credit tokens which are used to acquire such assets.'

In addition, the *Guide* specifies:

'payments that are not included on the deductions working sheet but must be returned at the end of the tax year [on form P11D],'

and lists these at para. E5.

Note that, having made the deductions, the employer must account for them to the Revenue. An attempt to establish that the liability was obviated by theft of the amount failed in *Attorney-General v Antoine* (1949) 31 TC 213. In that case, an employer who kept locked in a safe a sum of money equal to PAYE deductions from employees' wages was liable to account to the Revenue notwithstanding that the safe was burgled and the money stolen.

55.4.5 Returns for foreign secondees

An employer must, if required so to do, prepare and deliver to HMRC a return relating to persons who are or have been employed by him. Where a person performs the duties of an office or employment in the UK for a continuous period of at least 30 days and the employment is with a non-UK resident but the duties are performed for the benefit of a UK resident (or person carrying on a trade, profession or vocation in the UK), then the person benefiting from those services may be required to make a return of the name and address of the 'employee'.

Law: TIOPA 2010, Sch. 7, para. 12, 13 and 14

55.5 Trades, professions and vocations: foreign income

55.5.1 Charge on foreign income from trade, profession or vocation

Income of a UK resident derived from a trade, profession or vocation which is carried on wholly abroad is liable to tax only if it was remitted to the UK where he is:

- not domiciled in the UK; or
- a Commonwealth (including a British) citizen or a citizen of the Republic of Ireland and is not 'ordinarily resident' in the UK.

In all other cases the income of a resident is liable to tax whether or not the income is remitted. Income arising in the Republic of Ireland is treated as if it arose in the UK but is nevertheless entitled to the same deductions (and subject to the same limitation of reliefs) as apply to trades, etc. carried on abroad.

> **Planning point**
>
> Residence status is of vital importance for tax planning purposes (see **Chapter 60** for commentary on residence). The income of a non-resident derived from a trade carried on wholly abroad is not liable to tax. However, a non-resident trading in the UK through a branch or agency is liable to tax on consequent profits.

Law: ITTOIA 2005, s. 7, 269

55.5.2 Trading in the UK

A 'non-UK-resident' trading in the UK is only liable to UK tax where he is trading through a branch or agency.

Whether a person is trading in the UK through a branch or agency is a question of fact, but the distinction has to be made between trading with the UK and trading in the UK: soliciting orders in the UK will not by itself constitute trading in the UK. An important factor is whether the contract for sale or supply of services was made abroad, but the contract may not be conclusive.

Law: Firestone Tyre and Rubber Co Ltd v Lewellin (HMIT) [1957] 1 WLR 464; *FL Smidth & Co v Greenwood* (1922) 8 TC 193; *Grainger & Son v Gough* [1896] AC 325

55.5.3 UK resident trading wholly abroad

An individual who is resident in the UK and carries on a trade, profession or vocation wholly abroad, either alone or in partnership, is liable to tax on all his income from such a trade. The income is assessed on a current year basis. Losses, etc. can only be set off against the income of that or another overseas source, foreign emoluments, other overseas income and certain pensions.

However, a person who is not domiciled in the UK, or else is a Commonwealth (including a British) citizen (or a citizen of the Republic of Ireland) who is not ordinarily resident in the UK, is liable only on a remittance basis.

Changes in residence status will trigger a deemed commencement or cessation for the purposes of assessing business profits

> **Warning!**
>
> Where a member of a partnership either becomes resident, or ceases to be resident in the UK, then for tax purposes that partner is treated as having first

> ceased and then immediately recommenced as a partner. The rules ensure that resident partners are taxed on their share of the worldwide partnership profits, but non-resident partners only on their share of the profits earned in the UK.

Law: ITTOIA 2005, s. 17 and s. 858

55.5.4 Expenses connected with foreign trades

Special rules apply to travel expenses and board and lodging expenses incurred by an individual taxpayer whose trade, profession or vocation is carried on wholly outside the UK, and who has failed to satisfy the Revenue that he is not domiciled here or else, being a Commonwealth (including a British) citizen (or a citizen of the Republic of Ireland), is not ordinarily resident here.

Where the rules apply the travel and board and lodging expenses are to be treated as deductible provided that the taxpayer's absence from the UK is wholly and exclusively for the purpose of performing the function of the foreign trade.

In certain conditions travel expenses of the taxpayer's spouse and any child of his are deductible.

Travel between foreign trades is also deductible, subject to conditions.

Law: ITTOIA 2005, s. 92, 93, 94

55.5.5 Non-resident entertainers and sportsmen

The activities of a non-resident entertainer or sportsman (or sportswoman) performed in the UK will represent a trade, profession or vocation carried on in the UK. Consequently, a potential tax liability will arise in respect of prizes and appearance fees received by the entertainer or sportsman.

This provision is unnecessary and will not apply where:
- the entertainer or sportsman actually does exercise a trade, etc. in the UK of which the relevant activity is a part; or
- the entertainer or sportsman performs the relevant activity in the course of an employment or office. In such an instance the taxpayer is assessable anyway in his capacity as employee.

A withholding tax is applied to certain earnings of non-resident visiting entertainers and sportsmen and women. Broadly speaking, any person making a payment in relation to an appearance or performance in the UK by a non-resident entertainer or sports personality is required to withhold from that payment an amount equivalent to basic rate income tax upon it, no matter to whom the payment is made.

This particular system of deduction of tax at source was introduced to counter problems of non-payment of tax by such visitors who come to the UK often for short periods only and who can earn considerable sums of money in that time. Before that date, there were no problems either in identifying these visitors and their earnings in the UK, or in assessing them to tax. The difficulties actually arose in trying to collect the tax due on these earnings before the entertainer or sportsman left the country, and these difficulties were exacerbated following the abolition of exchange controls in 1979. It was calculated that, before the introduction in 1987 of the procedure for withholding income tax at source, the amount of tax lost to the Exchequer through non-payment of tax in such cases was running annually at £100m.

In fact, the provisions requiring deduction of tax at source merely brought UK tax law into line with established international practice, and they are consistent with the OECD model Double Taxation Convention 2005, art. 17 which assumes that international 'artistes and athletes' may be taxed on their earnings for acting as such by the state in which they perform their activities

Payment of tax by foreign entertainers and sportsmen

Where a payment is made in respect of an appearance by a non-resident entertainer or sportsman in the UK the payer must deduct tax at the basic rate. This rule does not apply if:

- the payment is below £1,000; or
- the recipient has agreed a lower or nil rate of withholding tax with HMRC.

Regulations give definitions of 'entertainers' and 'sportsmen', and detail the activities covered by the rules, the types of income subject to withholding, the deduction of expenses and the administration arrangements in connection with the procedure. The rules apply to fees and prize money, and also to associated income from advertising, sponsorship and endorsements. The deduction at source cannot be avoided by directing payment to a third party.

Tax is assessed on a current year basis.

Law: ITTOIA 2005, s. 13–14; Income Tax (Entertainers and Sportsmen) Regulations 1987 (SI 1987/530)

Other guidance: *A Guide to Paying Foreign Entertainers* (FEU 50; *Reduced Tax Payment Applications* (www.hmrc.gov.uk/feu/rtpa.htm); *Self-Assessment and Foreign Entertainers* (www.hmrc.gov.uk/feu/selfasst.htm); *List of approved promoters/agents and merchandisers* (www.hmrc.gov.uk/feu/appromers.htm).

55.6 Non-residents trading through a branch or agency

A non-resident individual who is trading in the UK is liable to UK tax on the profits of the trading operations in the UK. This is subject to possible double taxation relief. Whilst it is a simple matter to assess a non-resident, the collection of tax due from such an individual may prove more difficult.

Where non-residents are trading through UK representatives, the UK branch or agent is made jointly responsible with the non-resident trader for all that needs to be done in connection with self-assessment of the profits from, or connected with, the branch or agency.

Whether or not an individual is trading in the UK is a question of fact which often depends upon where the contract was made, i.e. if the contract was made overseas, then, in general, the trade is carried on overseas. There is a distinction between trading 'with' a country and trading 'within' that country. In *Grainger & Son v Gough* (1896) 3 TC 462 a French wine merchant appointed Grainger and Son, an English firm carrying on business in London, as his agents for the sale of his wines in England. The agents canvassed for orders and received a commission on all orders from Great Britain, if executed. When orders were received they were transmitted to France, where the French wine merchant exercised his discretion as to whether he should execute the orders or not. No orders were accepted in Great Britain. Payments for the most part were sent direct to France and all receipts were sent by the French wine merchant to the customers direct. On these facts the House of Lords held by a majority (Lord Morris dissenting) that no part of the trade was carried on in the UK. Lord Watson based his decision on the fact that the contracts were made in France and not in the UK. Lord Herschell drew the distinction between trading 'with' a country and trading 'within' it ([1896] AC at pp. 335–336):

> 'In the first place, I think there is a broad distinction between trading with a country, and carrying on a trade within a country. Many merchants and manufacturers export their goods to all parts of the world, yet I do not suppose anyone would dream of saying that they exercise or carry on their trade in every country in which their goods find customers ... Something more must be necessary in order to constitute the exercise of a trade within this country. How does a wine merchant exercise his trade? I take it, by making or buying wine and selling it again with a view to profit. If all that a merchant does in any particular country is to solicit orders, I do not think he can reasonably be said to exercise or carry on his trade in that country. What is done there is only ancillary to the exercise of his trade in the country where he buys or makes, stores, and sells his goods.'

Counsel for the Crown had argued that the appointment of English agents to solicit orders was the factor that rendered M Roederer, the French wine merchant, taxable as carrying on a trade within the UK. Lord Herschell rejected this argument (at p. 336):

'If in each case the other circumstances are the same, the contract of sale being made abroad and the delivery taking place there, I find myself quite unable to see how the mode in which orders are solicited and obtained, whether by an agent or by circulars or advertisements, can make the difference, and cause the trade in the one case to be exercised, and in the other not to be exercised, within this country.'

In *Tischler v Apthorpe* (1885) 2 TC 89 and in *Pommery and Greno v Apthorpe* (1885) 2 TC 182 the foreign wine merchant traded in the UK through an English agent who sold his wine in England, and received the price, making delivery to the buyer, either from the stock which had been sent to him by his principal, or by directing a consignment to be sent from Rheims. In *Werle & Co v Colquhoun* (1886) 2 TC 402 the decision of the Court of Appeal was based upon the express ground that the foreign wine merchant exercised his trade in England by making contracts there through his English agent.

It is clear that the mere purchase of goods in the UK for purposes of export and resale abroad is insufficient to constitute trading within the UK. In *Sulley v Attorney-General* (1860) 2 TC 149 an American firm carried on a business in New York which consisted of re-selling in New York goods purchased to their account in England. The Court of Exchequer Chamber held that the firm did not carry on its trade in the UK. However, where a non-resident individual, either by himself or through a UK representative, habitually does and contracts to do a thing capable of producing a profit and for the purpose of producing profit, he carries on a trade or business in the UK (see Jessel MR in *Erichsen v Last* (1881) 4 TC 422 at p. 415 and also Brett LJ at p. 418).

In ascertaining whether a non-resident is trading within the UK, the place of contracting will be an important factor. If the non-resident contracts in the UK himself or employs an agent in the UK to sell his goods or contract on his behalf, that non-resident will be trading within the UK (see *Pommery and Greno v Apthorpe* (1886) 2 TC 182 above; see also *Wilcock v Pinto* (1925) 10 TC 415 and *Nielsen, Andersen & Co v Collins* (1927) 13 TC 91). Conversely, if the contracts are made overseas, the presumption is that there is no trade within the UK (see *Grainger and Son v Gough*, above). In *Greenwood v FL Smidth & Co* (1922) 8 TC 193, Danish machine manufacturers had a London office from which an employee canvassed orders. Contracts, however, were only ever made in Denmark. It was held that the Danish manufacturers were not trading in the UK.

Whilst the place of contracting is an important factor (and thus careful consideration must be given to the rules of English contract law concerning methods of communicating acceptance, viz. postal rule: *Household Fire and Carriage Accident Insurance Co v Grant* (1879) 4 Ex D 216; telex: *Entores v Miles Far East Corporation* [1955] 2 QB 327; etc.), it is not paramount. In *Greenwood v FL Smidth and Co* (above), Atkin LJ observed (at pp. 203–204):

'The contracts in this case were made abroad. But I am not prepared to hold that this test is decisive. I can imagine cases where the contract of re-sale is made abroad, and yet the manufacture of the goods, some negotiation of the terms, and complete execution of the contract take place here under such circumstances that the trade was in truth exercised here. I think that the question is, where do the operations take place from which the profits in substance arise.'

In conclusion, place of contracting is an important, but not deciding, factor in determining whether a non-resident is trading within the UK. Other factors are also of importance (see Viscount Cave LC in *Maclaine & Co v Eccott* (1926) 10 TC 481 at p. 573). The issue is one of fact and is determined by reference to Atkin LJ's observation (above), i.e. where do the operations take place from which the profits in substance arise? (Cited with approval by the House of Lords in *Firestone Tyre and Rubber Co v Lewellin* (1957) 37 TC 111, where Lord Radcliffe stated that the place of contract was not a determining factor (at p. 142).)

Law: ITA 2007, s. 811-813; TIOPA 2010, Sch. 6, 4, 25, 26, 33

56 Working Overseas

56.1 Working abroad

56.1.1 Introduction

Very large numbers of British citizens go to live abroad for a substantial period of time, usually either at work or in retirement. Since tax is territorial there will inevitably be tax considerations and, as always, it is best to plan well in advance of departure.

The basis of liability to UK income tax and CGT is residence. As so often with key words in legislation, there is no statutory definition. The result is a mixture of case law and HMRC practice. Although many tax professionals do not agree with all the assertions made by HMRC in successive editions of their booklet HMRC 6 (formerly covered in IR20), for practical purposes it would be foolish to ignore it. **Chapter 60** covers the subject of residence and its implications for tax purposes in detail.

Other guidance: HMRC leaflet HMRC 6: *Residence, Domicile and the Remittance Basis* (*www.hmrc.gov.uk/cnr/hmrc6.pdf*)

56.1.2 Income tax

There is no substitute for detailed local advice on the tax system of the host country, and careful consideration of the double taxation agreement, where such an agreement exists. Many countries have more burdensome tax regimes than the UK. The traditional approach of UK tax advisers was to minimise the incidence of UK taxation. While income tax rates remain relatively low compared to the rest of Europe, advisers should consider whether they might devote some of their energies to maximising that proportion of their clients' income over which the UK has sole taxing rights.

Leaving the UK

In outline, anyone who is physically in the UK for 183 days or more in any tax year is resident here for the whole of that tax year. There is a further concept of 'ordinary residence' – broadly, habitual residence over a period of several years – which is sometimes relevant. The tax year is split by HMRC concession when an individual goes abroad under a contract of employment. The conditions are:

- the individual must be absent from the UK for an entire tax year;

- the employment must extend over an entire tax year;
- the individual must not spend more than 182 days in the UK in any tax year; and
- he must not spend 91 days or more in a tax year in the UK on average, over a period up to four years.

In these circumstances the person is treated as neither resident nor ordinarily resident with effect from the date of his departure. It is important to note that this is a HMRC concession, not a statutory right, and that it can be denied if HMRC perceive that it is being abused.

The taxation of the income of people who are domiciled in, but not resident in the UK (the normal case with those who go to work abroad for limited periods) is as follows:

Employment income	
– overseas duties	no liability
– UK duties	liable in respect of UK duties
Rent from UK property	taxable
UK-source taxed investment income	no further liability
FOTRA securities	no further liability

FOTRA = Free Of Tax to Residents Abroad

On leaving the UK, employees should complete Form P85. The form asks questions about the intended length of stay overseas, whether the departure is permanent, what continuing UK-source income is expected.

With the exception of the Republic of Ireland, other countries' fiscal years do not end on 5 April. It is possible to be resident in more than one country and in some cases there will be actual or potential double taxation of the same income. The UK has double taxation treaties with most countries and in most cases relief will be available; either the treaty will give one country the right to tax a particular type of income (for example, rent from property located in that country) or it will provide for credit relief (i.e. one jurisdiction will permit the set-off of tax paid in the other country).

The main income tax considerations for the ordinary British short-to-medium-term expatriate are to do with timing. After the date of his going abroad he will only be liable as indicated in the table above. It is quite easy to work abroad for nearly two years and remain within the UK income tax net.

It is worth remembering that employees are generally taxed on amounts received in a tax year. However, the employee's tax liability is determined by his residence status during the tax year when the remuneration was earned.

The position for the self-employed is quite different. The split year concession will only apply to the self-employed if they are going abroad for at least three years and will be not ordinarily resident in the UK following their departure. They will remain liable to UK tax to the extent that any part of the business is carried on in the UK. If the overseas country has a significantly more favourable tax regime it may be worthwhile incorporating an offshore company with non-resident directors so that the exposure to UK tax is limited to the profits of the UK branch.

There is no joint assessment on the partnership and each partner is responsible for the tax on his share of the firm's profits. Where the partnership carries on business partly in the UK and partly abroad, the non-resident partner's taxable share in the UK is limited to his share of the profits of the trade carried on in the UK.

Returning to the UK

Normally those who return to the UK from overseas postings will be resident and ordinarily resident in the UK from the date of return. Income tax planning will usually involve maximising pre-return income. As a matter of course all offshore accounts paying gross interest should be closed before return. There is a danger of double taxation and complex fractional calculations based on the amount of time spent between the date of return and the end of the tax year.

Law: ITEPA 2003, Pt. 2, Ch. 5; *Robert Gaines-Cooper v HMRC* (SpC 2006, 568); *Shepherd v HMRC* (2005) Sp C 484

Other guidance: HMRC leaflet HMRC 6: *Residence, Domicile and the Remittance Basis* (*www.hmrc.gov.uk/cnr/hmrc6.pdf*); Form P86: Leaving the United Kingdom (*www.hmrc.gov.uk/cnr/p85.pdf*)

56.1.3 Capital gains tax

The CGT regime differs so strongly from the income tax position that advice on the mitigation of one tax may conflict with advice about the other tax. A year's absence may be enough to avoid UK income tax; for CGT this is now usually five years.

An individual falls into the UK tax net if chargeable gains accrue to him:

'in a year of assessment during any part of which he is resident in the United Kingdom, or during which he is resident in the United Kingdom.'

Under the terms of the revised HMRC concession (ESC D2) the tax year can be split for CGT purposes if the individual was neither resident nor ordinarily resident in the UK for at least four out of the seven tax years preceding the year of departure. The concession thus will help temporary visitors to the UK but it is of absolutely no use to the ordinary person going to work abroad. The first planning point, therefore, for those going to work in a country with a generous CGT regime, is to defer capital gains as far as possible until after the next 5 April.

The basis of charge on short-term emigrants was greatly extended by the 1998 Budget. While this chapter seeks to avoid too detailed a discussion of the boundaries of residence and ordinary residence (see **Chapter 59** for more on this topic), absence from the UK for three whole tax years will always make an individual neither resident nor ordinarily resident. Dave Clark famously went to make his home and place of business in Los Angeles on 3 April, stayed there for a complete tax year, and escaped tax on a $450,000 sale of recording rights; the case established that one year might be enough to establish non-residence. HMRC believed that successful entrepreneurs were arranging employments, or merely going to live in countries such as Germany, where most long-term gains are tax free, and selling their companies from the safety of their absence. Non-resident trustees were also, under the old regime, able to distribute capital to non-resident beneficiaries and no CGT would be due. Besides, the concession was used to exempt from UK tax profits on disposals made after departure but in the same tax year by those who went to live abroad for three whole tax years.

The rules apply to an individual who was resident in the UK for at least four of the seven tax years preceding his departure. This catches most UK expatriates and spares most foreign visitors. The rules only apply to gains on assets acquired before the taxpayer's departure, and only apply if there are fewer than five whole tax years between departure and return. Their effect is to bring into the capital gains tax charge for the year of the taxpayer's return all gains (less allowable losses) realised in the interval.

Example 56.1

Gordon has spent all his life in Edinburgh. On 1 November 2006 he goes to work in Saudi Arabia under a three-year contract, and returns on 1 December 2009. He realises two capital gains: one of £10,000 on 1 December 2006 and one of £200,000 on 1 June 2008.

He is resident in the UK for part of 2006–07 and so the £10,000 gain is taxable for that year. He is not saved by the concession, as he has been resident in the UK for at least four of the seven preceding tax years.

The £200,000 gain is also taxable, this time in 2009–10, because his absence has not covered five complete tax years.

There is a proviso in the legislation which expressly makes it subject to the provisions of double taxation agreements. Most agreements contain a clause giving each country the sole taxing rights over its residents, with exceptions relating to business assets. The double taxation agreement with Ireland, however, which was revised in 1998, contains a further clause permitting the UK to levy CGT on gains realised by an Irish resident individual who was resident in the UK at any time in the three years preceding the sale. Many modern agreements contain similar clauses.

> **Example 56.2**
>
> Chris has lived in London all his life. He wants to sell his family company and the buyer is prepared to wait. He moves to Dublin on 1 December 2007. He will be liable to UK CGT if he sells the company before 1 December 2010.
>
> Before seeking to take advantage of a double taxation agreement, the taxpayer would be well advised to investigate the CGT regime of the country to which he hopes to emigrate.

Other guidance: Extra-statutory concession D2: '*Residence in the United Kingdom: Year of commencement or cessation of residence: Capital gains tax*'

56.1.4 Inheritance tax

Domicile is the main determinant of liability to Inheritance Tax (IHT) (See **Chapter 57** for commentary on domicile). It is a common law concept, without statutory definition. The country where an individual has his permanent home may be an adequate definition for these purposes. Everyone has a domicile. At birth a child acquires a domicile of origin, usually that of the father. If the father, mother, or person on whom the child is legally dependent, changes his or her domicile, the child acquires a new domicile of dependency. Since 1974 married women have been able to change domicile without reference to their husbands' domicile. At age 16 a person obtains the legal capacity to acquire a new domicile of choice.

It is difficult to displace domicile. There are scores of cases which underline the gap between going to live in another country and becoming a permanent dweller in it.

HMRC no longer issue domicile rulings. For a limited but substantial class of taxpayers, essentially foreigners who are long-term residents in the UK, this is unfortunate as it adds uncertainty to their affairs.

The general law of domicile recognises the different jurisdictions within the UK. An individual can therefore be domiciled in England and Wales, in Scotland, or in Northern Ireland. However, for IHT purposes, the concept of a UK domicile is used. A person domiciled in the UK is liable to IHT on all assets which he owns anywhere. In two cases a non-domiciled person's estate is brought into the IHT net.

(1) An individual who was domiciled in the UK within the three years preceding the transfer will be deemed to be domiciled in the UK at the time of the transfer.

(2) A person who has been resident in the UK for at least 17 out of the 20 income tax years ending with the year of the transfer is also deemed to be domiciled at the time of the transfer.

Working Overseas

> ### Planning points
>
> Forward planning is essential – the tax considerations should be considered well in advance of departure.
>
> Familiarise oneself with HMRC booklet HMRC 6.
>
> Obtain detailed knowledge of local tax system of host country.
>
> Consider timing and duration of visits to UK to avoid being classed as resident in a tax year if at all possible.
>
> Remember the UK is a relatively low tax rate country.
>
> Aim to minimise pre-return income when returning to UK.
>
> Consider interaction of income tax and capital gains tax – conflicts may arise.
>
> IHT liability depends on domicile, which is difficult to displace.

Law: TCGA 1992, s. 2, 10A; 112; *Reed (HMIT) v Clark* [1985] BTC 224

Other guidance: HMRC leaflet HMRC 6: *Residence, Domicile and the Remittance Basis*; ESC A11, '*Residence in the United Kingdom: year of commencement or cessation of residence*'; ESC D2, '*Residence in the United Kingdom: year of commencement or cessation of residence*'

57 Domicile and Non-Domicile

57.1 Relevance of domicile

UK income tax and capital gains tax are founded upon residence. Notwithstanding this fact, the domicile of an individual may also be of importance in determining his liability and the taxation of foreign emoluments under ITEPA 2003. Domicile is also important for the purposes of inheritance tax where it is given an extended meaning (see **58.13**). The concept of domicile is one of general law and within the jurisdiction of the UK domicile, is regarded as being the equivalent of a person's permanent home. Broadly speaking, therefore, a person is domiciled in that country in which he makes his permanent home. An individual is not domiciled in the UK as such but rather in one of the areas of jurisdiction that together constitute the UK, viz. England and Wales, Scotland, and Northern Ireland.

There are three kinds of domicile.

(1) Domicile of origin.

(2) Domicile of choice.

(3) Domicile of dependency.

At the outset it must be understood that there is a presumption of the continuance of an existing domicile. The burden of proving a change lies upon those who allege a change has occurred, and if the evidence is conflicting the court will usually decide in favour of the existing domicile.

Other guidance: Revenue leaflet HMRC 6: *Residence, Domicile and the Remittance Basis*

57.2 Domicile of origin

It is an established principle that every individual must have a domicile and that no person may be without one. Thus, each individual at his birth acquires a domicile of origin. In the case of a legitimate child this will be the domicile of his father, and in the instance of an illegitimate child that of his mother. It is apparent therefore that there need be no connection between an individual's place of birth and his domicile of origin, e.g. a legitimate child born in England to a father of Scottish domicile would acquire a Scottish domicile of origin.

No individual may have more than a single domicile. The domicile of origin subsists until it is displaced by a new domicile of either choice or dependency.

> **Warning!**
> Domicile of origin is characterised by two factors, its permanence and the heavy burden of proof required to displace it. Historically, it has been difficult for individuals to demonstrate a change of domicile, and this may prove particularly so where obtaining a tax advantage is one of the perceived reasons behind a change

In *IR Commrs v Bullock* (1976) 51 TC 522, the taxpayer was born in Nova Scotia, Canada, in 1910 and his domicile of origin was there. He came to England in 1932 to join the Royal Air Force. He married an English wife and they visited Canada on a number of occasions. He hoped to persuade his wife that they should live there after his retirement. He retired in 1961. His wife did not wish to reside in Canada and the couple continued to live in England. In 1966 he executed a will appointing a Nova Scotia corporation as executor. The will contained a declaration that his domicile was in Nova Scotia, Canada, and that he intended to return to that country upon his wife's death. All his assets were in Canada. The Court of Appeal held that for the taxpayer to have acquired a domicile of choice in England he must have intended to make his home there until the end of his days unless and until something happens (which was not indefinite or vague). The possibility that the taxpayer would survive his wife was not unreal. He had not formed the intention necessary to acquire a domicile of choice in England and therefore his domicile of origin still subsisted.

Thus, in Bullock's case, 40 years of residence in England was insufficient to displace the taxpayer's domicile of origin. The domicile of origin can never be completely lost. Since a person cannot be without a domicile, English law automatically assumes a domicile of origin. Thus, if an individual abandons a domicile of choice without acquiring a new domicile of choice, his domicile will be one of origin ensuring that he is not without a domicile. In *Udny v Udny* (1869) LR 1 Sc & Div 441, Colonel Udny had a domicile of origin in Scotland. He acquired an English domicile of choice and resided in that country for some 32 years. He then left England and went to live in France where he resided for the following nine years. On these facts the House of Lords held that upon his departure for France, Colonel Udny abandoned his English domicile of choice but did not acquire a French domicile of choice. In consequence his Scottish domicile of origin revived.

57.3 Domicile of choice

A domicile of choice is that domicile which an individual of legal capacity, not being dependent for his domicile upon another person, may acquire by taking up residence in another country with the intention of permanently residing there. In order to establish a domicile of choice an individual must demonstrate both residence and ordinary residence.

> **Example 57.1**
>
> If David, who had a domicile of origin in England, moves to Israel permanently he acquires a domicile of choice in Israel. Some years later he changes his mind and decides to leave. However, while he is still resident in Israel his domicile does not change. When he does leave Israel he lives in the USA, principally New York State and Delaware, but does not know whether he wishes to stay in either permanently. In such a case his domicile of choice in Israel is at an end and his domicile reverts to England (HMRC IHT Manual para. IHTM13022).

In *Plummer v IR Commrs* [1987] BTC 543 the taxpayer's family moved to Guernsey, and it was her intention also to settle there. However, she remained in the UK to continue her education at school and, later, university. Her claim to have established a Guernsey domicile of choice failed, since Guernsey had not become her chief place of residence.

In *Executors of Moore deceased v IR Commrs* (2002) Sp C 335, the taxpayer was a US citizen born in 1924, with a domicile of origin in the US. In 1942, he moved from Missouri to New York, where at some point he purchased an apartment which he sold in 1983. He then rented an apartment there. During the 1980s, the deceased and his partner spent time in England and the US. They purchased a holiday home in Ireland, which was sold in the early 1990s. In March 1991, the deceased was granted consent to enter the UK for the limited purposes of his employment as an artist. He purchased a flat in London. His leave to remain in the UK expired in March 1995 but he continued to live in London. There was no attempt to deport him. In October 1995, his partner died but the deceased continued to live in the UK. He renewed his US passport on which he travelled.

The deceased died in March 1997 in London, where his funeral took place. He had made US tax returns but no UK tax returns, although following his death, payment was made to the Revenue in respect of UK income tax and capital gains tax based upon his residency in the UK. He left two wills, one in US form dealing with his US assets and the other in English form disposing of the whole of his estate worldwide (apart from those assets in the US which were dealt with separately) to a wide range of beneficiaries and English charities. He also charged his UK estate with sole liability of all his just debts, funeral and testamentary expenses. The will was executed in London.

HMRC issued a notice of determination that the deceased died domiciled in England and Wales. The US executors supported the notice but the UK executors appealed, contending that the deceased died domiciled outside England.

The Special Commissioner, in allowing the appeal, said that the issue was whether the deceased had acquired a domicile of choice in England. That required that he had a fixed and determined purpose to make England his permanent home. The intention did not have to be immutable but an intention to make a home in a new country merely for a limited time or for some temporary or special purpose was insufficient. The true test was whether he intended to make his home in the new country until the end of his days unless and until something happened to make him change his mind. The burden of proof was on the Revenue to show on the balance of probabilities that the deceased acquired a domicile of choice in England (*IR Commrs v Bullock* applied).

On the evidence, it appeared that the deceased's living solely in London prior to his death was determined more by ill health than by a desire to make England his permanent home. His nomadic existence just happened to end up in London, rather than being the result of his forming the intention to stay, as was illustrated by his short-term immigration status. He never really gave up his New York connections. There was no clear evidence that he really had the necessary intention to acquire a domicile in England and quite a lot of evidence that he kept up his connections with New York. Accordingly, he did not die domiciled in England and Wales.

In *Surveyor v IR Commrs* (2002) Sp C 339, the taxpayer was born in England in 1958 and acquired from his father a domicile of origin in the UK. He went to work in Hong Kong in 1986 and until 1991, he returned to the UK once or twice a year for holidays. He married a UK national who had been resident in Hong Kong since 1984. In 1991, the taxpayer became a partner in his firm and was given the option of returning to the UK. He refused on the basis that he saw Hong Kong as his home and had no intention of returning to the UK to live. By 1994, he had three children and he purchased an apartment in Hong Kong for use as his family home. It was sold in 1995, as it was too small to accommodate a family but the taxpayer continued to live in rented accommodation in Hong Kong. After the early 1990s, the taxpayer rarely visited the UK, except on occasional business trips.

In 1997, when the handover of Hong Kong to China was imminent, the taxpayer and his wife applied for permanent resident status, as they desired to remain permanently in Hong Kong, even though it was not compulsory. In order to obtain that status, they had satisfied certain criteria, including seven years' continuous residence in Hong Kong and the possession of certain financial and academic or business qualifications. Thereafter, they were entitled to live and work in Hong Kong without needing a work permit and/or the sponsorship of an employer. The taxpayer could also travel in and out of Hong Kong using only his permanent resident's identity card and did not need a passport or visa. He would have been subject to restrictions if he had not acquired permanent resident status.

In 1999, the taxpayer built a holiday home in Thailand. From 2000 to 2002, he lived and worked in Singapore, because his employer relocated him there, although he returned to Hong Kong on a regular basis. In July 2002, the taxpayer left his job and returned to Hong Kong, where he purchased an apartment with the help of a Hong Kong-based mortgage.

In 1999 the taxpayer created a Jersey settlement which would have contained 'excluded property' for inheritance tax purposes if he was domiciled outside the UK at that time. The Revenue took the view that the taxpayer was domiciled in the UK but the taxpayer appealed to the Special Commissioners on the basis that he had established a domicile of choice in Hong Kong.

The Special Commissioner, in allowing the appeal, said that the intention to abandon a domicile had to be unequivocal and that the standard of proof was the balance of probabilities; however, so serious a matter as the acquisition of a domicile of choice was not to be lightly inferred from slight indications or casual words. There had to be 'convincing evidence' of a settled intention to reside in another place, otherwise the person remained domiciled in England. The test was whether the taxpayer intended to make his home in a new country until the end of his days unless and until something happened to make him change his mind.

Applying those principles to the present case, the evidence supported the conclusion that, at the date of the creation of the settlement in August 1999, the taxpayer had the intention to reside permanently in Hong Kong. At that time, his residence in Hong Kong was not for a limited period or for a particular purpose but was general and indefinite in its future contemplation. His intention was directed towards one country and that was Hong Kong. His family, social business and financial ties were all there.

The Revenue had argued that when the taxpayer completed Form DOM1 in 1999, he had stated that his intention for the future was to remain permanently in the Far East and that he was building a family residence in Thailand to meet those requirements. The Far East was not a territory and did not have a distinctive legal system, both of which were a requirement for domicile. However, the form also said that the taxpayer considered himself as domiciled in Hong Kong and the statements about the Thailand house had to be considered in that context. On the evidence, the existence of the house in Thailand did not alter the intention of the taxpayer to make Hong Kong his permanent home. It did not point to the conclusion that, in August 1999, it was the taxpayer's intention to reside permanently in more than one country; nor that he intended to settle in one of several countries. Moreover, the temporary move to Singapore did not affect the taxpayer's intention in August 1999 to reside permanently in Hong Kong.

Warning!

As detailed above, in order to establish a domicile of choice an individual must demonstrate both residence and ordinary residence – see **Chapter 56** for further commentary on residence status.

57.4 Residence

Residence is a matter of fact. Alone, without the necessary intention, it will be insufficient to establish domicile. However, intention may be inferred from the fact of residence since an individual's residence in a particular country is generally regarded as being *prima facie* evidence that he is also domiciled in that country. Thus, whilst no particular length of residence is required to establish a domicile of choice, the greater the period of residence the more strongly an intention to permanently reside is to be inferred.

In *IR Commrs v Duchess of Portland* [1982] BTC 65 Nourse J opined:

> 'Residence in a country for the purposes of the law of domicile is physical presence in that country as an inhabitant of it. If the necessary intention is also there, an existing domicile of choice can sometimes be abandoned and another domicile acquired or revived by a residence of short duration in a second country.'

However, in *IR Commrs v Bullock*, a period of 40 years' residence in England was insufficient to displace the taxpayer's domicile of origin. In *Ramsay v Liverpool Royal Infirmary* [1930] AC 588, a man born in Scotland in 1845 and thus with a Scottish domicile of origin, left that country in 1892 and henceforth resided in the city of Liverpool, in England. Whilst this individual often stated that he was proud to be a Glasgow man, he expressed a determination never to return to Glasgow. He resided in Liverpool for the final 36 years of his life leaving England on only two occasions during that period, once to visit the USA and once to visit the Isle of Man. He arranged for his own burial in Liverpool. On these facts, a unanimous House of Lords held that he had died domiciled in Scotland.

In *Anderson (Executor of Muriel S Anderson) v IR Commrs* (1997) Sp C 147, the deceased had lived in Scotland all her life until, in 1974, at the age of 64, she retired and sold her home in Scotland. She moved to a property which she acquired in Cornwall, where she died eight years later, and her ashes were scattered in Scotland. A Special Commissioner concluded that her domicile remained in Scotland.

Planning point

The cases referred to above illustrate that whilst residence is an essential element in establishing a domicile of choice, it is the *intention* of the individual that is the determining factor (see HMRC6 4.3.2 for HMRC's view).

57.5 Intention

The intention which is required for the acquisition of a domicile of choice in a particular country is the intention to reside permanently or for an unlimited time in that country.

In *Re Furse (deceased); Furse v IR Commrs* [1980] 3 All ER 838 the testator had a domicile of origin in Rhode Island, USA. In 1923, at the age of 40, the testator and his family came to England, and the following year they purchased a farm in Sussex where the testator resided until his death in 1963. During his periods of residence in England the testator indicated that he would not return to the USA until such time as he was rendered incapable of leading an active life on his farm in England. Fox J held that in view of the fact that the testator's intention was to go on living his accustomed life on the farm in England and only to leave when he was no longer able to lead an active physical life there, it was clear that he had no intention, save on a vague and indefinite contingency, of leaving England. It followed that at the time of his death the testator had acquired a domicile of choice in England.

> ### Planning point
>
> Although the merest possibility of a future contingency is probably insufficient to deny the acquisition of a domicile of choice, there is no doubt that a contingency which is both realistic and unambiguous (for example, the end of a job) will have that effect. In practice, it will be rare to find a person who has consciously formed the requisite intention to acquire a domicile of choice; consequently, such an intention will normally have to be inferred from the individual's conduct. The courts will look for any instance which is evidence of a person's residence or of his intention to reside permanently in a country.

As Scarman J observed in *In the Estate of Fuld (No. 3)* [1968] P 675:

> 'Domicile cases require for their decision a detailed analysis and assessment of facts arising within that most subjective of all fields of legal inquiry – a man's mind.'

At various times virtually every aspect of human existence that could conceivably be construed as indicating the intention of an individual has been considered by the courts. In *Attorney-General v Yule & the Mercantile Bank of India* [1931] All ER Rep 400, the dominant consideration was the fact that the testator's wife continued to live in England with the only child of the marriage, whilst in *Haldane v Eckford* (1869) LR 8 Eq 631, the court considered the fact that the testator had removed the remains of his children from France to Jersey to be of crucial importance. Such factors as the purchase of a house (*Moorhouse v Lord* (1863) 10 HL Cas 272); marriage to a native of the country (*Donaldson v Donaldson* [1949] P 363); naturalisation (*Wahl v Attorney-General* [1932] All ER Rep 922); and anglophobia (*Winans v Attorney-General* [1904] AC 287) have all been considered to be of importance by the courts. An individual's replies to a Revenue questionnaire have been held not to be a reliable indication as to his domiciliary intention (*Buswell v IR Commrs* (1974) 49 TC 334).

In the famous case of *Re Clore (deceased)* [1984] BTC 8,101 the testator had received professional advice to acquire a foreign domicile. He followed the advice received and started to make arrangements to sever his more important connections with the UK. He retired as company chairman, instructed the sale of his two residences, bought an apartment in Monaco to which he removed some furniture, and made a Monaco will. Despite these actions, it was held on the evidence that he had not formed a settled intention to reside permanently in Monaco, and thus had not lost his English domicile.

It is impossible to formulate a rule specifying the weight to be given to particular evidence. All that can be gathered from the case law in this respect is that more reliance is placed upon conduct than upon declarations of intention, especially if they are oral.

57.6 Abandonment of domicile of choice

A domicile of choice is less retentive, and therefore more easily abandoned, than a domicile of origin (*Qureshi v Qureshi* [1972] Fam 173 at p. 191). There is some dispute as to the required intention necessary to abandon a domicile of choice. In seeking to abandon a domicile of choice in a particular country an individual must clearly cease to reside there. The uncertainty concerns whether such cessation of residence must be accompanied by:

- a positive intention not to return; or
- mere absence of any intention to return.

It must be remembered that where a domicile of choice is abandoned, the domicile of origin will stand in its place unless and until it is replaced by a new domicile of choice.

57.7 Married women

Formerly the domicile of a married woman was dependent upon her husband's domicile. If he acquired a new domicile of choice then she acquired it too. She retained this domicile not only as long as her husband was alive and she was legally married to him but also during widowhood or following divorce unless and until it was changed by the acquisition of another domicile.

This former rule was abolished by the Domicile and Matrimonial Proceedings Act 1973, s. 1 (operative from 1 January 1974) and a married woman can now acquire a separate domicile from her husband.

Where a woman married prior to 1974, and thus acquired her husband's domicile upon marriage, she is treated as retaining that domicile, as a domicile of choice, or domicile of origin if it be so, until it is changed by the acquisition of a new domicile of choice or revival of the domicile of origin on or after 1 January 1974 (Domicile and Matrimonial Proceedings Act 1973, s. 1(2)).

> ### Planning point
>
> It would appear that a woman, living in England with her husband, who was married before 1 January 1974 will only be able to change her (now) domicile of choice by choosing to leave her husband for permanent residence abroad!

In *IRC Commrs v Duchess of Portland*, the taxpayer was a Canadian citizen with a domicile of origin in Quebec, Canada. In 1948 she married her husband and thereby acquired an English domicile of dependency. From the time of her marriage onwards she resided in England but visited Canada for 10–12 weeks each year. It was her intention to return to Canada should her husband predecease her, and she hoped to persuade him to live in Canada upon his retirement. Following the introduction of the Domicile and Matrimonial Proceedings Act 1973, the taxpayer maintained that her annual visit to Canada in July 1974 had the effect of instituting abandonment of her (now) domicile of choice in England which in turn effected the revival of her Quebec domicile of origin. In consequence, being now not domiciled in the UK, she was no longer liable to UK tax upon income accruing to her in Canada (see now ITTOIA 2005, s. 832). Nourse J held that the Domicile and Matrimonial Proceedings Act 1973, s. 1(2) obliged a woman who had married prior to 1974 to adopt her husband's domicile as a domicile of choice. The question of whether such a woman had abandoned that domicile on or after that date was determined by the test appropriate to the abandonment of a domicile of choice. On the facts of the present case the taxpayer had not abandoned her English domicile of choice. During such visits as she had made to Canada the taxpayer had not resided in that country as an inhabitant, and her intention to do so was a future one, not a present one. Indeed, in order to adopt another new domicile Nourse J was of the opinion that the taxpayer would have to leave her husband for permanent residence abroad.

American wives of UK-domiciled taxpayers

A unique and privileged situation is given to US wives of British tax residents where the marriage took place before 1 January 1974, the date of the coming into effect of the Domicile and Matrimonial Proceedings Act 1973. Under art. 4(4) of the US–UK double taxation Convention of 31 December 1975 (SI 1980/568), a pre-1974 marriage is regarded as having taken place on 1 January 1974, and thus the new law applies to the determination of the wife's domicile. The consequence is that a pre-1974 American wife has the best of both worlds. For income tax and capital gains tax purposes only, her domicile will be determined independently of her British husband's domicile, and she can claim to be domiciled in one of the states of the USA. If her claim is successful, her overseas income and capital gains will be assessed on the remittance basis. For capital transfer tax and inheritance tax purposes, a pre-1974 American wife will generally have her husband's UK domicile, and consequently enjoy the exemption for transfers between spouses. She will in any case have a deemed UK domicile for inheritance tax purposes after 17 out of 20 years of residence.

57.8 Miscellaneous considerations

In order to establish an individual's domicile of choice, it must be clear from the circumstances that an individual's residence in a particular country is a voluntary one, i.e. that it is exercised by free will rather than under some form of constraint. There are a number of miscellaneous cases concerning such individuals as prisoners, refugees, invalids and fugitives from whatever cause. Whether such an individual acquires a new domicile of choice or retains his old domicile will be a matter decided upon the particular facts of each case. If the requisites of residence and intention are present then a new domicile of choice will be acquired, irrespective of the fact that the individual is an invalid, prisoner or refugee. Conversely, if such an individual does not possess the requisite intention, no new domicile of choice will be acquired. In *National Provincial Bank v Evans* [1947] Ch 695, the testator had an English domicile of origin. In 1921 he and his family settled in Belgium where he acquired a domicile of choice. Following the German invasion of Belgium in 1940 the testator fled to England. Whilst in England he repeatedly expressed his intention of returning to Belgium as soon as circumstances permitted. He died in England in 1944 but was found to be domiciled in Belgium at the time of his death.

A person subject to a deportation order does not lose his English domicile of choice until he is actually deported (*Cruh v Cruh* [1945] 2 All ER 545). It is thought that a person who enters a country illegally cannot acquire a domicile there.

UK tax position of overseas voters

UK taxpayers resident abroad are required, if they wish to exercise their right to vote in the UK, to complete a declaration on their registration forms which states: 'I do not intend to reside permanently outside the United Kingdom'. In a Written Answer in the House of Lords on 17 October 1986 (*Hansard*, vol. 480, col. 1018) the Secretary of State for Employment considered the effect of signing such a declaration on the signatory's domicile and UK tax position. He said that making such a declaration would not affect the UK tax position of voters who were temporarily non-resident and maintained their links with the UK. However, where an individual with a UK domicile goes abroad and it becomes necessary to determine whether he retains his UK domicile or acquires a foreign domicile, any expression of his intentions (such as the declaration) would be only one of a number of factors to be taken into account, and the question of where he was domiciled would ultimately be resolved by looking at the extent to which he had in fact severed his ties with the UK so as to make his permanent home abroad.

Domicile for tax purposes of overseas electors

In order to determine, for inheritance tax, capital gains tax and income tax purposes, whether a person is domiciled in the UK on or after 6 April 1996, the following factors are to be ignored (FA 1996, s. 200(1), (2)):

- where a person does anything with a view to, or in connection with, being registered as an overseas elector; or
- where a person, when registered as an overseas elector, votes in any election in which he is entitled to vote by virtue of being registered.

The above rule is also applied for the purposes of establishing deemed domicile within IHTA 1984, s. 267(1)(a) from the earlier date of 6 April 1993.

A person is registered as an overseas elector if he is registered in any register mentioned in the Representation of the People Act 1983, s. 12(1) on account of an entitlement to vote conferred on him by the Representation of the People Act 1985, s. 1, or is registered under the Representation of the People Act 1985, s. 3 (FA 1996, s. 200(3)).

Where a person's domicile is to be established for tax purposes, he may require that the above-mentioned factors should be taken into account (FA 1996, s. 200(4)).

Fiscal domicile

The concept of a fiscal domicile (as opposed to a legal domicile) was introduced as an anti-avoidance measure in 1975. As a result, it is possible for a person to have a legal domicile in, say, France (accepted by both English and French courts), yet be treated for the purposes of British capital transfer tax as domiciled in the UK.

Where reference is made in other taxing provisions to a person's domicile, it is generally specified whether IHTA 1984, s. 267 applies, i.e. whether the reference is to legal or fiscal domicile.

IHTA 1984, s. 267 provides that a person who is not domiciled in the UK at any given time shall be treated for inheritance tax purposes as if he were domiciled in the UK (and not elsewhere) at that time if either:

- he was domiciled in the UK within the last three years; or
- he was resident in the UK in not less than 17 of the 20 years of assessment

ending with the present one (unless he has not been so resident at any time since 9 December 1974: IHTA 1984, s. 267(3)).

Example 57.2

Adam, who had lived in England all his life, emigrated to Australia, intending never to return. Adam died two years later in Australia. Under the general law, Adam is domiciled in Australia at the date of his death. For the purposes of UK inheritance tax, Adam is treated as domiciled in the UK. Accordingly, Adam's estate will suffer tax in Britain.

Example 57.3

Bob is an American citizen who has been living and working in Britain for the past 18 years, during which time he has made frequent visits to the USA and reiterated his desire to return there permanently. Bob makes a gift of £100,000 to his daughter. Under the general law, Bob is domiciled somewhere in the USA. For the purposes of UK inheritance tax, Bob is treated as domiciled in the UK. Accordingly, if Bob dies within seven years the gift will be liable to tax regardless of where the property gifted is located.

57.9 Domicile of dependency

The domicile of a dependent person is determined by the domicile of the person on whom he or she is dependent. Should the domicile of the latter change, then the domicile of the dependent person will change accordingly. There are two categories of dependent persons: children and mentally incapacitated persons.

Warning!

A dependent person cannot alone change his domicile.

57.10 Children

At birth a child acquires a domicile of origin. This will normally be the domicile of the father unless the child is either illegitimate, or born after the father's death in which case it will be the domicile of the mother. Between the time of his birth and attaining the age of sixteen, an unmarried child is incapable of acquiring a domicile of choice by his own act. He may, of course, acquire a new domicile of dependency if that person upon whom he is dependent does so (but note the decision in *Re Beaumont* [1893] 3 Ch 490 where the court took the child's welfare into account upon the re-marriage of her mother). Once a child reaches sixteen years of age, he becomes capable of acquiring a domicile of choice in his own right (Domicile and Matrimonial Proceedings Act 1973, s. 3). However, until he acquires an independent domicile he will retain his domicile of dependency as a (now) domicile of choice (note the decision in *IRC Commrs v Duchess of Portland*.

The Domicile and Matrimonial Proceedings Act 1973, s. 3 states that a married person under the age of sixteen is capable of acquiring an independent domicile. Whilst English domiciled children are incapable of contracting marriage below this age, the provision will be important in relation to a child below that age whose foreign marriage is recognised here.

> *Planning point*
>
> It may be of interest to some advisors that in Scotland, a minor with legal capacity, i.e. a girl of 12 years or over or a boy of 14 years or over, is capable of acquiring an independent domicile.

57.11 Mentally incapacitated persons

A mentally incapacitated person will be unable to acquire an independent domicile by his own act if he is incapable of forming the requisite intention. A mentally incapacitated child will, during infancy, continue to take his father's domicile as a domicile of dependency. Upon attaining majority such a person will probably continue to depend upon the domicile of his father. An adult who becomes mentally disordered probably retains the domicile he possessed prior to the disorder (cf. the position concerning ordinary residence; *Re Mackenzie* [1941] Ch 69).

57.12 Domicile of corporations

57.12.1 General

A corporation, being a separate person in its own right, is capable of maintaining a domicile of its own. Upon incorporation it acquires a domicile of origin, i.e. the domicile of the country in which it is incorporated. The law of that country determines all issues arising from the creation, continuance and dissolution of the corporation. Generally speaking the 'residence' of a company is far more important than its domicile since it is residence that establishes liability to UK tax. Subject to the rules introduced by FA 1988, s. 66, Sch. 7 (now contained in CTA 2009, s. 15(2)-(4) and Sch. 1, para. 309 and Sch. 2, paras. 13 to 15) concerning the residence of UK-incorporated companies, a company resides in that country where its central control and management abides. The domicile of origin adheres to a corporation throughout its existence. It cannot be converted into a domicile of choice (*Gasque v IR Commrs* [1940] 2 KB 80; see below).

HMRC have published flowcharts on understanding domicile at *HMRC6: Residence, Domicile And The Remittance Basis*, 4.4.

57.12.2 Tax

> **Planning point**
>
> The domicile of a company is largely irrelevant to its tax liability. It may, however, affect the tax liability of an individual ordinarily resident in the UK who transfers assets abroad whereby a company receives income. If that company is domiciled outside the UK the income may be assessable on the individual.

Before 1965 the domicile of a company determined whether its income from possessions abroad (Schedule D Case V) was assessable on the basis of amounts remitted to the UK or the amount arising from that source. However, such income is now taxable on the same basis as trading income.

The question of a company's domicile in the context of tax avoidance by an individual transferring assets out of the UK came before the court in *Gasque v IR Commrs* [1940] 2 KB. The company concerned was incorporated in Guernsey, where it had a registered office at which the company seal was kept. All directors meetings were held in London, and the company's business was conducted from there. Holding that the company was domiciled in Guernsey, Macnaghten J observed (at p. 84):

> 'It was suggested by Mr. Needham on behalf of the Appellant that by the law of England a body corporate has no domicile. It is quite true that a body corporate cannot have a domicile in the same sense as an individual any more than it can have a residence in the same sense as an individual. But by analogy with a natural person the attributes of residence, domicile, and nationality can be given, and are, I think, given by the law of England to a body corporate. It is not disputed that a company formed under the Companies Acts has British nationality, though unlike a natural person it cannot change its nationality. So, too, I think, such a company has a domicile – an English domicile if registered in England, and a Scottish domicile if registered in Scotland. The domicile of origin, or the domicile of birth, using with respect to a company a familiar metaphor, clings to it throughout its existence.'

He later supported his view by reference to an American authority, *Bergner and Engle Brewing Co v Dreyfus* 70 American State Reports 251, where it was also held that a company has a domicile which is 'in the jurisdiction of the State which created it, and, as a consequence, has no domicile anywhere else' (per Holmes J).

57.12.3 Change of company residence

Under the law as it stood on 14 March 1988 (see below), no company could emigrate (or migrate) from the UK without obtaining the consent of the Treasury. Criminal penalties were imposed for exporting a company without consent, though there is no record of proceedings ever having been taken.

These provisions were originally introduced in 1951 at a time of economic difficulty for the UK and at a time of protectionism amongst most of the major economies. After 14 March 1988 they were considered unnecessary.

Except in relation to existing applications (see below), the requirement to obtain consent ceased with effect from 15 March 1988. Thereafter such migration is permitted following appropriate notification and payment of outstanding tax although a special charge to corporation tax may arise on assets held by the company at the date of migration in addition to the other tax consequences involving the cessation of an accounting period, leaving group relationships and the effect on capital allowances, etc. There are monetary penalties for failure to comply with such notification or payment of tax; such penalties may be levied on any company, director or other person instructing the company, although there is an exception for certain professional advisers. The Revenue may also recover any unpaid tax from other group companies or controlling directors.

The export of a UK-resident company's trade or business is also freely permitted with effect from 15 March 1988. However, Treasury consent is required for a UK-resident company to permit a non-resident company which it controls to create or issue shares or debentures and for a UK-resident company generally to transfer, etc. shares or debentures in a non-resident company which it controls.

57.12.4 Permanent establishment (or branch or agency)

A company not resident in the UK is chargeable to corporation tax only if it carries on a trade in the UK through a 'permanent establishment' (PE; for accounting periods beginning before 1 January 2003, 'branch or agency'). It is therefore necessary to determine whether the company carries on a trade in the UK and if so, whether the trade is carried on through a PE/branch or agency. The use of the substituted term 'permanent establishment' instead of 'branch or agency', introduced by the Finance Act 2003, applies for accounting periods beginning after 31 December 2002, although the actual definition of 'permanent establishment' did not come into effect until 10 July 2003 (date of Royal Assent to the Finance Act 2003).

The change of terminology made by the Finance Act 2003 is not so drastic as it may seem. The concept of a 'permanent establishment' is much used in double taxation treaties, although it is defined slightly differently in various treaties. Now there is a statutory definition for tax purposes which is intended to accord, in large part, with that in common use in the UK's tax treaties. Furthermore, the new wording is not intended to affect the existing treatment of non-residents.

For corporation tax, a company has a PE in a territory if (and only if) either:

- it carries on business (wholly or partly) through a 'fixed place of business' in that territory; or
- there is an agent in the territory acting habitually on the company's behalf who is not acting in an independent capacity in the ordinary course of his own business,

but it will not be treated as having a PE if the activities carried on are merely of a 'preparatory or auxiliary character'.

A 'fixed place of business' can include a number of possible types of establishment, but is not exclusively:

- a place of management;
- a branch (hence, the continuity with the previous terminology);
- an office, factory or workshop;
- an installation or structure for the exploration of natural resources, as well as a mine, quarry, oil or gas well, or any other place where natural resources are extracted; and
- any project for construction or installation or building site.

'Activities of a preparatory or auxiliary character' can include (again, but are not exclusively such activities):

- storage, display or delivery facilities used by the company for its goods or merchandise together with the maintenance of a stock of goods, etc. for these purposes or for processing by someone else; and
- purchasing goods, etc. or collection of information for the company.

'Branch or agency' was already defined as any factorship, agency, receivership, branch or management. It is considered that a branch must have some degree of permanence and be in the nature of an establishment through which business is conducted.

Whether a non-resident company has an agency in the UK must be determined under the general law (*American Foreign Insurance Association v Davies* (1950) 32 TC 1). For example, there can be no agency in the UK of a person who is an alien enemy (*Boston Deep Sea Fishing and Ice Co Ltd v Farnham* [1957] 1 WLR 1051).

It should be noted that whether a person is an agent of a non-resident company for the purpose of making that company liable to corporation tax does not necessarily determine whether that person is the agent for the purpose of an assessment to tax on the company's profits being made on and in the name of the agent. For example, a broker is not so assessable (TMA 1970, s. 82) but may, nevertheless, be an agent for the purpose of bringing his principal within the charge to corporation tax (*Maclaine & Co v Eccott* [1926] AC 424).

Law: CTA 2009, s. 5(1)

57.12.5 Dual-resident companies

Because the criteria for determining a company's residence vary from country to country, it is possible for a company to be resident in more than one country. In the absence of double taxation relief this could be disadvantageous to the company, whose profits might be taxed twice; however, most UK double tax agreements include provisions determining the company's residence for the purposes of the agreement, and hence the taxing rights of the respective countries.

In 1984 the Revenue became concerned about possibilities for tax avoidance by multinational companies using dual-resident companies to create tax losses within the group. Typically this would involve a company incorporated in certain US states and resident in the UK. Such a company would borrow funds either from an unconnected lender or from another group member. According to the Revenue, this resulted in tax being lost in the UK because the dual-resident's tax loss (arising out of its interest payments on the loan) could be relieved twice: once through group relief in the UK and again through the US equivalent. A Consultative Document was issued on 15 November 1984, which proposed to deny dual-resident companies – other than those which were genuinely trading – the right to surrender losses to UK group members for group relief.

These proposals were strongly criticised. In their submissions, the Institute of Chartered Accountants in England and Wales suggested that no legislation was necessary. They considered that the proposals would result in no benefit to the UK Exchequer, although they would produce substantial benefit to the US Treasury, while discouraging multinational companies from seeking funds from UK lenders.

In the light of such criticisms, the Government announced on 19 March 1985 that no legislation on dual-resident companies would be introduced in the Finance Act 1985, but that the matter would be kept under review, to see whether there was evidence of growing exploitation at the Exchequer's expense.

On 5 December 1986 the Financial Secretary to the Treasury announced the publication of a further consultative document in the following terms:

> 'I have authorised the Inland Revenue to publish today a Consultative Document introducing draft clauses on the tax treatment of dual resident companies ... Recent legislation in the US and evidence of substantially increased use of dual resident companies at the expense of the UK Exchequer now make UK legislation necessary.

The Government intend to introduce provisions dealing with dual resident companies in the Finance Bill 1987.'

The draft clauses put forward by the consultative document precluded a dual-resident company from surrendering amounts eligible for group relief for use by other members of the UK group. The dual-resident would, however, be entitled to a full deduction for its interest payments and other costs against its own current or future income. Thus the effect of the draft clauses was merely to remove the tax advantage from deliberately setting up a dual-resident company financed by borrowing. The dual-resident which was not set up to create a tax loss but which had taxable profits (after all deductions and reliefs) would be protected. The consultative document also proposed that the contemplated legislation in the UK would complement similar legislation in this area in the US.

The professional bodies repeated their earlier criticisms but the government nevertheless introduced legislation in 1987 which virtually mirrored the draft clauses in the consultative paper. The provisions limit the extent to which a 'dual-resident investing company' can, for accounting periods on or after 1 April 1987, surrender losses, interest, charges on income and other expenses by way of group relief, and are intended to complement regulations passed in the USA under the Tax Reform Act 1986. They also restrict the application of certain other reliefs applicable to groups and consortia where one of the companies involved is a dual-resident investing company. The other reliefs affected are:

- election for substitution of written-down value for market value for purposes of capital allowances on a succession to a trade from a connected person and on certain transfers between connected persons;
- transfer of assets at written-down value where there is a company reconstruction without change of ownership;
- disposals and acquisitions of assets between members of a group on a no gain/no loss basis for corporation tax on chargeable gains;
- roll-over relief on disposals of business assets outside a group; and
- sale of machinery and plant at an undervalue, and relief from the provision which requires substitution of market value for actual price for purposes of capital allowances.

A dual-resident company is defined as one which, in any accounting period, is both resident in the UK for tax purposes, and also chargeable to tax in a territory outside the UK by virtue of certain laws of that territory (CTA 2010, s. 109(1)). This could be because it derives its status as a company from those laws, because its place of management is in that territory, or because the laws of that territory provide that the company is resident there for the purposes of the charge to tax. The term 'dual-resident investing company' is intended to cover all companies which are not genuine trading companies. Accordingly an 'investing' company can be an investment company, or one which carries on a trade which consists, broadly, of the making of investments. A company is an 'investing' company for an accounting period unless it has been a 'trading company' throughout that accounting period. Even 'trading company' is here defined restrictively: it is a company the business of which consists wholly or mainly in the carrying on of a trade or trades, but there are certain circumstances in which in any accounting period a dual-resident company which carries on a trade may nonetheless be regarded as an investing company. These are as follows:

- where the company engages in trading activities which consist mainly of acquiring and holding shares, securities and investments, including interests in companies, whether or not resident in the UK, with which the dual-resident is connected;
- for accounting periods ending after 31 March 1996, where the company's main trading activity, or one of its main trading activities, consists of making payments in relation to its loan relationship;
- where the trade consists mainly of making payments which are either charges on income (including discounts on bills of exchange and the income element of deep discount securities) or similar payments which are deductible in computing profits for purposes of corporation tax;
- where the trade consists mainly of obtaining funds, by borrowing or in any other way, for the purpose of, or in connection with any of the above activities;
- where the dual-resident, while not making a trade out of these activities, carries any or all of them on to an extent which does not appear to be justified by its actual trading activities, or for a purpose which does not appear to be appropriate to its actual trade; or
- where the company's main trading activity (or one of them) is to pay charges on income and, for accounting periods ending after 31 March 1996, interest on its debtor relationships, which exceed its profits for group relief purposes, and those charges include discounts on bills of exchange (and, for accounting periods ending before 1 April 1996, the income element of deep discount securities).

Planning point

The parliamentary debates during the committee stage of the Finance Bill introducing dual-resident investing companies revealed that genuine trading companies were never intended to be affected by the provisions, and the legislature believed that this end would be achieved, and the scope for abuse limited as far as possible, by providing an exhaustive definition of 'investing company', including various categories of non-genuine trading companies, and leaving those genuine trading companies to be excluded from the provisions as the residual class.

Law: Hansard, 15 July 1987, col. 1185–1188

57.12.6 Carrying on trade in the UK

A distinction has to be drawn between a company trading in the UK and one merely trading with the UK. Lord Herschell expressed the distinction in *Grainger & Son v Gough* ([1896] AC 325 at pp. 335–336):

> 'there is a broad distinction between trading with a country, and carrying on a trade within a country. Many merchants and manufacturers export their goods to all parts of the world, yet I do not suppose anyone would dream of saying that they exercise or carry on their trade in every country in which their goods find customers ... If all that a merchant does in any particular country is to solicit orders, I do not think he can reasonably be said to exercise or carry on his trade in that country ... [Counsel] relied on the circumstance that he [foreign principal] had appointed agents in this country who regularly solicited and received orders and transmitted them to [France]. If in each case the other circumstances are the same, the contract of sale being made abroad and the delivery taking place there, I find myself quite unable to see how the mode in which orders are solicited or obtained, whether by an agent or by circulars or advertisements, can make the difference, and cause the trade in the one case to be exercised, and in the other not to be exercised, within this country.'

Two main factors determine the place where trade is conducted, namely where the contracts constituting the trade are made, and where the trading operations giving rise to the profits take place (*Erichsen v Last* (1881) 8 QBD 414; *Grainger & Son v Gough*, above; *Firestone Tyre and Rubber Co Ltd v Llewellin* (1957) 37 TC 111). The question where a trade is carried on is one of fact to be determined according to the circumstances of each case (*Maclaine & Co v Eccott*).

In *Grainger & Son v Gough* (above) a French wine merchant obtained orders in the UK through its appointed English agent. The agent, who was paid commission, transmitted orders to the French merchant for acceptance and performance. The orders were accepted by the French merchant when the wine was shipped by the merchant. The House of Lords held that the French merchant did not trade in the UK as no contracts were made there on its behalf by the agent. All the agent did was to transmit orders to France and no contract was formed until the principal agreed to comply or complied with the orders.

One of the first expressions of doubt that the place where a contract is formed is decisive in determining whether the trade is carried on in the UK was made by Atkin LJ in *Greenwood v FL Smidth & Co* [1921] 3 KB 583 at p. 593:

> 'The contracts in this case were made abroad. But I am not prepared to hold that this test is decisive. I can imagine cases where the contract of re-sale is made abroad, and yet the manufacture of the goods, some negotiation of the terms, and complete execution of the contract take place here under such circumstances that the trade was in truth exercised here. I think that the question is, where do the operations take place from which the profits in substance arise?'

The House of Lords confirmed this view in *Firestone v Llewellin*. In that case the UK subsidiary of a US company manufactured tyres in the UK and supplied them to European agents of the US parent company at cost plus five per cent. The court held that both the UK company and its US parent company through the agency of the former, carried on the trade in the UK; and that the place where the master agreement was made between the subsidiary and the parent company, regulating the trade between them, was not conclusive. In the course of his opinion Lord Radcliffe said (37 TC at pp. 142–143):

> 'the law requires that great importance should be attached to the circumstance of the place of sale. It follows, then, that the place of sale will not be the determining factor if there are other circumstances present that outweigh its importance or unless there are no other circumstances that can. Since the Courts have not attempted to lay down what those other circumstances are or may be, singly or in combination, and it would be, I believe, neither right nor possible to try to do so, I think it true to say that, within wide limits which determine what is a permissible conclusion, the question whether a trade is exercised within the United Kingdom remains, as it began, a question of fact for the Special Commissioners. In my opinion, therefore, Harman, J, in the High Court and Lord Evershed MR, in the Court of Appeal were well founded in laying stress on the observation of Atkin LJ, in *F. L. Smidth & Co. v Greenwood*, 8 TC 193, at pages 203–204:
>
>> "The contracts in this case were made abroad. But I am not prepared to hold that this test is decisive. I can imagine cases where the contract of re-sale is made abroad, and yet the manufacture of the goods, some negotiation of the terms, and complete execution of the contract take place here under such circumstances that the trade was in truth exercised here. I think that the question is, where do the operations take place from which the profits in substance arise?"
>
> Now, in the present case the sales from which trading arose were the dealings by virtue of which Brentford disposed of Firestone tyres to the Swedish distributor in response to the orders received from the latter. It is, I think, the major fallacy of the Appellants' argument that it seeks to determine the locality of this trading by the locality which the law would attribute to the master agreement between Akron and that distributor. In my opinion, the master agreement has very little, if any, significance for this purpose. It was important, of course, for other purposes. It was one of the basic treaties upon which the international organisation of Akron was built up. It settled many particulars of the terms of trade upon which would take place the dealings of those who were to come within the operational range of that organisation. But it did not itself constitute the contracts of sale the locality of which was to be so important in deciding whether Akron was carrying on any trade inside the United Kingdom. The sales to look at for that purpose were the dealings which took place in the course of trade between Brentford and the Swedish distributor, and those dealings consisted of invitations to trade received by Brentford in England, the manufacture or appropriation of stock in England in response to those invitations, the delivery of the stock free alongside vessel in England in discharge of the order, and the receipt of the payment in a bank in England. Those operations constituted the exercising of a trade in England.'

What emerges from the authorities is that a trade is carried on where the operations which give rise to the profits of the trade are carried out. In determining that question of fact one of the important circumstances that has to be taken into consideration is the place where the contracts are made.

> **Planning point**
>
> Clearly this test does not apply to income other than from a trade or profession, which arises where the source of such income is located. In the case of such other income the location of the contract continues to be of major importance.

Law: Alloway v Phillips [1980] 1 WLR 888

57.13 Domicile and inheritance tax

57.13.1 General

If a person is domiciled in the UK, then inheritance tax is charged on his death on his whole estate wherever situated. In such cases, the locality of the assets is not of direct relevance for tax purposes, although it may be of importance in relation to other matters, e.g. the law of succession.

> **Warning!**
>
> The location of assets may in turn have an effect on tax payable, e.g. if the availability of an exemption depends upon the locality of the asset: 'I bequeath to my wife all my American property ... '

If a person is domiciled outside the UK, inheritance tax will be charged on his death only on property situated in the UK, since the rest will be 'excluded property' under IHTA 1984, s. 6(1). In such cases, the locality of assets is important.

The above applies equally to chargeable lifetime transfers, including potentially exempt transfers which become chargeable.

The locality of an asset is a matter to be determined by the general law. Sometimes this gives way to a special provision in an appropriate double taxation agreement, as discussed. The following paragraphs summarise the general law regarding the situation of the more common types of property, complicated by the fact that occasionally English and Scots law do not give the same result.

Law: IHTA 1984, s. 267(1)

57.13.2 Non-UK domiciled persons

A non-domiciled person is liable to inheritance tax on gifts, in lifetime or on death, of property situated in the UK but not property situated abroad. A person with an overseas domicile becomes domiciled in the UK for inheritance tax purposes only with effect from the beginning of the seventeenth year of residence in any consecutive 20 tax years. Domicile for inheritance tax continues for three years after domicile has been lost for other circumstances.

The spouse exemption is limited to £55,000 where the donor spouse is UK-domiciled and the recipient is not. The donor spouse could use the nil rate band to transfer more property to the other spouse. A larger gift could escape tax as a potentially exempt transfer.

57.13.3 Interests in land

Real property (in Scotland, heritable property) is situated where the land is located. This extends to interests in land, such as that of a mortgagee, and, in Scotland, that of a heritable creditor.

Double taxation agreements make a distinction between immovable and movable property. This corresponds to some extent with the distinction between real and personal property, and more closely with the distinction in Scotland between heritable and movable property. Any question as to whether an item of property is immovable is determined according to the *lex situs*.

57.13.4 Tangible movable property

Tangible movable property is normally regarded as situated where it is physically (see *Re Haig; Harris v Drayton* (1922) 17 ATC 635). Thus, the location of a movable item at the moment of transfer/death will be of great importance.

> **Warning!**
>
> A difficulty may arise as regards property temporarily in or out of the UK, because of the law as to incidence of tax under IHTA 1984, s. 211. The position regarding incidence of tax on property outside the UK is highly uncertain, but it is at least arguable that it continues to bear its own tax. Since the location of movable property is determined by physical situation, it would follow that such property might fortuitously bear its own tax, to the detriment of the person to whom it is bequeathed.

Works of art are treated in the same way as other items of movable property.

However, there is an extra-statutory concession (ESC F7) for works of art temporarily situated in the UK at the date of the owner's death. If the work of art becomes liable to inheritance tax solely because of its presence in the UK at that date, the liability is waived if the work was brought in solely for public exhibition, cleaning or restoring. (A similar concession applies in respect of the ten-year charge on property held on discretionary trusts.)

The Paymaster General announced, on 25 February 2003, an extension to ESC F7 in circumstances where, for example, a work of art is already in the UK when it is first acquired by a foreign buyer, and the new owner allows a period of loan to a public collection here before taking it to a permanent home abroad.

> **Warning!**
>
> The position as regards goods in transit between countries is unclear. There is authority that goods in transit to England are situated there (*Attorney-General v Pratt* (1874) LR 9 Ex 140), but with the change to capital transfer tax/inheritance tax this point may require to be considered afresh.

57.13.5 Business assets

The interest of a partner of a business is, as a rule, in an undivided share of the whole business, rather than in certain specific assets. Accordingly, an interest in a business, including goodwill, is situated where the business is carried on. Where a single business is carried on in the UK and abroad, the situation of the business will be that of the head office.

57.13.6 Shares and securities

Registered shares and securities are situated where the register is properly kept, which in turn is a matter of general law of the country of incorporation. The place where business is carried on is not relevant; nor is the residence or domicile of the directors. The test is: where could the shares be effectively dealt with as between the shareholder and the company, so that the transferee will be legally entitled to all the rights of a member? (*R v Williams* [1942] AC 541.)

In the case of companies with a dual register, the shares are situated with the principal register. If both registers are principal registers, so that shares can be transferred on either one, the shares will be situated where the transferor would have been most likely to deal with them (*Standard Chartered Bank Ltd v IR Commissioners* [1978] 3 All ER 644). The physical location of the share certificates is not conclusive.

British Government stock is situated in the UK, as are National Savings Income Bonds. Securities issued by the Inter-American Development Bank are treated for inheritance tax purposes as situated outside the UK (FA 1976, s. 131(2)).

57.13.7 Bearer securities

Since title to bearer securities is passed by delivery, they are situated where the share certificate is at the time of the transfer.

Eurobonds are a form of bearer security; however, a particular problem has arisen in respect that Eurobonds held through the Euroclear system cannot be identified as situated in any particular place. In these circumstances, it is understood that the Capital Taxes office are treating Eurobonds held through the Euroclear system as situated in the UK if they are so held through a UK broker, on the basis that the bond holder's rights against the broker are located where the broker carries on business.

57.13.8 Debts and other legal *choses*

As a rule, debts are situated where the debtor resides and hence where payment can be required (*English, Scottish and Australian Bank Ltd v IR Commissioners* [1932] AC 238). A corporate debtor which carries on business in a number of countries is resident in all of them and accordingly the debt may be regarded as situated in each place where the corporation carries on business: *New York Life Insurance Co v Public Trustee* [1924] 2 Ch 101 per Atkin LJ at p. 120. It may be, however, that the document creating the debt specifies the place at which the obligation to pay is to be performed in which case the debt is situated there: *Kwok v Commissioner of Estate Duty* [1988] BTC 8,073; (1988) 1 CTC 303.

This general rule is applicable to bank accounts, which are situated at the branch where the account is kept, rather than at the bank's head office.

Likewise, the proceeds of a life insurance policy are situated where payment may be demanded.

A negotiable instrument, being transferable by delivery, is situated wherever the instrument is, at least where there is an available market for its negotiation: *Kwok v Commr of Estate Duty* above, per Lord Oliver (delivering the Privy Council's judgment) at p. 8,077.

An exception to the rule is specialty debts, which are situated where the deed itself actually is. (This distinction is not recognised in Scotland.)

57.13.9 Equitable interests

An interest in an unadministered estate is situated at the *forum* of administration: either the domicile of the deceased or the residence of the personal representatives.

The situation of other equitable interests will depend upon whether the transferor had an absolute right to the trust assets *in specie* – in which case his interest is located with the assets themselves – or merely a right of action against a trustee or other person, in which case his interest is a *chose* in action and located where it could be enforced.

It is thought that the position in Scotland, as regards beneficiaries in executries and trusts, is similar.

57.14 Capital gains tax

57.14.1 General

An individual is domiciled in the country which is his permanent home. Every child acquires a domicile of origin at birth (normally that of the father). His later actions may lead to a new domicile of choice; should he abandon his domicile of choice, he will revert to his domicile of origin. Unlike residence, domicile is difficult to change. An individual is presumed to retain his domicile of origin unless there is strong evidence to the contrary. The general law of domicile is discussed in relation to inheritance tax.

> **Warning!**
>
> Proposals have been made for reform of the law of domicile. If enacted, the main effect would be to do away with the doctrines of domicile of origin and revival of domicile of origin. Instead, an individual who settles in a country with the intention of residing there indefinitely will be domiciled in that country.

A person's domicile status for, *inter alia*, capital gains tax purposes will not be affected, at any time on or after 6 April 1996, by any 'relevant action' taken in connection with UK electoral rights. A 'relevant action' occurs where a person takes any action in order to become registered as an 'overseas elector', or votes in any election which he or she is entitled to vote in, by virtue of being registered as an overseas elector.

A person is registered as an overseas elector if he or she is registered in any register mentioned in the Representation of the People Act 1983, s. 12(1), by virtue of s. 1, or is registered under s. 3 of the 1985 Act.

However, that person may require the above rule to be disregarded for the purposes of establishing his or her capital gains tax liability.

Thus, voting in UK elections will not prejudice a claim that an individual is not domiciled in the UK. However, anyone wanting to be regarded as UK-domiciled for the purposes of a particular liability may require their 'relevant actions' to be taken into account. Such a situation might arise where a resident but non-domiciled individual disposes of a foreign-sited asset at a loss, which is not an allowable loss. By trying to bring himself within the definition of 'domicile' for the purposes of that transaction, the individual may be entitled to an allowable loss to set against gains on UK-sited assets.

Whilst a company can have a domicile, which is where it is incorporated, the company's residence, as opposed to the company's domicile, is the relevant factor for the purposes of corporation tax.

Law: FA 1996, s. 200(2), (3), FA 1996, para. (4); TCGA 1992, s. 16(4)

57.14.2 Relief for non-domiciliaries

The relevance of domicile in the context of capital gains tax is in connection with gains arising on disposals of assets situated outside the UK.

For years up to and including 2007–08, gains on such assets were only within the charge to tax to the extent that they were remitted to the UK (TCGA 1992, s. 12, prior to amendment by FA 2008). Corresponding overseas losses were not available for relief against gains on either overseas or UK assets (TCGA 1992, s. 16(4), prior to its omission by FA 2008), presumably on the basis that, whilst it is possible to remit funds which represent a gain, it is not, by definition, possible to remit funds which represent a loss.

With the changes introduced by FA 2008, the universal right of a UK-resident but non-domiciled individual to be taxed on the remittance basis was withdrawn. Instead the automatic right to the basis is restricted to two categories of non-domiciliaries and the remainder are given the opportunity to make a claim.

For income tax purposes the remittance basis is available if the individual is UK-resident but either not ordinarily resident or not domiciled in the UK. However for the basis to be applicable for capital gains tax the individual must be non-domiciled; thus if he is UK-resident and domiciled but not ordinarily resident, the remittance basis will only be available in respect of income tax.

Those who make a claim for the remittance basis to apply for a particular year lose their entitlement to the annual exemption for that year regardless of whether there are remitted foreign gains in that year or not.

Where the remittance basis applies for capital gains tax for a tax year and an amount of 'foreign chargeable gains' has been remitted to the UK in that year, the individual is deemed to have realised chargeable gains equal to the amount of the remittance (TCGA 1992, s. 12(2), (3)). Foreign chargeable gains in this context are gains on the disposal of assets which are situated outside the UK.

As part of the changes introduced by FA 2008, non-domiciliaries were given a one-off opportunity to elect for a measure of relief for losses arising on disposals of assets situated outside the UK. The first year, from 2008–09, for which the individual makes a claim for the remittance basis to apply (as opposed being entitled to the basis without a claim) and for which he is non-domiciled, is termed the 'relevant year'. Losses arising on non-UK sited assets (termed 'foreign losses') in that year, and all subsequent years, will be available for relief if he makes an irrevocable election within five years of 31 January following the end of the relevant year. A failure to make such an election will mean that foreign losses for the relevant year and all subsequent years in which the individual is non-UK domiciled, will not be allowable losses.

Where an election is made, two specific provisions apply for the relevant year and all subsequent years:

Gains arising in one year remitted in a subsequent year

Where, for any year (termed the 'applicable tax year');

- foreign chargeable gains have arisen to the individual in a previous year (whether that is the 'relevant year' or any year subsequent to that year), and
- chargeable gains are treated as arising to him in the applicable tax year because of remittances of those earlier foreign gains in that year (termed the 'relevant gains'),

the amount on which he is chargeable is to be the sum of:

(a) the amount on which he would have been chargeable in respect of gains under TCGA 1992, s. 2(2) or s. 2(4) if the relevant gains were ignored. This amount therefore comprises:

- gains on UK sited assets;
- plus gains attributed to the individual as settlor of a non-resident settlement;
- less allowable losses (including foreign losses) of the current year and any unrelieved allowable losses of earlier years; and
- plus gains attributed to him as beneficiary of a non-resident settlement.

(b) the amount of the relevant gains.

This provision effectively 'ring-fences' the foreign gains so that the annual exemption, if due for the applicable year (because a claim to remittance basis has not been made for that year) cannot be set against foreign gains charged for the year but which arose in an earlier year for which the annual exemption was not due.

Remittance basis applying in years subsequent to the relevant year

Where an election has been made for the relevant year, then for that and any subsequent year for which the individual is entitled to the remittance basis (whether by means of a claim or otherwise) and for which he is non-UK domiciled, allowable losses are to be set against gains in the following order:

(a) foreign gains arising in the year to the extent that they have been remitted to the UK in that year;
(b) foreign gains arising in the year which have not been remitted; and
(c) all other gains arising in that year (i.e. on UK assets or gains attributed to the individual as a settlor of a non-resident settlement, but excluding gains attributed as a beneficiary of such a settlement).

Where losses are thus deductible against foreign gains in (b) above, and some part of those gains are unrelieved, the losses are to be deducted from those gains in reverse chronological order according to the dates on which they arose (in other words a 'last in-first out basis'. Where more than one gain arose on a particular day and the losses available to be set against them is less that the total of the gains, the loss is to be allocated to each gain on a proportionate basis.

Once this calculation has been performed, the amount on which the individual is taxable is determined under the normal rules, excluding the annual exemption (where appropriate) and only deducting the allowable losses attributed to the current years remitted foreign gains, and gains on UK assets or attributed as settlor of a non-resident settlement (items (a) and (c) above). The effect of this provision is to prevent the losses (including foreign losses) set against UK gains from being increased by a decision not to remit foreign gains in that year.

Where an amount of loss has been deducted from an unremitted foreign gain, the amount of that gain for future charging purposes is to be regarded as reduced by the amount of the loss. The effect therefore is that effective relief for that loss will only be obtained as and when that gain is remitted to the UK.

Law: TCGA 1992, s. 16ZD(3)

57.14.3 Remittances

The definition of 'received in the UK' follows that for income tax and covers gains used to settle debts incurred in the UK, debts incurred outside the UK where the money has been brought into the UK and debts replacing such original debts (TCGA 1992, s. 12(2)).

In practice, the Revenue do not normally seek to assess remittances of gains arising before a foreign domiciliary comes to take up residence in the UK.

> ### Planning point
>
> A non-domiciled UK resident needs to take particular care that his remittances of money to the UK cannot be categorised by HMRC as capital gains (or income). Such a person needs to maintain separate bank accounts abroad for.
>
> (1) Capital – this should contain the capital owned when the visitor arrives in the UK, and the proceeds of sale of an item giving rise to a capital loss.
>
> (2) Income – interest on bank deposit should be credited directly to the income account, so that the capital account cannot be treated as mixed.
>
> (3) Capital gains account – this should receive the sale proceeds of capital gains.

Careful segregation of bank accounts should protect non-domiciled residents from unjustified capital gains charges. Much has been written about the protection offered by *Clayton's Case* [1816] 1 Mer 529. Where a creditor (say, a bank) pays a debtor (e.g. a non-domiciled resident) a debt which consists of more than one item, the debts are cleared as follows:

- any debt which the debtor says he is clearing when he makes the payment, earlier items being taken before later; and
- in the absence of any statement by the debtor, in any order chosen by the creditor.

Thus, an instruction by the taxpayer to his overseas bank indicating that he is withdrawing capital from his capital account might protect him from a capital gains tax charge, even if the bank misinterpreted his instructions. A wise taxpayer would not rely on *Clayton's Case*; it does not accord with the Revenue's procedure, and it is safer to make sensible administrative arrangements.

57.14.4 Nationality

Nationality is not the same as domicile, but someone who ceases to be a citizen of one country and becomes a citizen of another country may well be acquiring a new domicile. Such an act is a strong indication of seeking to make a home in the new country.

Nationality can also be relevant in the context of double tax treaties, in particular that with the US, which taxes its citizens wherever they are. It is not generally important in domestic tax law, except for income tax provisions which tax Commonwealth citizens and citizens of the Republic of Ireland who have been ordinarily resident in the UK and have left the UK for occasional residence abroad.

57.15 Remittance basis

57.15.1 Outline

Finance Act 2008 introduced legislation that significantly changes the way that foreign income of people who are resident in the UK (see 55.2), but are not ordinarily resident (see 55.2.3) and/or not domiciled here, is taxed. The changes took effect from 6 April 2008.

Individuals who are resident in the UK, but who are not ordinarily resident and/or not domiciled here, are entitled to claim the remittance basis of taxation. This means that, while they are taxed on the same basis as resident UK taxpayers on income and gains arising in the UK, they are also taxed on any income or gains they 'remit' to this country (i.e. bring into the UK from overseas). They are not taxed on their foreign income and gains which remain outside the UK.

Where the remittance basis applies, it allows the taxpayer to defer tax on foreign income or gains that have arisen until amounts in respect of those income or gains are received in the UK (if they ever are). It does, however, have to be shown that what is received in the UK is 'in respect' of that income or gain.

Broadly, the legislation covers three categories of tax charge, namely relevant foreign income, employment income and capital gains. Historically, the remittance basis has applied automatically for both employment income and capital gains, but from 6 April 2008, the claims mechanism applies to all three categories of charge. It is therefore up to taxpayers who are UK resident but not domiciled or not ordinarily resident, to decide whether they wish to be taxed on the remittance basis for each tax year.

Self-assessment tax returns allow individuals who are entitled to use the remittance basis to make a claim if they so wish. Those eligible can choose from one tax year to the next whether they wish to be taxed on this basis.

> **Planning point**
>
> The changes do not apply to those non-UK domiciled individuals whose unremitted income and/or gains for a tax year are less than £2,000 (see 57.15.4). They will automatically be taxed on the remittance basis for that year, without the need for a claim (ITA 2007, s. 809C). In addition, individuals entitled to claim the remittance basis who have no UK income or gains, and who do not remit any foreign income or gains, will not have to claim the remittance basis in years they are not liable to the RBC. This avoids them having to complete a self-assessment return only so they can claim the remittance basis and then have no tax to pay.

> **Planning point**
>
> The obligation to file a self assessment return on individuals with small amounts of income from overseas employment has been removed with effect from 6 April 2008 where the overseas income is less than £10,000 and overseas bank interest is less than £100 in any tax year, all of which is subject to a foreign tax.

57.15.2 Personal allowances

From 6 April 2008, taxpayers who make a claim to be taxed on the remittance basis (under ITA 2007, s. 809B) will lose their entitlement to various personal tax allowances. Section s. 809G lists these as, for income tax purposes, personal allowance and blind person's allowance, tax reductions for married couples and civil partners, and payments for life insurance; and for capital gains tax (CGT), the annual exempt amount.

This does not, however, apply to individuals who are eligible to use the remittance basis without a claim in a tax year because they meet the conditions set out in s. 809C (because their unremitted income and gains for a tax year are less than £2,000). They retain their entitlement to all those various allowances and reliefs.

Law: FA 2008, Sch. 7

57.15.3 £30,000 annual charge

Eligible adults (individuals who are 18 in the relevant year) who choose to be taxed on the remittance basis and have been UK resident for longer than seven out of the past ten years will have to pay an additional tax charge. This charge, known as the remittance basis charge (RBC), is set at £30,000 (ITA 2007, s. 809H). The charge is in addition to the tax liability for the year in question on any income and gains remitted to the UK, and any UK income or gains taxed on the arising basis. The £30,000 will be paid on nominated income and gains not remitted to the UK in the year. (These income and gains are called 'nominated' income and gains because the taxpayer is free to nominate the income and gains not remitted to the UK in the year on which tax of £30,000 is payable. For example, this could be £75,000 of unremitted foreign deposit interest on which UK tax was due at 40 per cent, so leading to an income tax charge of £30,000.) If, in subsequent years, that 'nominated' income or gains upon which the RBC has been paid is, in fact, remitted to the UK, then that income or gains will not be taxed again.

However, there are ordering rules to ensure that if 'nominated' income or gains is, in fact, remitted when other untaxed income and gains remain unremitted, then that unremitted income and gains is treated as being remitted before the 'nominated' income and gains.

> **Planning point**
>
> The record keeping necessary for s. s. 809H and s. 809I can be avoided if individuals ensure that 'nominated' income or gains upon which the RBC is paid are not remitted to the UK, or only remitted after the remittance of all other unremitted income and gains since the first year of residence from April 2008. If an individual is confident they will never need to remit that 'nominated' income or gains, paying the RBC will not involve any extra complexity or record keeping.

The £30,000 charge is payable if the taxpayer has been resident in the UK for more than seven out of the last ten tax years up to and including the year in which a claim is made under s. 809B. The period of residence might be continuous or broken.

Law: ITA 2007, s. s. 809H and s. 809I

57.15.4 £2,000 de-minimis rule

The revised remittance basis procedures outlined above do not apply where an individual has unremitted foreign income and gains of less than £2,000 in any tax year. The remittance basis applies automatically to overseas income and gains without a claim. In addition, they will not lose personal allowances, or be required to pay the £30,000 tax charge.

> **Planning point**
>
> From 6 April 2008 onwards, HMRC will assume that taxpayers with unremitted foreign income and gains of less than £2,000 have used the remittance basis unless they are notified that the taxpayer wishes to be taxed under the arising basis. In addition, a claim to use the remittance basis will not be required where an individual has total UK income or gains of no more than £100 which has been taxed in the UK, provided they make no remittances to the UK in that tax year.

57.15.5 Anti-avoidance

Several measures have been brought into play from 6 April 2008, which are designed to close various loopholes and address certain flaws and anomalies in the way the rules previously operated. HMRC perceived that those eligible for the remittance basis could often arrange their affairs so that they received or enjoyed foreign income or gains in the UK without any liability to UK tax, even though they had in substance remitted the foreign income or gains to the UK. The general aim of the new measures is to ensure that income or gains to which the remittance basis applies are only excluded from charge to UK tax where they are genuinely kept offshore and not brought to the UK. Where they are in effect remitted to the UK in such a manner that the individual has the use or enjoyment of them in the UK, the individual will be liable to tax on them if he has effectively remitted them to the UK. The various measures are summarised in the following paragraphs.

57.15.6 Ceased sources

Under a long-standing interpretation of the legislation and case law in respect of relevant foreign income, HMRC have accepted that no tax liability arises if the source of the income benefiting from the remittance basis no longer exists in the year of remittance – the 'source doctrine'. This meant that if an individual arranged for a bank account to be closed at the end of one tax year and remitted the interest in the next tax year, there was generally no liability to tax. However, Finance Act 2008, Schedule 7 overturned this 'source doctrine', so that a charge can now be imposed where relevant foreign income that has benefited from the remittance basis is remitted, whether or not the source exists in the year of remittance. (That was already the case with employment income and capital gains, where the legislation was originally cast in terms preventing this outcome.)

57.15.7 Cash only

Previously, on the basis of case law, the general view was that relevant foreign income could only be taxed if it was brought into the UK as cash. This meant that if a taxpayer using the remittance basis turned relevant foreign income into an asset outside the UK and then imported that asset, it was unlikely that any charge would arise on the income (unless and until the asset was sold in the UK and there were cash proceeds). However, *Finance Act* 2008, Schedule 7 introduced a measure to ensure that money, property and services derived from relevant foreign income brought into the UK will, in future, be treated as a remittance and taxed as such.

Any asset purchased out of untaxed relevant foreign income which an individual or another relevant person owned on 11 March 2008 will be exempt from a charge under the remittance basis, for so long as that person owns it, even if the asset is outside the UK at that date and later imported.

Any asset purchased out of untaxed relevant foreign income and in the UK on 5 April 2008 will also be exempt from a charge under the remittance basis, for so long as the present owner owns it, even if the asset is later exported and then re-imported.

> **Planning point**
>
> For the future, the following exemptions are available to assets brought to the UK, purchased out of untaxed relevant foreign income:
>
> - the 'personal use rule', which applies to clothes, shoes, jewellery and watches, for the personal use of the individual or members of their immediate family;
> - the 'repair rule' for assets brought to the UK for repair and restoration;
> - the 'temporary importation rule' where assets are in the UK for less than a total period of 275 days; and
> - assets costing less than £1,000.
>
> There is also a new 'public access rule', allowing exemption for works of art, collectors' items and antiques brought into the UK for public display.
>
> If an asset is sold in the UK while any of these exemptions are in force, the exemption will cease at that point and the tax charge that arises under existing law will apply at that point.
>
> If an asset is sold in the UK while any of these exemptions is in force, the exemption will cease at that point and the tax charge that arises under existing law will apply at that point.
>
> If property meets the personal use rule, the repair rule or the public access rule then the time during which it meets any of those rules is taken into account in deciding whether it meets the temporary importation rule. So, for example, if an asset comes to the UK for repair, and that repair takes 75 days, then after the repair is complete it can be kept in the UK for a further 200 days under the temporary importation rule. Property to which the temporary importation rule applies remains exempt if, before the end of the 275-day period, it is then put on public display and meets the terms of the public access rule.

The existing rules for employment income and capital gains already tax assets brought into the UK where they were purchased out of untaxed foreign employment income or capital gains. Those rules remain unchanged (except in relation to the public access rule).

57.15.8 Overseas mortgages

Previously, taxpayers using the remittance basis who borrowed money from an overseas lender could repay the interest on that loan out of untaxed foreign income without giving rise to a tax charge on the remittance basis, even if the loan was advanced into the UK. Without special rules, the effect of other changes to the legislation made by Finance Act 2008, Schedule 7 would be that repayments on such loans advanced to the UK would be treated as a remittance on or after 6 April 2008. Schedule 7, Paragraph 86 therefore provides 'grandfathering' provisions for certain loans made before 12 March 2008. Subject to certain conditions, interest payments out of untaxed relevant foreign income will not therefore be treated as a remittance on or after 6 April 2008.

Broadly, the conditions are that the loan must be made to an individual outside the UK before 12 March 2008. It must be for the sole purpose of enabling the individual to purchase a residential property in the UK. Before 6 April 2008 the money had to be received in the UK and used to acquire the property, and repayment of the debt has to be secured on that property.

These rules apply to interest payments for the remaining period of the loan, or until 5 April 2028 if sooner. If the terms of the loan are varied or any further advances made after 12 March 2008, the repayments will be treated as remittances from that point.

57.15.9 Location of source of income or asset

It is clear from the foregoing that this is a matter of vital importance. There is a set of statutory rules for CGT. The rules for income tax and inheritance tax are based on case law but are not markedly different. For example, shares are located where they are registered or principally registered (if in more than one place) or where the certificates are kept if they are bearer shares. A debt is located where the debtor resides, an intangible right where it can be enforced or, as with patents or copyrights, where it is registered. A debt under seal is located where the document is kept (though the Revenue challenge this for income tax).

> **Planning point**
>
> By holding assets through a foreign company or trust rather than directly, an individual may be able to have a foreign source of income or asset separate from the underlying source or asset of the company or trust which may well be located in the UK. Anti-avoidance legislation exists. The capital gains of overseas companies that would be close companies if they were resident in the UK can be attributed to UK-resident shareholders. Shareholders must be domiciled in the UK and either resident or ordinarily resident.

57.16 Remittance of money

The remittance basis applies to actual sums received in the UK. This has caused difficulties. Clearly cash, i.e. notes and coins, will be chargeable, but beyond that the position is less certain. In *Gresham Life Assurance Society Ltd v Bishop* [1902] AC 287 the taxpayer company was registered in the UK. It held investments in a number of other countries. The interest on those investments was either:

(1) reinvested in those countries;

(2) remitted direct to other foreign countries for investment; or

(3) remitted to the UK.

All moneys in each of the three categories were included in the taxpayer's end of year accounts. The Crown contended that in view of the fact that the sums appeared in the end of year accounts, there was constructive remittance. The House of Lords unanimously rejected the notion of constructive remittance. Only sums actually remitted to the UK (item (3) above) were chargeable. In discussing items (1) and (2), Lord Halsbury LC opined (at pp. 291–292):

> 'In no way that I can give any reasonable interpretation to has the money reached this country or been received in this country ... I do not think any amount of book-keeping or treatment of these assets, wherever they may be, will be equivalent to or the same thing as receiving the amount in this country.'

Lord Shand noted that when the company entered the sums in its end of year accounts, it did so as property which the company had acquired abroad and which had not been brought to the UK or received there. It was part of their foreign assets ([1902] AC at p. 294). Thus, mere entry of a sum in a balance sheet will not amount to a remittance if the sum itself remains outside the UK. Whether the sum does actually remain outside the UK is a question of fact. In *Scottish Mortgage Company of New Mexico v McKelvie* (1886) 2 TC 165, the taxpayer company had a sum of income overseas available for remittance to the UK, and a capital sum available in the UK which it intended to transmit overseas for investment purposes. It made entries in its accounts to indicate that the overseas sum was remitted to the UK and the UK sum was transmitted overseas, although no money was actually transferred. It then proceeded to pay a dividend out of its UK profits. The cross entries in the books and the payment of dividend (which could only be paid out of income and not capital) were held sufficient to indicate remittance.

The issue of physical remittance has been further clouded by the use of loans and borrowed money, e.g. where the taxpayer borrows money in the UK and repays the debt overseas using funds that, if remitted to the UK, would fall liable to tax on the remittance basis. In *Thomson v Moyse* [1961] AC 967 the taxpayer, who was resident but not domiciled in the UK, was entitled to income from a trust in New York. At various times he sold cheques, drawn in dollars on his New York bank account, to banks in the UK. The UK bank then sold the dollar cheques to the Bank of England and the taxpayer's UK bank account was then credited with the sterling equivalent. The cheques were cleared at the New York bank and the proceeds credited to the account of the Bank of England with the Federal Reserve Bank. The taxpayer was assessed under (former) Case IV and V of Sch. D. He contended that the sterling sums received by him in the UK were not remittances of US income but arose from contracts concluded by him in the UK. The special commissioners accepted the taxpayer's argument, as did Wynn-Parry J and a majority of the Court of Appeal. The House of Lords, however, unanimously rejected it. (For discussion of this case and remittances generally see *Coles* [1979] British Tax Review 283.) The basis of the House of Lords decision was that the taxable income available to the taxpayer in New York had suffered a reduction whilst he had received a corresponding increase in funds available to him in the UK. The increase in UK funds was 'traceable' to the diminution in US funds. This fact was sufficient to render the UK sums chargeable, the House not concerning itself with the technical means by which the conversion of dollars into sterling was achieved (see Lord Reid at p. 990 and Lord Radcliffe at p. 993).

In *Harmel v Wright* (1974) 49 TC 149, the taxpayer was resident in the UK but domiciled in South Africa. He was in receipt of a substantial salary as an employee in South Africa, such salary being chargeable under Sch. E, Case III if remitted to the UK (from 2003–04, Sch. E, Case III is obsolete, the equivalent charging provisions for employment income are ITEPA 2003, s. 22 and s. 26). In order to avoid such a charge the taxpayer employed a scheme whereby his salary was invested in a company in South Africa. That company then lent the money received from the taxpayer to a second company which in turn lent the borrowed money to the taxpayer in the UK. In each case the loans were free of interest and repayable on demand. The taxpayer was assessed to Sch. E, Case III on the amount of the loans received in the UK. HMRC contended that the loans were in effect remitted income. The taxpayer contended that they were merely loans. Templeman J, applying *Thomson v Moyse* (above), held that the loans represented emoluments which, since they had been remitted, were chargeable to UK tax. Again the notion of tracing was applied; it was not necessary to pierce the corporate veil. Templeman J remarked (at p. 157):

> 'In my judgment, on the wording of [the section] one does not need to strip aside the corporate veil if you find that emoluments, which mean money, come in at one end of a conduit pipe and pass through certain traceable pipes until they come out at the other end to the taxpayer.'

Thus, the principle of tracing appears to have been accepted by the judiciary provided that, as in *Harmel v Wright* (above) there is a clear nexus between the loan and the income receipt. Despite this fact it has been doubted whether the wording of the legislation actually permits such tracing (see *Coles*, loc. cit., at p. 242). In *IR Commrs v Gordon* (1952) 33 TC 226, the taxpayer, a partner in a firm carrying on business in Ceylon, had an account with the Colombo branch of a bank that had its head office in London. By arrangement he was allowed to overdraw his London account, the overdrafts being transferred to the Colombo branch. At the Colombo branch they were converted into rupees and satisfied by periodic payments into the Colombo account from the taxpayer's firm, representing his share of the business profits. The Crown contended that the arrangement made with the bank was an arrangement for the remittance of money to the UK from Colombo, and that the sums so remitted were chargeable under Sch. D, Case V. The House of Lords held that there was no remittance payable in the UK. No property had been imported into the UK nor had there been received in the UK any sums of money or value arising from property not imported. Lord Cohen, who delivered the leading speech in the House, explained the case thus (33 TC at p. 242):

> 'it is attractive to suggest that, as the Respondent obtained and spent these loans in London and was, so far as the evidence goes, able to discharge them only from monies in Ceylon, part at any rate of which was income, and as the loan was in fact discharged, the money he received in England must have been received at least in part from remittances of income from Ceylon. Attractive though this may be it seems

to me quite impossible to bring what happened within the compass of the Rule. It is plain that the income receipts of the Respondent were all received in Ceylon. It is plain that the monies he received in London were advances of capital. There is no finding that those advances were made on credit or on account in respect of income in Ceylon which it was intended should be brought to London. On the contrary, the parties expressly agreed that the debt should be discharged in Ceylon; it was so discharged and there is no evidence that the rupees which the bank received in Ceylon were ever remitted to London.'

The decision in *IR Commrs v Gordon* resulted in statutory intervention designed to extend the meaning of remittance where loans had been utilised. Such intervention, however, applies only to those individuals who are ordinarily resident in the UK. Where an individual is not ordinarily resident, the question of whether a remittance has taken place or not will be decided by reference to the legislation and the applicable case law. In *Thomson v Moyse* (above), the earlier decision of *IR Commrs v Gordon* was distinguished, largely upon its facts (Lord Radcliffe doubting those facts: [1961] AC at p. 999) and also by virtue of the fact that the decision in *Gordon*'s case had been subsequently reversed by statute. It is therefore unclear as to whether *Gordon's* case still represents good law. This is unfortunate since in *Gordon* the taxpayer was able to avoid a charge to tax on the remittance basis, whilst in *Thomson v Moyse* he was not, due to the notion of tracing. In *Thomson v Moyse*, Lord Radcliffe remarked (at pp. 998–999):

> 'That leaves the two cases under the fourth branch, Hall v. Marians (No. 2), 19 T.C. 582, and Inland Revenue Commissioners v. Gordon, [1952] A.C. 552. They were cases of peculiar difficulty, depending on the relationship between loans made in this country and the foreign income out of which they were ultimately paid off. In essence the decisions adopted the view that you could, as it were, take the debt over to the income instead of bringing the income to the debt. Whether that is the right way to treat the facts when the creditor is a bank with London and overseas branches is not now of any importance, since the Legislature has intervened ... It would be a mistake, in those circumstances, to build any principles upon the basis of those two decisions.'

Notwithstanding Lord Radcliffe's remarks, the decision in *IR Commrs v Gordon* may still be of importance. The subsequent legislation applies only to individuals who are ordinarily resident in the UK. Thus, an individual who is resident, but neither ordinarily resident nor domiciled in the UK, may still avail himself of the decision in *IR Commrs v Gordon* if it remains a reliable authority. Of course it may be that the facts of the case would now provide a suitable situation for the application of the notion of tracing, dubious as that notion may be. But if that is not so, the case provides a method of avoiding a charge to tax under the remittance basis, assuming the taxpayer is neither domiciled nor ordinarily resident in the UK.

Planning point

The scope of exemptions which already allow individuals using the remittance basis to bring property, which has been purchased out of overseas investments and savings, into the UK, have been extended with effect from 6 April 2008 to include property purchased out of foreign employment income and foreign chargeable gains, as well as relevant foreign income.

58 Double Taxation Relief

58.1 Introduction

The UK has entered into numerous double tax treaties with other countries to mitigate the effect of double taxation of income and capital gains but far fewer in relation to gifts and inheritances.

Treaties are made with one country in each case but members of the OECD have subscribed to a model form and many treaties, for the most part, follow that form. Where a treaty applies it explains when UK domestic tax law applies and where the overseas tax law applies. The treaty does not override UK tax law in that the treaty cannot impose a liability. It can say which authority has the taxing rights if they exist and there would, otherwise, be double taxation. Double taxation arises because different countries employ different criteria to found their tax jurisdiction. For example, a US citizen who is taxable in the UK as a resident or because of a UK source of income will remain liable to US tax on worldwide income and gains by virtue of US citizenship.

> ***Planning point***
>
> A UK resident may claim double tax relief even where no treaty is in force. This relief is called unilateral relief. Relief will be given by a credit equal to the lower of the UK tax or foreign tax on the overseas income or capital gains. If there is no UK tax on the income such as where profits are covered by current year losses, the foreign tax can be deducted in calculating the income or gains for UK tax.

A treaty will normally go further than allowing credit by assigning exclusive taxing jurisdiction to one country or other by limiting withholding taxes (e.g. on dividends, interest and royalties). Treaties can apply to dual-residents but usually require an individual to be treated as a resident of only one country, determined by criteria in order of priority (e.g. permanent home, centre of vital interests, and nationality). They usually permit a country to tax business profits only if derived from a local permanent establishment. The permanent establishment is usually a fixed place of business defined in some detail. However, a permanent establishment might be a temporary site office or mobile home or caravan.

Double Taxation Relief

> ⚠️ **Warning!**
>
> The terms of the specific treaty must be checked. It is possible for a person to be taxed in one country on one type of income or profit but in another country for another type of income.

Credit is also available for overseas tax similar to inheritance tax charged on the gift of an asset, in lifetime or on death. Few treaties have been negotiated and many do not adequately cover lifetime gifts because they were negotiated when the former estate duty was in force. In addition to deductions and credit they also lay down useful criteria for determining and so resolving conflicts over the domicile of an individual and the location of assets.

There is also an agreement known as the arbitration convention, whereby different tax authorities will agree on corresponding adjustments if one country applies its transfer pricing rules to increase tax in that country.

> **Planning point**
>
> UK residents may claim double tax relief even where no treaty is in force. A credit equal to the lower of the UK tax or foreign tax on the overseas income or capital gains is given. If there is no UK tax on the income such as where profits are covered by current year losses, the foreign tax can be deducted in calculating the income or gains for UK tax.

58.2 Forms of double tax relief

Double tax relief may be given in several different forms. These can usefully be categorised as follows.

1. *Treaty exemption*: Income which has been taxed in one territory is specifically exempt by treaty from tax in another territory. This method does not generally prevent the second territory taking the amount of exempt income into account when computing the tax to be charged on the remaining taxable income.

2. *Credit relief*: Relief may be provided either by treaty or unilaterally. Income which has been taxed in one territory (usually the territory of source) is not exempt from tax in the second territory but the tax paid in the first territory in respect of that income is deductible from the tax payable in the second territory in respect of that income.

3. *Deduction*: Income which has been taxed in one territory is reduced by the amount of that tax in determining the amount of income which is taxed in the second territory.

4. *Other special reliefs*.

In addition, there is the question of transfer pricing as it applies to transactions between two countries. In 1998, the transfer pricing legislation was aligned with the OECD guidelines on transfer pricing, which are seen as representing international best practice (Transfer pricing is deal with in **Chapter 26**). Effect must be given to agreements, decisions or opinions in connection with transfer pricing made in accordance with the arbitration convention whether by assessment or discharge or repayment of tax.

The provisions made for double tax relief may also apply to capital gains and chargeable gains of companies.

Whether HMRC will admit a foreign tax for unilateral double taxation relief in relation to business profits is determined by examining the tax within its legislative context in the foreign territory and deciding whether it serves the same function as income tax and corporation tax serve in the UK in relation to such profits.

Law: TIOPA 2010, Pt. 2

58.3 Model treaty provisions as typically used in the UK

Two chief methods of relieving double taxation are adopted in 'tax treaties'. First, taxing rights over certain classes of income are reserved entirely to the country of residence of the person deriving the income. Second, all other income may be taxed (in some cases, only to a limited extent) by the country of origin of that income; if the country of residence of the recipient also taxes that income, it must grant a credit against its tax for the tax levied by the country of origin.

Many tax treaties are based on the 1977 or 1992 Model Convention published by the Organisation for Economic Cooperation and Development (OECD). They usually provide that a national from one territory should not be treated more harshly than a national from the other territory (a 'non-discrimination clause'). Though the EC Treaty requires similar treatment within the EC the matter in point must fall within the provision for the reliefs effected by arrangements agreed with foreign governments.

Some of the usual exemption provisions of treaties are noted below, but it is emphasised that each treaty must be looked at individually for its specific provisions.

Business profits

The profits of any business carried on by a resident of country A are taxable only in country A unless the business is carried on in country B through a permanent establishment (a fixed place of business, e.g. a branch, office, factory or mine) in country B. Where this is the case, the profits of the business are taxable in country B, but only to the extent that those profits are attributable to the permanent establishment.

Shipping, inland waterways and air transport

Profits from the operation of ships, aircraft or inland waterways transport are taxable only in the country in which the place of effective management of the relevant enterprise is situated.

Interest, dividends, royalties, non-government pensions

Interest, dividends, patent and copyright royalties, and non-government pensions are often taxable only in the country of residence or are taxed at a reduced rate in the other country (though it should be noted that, under the OECD Model, the circumstances in which each can be taxed (and the rates) in the other country differ dependent upon the type of payment). Recipients of dividends are often entitled to a proportion of the tax credit to which a UK resident would have been entitled. Where a tax credit on a dividend is to be determined subject to a deduction based on the aggregate of the dividend plus the tax credit, the deduction is calculated on the gross amount of the dividend and the tax credit, without any allowance for the deduction itself.

Professional services

The income of a person in respect of professional services is generally only taxable in the country in which he is resident, unless he has a fixed base regularly available to him in the other country for the purpose of providing his services. However, actors, musicians and athletes are generally liable to tax in both countries.

Salaries and wages

Article 15 of the OECD Model deals with the position of employees and, as its default position, allows a state to tax the remuneration arising to a non-resident individual in respect of services performed in that state. Special provision is made in other articles for:

- company directors;
- artists and sportspersons;
- pensioners; and
- those engaged on government service.

For any individuals remaining within the scope of art. 15 an exemption from 'host state' taxation is available under art. 15(2). This exemption applies where three conditions are satisfied.

(1) The individual is present in the host state for less than 183 days in any 12-month period which begins or ends in the fiscal year concerned.

(2) The remuneration is paid by, or on behalf of, a non-resident employer.

(3) The cost of that remuneration is not borne by a permanent establishment of the employer which is located in the host state.

The object is to exempt the remuneration of employees temporarily working in the host state for non-resident employers. It is not intended to apply where the employment services are rendered by its employees to an enterprise which is liable to tax in the host state, either on the grounds of residence or because of a business carried on via a permanent establishment there. Put in basic terms, the host state is saying 'if we allow a deduction in computing the profits of the enterprise for the cost of the remuneration of its employees, we want to balance that loss of tax by taxing that remuneration'.

Unfortunately, although the principle and the exemption are quite clear, doubts can exist over whether the individual is exercising an employment or not and if he is, just who is his employer? It is these aspects which are addressed by revisions to the OECD Commentary made in 2005.

> ⚠ **Warning!**
> The precise terms of each individual treaty must be examined as they do not all reflect the wording of the model agreement.

How is the 28 day period calculated?

The commentary on the OECD Model Tax Convention, discusses the different ways in which the 183 day period mentioned in art. 15(2)(a). There is only one way in which the period of 183 days can be calculated which is consistent with the wording of art. 15(2)(a) which is the 'days of physical presence' method; under this method for every day in which the individual is present in a country, including part days, days of arrival, days of departure and other days spent inside the State of activity, including weekends and national holidays.

Law: Art. 15, OECD Model Tax Convention

Other guidance: OECD Model Tax Convention commentary

Artistes and sportspersons

Article 17 of the OECD Model overrides the business profits article (art. 7) and the employment article (art. 15) in the case of entertainers and sportspersons. The income from the exercise of their personal activities as such may be taxed in the state in which those activities are exercised (the 'host state'). The right of the host state to tax the income is also given where the income accrues to person other than the entertainer/sportsperson.

> **Planning point**
>
> Most UK agreements in recent years contain such an article. Article 16(1) of the 2001 agreement with the USA, however, limits the host state's taxing rights to cases where the gross receipts in any tax year exceed $20,000.

Law: Art. 7, 15 and 17, OECD Model Tax Convention

Government salaries and pensions

Government salaries are generally taxable only in the country responsible for paying them. However, the income is only taxable in the other country if the services are rendered in that country and the taxpayer is resident in, or is a citizen of, that country.

Pensions paid on respect of private employment should only be taxed in the State of residence of the recipient, in accordance with Art 18 of the OECD Model Tax Convention. Pensions include not only pensions paid to former employees but also payments to other beneficiaries, and similar payments, e.g. annuities. Art 18 also applies to pensions provided by the State (or a political division or local authority thereof) which are not included in Art 19(2) of the OECD Model Tax Convention.

> ⚠ **Warning!**
>
> Not all countries accept that this principle should apply, and consequently adopt alternative articles. Therefore, the precise terms of each individual treaty must be examined as they do not all reflect the wording of the model agreement.

Law: Arts 18 and 19, OECD Model Tax Convention

Students

Students temporarily abroad for the purposes of education are generally not taxable on their grants and other income reasonably necessary for maintenance and education.

Law: Art 20, OECD Model Tax Convention

Teachers

Many double taxation agreements (but not all) contain an Article providing for exemption from UK tax of remuneration received by a teacher visiting the UK from an agreement country provided certain conditions are met.

> **Example 58.1**
>
> A resident of country A who visits country B for the purpose of teaching is usually exempt from tax in country B on the income derived from his teaching.

The normal proviso is that the period of temporary residence in country B does not exceed two years.

Foreign language assistants are usually undergraduates or recent graduates who come to the UK to support schools in teaching their own language and to improve their English. They are rarely trained teachers but it has been HMRC practice to accept that earnings from working as a language assistant in a school or college can be exempt under a 'Teacher Article' in a double taxation agreement. This has been reciprocated in other countries for United Kingdom residents working as language assistants abroad.

Other guidance: HMRC Double Taxation Relief Manual, paragraphs DT1935 – DT1937 (teachers) and HMRC Double Taxation Relief Manual, paragraph DT1938 (foreign language assistants)

Personal allowances and reliefs

Many double tax agreements provide that individuals who are resident in country A are entitled to the same personal allowances, reliefs, and deductions for the purposes of tax in country B as subjects of country B who are not resident in that country.

Often the double taxation agreement will exclude entitlement to the personal allowances, etc. where the income consists solely of dividends, interest or royalties.

Law: FA 1989, s. 115; TIOPA 2010, s. 6; *Getty Oil Co v Steele* [1990] BTC 312 (on the operation of FA 1989, s.115)

Dual resident individuals

Where an individual is regarded as resident under more than one country's domestic law, treaties which follow the OECD Model contain four 'tie-breaker' tests to be applied in order to determine the tax residence for the purposes of the agreement. The tests are to be applied in the following order until one of the contracting states can be clearly identified.

(1) In which state is the individual's permanent home located?

(2) If he has a permanent home in both states (but not otherwise), where is his 'centre of vital interests'?

(3) If the location of his centre of vital interests cannot be determined, where is his 'habitual abode'?

(4) If he has his habitual abode in both states or in neither of them, of which state is he a 'national'?

Where the answer to the 'nationality' test is that he is a national of both states or of none of them, the states are to settle the matter by mutual agreement.

Law: Art. 4(2) and (3), OECD Model Tax Convention

Permanent home

The commentary on art 4(2) observes that this test should frequently be sufficient to resolve the question. It also makes the point that the test need only be applied to the period when the individual's residence position affects tax liability and that this period may be less than an entire chargeable period.

Example 58.2

'For example, in one calendar year an individual is a resident in State A under that state's tax laws from 1 January to 31 March, then moves to State B. Because the individual resides in State B for more than 183 days, the individual is treated by the tax laws of State B as a State B resident for the entire year. Applying the special rules to the period 1 January to 31 March, the individual was a resident of State A. Therefore, both State A and State B should treat the individual as a State A resident for that period and as a State B resident from 1 April to 31 December.'

⚠ Warning!

Whilst it may be tempting to think that these tie-breaker tests are provided for globe-trotting millionaires who flit from one country to another at will, they are also needed in the more common situation of an individual taking up permanent residence in a new country part-way through a chargeable period.

In the special commissioners' decision of *Squirrell v R & C Commrs* (2005) Sp C 493, the taxpayer left the UK for permanent residence on 17 October 2000. By concession, he was regarded as resident in the UK only for that part of the tax year to 17 October. In the US, because his wife was a US citizen, they were able to file a joint return for the calendar year 2000 and elect to be treated as US residents for the whole of that year. The result was that for the period 1 January to 17 October 2000 Mr Squirrell was resident in both countries. In the event, his residence status had no bearing on the outcome of his appeal but it was suggested that under Art. 4 of the US Treaty his residence status should be determined separately for the periods before and after 17 October 2000. This view was based on the OECD Commentary quoted in **Example 58.1** above.

If an individual has two homes at any point in time, the question arises as to which, if any, is 'permanent' and what is meant by 'permanent' anyway? The OECD Commentary regards the concept of permanence as essential and defines this as existing where the individual has 'arranged and retained it for his permanent use as opposed to staying at a particular place under such conditions that it is evident that the stay is intended to be of short duration' and that the accommodation is 'available to him at all times continuously'.

The Commentary does not lay any great stress on the type of home or whether it is owned or rented, furnished or unfurnished, so any accommodation either owned outright or leased can be a permanent residence.

If the individual has such a residence in both countries, resort has to be had to the second test ('centre of vital interests'); on the other hand, if he does not have a permanent home in either state, then the third test ('habitual abode') is to be applied.

Law: OECD Model Tax Convention, Art 4(2), *Squirrell v R & C Commrs* (2005) Sp C 493

Other guidance: OECD Model Tax Convention commentary on art 4, para. 9–20

'Centre of vital interests'

This is the state with which the individual's personal and economic relations are the closest. The OECD Commentary requires a holistic approach to be taken, regard being had to the individual's family and social relations, his occupation and place of business, his political and cultural activities and the place from where he administers his property. It goes on to add:

> 'This is the state with which the individual's personal and economic relations are the closest. The OECD Commentary requires a holistic approach to be taken, regard being had to the individual's family and social relations, his occupation and place of business, his political and cultural activities and the place from where he administers his property. It goes on to add: "The circumstances must be examined as a whole, but it is nevertheless obvious that considerations based on personal acts of the individual must receive special attention. If a person who has a home in one State sets up a second home in the other State while retaining the first, the fact that he retains the first in the environment where he has always lived, where he has worked and where he has his family and possessions, can, together with other elements, go to demonstrate that he has retained his centre of vital interests in the first State."'

Guidance as to how to approach this test can be derived from a Canadian case, *Hertel v Minister of National Revenue* 93 DTC 712 (TCC), where the judge emphasised:

> 'In determining his centre of vital interests, it is not enough simply to weigh or count the number of factors or connectors on each side. The depth of the roots on one's centre of vital interests is more important than their number.'

In other words it is the durability and tenacity of the connectors which will be decisive. In the *Hertel* case the taxpayer was born in Germany in 1942 and emigrated to Canada in 1959, but returned to live in Germany in 1970. He started a business selling Canadian silver dollars to German Banks and visited Canada as much as 15 times per year. From 1970 he purchased several properties in Canada, one of which was used by him and his family for holidays and another where he intended to take up residence at a later date. He thus had a permanent home in both countries and his centre of vital interests had to be determined. All his family and friends were resident in Germany; the only relative living in Canada was a brother. His centre of vital interests was held to be in Germany because of the depth of those roots there, despite the fact that he visited Canada regularly, had a number of properties in Canada and intended to return to live in Canada at some future time.

This case was quoted with approval in a more recent Canadian case, *Yoon v The Queen* 2005 TCC 366, (*http://decision.tcc-cci.gc.ca/en/2005/2005tcc366/2005tcc366.html*), which involved a lady born in Korea, who moved to Canada in 1975, married and became a Canadian citizen. In 1984, with her husband and the two children of the marriage, she returned to live in Korea. In February 2000, Mr and Mrs Yoon bought a home in Canada where they planned to retire at some point in the future.

The appeal concerned her residence status for the calendar year 2001, during which she was working in Korea but spent 135 days in Canada. Her husband was living in Canada throughout that year. Mrs Yoon had numerous 'connectors' with Canada in 2001, e.g. four bank accounts, bank deposits, Canadian citizenship, passport, driver's licence, a car, two visa cards, a house and her husband was resident there.

Despite all these connectors, the Court placed greater emphasis on family ties and particularly the fact that her children were living with her in Korea in 2001 and were still in education. They 'relied on her considerably for support as they were entering a critical transition phase in their lives'. Mrs Yoon's social life in Canada centred exclusively around her husband as she had not yet established any substantial ties to the community in Canada. The centre of vital interests test was one to be applied to the connectors in that specific year. Therefore, her intention to retire to Canada at some point in the future was not a factor to be taken into account, following the *Hertel* decision mentioned above. Mrs Yoon, despite all the preliminary steps to move to Canada, continued to live in Korea in 2001 as she had done for the previous nine years. Her children continued to live and study in Korea and she continued with the social life she had established there. This was indicative of the fact that, for that year, her centre of vital interests was in Korea.

It is clear by definition that an individual cannot have more than one centre of vital interests. If that centre cannot be determined, the next test ('habitual abode') is to be applied.

Law: OECD Model Tax Convention, Art 4(2), *Hertel v Minister of National Revenue* 93 DTC 712 (TCC), *Yoon v The Queen* (2005) TCC 366

Other guidance: OECD Model Tax Convention commentary on Art 4, paras 9–20

'Habitual abode'

The OECD commentary offers little assistance in interpreting this term other than to say that the test 'tips the balance towards the State where he stays more frequently'. Regard must be had to periods spent by the individual at any place in the state, not just a permanent home. The comparison between the two states must be over a sufficiently long period to be able to determine whether the residence in any state is habitual.

In the *Yoon* case, mentioned earlier, although the appeal was decided on the centre of vital interest test, the court went on to cover all bases and looked at the habitual abode test. After considering the OECD commentary, the decision came down to a comparison of the number of days spent in each country in the year concerned and that clearly pointed to residence in Korea.

In most cases the habitual abode test should dispose of the question and establish one state as being the one to exercise taxing rights on the basis of residence. If not, then the final test ('nationality') is applied.

Nationality

This will be a question of fact. The individual will be resident in the state of which he is a national. Where he is either resident in both states or neither of them, the matter has to be decided by the two Contracting States by the mutual agreement procedure.

Person other than an individual

Where by the operation of art. 4(1) a person other than an individual is resident in more than one contracting state, the place of residence is the place where 'effective management' is situated. This test has recently been considered in the case of *Laerstate BV* [2009] TC 00162. This case highlights the important point that a company's effective management can be 'usurped' and where it is usurped, it will be the residence of the usurper (who has effective management of the company) whose residence will determine that of the company under the test in art. 4(3).

Law: OECD Model Tax Convention, art 4(3), *Laerstate BV* [2009] TC 00162

58.4 Effect of exemptions under double tax treaties

If a double tax treaty provides an exemption from tax or a partial exemption from tax in a particular territory, the amount in respect of which tax is exempt may nonetheless be brought fully into account in the UK – there is very little relief for 'tax spared' in the other territory, except in the case of transfers of foreign branches of UK-resident companies between EC member states (see below) and in the case of certain interest.

There is an element of tax sparing provided by virtue of EC provisions. A UK-resident company transferring a foreign branch activity between EC member states may be exempt from tax in the territory in which the branch subsisted (in accordance with the mergers Directive); chargeable gains in respect of the transfer may be netted with allowable losses and the resultant taxable amount may be subject to double tax relief on the basis of the tax which would have been payable but for the exemption.

> ⚠ **Warning!**
>
> Non-resident companies carrying on business in the UK are unable to claim relief for losses incurred as a result of the exemption of dividends, interest or royalty income under a double taxation convention. For accounting periods beginning before 30 November 1993, the restriction applied only to dividends and interest received by non-residents carrying on business as a bank, insurance company or dealer in securities.

*Law:*TIOPA 2010, s. 37, 38, 70, 122; CTA 2010, s. 54; EC Directive 90/434

58.5 Calculation of double tax credit relief available

In many cases, double tax agreements provide that where there is no deduction or exemption from UK tax, credit is to be given for any foreign tax which is paid and which corresponds to income tax whilst similar credit is given by 'unilateral relief'; this reduces the amount of UK tax chargeable except in certain cases where a non-resident company is connected with a state or province of a foreign territory which operates a 'unitary tax' regime. In general, a claim for relief by way of credit for foreign tax must be made within the period ending five years from 31 January following the end of the tax year within which the income falls to be charged to tax (before self assessment, a period of six full years).

For trades, professions and vocations, there are special rules relating to the years of commencement and cessation.

> ⚠ **Warning!**
>
> From 17 March 1998, taxpayers who have claimed relief for foreign tax must notify HMRC if there is an adjustment to the amount of foreign tax and the relief claimed has become excessive as a consequence. This requirement clarifies taxpayers' obligations under self assessment.

An overseas dividend manufacturer may have his right to double tax relief restricted, in particular, in respect of tax credits on overseas dividends received when the tax credits have been offset against tax due on manufactured overseas dividends paid or when the overseas dividends have been effectively paid on to a non-resident.

Where no credit is allowable the foreign tax may be deducted. A person may elect that any treaty provision giving credit is ignored.

Where transitional rules apply to average (or scale-down) profits or income under self assessment, double tax relief may be treated similarly.

Thin capitalisation

Some treaties contain thin capitalisation provisions, restricting relief or exemption where the size of loans is greater than would be expected between unrelated parties (or their terms are more beneficial to the lender). In this regard, it is specifically provided that, for interest paid after 14 May 1992, account should be taken in the UK of whether the loan would have been made at all, whether it would have been of such size and whether the rate and other terms would have been of that order. HMRC have confirmed that the absence of cross-default and cross-guarantee provisions, etc. in an intra-group loan will not be taken into account as regards the terms on which a loan is made.

Finance Act 2004 introduced measures to merge the current thin capitalisation requirements and subsume them within the general transfer pricing rules. The new rules end transfer pricing and thin capitalisation requirements for small and medium-sized enterprises in most circumstances from 1 April 2004 (see **Chapter 25** for further details).

Law: ICTA 1988, s. 8–15, 18, 19, 22–24, 26, 31, 32, 36, 40, 41–57, 60, 67, 81–83; 89, 90–103, 131; FA 2004, s. 30–37 and Sch. 5; *Yates (HMIT) v GCA International Ltd (formerly Gaffney Cline and Associates Ltd)*[1991] BTC 107; *Bayfine UK v R & C Commrs* [2010] BTC 467

Other guidance: SP 7/91, *Double taxation relief: business profits: unilateral relief*; IR 150, *Taxation of rents: a guide to property income*; Law Society's *Gazette*, 24 February 1993; TAX 5/93

58.6 Foreign tax as an expense

If no credit is allowable (or taken) the foreign tax may be deducted so that only the net income is charged to UK tax.

FA 2009 introduced new provisions in relation to payments from foreign tax authorities to a person who has received a reduction in their taxable income under TIOPA 2010, s. 112 with effect from 22 April 2009. The person's income is increased by the amount of the payment, which can be made directly to that person or to any person connected with them.

Law: FA 2009, s. 59; TIOPA 2010, s. 112

58.7 Companies and double tax relief

58.7.1 General

The commentary in this section deals only with those specific aspects of double taxation relief by way of credit that are exclusive to companies.

In the UK, the provisions relating to double tax relief are to be found in TIOPA 2010. A number of changes were made to these provisions by FA 2000, Sch. 30. The changes impact largely on companies. In the main, they affect relief for overseas tax suffered on income and gains taxable in the UK on companies receiving income from foreign subsidiaries or other non-resident companies in which they have significant investments.

Prior to TIOPA 2010, the provisions were found in ICTA 1988, and significant changes were made in FA 2009, primarily in relation to banks and manufactured overseas dividends and banks and the double tax relief credit rules. In relation to the former, relief for foreign withholding tax will be denied where the recipient of a manufactured overseas dividend has not borne the economic cost of the tax. These provisions are in FA 2009, Sch 29.

Currently legislation restricts the credit for foreign tax paid on trade receipts of a bank to the corporation tax arising on the relevant part of the trade profits. The new provisions make it clear that the credit restriction will apply where income is artificially diverted to a non-banking company in the bank's group, ensuring that the amount of DTR available is restricted with reference to a deduction of its average funding costs over all its transactions; this cannot be avoided by the bank allocating specific sources of funds to specific investments.

The provisions relating to double tax apply also to the chargeable gains of companies.

Law: FA 2009; TIOPA 2010, s. 2, 8, 9, 10–16, 18, 26, 29, 30, 42, 129, 134; CTA 2010, s. 1181, Sch. 3

58.7.2   Relief by way of credit against corporation tax

Where, under the terms of an agreement, income and gains are not exempted from tax in the UK by operation of a double taxation agreement and, accordingly, an item of income falls to be taxed both in the foreign country and the UK, the foreign tax charged on that income is allowed as a credit against UK corporation tax.

In these circumstances, relief for foreign tax is usually available in one of three forms.

(1) *Tax credit relief* against UK corporation tax for foreign tax payable directly on the profits, dividend, interest or other profits taxable in the UK. This can be by operation of a double tax agreement (treaty relief) or otherwise in the absence of any treaty (unilateral relief).

(2) *Credit relief* against UK corporation tax (either via a treaty or as unilateral relief) for tax suffered indirectly, usually on dividends from sizeable shareholdings (broadly with ten per cent or more of the votes) taxable in the UK. The foreign tax suffered ('underlying tax') is either on the profits out of which the dividend itself is payable, or on the profits, etc. of a company below the subsidiary.

(3) *Relief by deduction from profits* taxable in the UK where relief by credit is not available.

The amount of tax against which the foreign tax may be set as a credit is calculated in accordance with UK tax law and is normally grossed up to take into account foreign tax.

58.7.3   Claims and time limits

Claims for relief for foreign tax by means of a credit against UK income tax must be made either on or before:

(a) the fourth anniversary of the end of that tax year; or
(b) if later, the 31 January next following the year of assessment in which the foreign tax is paid.

Claims for relief for foreign tax by way of credit against UK corporation tax must be made not more than:

(a) four years after the end of that accounting period; or
(b) if later, one year after the end of the accounting period in which the foreign tax is paid.

These time limits were amended by FA 2008, s. 118, with effect from 1 April 2010. Prior to that date the time limits are the fifth anniversary and six years respectively. There are, however, transitional provisions which extend the start date of the new time limits to 1 April 2012, however these do not apply to companies.

There is an exception to the time limits above where there is any later adjustment made in the amount of foreign tax payable.

Law: FA 2008, s. 118 and Sch. 39, para. 24; TIOPA 2010, s. 19

Supplementary claims for and notification of adjustments to relief

Additional claims or assessments may be made where relief for foreign tax has become inadequate or excessive respectively, as a result of an adjustment to the amount of foreign tax. With effect from 17 March 1998, taxpayers who have claimed relief must notify the Revenue if there is an adjustment and the relief claimed has become excessive. This latter requirement does not apply to Lloyd's underwriters.

Insufficient relief

Where double tax credit relief (or foreign tax claimed as a deduction) has been rendered inadequate or excessive because of an adjustment to the foreign tax either in the UK or by the authorities in the territory of origin of the income, etc. then a claim for additional relief may be made within six years of the time when the adjustment was made.

Law: TIOPA 2010, s. 79

Obligation to notify excessive relief

Similarly, where double tax credit relief (or foreign tax claimed as a deduction) has been rendered excessive because of an adjustment to the foreign tax either in the UK or by the authorities in the territory of origin of the income, etc. then an assessment, adjustment or determination to correct relief already given may be made within six years of the time when the adjustment was made.

Law: TIOPA 2010, s. 80

Taxpayers who have claimed double tax credit relief must notify the Revenue if there is an adjustment to the amount of foreign tax and the double tax relief claimed has become excessive as a consequence. A similar notification must be made where foreign tax claimed as a deduction becomes excessive.

Notification must be made in writing within one year of the time the adjustment was made. A penalty up to the amount of the excessive relief (or tax payable as a result of the excessive adjustment where tax is claimed as a deduction) may be applied where there is a failure to notify in accordance with these provisions. It does not apply to Lloyd's underwriters (because they are already subject to separate requirements in regulations made under FA 1994, s. 229 (corporate members)).

For example, where foreign tax suffered on overseas income is reduced and the excess is then repaid by the fiscal authorities in the territory levying that tax, there is an obligation to notify HMRC that any previous claim for credit relief against UK income or corporation tax on the foreign income, based on the amount of foreign tax before adjustment, has become excessive.

HMRC have issued an interpretation of what is meant by an adjustment, and when it should be considered to have been made for these purposes (Revenue *Tax Bulletin*, Issue 41, June 1999, p. 673).

Law: FA 1994, s. 229; TIOPA 2010, s. 80

58.7.4 Duty to minimise tax available for claim

There is a burden on a claimant to have taken 'all reasonable steps' to keep to a minimum foreign tax for which relief can be claimed.

Law: TIOPA 2010, s. 33

58.7.5 Calculation of credit: companies

Attribution of corporation tax to income/gains

Where double tax relief is available, overseas income subject to UK corporation tax is grossed up by the amount of foreign tax. So, where in the exceptional case an item of income would normally be recognised under either of those provisions net of foreign tax, it will need to be grossed up for the purposes of arriving at the amount of double tax relief due. (Conversely, relief by way of expensing the foreign tax may be claimed, notwithstanding the gross measure of the charge under those provisions.)

The amount of credit for foreign tax which may be set off against UK corporation tax in respect of any income or chargeable gain may not exceed the corporation tax attributable to that income or gain. The corporation tax attributable to any income or gain is determined by applying to that income or gain the rate at which the company pays corporation tax on the whole of its income and chargeable gains (before any double taxation credit) for the accounting period in question. The amount of foreign tax is converted to sterling at the rate of exchange at the time when the tax becomes payable and not when it is paid: this is a matter of practice.

For accounting periods beginning after 31 December 2002, the amount of foreign tax available for relief against the profits of foreign permanent establishments of UK-resident companies is arrived at by calculating the profits of the permanent establishment in the same way as the profits of UK permanent establishments of non-resident companies.

The principles applying to tax relief by credit for companies are similar to those applying to individuals, except that a number of changes were made to the operation of relief for overseas tax suffered on income and gains taxable in the UK by the *Finance Act* 2000. In order for additional relief to be provided and be effective, these changes sometimes require the restriction by reference to corporation tax on certain types of income to be ignored. This makes it possible to determine the amount of excess foreign tax for which relief by way of credit is allowable over the relief actually given for that tax ('eligible unrelieved foreign tax').

Law: TIOPA 2010, s. 42, 43, 52–56

Set-off of deductions for purposes attributing tax

Deductions such as charges on income, management expenses of companies with investment business allowable under CTA 2009, s. 1219–1223, life insurance company expenses deductible under ICTA 1988, s. 76 and other amounts that can reduce 'profits of more than one description' may be allocated in whole or in part against any part of the company's profits for the accounting period in question, as the company thinks fit. Thus, it may allocate the maximum deductions to its UK profits, thereby maximising the corporation tax attributable to its foreign profits available for double taxation relief.

Special treatment applies to certain deductions for non-trading deficits under the loan relationships regime appropriate to companies. Where a company makes a claim (under CTA 2009, s. 459) for a non-trading deficit to be set against the company's current year profits then, for the purposes of calculating corporation tax on income available for double tax relief, it can be allocated only to those profits against which it is set off by the claim. Similarly, where TIOPA 2010, s. 54 does not apply, any unused non-trading deficits brought forward to an accounting period (under CTA 2009, s. 459) must be allocated to non-trading profits of the company for the period and cannot be allocated to any other profits.

Under TIOPA 2010, s. 54, credit is given, broadly, for foreign tax on a loan relationship on an accruals rather than a receipts basis, looking at the non-trading credits in isolation from any non-trading debits which offset them. This maximises the double tax relief position. There is a similar provision for non-trading credits in respect of intangible fixed assets. In accordance with these two sections, any non-trading debits/losses may be allocated to other sources of income instead, although once those sources have been exhausted, any remaining balance of debits must be set against credits.

Where non-trading debits/losses are carried forward, they do not have to be allocated for the purposes of double tax relief. For non-trading debits on loan relationships, this extends to include amounts carried back or surrendered as group relief. This extension is unnecessary for intangible assets as non-trading losses cannot be carried back and can only be surrendered as group relief once the profits for an accounting period have been eliminated.

Law: TIOPA 2010, s. 54

Transactions involving loan relationships

Special legislation applies to disposals and acquisitions of company loan relationships which alter the amount of foreign tax available for relief in situations where interest is paid to, or received from, the other party to the disposal or acquisition.

Broadly, double tax relief is still available while repo or stock lending arrangements have effect from the time when the rights under the loan relationship are first transferred, to the time when they are transferred back to the original transferor in pursuance of the arrangements. In other words, the transferor can claim relief for foreign tax paid on interest during the period of the transfer.

Where overseas interest on which foreign tax has been paid is taxable as a loan relationship non-trading credit, but falls to be paid to another person as a result of a transaction involving the disposal or acquisition of any rights or liabilities under the loan relationship, unilateral relief is given on the interest except where the 'related transaction' is the initial transfer under repo or stock lending arrangements involving that relationship.

These provisions were enhanced further to include within the scope of foreign tax which remains available for relief such tax attributable (on a reasonable apportionment), to a 'qualifying payment' under interest rate or currency contracts (but not options) in accordance with the special rules for such instruments. These amendments apply in respect of accounting periods ending after 20 March 2000 (FA 2000, Sch. 30, para. 7(4) and 24(4)).

Law: TIOPA 2010, s. 107–110

58.8 Unilateral relief

58.8.1 Introduction

Relief may still be given by way of credit against UK corporation tax charged on foreign income for taxes charged on that income in a foreign territory, even though there is no double taxation agreement between that territory and the UK or, similarly, where there is an agreement between the UK and a foreign territory, but that agreement does not include a particular tax or source of income. This is known as 'unilateral relief'.

Law: TIOPA 2010, s. 8–17

58.8.2 Unilateral relief for UK permanent establishments of non-resident companies

Unilateral relief is available in respect of tax charged in the country where the income or chargeable gain arises. Like treaty relief, unilateral relief used to be available only to persons resident in the UK throughout the chargeable period, subject to certain exceptions. However, after 20 March 2000, unilateral relief was extended to include UK permanent establishments (formerly branches) of non-resident companies.

Unilateral relief is allowed in exceptional cases.

(1) To UK permanent establishments of non-residents, for foreign tax suffered directly on the profits and dividends of the permanent establishment itself, as well as for underlying tax in relation to dividends received by the UK permanent establishment from sizeable shareholdings (broadly with ten per cent or more of the votes) providing:

   (a) the tax for which relief is claimed is not tax of the country where the person (whose permanent establishment it is) is normally taxed (by reason of domicile, residence or place of management); and
   (b) subject only to the restriction that such relief is not to exceed that available to a UK resident.

   This extension to UK permanent establishments applies for accounting periods ending after 20 March 2000.

(2) Prior to the introduction of the general relief for UK permanent establishments in (1) above (i.e. for accounting periods ending before 21 March 2000), there was a specific relief for UK branches of non-resident banks. Expressly, relief was available for tax paid in respect of interest on a loan, provided that the loan was made by a company which carried on a banking business in the UK through a branch throughout the chargeable

period and the loan was made through that branch (former ICTA 1988, s. 794(2)(c)) and:

(a) the foreign territory under whose law the tax was paid was not one in which the company was liable to tax by reason of domicile, residence, or place of management; and
(b) the relief was restricted to that available to a UK bank making a loan in similar circumstances in the course of its ordinary banking business.

> ⚠ **Warning!**
>
> Similar relief to that for banks was also available to overseas life assurance companies trading through a UK branch (not covered in this commentary).

UK branches of non-residents

The latter exception ((2) above) gave statutory effect to the previous concessionary practice of allowing UK branches of non-resident banks to claim unilateral relief against UK corporation tax for foreign tax paid in respect of a loan. Therefore where a UK branch had profits derived from non-UK business or investments, relief was only available for tax suffered on those non-UK profits where the business was banking or life insurance. Other industries could not claim relief, even though their branches were also taxable in the UK. The relief was repealed for accounting periods ending after 20 March 2000, having been rendered redundant by the broader relief in (1) above. Only the identification of the amount of tax suffered by a life assurance branch is retained, adjusted so that it refers to the general relief for foreign direct and underlying tax above.

> **Planning point**
>
> The repeal and replacement by a more general provision applicable to all UK branches (now permanent establishments) removed what had been perceived as a long standing anomaly. Thus, for the purposes of double tax relief, UK permanent establishment/branches are on the same footing as UK residents in respect of accounting periods ending after 20 March 2000 (FA 2000, Sch. 30, para. 4(14)).
>
> *Law:* TIOPA 2010, s. 30

58.8.3 The amount of foreign income assessable in the UK

Income of UK residents from foreign sources is assessable on the gross amount of the income with no deduction for any foreign tax suffered.

When certain conditions are satisfied individuals who are resident but not domiciled in the UK may make a claim for the remittance basis to apply. In those circumstances, they will be liable to UK tax on only that part of their foreign income which is remitted to the UK. In such a case the amount assessable is normally the full amount of the sums received in the UK. For the purposes of credit relief, however, that amount is to be increased by the foreign tax in respect of that income.

Law: ITTOIA 2005, s. 832; ITA 2007, Pt. 14, Ch A1; TIOPA 2010, s. 32

Example 58.3

Neville earns £5,000, on which he pays foreign tax at 20% (£1,000). He is taxed in the UK on a remittance basis. Neville remits £2,000 to the UK. The foreign tax attributable to this amount is calculated as follows:

$$\frac{\text{amount remitted}}{\text{gross overseas income} - \text{overseas tax on income}} \times \text{overseas tax on income}$$

$$\frac{£2,000}{£5,000 - £1,000} \times \text{overseas tax on income}$$

Neville will be taxed in the UK on £2,500.

Relief by credit is available in the usual way.

Underlying tax on dividends

Where foreign income is in the form of a dividend, the 'grossed-up' receipt or amount arising is to include any underlying tax which is to be taken into account under the double taxation agreement in considering whether a tax credit is to be allowed in respect of the dividend.

'Underlying tax' means, in relation to any dividend, tax which is not chargeable in respect of that dividend directly or by deduction. Underlying tax, therefore, is the tax charged upon the profits of a non-resident company in the foreign territory. If that company then makes a dividend, the foreign territory may additionally levy a tax on that dividend (withholding tax).

Generally, relief for underlying tax is restricted to dividends received by certain UK-resident companies or UK branches of non-resident companies.

So, where the recipient has the prescribed participation interest in the dividend-paying company (either under the applicable double taxation agreement or as unilateral relief where there is no treaty relief), foreign dividend income may be grossed up (in accordance with ICTA 1988, s. 795) to include underlying tax on the profits out of which the dividend has been paid and which is then to be taken into account in determining the level of credit relief.

Treaty relief for underlying tax: the required level of control

Underlying overseas tax is taken into account under treaty relief in establishing the extent of relief if the UK-resident company either:

- directly or indirectly controls; or
- is a subsidiary of a company which directly or indirectly controls

at least ten per cent of the voting power in the overseas company paying the dividend.

A company is a subsidiary of another if the second company controls, directly or indirectly, not less than 50 per cent of the voting power in the first company. Thus, a UK-resident company which controls ten per cent of the voting power in the overseas company paying the dividend is entitled to relief in respect of underlying tax. A subsidiary of such a company is similarly entitled to such relief.

Relief for underlying tax

If relief for underlying tax is due, then the underlying tax is taken into account in assessing the company's income.

Where a foreign company does not provide the shareholder with information as to the underlying tax paid, the inspector will refer the case to FICO (International) who has responsibility for agreeing computations of rates of foreign underlying tax. The taxpaying company is normally expected to provide specific documentation.

In certain circumstances the UK company may be entitled under foreign tax law to a credit in respect of the dividend (similar to a tax credit in the UK). In such cases the amount of the underlying tax taken into account in calculating double taxation relief is reduced by the amount of the foreign credit.

Calculation of underlying tax; split rate taxes and accumulated losses

A statement of practice (SP 3/01) has been published on the calculation of relief for underlying tax on foreign dividends received by companies. It provides guidance on how HMRC will treat claims for relief for underlying tax in two, separate, specific sets of circumstances where there might be some element of doubt as to the correct amount of relief:

- where the foreign company paying the dividend pays tax at different rates, one of which is dependent on how much of the profits are distributed, HMRC's view is that relief is available for the actual tax on the profits represented by the dividends, i.e. including the tax charged on the distribution, rather than the average rate up to that point; and
- where the foreign company paying the dividend has accumulated losses in its

accounts, the relevant profits for the purposes of calculating underlying tax are undistributed profits of the most recent available period (looked at in isolation) when the dividend is paid.

Calculation of available underlying tax: relevant profits

In order to establish the amount of underlying tax on a dividend, it is necessary to determine the tax paid on the profits out of which the dividend itself has been paid. If relief for underlying tax is due, then the amount of underlying tax to be taken into account is that amount of the foreign tax borne on the 'relevant profits' by the overseas company paying the dividend as is properly attributable to the proportion of the relevant profits represented by the dividend.

Underlying tax which is UK tax

In a chain of related companies, any UK income tax or corporation tax payable by the overseas company in respect of its profits (say, on UK permanent establishment profits) is available as if it were foreign tax in determining the available tax credit on a subsequent dividend paid out of those profits. Using the underlying tax formula, there may be a mismatch between a company's accounting profits and their corporation tax payable, which is calculated on their taxable profits. In a chain of companies, a company at the third or lower level may be a UK company (or a UK permanent establishment) and the underlying tax rate calculated may therefore be either greater than or less than the rate of UK corporation tax which the company has paid.

Law: TIOPA 2010, s. 63–66

58.9 Unrelieved foreign tax companies

58.9.1 Unrelieved double tax: introduction

The rules for unrelieved double tax, in relation to companies, have been subject to numerous changes (in form, if not substance) since the start of this century. Under the UK system of double tax relief there is potentially the loss of any relief which cannot be utilised in the year in which the income, profits or gains are taxable. This problem would not occur under an exemption system where foreign income is not taxed again in the country of residence of the recipient if it has already been taxed in the country of origin or source, regardless of the rate of that foreign tax. This method applies in many countries, particularly for shareholdings greater than mere portfolio level. This is sometimes known as a 'participation exemption'.

In the UK, however, the credit route applies instead. Therefore, where taxable amounts are reduced by reliefs, such as losses or management expenses, so that the UK tax is less than the foreign tax suffered, there was prior to March 2001, no mechanism for allowing that surplus of unrelieved foreign tax to be available in other periods. Companies unable to use foreign tax as a relief against corporation tax were required to write it off in their accounts as a direct expense of earning profits. This problem is now dealt with in TIOPA 2010, s. 72 et seq.

58.9.2 Outline of rules

The legislation provides for a relief for underlying tax on dividends received by UK companies directly from foreign subsidiaries by aggregation (TIOPA 2010, s. 71). There is also relief allowing for the carry-forward and carry-back of unrelieved foreign tax (TIOPA 2010, s. 73).

The relief is given by treating the excess as if:

(a) it were foreign tax paid in respect of, and calculated by reference to, the company's qualifying income from the permanent establishment in the accounting period; or
(b) as if it were foreign tax paid in respect of, and calculated by reference to, the company's qualifying income from the permanent establishment in one or more of the recent periods (in accordance with the rules set out in TIOPA 2010, s. 74); or
(c) by a combination of the methods set out in (a) and (b) above.

Law: TIOPA 2010, s. 71–77

58.9.3 Pre-FA 2009 rules: unrelieved foreign tax of companies

Prior to FA 2009, the rules for obtaining relief for unrelieved amounts were much more complex. They are set out below.

The provisions allow a company, on the making of a claim, to utilise both foreign tax available for credit and underlying tax which is unused due to insufficient corporation tax against which to set it, but only if arising on dividends or, separately, on foreign permanent establishment/branch profits. Relief is available in three ways:

- for dividends only – by offset against particular income of the same accounting period; or
- for trading, etc. profits, as well as dividends,
    (a) by carry-forward to succeeding accounting periods indefinitely; or else
    (b) by carry-back to accounting periods beginning within the three years preceding that in which the surplus arises,

or partly in one way and partly in one or both of the others (ICTA 1988, s. 806D(4), (5)).

Apparently generous, at least by comparison with the situation prevailing before the legislation applies, the provisions have their limitations.

(1) As indicated above, they only apply to companies (ICTA 1988, s. 806A(1)).

(2) They only cover foreign tax on specific income, namely:

    (a) dividends which are taxable under Schedule D Case V and which could not be trading income under the extended loss relief provisions including, for the avoidance of doubt, dividends where the relief claimed is underlying tax or as a deduction, but excluding certain types of dividends; and

    (b) profits from a trade carried on through a permanent establishment (formerly branch or agency) abroad.

(3) Relief for tax on dividends, including relief for any excess carried back or forward, can only be offset against corporation tax on specified 'pools' of 'related' and 'unrelated' dividends which are kept entirely separate for these purposes (hence, 'onshore pooling'), not against all foreign dividends (ICTA 1988, s. 806C).

(4) Similarly, relief for underlying tax on dividends is kept separate from relief for withholding tax (ICTA 1988, s. 806D).

(5) Each overseas permanent establishment (branch) stands on its own for relief purposes and if an overseas permanent establishment (branch) ceases, any surplus of unrelieved foreign tax dies with it.

(6) There are restrictions to the carry-back or forward of relief.

Law: ICTA 1988, s. 806C–806D

58.9.4 Unrelieved foreign tax on dividends

Where there is surplus foreign tax for which relief cannot be claimed against the dividend income on which it was suffered (or for which there is underlying tax), it may be available for additional relief (as 'eligible unrelieved foreign tax' or EUFT). An apparently complex structure of arrangements and calculations obscures a relatively straightforward principle. A modicum of extra relief is being made available by comparing the credit relief actually given, or the restricted underlying tax available, with a hypothetical regime where corporation tax is at a set rate (initially fixed at 45 per cent) higher than the full rate. To the extent that there is a difference, further relief may be possible as described below, up to the hypothetical higher rate, failing which, any excess can always be carried forward.

Surplus unrelieved foreign tax may be available for additional relief (as 'eligible unrelieved foreign tax' or EUFT) in two circumstances (ICTA 1988, s. 806A(3), (4)).

(1) Where the amount of foreign tax for which relief by way of credit is allowable

exceeds the relief actually given for that tax (ignoring the restriction by reference to corporation tax on the income in ICTA 1988, s. 797(1)) ('Case A').

(2) Where the amount of underlying tax (including tax at lower levels) for which relief is allowable exceeds the relief actually given for that tax (ignoring the restriction by reference to the underlying tax formula in ICTA 1988, s. 799(1)(b)) ('Case B').

In other words, the position where foreign or underlying tax is greater than the amount relieved, ignoring for the time being the normal statutory limits on the amount of such relief and, of course, also ignoring any relief under these new provisions.

Eligible unrelieved foreign tax

In those two instances, the amount of tax available for relief as 'eligible unrelieved foreign tax' is.

(1) **Actual tax (Case A)** the difference between the actual relief and the amount that would have been allowed, this time taking account of the restriction in ICTA 1988, s. 797(1), but as if the rate of corporation tax on the income were 45 per cent (the 'upper percentage'), i.e. EUFT is restricted to 15 per cent of the gross dividend.

(2) **Underlying tax (Case B)** either:

   (a) where the mixer cap in ICTA 1988, s. 799(1)(b) applies to restrict the amount of relief for underlying tax on the dividend received in the UK itself – the difference between that restricted relief and the amount that would have been allowed had the fraction used the 45 per cent 'upper percentage' rate instead of the main rate of corporation tax, i.e. EUFT is restricted to 15 per cent of the gross dividend.'M'; or

   (b) where the mixer cap applied to restrict the amount of relief for underlying tax on dividends at levels below the dividend received in the UK – must be streamed into its constituent components and the EUFT must be calculated on each portion separately. Again, this will be the difference between that restricted underlying tax and the amount arrived at by taking account of the mixer cap, but restricted to 15 per cent of the gross dividend out of which it was paid (ICTA 1988, s. 806B(6), (7)).

   (The 'upper percentage' is defined by ICTA 1988, s. 806J(7) and may be subject to adjustment in future.)

⚠ **Warning!**
FA 2009, Sch. 14, para. 9 removes the provisions of ICTA 1988, s. 806A–806K, i.e. the double taxation relief in relation to foreign dividends: onshore pooling and utilization of eligible unrelieved foreign tax. Thus these provisions will no

> longer apply from 22 April 2009. From that date, the simpler rules in TIOPA 2010 will apply to give relief for unrelieved amounts.

58.10 Capital gains tax

58.10.1 Double taxation relief on gains

Provision is made to give relief from double taxation by means of treaties and/or unilateral relief. This is done by applying the income tax provisions with the substitution of CGT for income tax as the context may require.

The provision relating to disclosure of information to foreign officials, etc. for purposes of double taxation applies in relation to CGT as it applies in relation to income tax.

The main requirement for the granting of credit for overseas tax against liability to CGT (or corporation tax on chargeable gains) is therefore that the overseas tax should be computed by reference to the same gain as the UK tax. There is no requirement that the respective tax liabilities should arise at the same time nor that they should be charged on the same person. In contrast, where 'roll-over' relief is claimed the gain on disposal of the old asset is not subjected to UK tax: the gain on realisation of the new asset remains a gain separate from that realised on sale of the old asset and overseas tax payable as a result of the sale of the old asset is not creditable against UK tax payable on the gain realised on sale of the new asset – however, in such circumstances the overseas tax can be claimed as a deduction in computing the gain for 'roll-over' relief purposes.

A HMRC statement of practice deals with double taxation relief and CGT. The statement provides clarification, particularly in respect of situations where charges to foreign and UK tax on the same gain do not arise at the same time. It gives the following useful examples.

- HMRC's view is that the following sets of circumstances fall within the terms of the standard credit article and may therefore give rise to a credit for overseas tax against CGT or UK corporation tax on chargeable gains.
- The overseas tax charges capital gains as income.
- Overseas tax is payable on a disposal falling within TCGA 1992, s. 170 (transfers within a group of companies treated as taking place on a no gain/no loss basis) and a liability to UK tax arises on a subsequent disposal.
- An overseas trade carried on through a branch or agency is domesticated (i.e. transferred to a local subsidiary) and relief is given under TCGA 1992, s. 140.
- There is a subsequent disposal of the securities (or the subsidiary disposes of the assets within six years) giving rise to a liability to UK tax and overseas tax

is charged in whole or in part by reference to the gain accruing at the date of domestication;
- Overseas tax is payable by reference to increases in the value of assets although there has been no disposal. There is a subsequent disposal of the assets on which a liability to UK tax arises.

Law: TIOPA 2010, Pt. 2

Other guidance: SP 6/88, *Double taxation relief: chargeable gains*

58.10.2 Special withholding tax and CGT

Relief for special withholding tax may be claimed through either TIOPA 2010, s. 137–140.

FA 2004, s. 108: income tax credit, etc. for special withholding tax

This credit is available where:

- a person is liable to income tax for a tax year in respect of a payment of savings income, or would be so liable for a tax year in respect of a payment of savings income but for any exemption or relief;
- special withholding tax is levied in respect of the payment; and
- the person concerned is resident in the UK for that tax year.

The definition of 'savings income' is given in TIOPA 2010, s. 136:

- where the special withholding tax is levied under the law of an EU member state in accordance with the EU Savings Income Directive (Directive 2003/48/EC), is the same as the definition of 'interest payment' which is set out in art. 6 of the Directive (see art. 15 of the Directive for exclusion of certain negotiable debt securities from debt claims for the purpose of the definition of interest payment); and
- where the special withholding tax is levied under the law of a territory other than an EU member state, is the same as the definition of the corresponding expression within any 'international arrangements' concerning that territory and the UK.

The expression 'international arrangements', in relation to a territory, means arrangements in relation to that territory with a view to ensuring the effective taxation of savings income under either UK law or UK law and the law of the territory concerned.

On making a claim, the special withholding tax is treated, under TIOPA 2010, s. 137(5), as being an amount of income tax ('the deemed tax') that has been:

- paid by or on behalf of the person for that tax year; and
- deducted at source for that tax year for the purposes of:

(a) TMA 1970, s. 7 (notice of liability to income tax and capital gains tax);
(b) TMA 1970, s. 8 (personal return);
(c) TMA 1970, s. 8A (trustee's return);
(d) TMA 1970, s. 9 (returns to include self assessment);
(e) TMA 1970, s. 59A (payments on account of income tax);
(f) TMA 1970, s. 59B (payments of income tax and capital gains tax); and
(g) ICTA 1988, s. 824(3) (repayment supplements: determination of relevant time).

Where 'the deemed tax' (i.e. special withholding tax deemed to be an amount of income tax) exceeds the amount of income tax for which the person is liable for the tax year:

- first, the excess is set off against any capital gains tax liability for that tax year; and
- if some excess remains after set-off against that capital gains tax, the excess remaining can be repaid to the person (TIOPA 2010, s. 138(4)).

A claim to deem the special withholding tax to be an amount of income tax (i.e. to have deemed tax) does not take effect if:

- the person has obtained double tax relief in respect of the special withholding tax under the law of a territory outside the UK; and
- the person was resident in that territory, or was treated as being so resident under any double taxation arrangements, in the tax year concerned.

TIOPA 2010, s. 21(1) provides that double taxation relief in respect of special withholding tax is not to be available under the UK legislation (TIOPA 2010, Pt. 2).

Planning point

By virtue of TIOPA 2010, s. 141, any credit for foreign tax that is allowed against income tax or capital gains tax takes effect before the special withholding tax provisions take effect. This order of precedence is advantageous for the taxpayer because excess 'deemed tax', after set-off against income tax and capital gains tax, is repayable to the taxpayer whereas any excess foreign tax, after set-off against UK tax, is not repayable.

Example 58.5

Samuel, who is resident and ordinarily resident in the UK, received in the tax year a cheque for £1,700 in respect of interest on his Austrian Government securities. Special withholding tax of £300 had been levied. For that tax year, Samuel's income tax liability is £100 and his capital gains tax liability is £600.

If Samuel makes a claim under TIOPA 2010, s. 135 et seq, then income tax ('the deemed tax') of an amount equal to the amount of the special withholding tax (i.e. £300) is treated as having been deducted at source and paid by or on behalf of Samuel in the tax year.

Accordingly, the deemed tax of £300 is set against the income tax liability of £50, leaving the excess amount of the deemed tax (i.e. £250) to be set against the capital gains tax liability. Therefore, Samuel's capital gains tax liability for the tax year is reduced from £600 to £350.

Capital gains tax credit, etc. for special withholding tax

TIOPA 2010, s. 139 applies where:

(1) a person disposes of an asset in a tax year;

(2) on the assumption that if a chargeable gain were to accrue on this disposal, then:

    (a) the chargeable gain would accrue to the person making the disposal; and

    (b) that person would be chargeable to capital gains tax in respect of that gain.

(3) the disposal consideration consists of, or includes, an amount of savings income and special withholding tax is levied in respect of all or some of the disposal consideration; and

(4) the person making the disposal is resident in the UK for that tax year.

With regard to the person being chargeable to capital gains tax in respect of the gain, the following provisions are to be disregarded:

- TCGA 1992, s. 2(2), which covers the deduction of allowable losses; and
- TCGA 1992, s. 3, which covers the annual exempt amount.

On making a claim, the special withholding tax is treated as being an amount of capital gains tax ('the deemed tax') that has been paid by or on behalf of the person for that tax year. For the purposes of computing a repayment supplement under TCGA 1992, s. 283, 'the deemed tax' is treated as having been paid on 31 January next following the tax year.

Where 'the deemed tax' (i.e. special withholding tax deemed to be an amount of capital gains tax) exceeds the amount of capital gains tax for which the person is liable for the tax year:

- first, the excess is set off against any income tax liability for that tax year; and
- if some excess remains after set-off against that income tax, the excess remaining can be repaid to the person (TIOPA 2010, s. 140).

A claim to deem the special withholding tax to be an amount of capital gains tax (i.e. to have deemed tax) does not take effect if:

- the person has obtained double tax relief in respect of the special withholding tax under the law of a territory outside the UK; and

Double Taxation Relief

- the person was resident in that territory, or was treated as being so resident under any double taxation arrangements, in the tax year concerned.

Double taxation relief in respect of the special withholding tax is not to be available under the UK legislation (TIOPA 2010, Pt. 2). Furthermore, the special withholding tax is not to be regarded as foreign tax for the purposes of the UK legislation (TIOPA 2010, s. 21).

By TIOPA 2010, s. 140, the special withholding tax cannot be claimed to be treated as capital gains tax to the extent that a claim under TIOPA 2010, s. 137 has been made or could be made.

Planning point

Any credit for foreign tax that is allowed against income tax or capital gains tax takes effect before TIOPA 2010, s. 135–141 take effect. This order of precedence is advantageous for the taxpayer because excess 'deemed tax', after set-off against income tax and capital gains tax, is repayable to the taxpayer whereas any excess foreign tax, after set-off against UK tax, is not repayable.

Computing chargeable gain subject to special withholding tax only

Where just the special withholding tax has been levied, the provisions for computing the amount of income or gain for the purposes of income tax and for computing the amount of chargeable gain for the purposes of capital gains tax are set out in TIOPA 2010, s. 142–143. TIOPA 2010, s. 144, which is dealt with below, contains the provisions for computing the income or gain for income tax purposes and for computing the chargeable gain for capital gains tax purposes where the income, gain or chargeable gain, as the case may be, has been subject to both special withholding tax and foreign tax.

TIOPA 2010, s. 142–143 apply where:

- a person is chargeable to income tax in respect of a payment of savings income, or a chargeable gain accrues to a person on a disposal made by that person of assets in circumstances where the disposal consideration consists of or includes an amount of savings income; and
- the following two conditions are satisfied:
    (a) the first condition is that the special withholding tax is levied in respect of the payment of savings income or in respect of the whole or any part of the disposal consideration; and
    (b) the second condition is that no credit for foreign tax in respect of the savings income or chargeable gain concerned falls to be allowed otherwise.

Remittance basis

If capital gains tax is payable by reference to the amount of chargeable gain received in, or remitted to, the UK then, under TIOPA 2010, s. 143, the amount received is treated for the purposes of capital gains tax as increased by an amount equal to:

$$SWT \times GUK / (G - SWT),$$

where:

SWT = the amount of special withholding tax levied in respect of the whole or any part of the disposal consideration;
GUK = the amount of the chargeable gain received in the UK; and
G = the amount of the chargeable gain accruing to the person on the disposal.

TCGA 1992, s. 12 sets out the remittance basis for the purposes of the taxation of certain chargeable gains of persons who are resident but not domiciled in the UK who can claim the remittance basis. It applies the provisions of ITA 2007, s. 809L to 809T to determine the meaning of 'remitted to the United Kingdom'.

Example 58.6

Benjamin, who is resident and ordinarily resident in the UK but domiciled outside the UK, made a claim for the remittance basis to apply. He disposed of certain overseas securities. With regard to this disposal, savings income is included in the disposal consideration, special withholding tax (SWT) of £150 (which is the subject of a claim made by Benjamin) was levied on part of the disposal consideration, the amount of the gain accruing to him is £15,000 (G) and the amount of the gain received in the UK (GUK) is £5,000. The gain accruing to Benjamin on his disposal has not given rise to any foreign tax liability.

Therefore, the amount of the gain that is subject to UK capital gains tax is £5,050, being:

£5,000 + [£150 × (£5,000 / (£15,000 − £150))].

Finally, TIOPA 2010, s. 143 provides that, where income tax is charged on income received in the UK (i.e. remittance basis) instead of on income accrued, the amount of savings income received in the UK is treated for the purposes of income tax as increased by the amount of special withholding tax levied in respect of it.

Accruals basis

If the remittance basis does not apply then no special withholding tax is deducted from the amount of the chargeable gain for the purposes of capital gains tax.

The amount of the chargeable gain for the purposes of capital gains tax is computed in accordance with the provisions of the *Taxation of Chargeable Gains Act* 1992

(TCGA 1992). In particular, TCGA 1992, s. 37, exclusion of consideration chargeable to income tax, applies.

Finally, as with the chargeable gain for capital gains tax purposes, no special withholding tax is deducted from the amount of the income or gain in question for the purposes of income tax.

Law: TIOPA 2010, s. 143

Computing chargeable gain subject to foreign tax and special withholding tax

Background

Foreign tax may be used to reduce UK tax in order to avoid double taxation. In this regard, foreign tax is distinct from the special withholding tax – TIOPA 2010, s. 6(5) and s. 21 provide that:

- relief from double taxation in respect of special withholding tax is not available under TIOPA 2010, Pt. 2; and
- special withholding tax is not regarded as foreign tax for the purposes of TIOPA 2010, Pt. 2.

Details on the computation

Remittance basis

Where:

- a chargeable gain accrues to a person on a disposal by that person of assets in circumstances where the disposal consideration consists of or includes an amount of savings income; and
- special withholding tax is levied in respect of the whole or any part of the disposal consideration, then, under TIOPA 2010, s. 31–32, as applied (or modified) by TCGA 1992, s. 277(1B), the amount of the chargeable gain that has been received in the UK is increased by:
- the amount of foreign tax charged in respect of the amount of chargeable gain received in the UK; and
- an amount of special withholding tax equal to:

$$AWT \times [GUK / (G - SWT)],$$

where:

AWT = the amount of special withholding tax levied in respect of the whole or the part of the disposal consideration;
GUK = the amount of the chargeable gain received in the UK; and
G = the amount of the chargeable gain accruing to the person on the disposal.

Finally, with regard to income tax where the remittance basis applies, under TIOPA 2010, s.s. 32, the amount of income received in the UK is increased by:

- the amount of foreign tax charged; and
- the amount of the special withholding tax levied,

in respect of the amount of income that has been received in the UK.

Accruals basis

Where the remittance basis is not or cannot be claimed, the normal accruals basis applies. Under ICTA 1988, s. 795(2)(a) as amended by FA 2004, s. 112(3). No foreign tax and no special withholding tax are deducted from the amount of chargeable gain for the purposes of capital gains tax. Similarly, no foreign tax and no special withholding tax are deducted from the amount of income or gain in question for the purposes of income tax.

59 Residence Status of Individuals

59.1 Introduction

The tax liabilities of individuals can vary enormously depending on whether they are resident or not in the United Kingdom. This chapter discusses what is meant by residence status for these purposes; it does not purport to summarise the various tax advantages (and disadvantages) of being classified as resident or non-resident for any particular tax year.

> ⚠ *Warning!*
>
> If an individual is not resident in the UK in any one tax year (and even if the individual is resident in the UK in that tax year), income arising and gains realised might nevertheless be taxed in other jurisdictions. Therefore, it would be foolhardy to consider the UK consequences on their own.

> *Planning point*
>
> The tie-breaker provisions in the near-comprehensive range of double taxation agreements entered into between the UK and other nations will often mean that an individual will not be treated as resident in more than one jurisdiction at any one time.
>
> Treaty relief and unilateral relief provided for in the UK will also minimise the impact of double taxation.

> ⚠ *Warning!*
>
> However, double taxation agreements are not necessarily comprehensive. For example, income arising in an ISA will generally be tax-free in the UK. However, there is no reason to suggest that such income will escape tax overseas.

59.2 General principles

59.2.1 Sources of definitions

The concept of an individual's residence is subject to common law principles. However, in the tax context, statute often supplements (or overrides) the common law.

For many years, HMRC (and its predecessor, the Inland Revenue) had a practice that was based upon a booklet, known generally as 'IR20'. Until 5 April 2009, HMRC maintained that the IR20 guidance remained operative although recent cases suggested that HMRC had reinterpreted their own guidance. Their ability to change their practice in this way is currently subject to judicial review proceedings, with the outcome expected to be known early in 2010.

Anticipating further complaints, as well as the fact that IR20 had become sorely out of date – it was last published in December 1999 – HMRC officially withdrew the guidance with effect from 6 April 2009. They have published in its place guidance known as HMRC6. However, that falls short of offering anything that they can base any reasonable reliance in borderline cases.

59.2.2 The types of residence

The tax statutes refer to two types of residence: 'residence' and 'ordinary residence'.

Generally speaking, 'ordinary residence' relates to an individual's residence status over the longer term. However, practice and some case law suggests that an individual cannot be ordinarily resident in the UK unless that individual is also resident in the UK.

Other guidance: *Levene v IR Commrs*(1928) 13 TC 486

59.3 Residence

59.3.1 Common law meaning

59.3.1.1 Introduction

Contrary to what one might expect, there is nothing complicated about the meaning of 'residence'. In one of the leading cases in this area (*Levene*), Viscount Cave held:

> 'My Lords, the word 'reside' is a familiar English word and is defined in the Oxford English Dictionary as meaning 'to dwell permanently or for a considerable time, to have one's settled or usual abode, to live in or at a particular place'.'
>
> 'In most cases there is no difficulty in determining where a man has his settled or usual abode, and if that is ascertained he is not the less resident there because from time to time he leaves it for the purpose of business or pleasure. Thus, a master mariner who had his home at Glasgow where his wife and family lived, and to which he returned during the intervals between his sea voyages, was held to reside there, although he actually spent the greater part of the year at sea (*Re Young* (1875) 1 TC 57; *Rogers v Inland Revenue* (1879) 1 TC 225). Similarly a person who has his home abroad and visits the United Kingdom from time to time for temporary purposes without setting up an establishment in this country is not considered to be resident here'

The same logic is used to determine whether a particular house (or other dwelling) constitutes an individual's place of residence (for example, for the main residence relief rules). However, it is important to realise that an individual need not be attached to a particular property or location to be considered a resident in the UK. In another case (*Reid*), the Lord President held:

> 'Take the case of a homeless tramp, who shelters tonight under a bridge, tomorrow in the greenwood and as the unwelcome occupant of a farm outhouse the night after. He wanders in this way all over the United Kingdom. But will anyone say he does not live in the United Kingdom? And will anyone regard it as a misuse of language to say he resides in the United Kingdom? In his case there may be no relations with family or friends, no business ties, and none of the ordinary circumstances which create a link between the life of a British subject and the United Kingdom; but, even so, I do not think it could be disputed that he resides in the United Kingdom. There are other and very different kinds of tramps, who–being possessed of ample means, and having the ordinary ties of birth, family, and affairs with the United Kingdom or some part of it–yet prefer to enjoy those means without undertaking the domestic responsibility of a home, and who move about from one house of public entertainment to another–in London today, in the provinces tomorrow, and in the Highlands the day after. They too are homeless wanderers in the United Kingdom. But surely it is true to say that they live in the United Kingdom, and reside there? The Section of the Act of Parliament with which we are dealing speaks of persons 'residing,' not at a particular locality, but in a region so extensive as the United Kingdom.'

In the other main case in this area, Lord Buckmaster held:

> 'It may be true that the word 'reside' or 'residence' in other Acts may have special meanings, but in the Income Tax Acts it is, I think, used in its common sense and it is essentially a question of fact whether a man does or does not comply with its meaning.'

In the *Grace* case (and subsequently endorsed by the Court of Appeal), Lewison J listed a number of other propositions that were relevant in determining a person's residence status including:

- Physical presence in a particular place does not necessarily amount to residence

in that place where, for example, a person's physical presence there is no more than a stop gap measure: *Goodwin v Curtis* [1998] BTC 176, 180.
- In considering whether a person's presence in a particular place amounts to residence there, one must consider the amount of time that he spends in that place, the nature of his presence there and his connection with that place: *IR Commrs v Zorab* (1926) 11 TC 289.
- Residence in a place connotes some degree of permanence, some degree of continuity or some expectation of continuity: *Fox v Stirk* [1970] 2 QB 463, 477; *Goodwin v Curtis* [1998] BTC 176, 180.
- However, short but regular periods of physical presence may amount to residence, especially if they stem from performance of a continuous obligation (such as business obligations) and the sequence of visits excludes the elements of chance and of occasion: *Lysaght v IR Commrs* (1928) 13 TC 511.
- Although a person can have only one domicile at a time, he may simultaneously reside in more than one place, or in more than one country: *Levene v IR Commrs* (1928) 13 TC 486.
- Where a person has had his sole residence in the United Kingdom he is unlikely to be held to have ceased to reside in the United Kingdom (or to have 'left' the United Kingdom) unless there has been a definite break in his pattern of life: *IR Commrs v Combe* (1932) 17 TC 405, 411.

Other guidance: *Levene v IR Commrs* (1928) 13 TC 486; *Reid v IR Commrs*(1926) 10 TC 673; *Lysaght v IR Commrs* (1928) 13 TC 511; *R & C Commrs v Grace* [2009] BTC 704

59.3.1.2 Time spent in the UK

By far the most important factor determining an individual's residence status is the amount of time spent in the UK.

> ⚠ **Warning!**
>
> However, this factor is not itself determinative of the matter.
>
> The mariner cases referred to above show that it is possible for an individual to be treated as resident in the UK in a tax year in which the individual does not spend any time in the UK.

In the *Lysaght* case, an individual who had retired to the Irish Free State made frequent business trips to the UK in his capacity as advisory director to his former company. Over a number of years, his visits averaged approximately 91 days each year. It was held that he had remained resident in the UK in those years.

It was the conclusion of this case that has led to the HMRC practice (found in the former IR20 guidance) that will treat an individual as resident if their visits average 91 days or more over a number of years.

> **Planning point**
>
> The 91-day rule is not statutory. Depending on the circumstances of the case, there is no reason why every taxpayer who spends 91 days on average will be held to be resident.
>
> Furthermore, the validity of the decision in *Lysaght* is not the most convincing. The House of Lords was not unanimous in its decision. More importantly, one of the Lordships in the majority noted that he would personally not have found the individual to have been resident on the facts presented but he felt unable to overturn the finding of fact made by the Special Commissioners.

Much of the recent controversy concerning HMRC's treatment of individuals' residence status relates to the application of the 91-day rule. Hitherto, HMRC appeared in practice to accept an individual as non-resident if they spent fewer than 91 days in the UK on average. However, they have made it clear that they will consider the *quality* of an individual's presence in the UK as well as the *quantity*.

59.3.1.3 Other factors indicating residence

Subsequent case law has determined that an individual's residence status must be determined by considering all the relevant facts.

Factors that ought to be considered include:

- the duration of an individual's presence in the UK;
- the regularity and frequency of visits;
- birth, family and business ties;
- the nature of visits;
- the connections with this country; and
- whether or not the individual had previously established a residence in the UK.

> **Planning point**
>
> It has been held that an individual's desire to avoid UK taxes is not a relevant factor in determining whether or not the individual has ceased to be resident in the UK.

> ⚠ **Warning!**
>
> It is often assumed that the availability of UK accommodation is not a factor that need be considered when determining an individual's residence status. That assumption follows a change in the law in 1993.
>
> The assumption is, however, wrong.

> The change made in 1993 is much more limited in scope and relates to one of the statutory modifications to the rules, discussed below. As a general rule, the availability of UK accommodation continues to be a relevant factor.

Other guidance: Shepherd v R & C Commrs [2007] BTC 426; Reed (HMIT) v Clark [1985] BTC 224

59.3.1.4 Differences between leavers and those arriving in the UK

It has long been accepted that individuals who seek to leave the UK will often find it more difficult to abandon a UK-resident status than for individuals, who come from overseas, to avoid acquiring one. The cases of *Zorab* and *Brown*, though superficially similar to that of *Levene* will demonstrate this. The *Brown* case is particularly telling as Mr Brown had spent the previous 25 years living in the UK before the tax years in question.

Following those precedents, it would have been thought that one could discern a sufficient difference in relevant facts to justify the (same) Special Commissioner's different conclusions in the cases of *Shepherd v R & C Commrs* and *R & C Commrs v Grace*. However, when the latter was subject to an appeal by HMRC at the High Court, the judge felt that the facts found could lead only to the conclusion that Mr Grace was in fact resident for the years in question. This seemed to contradict the decision by another High Court judge, only one week previously, in the non-tax case involving the Russian oligarch, Roman Abramovich that suggested that significant presence by an overseas visitor (even one with living accommodation in the UK) would not necessitate the acquisition of common law residence status. The *Grace* case was subsequently heard by the Court of Appeal in late 2009 and has been remitted to the First-tier Tribunal for further consideration.

Other guidance: IR Commrs v Zorab (1926) 11 TC 289; IR Commrs v Brown (1926) 11 TC 292; Shepherd v R & C Commrs [2007] BTC 426; Grace v R & C Commrs [2009] BTC 704; OJSC Oil Company Yugraneft (in liquidation) v Abramovich [2008] EWHC 2613 (Comm)

59.3.2 Statutory provisions

59.3.2.1 Introduction

In addition to the common law test, statute has provided supplementary tests that need to be considered for tax purposes. They are similarly worded for income tax purposes and capital gains tax purposes. This chapter will consider only the former set of provisions.

Law: ITA 2007, Pt. 14, Ch. 2; TCGA 1992, s. 9

59.3.2.2 The 183-day rule

The most well-known rule is the 183-day rule. Until 5 April 2007, the test referred to 'six months'. However, it has almost universally been applied as if it were a 183-day rule and that practice was reflected in the rewrite of the rules with effect from 6 April 2007.

The rule provides that, in certain cases:

- individuals who spend 183 or more days in the UK are taxed as if they were resident in the UK; and
- individuals who spend fewer than 183 days in the UK are taxed as if they were not resident in the UK; and

The 183-day rule is not of universal relevance. It applies only in respect of individuals:

- who are in the UK for some temporary purpose only; and
- who are not in the UK with a view to establishing a residence in the UK.

> ⚠ **Warning!**
>
> The 183-day rule does not apply for all tax purposes. It is relevant only in respect of employment income and those purposes listed in s. 831(2).

Counting the 183 days

The practice before 6 April 2008

Until 5 April 2008, HMRC practice was for days of departure and arrival to be ignored when counting the 183 days. This was a pragmatic solution to the decision in a case in the 1950s in which it was held that, strictly, the time spent in the UK should be calculated on the basis of fractions of the day.

> **Example 59.1**
>
> Suppose David arrived in the UK at noon on 6 April. In order not to be caught by the 183-day rule, he would strictly needed to have left the UK before noon on 6 October (183 days later).
>
> Under HMRC practice, however, the time spent in the UK on 6 April would not have counted. Nor would the time spent in the UK on the date of departure. Consequently, David could have remained in the UK until midnight on 7 October to avoid the application of the 183-day rule.

The rules from 6 April 2008

From 6 April 2008, the method for calculating the number of days has been revised. In brief, a day is counted if and only if the individual is present at midnight at the end of the day in question: thus, days of arrival are counted, but days of departure are excluded and days on which an individual both arrives and leaves are also excluded.

> ### Planning point
>
> HMRC's guidance will indicate that the new counting rules will apply equally for the purposes of the 91-day and 183-day rules. However, strictly, they are relevant only to the 183-day rule because the 91-day rule is non-statutory and cannot be amended 'by implication'.
>
> Given the doubts concerning the 91-day threshold (referred to above) any over-zealous application of the 91-day rule should be referred to the tax tribunal.

Under the 2008 rules, however, there is a statutory concession for visitors to the UK who spend only one night in the country. The concession is designed to protect individuals who spend the night in the UK in transit and applies only to individuals who, whilst in the UK do not 'engage in activities that are to a substantial extent unrelated to the individual's passage through the United Kingdom'.

Guidance published in HMRC6:

- arranging to meet a business contact for dinner would mean that the night spent in the UK would be counted under the 183-day rule; but
- a drink in the airport or hotel with an acquaintance whom one meets by chance would not.

> ### ⚠ Warning!
>
> The application of this test in practice will need to evolve over time. However, the following should be noted:
>
> - If an individual plans to spend the working day in the UK but to take a late flight out of the country, that should allow the day to be excluded from the 183-day test. However, the day will count if the departure is delayed until the next day (for any reason).
> - If an individual plans to be in the UK overnight but is strictly in transit, that night will not count if the individual does not engage in any non-incidental activities whilst in the UK. However, if the outbound journey is delayed until the following day, the individual will have to count both the day of arrival and the following day.
>
> In addition, it is not yet certain what constitutes departure from the UK.
>
> - Is it passing through passport control?
> - Is it the time of boarding?

- Is it the time of departure?
  - If so, is it the scheduled departure?
  - Or is it actual departure?
- Or is it time that one leaves territorial waters or airspace?
- Additionally, for departures on Eurostar, are there special definitions of what constitutes the UK?

Law: ITA 2007, s. 831, 832

59.3.2.3 Temporary absences

The 183-day rule (which applies to temporary visitors to the UK) is often considered to be the converse of the rule which considers temporary absences from the UK.

It applies if an individual was both UK resident and ordinarily resident and then leaves the UK. If that departure is only 'for the purposes of occasional residence abroad' then the individual will continue to be treated as resident for income tax purposes.

In one celebrated case, involving the singer Dave Clark, it was held that absence abroad for an entire tax year would constitute more than a temporary absence if:

- the individual establishes a residence overseas;
- the individual is working full-time overseas; and
- the individual makes no return visits to the UK in the meantime.

Law: ITA 2007, s. 829

Other guidance: Reed (HMIT) v Clark [1985] BTC 224

59.4 Ordinary residence

59.4.1 Meaning of ordinary residence

There is no statutory definition given to the term 'ordinary residence'. However, it is widely accepted that it bears the same meaning as that applied in education law and the term 'habitual resident' used in social security law.

In the leading authority on the former term, Lord Scarman held:

> 'Unless, therefore, it can be shown that the statutory framework or the legal context in which the words are used requires a different meaning, I unhesitatingly subscribe to the view that "ordinarily resident" refers to a man's abode in a particular place or

country which he has adopted voluntarily and for settled purposes as part of the regular order of his life for the time being, whether of short or of long duration.

All that is necessary is that the purpose of living where one does has a sufficient degree of continuity to be properly described as settled.'

As noted above, it is unclear as to whether an individual can be non-resident in the UK yet ordinarily resident here. *Levene* suggests no but the above extract from Lord Scarman does not necessarily support that conclusion.

In the *Grace* case in the High Court (and endorsed by the Court of Appeal), Lewison J listed a number of other propositions that were relevant in determining a person's ordinary residence status including:

- Just as a person may be resident in two countries at the same time, he may be ordinarily resident in two countries at the same time: *Re Norris* (1888) 4 TLR 452; *R v Barnet London Borough Council, ex parte Shah* [1983] 2 AC 309, 342;
- It is wrong to conduct a search for the place where a person has his permanent base or centre adopted for general purposes; or, in other words to look for his 'real home': *R v Barnet London Borough Council, ex parte Shah* [1983] 2 AC 309, 345 and 348
- There are only two respects in which a person's state of mind is relevant in determining ordinary residence. First, the residence must be voluntarily adopted; and second, there must be a degree of settled purpose: *R v Barnet London Borough Council, ex parte Shah* [1983] 2 AC 309, 344;
- Although residence must be voluntarily adopted, a residence dictated by the exigencies of business will count as voluntary residence: *Lysaght v IR Commrs* (1928) 13 TC 511
- The purpose, while settled, may be for a limited period; and the relevant purposes may include education, business or profession as well as a love of a place: *R v Barnet London Borough Council, ex parte Shah* [1983] 2 AC 309, 344.

Two conflicting cases have emerged recently on the meaning of 'ordinary residence'. They both featured overseas bankers who had come to live and work in the United Kingdom but whose initial plans were uncertain. In *Genovese*, the Special Commissioner considered that an individual who had no firm plans upon arrival would generally become ordinarily resident about three years after arrival. However, the same Special Commissioner (by now sitting as a Judge of the First-tier Tribunal) decided in *Tuczka* that once one became ordinarily resident, that status could then be backdated to the time that the circumstances that led to the finding of ordinary residence first arose. It is understood that both cases are subject to appeal in the Upper Tribunal.

A further case concerning ordinary residence, *Turberville*, made the point that one should look at all the relevant facts in their proper context when determining an individual's residence status –normal pointers towards ordinary residence in the

UK (such as a house and a relatively short absence abroad) were not sufficient to displace a finding that Mr Turberville was not ordinarily resident in the UK when those facts were considered in the light of his working life over the previous thirty years.

Other guidance: *R v Barnet London Borough Council, ex parte Shah* [1983] 2 AC 309; *Grace v R & C Commrs* [2009] BTC 704; *Genovese v R & C Commrs* (2009) Sp C 741; *Tuczka v R & C Commrs* [2010] UKFTT 53 (TC); *Turberville v R & C Commrs* [2010] UKFTT 69 (TC)

60 Offshore Tax Planning Through Trusts

60.1 History of the taxation of offshore trusts

Like individuals, trustees are not generally liable to capital gains tax on disposals of trust assets, unless they are resident or ordinarily resident in the UK.

Historically, persons wishing to avoid tax have taken advantage of settlements and, in turn, maximum advantage has been taken of the additional planning opportunities afforded by non-UK settlements. As a result, a series of complicated anti-avoidance provisions have been introduced over the years to counter avoidance through the use of offshore settlements. This means that when using offshore settlements, it is essential to obtain appropriate legal advice in order to understand how the anti-avoidance provisions will apply, and the limitations that such provisions impose on any offshore settlement.

Since the introduction of capital gains tax in 1965, the legislation has attempted to tax the gains of non-resident trusts on the UK beneficiaries of such trusts. Originally, this was done by a method of apportionment, and gains which would have been charged on the trustees had they been UK-resident were apportioned between beneficiaries on a just and reasonable basis (CGTA 1979, s. 17). This method was considered to be unsatisfactory as, whilst a tax charge could quite easily be avoided, it could also result in the unfair treatment of certain beneficiaries, who could be taxed on an apportioned gain even though no benefit had been received from the settlement.

In 1981, the original legislation was repealed and FA 1981, s. 80 (see now TCGA 1992, s. 87) was introduced, which assessed trust gains on beneficiaries receiving capital payments. The 1981 rules, whilst making the basis of taxation of beneficiaries more equitable (because the tax charge was by reference to a capital payment received), did, however, allow for the deferral of gains through the non-repatriation of capital.

Throughout the 1980s, offshore trusts became extremely popular tax avoidance vehicles. What were termed 'freezer trusts' were increasingly used to shelter gains whereby low value assets were put into trust and before the value of the assets had substantially appreciated, the trust exported. In the year(s) following export, gains would be realised effectively free of tax if the ultimate beneficiary were prepared to go offshore to benefit from the gain. Increasing adverse publicity ultimately put pressure on the government to review the situation and in the Finance Act 1991 new measures applying to both non-resident and dual resident trusts, were announced. As a result of those changes it is now necessary to distinguish between trusts that emigrated pre-19 March 1991 and those that emigrate after that date. In 1998 legislation imposed additional charges on pre-1991 offshore trusts where the settlor retained an interest.

> **Planning point**
>
> *Finance Act* 2006 contained changes to the capital gains tax definition of offshore trust, which took effect on 6 April 2007. Under the new definition, the trustees are treated as resident and ordinarily resident in the UK at any time if either:
>
> - all the trustees are UK resident; or
> - the following three conditions are met:
>
>   (a) at least one of the trustees is resident in the UK,
>   (b) at least one of the trustees is not resident in the UK, and
>   (c) the settlor was either resident, ordinarily resident or domiciled in the UK when the settlement was made (or, in the case of a settlement arising on the settlor's death, immediately before death).

Finally, the changes made to the remittance basis in FA 2008 had knock-on effects on the taxation of offshore trusts.

60.2 Creation of offshore trust

An offshore trust can be created by the initial appointment of non-resident trustees. The chargeable gains consequences of creating an offshore settlement will depend on the domicile and residence status of the settlor. A non-resident settlor can dispose of assets situated abroad to a non-resident trust without any charge to capital gains tax. When creating an offshore trust it is important to consider the power of appointment of new and additional trustees, which should be restricted so as to prevent the appointment of UK resident trustees.

> **Example 60.1**
>
> Tom, who has a Californian domicile and who is resident in Switzerland, transfers US-situs shares to a trust, resident in Guernsey.
>
> Unsurprisingly, there is no charge to capital gains tax on the disposal.

From 6 April 2008, the capital gains tax position of UK-residents has depended on whether or not the individual is entitled to the remittance basis.

60.3 HMRC information powers

HMRC are given extensive information powers in connection with the attribution of gains of non-resident trusts to settlors. Those powers are outlined below.

(1) An inspector may make a written demand for information to be supplied (within as little as 28 days) from any party to a settlement. Penalties may be imposed for failure to comply with a notice making such a demand.

Law: ITTOIA 2005, s. 647; TMA 1970, s. 98

(2) Where a settlement was created before 17 March 1998 and property is transferred to that settlement on or after 3 May 1994 by way of a transaction other than at arm's length (except in pursuance of a liability incurred before 3 May 1994) to trustees who are at the date of transfer neither resident nor ordinarily resident in the UK, that person is required to supply HMRC with specified details within 12 months of the transfer; this requirement applies even where the transferor only has reason to believe that the trustees are not resident. The details specified are:

(a) details which identify the settlement;
(b) the property transferred;
(c) the day on which the transfer was made;
(d) the consideration for the transfer.

Law: TCGA 1992, Sch. 5A, para. 2

(3) Where a trust has trustees that are neither UK resident nor ordinarily resident, or are UK resident or ordinarily resident but fall to be regarded as resident outside the UK for double taxation relief, is created on or after 3 May 1994, a settlor who is UK-domiciled and either UK-resident or ordinarily resident at the time the settlement is created must supply HMRC with specified details within three months of the date of the creation of the settlement. The details specified are:

(a) the day on which the settlement was created;
(b) the name and address of the person delivering the return;
(c) the names and addresses of the persons who are the trustees immediately before the delivery of the return.

Law: TCGA 1992, Sch. 5A, para. 3

(4) Where a trust has trustees that are neither UK resident nor ordinarily resident, or are UK resident or ordinarily resident but fall to be regarded as resident outside the UK for double taxation relief, is created after 18 March 1991, a settlor who is not UK-domiciled and resident or ordinarily resident at the time the settlement is created but subsequently, at a time after 3 May 1994, becomes so must supply specified details to the HMRC within 12 months of becoming so domiciled and resident.

Law: TCGA 1992, Sch. 5A, para. 4

(5) Where trustees become non-resident or dual-resident on or after 3 May 1994, anyone who was a trustee immediately before the trust became non-resident or dual-resident must supply specified details of the settlement to HMRC within 12 months of the trust becoming non-resident. The specified details are:

- the date on which the settlement was created;
- the name and address of the settlor (or settlors, where more than one) in relation to the trust immediately before the submission of the return; and
- the names and address of the trustees immediately before the submission of the return.

Law: TCGA 1992, Sch. 5A, para. 5

Where information has already been supplied as the result of another provision, there is no need to supply further information under Sch. 5A (TCGA 1992, Sch. 5A, para. 6).

Penalties under TMA 1970, s. 98 apply for failure to provide the required information, although no such failure arises if the HMRC receive the necessary information under other provisions.

Capital payments

An inspector may require any person to supply him with information (in as short a period as 28 days) pertaining to capital payments under TCGA 1992, s. 87–90. HMRC's powers to obtain information in relation to capital payments are the same as their powers under ITA 2007, s. 748.

> ⚠ **Warning!**
>
> A professional adviser, other than a barrister, who is concerned with the making of a settlement who is aware that:
>
> - the settlor is UK-domiciled; and
> - the trustees are not UK-resident, or will not be UK-resident,
>
> is required to notify HMRC, by way of return, of the names and addresses of the settlor and trustees. This obligation, which applies by virtue of IHTA 1984, s. 218, requires that the return be made three months from the making of the settlement.

Law: TCGA 1992, Sch. 5 and 5A

60.4 Migrant settlements

The 1981 regime sought to prevent the avoidance of capital gains tax through a change in the residence status of trustees. These rules were amended by the Finance Act 1991 and are now contained in TCGA 1992, s. 89.

Where a settlement is non-resident for one or more tax years and that period of non-residence (a 'non-resident period') follows a period of one or more years of assessment to which the s. 87 rules attributing gains to beneficiaries do not apply (a 'resident period'), capital payments received by a beneficiary during the resident period are disregarded for the purpose of attributing capital payments to beneficiaries, provided that they were not made in anticipation of a disposal by the trustee when non-resident. The legislation does not attempt to define 'in anticipation of a disposal ...'.

Where a trust which has been non-resident becomes resident and the trust gains for the last year of the non-resident period are not treated (or not wholly treated) as accruing to beneficiaries in that year, any balance is to be carried forward and treated as chargeable gains accruing to beneficiaries who receive capital payments in the first year of residence. Gains are attributed to beneficiaries in proportion to capital payments made. The unattributed gains of the non-resident period continue to be allocated until the amount treated as accruing to the beneficiaries equals the amount of trust gains for the last year of non-residence.

Where there is a subsequent period of non-residence and gains brought forward from the previous non-resident period have still not been exhausted, they will be taken into account in the first year of the subsequent non-resident period.

> **Planning point**
>
> The former exemption for non-domiciliaries continues to operate in respect of certain amounts arising before 6 April 2008.

Law: TCGA 1992, s. 89; FA 2008, Sch. 7, para. 124

60.5 Export of UK trusts

60.5.1 Export of UK trusts: the March 1991 watershed

Where a trust was exported before 19 March 1991 then, unless it became a 'qualifying settlement' the only change introduced by the Finance Act 1991 that affected such a trust is the supplementary charge.

Where a trust was exported before 19 March 1991 it is not, unless it becomes a 'qualifying settlement', subject to the regime whereby settlement gains are attributed to the settlor. As a result such trusts enjoyed privileged status and it was generally the case that the trustees of such a trust wished to ensure that that status was maintained.

From 6 April 1999, pre-1991 trusts were brought within the terms of the 1991 regime even if there had been no change in circumstances.

⚠ Warning!

Some pre-1991 trusts remained protected from the 1991 rules. However, this protection is lost if:

- funds are added to the settlement otherwise than at arm's length;
- the trustees become non-resident (or treated as such); or
- the class of potential beneficiaries is varied so that a disallowed person becomes a beneficiary for the first time.

⚠ Warning!

The list of disallowed beneficiaries was extended from 6 April 1999. Previously, such beneficiaries were the settlor, the settlor's spouse, the child of a settlor or the settlor's spouse, a company controlled by such a person or a company associated with such a company.

From 6 April 1999, grandchildren of the settlor and spouses of such grandchildren were added to the list of disallowed beneficiaries.

⚠ Warning!

The extension of references to spouses so as to cover civil partners with effect from 5 December 2005 causes yet further problems. If a trust has the *potential* of benefiting a civil partner of the settlor (for example), it will lose its protection.

Most pre-1991 trusts were not drafted so as to exclude civil partners and consequently, such trusts would have lost their protection on 5 December 2005.

60.5.2 Gift hold-over relief: emigration of recipient trust

Where trustees ceased to be either UK-resident or ordinarily resident in the UK and at that time the settled property included one or more assets in which hold-over relief had been given, a chargeable gain equal to the held-over gain was deemed to crystallise immediately before the trust was exported (FA 1981, s. 79). The charge on emigration applies to all hold-overs whether under the old gift relief or the later provisions for hold-over of business assets or assets on which inheritance tax is chargeable.

60.5.3 Gift of business asset to company: emigration of controlling trustees

Where trusts were exported before 19 March 1991 a chargeable gain would be deemed to accrue where (CGTA 1979, s. 126C):

- trustees ceased to be either UK-resident or ordinarily resident in the UK;
- before that time (but after 13 March 1989), a connected person disposed of an asset to a company which was controlled by the trustees;
- hold-over relief for business assets had been claimed; and
- at the time of the trust's migration the trustees still controlled the company and the company still owned the asset.

This provision was repealed in 1991 so that CGTA 1979, s. 126C ceased to have effect where trustees become neither UK-resident nor ordinarily resident after 18 March 1991. When the repeal of CGTA 1979, s. 126C was announced, it was referred to by the government as an 'anti-avoidance provision which is no longer necessary in the light of the new provisions'. It is in fact questionable whether that is in fact the case as there would appear to be nothing in the 1991 provisions which would impose a charge to tax in these circumstances.

60.5.4 Attribution of trust gains to beneficiaries

In relation to trusts exported before 19 March 1991, beneficiaries can be taxed in respect of trust gains; gains are assessed on the basis of capital payments received by beneficiaries.

> ⚠ **Warning!**
>
> In certain circumstances, the disposal of a beneficiary's interest in a non-resident trust, or a trust that became non-resident before 19 March 1991, would give rise to a chargeable gain.

60.6 UK trusts exported on or after March 1991

60.6.1 Exit charge: general

Where on or after 19 March 1991 the trustees of a settlement become neither UK-resident or ordinarily resident then at that time – 'the relevant time' – they are deemed for capital gains tax purposes to have disposed of all the 'defined assets' in the trust and immediately re-acquired them at market value.

The assets which the trustees are deemed to dispose of (the 'defined assets') are all of the assets constituted in the trust immediately before the trustees became non-resident, with the exception of:

- assets situated in the UK and used in (or for the purposes of) a trade which, immediately after the 'relevant time', the trustees carry on in the UK through a branch or agency; or
- assets specified in a double tax relief arrangement which would not be regarded as liable to capital gains tax in the UK if the trustees disposed of them immediately before the relevant time.

Where the settlor retains an interest in the settlement, the gain will be assessed on him and not on the trustees.

Trustees who became not resident and not ordinarily resident in the UK between 6 April 1990 and 18 March 1991 (inclusive) and who remained so after 5 April 1991 are not liable to a charge under s. 80 (SP 5/92, para. 3).

Special rules apply where the exit charge provisions are brought into play where emigration occurs as a result of the death of a trustee.

> **Planning point**
>
> The exit charge will no longer allow high gain assets to be exported without charge. However, where a trust contains exempt assets (for example cash, gilts, etc.) or any potential gain on export is low there may still be advantages in exporting the trust given that there would be no charge on migration in the first instance and a low charge in the latter case. This must, however, be considered in the light of the rules attributing gains to settlors.

> **⚠ Warning!**
>
> The exit charge was successfully avoided in the case of *Davies v Hicks*. The UK trustees held quoted shares which were sold before migration of the trust. There was therefore no chargeable asset at the date of migration. The gain that would have arisen in respect of the trustees' actual disposal, however, was avoided by the non-resident trustees reacquiring the shares within 30 days (taking advantage of the anti-bed and breakfasting rules introduced in 1998).
>
> This is no longer effective, however, in respect of any reacquisition taking place on or after 22 March 2006.

Law: TCGA 1992, s. 80

Cases: Davies (HMIT) v Hicks [2005] BTC 331

60.6.2 Export of trusts: assets subject to roll-over relief

In relation to the exit charge where a trust becomes non-resident after 18 March 1991, roll-over relief (under TCGA 1992, s. 152) on replacement of business assets is not available where the old assets are disposed of before the relevant time and the new assets are acquired after that time, except where the new assets are situated in the UK when they are acquired and are used in (or for the purposes of) a trade carried on by the trustees in the UK through a branch or agency, or used or held for the purposes of the branch or agency.

In this context 'old' and 'new' assets have the usual meaning assigned to them under the roll-over relief provisions.

> ⚠ *Warning!*
>
> Rollover relief on replacement of business assets may not be available where the old assets are disposed of before the relevant time and the new assets are acquired after that time.

Law: TCGA 1992, s. 152 and 80(6), (7)

60.6.3 Trustees ceasing to be liable to UK tax

Where, on or after 19 March 1991, trustees of a settlement become dual-resident and by virtue of double taxation relief arrangements they are consequently treated as non-UK-resident for tax purposes, there is deemed to be a disposal and re-acquisition at market value of all the trustees' relevant assets.

'Relevant assets' means all of the assets which are settled property and which are covered by the double taxation relief arrangements.

> ⚠ *Warning!*
>
> This deemed disposal and re-acquisition can arise even if the trustees do nothing to cause the change. For example, if the terms of a double taxation agreement are renegotiated so that, under the new arrangements, the trustees are treated as non-UK-resident, the coming into force of the new arrangements would trigger a deemed disposal and re-acquisition.

Law: TCGA 1992, s. 83

60.6.4 Liability of former trustees on export of trust

Where a trust has been exported, there may be practical problems in recovering tax from the current trustees. To counter this, provision is made that tax may in certain circumstances be claimed from a former trustee.

Where there is an exit charge on a migrating trust (see **56.6.1**) and the capital gains tax which is payable remains unpaid six months from the due date, provision is made for the outstanding tax to be recovered from past trustees.

HMRC may demand the unpaid tax from anyone who had been a trustee in the 12-month period before the date the trust was exported, but excluding the period before 19 March 1991. There is one statutory exception, so that tax cannot be recovered from a person who ceased to be a trustee before the end of the relevant period if he can demonstrate that there was at that time no proposal for the trustees to become not resident or ordinarily resident in the UK. How useful an exception this may be is difficult to judge, as the onus of proof lies with the former trustee to prove that he was not aware of any proposal that the trust should be exported. HMRC have also indicated that no liability can be sought from the personal representatives of a former trustee who dies before a notice of liability has been served on him.

A notice requiring payment of tax by a former trustee may be served within three years of the date when that tax is finally determined and the tax is recoverable from the former trustee. Any notice served under these provisions must state:

- particulars of the tax payable, the amount unpaid and the date when the tax became due;
- particulars of any interest payable, any interest unpaid and the date when it became payable; and
- the requirement that the person must pay the unpaid tax and where appropriate interest within 30 days of the notice being served.

Tax is due from the former trustee under these provision as if it were a personal liability and no deduction is permitted in computing profits, etc. for tax purposes. The latter rule has been criticised by many as being unduly harsh on professional trustees.

The former trustee may recover any amount paid by him from the migrating trustees (TCGA 1992, s. 82(4)). HMRC have indicated that any amount recovered by a former trustee under these provisions will not be treated as a capital payment. Furthermore, HMRC have indicated that amounts recovered under this provision would not give rise to any income tax consequences under ITA 2007, Pt. 13, Ch. 2 and that there are no 'inheritance tax consequences'. As the statement of practice concerns the recovery of tax, the question of whether a failure to seek reimbursement of the tax paid by a former trustee could result in a claim for inheritance tax (IHT) under IHTA 1984, s. 3(3) is left unanswered. Paragraph 9 of

SP 5/92 deals with the situation in the context of the settlor charge where it is stated that a failure by the settlor to seek reimbursement 'may' give rise to an IHT claim. The more prudent approach would be that a claim should be made under TCGA 1992, s. 82(4) to put the position beyond doubt.

Although each case is considered on its facts, HMRC have stated that in seeking payment of tax from former trustees they will generally first pursue those persons who resigned as trustees, immediately before the trust migrated and then earlier trustees.

> **Planning point**
>
> Any retiring trustee might be well advised to ensure that he is suitably indemnified against the possibility of the migration of the trust and any consequential tax liability falling upon him. There is a particular need for this where professional trustees resign in favour of, say, family members who may as a result of a change in their own residence status alter the residence status of the trust.

Law: TCGA 1992, s. 82

Other guidance: SP 5/92, para. 4–6

60.6.5 Export of trust on death of trustee

The 'exit charge' provisions (see **56.6.1**) may have a more limited application where a trustee dies.

Where the trustees of a settlement cease to be UK-resident or ordinarily resident as a result of the death of a trustee the charge applies in the usual way, except where the trustees become resident and ordinarily resident in the UK within six months of the death of the trustee concerned.

In that case, the exit charge provisions are modified so that the deemed disposal and reacquisition apply in respect of 'defined assets':

- which are disposed of by the trustees during the period of non-residence resulting from the trustees' death; or
- which by virtue of a double tax relief arrangement become exempt from capital gains tax after the trustees again become UK-resident.

Trustees becoming UK-resident on death of trustee

Where trustees of a settlement become UK-resident and ordinarily resident as a result of the death of a trustee, but subsequently, after 18 March 1991 and within six months of becoming so resident, the trustees cease to be either UK-resident or ordinarily resident, the exit charge will apply at the later date (the 'relevant time') in relation to 'defined assets' which:

- were acquired by the trustees in the period beginning with the death and ending with the relevant time; and
- were gifted assets which were acquired by way of a gift where the gain was held over because the assets in question were business assets or assets on which inheritance tax was chargeable.

> **Planning point**
>
> Keep a note of the residence of a trust as this can change upon the death of a trustee. If a settlement becomes UK resident because of the death of a non-resident trustee, appoint a replacement trustee within six months. In the meantime try to ensure that the trust does not acquire chargeable assets subject to a hold-over relief claim.

Law: TCGA 1992, s. 81

60.6.6 Acquisitions by dual-resident trustees

In relation to assets, which would normally qualify for roll-over relief under TCGA 1992, s. 152, acquired on or after 19 March 1991 by dual-resident trustees, roll-over relief will not be available if the 'new' assets are covered by double taxation relief arrangements at the time of the acquisition. 'New' assets are defined according to the roll-over relief provisions on replacement of business assets.

> **Planning point**
>
> Dual-resident trustees are trustees who are UK-resident and ordinarily resident but who, by virtue of a double taxation relief arrangement, are resident in a territory outside of the UK. This provision prevents dual-resident trustees obtaining roll-over relief where any subsequent disposal would not be within the capital gains tax net.

Law: TCGA 1992, s. 84

60.7 Beneficiaries of offshore trusts

60.7.1 Capital payments charged on beneficiaries: general

Non-resident trustees are outside the scope of UK capital gains tax. As a result, offshore trusts would be set up, gains realised by the trustees and beneficiaries could then benefit from the gains by means of receiving payments which would not be taxable in their hands. To counteract this, specific legislation was introduced in 1981. Where this applies, the gains of the trustees are attributed to the beneficiaries to the extent that they receive 'capital payments' and capital gains tax charged accordingly.

The conditions for this charge to apply are that, for a year of assessment:

- the trustees are non-resident and not ordinarily resident in the UK throughout the year;
- 'trust gains' have arisen to the trustees in that year or any earlier year, which have not previously been attributed to beneficiaries; and
- a UK-resident and domiciled beneficiary receives a 'capital payment'.

When the capital payments provisions were first enacted, the definitions of 'settlement' and 'settlor' were imported from ICTA 1988, s. 681(4) so that a settlement was 'any disposition, trust, covenant, agreement or arrangement', and a settlor was 'any person by whom the settlement was made'. When the income tax settlement anti-avoidance code was revised in 1995, the corresponding definitions in ICTA 1988, s. 660G(1), (2) (now found in ITTOIA 2005, s. 620) were substituted, so that a 'transfer of assets' was added to the scope of 'settlement'. In *Tax Bulletin*, April 1995, p. 204, the Revenue draw attention to the point demonstrated by case law, that an element of bounty is needed for there to be a settlement under that definition. They make the same point with regard to the 'settlor' identified by TCGA 1992, Sch. 5, para. 7, 8. They therefore accept that a trust devoid of bounty is not within either the beneficiary or the settlor charge legislation, citing as an example a genuine commercial arrangement by a company to attract, retain and motivate good-quality staff.

Where a settlement arises as a result of a will or intestacy it is treated as made by the deceased at the date of his death.

Where there is more than one settlor the rules will apply provided any one of the settlors satisfies the above conditions.

A supplementary charge may be made where trustees delay in making capital payments (see **56.9**).

Law: TCGA 1992, s. 87–87C

60.7.2 Deduction of personal losses from gains attributed to beneficiaries

Changes in the set-off of personal losses, which were introduced by FA 2002, Sch. 11 affect only settlors (i.e. gains of a settlor-interested settlement that are attributed to the settlor under TCGA 1992, s. 86). The gains that have been attributed to a beneficiary of a non-resident or dual-resident settlement form part of the amounts that are stated in TCGA 1992, s. 2(5)(b) and are charged to capital gains tax without any deduction of the beneficiary's personal losses.

Law: TCGA 1992, s. 2 and 86

60.7.3 Consequences of FA 2008 reforms

FA 2008 saw the recasting of s. 87 and the introduction of supplementary provisions in s. 87A detailing how gains are to be matched with capital payments.

> **Planning point**
>
> There are a number of transitional measures to protect individuals from retrospective charges and elections for cases where s. 87 applies for 2008–09 or in earlier years.

> ⚠ **Warning!**
>
> An election for cases where s. 87 applies for 2008–09 is irrevocable.

Law: FA 2008, Sch. 7, para. 116–126

60.7.4 The meaning of 'capital payments'

Certain capital payments may be attributed to beneficiaries of a non-resident trust. For the purposes of TCGA 1992, s. 86A–96 and Sch 4C, a 'capital payment':

- is any payment (as defined) on which a UK-resident and ordinarily resident beneficiary is not chargeable to income tax;
- is any payment (as defined) which a non-UK resident nor ordinarily resident beneficiary receives other than as income, but
- does not include any payment received after 18 March 1991 by way of an arm's length transaction.

> ⚠ **Warning!**
> 'Payment' does not necessarily mean money. It includes the transfer of an asset, the conferring of any other benefit or the occasion on which a beneficiary becomes absolutely entitled as against the trustees.

A beneficiary shall be regarded as receiving a capital payment from trustees where:

- such a payment is made directly or indirectly;
- such a payment is applied directly or indirectly in payment of a debt of the beneficiary or otherwise for his benefit; or
- such a payment is made to another person at the beneficiary's discretion.

Where a settlor recovers tax from trustees under the recovery provisions it is understood that HMRC do not in practice regard such a payment as a capital payment.

Law: TCGA 1992, s. 97

Other guidance: SP 5/92, para. 4

60.7.5 Valuation of capital payments

Where a capital payment is made by way of a loan or the transfer of an asset, the amount of that payment is the value of the benefit conferred.

In the case of *Billingham v Cooper*; *Edwards v Fisher* [2001] BTC 282, the Court of Appeal held that CGT was attributable, under TCGA 1992, s. 87(4), to UK-resident beneficiaries of non-resident trusts, who received substantial interest free loans from the trustees repayable on demand.

The Special Commissioners allowed appeals by both taxpayers against assessments to capital gains tax under TCGA 1992, s. 87(4), calculated on the basis that the benefit conferred by the loans was equivalent to the interest that would have had to be paid to a commercial lender. Both taxpayers appealed to the High Court.

The taxpayer contended that there were no capital payments where the trustees simply refrained from calling in a loan payable on demand. A capital payment had to be the result of an identifiable action by the trustees, at an identifiable time, having the result of conferring an immediately quantifiable benefit on the recipient. If the beneficiary could be said to receive a benefit, nevertheless, the absence of a single action of the trustees on a given date precluded the existence of a 'payment' and therefore of a 'capital payment' within the meaning of TCGA 1992, s. 97(2).

Alternatively, the taxpayer argued that the beneficiaries, who were in any event entitled to the income of the settlements, received no benefit from the loans, because their income from the capital would be correspondingly reduced.

Lloyd J said that although any benefit derived from a loan repayable on demand could be ascertained only in retrospect, it was nevertheless a benefit conferred day by day, as long as the loan remained outstanding. By conferring such a benefit day by day, the trustees made what TCGA 1992, s. 92(2) treated as a 'payment'.

The argument that any benefit derived by the beneficiary under the loan would be, in effect, conferred by the beneficiary on himself also failed. If the loan had not been made, the recipient would not have had the immediate use of the money lent. The recipient's existing interest under the trust had to be left out of the calculation for the purpose of valuing the benefit conferred under TCGA 1992, s. 97(4) and the benefit was conferred by the trustees, not by the beneficiary on himself, since it was they who refrained from calling in the loan. The Revenue's appeal was allowed by the High Court and this decision was confirmed by the Court of Appeal.

Law: TCGA 1992, s. 87(4), 92 and 97

60.7.6 Exempt beneficiaries

In general, gains accruing to charities are exempt from tax. However, this exemption has previously not been available for gains treated as accruing to charities as the beneficiary of an offshore settlement. Following legal advice on the application of the legislation, HMRC accept that the exemption may be applied to UK charities who receive capital payments as the beneficiary of an offshore settlement. The exemption applies only to the extent that the capital payment is applicable and applied for charitable purposes.

Other guidance: Tax Bulletin, Issue 36, August 1998

60.8 Disposal of settled interests

60.8.1 Disposal of settled interests

A beneficiary's interest in settled property is an asset in its own right and would, in the absence of any specific provisions, give rise to a capital gain or allowable loss on disposal. However, a specific exemption provides that no chargeable gain will accrue on the disposal of a settled interest, provided the beneficiary did not acquire that interest for a consideration in money or money's worth (or from someone who did).

> **Example 60.4**
>
> In 1995, Adam purchased a life interest in a settlement. In 2000, he assigned the interest to Scott.

> On disposal of his interest, Scott will make a disposal for capital gains tax purposes.

⚠ Warning!

> The exemption is disapplied in the case of settlements where the trustees were neither UK-resident nor ordinarily resident in the UK at the time of the disposal of the settled interest.

Disposals of interests from March 1998

TCGA 1992, s. 76(1) does not apply to exempt disposals of settled interests on or after 6 March 1998 if either:

- the settlement has at any time been non-UK resident; or
- the property comprised in the settlement is, or includes, property deriving directly or indirectly from a settlement which has at any time been non-UK-resident.

As a result, the disposal of an interest in any trust which has been non-resident at any time in the past will be caught under the new provisions. Although the new rules apply only to disposals made on or after 6 March 1998, they can apply regardless of when the settlement immigrated into the UK.

It is, however, specifically provided that a disposal occasioned by the beneficiary becoming absolutely entitled as against the trustees still remains within the general exemption.

Law: TCGA 1992, s. 76

60.8.2 Disposal of settled interest where trust migrates after March 1991

The general exemption afforded to beneficiaries disposing of interests under UK-resident settlements does not extend to non-resident trusts, so that the disposal of an interest in a non-resident trust will result in a charge to capital gains tax.

Where a UK-resident trust becomes non-resident, so that the exit charge provisions apply (see **53.6.1**) and after the migration, a beneficiary disposes of an interest which was created for or acquired by him before that time, provision is made to mitigate the charge on the disposal of the interest. This is in order to mitigate the double taxation which would otherwise occur; once on the value of the settled property on the trustees and once on the beneficiary's disposal of his or her interest.

In such circumstances, the chargeable gain on the disposal of the interest is to be calculated on the basis that the interest was disposed of and immediately reacquired at market value immediately before the migration of the trust.

These provisions do not apply if:

- the trustees had become dual-resident and subject to a CGT charge by virtue of their ceasing to be liable to UK tax before the interest disposed of was created for or acquired by the person disposing of it; or
- the trustees become dual-resident so as to be not liable to UK tax by virtue of double taxation relief arrangements between the creation or acquisition of the interest and the relevant time.

In the latter case, any chargeable gain on the disposal of the interest is computed on the basis that the interest had been disposed of and reacquired at its market value at the time when the trustees became dual-resident – or at the time they first became dual-resident if that happened more than once.

Law: TCGA 1992, s. 85

60.8.3 Disposals of interests following emigration of trust on or after March 2000

The rules in TCGA 1992, s. 85 have been exploited by offshore trusts, using what was known as the 'import-export' scheme. The non-resident trust would have realised gains which have not been charged to tax on either the settlor or beneficiaries of the trust (stockpiled gains). Its current trust assets would comprise almost entirely cash and not show any significant unrealised gains. The trusts were brought onshore by appointing UK trustees and then taken offshore again by replacing the UK trustees with non-resident trustees. The gains on the trust property escaped a tax charge, because they were realised while the trust was offshore. The beneficiary paid little tax on the subsequent sale of his interest in the trust, because on the exportation of the trust, the base cost of the beneficiary's interest is uplifted to the then market value by TCGA 1992, s. 85(3).

This uplift is now denied where a settlement has 'relevant offshore gains' at the 'material time'.

A settlement has 'relevant offshore gains' at any time if, were the tax year to end at that time, there would be an amount of trust gains which by virtue of TCGA 1992, s. 89(2) or TCGA 1992, Sch. 4C, para. 8 would be available to be treated as chargeable gains accruing to beneficiaries in the following tax year.

The provisions of TCGA 1992, s. 89(1A) above ensure that trust gains of a non-resident settlement which becomes a resident settlement are attributed to beneficiaries who receive capital payments from the resident trustees. The provisions in TCGA 1992, Sch. 4C, para. 8(3) deal with 'flip flop' deemed gains.

To the extent that such deemed gains are not attributed to beneficiaries under TCGA 1992, s. 87, they become trust gains.

The 'material time' is the time on or after 21 March 2000 when the UK trustees are replaced by trustees neither resident nor ordinarily resident in the UK.

If a trust does not have stockpiled gains, then the section does not apply. Thus if the trust has assets with unrealised gains, such gains will be crystallised on export. If the trust assets do not show gains, they could be appointed to the beneficiary.

> *Planning point*
>
> Although personal losses suffered by an individual cannot be set against gains attributed to him under TCGA 1992, s. 87, he could set such personal losses against gains realised on the sale of an interest under a trust. He could still sell his interest, where there are stockpiled gains and set those gains on such a sale against his personal losses. He will have a nil base cost on his trust interest, but at least he can use his personal losses.

60.8.4 Disposals of interests after 5 April 2008

These provisions were altered again with effect from 5 April 2008 by FA 2008. A chargeable gain will be treated as accruing to a beneficiary where a capital payment made to the beneficiary by the trustees is matched with 'the section 2(2) amount' of the current or a previous year. The section 2(2) amount is defined as being the amount upon which the trustees of the settlement would be chargeable to tax under section 2(2) for that year if they were resident and ordinarily resident in the United Kingdom in that year, or if section 86 applies to the settlement for that year, that amount minus the total amount of chargeable gains treated under that section as accruing in that year. The rules for matching trust gains with capital payments are complex, and can be found in TCGA 1992, s. 87A.

60.8.5 Gains of dual-resident trusts attributed to beneficiaries

The capital payments provisions are extended to apply to dual-resident trusts (i.e. those trusts which are either UK resident or ordinarily but are treated as such for the purposes of any double taxation arrangements). Capital payments made before 6 April 1991 are to be ignored for these purposes.

The provisions apply where:

- trustees are UK-resident and ordinarily resident for part of a tax year; and
- at any time during that residence and ordinary residence the trustees are

regarded by virtue of a double taxation relief arrangement as resident outside the UK.

For the purposes of this provision, the section 2(2) amount for a tax year for which s. 87 applies by virtue of s. 88 is what it would be if the amount mentioned in s. 87(4)(a) were the assumed chargeable amount (i.e. the amount upon which the trustees of the settlement would be chargeable to tax under s. 2(2) for that year). The assumed chargeable amount in respect of a year of assessment is the lesser of the following 2 amounts:

- the amount on which the trustees would be chargeable to tax for the year under s. 2(2) on the assumption that the double taxation relief arrangements did not apply;
- the amount on which, by virtue of disposals of protected assets, the trustees would be chargeable to tax for the year under s. 2(2) on the assumption that those arrangements did not apply.

'Protected assets' are assets specified in a double taxation relief arrangement which by virtue of the arrangement would not be taxable in the UK at any time in the tax year of migration of the trust.

In computing the chargeable amount in relation to any tax year under these provisions the provisions attributing gains to a settlor shall be ignored.

Law: TCGA 1992, s. 88

60.8.6 Transfers between settlements

Under the 'capital payments' rules (see **56.7.1**) a person is liable to capital gains tax only to the extent that capital payments are made to him (for the definition of capital payments, see **56.7.5**). As it would be possible to circumvent these rules, provision is made to trace settled property between settlements in so far as a transfer is made otherwise than for consideration in money or money's worth.

The relevant legislation uses the terminology 'transferor settlement' to refer to a non-resident or migrant settlement transferring money to another settlement, the 'transferee settlement'. Where, in a tax year, the capital payment rules apply to a non-resident or migrant settlement ('the transferor settlement') and property is transferred from that settlement to another ('the transferee settlement') trust gains for the year are adjusted as follows:

- if the transferee settlement is subject to the capital payments provisions its trust gains for the year of transfer are increased by the amount of the transferor's outstanding trust gains for the year (apportioned as appropriate where only part of the settled property is transferred);
- if the transferee settlement is a migrant settlement subject to the provisions outlined at **56.6.1**ff. a similar increase applies to its gains for the tax year; and

- if the transferee settlement is not within the capital payments or migrant settlements provisions in that tax year then the migrant settlements provisions (see **56.6.1**ff.) are to apply to the transferee company in the same way as when trustees of a settlement become resident in the UK after a period of non-residence; a charge to tax will therefore arise whenever beneficiaries of the transferee settlement receive capital payments.

Where the transfer between settlements is a 'transfer of value' within TCGA 1992, Sch. 4B, (transfers of value by trustees linked with trustee borrowing) or involves a section 2(2) amount within a Schedule 4C pool (transfers of value: attribution of gains to beneficiaries) it is ignored for these purposes and does not have the effect of increasing the transferee settlement's trust gains.

The transferor settlement's outstanding trust gains for the year are trust gains of the year other than amounts attributed to beneficiaries in the year (in effect this is the amount of gains to be carried forward) or, in the case of migrant settlements, the amount not treated as beneficiaries' gains in that or an earlier year.

Law: TCGA 1992, s. 90, 90A

60.9 The supplementary charge

60.9.1 The supplementary charge: general

The Finance Act 1991 introduced a new charge – 'the supplementary charge' – in relation to settlements whose beneficiaries are charged to tax in respect of capital payments (see **55.7.1**).

The provisions are intended to act as a disincentive to the deferral of a capital gains tax charge as a result of delaying the distribution of trust gains by way of capital payments to beneficiaries. Broadly the effect of the provisions, which are now contained in TCGA 1992, s. 91, is to increase the capital gains tax payable by beneficiaries by ten per cent for each complete tax year for which the trust gains remain undistributed, where a trust gain is matched with a capital payments made later.

There is a maximum period of six years beyond which the charge may be levied.

The supplementary charge provisions apply where:
- a capital payment is made by the trustees of a settlement on or after 6 April 1992;
- the payment is made in a year of assessment during which the capital payments provisions (see **56.7.1**) apply or where the migrant settlement provisions apply to treat a chargeable gain as accruing in respect of the payment;
- the whole of the capital payment is 'matched' with a 'qualifying payment' of

the settlement for a tax year before the year immediately preceding the year of payment; and
- a beneficiary is liable to capital gains tax in respect of the capital payment.

Two points are worth noting here:

- first, the supplementary charge will not be levied where all of a trust's gains are matched with capital payments made in the same or following tax year; and
- second, the charge appears only capable of being levied on an actual beneficiary even though non-beneficiaries can in some circumstances be charged to tax in respect of capital payments.

The charge is a quasi-interest type charge and runs from a date determined by reference to the matching of the trust gains with capital payments (see **56.7.1**).

60.9.2 Rate of supplementary charge

The supplementary charge increases the amount of tax payable by a beneficiary in respect of a capital payment by an:

> 'amount equal to the interest that would be yielded if an amount equal to the tax which would be payable by the beneficiary in respect of the payment ... carried interest for the chargeable period at the rate of 10 per cent per annum.'

The specified percentage rate of the supplementary charge, which is initially set at ten per cent, may be altered by the Treasury.

Law: TCGA 1992, s. 91(3)

60.9.3 'Qualifying amount': period for which supplementary charge runs

For the purpose of the supplementary charge, the chargeable period in respect of which it is levied begins on the later of:

- 1 December in the tax year immediately after the relevant tax year; and
- 1 December falling six years before 1 December in the tax year following that in which the capital payment is made,

and ends on 30 November in the tax year following that in which the capital payment is made.

'Qualifying amounts' are determined as follows:

- in relation to 1992–93 and subsequent years, the qualifying amount is the amount computed for the settlement as trust gains for the year by virtue of TCGA 1992, s. 87(2);
- in relation to 1990–91 and 1991–92, a settlement has the same qualifying

amount as it did by virtue of FA 1991, Sch. 17, para. 2; for 1991–92 this is the amount of trust gains for the year; and
- for 1990–91, the qualifying amount is the trust gains for the year less any amounts treated as gains accruing to beneficiaries in that year by virtue of what is now TCGA 1992, s. 87; and
- in relation to a settlement which was not subject to what is now s. 87 in 1990–91, but in relation to which before that year there was a period of one or more years of non-residence to which that provision did apply, and for the last year of that period there were trust gains not treated as wholly accruing to beneficiaries, then the amount of those gains less any amounts attributed to beneficiaries is the qualifying amount for 1990–91 (FA 1991, Sch. 17, para. 2; TCGA 1992, s. 92(2)).

Example 60.5

Charles, who is UK-resident, is a beneficiary of the White trust which is non-resident. Charles is a higher rate taxpayer. In March 2005 the trustees make gains of £150,000. In March 2009 a capital payment of £50,000 is made to Charles. Assume that the annual exemption has been used. Charles will be charged to tax and a supplementary charge will apply as follows:

Chargeable gain £50,000 Tax thereon at say 18% £9,000 Supplementary charge is £9,000 × 10% × 4 (see note) = £8,000.

Note: The supplementary charge applies for the period beginning 1 December 2005 (the year in which the qualifying amount arises) and continues to run until 30 November in the tax year after which the capital payment is made, i.e. 1 December 2009. The charge is therefore for four years.

Planning point

Although the supplementary charge begins to run from 1 December after the end of the tax year in which the trust makes a gain, it cannot continue to increase beyond the six-year maximum period. Based on a ten per cent supplementary charge and top rate of capital gains tax of 18 per cent, the maximum amount of the supplementary charge is therefore 28.8 per cent (i.e. 18% + 6 (10% × 18%) = 28.8%).

Example 60.6

Assuming facts as in **Example 60.5** above but that the capital payment is not made to Charles until March 2012. In those circumstances the supplementary charge could not exceed the maximum charge based on the six year period of: £9,000 × 10% × 6 = £5,400.

Other guidance: Revenue *Tax Bulletin*, Issue 16, April 1995, p. 205

60.10 Matching capital payments with gains

60.10.1 Matching: general

The matching rules were overhauled by FA 2008. The previous rules in TCGA 1992, s. 93–96 were replaced by s. 87A.

The new rules are drafted in a complex fashion but operate so as to match capital payments with gains of the same tax year and, where surpluses remain, matching the surpluses with unmatched surpluses from earlier years.

Law: TCGA 1992, s. 87A

60.10.2 Interaction of capital payments charge and ITA 2007, Pt. 13, Ch. 2 charge

Where a UK-resident beneficiary receives a capital payment there may be a potential charge on the beneficiary in respect of capital gains tax (see **56.7.1**) if the trustees have made gains and an income tax charge under ITA 2007, Pt. 13, Ch. 2 is in point because the trust has 'relevant income'. Generally, the charge to income tax will take priority so that the capital sum will be charged to income tax under ITA 2007, s. 733.

To the extent that capital payments exceed available relevant income for the purposes of the income tax charge (relevant income of tax years up to and including the year in which the capital payment is received), the payment will be apportioned under TCGA 1992, s. 87 (see **56.7.1**) to the extent that there are any gains available. Where the capital payment is not then exhausted, the balance can only be carried forward to be treated as income of the beneficiary when further relevant income arises under the settlement.

The recovery of tax by a former trustee is not treated as a capital payment and any amount so recovered does not fall within the provisions of ITA 2007, Pt. 13, Ch. 2.

Law: TCGA 1992, s. 87 and 97; ITA 2007, Pt. 13, Ch. 2

Other guidance: SP 5/92, para. 6

60.10.3 Transfers of value: attribution of gains to beneficiaries

The *Finance Act* 2000 introduced a charging regime to counter avoidance schemes which aimed, *inter alia*, to allow beneficiaries of non-resident settlements to enjoy the benefits of capital gains made by the trustees outside the scope of UK capital gains tax, without receiving a capital payment within TCGA 1992, s. 87. These avoidance schemes involved the trustees borrowing funds against the value of the settled property and advancing funds to a new settlement with identical beneficiaries which then makes a loan to one or more of those beneficiaries. As the new settlement would not have any trust gains, the loan to the beneficiary would not otherwise be caught by TCGA 1992, s. 87.

The provisions in TCGA 1992, Sch. 4B impose a deemed disposal and re-acquisition of settled property where 'transfers of value' are made by trustees which can be identified with trust borrowings.

In the case of settlements falling within TCGA 1992, s. 87 (see **56.7.1**) further charging provisions have been introduced to attribute these 'Sch. 4B' gains to UK-resident and domiciled beneficiaries who receive capital payments. These new provisions are contained in TCGA 1992, Sch. 4C and run in parallel with the existing provisions of TCGA 1992, s. 87. By virtue of FA 2003, Sch. 29, para. 1(2) and 7A, the outstanding TCGA 1992, s. 87–89 gains are added to the Sch. 4C pool at the end of the tax year in which a transfer of value, to which TCGA 1992, Sch. 4B applies, is made. The outstanding TCGA 1992, s. 87–89 gains, which are within the Sch. 4C pool, can be attributed only in accordance with the provisions of TCGA 1992, Sch. 4C to beneficiaries who received capital payments on or after 9 April 2003.

The determination of the outstanding TCGA 1992, s. 87–89 gains to be added to the Sch. 4C pool is set out below (see **56.10.6**).

Law: TCGA 1992, s. 87–89, Sch. 4C

60.10.4 The charge to tax

Schedule 4C pool

Gains in the Schedule 4C pool

If a transfer of value, which is linked to trustee borrowing, is made in a tax year during which the trustees of the transferor settlement are at no time resident or ordinarily resident in the UK, the chargeable amount is the amount of the deemed gain arising under TCGA 1992, Sch. 4B.

If the transfer of value (linked to trustee borrowing) is made in a tax year where:

- during any part of that year the trustees are UK-resident, or ordinarily resident; and
- at any time of such residence they are regarded as resident outside the UK by virtue of any double taxation relief arrangements,

the chargeable amount is the lesser of:

(a) the amount of the deemed gain arising under TCGA 1992, Sch. 4B on the assumption that the double taxation relief arrangements did not apply; and
(b) the amount on which the trustees would be so chargeable to tax by virtue of disposals of protected assets within TCGA 1992, s. 88(4)).

The chargeable gains arising from the deemed disposal of the remaining chargeable assets or remaining protected assets are referred to as the 'Sch. 4B trust gains' and these gains will be put into a Sch. 4C pool.

The 'Sch. 4B trust gains' are computed in relation to each transfer of value to which TCGA 1992, Sch. 4B applies.

Gains and allowable losses arising under TCGA 1992, Sch. 4B are 'ring-fenced' and therefore are not to be taken into account for the purpose of attributing trust gains in the TCGA 1992, s. 87–89 pool under TCGA 1992, s. 87–89. Any allowable loss accruing by virtue of Sch. 4B may only be set against a chargeable gain so accruing, within the Sch. 4C pool.

Calculation – attribution to beneficiaries

The amount of the Sch. 4B trust gains for the purposes of the attribution to beneficiaries is given by the formula:

$(CA - SG) - AL$

where

CA is the chargeable amount,
SG is the amount of any gains attributed to the settlor; and
AL is the amount of any allowable losses which may be deducted under TCGA 1992, Sch. 4C, para. 7.

With regards to the amount of SG, this was always the tapered amount (i.e. after reduction of trustees' taper relief) of the gains, in a Sch. 4C pool, which have been attributed to a settlor with an interest in the settlement under TCGA 1992, s. 86(4), or Sch. 4C, para. 12 where TCGA 1992, s. 10A applies. This is so even if the amount actually attributed to the settlor for the purposes of his or her capital gains tax was untapered (i.e. without reduction for trustees' taper relief). For tax years after 2002–03, the settlor's attributed gains are untapered (i.e. without reduction for trustees' taper relief). Hence, in this case, SG is still the tapered amount. The untapered gains attributed to the settlor under TCGA 1992, s. 86(4) or TCGA 1992, Sch. 4C, para. 12 are combined with any gains attributed to the settlor under TCGA 1992, s. 77 (i.e. gains of a UK-resident settlor-interested settlement) and subject to capital gains tax under TCGA 1992, s. 2(5)(aa). Under TCGA 1992, s. 2(5)(aa)(i), the settlor was able to set his or her personal allowable losses against these combined gains, after first setting the personal allowable losses against the settlor's own gains under TCGA 1992, s. 2(5)(a)(i) The provisions of TCGA 1992, s. 2(5) were repealed and replaced by FA 2008 with effect for gains treated as accruing in 2008–09 and subsequent tax years.

With regards to the amount of AL, under TCGA 1992, Sch. 4C, para. 7 allowable losses arising on a transfer of value that is linked to trustee borrowing may be.

(1) First set against chargeable gains arising from other transfers of value (linked to trustee borrowing) made in the same tax year.

(2) Then set against chargeable gains arising from transfers of value (linked to trustee borrowing) made in the next tax year, and so on until the losses have been wholly used.

Where, in any tax year, the total amount of the chargeable gains arising from two or more transfers of value (linked to trustee borrowing) exceed the total amount of allowable losses available, then the total amount of allowable losses available shall be set against each chargeable gain in the same proportion as that to which each chargeable gain bears to the total amount of chargeable gains in the tax year concerned.

If the transferor settlement has a TCGA 1992, s. 87–89 pool at any time in the tax year in which the settlement makes a transfer of value (linked to trustee borrowing) then the outstanding TCGA 1992, s. 87–89 gains will be added to the Sch. 4C pool at the end of the tax year in which the transfer of value was made.

The settlement's actual gains, which fall to be placed in a TCGA 1992, s. 87–89 pool and which accrue after the tax year in which the transfer of value was made, will form a new TCGA 1992, s. 87–89 pool. The new TCGA 1992, s. 87–89 pool is separate from the Sch. 4C pool.

Subsequent transfer of value

On a subsequent transfer of value within Sch. 4B in a further tax year, para. 7B (as substituted by FA 2008) provides for the following.

Scenario	Matching
If the settlement has a Sch. 4C pool at the beginning of the later tax year	1. The section 2(2) amounts in the Sch. 4C pool are increased by the s. 2(2) amounts outstanding at the end of the tax year. 2. The s. 2(2) amount in the pool for that year is (further) increased by the Sch. 4B trust gains arising as a result of the further transfer.
If the settlement does not have a Sch. 4C pool at the beginning of the later tax year	Sch. 4C applies as it did in respect of the original transfer.

Law: TCGA 1992, s. 87–89, Sch. 4B and Sch. 4C, para. 7B

Attributing gains in the Sch. 4C pool to settlors

Attribution of gains to settlor who is UK resident

The gains arising under Sch. 4B on a transfer of value, linked to trustee borrowing, where the transfer is made by a non-resident or dual-resident settlement, are attributed to the UK-resident settlor who has an interest in that settlement. The gains which are attributable to beneficiaries are the chargeable amount (CA) minus the gains attributed to the settlor (SG) and minus any allowable losses (AL); see above. Hence gains are attributed to the settlor before any gains are attributed to beneficiaries of a relevant settlement (i.e. a relevant settlement in relation to the Sch. 4C pool).

Where the outstanding TCGA 1992, s. 87–89 gains are brought into the Sch. 4C pool, these gains would already exclude any gains attributed to the settlor with an interest in the settlement. The attribution of gains to the settlor occurs under TCGA 1992, s. 86(4).

Attributing gains in the Sch. 4C pool to beneficiaries
If:

(1) a beneficiary receives a capital payment in a tax year (or has received a capital payment in an earlier tax year); and

(2) all or part of the capital payment is matched (under s. 87A) with the s. 2(2) amount in the Sch. 4C pool for that tax year *or any earlier tax year*,

then the amount of the capital payment (or the matched part, if less) is treated as accruing to the beneficiary in the tax year.

For these purposes, para. 8(3) provides that s. 87A applies as follows:

(1) references to 's. 2(2) amounts' are to be read as references to 's. 2(2) amounts in the Sch. 4C pool';

(2) references to 'capital payments received by a beneficiary from the trustees' are to be read as 'capital payments received from the trustees by a beneficiary who is chargeable to tax for that year'.

Para. 8(4) provides that the application of s. 87A by virtue of para. 8 applies in priority to its application otherwise. However, that is subject to the one exception: the application of s. 87A by virtue of ICTA 1988, s. 762(3).

Para. 8AA provides that s. 87B, which deals with the remittance basis, applies in relation to para. 8 in the same way as it applies to s. 87A in the ordinary way.

Law: TCGA 1992, Sch. 4C, para. 8, para. 8AA

Disregard of certain capital payments

From 6 April 2008, certain capital payments are to be disregarded. These are:

(1) Capital payments received before the tax year preceding the tax year in which the original transfer is made.

(2) Capital payments that are:
   (a) received by a beneficiary of a settlement in a tax year during the *whole* of which the trustees were resident and ordinarily resident in the UK and were *not* treated as not resident by any double taxation treaty;
   (b) made before any transfer of value to which Sch. 4B applies; and
   (c) not made in anticipation of the making of any such transfer of value or chargeable gains accruing under Sch. 4B.

(3) Capital payments received (or treated as received) from the trustees of a company that:
   (a) is not resident in the UK in that tax year; but
   (b) would be a close company if resident in the UK

In the case of (3), if only part of the capital payment satisfies the conditions, then only that part of the capital payment is to be disregarded.

> ⚠ **Warning!**
> If the original transfer is to be made in 2010–11, the capital payment will not be disregarded if it was made on or after 6 April 2009.

Law: TCGA 1992, Sch. 4C, para. 9

Relevant settlement

Relevant settlements, in relation to a Sch. 4C pool, are identified (defined) as follows.

(1) The transferor and transferee settlements, in the context of the original transfer of value that is linked to trustee borrowing, are relevant settlements (Sch. 4C, para. 8A(2)) – i.e. the transferor settlement is a relevant settlement in relation to the Sch. 4C pool that was formed on the original transfer of value and the transferee settlement is also a relevant settlement in relation to that Sch. 4C pool.

(2) If the trustees of any settlement that is a relevant settlement in relation to an existing Sch. 4C pool:
   (a) make a transfer of value to which TCGA 1992, Sch. 4B applies; or
   (b) make a transfer of settled property to which TCGA 1992, s. 90 applies,

then any settlement that is a transferee settlement in the context of the transfer of value or transfer of settled property is also a relevant settlement in relation to the existing Sch. 4C pool (Sch. 4C, para. 8A(3)).

(3) If the trustees of a settlement, that is a relevant settlement in relation to a Sch. 4C pool, make a transfer of value to which TCGA 1992, Sch. 4B applies, then any other settlement that is a relevant settlement in relation to that Sch. 4C pool is also a relevant settlement in relation to the Sch. 4C pool arising from the further transfer of value (Sch. 4C, para. 8A(4)).

The definition of a relevant settlement given in (1) above applies for transfers of value (i.e. as mentioned in (1) above) that are made on or after 21 March 2000. However, the inclusion of (2) and (3) above in the definition of a relevant settlement applies only where the transfers of value or transfers of settled property (i.e. as mentioned in (2) or (3) above, as the case may be) occur on or after 9 April 2003 (FA 2003, s. 163(5)).

For the purposes of TCGA 1992, Sch. 4C, references:

- to a transfer of value are to a transfer of value as defined in TCGA 1992, Sch. 4B;
- to the time at which a transfer of value was made are to the time when the loan is made, the transfer is effectively completed or the security is issued ('material time') – the effective completion of a transfer means the point at which the person acquiring the asset becomes, for practical purposes, unconditionally entitled to the whole of the intended subject matter of the transfer (TCGA 1992, Sch. 4B, para. 2(2) and Sch. 4C, para. 14(1));
- to the 'transferor settlement', in relation to a transfer of value, are to the settlement that made, through its trustees, the transfer of value (TCGA 1992, Sch. 4C, para. 14(2)(a)); and
- to the 'transferee settlement', in relation to a transfer of value, are to any settlement of which the settled property includes property representing, directly or indirectly, the proceeds of the transfer of value (TCGA 1992, Sch. 4C, para. 14(2)(b)).

Law: TCGA 1992, Sch. 4C, para. 14

Interest added to tax charge on Sch. 4C gains

In accordance with TCGA 1992, Sch. 4C, para. 13, where gains in a Sch. 4C pool are attributed to beneficiaries, the tax charged on those gains is increased (though not beyond the amount of the capital payment received) by an amount representing interest at the rate for the time being specified by TCGA 1992, s. 91(3) for the chargeable period (TCGA 1992, Sch. 4C, para. 13); at present, the rate is ten per cent per annum. The provisions in TCGA 1992, Sch. 4C, para. 13 replicate the provisions of TCGA 1992, s. 91 in charging interest on the tax charge on gains in a TCGA 1992, s. 87–89 pool that have been attributed to beneficiaries.

The 'chargeable period' is the period which:

- begins with the later of:
  (a) 1 December in the tax year immediately after the relevant tax year; and
  (b) 1 December falling six years before 1 December in the tax year following that in which the capital payment is made; and
- ends with 30 November in the tax year following that in which the capital payment is made (TCGA 1992, Sch. 4C, para. 13(4), (5)).

Where a capital payment is deemed to have been made in the year of return, in the case of TCGA 1992, s. 10A applying, the date on which the actual capital payment was made is used (TCGA 1992, Sch. 4C, para. 13).

Hence, in this case, interest at the rate specified in TCGA 1992, s. 91(3) is applied to the tax charge during the period:

- from the later of:
  (a) 1 December in the tax year following that in which the transfer of value was made; and
  (b) 1 December falling six years before 1 December in the tax year following that in which the actual capital payment was made,
- to 30 November in the tax year following that in which the actual capital payment was made.

Law: TCGA 1992, Sch. 4C, para. 13

Gains attributed to beneficiaries in section 10A cases

Basically and in general terms, under TCGA 1992, s. 10A, gains accruing to an individual, while he or she is not resident in the UK, on the disposal of assets acquired before he or she became not resident, are, on the satisfaction of the conditions set out in TCGA 1992, s. 10A(1), treated as accruing in the tax year in which the individual resumes his or her UK residence for tax purposes; for details on the operation of TCGA 1992, s. 10A.

Where the individual is a beneficiary, the gains to be attributed to that beneficiary are based on the capital payments received by the beneficiary from a relevant settlement during the intervening years. Where the gains to be attributed are within a Sch. 4C pool, capital payments made on or after 9 April 2003 can be used only for the attribution of those gains if they are received by beneficiaries who are chargeable to tax. If the capital payments were received before 9 April 2003, then capital payments received by any beneficiary (whether or not he or she is chargeable to tax) can be taken into account in the attribution of the deemed gains arising under Sch. 4B (i.e. for the purposes of attributing the Sch. 4B trust gains that are within the Sch. 4C pool); the gains attributed to beneficiaries who are not chargeable to tax will of course not be subject to capital gains tax in the hands of those beneficiaries.

Unlike the attribution of gains within the Sch. 4C pool, where the gains to be attributed to beneficiaries are actual trust gains in a TCGA 1992, s. 87–89 pool, then capital payments received by non-resident or UK-resident beneficiaries, whether or not received on or after 9 April 2003, may be taken into account in the attribution; but, again, the gains attributed to beneficiaries who are not chargeable to tax will not be subject to capital gains tax in the hands of those beneficiaries.

Where the gains to be attributed are in the Sch. 4C pool, and s. 10A applies, then the beneficiary concerned who receives a capital payment during the intervening years would be non-resident for tax purposes during those years. If such capital payments were received on or after 9 April 2003 (i.e. during the intervening years) then, normally, the capital payments would not be taken into account. However, under TCGA 1992, Sch. 4C, para. 12A(2), a capital payment, equal to the total amount of the capital payments received during the intervening years minus any amounts taken into account for the purposes of attributing actual trust gains in the settlement's TCGA 1992, s. 87–89 pool, is deemed to have been received in the year of return (i.e. when the beneficiary resumes his or her UK residency for tax purposes).

For the purposes of adding interest on to the tax charge arising from the attribution of Sch. 4C gains (TCGA 1992, Sch. 4C, para. 13), the deemed capital payment will be treated as having been made when the actual capital payments were received; for further details, see above.

60.11 Liability of settlors of non-resident trusts

60.11.1 Liability of settlors of non-resident trusts: general

The provisions introduced by the *Finance Act* 1991 introduced a charge on certain UK-domiciled and resident settlors of non-resident trusts where the following conditions are met:

- the settlement is a 'qualifying settlement' in the tax year concerned;
- the trustees are not UK-resident or ordinarily resident or dual-resident at any time in the tax year;
- the settlor (or one of them, where there is more than one) is UK-domiciled at some time in the tax year and either resident for any part of that tax year or ordinarily resident for that tax year;
- at any time in the tax year the settlor has an interest in the settlement; and
- that property originating from the settlor is disposed of by the trustees in respect of which a charge to capital gains tax would arise if the trustees were

resident or ordinarily resident in the UK throughout the tax year and if no double taxation arrangements applied.

> ⚠ **Warning!**
>
> In ascertaining the settlor's residence status it should be noted that the concession whereby individuals may split the tax year for capital gains tax purposes (ESC D2) is specifically disapplied where the individual is a settlor who is caught under the above provisions.

The provisions do not apply where the settlor dies in the tax year.

In practice, the provisions introduced in 1991, which are now contained in TCGA 1992, s. 86 and Sch. 5, have given rise to difficulties of interpretation which have been addressed, although not perhaps fully resolved, by the publication of two extra-statutory concessions and a detailed statement of practice.

Law: TCGA 1992, s. 86 and Sch. 5

> ⚠ **Warning!**
>
> Tax practitioners should, where possible, familiarise themselves with the rules, so as to be alert to ensuring that events that may jeopardise the status of a trust exported before 19 March 1991 do not occur and thereby to bring the settlement within the 'qualifying settlements' regime.

60.11.2 Circumstances in which settlor has an interest

A person is a settler in relation to a settlement if the settled property consists of or includes property originating from him. For the purpose of attributing, to a settlor, the gains of a 'qualifying' settlement, a 'settlor' has an interest in a settlement if he satisfies the following tests.

(1) Any property which may be comprised in the settlement or any income which may arise under the settlement is, or will or may become, applicable for the benefit of or payable to a defined person in any circumstances.

(2) Any relevant income which arises or may arise under the settlement or any income which may arise under the settlement is, or will or may become, applicable for the benefit of or payable to a defined person in any circumstances.

(3) Any defined person enjoys a benefit directly or indirectly from any relevant property which is comprised in the settlement or income arising under it.

A 'defined person' is:

- the settlor;
- the settlor's spouse/civil partner;
- any child of the settlor or of the settlor's spouse/civil partner or the spouse/civil partner of any such child;
- any grandchild of the settlor or the settlor's spouse/civil partner;
- any spouse/civil partner of such a grandchild; or
- a company controlled by any one of the above or a company associated with such a company.

> ⚠ **Warning!**
>
> The list of defined persons does not explicitly refer to adopted children. However, the effect of adoption is that the child is treated, in law, as if he or she were the child of the adopted parent(s). Consequently, an adopted child *does* fall within the meaning of 'defined person'.

'Control' of a company and the question of association is to be determined in accordance with CTA 2010, s. 450, but in either case no rights or powers of associates of a person are to be attributed to a person unless he is a participator (as defined by CTA 2010, s. 454) in the company.

'Relevant property' and 'relevant income' are property and income originating from the settlor.

A settlor does not, however, have an interest in a settlement if none of the settlement property or income can become payable to the settlor, except in the event of:

- the bankruptcy of a person who is or may be beneficially entitled to the property or income;
- any assignment of or charge on that property or income being made or given by such a person;
- in the case of marriage or civil partnership settlements, the death of both parties to the marriage and of all or any of the children to the marriage;
- the death at 25 or a lower age of a beneficiary who would become beneficially entitled at 25 or that lower age; or
- the bankruptcy, or assignment or charging of the interest during the lifetime of a person under the age of 25.

Law: TCGA 1992, Sch. 5, para. 2 and 7; CTA 2010, s. 450, 454

Other guidance: ICAEW Tax Faculty, Guidance Note TAX 20/92, para. 24: 'Charge on the settlor: other issues'

60.12 Qualifying settlements

60.12.1 Meaning of 'qualifying settlement'

A 'qualifying settlement', for the purposes of the provisions attributing gains of non-resident trusts to settlors, is one which is:

- created on or after 19 March 1991; and is a qualifying settlement for the tax year in which it is created and subsequent tax years;
- created before 19 March 1991 (other than a 'protected settlement' (see **56.12.2**); and is a qualifying settlement for 1999–2000 and subsequent years;
- created before 19 March 1991 fulfilling for any of the years up to 1998–99, any one of the following four conditions in a tax year (in that case the settlement is a qualifying settlement for that tax year and all subsequent tax years); or
- a 'protected settlement' which satisfies the five conditions set out below.

A pre-19 March 1991 trust will become a qualifying settlement for years up to 1998–99 or a post-18 March 1991 'protected settlement' will become a qualifying settlement for any year from 1999–2000, where any one of the following five conditions triggers the change in status.

(1) Subject to certain exclusions, property or income is provided directly or indirectly for the purposes of the settlement other than under a transaction entered into at arm's length, and other than in pursuance of a liability incurred by a person before 19 March 1991.

(2) The trustees become non-UK resident or ordinarily resident or dual-resident.

(3) There is a variation in the terms of the settlement so that for the first time certain new beneficiaries might be admitted.

(4) A defined person enjoys a benefit from the settlement for the first time, not being such a person who (looking at the terms of the settlement at 18 March 1991) would be capable of enjoying a benefit from the settlement on or after that time.

(5) The settlement ceases to be a protected settlement on or after 6 April 1999.

The second 'trigger' is the easiest to comprehend and leaves no room for debate. However, it may be considered unduly harsh as any period of residence, however short, will result in the settlement being caught. Unlike the emigration charge imposed by Finance Act 1991 there is no safety net to cover the situation where the trust becomes resident through the death of a trustee.

In practice, the so-called triggers have caused a considerable degree of problem in interpretation. The Revenue, in response to these problems, issued a detailed statement of practice – SP 5/92 – which was intended to clarify the problem areas.

Law: TCGA 1992, Sch. 5, para. 9(9)

Other guidance: SP 5/92

60.12.2 'Protected settlements'

A 'protected settlement' is defined as a pre-1991 trust where all the actual or potential beneficiaries are confined to:

- a future spouse/civil partner of the settlor;
- children of the settlor or a spouse/civil partner of the settlor, aged under 18;
- future children of the settlor or of the settlor's current or future spouse/civil partner;
- future spouses/civil partner of any child or future child of the settlor, or of any current or future spouse/civil partner of the settlor; or
- other persons who are not defined persons at all.

> ⚠ **Warning!**
>
> In 1991, the class of defined persons did not include grandchildren of the settlor. Therefore, a settlement that was for the benefit of the settlor's grandchildren could be a protected settlement. Since 1997–98, however, grandchildren and their spouses (and since 5 December 2005, their civil partners) have come within the class of defined persons. Therefore, such settlements have ceased to be protected settlements.

Law: TCGA 1992, Sch. 5, para. 9(10A)

Other guidance: Revenue *Tax Bulletin*, Issue 38, December 1998

60.12.3 Property or income provided for the purposes of a settlement exported pre-19 March 1991

The first trigger whereby a trust exported before 19 March 1991 may become a qualifying trust applies where property or income is provided directly or indirectly for the purposes of the settlement other than under a transaction entered into at arm's length, and other than in pursuance of a liability incurred by an person before 19 March 1991.

There is only one statutory exception, which concerns the payment of 'taxation' and 'administration' expenses. The legislation states that (TCGA 1992, Sch. 5, para. 9(3) (closing words)):

> 'if ... expenses relating to administration and taxation for a year of assessment exceed its [the settlement's] income for the year, property or income provided towards meeting those expenses shall be ignored for the purposes of this condition if the value of the property or income so provided does not exceed the difference between the amount of those expenses and the amount of the settlement's income for the year.'

Paragraph 9(3) caused a great deal of consternation when first published and the exception for expenses was added in response to strong lobbying by professional advisers, etc. The condition as drafted still causes problems and on 21 May 1992 the Revenue issued SP 5/92, much of which is concerned with the operation of this provision. The various points in SP 5/92 in relation to this provision are considered below.

Transactions entered into at arm's length

Paragraph 9(3) does not apply if it can be shown that property or income is provided by way of an arm's length transaction. Guidance on this matter is available in (SP 5/92, para. 12–15).

Any transaction is of course dependent on the facts but where property or income is to be provided in this way, it will be prudent to ensure that transaction is properly documented to support the contention that the parties have acted in commercial bargain.

The ICAEW raised the situation where an adjuster clause deals not only with the provision of compensating interest at a commercial rate but for the provision for issued shares to be cancelled. The Revenue response stated (TAX 20/92):

> 'The practice does not encompass situations to which you refer. It would, of course, be possible for the parties to the transaction to show that the transaction was carried out on arm's length terms.'

In *Tax Bulletin*, Issue 16, April 1995, p. 204, it says that including an 'adjuster clause' of the kind suggested in paras. 13, 14 in appropriate circumstances brings the certainty that HMRC will not argue that value has been added to the trust provided all necessary steps have been taken. In the absence of an adjuster clause, the parties could still demonstrate that the transaction was on arm's-length terms, but it might be more difficult for them to do so. 'One-way' adjuster clauses are satisfactory provided that the parties are not concerned that they might face a claim that a 'capital payment' had been made by the trustees if more passed out of the trust than was received in return.

Close companies

The conditions in para. 9(3) may, it seems, be satisfied where property or income is provided to a close company in which the trustees are participators. The HMRC practice is that such transactions will be disregarded in certain circumstances (SP 5/92, para. 16–17).

Transactions with wholly-owned companies

Transactions between trustees and companies wholly-owned by them will generally be ignored for the purposes of para. 9(3), except where a particular transaction has been entered into mainly or solely to secure a UK tax advantage (SP 5/92, para. 18).

Loans

The conditions of para. 9(3) will be met where a loan is made to a settlement after 19 March 1991 on other than commercial terms. Any continued provision of a loan on better than commercial terms after it could have been recalled and the 'benefit' to the settlement terminated is, according to HMRC, clearly within the ambit of para. 9(3) (ICAEW Guidance Note TAX 20/92, para. 10).

Failure to exercise the right to reimbursement

The failure to exercise a right to reimbursement may constitute the provision of property for the purposes of the settlement and cause the conditions of para. 9(3) to be met (SP 5/92, para. 24).

Administration and taxation expenses

In certain circumstances the payment of administration or taxation expenses by any person, including the settlor, will not bring a settlement within the scope of the 'qualifying settlement' provisions. This exception was added in response to representations made by professional advisors who instantly recognised the potential problem that would exist in relation to a settlement with no or low income producing assets, unable to pay the annual costs of administration and any tax liabilities. The terms of the exception appear rather hastily drawn and the wording causes practical difficulties as to exactly what is covered. The Revenue have attempted to define the exact terms of the exception (SP 5/92).

The appropriate rate of interest at which funds borrowed from the income fund to defray trust expenses should be repaid is considered to be the rate payable on the Basic Account administered by the Court Office of the Supreme Courts of Justice (*Tax Bulletin*, Issue 16, April 1995, p. 204). Where a trustee's annual fee is consistently paid out of income, and no part of the fee is identifiable as relating to duties of a capital nature, HMRC will raise no objection.

It is worth noting that payments provided that exactly match, or are smaller than the taxation liabilities or administration expenses of a trust within a tax year will not cause the para. 9(3) trigger to operate. Any amounts exceeding such liabilities, however inadvertently applied, will be sufficient to bring the settlement within the scope of TCGA 1992, Sch. 5. The timing of amounts provided for such purposes will be important, particularly given the seemingly vague requirement in the statement of practice that there must be a 'clear connection' with the amounts added and the shortfall of expenses from income.

Provision of funds by a life tenant

The express direction by a life tenant to retain income would constitute the provision of property within the terms of para. 9(3) although an administrative delay in payment would not (SP 5/92, para. 33).

Tax Bulletin, Issue 16, April 1995, p. 204 states the HMRC view that considering whether the giving of a guarantee or indemnity, etc. by a third party would enable the trustees to sell at a better price, or whether the sale would go through at all without the guarantee, might help resolve cases of difficulty. They also repeat that the question whether the trust assets are to be exposed to the same degree of risk that other vendors will have to accept is a factor for consideration.

Other guidance: SP 5/92, ICAEW Guidance Note TAX 20/92, para. 10; *Tax Bulletin*, Issue 16, April 1995, p. 204

60.12.4 Variation in terms of settlement exported before March 1991

A trust exported before 19 March 1991 may become a qualifying settlement, after that date, where there is a variation in the terms of the settlement so that for the first time there becomes a person who will or might benefit from the settlement that is included in the following list:

- a settlor;
- the spouse/civil partner of a settlor;
- any child of a settlor or a settlor's spouse/civil partner;
- any grandchild of the settlor or the settlor's spouse/civil partner;
- any spouse/civil partner of such a grandchild;
- a company controlled by one or more of the above; and
- a company associated with such a company.

> ⚠ **Warning!**
>
> Again, care needs to be taken if the class of potential beneficiaries includes a civil partner (or future civil partner) of the spouse (or the settlor's child etc.). Many trusts are drafted so that a wide number of individuals can theoretically benefit (often in the absence of other beneficiaries closer to the settlor and within the settlor's contemplation). If such a person could become a civil partner (however remote a prospect) the trust will have become a qualifying settlement on 5 December 2005.
>
> It should also be noted that the definition of civil partner includes a person who is a party to an equivalent union registered in countries outside the UK.

Law: TCGA 1992, Sch. 5, para. 9(5) and 9(7)

60.12.5 *Ultra vires* payments in connection with settlements exported before March 1991

A trust exported before 19 March 1991 may become a qualifying settlement where a person mentioned in the following list enjoys a benefit from the settlement for the first time, where that person is when looking at the terms of the settlement at 18 March 1991 not a person who would be capable of enjoying a benefit from the settlement on or after that time. The following is the list of persons that must be considered:

- a settlor;
- the spouse/civil partner of a settlor;
- any child or stepchild of a settlor or a settlor's spouse/civil partner;
- any grandchild of the settlor or the settlor's spouse/civil partner;
- any spouse/civil partner of such a grandchild;
- a company controlled by one or more of the above; and
- a company associated with such a company.

The sixth trigger has been widely criticised, if for no other reason than that commentators appear to be at something of a loss as to what exactly it is aimed at.

Law: TCGA 1992, Sch. 5, para. 9(6)–(7)

60.12.6 Definition of 'settlor' for the purposes of attributing gains of non-resident settlements

A 'settlor' for the purpose of attributing the gains of a non-resident settlement to a settlor is defined as follows:

> 'a person is a settlor in relation to a settlement if the settled property consists of or includes property originating from him.'

The meaning of 'originating' is considered in some detail in TCGA 1992, Sch. 5, para. 8 so that property and income are treated as originating from the settlor as follows:

- property is provided (directly or indirectly) by or represents property (including property representing accumulated income) provided by the settlor;
- so much of any property representing such property as well as any other property which on the basis of a just and reasonable apportionment can be taken to represent property from the settlor; and
- income arises from property provided by the settlor or income provided by him.

The above definition of 'settlement' corresponds with that in ITTOIA 2005, s. 620 for the purposes of the income tax settlement anti-avoidance provisions.

Reciprocal arrangements are specifically covered so that property or income provided by another party to such an arrangement is treated as provided by the settlor and property or income provided by the settlor in pursuance of such an agreement is treated as not provided by him but by the other person.

Where property is provided by a qualifying company it is treated as provided by the participators (within the definition in ICTA 1988, s. 417), broadly, according to their respective interests in the company. A person shall not be treated as providing property in circumstances where less than one-twentieth would be justly apportioned.

By concession, in applying TCGA 1992, Sch. 5, para. 8, a trust beneficiary is not regarded as a participator solely because of his beneficiary status.

Law: TCGA 1992, Sch. 5, para. 7 and 8; *IR Commrs v Leiner* (1964) 41 TC 589

60.12.7 Charge on settlor

Where gains of a non-resident or dual-resident settlor-interested settlement are to be attributed to the settlor, the settlor is subject to capital gains tax on those gains in the tax year in which the gains are attributed to that settlor.

In the case of settlor-attributed gains, the settlor is able to recover from the trustees of the settlement concerned the tax charged on the settlor-attributed gains, provided the settlor has paid the tax and has a certificate from a tax inspector which verifies the amount of the gain(s) attributed and the amount of tax paid. For non-resident or dual-resident settlor-interested settlements, the settlor's right of recovery of tax from the trustees is set out in TCGA 1992, Sch. 5, para. 6. For beneficiaries, there is no right of recovery of tax from the trustees.

In ascertaining the amount of gains of a non-resident trust on which the settlor is to be charged, it is provided that (TCGA 1992, Sch. 5, para. 1(1), (2)(a)):

- the annual exemption is ignored;
- the effect of the provisions which attribute the gains of a UK-resident trust to a settlor are ignored;
- a deduction may be made for losses of the tax year or losses brought forward insofar as they relate to property originating from the settlor; for this purpose, the provisions which disallow losses of non-residents are ignored and gains or losses in respect of disposals before 19 March 1991 are not to be taken into account (TCGA 1992, Sch. 5, para. 1(2)(b), (7)); and
- if the trustees are participators in (or, in relation to gains accruing before 28 November 1996, hold shares in) a non-resident company which originated from the settlor, any gains or losses which would have been treated as accruing to the trustees had they been UK-resident and ordinarily resident may be taken into account but gains or losses in respect of disposals before 19 March 1991 are not to be taken into account (TCGA 1992, Sch. 5, para. 1(3), (7)

Special rules apply where the trustees are dual-resident and part of the settled property is represented by 'protected assets' (assets held by dual-resident trustees gains from which would not be liable to UK tax by virtue of double taxation relief arrangements if disposed of at the relevant time): the charge on the settlor may be reduced or eliminated entirely. It is necessary to calculate gains chargeable on the settlor according to the rules and compare that with the amount of the gain if only protected assets are taken into account. If the latter produces a smaller gain, that figure is the chargeable amount and if it produces no gain then there is no charge on the settlor.

Law: TCGA 1992, Sch 5, para. 1 and 6

Attribution of gains to settlor in TCGA 1992, s. 10A cases

As a result of the capital gains tax charge imposed on non-residents, non-resident settlors who return to the UK after a period of temporary residence abroad (broadly, less than five years) will suffer a capital gains tax charge in the year of return in respect of gains realised by offshore trusts during that period of non-residence (TCGA 1992, s. 86A(1)). However, UK-resident beneficiaries may have already paid tax on some of those gains under TCGA 1992, s. 87 if capital payments have been made to them while the settlor was abroad.

In these circumstances, the gains which would fall to be charged on the settlor on his return to the UK will be reduced by the amount of the gains realised by the trustees in his absence which have already been charged under TCGA 1992, s. 87 on UK-resident beneficiaries during that period of absence.

In order to obtain the relief, two requirements must be satisfied (TCGA 1992, s. 86A(1)–(4)):

- gains of a non-resident settlement are realised during the settlor's period of temporary non-residence which are taxable in the year of return (i.e. the tax year in which the settlor resumes his or her UK residency for tax purposes) by virtue of TCGA 1992, s. 86 and s. 10A; and
- amounts are charged on beneficiaries receiving capital payments from the settlement (by virtue of TCGA 1992, s. 87) which are attributable to gains arising in the period of the settlor's non-residence. (It is only gains arising while the settlor is abroad not gains arising before departure which are eligible for relief.)

Therefore only the amount of gains arising during the settlor's period of temporary non-residence (i.e. intervening years, being tax years) that have not already been charged on UK-resident beneficiaries under TCGA 1992, s. 87 are to be charged on the settlor under s. 86. Any gains that have been attributed to non-resident beneficiaries in the tax years during which the settlor was temporarily non-resident are available for attribution to that settlor in the year of return.

Where there are multiple settlors, only capital payments from and gains arising to property originating from a particular settlor are to be taken into account.

If a settlor is taxed in the year of return under TCGA 1992, s. 86A on gains realised by the offshore trust during his period of non-residence (i.e. intervening years), the pool of gains carried forward, on which a beneficiary can in future years be taxed under TCGA 1992, s. 87, is reduced accordingly. Thus, the section also provides a mechanism to ensure that any gains arising during the settlor's period of absence which are charged on the settlor on his return cannot also be taken into account in attributing gains to beneficiaries. Further, TCGA 1992, s. 86A does not allow capital distributions assessed to income tax under ITA 2007, s. 727–729 as relevant income to be deducted from the gains assessed as the settlor's in the year of return.

60.12.8 Charge on settlors of settlements for grandchildren

When the 1991 provisions came into force, they did not extend to settlements for the benefit of the settlor's grandchildren, as they were not included in the list of 'defined persons' set out in TCGA 1992, Sch. 5, para. 2(3).

That list was amended by the *Finance Act* 1998 to include:

- any grandchild of the settlor or the settlor's spouse; and
- the spouse of any such grandchild.

This amendment applies to trusts created on or after 17 March 1998 but the charge will not apply if the settlor is non-UK-domiciled, or the settlor is UK-domiciled but non-resident for more than five years.

The new definition does not apply to settlements created before 17 March 1998 unless they become 'tainted', i.e. one of the following occurs.

(1) Property is added to the trust on or after 17 March 1998 (with the usual exemption for administrative expenses where the income is insufficient to pay these and property has to be added).

(2) The trustees become non-resident on or after 17 March 1998.

(3) On or after 17 March 1998 the terms of the settlement are varied so that one of the new defined persons (grandchildren, their spouses, etc.) is admitted for the first time as actual or potential beneficiaries.

(4) One of the new defined persons benefits from the settlement without being a beneficiary under the terms of the settlement (i.e. trustees make an *ultra vires* payment).

Even if the trust becomes tainted, gains or losses on disposals made before 17 March 1998 or (if later), before the beginning of the tax year in which the trust becomes tainted are not taken into account.

Law: TCGA 1992, Sch. 5, para. 2–2A

Reporting requirements

TCGA 1992, Sch. 5A, para. 2(1) (returns in relation to dealings involving settlements created before 19 March 1991) is amended to require information to be provided about a settlement within 12 months where, on or after 17 March 1998, property is transferred to an offshore trust created before 17 March 1998.

Law: TCGA 1992, Sch. 5A, para. 2(1)

60.12.9 Exceptions to settlor charge

There are a number of exceptions to the provisions whereby gains of a non-resident trust are attributed to the settlor. The provisions do not apply where:

- the settlor dies during the tax year;
- the only defined person by reason of whom the settlor has an interest in the settlement dies during the year, or if the defined person concerned is only a defined person by virtue of being a spouse of a defined person if that person ceases to be married to the settlor or the defined person concerned; or
- the settlor has an interest in the settlement by virtue of more than one defined person, but they all die in the tax year.

Law: TCGA 1992, Sch. 5, para. 3–5

60.12.10 Right of settlor to recover tax paid

Where a settlor is charged to tax as a result of gains made by non-resident trustees being attributed to him the settlor is entitled to recover the tax paid in respect of those gains from anyone who is a trustee of the settlement.

In order that the tax might be recovered the settlor can require the inspector to provide him with a certificate stating:

- the amount of the gain on which he is charged; and
- the amount of the tax paid.

It is understood that where a settlor exercises his right to reimbursement any payment is not a capital payment.

Law: TCGA 1992, Sch. 5, para. 6

Section 7 – Specialist

Section 7 – Specialist – What's New

- 63.2.6: New obligations on intermediaries to identify originators of schemes
- 63.6.2: Wider definition of promoter as introduced by FA 2010
- 63.8.8: New promoters rules requiring details to be provided to clients
- 63.12.2: New SDLT DOTAS rules
- 63.12.3: New hallmarks for income tax, corporation tax, capital gains tax
- 64.1.2: Proposed changes to Enterprise Investment Scheme
- 64.1.3: Proposed changes to Enterprise Investment Scheme
- 64.3.2: EIS and changes to CGT rates
- 64.3.2: New guidance on reduction of the penalty for disclosure
- 66.1.6: New series of HMRC fact sheets on compliance checks
- 66.3.6: New power for HMRC to correct tax returns for information they hold
- 66.4.3: Application of new information and inspection powers to statutory records
- 66.4.3: New guidance on refusing an inspection visit
- 66.9.5: The start of the new penalty provisions for incorrect returns
- 66.9.5: New guidance on calculating the penalty for incorrect returns; new guidance on reduction of the penalty for disclosure; new guidance on calculating the penalty for incorrect returns; and new provisions for penalties involving certain off-shore income
- 72.7.2: Changes to rules on capital allowances
- 72.9.8: Proposed changes to tax rules for furnished holiday lettings
- 76.2.1: Review of EFRBS to be enacted in Finance Bill 2011
- 76.2.2: and 76.6.4: Replacement of Personal Account by NEST (National Employment Savings Trust)
- 76.3.1: Change of earliest pension benefit age to 55
- 76.4.2: Freezing of annual allowance
- 76.4.3: Latest annuitisation age changed to 77 and freezing of lifetime allowance
- The following are also updated throughout chapter 76, Pensions, where applicable: anti-forestalling rules for pension contributions; the pension contributions to be enacted in Finance Bill 2011; and the review of the format of pension benefit payments in Finance Bill 2011
- 77.1.3: Proposed changes to Venture Capital Trusts

61 A Practical Guide to Trusts

61.1 Introduction

The aim of this chapter is to give non-specialists an introduction to trusts and their implications so that they can recognise, and advise their clients on, the uses of trusts and be aware of some of the most common opportunities and pitfalls.

61.2 What is a trust?

A trust is a relationship that exists where a person or persons hold property for the benefit of another or others. A trust is generally created by a person, known as a settlor, who transfers funds or other property to trustees stipulating in a trust deed or other written instrument (such as a will) the manner in which the property should be held.

The persons who hold the property are known as *trustees* and those for whom the property is held are termed *beneficiaries*. A fiduciary duty is owed by the trustees to deal with the property vested in the trust according to the terms of the trust. A breach of trust may, amongst other things, arise when a trustee uses trust property for his own benefit, for the benefit of someone other than a beneficiary or in a manner not authorised by the trust.

Where property is held on trust for beneficiaries the property may be referred to as settled, the term 'settlement' often being used interchangeably with trust. In recent years the term 'settlement' seems to be used with increasing frequency in tax-related legislation. Historically, the Income Tax Acts have set out the meaning of the word 'settlement' in various contexts, and there are still a number of definitions in different taxing acts which need to be borne in mind. In practice, the term 'settlement' can potentially embrace any situation where a person arranges for money or property to be held by or for the benefit of another otherwise than for full and valuable consideration and therefore includes any disposition, trust, covenant, agreement, arrangement or transfer of assets. As part of the trust reform process some terminology relating to the concept of settlement has been refined. To the extent that a settlement can involve the outright transfer of assets from settlor to beneficiary the term is strictly wider than trust.

> ⚠ **Warning!**
> The definition of 'settlement' is not the same for all taxes, and is not necessarily the same in relation to different parts of the same act. Therefore it is important to

> check that a specific set of circumstances does or does not fall within the settlement provisions for each different purpose, dependent on the relevant definition of 'settlement'.

Terminology is not always consistent so, for example, a trust established by will may often be referred to as a 'will trust', whereas a trust established *inter vivos* by deed may be referred to as a settlement or a trust. Unless otherwise stated, the use of the term 'trust' in this division refers equally to a lifetime trust, settlement or will trust.

> ⚠ **Warning!**
> The definition of 'settlement', 'settled property' and 'trust' (where applicable) vary drastically between different legislative regimes. For example, ITTOIA 2005, s. 620 has an exceedingly wide definition of 'settlement'. IHTA 1984, s. 43 has a wide, but different, definition of 'settlement' while for the most part TCGA 1992 applies the comparatively narrow definition of 'settled property' in s. 68. This means that a certain set of circumstances could be a settlement for the purposes of one tax and not the other. The circumstances must be considered in the light of each relevant definition in each instance to determine whether or not the circumstances will be treated as a settlement and the relevant rules applied.

Bare trusts

A bare trust occurs generally when the beneficiary is absolutely entitled to the trust property as against the trustees. The beneficiary has an indefeasible interest in the whole of the property, and is entitled to the property vesting in him absolutely, other than for a deduction for trustee's expenses. In these circumstances the trustee's powers are purely administrative (see **61.5.2**).

Interest in possession trusts

A trust may be for the benefit of a named person or persons who may be given an 'immediate' or 'contingent' interest in the income of the trust fund, or the right to use trust assets for a defined period or for life. This will generally create an *interest in possession* or *life interest*; the beneficiary in such circumstances is often referred to as the 'life tenant'. On the termination of the life interest – on the death of the life tenant or on his relinquishing his interest – other interests succeed and these are known as *interests in remainder* (see **61.5.2**).

Discretionary trusts

Property may be put into trust for trustees to apply according to their discretion for any one or more of a number of stated purposes in connection with a class of beneficiaries. No such beneficiaries have an indefeasible right to the trust property, as their entitlement is dependent entirely on the exercise by the trustees of the discretion afforded them by the trust instrument. Trusts of this type are often referred to as discretionary trusts and the exercise by the trustees of their discretion in favour of any one or more of the objects of the trust is known as an *appointment* (see **61.5.4**).

Protective trusts

A protective trust (Trustee Act 1925, s. 33) is one under which an interest in possession may terminate on the bankruptcy of the life tenant or on his attempting to assign his life interest. In these circumstances, the interest in possession will be superseded by a discretionary trust for the maintenance of the beneficiary and his family. Protective trusts are relatively uncommon, and are used primarily for purposes of asset protection.

Law: Trustee Act 1925, s. 33

Implied trusts

As well as express trusts created by deed or will or some other deliberate act of the settlor, there are various 'implied' trusts. Of particular significance for tax purposes is the 'resulting' trust which arises, for instance, where the initial objects of a trust fail and, in the absence of any other defined objects, the property reverts to the settlor (see, for example, '*Haworth v IRC*' (1974) 49 TC 489. A resulting trust may also arise where the settlor fails to make an effective gift of the trust property to the donee, or where the trusts are undefined or uncertain (*Vandervell v IRC* [1967] 2 AC 291). HMRC are alert to finding hidden resulting trusts within the terms of an express trust, since where the settlor may benefit, the income will be treated as the settlor's for tax purposes.

Law: Vandervell v IRC [1967] 2 AC 291; *Haworth v IRC* (1974) 49 TC 489

Charitable trusts

Special tax treatment is afforded to charitable trusts which enjoy a number of exemptions and reliefs from income tax, tax on chargeable gains, inheritance tax, stamp duty land tax etc.

Vested and contingent interests

A beneficiary has a vested interest in trust property if his entitlement is indefeasible. For example, he may be entitled to the income of the trust as it arises, or the trust may provide for him to become entitled at a future date on attaining a certain age. A beneficiary has a contingent interest if his entitlement is dependent on an event which may or may not occur: for example, a beneficiary's entitlement may be dependent on his marriage. There is sometimes a thin dividing line between a vested and contingent interest but essentially the distinction is between becoming entitled *when* something occurs (vested) or becoming entitled *if* something occurs (contingent). In *Stanley v IR Commrs* (1944) 26 TC 12, the trustees were directed by the *Trustee Act* 1925, s. 31(2), in the event of the beneficiary's death before attaining twenty-one (the age in *Trustee Act* 1925, s. 31 is now eighteen), to hold income accumulated during his minority as an accretion to capital. This converted his interest in that income to a contingent one, even though his interest in the remainder of the trust company was vested on his attaining twenty-one.

Law: Stanley v IR Commrs (1944) 26 TC 12

Trusts with vulnerable beneficiaries

FA 2005, s. 23–45 introduced a special tax regime for certain trusts with 'vulnerable beneficiaries', with effect from 6 April 2004. The intent of the new scheme is to ensure that qualifying trusts pay no more tax on the income that accrues for the benefit of vulnerable beneficiaries than the beneficiary would themselves pay if the income had arisen directly in their own hands (see **61.5.5**).

Law: TCGA 1992, s. 60; FA 2005, s. 23–45; FA 2006, s. 88, s. 89, , and Sch. 12, 13

61.3 The rules against perpetuities and the restriction of accumulation periods

61.3.1 Introduction

The rules in relation to perpetuities and accumulations in England and Wales have recently changed. The previous legislation was the *Perpetuity and Accumulations Act* 1964 and the *Law of Property Act* 1925 (s. 164–165). This has been significantly amended by the *Perpetuities and Accumulations Act* 2009, but the *Perpetuities and Accumulations Act* 1964 remains in force to some extent. It is important to note that the Perpetuities and Accumulations Act 2009 is mostly prospective, i.e. it fails to sweep away the complexity and uncertainty of the old rules which will continue to apply to dispositions made before 6 April 2010. Thus it is necessary, given the duration of trusts generally, to be familiar with both the previous and the current rules. It is now, more than ever, important to obtain competent legal advice where there is a concern about perpetuity and accumulation periods, especially where there are concerns about how the two sets of rules interact.

In the Law Commission Report 251, published 31 March 1998, the authors recommend that the existing law is too complex and that the period for perpetuities be made 125 years and that the accumulation period should be abolished. While it was a long time in the making, this is largely the effect of the Perpetuities and Accumulations Act 2009, at least with respect to property settled after 6 April 2010.

61.3.2 The rules prior to 6 April 2010

Section 1 of the *Perpetuity and Accumulations Act* 1964 set the term for settlements, other than charitable trusts, at 80 years. Section 3(4) *Perpetuity and Accumulations Act* 1964 extended the period for lives in being (which includes foetuses) of the settlor and most beneficiaries and potential beneficiaries. Section 13 *Perpetuity and Accumulations Act* 1964 extended the period formerly set in s. 164(1) *Law of Property Act* 1925 so that accumulations could be for the longest of:

- the life of the settlor;
- 21 years from the death of the settlor;
- the duration of the minority of any person living (or a foetus) at the death of the settlor;
- the duration of the minority of persons under a limitation who would be entitled if they were of full age;
- 21 years from the date of the settlement; and
- the duration of the minority of persons in living (or a foetus) at the date of the settlement.

Note that for the above purposes a disposition made by will is deemed to be made on the date of the death of the settlor.

61.3.3 The Perpetuities and Accumulations Act 2009

The *Perpetuities and Accumulations Act* 2009 provides for a single period of 125 years to be the perpetuity period for all dispositions made after 6 April 2010, notwithstanding any contrary intention expressed in the instrument effecting the disposition. Interests created so as to vest in a charity, and interests or rights arising under a relevant pension scheme, but not including interests or rights arising as a result of a letter of nomination or an advancement, are stated to be excepted from the application of the rule against perpetuities. Thus a trust for charitable purposes is not subject to the rule against perpetuities and this must be borne in mind when making dispositions to both charitable and non-charitable objects.

The rule against excessive accumulations of income is abolished from 6 April 2010, except in the case of charities. Thus an instrument may specify any period up to the perpetuity period of 125 years as the applicable accumulation period. For charities, the previous 21-year period will still apply in order to ensure that funds held by charities are applied for the public benefit within a reasonable time of receipt.

Law: *Law of Property Act* 1925, s. 164–165; *Perpetuities and Accumulations Act* 1964; *Perpetuities and Accumulations Act* 2009, s. 2, 5, 12, 13, 14 and 15

> ⚠ **Warning!**
>
> A special power of appointment is bound by the same perpetuity period as in the instrument giving the power. This means that for a pre-6 April 2010 trust, it is not possible to extend the perpetuity period simply by using a power of appointment in the trust instrument. One possibility for trustees in this position is to consider the approach taken in *Wyndham v Egremont* [2009] EWHC 2076 (Ch).

61.4 Management of the trust

61.4.1 Who should be the trustees?

This is frequently one of the most difficult problems in creating a trust. Once trusts are established the trustees will have obligations both to the beneficiaries and to external parties, such as HM Revenue & Customs (HMRC). In trusts of any complexity, accounts will have to be prepared for the beneficiaries and there may be the need for financial or legal advice in the management of the assets and income of the trust. Therefore, it will often be advisable to have the advice of accountants, lawyers and financial advisers. However, this advice may be given by such professionals without their being trustees. On the other hand, it might be felt that they will feel more involved if they become trustees. The alternative to professionals is the settlor himself while he lives and members of his family or friends. This will obviously have to be persons younger than the settlor who may be expected to survive the settlor and last long enough to run the trust at least for a few years. If the settlor is to be a trustee, he must ensure that he receives no remuneration and if he is settling shares in his family company, consideration should be given as to the extent to which his remuneration and his voting rights constitute a gift with reservation. In most cases they will not.

> ⚠ **Warning!**
>
> Where the settlor is also a trustee or beneficiary there may be adverse tax consequences. Therefore where tax is a consideration it is important to take advice on the tax implications of the proposed trust structure and trust officers.

There may also be a mixture of family, etc. and professionals. If family or friends are to be trustees care may need to be taken, especially where trustees have discretion, that conflicts of interest do not arise between trustees in their capacity as trustees and trustees in their capacity as beneficiaries or potential beneficiaries. It is not uncommon for the settlor to be a trustee while he lives (but see above). Normally, non-professional trustees are not allowed to be remunerated for their services as trustees; however, where professionals are involved they can be paid their normal professional remuneration, but only if the document creating the trust includes a 'charging clause'. Any professional being considered for the role of trustee (or executor) will insist on the insertion of such a clause. There should be no possibility of remuneration for the settlor even if he is a professional.

> ⚠ **Warning!**
>
> It should be noted that the beneficiaries may include the settlor even though he is also the trustee. For tax reasons, however, this is often inadvisable. Where a trust is to be created by a will, no beneficiary should witness the will since that will exclude the witness from benefit.

It is possible to have only one trustee, but this is generally inadvisable since the single trustee may die or be unable to act at any given time and getting a new trustee appointed when there is no existing trustee is more difficult. In the case of trusts where the settled property includes land, at least two trustees are required, unless a trust corporation (e.g. a bank) is appointed.

> ⚠ **Warning!**
>
> Where there is a charitable trust, the trustees must meet the requirements of the management condition (basically, a 'fit and proper person' test) in FA 2010, Sch. 6, para. 4. Where the trustees do not meet that condition, the trust will fall outside the definition of 'charity' and will not be eligible for the charitable tax reliefs.

61.4.2 Should there be a trust protector?

The purpose of a trust protector is to exercise a restraining influence on trustees when they exercise their discretion, though the role of protector is flexible and its scope may be specified in the trust instrument. The protector is appointed by the settlement and he must normally give his prior written consent before the trustees can do certain things named in the deed (e.g. make investments, lend or borrow, advance capital to beneficiaries, etc.). This may be particularly important where the trustees are non-resident. However, the protector must not usually be an active administrator.

61.5 Types of trust

61.5.1 The main types

Trusts have a variety of descriptions. Non-technical terms include:

(a) *The bare trust*, where the beneficiary is fully entitled to the assets in his own

right and the trustee merely administers them as nominee – it is also possible to hold assets for minor children in this way, though the minor child could not call for the trust assets.
(b) *The life interest trust* where assets are held for the life of one or more persons and then, on the death of the last of them, the capital passes to someone else. It is possible for there to be successive life interests.
(c) *The pure discretionary trust* where the trustees have power to give income or capital to any of a clearly defined set of beneficiaries. The trustees (or other person) may also have the power to alter the class of beneficiaries by adding to it, or excluding individuals from it.
(d) Trusts with vulnerable beneficiaries.

For tax purposes, trusts are divided into two main types:

- those with interests in possession, and
- those without interests in possession.

When a trust is set up, the trustees or their advisers are required to complete form 41G (Trusts) for HMRC to set up a reference and issue returns, etc. To some extent, the form fixes the nature of the trust, whereas previously the Revenue required the trust deed and determined the nature of the trust themselves. This means that the responsibility for determining the nature of the trust rests entirely with the trustees who can be liable for penalties and interest if they get it wrong.

61.5.2 Trusts with interests in possession – 'life interest trusts'

Ordinary life interest trusts

In the first type of trust, the deed creating the trust states that the income will be paid to a given person or will be shared among a number of persons either for a limited period or for their lifetimes. Such persons have interests in possession in that, while the period of their interest lasts, the income must be paid to them and, if it is not, they can sue the trustees for it. Frequently at the end of such periods other 'life interests' may arise.

However, the rule against perpetuities ensures that trusts cannot last for ever. The broad effect of the law is to restrict the lives of settlements to around 80 years. This means that the capital must be given to some beneficiaries at the end of that period and they become 'absolutely entitled as against the trustees'. In other words, the trusts come to an end and the beneficiaries receive the legal ownership of the property in the settlement and can do what they like with it. The persons who receive the income are known as 'life-tenants' and those who receive the capital are known as 'remaindermen'. They may be the same persons or they may not depending on the terms of the trust. Quite often children may receive the income until they reach a certain age and then they become entitled to the capital.

Trusts that are treated as life interest trusts

Two particular types of trust, the protective trust under the *Trustee Act* 1925, s. 31(1) and the trust for the disabled, may in fact be discretionary because the right to income has been taken away. However, where the bulk of the income is in fact applied for the benefit of the beneficiary at the discretion of the trustee, the trusts are treated as life interest trusts (IHTA 1984, s. 88 and 89).

Bare trusts

These can arise when a beneficiary has become absolutely entitled both to income and capital but the trustees continue to hold the assets. This may happen, for instance, where one beneficiary to a property has come of age but the other beneficiaries have not done so. Note the powers of the trustees, given by the *Trusts of Land and Appointment of Trustees Act* 1996, to partition land where beneficiaries have become absolutely entitled. Bare trusts may also arise where it is required that a minor should be absolutely entitled to property but an adult is needed to manage it on his behalf. The adult can be appointed a bare trustee. Such trustees are treated as merely nominees of the beneficiaries.

Example 61.1

In her Will, Mrs Jones left the residue of her estate to such of her grandchildren as were alive at the date of her death.

She directed that the funds should not be paid to the grandchildren until they respectively attain age 21 years.

All of the grandchildren who were alive when Mrs Jones died are entitled to an equal share in the residue of the estate. There are no other conditions that they must fulfil before they become entitled. The direction about payment does not affect this basic position.

The beneficiaries have a vested interest and the trust is a bare trust.

Example 61.2

Mr Barnes left the residue of his estate to 'such of my grandchildren as survive me and attain age 21 years'. If any grandchild dies before age 21, his/her prospective share goes to the other grandchildren who do attain that age.

Here there are two conditions to be met before the grandchildren become entitled to their shares in the estate:

- they must survive Mr Barnes; and
- they must attain age 21 years.

Here the grandchildren did not take immediate vested interests at the death of the testator.

> This is not a bare trust and the trustees must make a tax return.

61.5.3 Reversionary interests

In the case of a trust that takes the form of 'To A for life, then to B for life, with remainder to C' the interests of B and C are said to be 'reversionary' on the life of A while he lives. C's interest is reversionary both on the lives of A and B. When A dies B's interest is said to 'fall in' and likewise C's interest when B dies.

61.5.4 Trusts without interests in possession

These are 'discretionary' trusts, so called because the trustees have discretion as to which of a specified set of beneficiaries shall receive benefits from the trust. Discretion of the trustees may extend to income or capital or both. Care must be taken in specifying the class of beneficiaries because if the description of the class is imprecise the trust may fail and result in reversion of the property to the settler, or result in adverse tax consequences for the settlor, or a member of the beneficial class.

It is not necessary that the class should be described in such a way that a complete list of its members can be drawn up, but when a person presents himself as a potential beneficiary he must be able to be identified as a beneficiary. An example of a class might be 'sons born in Hertfordshire to ordained clergymen of the Church of England'. However, in most family trusts the class normally extends to sons and daughters of the settlor and their offspring, and may include a surviving spouse.

The discretionary trust

The pure discretionary trust may give the trustees discretion to pay the income to certain beneficiaries during the trust period (say 80 years) and then to share the capital at their discretion between certain other beneficiaries. However, most trusts carry a mixture of interests in possession coupled with discretion of the trustees with regard to certain aspects of the trust. For instance, a widow might be given a life interest in her husband's estate and the trustees may be given discretion to advance capital to her during her lifetime and then to distribute the remainder as they think fit among the family after her death.

> **Planning point**
>
> In practice, too, many trusts, although discretionary in form, are less discretionary than they appear since the settlor can give his trustees a memorandum of wishes, advising his trustees of the principles on which they should exercise their discretion. This memorandum is not, however, mandatory on the trustees and it legally enforceable and must not in any way be possible to

> construe it as part of the trust deed. Notwithstanding that a letter of wishes is not legally enforceable trustees will generally try and follow one.

The accumulation and maintenance trust

This type of trust was especially favoured for inheritance tax purposes. It was a special kind of discretionary trust, generally used for children. Such trusts used to generally be for children up to the age of 25, but since FA 2006 favourable treatment for such trusts has been restricted to those for individuals 18 years or under. Income is normally accumulated for a given period. Subsequently, the children will come into an interest in possession (see **61.5.2** above) thereby becoming entitled to a share of income in their own right and then, perhaps at some later date, they will become absolutely entitled to the capital. In order to qualify for the benefits of this status there are stringent requirements laid down in IHTA 1984, s. 71, which requires that:

(a) one or more persons (referred to as beneficiaries) will, on or before attaining a specified age not exceeding 18, become beneficially entitled to it [the settled property] or to an interest in possession in it, and
(b) no interest in possession subsists in it and the income from it is to be accumulated so far as it is not applied for the maintenance, education or benefit of a beneficiary.

IHTA 1984, s. 71(1A) and 71(1B) were added by the *Finance Act* 2006; these provisions mean that after 22 March 2006 new accumulation and maintenance trusts cannot be created so as to benefit from the beneficial tax treatment accorded to such settlements in existence prior to that date.

Law: IHTA 1984, s. 71

61.5.5 Trusts with vulnerable beneficiaries

Finance Act 2005, Sch. 1, s. 23–45 introduced new rules for trusts which involve a vulnerable person. The term 'vulnerable person' (VP) includes 'disabled persons' and 'relevant minors'. The definition of 'disabled persons' has been taken from IHT 1984), s. 74(4) (which provides for pre-1981 trusts for disabled persons), and repeated in FA 2005, s. 38 with a slight relaxation. They include sufferers from mental disorder, within the meaning of the *Mental Health Act* 1983, who cannot manage their own affairs, and recipients of attendance allowance or disability living allowance entitled to the care component at the highest or middle rate. If they do not receive these allowances only by reason of their receiving kidney treatment or of the provision of certain accommodation, they may still qualify as disabled – this being the relaxation mentioned above. A 'relevant minor' is a person under 18 at least one of whose parents is dead. The remarriage of a surviving parent does not affect the status (s. 39).

The VP must be a beneficiary under a 'qualifying trust' (FA 2005, s. 34 and 35). In the case of a disabled person, the definition is a tighter version of that contained in IHTA 1984, s. 74(1). Where any trust property (at all) is applied for the benefit of a beneficiary (other than under a statutory power of advancement under the *English Trustee Act* 2000 or *Trustee Act (Northern Ireland)* 1958 – a relaxation not available in Scotland) it must be applied for the disabled person's benefit.

A protective trust may qualify, unless and until the disabled person's entitlement to income fails or determines. In the case of a relevant minor, a qualifying trust may be a statutory trust arising on intestacy, or a will trust (or one established under the Criminal Injuries Compensation Scheme) which secures that the relevant minor takes capital, income and accumulations absolutely at 18, and that prior to such entitlement, and during his or her lifetime, none of the trust property or its income is applicable for the benefit of any other person. Again, (except in Scotland) a statutory power of advancement can be exercised without breaching these conditions. Section 42 modifies the rules in Scotland, substituting references to 'in trust' for 'on trusts' and similar, and changing the language concerning intestacy.

The regime is elective (by FA 2005, s. 37) and, the election must be made no later than 31 January in the tax year following that in which the date from which election is to have effect falls. Both the trustees and the VP must elect, which is somewhat curious, given that many VPs will be either mentally incapable or very young indeed. HMRC may specify the information to be contained in the election, which will include details of the trusts, the trustees, the VP and any other person connected with the trust, a statement that the trust is a qualifying trust, a declaration of accuracy of the information provided and a declaration by the VP authorising the trustees to claim under the rules, and 'such other declarations as the ... Revenue may reasonably require'. The election is irrevocable, but ceases to have effect on the ceasing of the person's vulnerability (for example on recovery from a disabling condition), the failure of the trust to be qualifying or the termination of the trust. When such an event occurs the trustees must inform HMRC within 90 days.

Example 61.3

A qualifying trust has had a vulnerable beneficiary since 2003. The earliest 'effective date' for the trust will be 6 April 2006, being the date from which the provisions are effective. The 'vulnerable person' election must be made no later than 31 January 2009. That is 12 months after the 31 January next following the end of the tax year in which the 'effective date' falls (i.e. 31 January 2008, which next follows the end of the tax year 2006–07).

Law: FA 2005, Sch. 1, s. 23–45

61.5.6 Special income tax treatment

The intention of the regime is to make the VP's personal allowances and lower rate bands available to the trustees. What is referred to as 'special income tax treatment' is described in FA 2005, s. 25–29, and must be claimed for each tax year. It is not available where the trust income is taxable on the settlor by virtue of ITTOIA 2005, s. 624. The starting point is the computation of the vulnerable person's liability', known as 'VQTI'.

First, compute the VP's liability for income and capital gains tax (CGT) on the assumption that any income distributed to him by the trustees is disregarded and that any relief given by way of an income tax deduction (say, married couple's allowance) is also disregarded, and call it TLV2. Now find TLV1, which is TLV2 plus tax chargeable on the VP on the assumption that the trust income was the VP's income. Subtract TLV2 from TLV1 and the answer is VQTI. The next step is to determine the 'trustees' liability': TQTI. This is done by assuming that the trustees are liable to tax without the benefit of the VP provisions. Now perform the calculation TQTI – VQTI to find the amount by which the trustees' income tax liability is reduced.

Special provision is made for cases where the VP is non-UK-resident by deeming him resident for income tax and calculating his deemed capital gains as more particularly described below. Where the trustees have other income to which the VP provisions do not apply management expenses chargeable against income have to be apportioned. Where the VP election has effect for only part of a tax year, only the income for that part of the year to which the election applies is relieved, and the apportionment of expenses applies only to the elected part of the year.

Law: FA 2005, s. 25–29; ITTOIA 2005, s. 624

61.5.7 Special capital gains tax treatment

Capital gains tax is dealt with in FA 2005, s. 30–33. Again, relief must be claimed and different provisions apply depending on whether the VP is UK-resident or non-resident. (The legislation provides definitions of residence and non-residence by reference to residence in any part of the tax year and ordinary residence during the tax year, which causes no surprise, according with the CGT charging provisions in *Taxation of Chargeable Gains Act* 1992 (TCGA 1992), s. 2(1)) No claim may be made where the VP dies in the relevant tax year and gains include gains imputed to shareholders of non-resident companies.

The rules were overhauled from 6 April 2008, due to the standard rate of 18 per cent for the charge on capital gains. Therefore there are now two sets of relevant provisions: those applicable in 2007–08 and earlier tax years and those applicable in subsequent years.

The rules for 2007–08 and earlier years

Where the VP is UK-resident, he is treated as if he were the settlor interested in the settlement and as if the provisions charging CGT on him (TCGA 1992, s. 77–79, less the information provision) applied.

Where the VP is non-resident things become a lot more complicated. The first resort is to the definitions in FA 2005, Sch. 1. The basic building blocks are 'actual gains and losses' and 'assumed gains and losses'. Actual gains are gains accruing to the VP on which he is taxable and actual losses are losses of the year together with losses brought forward from previous years. To understand assumed gains and losses, however, it is first necessary to comprehend the 'relevant assumptions'. These are:

- that the VP is resident and domiciled in the UK throughout the year, and
- that he has given the notice necessary to claim relief for allowable losses (since he is non-resident he could not have actually given notice because the losses of a non-resident are not allowable).

Assumed gains are those taxable on the relevant assumptions and assumed losses are those which would be available on the relevant assumptions. The actual gains and the assumed gains are then aggregated and together form the VP's 'deemed taxable amount'. Now it is possible to compute TLVB: the total amount of income tax and CGT to which the VP would be liable if his income included his actual income and the trustees specially taxed income and his capital gains equalled his deemed taxable amount for the year.

The next step is to calculate TLVA. Here, one takes the deemed taxable amount (above) and adds to it the 'notional section 77 gains'. For these, back to Sch. 1, para. 4: make the 'relevant assumptions' (above) and calculate the gains that would accrue to the VP if he were deemed to be the settlor chargeable under the settlor-interested trust provisions. Finally, the figure for TLVB is subtracted from TLVA. The result is called VQTG. To get the amount of the VP relief, take VQTG away from TQTG. TQTG is simply the amount of CGT for which the trustees would be liable without VP relief.

The rules in 2008–09 and subsequent years

In 2008–09 and subsequent years the calculation is as follows:

- The trustees' liability to capital gains tax for the tax year is to be reduced by an amount equal to TQTG − VQTG. TQTG is the amount of capital gains tax to which the trustees would (apart from this Chapter) be liable for the tax year in respect of the qualifying trust gains, and VQTG is the amount arrived at using the calculation: TLVA − TLVB.
- TLVB is the total amount of capital gains tax to which the vulnerable person is liable for the tax year, and TLVA is what TLVB would be if the qualifying

trust gains accrued to the vulnerable person (instead of to the trustees) and no allowable losses were deducted from the qualifying trust gains.

Law: TCGA 1992, s. 77–79; FA 2005, s. 30–33; FA 2008, s. 8 and Sch. 2

61.5.8 Administration and information

HMRC may seek such particulars as they reasonably require to check that the beneficiary is vulnerable and that the trusts are qualifying trusts, giving a minimum 60 days' notice. If they determine that the requirements were not met or that an event has occurred since the effective date of the election which terminates its validity, they may give notice that the election never had, or ceased to have, effect, as the case may be. An appeal lies to the General Commissioners only and must be made within 30 days after the notice was given. Steps may be taken to recover additional income or CGT consequent on the giving of the notice.

Law: FA 2005, s. 40

61.6 The uses of trusts

61.6.1 Life interest settlements

The traditional uses for life interest settlements include:

- 'the flighty widow' – where the widow, who might remarry and take the family estate elsewhere, was given a life interest only and on her death or remarriage the capital went to the children of the marriage (or of a former marriage);
- 'the desirable heiress' – in order to protect the wealthy daughter from the predations of fortune-hunters, the daughter was given a life interest only so that she could not give or leave her money to any husband or other predatory young men;
- 'the prodigal son' – where the son was considered not fit to have the capital, he could be given an income only until such time as he became of more mature habits when he might come into the capital;
- 'the handicapped child' – where a child suffers from mental incapacity, a trust may be set up to maintain him or her for life; or
- 'the vulnerable settlor' – occasionally a settlor may make himself (or his spouse) life tenant of his own property where he feels that, if property is held in trust, it will be protected from creditors or governments, etc. However, most regimes will see through such trusts.

61.6.2 Discretionary settlements

These are more obviously of use where the settlor wishes to benefit a class of persons but does not know in what proportions he wishes to do so. In particular, he will not know which members of his family after his death will have most need of the funds. Therefore, he can leave those decisions to his trustees. The accumulation and maintenance settlement is merely an extension of this, except that the beneficiaries will tend to be younger children.

While the above are the traditional uses for trusts and, to a large extent, are still worthwhile uses, the late Professor Wheatcroft was of the opinion that 90 per cent of trusts were formed for tax purposes. This is probably still the case. If it were not for the tax advantages of trusts, far more gifts would be outright gifts to individuals and the relatively high costs of trusts in terms of compliance, accountancy and legal fees would not be incurred. Simple trusts may be acquired comparatively cheaply from insurance companies engaged in inheritance tax (IHT) planning, but these are normally tied to the purchase of a product (usually a bond) and even then the purchaser normally has to provide his own trustees.

61.7 Tax aspects of trusts

61.7.1 Benefits

Before proceeding to consider the taxation aspects of trusts in some detail, it is worth considering the main tax benefits that arise from trusts.

(1) The alienation of property out of large estates for the purposes of inheritance tax. The general rule is that once the period for gifts has expired (currently seven years) the property given to the trust is in a separate estate and is subject to a different regime of taxation. In the past, the settlor could often continue to control that property and even benefit from it without it being in his estate. The 'gifts with reservation' rules have made that more difficult, but still not impossible.

(2) Freezing the value of gifts for inheritance tax to the value of the property at the time of its settlement where cash is given to trustees who then acquire investments or property. The growth arises in the trust free of inheritance tax.

61.7.2 The lower rates band

Finance Act 2005, s. 14 introduced a new ICTA s. 686D (now ITA 2007, s. 491). This disapplies 'special trust rates' to the first slice of trust income. FA 2009 set the trust rate at 50 per cent and the trust dividend rate at 42.5 per cent.

Law: ITA 2007, s. 9

61.8 Some important legal considerations

61.8.1 Introduction

Readers should ensure that they understand the distinction between trustees and executors. In many cases they will be the same persons, but their roles will be quite different and they are subject to different tax regimes. The duty of the executors is to gather in the assets and pay the liabilities and then to distribute the surplus according to the will. At that point, if any of the surplus is to be held on trust, the trustees will take over in respect of that part. The date at which that is deemed to happen may be important for some tax and other purposes, but for many tax purposes the fiction that the trustees inherited as at the time of death will be maintained.

There are three significant pieces of legislation to take note of:

- the *Trustee Act* 1925;
- the *Trusts of Land and Appointment of Trustees Act* 1996, and
- the *Trustee Act* 2000.

61.8.2 The Trustee Act 1925

This Act is still the main piece of statutory legislation governing trusts. It is a curious mixture and most modern trust deeds tend to override it or amend its provisions for the purposes of the settlement in hand. This can be done in respect of trustees' powers by expressing a clear contrary intention in the trust instrument (*Trustee Act* 1925, s. 69(2)). Two clauses, however, are particularly relevant, namely s. 31 and 32, which give the trustees obligations or powers that have a bearing on the rights of beneficiaries.

Trustee Act 1925, s. 31(1)(i) empowers trustees to advance income during the minority of children to parents, guardians, etc. for the child's education, maintenance, etc. This applies whether or not the child has a vested or a contingent interest. There is also a complex proviso which is normally overridden.

Trustee Act 1925, s. 31(1)(ii) provides that when the child reaches the age of 21 (though for this we must now read 18 because of the *Family Law Reform Act* 1969, s. 1) the trustees are to pay his share of the income to him whether or not he has a vested interest (but see **61.9.4** below).

The significance of this is that the child generally obtains an interest in possession at the age of 18 and not at a later age unless this part of *Trustee Act* 1925, s. 31 is overridden (see **61.9.4** below). It also means that until that time the trust is effectively discretionary in respect of the rate applicable to trusts.

It is also particularly important with regard to hold-over relief for capital gains on property coming out of an accumulation and maintenance trust, since unless the property is 'business' or agricultural property, the relief only applies where the child becomes entitled to the income and the capital at the same time (TCGA 1992, s. 260(2)(d)).

Trustee Act 1925, s. 31(2) authorises the trustees to accumulate the balance of any income during the minority of the child, though the accumulations can be advanced for the maintenance of the child.

Thus, unless it is overridden, *Trustee Act* 1925, s. 31 tends to create an effective accumulation and maintenance settlement, with the child becoming entitled to an interest in possession at the age of 18.

Trustee Act 1925, s. 32 allows trustees to advance capital to beneficiaries, whether or not they have a vested interest, up to one-half of their share or their prospective share. Most trust deeds tend to delete the words 'one-half' in this section.

61.8.3 The Trusts of Land and Appointment of Trustees Act 1996

The *Trusts of Land and Appointment of Trustees Act* 1996, as its name suggests, deals with trusts of land (which includes buildings) for which either two trustees are required or a trust corporation. This Act repeals the former legislation dealing with settled land and deals with express and implied trusts for sale (that is, where land is owned jointly by more than one person). It also covers the powers of trustees, including the right to partition land (for example, where one or more beneficiaries have become absolutely entitled as against the trustees) and the powers to delegate together with the requirement to consult beneficiaries and the right of beneficiaries to occupy the land in appropriate circumstances. The second part of the Act gives beneficiaries the right to appoint new trustees or to require current trustees to retire. Thus, the Act empowers beneficiaries to a more considerable extent than previously.

61.8.4 The Trustee Act 2000

The principal purpose of the *Trustee Act* 2000 is to relax the provisions of the *Trustee Investment Act* 1961. The 1961 Act, unless overridden in the trust document, required trustees to divide the trust fund into wider- and narrower-range investments, where the latter consisted of safer investments (for example, Government securities) and the former of more dangerous investments, such as equities. The Act laid down proportions of each which trustees were allowed to hold. The *Trustee Act* 2000 removes the need to split the fund and allows trustees to make investments as they think fit. However, the Act requires them to observe the standard investment criteria and to take advice from a person whom the trustees believe is qualified to give it by his ability and practical experience in the appropriate area of financial matters, although it allows them not to where they judge it reasonable in all the circumstances not to do so.

'The standard investment criteria, in relation to a trust, are–

the suitability to the trust of investments of the same kind as any particular investment proposed to be made or retained and of that particular investment as an investment of that kind, and

the need for diversification of investments of the trust, in so far as is appropriate to the circumstances of the trust.'

The above rules do not apply to purchases of land but these too are dealt with in Trustee Act 2000, s. 8.

The *Trustee Act* 2000 also deals with the powers of trustees to delegate some, but not all, of their functions, including the appointment of agents, nominees and custodians of assets. This is a considerable extension of the ability of trustees to delegate some of their administrative functions since trusts were previously ruled by the slogan '*delegatus non potest delegare*' (one who is himself a delegate cannot delegate). However, trustees are not generally permitted to delegate their functions of exercising discretion between beneficiaries. The *Trustee Act* 2000 also covers remuneration of trustees, nominees, etc. although it does not generally change the rules about remuneration of professional trustees and non-remuneration of lay trustees.

61.8.5 The age of majority

By reason of the *Family Law Reform Act* 1969, s. 1 the age of majority became 18 instead of 21 and any statute made before that date is to be construed accordingly. However, this does not affect non-statutory instruments made before 1 January 1970 which are still read as implying 21 as the age of majority in references to 'infant' or 'minor' children. In the case of wills made before that date (and any codicils to them even if made later) the age is deemed to be 21 even where the testator dies after 1 January 1970 and for such wills any entitlement under the *Trustee Act* 1925, s. 31 is taken also to be 21 and not 18 (*Family Law Reform Act* 1969, s. 1(7)). Where an appointment is made out of a trust after 1 January 1970 but the trust itself was formed before that date, Revenue practice (SP E8 1 June 1977) has been to treat the age of majority under the deed of appointment as 18. Since this view was confirmed by the High Court in *Begg-McBrearty (HMIT) v Sitwell* [1996] BTC 269 the Revenue have withdrawn their statement of practice in favour of the case law (Inland Revenue Press Release, 30 September 1996).

61.9 Tax planning opportunities with trusts

Prior to 9 October 2007 trusts were a popular way to avoid wasting the inheritance tax nil-rate band on a straight gift to spouse, or civil partner. Instead of leaving assets directly to the surviving spouse or civil partner, a discretionary trust equal to the amount of the nil-rate band (or unused nil-rate band) for inheritance tax was often created. Then, at the time of the settlor's death, the trustees could see who needed the assets most. If they distributed the assets to the spouse or civil partner (later than three months but earlier than two years after the death) the spouse (or civil partner) exemption could be obtained, otherwise they could distribute the assets to other beneficiaries and not waste the nil-rate band. For the significance of the three months see the case of *Figg v Clarke* [1997] BTC 157.

Since 9 October 2007, it has been possible for all, or part, of an inheritance tax nil rate band, which has not been used on the death of a spouse or civil partner, to be transferred to the surviving spouse or partner (IHTA 1984, s. 8A-C).

Give the spouse a life interest in the assets but give the trustees wide powers to withdraw the life interest and make it a discretionary trust if they think fit. The spouse will be a beneficiary of the discretionary trust. Since the surviving spouse has the life interest he or she is deemed to be the settlor, but gifts with reservation cannot apply since the surviving spouse did not make the original gift.

Obtain capital gains tax private residence relief on a property occupied by someone for which the relief might otherwise not be available. The relief is available for a property occupied by a beneficiary under the terms of a settlement.

Use a discretionary trust to obtain capital gains tax hold-over relief on an asset which is neither 'business' nor agricultural, using the nil-rate band but ensure that the trust is truly discretionary.

Use a new trust to receive a reversionary interest in another trust where the beneficiary of the reversionary interest does not need it.

Use the normal gifts out of income provisions to fund a life policy written in trust which will help to provide funds for potential beneficiaries or help to pay inheritance tax.

Consider the use of stock dividends paid to trustees in private companies in conjunction with ITTOIA 2005, Pt. 4, Ch. 5 (Stock dividends from UK resident companies), ITTOIA 2005, s. 568 (application of rate applicable to trusts to trust income) and TCGA 1992, s. 142, as amended by FA 1998 (capital gains tax treatment of stock dividends).

> **Planning point**
>
> The planning opportunities set out above can be summarised as follows:
>
> (a) the spouse (or civil partner) should be given a life interest in the assets, but the trustees should also be given wide powers to withdraw that interest and make it a discretionary trust if they think fit;
> (b) fully utilise the CGT private residence exemption;
> (c) a discretionary trust may be used to obtain capital gains tax hold-over relief;
> (d) use a new trust to receive a reversionary interest in another trust where the beneficiary of the reversionary interest does not need it;
> (e) the normal gifts out of income provisions may be used to fund a life policy written in trust; and
> (f) consider stock dividends paid to trustess (see (9) above).

61.10 Checklist of considerations on using trusts

(1) Are there good reasons for having a trust or trusts?

(a) Does the trust fulfil a family need?
(b) Is the trust for tax saving?
(c) If the latter, does it also fit in with family needs?
(d) Could the same needs not be met without a trust?

(2) Can the client afford a trust?

(a) Is the trust fund going to be able to provide the requisite income to pay trust expenses (frequently quite high legal and accountancy fees, maintenance of assets, etc.) and provide a return for the beneficiaries?
(b) If the trust is to be a lifetime trust can the client afford to lose the funds and the income, bearing in mind his own current and future needs and possibly those of his spouse, partner, etc.?
(c) Will there be a serious loss of taper relief on any assets transferred to the trust?
(d) If the trust is to be a death trust will there be enough money after paying fees, etc. to support those who need to be supported?

(3) Can the family live with a trust?

(a) Will the settlor be happy to lose some benefit from the assets put into the settlement (though by being a trustee he may be able to keep some control)?
(b) Will spouses, children, etc. be content to live with the decisions of the trustees (who may partly be some of their own number)?
(c) Will the trust be flexible enough (e.g. to provide income or capital where it is

most needed, to cope with the unexpected such as deaths in the wrong order, new births, etc.)?
(d) Are assets to be given to children too young or are assets to be tied up too long?
(e) Consider the above especially where the trust is purely for tax reasons – is the tax reasons tail wagging the family dog?

(4) If the trust is for family reasons:

(a) Does the trust as designed fulfil all the needs and allow for contingencies? When it does not, give the trustees powers to wind it up.
(b) Have the trustees sufficient powers to do what they might need to do?
(c) Does the trust have any tax pitfalls or disadvantages and can they be overcome? Be especially careful of allowing settlors or their spouses (but not widows or widowers) to be beneficiaries.
(d) And the trust is to be discretionary consider the settlor leaving a memorandum of wishes, which must not be part of the settlement deed. The trustees do not have to follow it but, unless it conflicts with their duties, they probably will.

(5) If the trust is for tax reasons:

(a) Does it meet the tax reasons (e.g. bare trusts might have a lower rate of capital gains tax than accumulation and maintenance trusts, so should you have a bare trust for minor children, but then lose the inheritance tax advantages)?
(b) Does it save tax at the expense of increasing some other tax or otherwise losing more than the tax saved (e.g. tax can be saved by gifts to charities, etc. but you lose the whole asset to save the tax!)?
(c) And it is purely for tax reasons is it vulnerable to any of the anti-avoidance provisions, not only those mentioned in this chapter but also the *Ramsay* doctrine concerning a pre-ordained series of transactions?
(d) And it is purely for tax reasons will the trustees, beneficiaries, etc. know what is expected of them and follow it through?
(e) Have you explored the effects of various scenarios (e.g. deaths in the wrong order, unexpected births, divorce, etc.)? Does the trust still work?

(6) Who will be the trustees?

(a) If the trust is for tax reasons it is advisable to have a professional who understands the implications of what has been done and why or, alternatively, a family member who will do what the professional advises.
(b) Family members are much cheaper but beware of conflicts of interest and gifts with reservation.
(c) Will the appointment of anyone as a trustee taint the trust for tax purposes?

(7) Drafting the deed and implementing it

Get the trust deed (or will) drafted and make sure that the timing is right especially if the end of a tax year or some important birthday is approaching.

(8) Documentation and diary system

Ensure that the thinking behind the plan is fully documented. Trusts last a long time, memories are short and staff changes are frequent. Leave good details. Also, arrange a diary system to remind yourself of important dates for tax elections, numbers of years elapsed between gifts and deaths, ten-year anniversaries, birthdays of beneficiaries, current addresses of all relevant parties, etc.

(9) Periodic review

Arrange to review the trust at least annually and preferably before tax liabilities on the trust will fall due.

(7) Drafting the deed and implementing it

(8) Documentation and diary system

(9) Periodic review

62 Construction Industry Scheme

62.1 Introduction

Businesses operating in the construction industry are known as contractors and subcontractors and they may be companies, partnerships or self-employed individuals. A contractor will pay a subcontractor for construction operations. Subcontractors are those businesses that carry out building work for contractors.

Most contractors and subcontractors in the construction industry are affected by the CIS, but these terms go much wider than the meanings they normally have. Contractors include not just construction companies and building firms but also some government departments and local authorities, and many other businesses usually referred to in the industry as 'clients' (see **62.4.1**).

> ⚠ **Warning!**
>
> Private householders, and non-construction-related businesses spending less than £1m a year on construction work are NOT contractors and are not covered by the Construction Industry Scheme.

The scheme applies to workers who for particular contracts are self-employed and are not employees subject to PAYE. For a contract to fall within the scheme, it must be one that is 'not one of employment'. Employment status depends on general law.

Other guidance: Construction Industry Scheme (CIS340)

62.1.1 CIS online

Contractors can file online using HMRC's CIS Online service. Contractors can use CIS Online to file monthly returns and perform verifications over the Internet or using Electronic Data Interchange (EDI). Agents that administer CIS payments on behalf of contractors may use the PAYE/CIS Online for Agents service.

HMRC also provides an online registration service for subcontractors wishing to register for payment under deduction. This is a one-off process and subcontractors wanting to use this service do NOT need to register and enrol beforehand.

The CIS Online – Internet service allows contractors to file monthly returns and perform verifications over the Internet. Once logged onto the service users will need relevant software and they will be able to choose between HMRC's free 'Online Return and Forms – CIS' product, or from a list of Internet filing enabled third party software products.

> ### Planning point
>
> The CIS Online – EDI service is a way of submitting large amounts of data online using a secure communication link. Large contractors and those who already use EDI to send data to HMRC may in particular find it cost-effective. EDI is ideal for:
>
> - any organisation that handles larger volumes of CIS payments and verifications, e.g. contractors who pay a large number of subcontractors monthly, typically in the hundreds; or
> - bureaux that will handle CIS Returns or verifications for several contractors.

62.2 Background

The Construction Industry Scheme (CIS) first came into operation in 1971. However, extensive amendments were made in 1975 and full operation of the revised scheme commenced from 6 April 1977. Problems within the industry regarding the scheme continued to arise and led to certain changes contained in Finance Acts 1995 and 1996.

A consultation paper was published in the 2002 Pre-Budget Report, proposing major reform of the scheme and the resulting legislation is contained in Finance Act 2004. The proposals included replacing existing documentation with a verification service run by HMRC, periodic returns and a new employment status declaration. It is originally planned that the new scheme would come into effect from April 2006, but this was subsequently delayed until 6 April 2007.

Broadly, the CIS is a quasi PAYE system designed to counter tax evasion in the construction industry by imposing responsibility for making a deduction at source from payments made for labour services provided by self-employed building subcontractors and companies unless those persons have received prior verification from HMRC. The CIS, however, is not, and never has been, a system designed to replace the PAYE system with respect to the employees of firms in the construction industry although this is a common misconception brought about partly by the way in which HMRC has operated the scheme in practice. Nevertheless, since its inception, PAYE auditors have been charged with the responsibility for ensuring that the scheme is being operated properly by building contractors and many of the regulations providing the rules for operating the scheme have parallels within the PAYE regulations.

In essence, the scheme requires a contractor to make tax deductions at a prescribed rate from amounts payable to subcontractors for services unless HMRC have provided a verification reference number.

The rules governing the CIS from 6 April 2007 are dealt with in the following paragraphs.

Other guidance: Construction Industry Scheme (CIS340)

62.3 Employment status

Under the CIS, contractors must check or 'verify' new subcontractors with HM Revenue and Customs (HMRC). Broadly, this means that HMRC check the employment status of the subcontractor and ensure that he is properly registered for income tax and national insurance contributions purposes.

A worker's employment status, that is whether they are employed or self-employed, is not a matter of choice. Whether someone is employed or self-employed depends upon the terms and conditions of the relevant engagement. The tax and National Insurance contributions (NICs) rules do, however, contain some special rules that apply to certain categories of worker in certain circumstances. A worker's employment status will determine the charge to tax on income from that employment or self-employment. It will also determine the class of NICs, which are to be paid.

HMRC provide an 'Employment Status Indicator (ESI) Tool' on their website (*www.hmrc.gov.uk/calcs/esi.htm*). Employers and contractors may use the tool to obtain a HMRC 'view' of the employment status of their workers. It should be noted that the tool will provide a general guide only which would not be binding on HMRC. To obtain a written 'opinion' of employment status in the construction industry, the contractor will need to telephone the CIS Helpline on 0845 366 7899.

62.4 Contractors

62.4.1 What is a contractor?

The following are included in the definition of contractor.

(1) Any person carrying on a business which includes construction operations. These are known as 'mainstream contractors' (see below).

(2) Any public office or department of the Crown (including any Northern Ireland department).

(3) Any local authority.

(4) Any development corporation (within the New Towns Act 1981, or the New Towns (Scotland) Act 1968) or new town commission (within the New Towns Act (Northern Ireland) 1965.

(5) The Commission for the New Towns.

(6) The Housing Corporation, Housing for Wales, a housing association (within the Housing Associations Act 1985 or the Housing (Northern Ireland) Order 1981 (SI 1981/156)), a housing trust (within the Housing Associations Act 1985), the Scottish Special Housing Association, and the Northern Ireland Housing Executive.

(7) A person carrying on a business at any time, if:
   (a) his average annual expenditure on construction operations in the period of three years ending with the end of the last period of account before that time exceeds £1m; or
   (b) where he was not carrying on the business at the beginning of that period of three years, one-third of his total expenditure on construction operations for the part of that period during which he has been carrying on the business exceeds £1m.

In (6) above, 'period of account' means a period for which an account is made up in relation to the business in question.

The definition of 'contractor' includes government departments, public offices, and any body carrying out statutory functions and designated in regulations.

It should be emphasised that businesses which would not normally be regarded as contractors because their trading activities are not in construction areas will be regarded as contractors if the average annual expenditure of the business on construction operations in the three years ending with its last accounting date exceeds £1m; if the business has been carried on for less than three years it will be regarded as a contractor for the purposes of the scheme if its total expenditure on construction operations during the period it has been trading exceeds £1m. A business which is so regarded as a 'deemed contractor' (see below) because of its expenditure on construction operations will continue to be regarded as a contractor until it satisfies HMRC that subsequently the expenditure on construction operations has been less than £1m in each of three successive years commencing in or after the period for which it is first so regarded.

Example 62.1

Egg Ltd commences a new trade, having built new multi-storeyed premises, in February 2008. In earlier years Egg Ltd had traded as a retail store but had no expenditure on construction.

Construction expenditure year ended	£
31/12/08	250,000
31/12/09	1,000,000
31/12/10	1,440,000
31/12/11	800,000
31/12/12	800,000
31/12/13	500,000
31/12/14	200,000

Egg Ltd will be required to comply as a 'contractor' with the provisions of the construction industry deduction scheme from January 2011 and will not be able to satisfy HMRC that they are no longer within those requirements until some time in the year ending 31 December 2013.

Law: FA 2004, s. 59

Other guidance: Construction Industry Scheme (CIS340)

62.4.2 Mainstream contractors

These are businesses which carry out construction work, or supply labour for carrying out construction work. They include construction businesses, property developers or speculative builders and gang leaders. These businesses are liable to operate the CIS whatever the level of their expenditure on construction operations.

Construction businesses are businesses whose activities consist of or include carrying out construction operations for other parties and which use subcontract labour for this purpose.

Property developers are included within the meaning of mainstream contractors because their principal business activity is the creation of buildings or other civil engineering works. The same is true of a speculative builder.

A property investment business is not, however, the same thing as a property developer. A property investment business acquires and disposes of buildings for capital gain or uses the buildings for rental. It need not be involved in the construction of buildings. Even so, if its property estate is substantial enough, its expenditure on construction operations may well cause it to fall within the meaning of 'deemed contractor'.

Where a contractor negotiates with a gang leader to pay him/her for work done by the gang and the gang leader shares out the money amongst the gang, the gang leader is contractor for the other gang members and the original contractor only deals with one subcontractor, the gang leader.

Generally labour agencies are not contractors under the scheme although they can be subcontractors. Since 6 April 1998 a labour agency supplying workers to a contractor has been obliged to operate PAYE where the contract between the agency and the worker is a contract for services. This means that circumstances in which an agency has to operate the CIS in the role of contractor are likely to be rare.

Law: ITEPA 2003, Pt. 2, Ch. 7

Other guidance: Construction Industry Scheme (CIS340)

62.4.3 Deemed contractors

Under the CIS, some businesses, public bodies and other concerns outside the mainstream construction industry but who regularly carry out or commission construction work on their own premises or investment properties are deemed to be contractors. These concerns are deemed to be contractors if their average annual expenditure on construction operations in the period of three years ending with their last accounting date exceeds £1m.

If these concerns have not been trading for the whole of the last three years, they are contractors if their total expenditure on construction operations for the part of that period of three years during which they were trading exceeds £3m.

Any concern that is deemed to be a contractor because one of the above conditions is met will continue to be deemed a contractor until it can satisfy HMRC that its expenditure on construction operations has been less than £1m in each of three successive years.

> **Planning point**
>
> Since it is more difficult for businesses outside the mainstream construction industry to gear their tax administration around the needs of the CIS, HMRC will make concessions for small payments. HMRC can authorise deemed contractors not to apply the scheme to small contracts for construction operations amounting to less than £1,000, excluding the cost of materials. (This arrangement does not apply to mainstream contractors (see **62.4.2**).

62.4.4 Construction operations

Construction operations, as defined in the tax legislation, are those described below, excluding certain specified activities but so that in all circumstances references to construction operations are to be taken:

Contractors 62.4.4

- except where contrary to the context of the term, as including references to the work of individuals participating in the carrying on of such operations; and
- except in the case of offshore installations, as not including references to operations outside the UK.

Operations included are as follows.

(1) The construction, alteration, repair, extension, demolition or dismantling of buildings and structures (whether permanent or not), including offshore installations (that is to say, installations which are maintained, or are intended to be established, for underwater exploitation or exploration to which the Mineral Workings (Offshore Installations) Act 1971 applies. (The 1971 Act applies to offshore installations for underwater exploration and exploitation of mineral resources in or under the shore or bed of waters in or adjacent to the UK up to the limit of territorial waters and the waters in any designated area of the continental shelf.)

(2) The construction, alteration, repair, extension or demolition of any works forming, or to form, part of the land, including (without prejudice to the foregoing) walls, roadworks, power lines, telecommunication apparatus, aircraft runways, docks and harbours, railways, inland waterways, pipelines, reservoirs, water mains, wells, sewers, industrial plant and installations for purposes of land drainage, coast protection or defence.

(3) The installation in any building or structure of systems of heating, lighting, air conditioning, ventilation, power supply, drainage, sanitation, water supply or fire protection.

(4) The internal cleaning of buildings and structures, so far as carried out in the course of their construction, alteration, extension, repair or restoration.

(5) Operations which form an integral part of, or are preparatory to, or are for rendering complete, such operations as are previously described in the Schedule, including site clearance, earth moving, excavation, tunnelling and boring, laying of foundations, erection of scaffolding, site restoration, landscaping and the provision of roadways and other access works.

(6) The painting or decorating of the internal or external surfaces of any building or structure.

Excluded operations are as follows:

- drilling for, or extraction of, oil or natural gas;
- extraction (whether by underground or surface working) of minerals and tunnelling or boring, or construction of underground works, for that purpose;
- manufacture of building or engineering components or equipment, materials, plant or machinery and delivery of any of those things to site;
- manufacture of components for systems of heating, lighting, air conditioning, ventilation, power supply, drainage, sanitation, water supply or fire protection and delivery of any of those things to site;

- the professional work of architects or surveyors, or of consultants in building, engineering, interior or exterior decoration or in the laying out of landscape;
- the making, installation and repair of artistic works, being sculptures, murals and other works which are wholly artistic in nature;
- signwriting and erecting, installing and repairing signboards and advertisements;
- the installation of seating, blinds and shutters; and
- the installation of security systems, including burglar alarms, closed circuit television and public address systems.

The Treasury may also, by an Order approved by the House of Commons, extend the above list should they wish to do so.

> **Planning point**
>
> HMRC takes the view that carpet fitting is an operation outside the scope of the construction industry scheme.

Law: FA 2004, s. 74

Other guidance: HMRC leaflet CIS340: *Construction Industry Scheme*

62.4.5 Construction payments

The term 'contract payment' means any payment which is made under a construction contract made by a contractor to:

- a subcontractor;
- a person nominated by the subcontractor or the contractor; or
- a person nominated by a person who is a subcontractor under another such contract relating to all or any of the construction operations.

A payment made under a construction contract is not, however, a 'contract payment' if the payment is treated as earnings from employment under ITEPA 2003, Part 2, Chapter 7 (Agency workers).

A payment is also not treated as a 'contract payment' if the person to whom the payment is made or, in the case of a payment made to a nominee, each of the following persons:

- the nominee;
- the person who nominated him; and
- the person for whose labour (or, where that person is a company, for whose employees' or officers' labour) the payment is made,

is registered for gross payment when the payment is made.

> ⚠ **Warning!**
>
> Where a person is registered for gross payment as a partner in a firm, the above exemption applies only in relation to payments made under contracts under which the firm is a subcontractor, or, where a person has nominated the firm to receive payments, the person who has nominated the firm is a subcontractor.
>
> Where a person is registered for gross payment otherwise than as a partner in a firm but he is, or becomes, a partner in a firm, the above exemption does not apply in relation to payments made under contracts under which the firm is a subcontractor, or, where a person has nominated the firm to receive payments, the person who has nominated the firm is a subcontractor.

Law: FA 2004, s. 60

62.4.6 IR35 and the construction industry

Construction industry workers who operate through their own personal service companies may be caught by the IR35 legislation. This can potentially result in tax being paid twice on the same income, once as a CIS deduction and once as PAYE on a deemed payment. Although the CIS deductions can be repaid once a company has submitted its accounts, the timing of the repayment may cause cash flow difficulties for those affected.

> **Planning point**
>
> To relieve these potential cash flow problems, in April 2001, HMRC announced details of a concession (ESC C32) to avoid the double taxation trap. FA 2004, Sch. 12, para 17 gives this concession a statutory footing (rendering ESC C32 obsolete).
>
> Broadly, if the company claims a repayment of CIS deductions before 31 January following the end of the tax year for which the deemed salary payment has been calculated, the double taxation may be avoided. The service company must inform HMRC, when it sends in its end-of-year employer's return, that it wishes to defer paying the tax due under the IR35 rules. It will then be able to set the CIS repayment against the PAYE and NIC deductions it owes, so that it will not have to pay two lots of tax.

Where such a claim is made and accepted by HMRC, interest will not be charged on any late-paid tax and NICs due under the IR35 rules to the extent that the late-paid tax and NICs is matched by the corporation tax repayment due to the company, up to the date of the repayment of the corporation tax.

62.4.7 Multiple contractors

Construction businesses sometimes find it administratively beneficial to divide up their businesses for CIS purposes. It might be because they operate through a branch or divisional structure and find it easier for each branch or division to have its own contractor scheme identity for CIS than to collate the information from the different sources into a single consolidated return and payment. The business can do this by electing to become a multiple contractor. Once the election has been made, a separate scheme will be created for each division and each scheme is treated as if it were a contractor in its own right.

The business must submit a written notice to the HMRC office which would normally deal with queries on their returns. This must be done before the start of the tax year in which the election is to take effect.

> ***Planning point***
>
> If the business wishes to revoke the election it can do so by notifying HMRC before the beginning of the tax year in which the election is to be discontinued. Otherwise the election will have continuing effect. Revoking an election does not prevent the business making another election either before the start of the next or a future tax year.

A business may acquire the whole or part of another contractor's business during the course of the tax year. If the business continues to operate the acquired business's own contractor scheme, nothing need be done (other than to notify HMRC of the change of control, if the acquired business is a limited company). But, if the business is absorbing some, or all, of the acquired business's subcontractors into its own business and there is a multiple contractor election in place, it must notify HMRC within 90 days of the acquisition on how it wishes the acquired subcontractors to be treated – as separate to the existing divisions, or allocated to the existing divisions. If the election is accepted, the separate schemes will come into effect from the start date of the business. Verifications made by the acquired business will generally not be valid for the existing divisions.

62.5 Non-resident contractors and subcontractors

Construction operations may be carried out on a construction site in the UK or within its territorial waters (see **62.4.5**). Where operations are within the UK, it is clear that non-resident contractors and non-resident subcontractors are obliged to comply with the scheme's requirements. Similarly, it is clear that non-resident subcontractors will be subject to the scheme even if their sub-contracting activities are limited to UK territorial waters.

Different considerations may apply where a contractor is operating in UK territorial waters. The House of Lords considered the issues in the context of liability to PAYE in *Clark (HMIT) v Oceanic Contractors Inc* [1982] BTC 417. A non-resident taxpayer company claimed that it was not obliged to operate the UK PAYE system of tax collection in respect of those of its employees who were engaged in exploration activities which were controlled out of Belgium and took place in the UK sector of the North Sea. Their Lordships held by a majority that the company was required to operate the PAYE system in respect of its North Sea employees because it had a sufficient 'tax presence' in the UK to justify the imposition of a liability to comply with the PAYE regulations. The company's 'tax presence' in the UK was reinforced by the fact that it also had an address for service in the UK, so that there were perceived to be no practical difficulties in operating PAYE. Lord Scarman said that, unless there is clear evidence to the contrary, UK legislation is applicable only to British subjects, or to foreigners who, by coming to the UK (whether for a short or long time), have subjected themselves to British jurisdiction.

> **Planning point**
>
> If the contractor, or the company, is resident in a country that has a Double Taxation Agreement (DTA) with the UK, it may be possible to claim exemption from UK tax. This will be the case where UK business profits are not attributable to a permanent establishment in the country through which the business is being carried on. Claims for exemption under the terms of a DTA should be sent to HMRC Centre for Non-Residents.

The term 'permanent establishment' generally includes:

- a place of management;
- a branch;
- an office;
- a factory;
- a workshop;
- a mine;
- an oil or tar well; or
- a quarry or any other place of extraction of natural resources.

A building site or construction project counts as a permanent establishment if it lasts longer than a stated period – usually between three and twenty-four months.

> **⚠ Warning!**
>
> The existence of a DTA does not mean that the contractor does not have to operate the CIS. He must still register and operate the Scheme as normal.

If HMRC agree that the contractor is exempt from UK tax under a DTA, they will repay any deductions made under the Scheme as follows:

- company subcontractors should set off any deductions made from payments they receive from contractors against their own liability for PAYE/NICs and subcontractors' deductions, where they have such liabilities. Any balance of deductions that cannot be set off in this way may be repaid on submission of the company's annual return on form P35;
- individuals and partnership subcontractors wanting to claim a refund should contact the HMRC office at which they registered for the Scheme.

Generally, for individuals or partners in a firm, any deductions made by contractors from the amounts they pay are allowable against UK tax liability. However, there may be times when the individual or firm makes little or no profit in the tax year, and the deductions exceed liability. When this happens, a repayment of the excess deductions may be claimed from HMRC.

62.6 Subcontractors

62.6.1 What is a subcontractor?

A subcontractor is any business which has agreed to carry out construction operations for another business or body which is a contractor or deemed contractor – whether by doing the operations itself, or by having them done by its own subcontractors or employees, or in any other way. Subcontractors include concerns normally known as main contractors, where they are engaged by a client who is a contractor, for example, a local authority.

The term 'subcontractor' includes:

- a company, including any corporate body or public body, as well as any individual self-employed person(s) running a business or partnership;
- a labour agency or staff bureau which contracts either to get work done with its own workforce, or to supply workers to a contractor;
- a foreign business if the construction operations for which it is being paid take place in the United Kingdom or within United Kingdom territorial waters (up to the 12 mile limit);
- a local authority or public body if they are engaged on construction operations for someone else; and
- a gang-leader who agrees with a contractor on the work to be done, and in turn receives payment for the work of the gang.

> **Planning point**
>
> Some businesses may act solely as contractors or as subcontractors but many act as both. This means that they both pay businesses below them and are paid by businesses above them in a chain. So for some of their transactions they will have to follow the rules for contractors and for others the rules for

> subcontractors. Appropriate administrative procedures to comply with both sets of rules should be considered.

62.6.2 Labour-only subcontractors

The term 'labour-only subcontractor' includes arrangements where the subcontractor may be required to supply his own tools. A subcontractor may also be required to supply materials connected with the contract the cost of which will be deducted prior to the calculation of the deduction on account of tax made from payments to subcontractors.

62.6.3 Agencies as subcontractors

Where a worker is supplied to a contractor by or through an agency and the worker carries out construction operations under the terms of a contract they have with the agency, the agency supplying the worker will be a subcontractor as far as the contractor is concerned. The contractor must always apply the scheme when making payment to the agency.

> ⚠ **Warning!**
> Where a worker is merely introduced to the contractor by an agency and subsequently carries out construction operations under the terms of a contract they have with the contractor, the agency is not a subcontractor in this case.

Special rules apply to agency workers who normally treat the worker as an employee for tax and National Insurance contribution (NICs) purposes. The business paying the worker should normally deduct tax under PAYE and account for Class 1 NICs. Very exceptionally, the special rules for agency workers do not apply and any payments for construction work will fall within the scheme. The agency will then be a contractor and will need to fulfil its obligations in that role.

62.6.4 Gangs

The contractor must meet their obligations under the scheme for payment to the gang-leader. The contractor does not need to be concerned with the transactions between the gang-leader and the other members of the gang. Any deductions from payments to the members of the gang are the responsibility of the gang-leader.

> ⚠ **Warning!**
> If the contractor makes a separate agreement with any other member of the gang, then that member will be a subcontractor or employee of the contractor. A

> contractor who pays each member of the gang separately must treat each as a separate subcontractor or employee and apply the deduction scheme or PAYE in each case.

62.7 Payments to subcontractors

This section explains what contractors must do before payments can be made to subcontractors and how payments are made. The following table summarises a contractor's obligations under the CIS:

Action	Due date	Legislation
Monthly returns	Within 14 days of the end of the tax month (that is by the 19th).	SI 2005/2045, reg. 4(1)
	If no payments made, contractor obliged to make a nil return within 14 days of the end of the tax month, unless contractor has notified HMRC that he will make no further payments in next 6 months.	SI 2005/2045, reg. 4(10), (11)
Subcontractor information to be provided	Information in writing to be provided within 14 days after the end of the tax month either in respect of the total payments made in that month or in respect of each payment made in that month.	SI 2005/2045, reg. 4(8)
Payment and recovery	The contractor must pay any amounts deducted from sub-contractors to HMRC within 17 days after the end of the tax period, where payment is made by an approved method of electronic communications, or within 14 days after the end of the tax period, in any other case.	SI 2005/2045, reg. 7(1)
Quarterly payments	Contractors may use quarterly tax periods if there are reasonable grounds for believing that the average monthly amount will be less than £1,500.	SI 2005/2045, reg. 8

62.7.1 Verification

Verification is the process HMRC use to make sure that subcontractors have the correct rate of deduction applied to their payments under the CIS. There are three main steps to the process:

- the contractor contacts HMRC with details of the subcontractor;
- HMRC check that the subcontractor is registered with them;
- HMRC tell the contractor what rate of deduction to apply, if any.

Before a contractor can make a payment for construction work to a subcontractor, they must decide whether they need to verify the subcontractor.

The general rule is that a contractor does not have to verify a subcontractor if they last included that subcontractor on a return in the current or two previous tax years.

> ⚠ **Warning!**
>
> If a contractor does not have to verify a subcontractor they must pay the subcontractor on the same basis as the last payment made to them. This means that if the subcontractor was last paid under the standard rate of deduction, the current payment must also be made under the standard rate of deduction. If the last payment was made gross, because a deduction was not required, the current payment must also be made gross.

62.7.2 Verification reference number

Once HMRC have received the above information they will check their records to see if the subcontractor is registered for tax and then tell the contractor to pay the subcontractor in one of the following ways:

- gross – i.e. without any deductions taken from the payment;
- net of a deduction at the standard rate; or
- net of a deduction at the higher rate because HMRC have no record of that subcontractor's registration, or are unable to verify the details for any other reason.

When HMRC verify a subcontractor, they will give the contractor a verification reference number. The verification reference number will be the same for each subcontractor that they have verified at the same time. If it is not possible to verify a subcontractor, HMRC will add one or two letters to the end of the number so that it is unique to that subcontractor.

62.7.3 Rate of deduction

The *Finance Act 2004, Section 61(2), (Relevant Percentage) Order* 2007 (SI 2007/46) sets the rates of deduction to be made from subcontractors in the construction industry. The rates from 6 April 2007 are:

- registered subcontractors: 20 per cent; and
- non-registered subcontractors: 30 per cent.

The rates remain unchanged for 2008–09 to 2010–11.

> **Example 62.2**
>
> The following example shows deductions at the higher rate of 30 per cent.
>
> Where no materials are supplied ('labour-only')
>
> A labour-only subcontractor does work on site for £200
>
> Total payment ... £200
>
> Amount deducted at 30% ... 60
>
> Net payment to subcontractor... £140
>
> The contractor calculates the deduction (£60), which has to be paid to our Accounts Office. The labour-only subcontractor receives the balance of £140.

If HMRC need to change a subcontractor's payment status from gross payment to payment under deduction, they will write and tell the subcontractor giving 90 days' notice of any change to allow the subcontractor to appeal, if required.

Sometimes a subcontractor's payment status will change from payment under deduction to gross payment. If this happens, HMRC will tell the subcontractor and any contractors who have verified or used the subcontractor in the current or previous two tax years. The revised payment status should then be applied to all subsequent payments to the subcontractor as soon as it is practical for the contractor to do so.

Law: A Longworth & Sons Ltd [2009] TC 00230; *Mutch* [2009] TC 00232

62.7.4 Payments under deduction

Deductions must only be made from that part of the payment that does not represent the cost of materials incurred by the subcontractor.

Any travelling expenses (including fuel costs) and subsistence paid to the subcontractor must be included in the gross amount of payment and the amount from which the deduction is made.

There are two steps that contractors must follow.

(1) Calculate the gross amount from which a deduction will be made by excluding VAT charged by the subcontractor if he is registered, and any amount equal to the Construction Industry Training Board (CITB) levy.

The contractor will need to keep a record of the gross payment amounts so that they can enter these on their monthly return.

(2) Deduct from the gross payment the amount the subcontractor actually paid for

the following items used in the construction operations, including VAT paid if the subcontractor is not registered for VAT:

(a) materials – the contractor can ask the subcontractor for evidence of the direct cost of materials. If the subcontractor fails to give this information, the contractor must make a fair estimate of the actual cost of materials. The contractor must always check, as far as possible, that the part of the payment for materials supplied is not overstated. If the materials element looks to be excessive, HMRC may ask the contractor to explain why;
(b) consumable stores;
(c) fuel (except fuel for travelling);
(d) plant hire; and
(e) the cost of manufacture or prefabrication of materials.

⚠ Warning!

The contractor must provide a written statement to every subcontractor from whom a deduction has been made within 14 days of the end of each tax month. A tax month runs from the 6th of one month to the 5th of the next month so the statement must be provided by the 19th of the month.

The statement may be issued by electronic means but only where the contractor and subcontractor agree to this method, and it is in a form that allows the subcontractor to store and print it.

The statement can be issued on the basis of one for each tax month or one for each payment if this is more frequent.

Example 62.3

Where no materials are supplied ('labour-only').

An uncertificated labour-only subcontractor does work on site for £200.

Gross payment £200

20% deduction ....(40)

Net payment to subcontractor ...160

The contractor calculates the deduction (£40) that has to be paid to HMRC Accounts Office. The labour-only subcontractor receives the balance of £160.

Example 62.4

The following is an example of a calculation where materials as well as labour are supplied ('supply and fix').

Where the subcontractor is not registered for VAT, any VAT he or she had to pay on materials should be included in the cost of materials when calculating the CIS deduction.

An uncertificated tiling subcontractor, who is not VAT-registered, agrees to tile a wall and to supply the necessary materials for £535. The materials cost the subcontractor a total of £235 (£200 + £35 for VAT).

	£
Gross payment	535
Less materials	235
Total	300
20% deduction	(60)
Payment excluding materials and deduction	240
Add back cost of materials	235
Net payment to subcontractor	475

The contractor deducts the cost of materials from the price for the whole job and calculates the deduction on the difference of £300.

The contractor has to pay £60 to HMRC Accounts Office and pays £475 (£535-£60) to the tiler.

Example 62.5

The following is an example of a calculation where materials as well as labour are supplied ('supply and fix').

Where the subcontractor is registered for VAT, any VAT they had to pay on materials should be excluded from the cost of materials when calculating the CIS deduction.

For the total cost of £600, a subcontractor who is a taxable person for VAT purposes, agrees to paint the interior of a building and to supply the materials. The painter pays £235 for the materials, which includes VAT of £35.

	£
Labour charge	400
Materials	200
Gross payment	600
Add VAT	105
Amount due (invoice amount)	705
Calculation of deduction	
Total payment (exclusive of VAT)	600
Less cost of materials (exclusive of VAT)	(200)
Amount liable to deduction	400
Amount deducted at 20%	(80)
Net payment to subcontractor	625

> The subcontractor is paid £625, which is the invoice amount (£705) less the deduction (£80).

62.7.5 Monthly returns

Each month, contractors must send HMRC a complete return of all payments made to all subcontractors within the CIS in the preceding tax month. This is regardless of whether the subcontractors were paid gross or net of either the standard or higher deduction. Monthly returns must reach HMRC within 14 days of the end of the tax month they are for. Returns may be made electronically or by post.

> ⚠ **Warning!**
>
> Contractors who have not paid any subcontractors in a particular month must submit a 'Nil return'.

Contractors must pay the amount deductible from payments to subcontractors to HMRC Accounts Office monthly. They must pay deductions due to be made in each tax month within 14 days of the end of that month or within 17 days where payment is made electronically, whether or not these deductions have actually been made. This means that where a required deduction has not actually been made from the subcontractor's payment, for whatever reason, the contractor is still responsible for paying that amount over to HMRC.

> *Planning point*
>
> There are no annual returns within the Construction Industry Scheme. Contractors who are required to submit an Employer's Annual Return on form P35 should remember to include on that form the total amount of CIS deductions they are due to pay so they can reconcile the total payments made during the year.

Law: FA 2004, s. 70–71; SI 2005/2045, reg. 7; *Leeds Lifts Ltd* [2009] TC 00231; *Jonathan David Ltd* [2009] TC 00233

Other guidance: HMRC booklet CIS340, Chapter 4

62.7.6 Penalties

Finance Act 2009 introduced revised penalties for late filing of CIS returns. The penalties include:

- a fixed penalty of £100 for failure to submit any return by the filing date;

Construction Industry Scheme

- an additional fixed penalty of £200 if any return is outstanding more than three months after the filing date;
- penalties of five per cent of deductions due for the return period for prolonged failures (over six months and again at 12 months); and
- higher penalties of 70 per cent of the deductions due where a person fails to submit a return for over 12 months and has deliberately withheld information necessary for HMRC to assess the tax due (100 per cent penalty if deliberate with concealment).

If a contractor submits a monthly return that is incomplete or incorrect, HMRC may charge penalties where they believe the error or omission has been caused by negligence or intent on the part of the contractor.

Incomplete or incorrect returns include:

- persons or payments omitted from the return;
- persons or payments incorrectly entered onto the return;
- failing to make a declaration in respect of verification or employment status; and
- incorrectly making a declaration in respect of verification or employment status.

If a contractor fails to produce records relating to payments made under the CIS when asked to do so, HMRC may charge penalties up to £3,000. Penalties of up to £3,000 may be charged where a contractor:

- fails to give statements to subcontractors registered for payment under deduction recording their payments and deductions; or
- negligently or deliberately provides incorrect information in such statements.

Law: FA 2009, Sch. 55; FA 2004, s. 72; the *Finance Act 2009, Schedule 56 (Appointed Day and Consequential Provisions) Order* 2010 (SI 2010/466)

62.8 Registration

Subcontractors who were registered under the previous CIS (before 6 April 2007) did not need to need to register for new CIS if they, or their business, had one of the following:

- a tax certificate CIS5, CIS5(Partner) or CIS6;
- a permanent registration card CIS4(P); or
- a temporary registration card CIS4(T) with an expiry date of 04–2007 or later.

> **Planning point**
>
> A new subcontractor, starting working in the construction industry on a self-employed basis for the first time after 5 April 2007, or an existing subcontractor who last had a temporary registration card CIS4(T) that expired on or before

> March 2007, should register for new CIS if they do not want deductions at the higher rate made from their payments.

HMRC will only authorise a contractor to make gross payments to a subcontractor where the following conditions are satisfied.

The business test

To satisfy this condition, the subcontractor must provide evidence that he is carrying on a business in the UK which:

(1) consists of or includes the carrying out of construction operations or the furnishing or arranging for the furnishing of labour in carrying out construction operations; and

(2) is, to a substantial extent, carried on by means of an account with a bank.

Evidence prescribed to satisfy the business test is as follows:

- the business address;
- invoices, contracts or purchase orders for construction work carried out by the applicant;
- details of payments for construction work;
- the books and accounts of the business; and
- details of the business bank account, including bank statements.

Law: SI 2005/2045, reg. 27

The turnover test

The applicant must satisfy HMRC that in the year following the making of the application:

- as an individual, his net business turnover from construction work (that is, after the cost of any materials used to earn that income) is £30,000 a year or more; or
- as a partnership or company, the net business turnover from construction work (that is, after deducting the cost of any materials) is £30,000 a year or more multiplied by the number of partners or directors.

In the case of 'close companies' (broadly, companies controlled by five or fewer individuals), the figure will be multiplied by the number of individuals who are directors and/or shareholders. For a husband and wife team, for instance, it would be £60,000.

An alternative test for partnerships and companies is that the business has an annual net turnover from construction work (after deducting the cost of materials) of £200,000 or more.

Law: SI 2005/2045, reg. 28

Construction Industry Scheme

The compliance test

The subcontractor must have kept all your tax affairs up to date during the 'qualifying period' (the period of 12 months ending with the date of the application in question). This means he must have paid all tax liabilities, including any PAYE and subcontractor deductions, and submitted all tax returns on time. HMRC will not accept an application from a subcontractor who brings his tax affairs up to date just prior to submitting that application.

The *Income Tax (Construction Industry Scheme) (Amendment No. 2) Regulations* 2008 (SI 2008/1282) came into force from 3 June 2008 and amended the *Income Tax (Construction Industry Scheme) Regulations* 2005 (SI 2005/2045). The amendment means that applicants seeking registration for gross payment will be able to pass the compliance test even though they have failed to pay, or have paid late, an amount of tax due under the Taxes Acts or *Taxes Management Act* 1970, where that amount is small. In this situation, 'small' is taken to mean less than £100.

Law: *Munns* [2009] TC 00234; *Strongwork Construction Ltd* [2009] TC 00236; *Prior Roofing Ltd* [2009] TC 00246; *Grosvenor* [2009] TC 00227; *Bruns (t/a TK Fabrications)* [2010] TC 00371

62.9 Compliance

62.9.1 Background

Following the boom years of the mid to late 1980s, there was a significant slump in the construction industry, which was felt by most large and small building firms alike, as well as labour-only subcontractors, who probably suffered most from this slump. Many industrial tribunal cases in the industry at that time centred on whether the worker whose grievance was being heard was an employee of the company or self-employed at the time the grievance occurred. It was in the workers' interests to argue that they were in fact employees since this would create the right medium for a successful claim to damages.

In several cases, it was held that workers who had been treated as self-employed and therefore taxed under the CIS were in fact employees who should have been taxed via the PAYE/NIC legislation. This threw the tax status of many thousands of workers into doubt, even though it should be borne in mind that every worker in the industry who possessed a 714 certificate at the time had to pass the Revenue's test as to whether he was or was not in self-employment. Be that as it may, in 1994, representatives of the construction industry made representations to the Revenue and the former Contributions Agency and requested that the matter of the true status of workers in the industry be clarified. This resulted in the joint issue of a leaflet by the Revenue and Contributions Agency (IR148/CA69) entitled *Are your workers employed or self-employed?*

The contact between the construction industry and the Revenue and Contributions Agency subsequently resulted in change in the way that these government departments were to treat the industry's workers both in terms of administration and legislation from then on. Not only did *Finance Act* 1995 and *Finance Act* 1996 contain legislation which eventually resulted in many small building subcontractors being excluded from the CIS, but this contact heralded a concerted drive by the Revenue and Contributions Agency against small contractors in the industry who had come to rely on the relatively relaxed attitude displayed by the Revenue in previous years. These contractors used the CIS to replace the proper functioning of the PAYE and NIC regulations with their attendant costly administrative burdens.

In November 1996 a joint statement by the Treasury and the DSS was published, which gave notice to the construction industry that contractors in the industry should review the status of their workers and apply PAYE to payments made to their workers from 6 April 1997. Both departments pledged that where contractors were found to be failing to operate PAYE after 6 April 1997 they would only seek arrears going back to that date unless there was clear evidence of evasion (see the Revenue's *Tax Bulletin*, issue 28, April 1997). To date, neither department seems to have clarified what they mean by the phrase 'clear evidence of evasion'.

The strength and purpose of the drive against the traditional use of labour-only and small scale subcontractors under the umbrella of the CIS can be gauged by the impressively speedy response by the Revenue to a loophole in the agency legislation which was apparently 'created' (it was always there but there was never previously a need to exploit it) by its U-turn on subcontractors.

The agency legislation (see **62.6.3**) was designed to tax self-employed persons who are being supplied by agencies to contractors in any industry. It does this by the simple expedient of deeming that an individual is to be treated as if he or she were taxable under ITEPA 2003 if certain contractual conditions apply, when all other factors would point to that person being self-employed and therefore taxable under ITTOIA 2005 (formerly Schedule D). If the charge on employment income provisions of ITEPA 2003 are to apply then the PAYE/NIC regulations must be observed when payment is made to the worker in question.

Workers in the construction industry who are 'sub-contractors' are, however, exempt from this legislation because, of course, they are subject to similar legislation of their own – namely the CIS. Consequently, there was a wellspring of opinion in the industry and professional advisers that the Revenue's push to make contractors take on small-time certificated and uncertificated building workers as full-time employees taxable under the PAYE/NIC regulations, could be circumvented for the time being.

If these workers were hired from agencies under the correct contractual conditions then the agency legislation would serve to exempt either the agencies or the ultimate contractors from having to operate PAYE/NIC. All parties to this thought process tended to forget (or did not recognise) that both the agency legislation and the CIS only operate in circumstances where the worker is taken on by the contractor in circumstances where he is carrying out a task under self-employed conditions. Therefore, the fundamental question as to whether the worker was or was not self-employed at any given point was not avoided by this mechanism.

Nevertheless, the Revenue recognised the dangers inherent in this strategy as serving to weaken its drive to get the industry into line. In August 1997 the Treasury announced that the Inland Revenue would bring in measures to end the exemption in the agency legislation for construction industry workers which seemed to provide the panacea that the industry was looking for. The *Finance Act 1998* contained the necessary changes to the agency legislation to achieve this end.

62.9.2 Auditing the CIS

The auditing of the CIS is carried out by HMRC in parallel with the normal PAYE/NIC auditing process. There is no separate group dedicated to the construction industry as such, although, until the early 1990s, HMRC's Investigations Office was charged with investigating and prosecuting frauds on the CIS alongside its role in investigation frauds on the PAYE/NIC system. This section was subsumed into the prosecutions arm of SCO, so that the manpower of this section and its surveillance and interviewing techniques learned in investigating such fraud became available to Inspectors in SCO who previously had concentrated on investigating corporation tax and income tax fraud.

The audit of the CIS is so closely allied to the audit of an employer's compliance with the PAYE/NIC regulations that the two processes should be considered as one if the employer is also a contractor and/or subcontractor in the construction industry. This is unsurprising because the CIS is, after all, a quasi PAYE system applied to the payment of self-employed people. It has its own set of monthly and annual (until 2007) forms – analogous to the monthly and annual PAYE returns – and it shares the PAYE/NIC penalty regime. The contractor should consider himself to be in almost exactly the same position legislatively when paying money to subcontractors as when paying money to his own employees. Consequently, failure to operate the scheme correctly will invite claims for tax just as if the contractor had not operated the PAYE rules correctly. The only real difference is that he does not have to account for employers' or employees' NICs on such payments so long as the contract between himself and the subcontractor giving rise to the payment is one for services and not of service.

HMRC officers also provide information through the in-depth review of contractors' and subcontractors' accounts. The officer will check that returns from

Compliance 62.9.2

the Construction Industry Processing Centre which deals with the collation of data from the CIS match up with the turnover or labour costs declared by the subcontractor or contractor for any accounting period. For example, the turnover of a labour-only subcontractor should, in theory, coincide with the returns made by contractors to HMRC, or the amount of payments made under deduction in paying an unverified subcontractor. Clearly, the problems associated with accounts year-ends which are not coterminous with the CIS returns periods have to be taken into account in the review process.

The auditor seeks to check the following matters:

(1) that payments have not been made under deduction of tax to unverified subcontractors;

(2) that where payments to subcontractors have been made without deduction, proper checks were made to verify the bona fides of the subcontractor; and

(3) that neither the contractor nor the subcontractor have previously been associated with forged or misappropriated tax certificates and vouchers.

These checks are achieved both through examination of the contractor or subcontractor's records and discussion with the relevant party. The auditor has an initial interview with the contractor using an aide memoir which covers all matters of fundamental importance to the CIS including the nature of the system in use to record payments to subcontractors and the standard of the records being kept.

The auditor carries out several 'core checks' on the systems as follows:

(1) a check to ensure that the appropriate rate has been used when calculating deductions;

(2) a check to ensure that there has been no payment for labour recorded as payment for materials (bearing in mind that as payment for materials is not part of the CIS per se, there is a temptation to describe a payment for labour as a payment for materials);

(3) a check to ensure that all payments to unverified subcontractors have been identified and that these payments have been accurately recorded;

(4) a comparison of the amounts shown in the monthly returns as payable with the amounts actually paid;

(5) a check to ensure that at the time that a payment was made to a verified subcontractor, the verification was properly authorised by HMRC; and

(6) a check of payments to overseas parent companies using subsidiary companies to provide subcontract labour to the contractor without the contractor observing the rules of the scheme in making payments to the subcontractor, or where payments have been made to an offshore individual who has used a company registered offshore to provide the labour.

219

> ⚠ **Warning!**
>
> If the auditor discovers that the contractor has failed to make deductions from payments to unverified subcontractors in a current year (having first satisfied himself that the subcontractors were indeed self-employed) then he is entitled to agree a calculation of the under-deduction and make arrangements with the contractor to account for the liability through the normal accounting procedure for that year. If the failure extends to earlier years then the auditor can effect a settlement to include interest and penalties on the under-deduction.

Relief from payment of under-deducted amounts is possible if the Collector of Taxes directs that the contractor is so relieved. In order to make such a direction the Collector must be satisfied that the contractor took reasonable care in operating the CIS and that the failure was either due to an error made in good faith or no deduction was made because the contractor genuinely believed that no deduction was necessary.

If it is discovered that the contractor did not pay due care and attention to his responsibilities under the CIS, then HMRC may cancel the contractor's gross payment status.

Cases of fraud are dealt with severely for the same reasons as cases of fraud on the PAYE system. Contractors are required to oversee the CIS and to collect deductions from those who have been unable or unwilling to register for verification. Consequently, the prosecution for fraud on the system is seen as a justifiable deterrent to unscrupulous contractors and subcontractors. Apart from offences under the Theft Act, Forgery Act and prosecutions under common law, the tax legislation provides for fines upon summary conviction for:

(1) persons making false statements in order to obtain a certificate;

(2) the unauthorised disposal of a certificate or voucher; and

(3) the unauthorised possession of a certificate or voucher.

In the past, the number of prosecutions for misuse of certificates and the sale of 714C, P, or I vouchers to uncertified subcontractors far outweighed all other HMRC prosecutions each year. However, the number carried out has fallen substantially, possibly because of recent legislation, which will cut out many of the perpetrators of subcontractor fraud by integrating them within the PAYE system.

63 Disclosure of Direct Tax Avoidance Schemes

63.1 Introduction

63.1.1 Generally

This chapter considers the provisions set out in the Finance Act 2004 and in secondary legislation which seek to minimise the use and effectiveness of tax avoidance schemes. These rules came into force on 1 August 2004, but the effective start date for different types of scheme cannot be so simply stated.

All references to section numbers, unless stated otherwise, are to sections of the Finance Act 2004. All references to HM Revenue and Customs (HMRC) guidance are, unless stated otherwise, to the document *Tackling Tax Avoidance – Guidance* originally published 29 July 2004 and available at www.hmrc.gov.uk/aiu/guidance.pdf.

Initially, the rules covered certain limited schemes relating to income tax, corporation tax and capital gains tax. There was also a parallel scheme applying to VAT avoidance. In 2005, the disclosure rules were extended to Stamp Duty Land Tax. Following the passing of the National Insurance Contributions Act 2006, disclosures have been required (since 1 May 2007) in relation to any arrangement which will or is expected to give rise to a National Insurance advantage. Also in 2006, the rules relating to income tax, corporation tax and capital gains tax were widened.

> ⚠ **Warning!**
> Different criteria apply depending on whether the disclosure relates to a notifiable proposal or arrangement and also depending on who is required to make the disclosure.

63.1.2 Avoidance – a summary of start-dates

The introduction of the rules in Finance Act 2004, combined with the confusion that surrounded certain of the provisions therein, led to a rather haphazard series of starting dates. For reference, these are summarised below.

The various terms used in this section will be explained in the text that follows.

Disclosure by promoters

No disclosure is necessary in respect of any arrangement which includes a transaction entered into before 18 March 2004. This date applies to all schemes.

Notifiable proposals relating to employment-related schemes did not need to be disclosed if the promoter made the proposal available for implementation by another person before 18 March 2004.

Notifiable proposals relating to financial products schemes did not need to be disclosed if the promoter made the proposal available for implementation by another person before 22 June 2004.

Notifiable proposals relating to stamp duty land tax schemes did not need to be disclosed if the promoter made the proposal available for implementation by another person before 1 August 2005.

Notifiable arrangements relating to employment-related schemes did not need to be disclosed if the promoter first became aware before 18 March 2004 of a transaction forming part of a notifiable arrangement implementing the notifiable proposal.

Notifiable arrangements relating to financial products schemes did not need to be disclosed if the promoter first became aware before 22 June 2004 of a transaction forming part of a notifiable arrangement implementing the notifiable proposal.

Notifiable arrangements relating to stamp duty land tax schemes did not need to be disclosed if the promoter first became aware before 1 August 2005 of a transaction forming part of a notifiable arrangement implementing the notifiable proposal.

In cases where the notifiable proposal preceded the key date (18 March or 22 June 2004 or 1 August 2005) but the promoter first became aware of it being implemented on or after that date, no disclosure is necessary.

Example 63.1

Suppose a scheme involving financial products were developed in August 2004 but included a transaction entered into in May 2004.

The scheme would be notifiable even though the key date for financial products is usually 22 June 2004.

Proposals caught under the 'hallmark rules' (which apply to income tax, corporation tax and capital gains tax) did not need to be disclosed if the promoter made the proposal available for implementation by another person (or the promoter first became aware of any transaction forming part of notifiable arrangements implementing the proposal) before 1 August 2006 (unless the scheme was employment-related or involved a financial product and was also subject to the pre-2006 rules).

Arrangements caught under the 'hallmark rules' and involving UK promoters did not need to be disclosed if the promoter first became aware of any transaction forming part of notifiable arrangements implementing the proposal before 1 August 2006 (unless the scheme was employment-related or involved a financial product and was also subject to the pre-2006 rules).

National insurance schemes did not become notifiable until 1 May 2007. However, HMRC has suggested that the let-out for existing standardised products applies only in respect of schemes made available before 1 August 2006.

Law: FA 2004, s. 308(2) and 319(3); Tax Avoidance Schemes (Information) Regulations (SI 2004/1864), reg. 1(2); Tax Avoidance Schemes (Prescribed Descriptions of Arrangements) Regulations (SI 2006/1543), reg. 1(2); National Insurance Contributions (Application of Part 7 of the Finance Act 2004) Regulations 2007 (SI 2007/785)

Other guidance: www.hmrc.gov.uk/aiu/nics-disclosure.htm

Disclosure by parties

Parties are not required to make any disclosure in respect of any arrangement which includes a transaction entered into before 23 April 2004.

Nor does a return need to include a reference number on a tax return in respect of any arrangement where there was no duty on the promoter to disclose the scheme (whether as a proposal or arrangement) or on the party itself (either because there was no promoter or because the promoter was outside the UK). Therefore, if a promoter made a scheme available to a client in February 2004 but the client did not implement it until July 2004, no subsequent disclosure is necessary by the client.

Furthermore, in respect of schemes involving financial products, no disclosure is necessary if any transaction forming part of the arrangements is entered into before 22 June 2004.

No disclosure is necessary by a party in respect of any stamp duty land tax transaction forming part of arrangements entered into before 1 August 2005.

For 'hallmark schemes', no disclosure is necessary by a party if the first transaction forming part of notifiable arrangements was entered into before 1 August 2006 (unless the scheme was employment-related or involved a financial product and was also subject to the pre-2006 rules).

Law: FA 2004, s. 319(4), (5); Tax Avoidance Schemes (Information) Regulations (SI 2004/1864), reg. 1(2); Tax Avoidance Schemes (Information) Regulations (SI 2005/1869), reg. 1(2); Tax Avoidance Schemes (Prescribed Descriptions of Arrangements) Regulations (SI 2006/1543), reg. 1(2)

Disclosure by parties where legal professional privilege applies

In some circumstances a disclosure must be made by a party because the promoter's duty to make a disclosure is curtailed by legal professional privilege. However, that duty first arose on 14 October 2004. In such circumstances, the first disclosure was not due until 19 November 2004.

Law: Tax Avoidance Schemes (Promoters, Prescribed Circumstances and Information) (Amendment) Regulations 2004 (SI 2004/2613), reg. 1(3)

63.1.3 Avoidance – a brief history

Tax avoidance is not a new phenomenon in the United Kingdom. Indeed, one of the leading cases on avoidance (*IR Commrs v Duke of Westminster* (1935) 19 TC 490) was heard by the House of Lords over 70 years ago in 1935. In that case, the Duke of Westminster sought to minimise his exposure to surtax by covenanting with his gardener that he would pay the gardener an annuity in lieu of some of his wages. Payments made under deed of covenant were then tax-deductible even if not paid to charities.

In a much quoted speech, Lord Tomlin said at p. 19 that:

> 'Every man is entitled if he can to order his affairs so that the tax attaching under the appropriate Acts is less than it otherwise would be.'

In other words, the majority of the House of Lords endorsed the view that taking advantage of loopholes and statutory reliefs was a perfectly acceptable form of tax planning. The House of Lords' decision did no more than echo the more colourful statement of Lord Clyde in the Scottish case of *Ayrshire Pullman Motor Services v IR Commrs* (1929) 14 TC 754. There, at p. 763, the Lord President said:

> 'No man in this country is under the smallest obligation, moral or other, so to arrange his legal relations to his business or to his property as to enable the Inland Revenue to put the largest possible shovel into his stores.'

Largely fuelled by these sentiments, the tax planning 'industry' blossomed in the 1970s as a direct reaction to the punitive tax rates then in place. Whilst the *Duke of Westminster* and *Ayrshire* cases remain good law, the Courts have limited the effect of these cases by revising the courts' approach to statutory interpretation. This new approach was heralded by the House of Lords' decision in *Ramsay (WT) Ltd v IR Commrs* [1982] AC 300 and confirmed in subsequent cases heard during the following two decades.

The *Ramsay* 'doctrine' was dealt a minor, but significant, blow by Lord Hoffmann in *Westmoreland Investments Ltd v MacNiven (HMIT)* [2001] BTC 44 – in part by being downgraded from a doctrine to an approach. However, the more recent Hong Kong case of *The Collector of Stamp Revenue v Arrowtown Assets Ltd* (2003) has in turn suggested that Lord Hoffmann's speech in *Westmoreland* is of limited application. These issues were once again argued in front of the House of Lords in

October 2004. In *Barclays Mercantile Business Finance Ltd v Mawson* [2004] BTC 414 and *IR Commrs v Scottish Provident Institution* [2004] BTC 426, their Lordships held that *Ramsay* did not represent a new principle, but merely illustrated that tax statutes should be interpreted less rigidly. In the first, a circular leasing scheme was held to be valid as it came within the terms of the legislation; in the second case, the House of Lords held that a self-cancelling set of options would be treated as part of a single transaction.

However, even if the taxpayers lose a particular round of this battle, the Government realised that success in one case does not guarantee revenues in the future. More importantly, the Government is concerned to maximise the current tax take (to fund its expenditure programme) whilst maintaining what are relatively low headline rates of tax. In particular, the Government recognised that a typical avoidance scheme would often be marketed for over a year before HMRC ever got wind of it. This means that by the time that countering legislation is announced, the scheme has already been widely used.

The Government therefore adopted a new weapon in its battle against what it considers 'unacceptable' tax avoidance. The tax profession must provide the Government with the details of avoidance schemes as soon as they come off the drawing board.

Hitherto, tax avoidance was distinguished from tax evasion by virtue of the former being legal and the latter illegal. Recent pronouncements by Government ministers and some civil servants appear to have blurred this distinction with morality being added to the list of ingredients (notwithstanding Lord Tomlin's words in *Duke of Westminster*). This discussion has been much publicised in the professional press and interested readers are recommended to refer to these articles for fuller details.

> ⚠ **Warning!**
>
> Any tax avoidance scheme (however effective, technically) can always be undone by legislation. The Human Rights cases make it clear that retroactive legislation can legitimately be deployed to counter avoidance.
>
> Additionally, the Government made a clear announcement in December 2004 announcing that the 'unacceptable' use of employment-related securities would be countered retrospectively to that date and subsequent Finance Acts have included provisions with that effect.
>
> However, the most unpredictable factor in any avoidance scheme is the attitude of the Courts. Whilst a scheme in 2009, say, might appear to fall on the right side of the judicial line when it is devised and implemented, it can often take ten years (sometimes, even longer) for an element of tax planning to find its way to the House of Lords. In that time, judicial attitudes can change and judgment will depend, partly, on the attitude at the time of the hearing (not that prevailing when the scheme was implemented).

63.1.4 Overview of the disclosure rules

The Finance Act 2004 provides two sets of rules – one (found in s. 19 and Sch. 2 which in turn inserted Sch. 11A into the Value Added Tax Act 1994) deals with Value Added Tax; the other (located in s. 306–319) potentially covers income tax, capital gains tax, corporation tax, petroleum revenue tax, inheritance tax, stamp duty land tax and stamp duty reserve tax. This chapter will not consider the rules as they apply to Value Added Tax.

It must be added, however, that the Finance Act 2004 provides only the skeleton for the new regime. For example, the definition of 'notifiable arrangements' in s. 306(1) reads:

> 'In this Part "notifiable arrangements" means any arrangements which:
> (a) fall within any *description prescribed* by the Treasury by regulations;
> (b) enable, or might be expected to enable, any person to obtain an advantage in relation to *any tax that is so prescribed* in relation to arrangements of that description; and
> (c) are such that the main benefit, or one of the main benefits, that might be expected to arise from the arrangements is the obtaining of that advantage.'

[emphasis added]

Just as cryptically, s. 308–310 provide that various persons involved with such a scheme must 'within the *prescribed period* after the relevant date, provide HMRC with *prescribed information* relating to any notifiable proposal'. In the first incarnation of the rules, the provision of the prescribed information had also to be in the *prescribed manner*. But this was changed to require that the information be provided merely 'in a form and manner specified by [HMRC]'.

FA 2008 provides that, from 1 April 2009, HMRC need not specify the form and manner in which information is to be provided. However, if they do specify the form and/or manner, then promoters and taxpayers will be obliged to comply with the specifications.

> ⚠ **Warning!**
>
> For the details (as prescribed), one must therefore look at the secondary legislation issued in accordance with the Finance Act and other guidance issued by HMRC. Such legislation and guidance can be changed relatively swiftly and therefore readers are advised to ensure that the most up-to-date version is considered when advising on any particular case.

Law: FA 2004, s. 316

63.2 Notifiable arrangements

63.2.1 Introduction

At the heart of the regime is the requirement for details of avoidance schemes to be notified to HMRC. With this in mind, the following paragraphs consider the definitions of the various concepts employed by the legislation.

63.2.2 The limits on what needs to be notified

As one would expect (or at least hope) not everything that a taxpayer does needs to be related to HMRC. Instead, the legislation focuses on what it calls 'notifiable arrangements'. The definition of notifiable arrangements has been set out at **59.1.4** above. However, it merits closer examination.

First, it concerns 'any arrangements' which satisfy the three conditions reproduced above. The word 'arrangements' is defined widely to include 'any scheme, transaction or series of transactions'.

It is not immediately obvious whether any non-binding agreement between two individuals, say, would come within the natural meaning of 'any scheme, transaction or series of transactions'. However, it is suggested that an agreement can fall within the normal meaning of 'arrangement'. Consequently, such an agreement would therefore appear to come within the scope of the legislation.

> **Planning point**
>
> On the other hand, by using the word 'arrangements', the legislation provides that not every situation is covered by the rules. For example, events arising which are beyond an individual's control would not appear to come within the meaning of arrangement, or 'any scheme, transaction or series of transactions'. So, if a tax saving simply arose (perhaps because of an individual's death) such an eventuality would not come within the definition of an arrangement, and therefore would not be a 'notifiable arrangement'.

Second, to be notifiable, the arrangement must fall within a category prescribed by the Treasury (rather than HMRC) through regulations. The primary legislation provides no limit on the type of scheme that may be included in such regulations, and one suspects that the scope of these rules will be widened in due course.

On 22 July 2004 (the day that the Finance Act 2004 obtained Royal Assent), the Treasury laid regulations in accordance with its powers under s. 306(1)(a). It set out broadly two types of arrangements to which the disclosure rules apply – arrangements connected with employment and arrangements concerning financial products. As these rules are now of only a historical relevance, they are not reproduced here. They are discussed in the 2007/08 edition of this work.

From 1 August 2006, the restriction to employment and financial-product schemes was lifted. Instead, arrangements are subject to the disclosure if they fall within one of the 'descriptions' set out in the regulations. Whilst the legislation refers to these as 'descriptions', most commentaries (including those prepared by HMRC) refer to them as 'hallmarks'.

Law: FA 2004, s. 306(1), 318(1); the Tax Avoidance Schemes (Prescribed Descriptions of Arrangements) Regulations 2004 (SI 2004/1863); Tax Avoidance Schemes (Prescribed Descriptions of Arrangements) Regulations (SI 2006/1543), reg. 1(2)

63.2.3 Pre-disclosure enquiry

FA 2007 introduced provisions that permit HMRC to enquire into a person whom they suspect of being a promoter of a particular scheme. The subject of the enquiry must then state whether or not (in its opinion) the scheme is notifiable by it and, if not, why not.

> ⚠ **Warning!**
>
> The subject of a pre-disclosure enquiry cannot say that it does not believe that the scheme is notifiable because it has been so advised. The response to the enquiry must be sufficiently comprehensive to allow HMRC to reach a reasoned conclusion on the matter.

The subject of the enquiry will be required to respond within ten working days starting with the day *after* the notice is issued or such longer time as HMRC may direct.

If the response states that a scheme is not notifiable, HMRC can then ask for specified information or documents to support the reasons for this conclusion. Although HMRC would probably initially seek this information voluntarily, they can apply to the Special Commissioners for an order requiring the papers or information to be supplied. If such an order is given, the subject of the enquiry will be required to respond within fourteen working days starting with the day *after* the order is made or such longer time as HMRC may direct.

> ⚠ **Warning!**
>
> Failure to comply with such requests will give rise to a penalty of up to £5,000 and daily penalties of up to £600.

Law: TMA 1970, s. 98C; FA 2004, s. 313A, s. 313B; Tax Avoidance Schemes (Information) Regulations (SI 2004/1864), reg. 8A(1), reg. 8A(2)

63.2.4 Doubt as to notifiability

FA 2007 introduced provisions that permit HMRC to seek a ruling from the Special Commissioners that a particular scheme is to be treated as notifiable. Such an application must specify the (would-be) promoter as well as the details of the scheme itself. However, HMRC may not seek such an order if:

- they have not taken all reasonable steps to establish whether or not the scheme is notifiable; or
- they do not have reasonable grounds for suspecting that the scheme may be notifiable.

Although HMRC will not be obliged to have taken proceedings under either s. 313A or s. 313B, those provisions are listed as ones that might constitute reasonable steps. Equally, a person's failure to comply with those provisions could be grounds for suspicion that the scheme might be notifiable.

> ⚠ *Warning!*
> If a person fails to comply with the obligations under the disclosure rules in respect of a scheme which is subject to an order under this rule, any daily penalties subsequently chargeable are increased by a sum to be prescribed.

Law: TMA 1970, s. 98C(2A); FA 2004, s. 306A

63.2.5 Order that scheme notifiable

The provisions under s. 306A merely provide that a scheme is to be deemed to be notifiable in the absence of fuller information.

Once the details of the scheme are known, HMRC can approach the Special Commissioners who can determine whether or not the scheme is notifiable.

> ⚠ *Warning!*
> If a person fails to comply with the obligations under the disclosure rules in respect of a scheme which is subject to an order under this rule, any daily penalties subsequently chargeable are increased by a sum to be prescribed.

Law: TMA 1970, s. 98C(2B); FA 2004, s. 314A

63.2.6 Information provided to introducers

FA 2010 introduced a further requirement from a date to be appointed.

If HMRC suspect that a person is an introducer in relation to a proposal and that the proposal may be notifiable, then they may require that person to provide HMRC with information to be prescribed in relation to each person who has provided the person with any information relating to the proposal.

Such a requirement must be in writing and specify the proposal to which it relates.

The purpose of this is to ensure that arrangements put forward to clients can be traced back to the originators of the arrangements and not merely the intermediaries.

Law: FA 2004, s. 313C

63.3 Notifiable proposals

The legislation, however, does not cover only arrangements which have already been effected. Also within the scope of the rules are 'notifiable proposals'. Notifiable proposals are proposals that would be notifiable arrangements (and, hence, satisfy the three conditions above) once entered into. To be notifiable, a proposal need not relate to any particular person or have any person in contemplation.

Law: FA 2004, s. 306(2)

63.4 A tax advantage must arise

63.4.1 Introduction

Not surprisingly, HMRC are not interested in every arrangement entered into which falls within the prescribed categories. In particular, an arrangement is notifiable only if either:

- the arrangement will enable a person to obtain a tax advantage; or
- the arrangement might be expected to enable a person to obtain a tax advantage.

Law: FA 2004, s. 306(1)(b)

63.4.2 What is a tax advantage?

A tax advantage is one which provides:

- relief, or increased relief, from tax;
- the repayment, or increased repayment, of tax;
- the avoidance or reduction of a charge to tax or an assessment to tax;
- the avoidance of a possible assessment to tax;
- the deferral of any payment of tax;
- the advancement of any repayment of tax;
- the avoidance of any obligation to deduct a tax; or
- the avoidance of any obligation to account for tax.

The broad wording of the legislation means that it is not necessary for the tax advantage to arise to the person who enters (or would enter) into the arrangements. In addition, it would appear that there is no need for a tax advantage actually to materialise. It is sufficient for the scheme to 'enable or be expected to enable' a person to obtain a tax advantage. See **Example 63.2** below. It remains to be seen whether 'expected' will in due course be interpreted as 'hoped'. It is submitted that 'expected' will to an extent be a subjective issue but should not to be given such a wide meaning so as to include tax advantages that are hoped for but not realistically expected.

> ### Example 63.2
>
> An arrangement is entered into which would allow a taxpayer to reduce his or her taxable income by £4,000. However, the only taxpayer to purchase the scheme happens to have taxable income for the year of only £4,500.
>
> In this scenario (unlikely though it is), the effect of entering into the arrangement is that no tax is saved. Nevertheless, the arrangement 'might be expected to enable' an individual to save tax and, therefore, the arrangement would be notifiable if the other conditions are met.

When the rules were first announced, there were suggestions that the operation of the rules would be highly subjective as one person's 'unacceptable' tax advantage could be another's 'acceptable' tax mitigation. (The use of the words 'acceptable' and 'unacceptable' is to give a flavour of the Government's rhetoric and is not intended to cast any aspersions on those who choose to mitigate their exposure to tax in a lawful manner as well as those who do not.)

Consequently, it was feared that it would be difficult to determine whether any particular arrangement would fall within or outside the rules. However, as the above definition makes clear, each arrangement entered into (or proposed) must be judged against the alternative of not entering into such an arrangement. There is no test of 'moral acceptability'; nor is there any comparison with the commercial norm. If an arrangement gives rise to a tax advantage (as defined) which would not

Disclosure of Direct Tax Avoidance Schemes

exist (or would not exist to such a great extent) but for the arrangement being entered into, then the statutory test is satisfied. However, the other tests must also be considered, for example by ascertaining whether a particular scheme comes within one of the definitions of prescribed arrangements set out at **59.12** below.

HMRC recognise this point in their guidance (para. 2A(iii)(b)). That reads:

> 'We do not intend that this should catch everyday tax advice and in our view the overall disclosure rules will filter such advice out. We will be updating our guidance regularly to ensure that unnecessary disclosures are not made.'

Of course, updating guidance is no substitute for ensuring that the law does what the Government actually wants it to do.

Law: FA 2004, s. 318(1)

Other guidance: www.hmrc.gov.uk/aiu/guidance.pdf

63.4.3 Which taxes are covered by the rules?

As stated above, the direct tax rules potentially cover income tax, capital gains tax, corporation tax, petroleum revenue tax, inheritance tax, stamp duty land tax and stamp duty reserve tax. However, possibly as a concession to the tax profession, the only taxes that are currently prescribed are:

- income tax;
- corporation tax;
- capital gains tax; and
- stamp duty land tax.

It should also be noted that elsewhere in the Finance Act 2004, provisions were introduced that severely restrict inheritance tax planning schemes (see **Chapter 49**).

Schemes relating to National Insurance are not covered by FA 2004. However, the statute provides that a parallel scheme may operate for NICs purposes.

Law: SI 2004/1864 reg. 2(1); SI 2005/1868; SSAA 1992, s. 132A (inserted by the National Insurance Contributions Act 2006, s. 7(2))

63.5 The tax advantage must be a main benefit

The final condition is that the tax advantage must be either the main benefit or one of the main benefits that might be expected to arise from the arrangements. This 'main benefit' test is not new to tax legislation; it is used in a number of anti-avoidance provisions. However, the test here is unusual because it must be applied in conjunction with the condition (see **59.4** above) that a tax advantage has been (or can be) obtained. Normally, the test stands alone.

It is arguable that the conjunction of the two tests means that the 'main benefit' test can be read rather more narrowly than would usually be the case. Alternatively, the use of the two tests might be viewed by the courts rather more as a 'belt and braces' approach.

HMRC have emphasised in para. 2A(iii)(d) of their guidance that whether a benefit is a main benefit 'is a question of fact'.

Law: FA 2004, s. 306(1)(c)

Other guidance: www.hmrc.gov.uk/aiu/guidance.pdf

63.6 Duties to disclose

63.6.1 Generally

The clear purpose of the rules is to ensure that HMRC have details of the mischief at an early stage in the life of any tax avoidance scheme. Consequently, there are a number of duties to provide HMRC with information concerning notifiable arrangements. At the heart of these requirements, are the duties on 'promoters'.

63.6.2 Promoters

The meaning of the term 'promoter' depends on whether the notifiable matter constitutes a notifiable arrangement or merely a notifiable proposal (see **59.3** above). However, no person is a promoter of a notifiable proposal or arrangement if that person's disclosure obligations are restricted by virtue of FA 2004, s. 314, which provides that material subject to legal professional privilege need not be disclosed (see **59.10** below).

Promoters in relation to notifiable proposals

In relation to a notifiable proposal, a person is a promoter if that person:

- is involved in the course of a trade, profession or business which:

    (a) involves the provision of tax services to others; or
    (b) is carried on by a bank or securities house (as defined by the Corporation Tax Act 2010, s. 1120 or 1009(3) respectively); and

- either:

(a) is to any extent responsible for the design of the proposed arrangements; or
(b) makes the notifiable proposal available for others to implement.

In other words, a person who provides tax services by way of a business (or bank or securities house) is a promoter in relation to a notifiable proposal if that person either:

- helps to design the scheme to any extent; or
- markets it to others.

HMRC have commented in para 2A(iv)(a) of their guidance on the scope of the word 'design':

> 'In this context, the design requires the application of thought to a problem. Merely documenting or pricing a financial product to someone else's design is not itself design. But developing a solution to a requirement is.'

However, a limit on the effect of this rule as it affects persons partly responsible for the design of proposed arrangements has been introduced by HMRC. See *Involvement in a peripheral part of the arrangements* below.

From a date to be appointed, FA 2010 extends the definition of 'promoter' so as to catch marketing approaches by firms when an arrangement is more or less in a finished state. The statutory definition will catch anyone who:

> 'makes a firm approach to another person in relation to a notifiable proposal with a view to making the notifiable proposal available for implementation'

For these purposes:

- a firm approach is a marketing proposal at a time when the proposed arrangements have been substantially designed; and
- proposed arrangements have been substantially designed if they are sufficiently developed for implementation in their current form or in a form not substantially different.

Law: FA 2004, s. 307(1), (1A), (2), (4A)–(4C)

Other guidance: www.hmrc.gov.uk/aiu/guidance.pdf

Promoters in relation to notifiable arrangements

In relation to a notifiable arrangement, a person is a promoter if that person was a promoter in relation to the scheme when it was merely a notifiable proposal because that person was involved in the marketing of the scheme.

Additionally, a person is also a promoter in relation to a notifiable arrangement if that person:

- is involved in the course of a trade, profession or business which:

(a) involves the provision of tax services to others; or
(b) is carried on by a bank or securities house (as defined by the Corporation Tax Act 2010, s. 1120 or 1009(3) respectively); and

- is to any extent responsible for either:

(a) the design of the arrangements; or
(b) the organisation or management of the arrangements.

In other words, the evolution from notifiable proposal to notifiable arrangement does not prevent a person from continuing to be a promoter. But, in the course of this evolution, additional persons become promoters if they assume any responsibility for the organisation or management of the scheme.

Planning point

The only way to avoid being a promoter is by ensuring that one's involvement in the scheme is otherwise than in the course of a trade, profession or business providing tax services, banking or the business of a securities house. For example, an individual who provides gratuitous tax advice for family members will fall outside the definition of promoter.

The legislation refers to a trade, profession or business providing tax services or that of a bank or security house as a '*relevant business*'. This term is used below as a convenient shorthand.

However, limits on the effect of this rule as it affects persons partly responsible for:

- the design of arrangements; or
- their organisation or management,

have been introduced by HMRC. See *Involvement in a peripheral part of the arrangements* and *Unconnected persons organising or marketing the arrangements* respectively below. The relaxation in respect of persons involved in the organisation and/or management of a scheme is particularly useful.

Law: FA 2004, s. 307(1) and (2)

Group companies

It would be relatively easy for a banking company (or a securities house) to set up a subsidiary (or further subsidiary) to carry out the functions of designing, marketing, organising or managing a scheme. Without any special provisions, this division of roles would be sufficient for these activities to be carried out by a person which was not carrying on a business of a bank or securities house and therefore would ensure that the activities did not allow the subsidiary to become a promoter.

However, FA 2004, s. 307(3) ensures that activities by one company are caught by the rules if these activities are done for the purposes of a banking or securities house business carried on by another company within the same group.

For these purposes, the definition of group company is based on that in TCGA 1992, s. 170. However, this definition is modified. In particular:

- a subsidiary need be only a 51 per cent subsidiary (rather than a 75 per cent subsidiary); and
- there is no need for the subsidiary company to be an effective 51 per cent subsidiary of the parent.

For this purpose, TCGA 1992, s. 170(6)–(8) are treated as omitted.

Law: FA 2004, s. 307(4)

Exceptions from the definition of 'promoter'

The broad definition of promoter – in particular the fact that any involvement in a scheme would be sufficient to bring a person within the definition – could cause unnecessary problems (and reams of unnecessary paperwork). Consequently, HMRC have power to ensure that certain activities (as prescribed) would not make a person a promoter. These exceptions come under discrete headings.

Law: FA 2004, s. 307(5)

Groups

A company is not a promoter if:

- it is carrying on a relevant business (see above);
- it provides services in connection with a notifiable proposal or a notifiable arrangement;
- these services are provided to a company which is a member of the same group; and
- these services are provided on:

    (a) in the case of a notifiable proposal, the earlier of:

    - the date on which the company makes the proposal available for implementation by another person; and
    - the date on which the company first becomes aware of any transaction which forms part of notifiable arrangements which implement the proposal; or

    (b) in case of a notifiable arrangement, the date on which the company first becomes aware of any transaction which forms part of the notifiable arrangement.

The broad definition of group set out at *Group Companies* in this section above is also applied here.

Law: FA 2004, s. 307(2), (3); Tax Avoidance Schemes (Promoters and Prescribed Circumstances) Regulations 2004, SI 2004/1865, reg. 2

Employees

A similar exemption applies to individuals who would otherwise be promoters simply by virtue of being employees (or officers). This exemption covers:

- employees of actual promoters (so that only the employer promoter is under any obligations in respect of the arrangements);
- (in the case of notifiable proposals) employees of any person who is to enter into a transaction forming part of a proposed arrangement; and
- (in the case of notifiable arrangements) employees of any person who enters into a transaction forming part of the arrangement.

The word 'employee' has the same meaning as in ITEPA 2003, s. 4 and is also expressly extended to cover directors and other office holders. Furthermore, an employee of one employer 'E' will be treated as an employee of all persons connected with E.

Example 63.3

X Ltd owns 60 per cent of the share capital of Y Ltd which in turn owns 60 per cent of the share capital of Z Ltd – all other shares are owned by unconnected individuals.

Furthermore:

A is a director of X Ltd;

B was a director of Y Ltd; and

C is to be a director of Z Ltd.

A, B and C have had no other employments/offices with the other companies.

B and C are not protected by SI 2004 No. 1865 since they are not current employees (as defined by regulation 3).

A, however, is protected by reg. 3. Whilst an employee of X Ltd, A is also treated as an employee of Y Ltd and Z Ltd.

Incidentally, X Ltd, Y Ltd and Z Ltd are all treated as members of the same group for the purposes of the disclosure rules (see *Group companies* and *Groups* in this section above).

Law: SI 2004/1865, reg. 3

Involvement in a peripheral part of the arrangements

It will be recalled (see above) that a person can become a promoter simply by being 'to any extent responsible for the design of the proposed arrangements'. This wording means that every person involved in any part of the scheme would be a promoter – even if that person's input had nothing to do with any tax advantage that might arise.

This situation is mitigated by SI 2004/1865, reg. 4 which provides three sets of circumstances in which a person would not be treated as a promoter despite their participation in the design of a scheme.

1. The first circumstance applies to tax advisers. Tax advisers are kept outside the meaning of promoter if they are not responsible for any element of the scheme from which the expected tax advantage would arise.

    In other words, if a tax adviser is asked to approve one element of the scheme (for example, because the adviser has a particularly specialist knowledge of one particular aspect of tax law), the adviser would not be treated as a promoter under this heading if this involvement does not relate to any part of the scheme which gives rise to a tax advantage.

2. The second circumstance applies to any person carrying on a relevant business (i.e. tax services or the business of a bank or securities house – see above). Such persons are outside the meaning of promoter if:

    (a) they are responsible to any extent for the design of the scheme; and
    (b) such involvement is in the course of the relevant business; but
    (c) they do not provide any tax advice in the course of this involvement.

    In other words, a person will not be caught under the heading of responsibility for the design of the scheme if their involvement is merely administrative and does not amount to the provision of tax advice.

3. The final circumstance covers all other persons. It ensures that they are outside the meaning of promoter if:

    (a) they are not responsible for any element of the scheme from which the expected tax advantage would arise; and
    (b) could not reasonably be expected to have sufficient information about the scheme either to:

        (i) know that the scheme represented a notifiable proposal or notifiable arrangement; or
        (ii) be able to comply with the notification duty.

It is submitted that 'could not reasonably be expected' gives rise to a relatively low threshold. In other words, a person in such situations would be a promoter if:

- it was fairly obvious that the scheme was notifiable; and
- it would have been relatively easy to comply with the notification obligations.

Law: SI 2004/1865, reg. 4

Other guidance: Taxation 5 August 2004 at pp. 478–479

Unconnected persons organising or marketing the arrangements

A similar relaxation of the rules benefits persons who, in the course of a relevant business (i.e. tax services or the business of a bank or securities house – see above) are to an extent responsible for the organisation or management of a notifiable arrangement.

Under the relaxed version of the rule, a person involved in the organisation or management of a notifiable arrangement is a promoter only if connected (as defined by CTA 2010, s. 1122) with any other person who:

- is a promoter in respect of the notifiable arrangement (by being responsible for the design (or some of it) of the arrangement);
- was a promoter in respect of the scheme (again by being responsible for the design (or some of it) of the arrangement) from the time when it was merely a notifiable proposal; or
- is or was a promoter in respect of any other scheme which is substantially the same as the one under consideration.

In other words, if the marketing or organisation of the scheme is carried out by a person which is unconnected with the devisers of the scheme (because, for example, the person is merely an independent marketing company), then that person will not be a promoter.

Law: SI 2004/1865, reg. 1(3) and 5

Promoters' duty of disclosure

FA 2004, s. 308 (as expanded upon by SI 2004/1864) sets out the duties of promoters in respect of notifiable proposals and arrangements.

Under the original rules (still currently in force). if there are two or more promoters in relation to the same scheme, notification by any one of them would suffice.

> ⚠ **Warning!**
>
> Where agreements are made for one promoter to make the disclosure, co-promoters would need to be certain that the disclosure rules have been properly complied with. In view of the five-day reporting period, it would be advisable for most co-promoters operating at arm's length to make independent reports if they wish to avoid the risk of a penalty.

The legislation is not totally free from ambiguity, but it would appear that the notification by one co-promoter in respect of a notifiable proposal would exempt other co-promoters from the notification duty even when the proposal is transformed into a notifiable arrangement. This would be consistent with the rule that provides that a promoter in respect of a notifiable proposal (who makes a disclosure in respect of the proposal) need not make a further disclosure if the scheme subsequently becomes a notifiable arrangement.

> **Planning point**
>
> It may be safer to make an unnecessary disclosure than to risk a penalty (especially if, due to the short time frame, one does not have independent confirmation that the earlier notification had been properly made).

Similarly, a promoter is not under any obligation to make a disclosure in respect of two schemes which are substantially the same – provided, of course, that a notification has been made in respect of at least one of them. It does not matter if the schemes are entered into by different parties. HMRC considers in para. 2A(viii)(b) of their guidance two schemes to be no longer substantially the same if the disclosure in respect of the first would be misleading in respect of the second. This includes a change in the tax analysis. It is possible that HMRC consider that a new disclosure is necessary if, as a result of legislative changes (not merely the consolidation or restatement of earlier statutes), the tax analysis has to be revised. However, it is suggested that no such disclosure is necessary if, despite the changes to the analysis, the actual working of the scheme remains unaltered.

> ⚠ **Warning!**
>
> HMRC state in para. 2A(viii)(a) of their guidance that a scheme which predated one of the commencement dates still needs to be disclosed if it is re-used with a new client after the relevant commencement date.
>
> It is submitted that this is not wholly correct. Section 319(3)(b) appears pretty clear that a promoter is under no obligation to make a disclosure in respect of any arrangement which was made available for implementation before 18 March 2004 even if the arrangement was implemented after that date.

Law: FA 2004, s. 308 and 319(3); SI 2004/1864 reg. 3(5), 4(7) and 6

Other guidance: www.hmrc.gov.uk/aiu/guidance.pdf

Change introduced by FA 2008

From 1 November 2008, the procedure for cases involving more than one promoter was revised. They apply where there are different promoters in respect of the same scheme or different schemes that are substantially the same (whether or not they relate to the same parties).

Under the new rules, the duty of one promoter ('P1') is discharged if:

(1) either:

(a) the other promoter ('P2') has notified HMRC of the identity and address of P1; or

(b) P1 has the reference number allocated to the scheme; and

(2) P1 holds the information provided to HMRC.

Law: FA 2004, s. 308(4)–(4C)

Promoters' duty in relation to notifiable proposals – what must be provided

A promoter in relation to a notifiable proposal must provide HMRC with 'sufficient information as might reasonably be expected to enable an officer of the Board to comprehend the manner in which the proposal is intended to operate'. It is submitted that the words 'reasonably be expected' suggest that the information should be comprehensive enough to allow most reasonably competent tax inspectors to understand what is going on.

The information must include, however, the following:

- the promoter's name and address;
- details of the provision of SI 2004/1863 (see **59.12** below) by virtue of which the proposal is notifiable;
- a summary of the proposal and the name (if any) by which it is known;
- information explaining each element of the proposed arrangements (including the way in which they are structured) from which the tax advantage expected to be obtained under those arrangements arises; and
- the statutory provisions, relating to any of the prescribed taxes (see **59.4.2** above), on which that tax advantage is based.

HMRC have confirmed in para 2A(vii) of their guidance that clients' details need not be shown nor any arguments that HMRC might use to counter the scheme without introducing new legislation. They also say that nothing subject to legal professional privilege needs to be disclosed. For further comments on privilege, see **59.10** below.

A standard form, AIU1, is provided by HMRC for reporting this information. This standard form must be used unless the disclosure is made by an approved form of electronic communication.

The form should be sent to:

Anti-Avoidance Group (Intelligence)
1st Floor South
22 Kingsway
London WC2B 6NR
Tel: 020 7438 6733
Email: *aag@hmrc.gov.uk*

Since 1 August 2006, notifications can also be made online.

Law: FA 2004, s. 316; SI 2004 No. 1864, reg. 3 and 10

Other guidance: www.hmrc.gov.uk/aiu/guidance.pdf

Promoters' duty in relation to notifiable proposals – time limit

Ordinarily, this information must be provided to HMRC by the fifth working day after the earlier of:

- the date on which the promoter makes the proposal available for implementation by another person; and
- the date on which the promoter first becomes aware of any transaction which forms part of notifiable arrangements which implement the proposal.

A working day is any day other than Saturdays, Sundays, bank holidays, Good Friday, Christmas Day and any other day declared to be a bank holiday or so appointed by Royal Proclamation (e.g. in England and Wales, New Year's Day and the early May Bank Holiday).

> **Example 63.4**
>
> A promoter first makes a proposal available for implementation on Thursday 15 May and first learns of its implementation in a transaction which forms part of a notifiable arrangement on 23 May.
>
> The fifth working day (assuming no public holidays in the meantime) after 15 May is Thursday 22 May. Thus, the disclosure is due to be made by midnight at the end of that day.

However, a later disclosure is allowed in cases where a statutory clearance is expected to be sought. See *Later disclosure in statutory clearance cases* below.

Law: FA 2004, s. 308(1) and (2); SI 2004 No. 1864, reg. 4(2) and (6)

Later disclosure in statutory clearance cases

A promoter may defer disclosure of a notifiable proposal if:

- the promoter makes the proposal available for implementation by another person before the promoter first becomes aware of any transaction which forms part of notifiable arrangements implementing the proposal; and
- the promoter reasonably expects to make an application on behalf of a client under any of the following provisions allowing for statutory clearances:

    (a) CTA 2010, s. 1091 (exempt distributions);
    (b) CTA 2010, s. 1044 (purchase of own shares);
    (c) ICTA 1988, s. 444A (transfers of insurance business);
    (d) CTA 2010, s. 748 and ITA 2007; s. 701 (transactions in securities);
    (e) TCGA 1992, s. 138 (reorganisation of share capital);
    (f) TCGA 1992, s. 139 (reconstructions involving transfer of business);
    (g) TCGA 1992, s. 140B (transfers of UK trade to another EU member state);
    (h) TCGA 1992, s. 140D (transfers of non-UK trade to another EU member state).

In such cases, the disclosure must be made between:
- the day after the day the promoter makes the proposal available for implementation by another person; and
- the applicable date, which is defined as:
  (a) the date on which the first transaction occurs in pursuance of the arrangements; or
  (b) if the promoter ceases to hold the reasonable expectation to apply for the statutory clearance, five working days after he ceases to hold it.

> ⚠ **Warning!**
> Remarkably, disclosure may not be made on the same day that the promoter makes the proposal available for implementation. Whilst HMRC would probably not take the point, it would be safer, if one is in these circumstances, to delay making the disclosure by 24 hours. Alternatively, the HMRC guidance (at para. 2A(x)(a)) suggests that the clearance application should incorporate the disclosure requirement, but there is no statutory authority for this.

> **Planning point**
> Furthermore, the definition of 'applicable date' does not operate on the basis of 'the earlier' or 'the later' of the two dates cited. It would therefore seem that the first transaction date is the applicable date in any situation where the promoter intends to make a statutory clearance application. In cases where the expectation to make the application ceases to be held, the applicable date is five working days after this event. Consequently, a promoter could arguably delay the applicable date by deciding latterly not to seek a statutory clearance.

> **Example 63.5**
>
> A promoter is dealing with a notifiable proposal. The promoter reasonably expects to seek a statutory clearance in respect of the proposal.
>
> On 3 May, the promoter first makes the proposal available for implementation by another person. On 9 May, the promoter decides not to seek a statutory clearance and the first transaction in accordance with the arrangements occurs on 10 May.
>
> Had the promoter not decided against seeking a statutory clearance, the disclosure would have fallen due between 4 May and 10 May inclusive.
>
> But the decision not to seek the clearance has the effect of extending the disclosure period to 16 May.

In most cases this will be of only marginal interest since seven of the statutory provisions deal with pre-transaction rulings. However, the transactions in securities clearance procedures can operate to give post-transaction rulings (despite being headed 'Procedure for clearance in advance'). Arguably, this can allow the disclosure window to be extended for far longer than a week, provided that there remains the reasonable expectation that statutory clearance would be sought. It would appear that this was an oversight as the HMRC guidance at para. 2A(x)(a) clearly indicates that the intention was to require pre-transaction rulings.

Additionally, the regulations require only that the promoter should 'reasonably expect to make an application *on behalf of a client* [emphasis added]'. So technically, the intended clearance application need not necessarily be connected with the notifiable proposal. However, it is difficult to expect a court to be keen to reach such a conclusion.

Law: SI 2004/1864 regs. 4(6) and 5

Promoters' duty in relation to notifiable arrangements – what must be provided

A promoter in relation to a notifiable arrangement must provide HMRC with 'sufficient information as might reasonably be expected to enable an officer of the Board to comprehend the manner in which the arrangement is intended to operate'. (See *Promoters' duty in relation to notifiable proposals – what must be provided* above for comments on the meaning of this phrase.)

The information must include the following:

- the promoter's name and address;
- details of the provision of SI 2004/1863 (see **59.12** below) by virtue of which the arrangement is notifiable;
- a summary of the arrangement and the name (if any) by which it is known;
- information explaining each element of the arrangement (including the way in which it is structured) from which the tax advantage expected to be obtained under the arrangement arises; and
- the statutory provisions, relating to any of the prescribed taxes (see **59.4.3** above), on which that tax advantage is based.

HMRC have confirmed that clients' details need not be shown nor any arguments that the HMRC might use to counter the scheme without introducing new legislation. They also say that nothing subject to legal professional privilege needs to be disclosed. For further comments on privilege, see **59.10** below.

Again form AAG1 can be used to report this information. The form is provided by HMRC. This standard form must be used unless the disclosure is made by an approved form of electronic communication.

The form should be sent to:

Anti-Avoidance Group (Intelligence)
1st Floor South
22 Kingsway
London WC2B 6NR
Tel: 020 7438 6733
Email: *aag@hmrc.gov.uk*

Since 1 August 2006, notifications can also be made online.

This information is not needed, however, if the promoter has already made a disclosure of the equivalent information in respect of the scheme when it was only a notifiable proposal.

Law: FA 2004, s. 308(3) and 316; SI 2004 No. 1864, reg. 3(2) and (10)

Other guidance: www.hmrc.gov.uk/aiu/guidance.htm

Promoters' duty in relation to notifiable arrangements – time limit

The information must be provided to HMRC by the fifth working day after the date on which the promoter first becomes aware of any transaction which forms part of the notifiable arrangement.

See **Example 63.6** for how to calculate the five days.

Law: FA 2004, s. 308(1) and (3); SI 2004/1864, reg. 4(3) and (6)

Where the duty arises following an order of the Special Commissioners, the information must be provided within ten days starting with the day *after* that on which the order is made.

Law: FA 2004, s. 306A(6); SI 2004/1864, reg. 4(1A)

Request for further information

FA 2007 introduced provisions that permit HMRC to request from the Special Commissioners for an order requiring a promoter to provide specified information or documents relating to a particular notifiable scheme.

The information must be provided within ten days starting with the day *after* that on which the order is made.

Law: FA 2004, s. 308A; SI 2004/1864, reg. 4(3B)

63.6.3 Clients' duty to disclose arrangements

HMRC naturally would not wish these rules merely to lead to the provision of tax avoidance schemes by overseas promoters against whom the rules would not be enforceable.

Consequently, the Finance Act 2004 includes provisions whereby the clients of such schemes (i.e. any person who has entered into a transaction which forms part of a notifiable arrangement) are required to make a disclosure.

No such disclosure is necessary if:

- there is at least one promoter resident in the UK; or
- a promoter has nevertheless made a disclosure in respect of the scheme when it was a notifiable proposal.

This last point is significant in that it appears only to relate to notifiable proposals and not notifiable arrangements. It is not clear, however, whether HMRC would pursue this point.

> ### Example 63.7
>
> A scheme is developed by an overseas promoter so that it comes within the definition of a notifiable proposal. The promoter fails to make a disclosure in respect of the proposal (i.e. fails to comply with FA 2004, s. 308(1)).
>
> However, the promoter subsequently sells the scheme to a client in the UK who enters into arrangements under the scheme. The promoter agrees with the client that the promoter will make a timely disclosure of the (now) notifiable arrangements (under s. 308(3)).
>
> The promoter is obliged to make this disclosure (even though the rules are not enforceable against non-residents) and does indeed make the required disclosure. Had the promoter also been UK-resident, the client would not have been required to make a disclosure (because of the limited scope of s. 309(1)).
>
> However, the promoter's disclosure would now be under s. 308(3) and not s. 308(1). Consequently, the circumstances fall outside the terms of s. 309(2). Therefore, the punter is still required to make a disclosure under s. 309(1).
>
> The HMRC guidance (para. 2A(i) (penultimate bullet) and 2A(iv)(b)), however, implies that disclosure by the promoter would mean that the punter is not required to disclose the arrangements.

Law: FA 2004, s. 309

Other guidance: www.hmrc.gov.uk/aiu/guidance.pdf

Clients' duty in relation to notifiable arrangements – what must be provided

Any client who is obliged to make a disclosure in relation to a notifiable arrangement must provide HMRC with 'sufficient information as might reasonably be expected to enable an officer of the Board to comprehend the manner in which the arrangement is intended to operate'.

The information must include the following:

- the client's name and address;
- the promoter's name and address;
- details of the provision of SI 2004/1863 (see **63.12** below) by virtue of which the arrangement is notifiable;
- a summary of the arrangement and the name (if any) by which it is known;
- information explaining each element of the arrangement (including the way in which it is structured) from which the tax advantage expected to be obtained under the arrangement arises; and
- the statutory provisions, relating to any of the prescribed taxes (see **63.4.3** above), on which that tax advantage is based.

A standard form, AAG2, is provided by HMRC for reporting this information. This standard form must be used unless the disclosure is made by an approved form of electronic communication.

The form should be sent to:

Anti-Avoidance Group (Intelligence)
1st Floor South
22 Kingsway
London WC2B 6NR
Tel: 020 7438 6733
Email: aag@hmrc.gov.uk

Since 1 August 2006, notifications can also be made online.

Law: FA 2004, s. 316; SI 2004/1864, reg. 3(3) and 10

Other guidance: www.hmrc.gov.uk/aiu/aiu2.pdf

Clients' duty in relation to notifiable arrangements – time limits

The information must be provided to HMRC by the fifth working day after the client enters into the first transaction which forms part of the notifiable arrangement.

See **Example 63.4** above for how to calculate the five days.

Law: FA 2004, s. 310

63.6.4 Parties' duty where no promoter is involved

Similarly, there is an obligation on parties entering into any transaction which forms part of a notifiable arrangement to make a disclosure if there is no person required to make a disclosure under either of the rules set out at **59.6.1** and **59.6.2** above. In such circumstances it is unlikely that HMRC would issue a reference number in relation to the scheme (see paragraph 1(iii)(c) of the HMRC guidance).

Law: FA 2004, s. 309(1); SI 2004/1864 reg. 4(4) and (6)

Other guidance: www.hmrc.gov.uk/aiu/guidance.pdf

Parties' duty in relation to notifiable arrangements – what must be provided

Any person who is obliged to make such a disclosure in relation to a notifiable arrangement must provide HMRC with 'sufficient information as might reasonably be expected to enable an officer of the Board to comprehend the manner in which the arrangement is intended to operate'.

The information must include the following:

- the name and address of the person entering into the transaction;
- details of the provision of SI 2004/1863 (see **59.12** below) by virtue of which the arrangement is notifiable;
- a summary of the arrangement and the name (if any) by which it is known;
- information explaining each element of the arrangement (including the way in which it is structured) from which the tax advantage is expected to be obtained under the arrangement arises; and
- the statutory provisions, relating to any of the prescribed taxes (see **59.4.2** above), on which that tax advantage is based.

A standard form, AAG3, is provided by HMRC for reporting this information. This standard form must be used unless the disclosure is made by an approved form of electronic communication. It was previously requested that the form should be sent to the party's normal tax office (or, in relation to employment schemes, to the party's PAYE tax office). However, HMRC issued a statement on 19 May 2005 requesting such forms to be sent to the office dealing with all other disclosures. Therefore, AAG3s should now be sent to:

Anti-Avoidance Group (Intelligence)
1st Floor South
22 Kingsway
London WC2B 6NR
Tel: 020 7438 6733
Email: *aag@hmrc.gov.uk*

Law: FA 2004, s. 316; SI 2004/1864 reg. 3(4) and 10

Other guidance: www.hmrc.gov.uk/aiu/forms-tax-schemes.htm

Parties' duty in relation to notifiable arrangements – time limits

Since 1 August 2006 (or where a notification is due in relation to stamp duty land tax), the disclosure must be made in the 30 days after the day on which the person enters into the first transaction forming part of the notifiable arrangements.

> ⚠ **Warning!**
>
> It seems odd that a disclosure on the day on which the party enters into the first transaction which forms part of the notifiable arrangement is technically invalid. The author understands that HMRC would not take this point, but to avoid the risk of a penalty, it would be safer to delay disclosure by 24 hours.

Law: FA 2004, s. 316; SI 2004/1864 reg. 3(4), 4(5) and (5ZA) and 8

63.6.5 Parties' duty where promoter's disclosure restricted by legal professional privilege

After some discussions with the legal and accountancy profession, it became clear that difficulties arose where a promoter's disclosure was subject to legal professional privilege. The consequence is that parties now have to make a disclosure within five working days of entering into a notifiable arrangement. This is discussed in more detail at **59.10** below.

63.7 HMRC's response to a disclosure

The terms of FA 2004, s. 311 are particularly vague and provide little reassurance to taxpayers and their advisers.

The section provides that, once notified of a notifiable arrangement or proposal, HMRC *may* allocate a reference number to the arrangement or proposal within 30 days. If they do so, they may also notify the person making the disclosure of the reference number.

There is no obligation for HMRC to allocate a reference number to any scheme – possibly to ensure that it is not overrun with what it considers to be trivial disclosures. In particular, they do not propose to issue reference numbers in respect of SDLT schemes which were brought within the disclosure rules on 1 August 2005.

It would therefore be possible that someone who makes a disclosure will never be sure that a reference number has not been allocated and not merely mislaid in the post. However, HMRC previously stated in their guidance (at paragraph 1(iii)(c)) that a letter will be issued in respect of all cases where no reference number is to be allocated. It is not clear whether this will apply in respect of SDLT cases.

According to a strict interpretation of FA 2004, s. 311, HMRC may not allocate a reference number more than 30 days after the relevant disclosure. Nor may they allocate a reference number in respect of any disclosure made late (since the wording of s. 311(1) requires there to have been compliance with the relevant duty to make a disclosure and that duty includes a time limit). Nor may HMRC notify the person making the disclosure of the reference number outside the 30-day period.

> ⚠ **Warning!**
> What is clear, however, is that the allocation of a reference number does not necessarily imply that the scheme so notified confers the tax advantage as disclosed.

FA 2008 has modified s. 311 slightly from 1 November 2008. It provides that, if HMRC allocate a reference number, they *must* notify the person who made the disclosure of that number. And, where, the disclosure was by a promoter, they must also notify any other person who is also a promoter in relation to that arrangement whose identity and address have been notified to HMRC by the first promoter.

Law: FA 2004, s. 311(1), (2)

63.8 Duties with respect to reference numbers

63.8.1 Introduction

Whilst HMRC have no obligation to allocate a reference number to a particular proposal or arrangement, there are firm obligations on promoters.

> **Planning point**
>
> It is stated in the legislation that all references to 'reference numbers' are to be read as referring to reference numbers allocated under FA 2004, s. 311. For example, a reference number may not be allocated outside the 30-day limit or if there has been a compliance failure with regards to FA 2004, s. 308, 309 or 310. It is arguable, therefore, that there is no obligation on promoters to comply with its obligations with respect to a reference number allocated *ultra vires*.

Law: FA 2004, s. 311(3)

63.8.2 Promoters' duty in relation to reference numbers – who must provide information

A promoter is obliged to comply with these obligations only if:

- the promoter is providing services to another person ('the client'); and
- those services are provided in connection with notifiable arrangements.

By the use of the present continuous tense, it would appear, therefore, that a promoter whose involvement with their client ended before receiving notification of the reference number is not under any obligation to comply with FA 2004, s. 312.

Law: FA 2004, s. 312(1)

63.8.3 Promoters' duty in relation to reference numbers – what must be provided

The promoter must provide the client with the reference number in relation to the notifiable arrangements. Of course, if no reference number is given, then there is no such obligation on the promoter.

If the arrangements are substantially the same as other arrangements (not necessarily made by the same parties), the promoter is also obliged to notify the client of any reference number in relation to the other arrangements.

Law: FA 2004, s. 312(1); SI 2004/1864 reg. 7

63.8.4 Promoters' duty in relation to reference numbers – time limits

The promoter must so notify the client within 30 days of the later of:

- the date on which the promoter first becomes aware of any transaction which forms part of the notifiable arrangements; and
- the date on which the reference number is notified to the promoter.

Law: FA 2004, s. 312(2)

63.8.5 Promoters' duty in relation to reference numbers – form of notification

FA 2004, s. 316 requires the promoter to notify the client of the reference number 'in a form and manner specified by [HMRC]'. However, there is, as yet, no such specified form and manner by HMRC. This point has been raised by the author of this chapter with HMRC who have responded in the following terms:

> '[T]he form of communicating the reference number issued is not specified by the Board. Therefore until and unless the form of communication is so specified, promoters may use the form that is most convenient to them.'

FA 2008 modifies s. 316 to ensure that notifications are still able to be made in the absence of specific forms. That revised version came into force on 1 November 2008.

63.8.6 Removal of requirement to notify reference number

From 1 November 2008, s. 312(6) (introduced by FA 2008) provides that HMRC can notify promoters that there will be no need to notify clients of reference numbers.

Law: FA 2004, s. 312(6)

63.8.7 Clients' duties with reference numbers

From 1 November 2008, clients to whom a reference number has been provided by a promoter must notify other parties to the arrangements and whom might be expected to obtain a tax advantage as a result. This must be done within 30 days.

Again HMRC can notify the clients that this duty need not be complied with in particular cases. Furthermore, regulations can be introduced to dispense with this duty in prescribed circumstances. For example, regulations have provided that there is no obligation for employees who are expected to receive a tax advantage arising from that employment.

Law: FA 2004, s. 312A; SI 2004/1864, reg. 7A, 7B

63.8.8 Promoters' duty to provide details to clients

From a date to be appointed, FA 2010 introduces a new obligation on promoters. If the promoter is subject to the reference number information requirement in FA 2004, s. 312(2), or has failed to notify HMRC of the arrangements under s. 308 (and would be subject to the reference number information requirement had a reference number been allocated to the arrangements), then the promoter must provide HMRC with information (to be prescribed) in relation to the client.

The purpose of this requirement is to enable HMRC to ascertain how widely a scheme is being used long before the tax returns on which the scheme reference number is cited are submitted.

Law: FA 2004, s. 313ZA

63.9 Parties' duties with respect to notifiable arrangements

63.9.1 Introduction

A party to a notifiable arrangement is obliged to provide information to HMRC. This requirement exists whether or not there is any other disclosure by the party or another person in respect of the arrangements.

From 1 November 2008, HMRC can give notice to dispense with this requirement.

Law: FA 2004, s. 313(1), (5)

63.9.2 Parties' duties – what needs to be disclosed

If the party has been notified of a reference number in relation to the arrangements either by the promoter (see **59.8.3** above) or by HMRC (see **59.6.4** above), then that person must provide this information to HMRC. In other words, this information must be provided to HMRC even if the party was notified of the number by HMRC itself.

The reason for this peculiar state of affairs is that the party must also provide additional information and the reference number merely enables HMRC to keep track of the arrangements in circulation. This additional information is needed whether or not a reference number has been notified to the party.

This additional information required by HMRC is the time of the expected tax advantage. This 'time' will be a tax year, an accounting period or a particular date.

Law: FA 2004, s. 313(1); SI 2004/1864 reg. 8(1)(a)

63.9.3 Parties' duties – how should disclosure be made

The Finance Act 2004 provides for two methods of disclosure:
- by including the disclosure as part of a return which would otherwise be made in any event; and
- a stand-alone disclosure.

The type of disclosure depends on the particular circumstance of the case.

Law: FA 2004, s. 313(3)

Disclosure as part of a return

Where a tax return is being made by the party, it is sufficient to disclose the reference number of the arrangement and the tax year (or accounting period) in which the tax advantage is expected to be obtained.

Law: SI 2004/1864 reg. 8(1)

Other guidance: www.hmrc.gov.uk/aiu/aiu4.pdf

Stand-alone disclosures

If the party does not prepare a tax return, disclosure is still required of:
- the name and address of the person making the disclosure;
- any National Insurance number, tax reference number, PAYE reference number or other identifier relating to that person;
- the reference number allocated to the scheme by HMRC;
- the year of assessment, accounting period or tax year in which, or the date on which, the person expects to obtain the tax advantage;
- the name of the person providing the declaration as to the accuracy and completeness of the notification (for example the director of the company making the disclosure); and
- the capacity in which the person making the declaration is acting.

The statutory provision listing this information suggests in places that the disclosure might be made by a person other than the party to the transaction – in other words one makes a formal disclosure on behalf of another. However, this would be inconsistent with certain other provisions; furthermore, the standard form (AAG4) prepared by HMRC does not envisage this. This form must be used unless the disclosure is made by an approved form of electronic communication.

Stand-alone disclosures are required by the earliest day a tax return (or P35) for the period in question would have been due. So, an individual who is required to make a stand-alone disclosure in respect of the 2004/05 tax year must do so by 31 January 2006 notwithstanding the fact that no section 8 notice to file a return has been issued.

Law: FA 2004, s. 316; SI 2004/1864 reg. 8 and 10

Other guidance: www.hmrc.gov.uk/aiu/aiu4.pdf

63.9.4 Duty to disclose when no reference number given

According to the HMRC guidance (at paragraph 2.B(i)), there is no obligation on a party to make any such disclosure if no reference number has been allocated to the party. The guidance reads:

> Users of schemes and arrangements are required to inform the Inland Revenue that they have used a registered scheme or arrangement, normally when submitting the income tax, corporation tax or P35 return. Users should provide both the scheme reference number and the year in which the tax advantage is expected to arise. *There is no obligation on a user if the promoter does not inform them of a reference number.*

[emphasis added]

Whilst this probably makes sense from a practical perspective, it does not appear to accord with the wording of FA 2004, s. 313.

It would appear that the HMRC guidance nevertheless represents the Government's intention as FA 2004, s. 313(3) refers to the provision of 'the number and other information' (suggesting that HMRC expects both pieces of information or neither).

On the other hand, the transitional rule in FA 2004, s. 319(5) purports to provide that the disclosure of this information is not necessary in cases where there was no obligation for a promoter or party to a transaction to make a disclosure of the arrangement or proposal under the rules set out at **59.6** above. Making this rule explicit suggests that parties would otherwise be obliged to make these disclosures in the absence of a reference number.

Furthermore, SI 2004/1864 reg. 8(2) refers to the provision of the relevant information to HMRC:

> 'in the return ... which relates to the year of assessment in which [the party] is notified of the reference number ..., or in which the advantage is expected to arise if earlier.'

That timing requirement seems to suggest that tax advantages should, in some situations, be returned in advance of the allocation of the reference number and therefore anticipates the situation in which no reference number at all has been issued.

Alternatively, it is equally arguable that the words 'if earlier' have no logical meaning unless there is an actual later event (i.e. the issue to the party of the reference number).

Whilst it would seem that HMRC does not actually want a return from parties to arrangements in cases where no reference number has been issued to them, parties are recommended to consider providing this information unless:

- they fall squarely within the terms of the HMRC guidance reproduced above (i.e. the party would ordinarily have received the reference number from the promoter and not directly from HMRC); or
- firmer instructions from HMRC are subsequently given supporting the stance being taken.

This ensures that there can be no risk of a penalty charge from HMRC and avoids problems which would occur if the notification had merely been mislaid in the post.

If the form AIU4 (for use where returns are not to be used for disclosure purposes) is anything to go by, however, a return without a reference number will consist only of the expected timing of the expected tax advantage. It is of course recognised that this information will be of little use to HMRC and would almost inevitably lead to an enquiry.

63.10 Legal professional privilege

FA 2004, s. 314 provides what appears to be a comforting reassurance:

'314(1) Nothing in this Part requires any person to disclose to the Board any privileged information.

(2) In this Part "privileged information" means information with respect to which a claim to legal professional privilege, or, in Scotland, to confidentiality of communications, could be maintained in legal proceedings.'

Legal professional privilege is a common law right which the courts jealously guard on behalf of citizens. For example, see the House of Lords' decision in *R v Special Commissioner, ex parte Morgan Grenfell & Co Ltd* [2002] BTC 223 and *Three Rivers District Council v Bank of England* [2004] UKHL 48. The right ensures that disclosure of the following cannot be compelled:

- communications between a professional legal adviser and a client made in connection with the provision of legal advice;
- communications (not necessarily between a legal adviser and a client) made in connection with, or in contemplation of, or for the purposes of, legal proceedings; and
- items enclosed with or referred to in such communications and made:
  (a) in connection with the giving of legal advice; or

(b) in contemplation of, in connection, or for the purposes of legal proceedings.

It is worth emphasising that communications between a client and an accountant or other tax adviser (not being a lawyer) are not currently privileged. (Or, perhaps more correctly, such communications are not thought to be privileged pending a successful challenge to this rather arbitrary distinction in the courts.)

The clear aim of FA 2004, s. 314 is to ensure that legal professional privilege is not eroded by the new rules. However, concern was raised at HMRC's understanding of what constituted privileged information and what was nevertheless subject to disclosure under the new rules.

In the draft guidance published in May 2004, the then Inland Revenue stated:

> 'The disclosure rules do not in any way override LPP [legal professional privilege]. However, LPP does not in itself provide justification for not disclosing a scheme if it meets the criteria for disclosure. There is no requirement upon an accountant or lawyer to identify the client or to provide copies of actual documents or planning advice. The rules are intended to obtain details of the product and not the technical or legal advice given to the client. Solicitors and barristers in particular should be able to meet the requirements through normal redactive processes.'

In other words, the Revenue's position was that the workings of any scheme could be disclosed by legal advisers (and, in fact, must be disclosed by them) and such a disclosure would not breach a client's privilege. (Whilst many papers might be in the control of a legal adviser, it is only the client who may waive the right to privilege.) By the time the final guidance was published (on 29 July 2004), the Revenue had retreated somewhat although one could by no means call it a surrender. The guidance now reads:

> 'Lawyers are subject to the disclosure rules in the same way as other professional advisers. The rules do not require the disclosure of any information which would be subject to legal professional privilege (in Scotland, confidentiality of communications) in legal proceedings). The ambit of legal professional privilege is under discussion with the Law Society following which we shall add further guidance.'

On 6 October 2004, the then Inland Revenue announced the resolution of these discussions. This resolution provides that a person is not to be considered as a promoter of a particular scheme if legal professional privilege would otherwise prevent that person's full disclosure of scheme. For example, if a lawyer:

- would ordinarily be a promoter of a scheme; but
- is protected by s. 314 from disclosing information:

    (a) which is subject to legal professional privilege; but
    (b) which would otherwise be required (see *Promoters' duty in relation to notifiable proposals – what must be provided* and *Promoters' duty in relation to notifiable arrangements – what must be provided* in section **59.6** above with respect to notifiable proposals and arrangements respectively),

then the lawyer is not to be treated at all as a promoter.

It would appear that co-promoters (not being lawyers) may similarly be excused from making any notification if their notification would otherwise be based on legal advice provided to them.

> ⚠ **Warning!**
>
> The consequence of a person escaping treatment as a promoter is that it leaves a greater responsibility on the other parties to report matters where necessary. In particular, where no promoter is under any obligation to make a notification because of legal professional privilege, a party to a transaction is required to make a disclosure under the provisions discussed at **59.6** above. However, the relatively relaxed time limit for making a disclosure (effectively, the due date for making the relevant return) is not retained. Instead, such a disclosure must be made in the five working days after the person enters into the first transaction forming part of the notifiable arrangements. However, no such disclosure needed be made in these circumstances any earlier than 19 November 2004.

It would also appear that s. 314 still provides protection to the parties from any obligation to make a disclosure of material subject to legal professional privilege. As a result, the October amendments have simply ensured that the 'incomplete' disclosure is now made by the party to the transaction rather than the promoter.

> ⚠ **Warning!**
>
> Although the legal professional privilege exemption is not qualified, it is sometimes disregarded when determining whether or not an arrangement is to be treated as prescribed. The reason for this is to determine whether or not there is a promoter in particular circumstances. As the exemption operates by treating a person as if they were not a promoter (and so removing the obligation on that person to make a disclosure), the exemption must be disapplied when determining the whether a particular scheme is subject to a duty to notify. Once a scheme has been determined as notifiable then the exemption for legal professional privilege reverts.

Law: SI 2004/1864 reg. 4(5A); SI 2004/2613 reg. 1(3); Tax Avoidance Schemes (Prescribed Descriptions of Arrangements) Regulations 2006 (SI 2006/1543), reg. 5(3)

63.11 Penalties

63.11.1 Introduction

FA 2004, s. 313(4) makes it clear that if:

Disclosure of Direct Tax Avoidance Schemes

- a disclosure is required to be made under FA 2004, s. 313 as part of a return; and
- the disclosure is not so made or is not fully made; butr
- the return would otherwise not attract a penalty,

then no penalty will be charged even though the return was not complete. This rule is extended to penalties under TMA 1970, s. 98A(4) in respect of incorrect P35s.

However, this apparent generosity exists only because more stringent penalties apply in respect of failures to comply with these rules.

Law: FA 2004, s. 313(4)(g); SI 2004/1864 reg. 9

63.11.2 Failure to provide details of a notifiable proposal or arrangement

If a promoter or party fails to disclose the details of a notifiable proposal or arrangement (see **59.6** above) that person will be liable to a penalty. The maximum penalty which may be levied is:

- £5,000 for the initial failure; and
- daily penalties of £600 if, after a penalty is imposed for the initial failure, the disclosure remains due.

If it is of any consolation, only one daily penalty may be imposed on any person in respect of any one day even if there are a number of overdue disclosures on that particular day. It is suggested that the intention of this rule was to ensure that a daily penalty would not be imposed in respect of the same day in relation to a scheme which was a notifiable proposal and has subsequently become a notifiable arrangement, but where no disclosure was made under either heading. However, it is possible to argue that there cannot be more than one daily penalty in respect of any one day even if the disclosure failure relates to wholly different schemes.

> ⚠ **Warning!**
>
> It should be remembered that these penalties do not relate only to late compliance. They can be imposed in respect of failures to use the correct forms or even in respect of premature notification.

HMRC have stated in para. 2A(xiii) of their guidance that they would not seek penalties if satisfied that either:

- a promoter has made a judgment on a reasonable basis in determining whether or not a disclosure is required; or
- the promoter can demonstrate there is a reasonable excuse for the failure to comply.

Law: TMA 1970, s. 98C

63.11.3 Failure to provide reference number and timing of tax advantage

Where a person is required to disclose a scheme's reference number and the time a tax advantage is expected to arise (see **59.9** above), the following penalties apply. It does not matter whether the disclosure is due as part of a return or in a stand-alone form.

The amount of the penalty depends on whether the person has failed to provide this information in respect of the same or another scheme in the previous three years.

(1) For the person's first such failure, the penalty is £100 per scheme to which the failure relates.

(2) For the person's second such failure, the penalty is £500 per scheme to which the failure relates.

(3) In all other cases, the penalty is £1,000 per scheme to which the failure relates.

Law: TMA 1970, s. 98C(3), (4)

63.12 What schemes are prescribed?

63.12.1 Introduction

As explained at **59.2** above, a scheme is notifiable only if it comes within the description prescribed by the Treasury. The initial targets of the rules are arrangements connected with employment and arrangements concerning financial products. Following the 2005 Budget, the scope of the disclosure rules was extended to certain Stamp Duty Land Tax transactions. These are considered in turn below.

The following discusses only the rules applying since 2006. For the earlier rules, the reader is referred to the 2007/08 edition of this work.

SDLT

63.12.2 Stamp Duty Land Tax schemes

The 2005 Budget announced that the disclosure rules were to be extended to SDLT arrangements with effect from 1 July 2005. In the end the implementation of the rules was delayed until 1 August 2005.

Schemes which come within the disclosure rules are set out as follows:

- schemes which might be expected to provide, as a main benefit of using the scheme, an SDLT advantage where it concerns property which is not wholly

residential property (as defined in FA 2003, s. 116), and in respect of which the applicable value is at least £5,000,000 at the time any requirement to notify would otherwise arise;
- (from 1 April 2010) residential property in respect of which the applicable value is at least £1,000,000; and
- a mixture of non-residential and residential property where either:
    - (from 1 April 2010) the applicable value of the residential property is at least £1,000,000; or
    - the applicable value of all the property is at least £5,000,000.

This test applies whether or not the duty to make the disclosure is on a promoter or the party to any transaction.

The applicable value is the aggregate market value of all of the chargeable interests in non-residential property subject to the arrangements. The market value is to be determined in accordance with FA 2003, s. 118 and, for the purposes of ascertaining that value, all chargeable interests held by the same person or connected persons shall be taken into account.

Certain arrangements are excluded from the provisions and these are discussed below.

Law: SI 2005/1868 reg. 2(1)–(3)

Assumptions made

In some cases, a promoter might not know whether the subject matter of an arrangement will consist at least in part of non-residential property. In such circumstances, it is to be assumed that the arrangement will involve property that is not wholly residential property.

Similarly, a promoter might make a notifiable proposal available generally without knowing the applicable value. In such cases, the applicable value is assumed to be at least £5,000,000.

Similarly, a person is required to assume that the applicable value is at least £5,000,000 if:
- the applicable value is not otherwise known; and
- either:
    (a) a promoter makes available a proposal for arrangements in circumstances where he knows the identity of at least one of the persons who it is proposed should be a party to the arrangements;
    (b) a promoter becomes aware of a transaction entered into in pursuance of arrangements in circumstances where he knows the identity of at least one of the persons who it is proposed should be a party to the arrangements; or
    (c) a person becomes a party to any transaction forming part of notifiable arrangement and liable to comply with either s. 309 or 310.

This last assumption is rather meaningless – but it does remove one possible (albeit unjustified) argument that might be made. Either the applicable value is at least £5,000,000 or it isn't. If it is at least £5,000,000 then a duty to make a disclosure will then follow (provided that the other conditions are met). There is no need for the applicable value to be deemed to be at least £5,000,000. Conversely, if the applicable value is less than £5,000,000 then no duty to make a disclosure exists in any event.

Law: SI 2005/1868 reg. 2(4)–(6)

The excluded arrangements

The exclusions are framed by reference to certain steps. Although the legislation refers to two rules referring to these steps, there are in fact three such rules.

The harsh rule (rule 2 per the legislation)
Arrangements are not excluded arrangements if they:

- include all, or at least two of, steps A, C and D; or
- involve more than one instance of either step A, C or D.

The more relaxed rule (rule 1 per the legislation)
Where the harsh rule does not apply, any arrangements involving Steps B, D, E and F are excluded arrangements.

The general rule
Subject to the above two rules, arrangements are excluded from being prescribed arrangements if they:

- comprise one or more of the following steps A to F; and
- do not include any other step, which is necessary for the purpose of securing a tax advantage.

Step A: Acquisition of a chargeable interest by special purpose vehicle
The acquisition of a chargeable interest in land by a company created for that purpose ('a special purpose vehicle').

Step B: Claims to relief
Making:

1. A single claim to relief under any of the following provisions of the Finance Act 2003:
    - s. 57A (sale and leaseback arrangements);
    - s. 60 (compulsory purchase facilitating development);
    - s. 61 (compliance with planning obligation);
    - s. 64 (demutualisation of building society);
    - s. 64A (initial transfer of assets to trustees of unit trust scheme);
    - s. 65 (incorporation of limited liability partnership);

- s. 66 (transfers involving public bodies);
- s. 67 (transfer in consequence of reorganisation of parliamentary constituencies);
- s. 69 (acquisition by bodies established for national purposes);
- s. 71 (certain acquisitions by registered social landlords);
- s. 74 (collective enfranchisement by leaseholders);
- s. 75 (crofting community right to buy);
- Sch. 6 (disadvantaged areas relief);
- Sch. 6A (relief for certain acquisitions of residential property);
- Sch. 7 (group relief and reconstruction acquisition reliefs);
- Sch. 8 (charities relief); or
- Sch. 9 (right to buy, shared ownership leases, etc.).

2. One or more claims to relief under any one of the following provisions of the Finance Act 2003:
   - s. 71A (alternative property finance: land sold to financial institution and leased to individual);
   - s. 72 (alternative property finance in Scotland: land sold to financial institution and leased to individual);
   - s. 72A (alternative property finance in Scotland: land sold to financial institution and individual in common); or
   - s. 73 (alternative property finance: land sold to financial institution and re-sold to individual).

Step C: Sale of shares in special purpose vehicle
The sale of shares in a special purpose vehicle, which holds a chargeable interest in land, to a person with whom neither the special purpose vehicle, nor the vendor, is connected.

Step D: Not exercising election to waive exemption from VAT
No election is made to waive exemption from value added tax contained in VATA 1994, Sch. 10, para. 2 (treatment of buildings and land for value added tax purposes).

Step E: Transfer of a business as a going concern
Arranging the transfer of a business, connected with the land which is the subject of the arrangements, in such a way that it is treated for the purposes of value added tax as the transfer of a going concern.

Step F: Undertaking a joint venture
The creation of a partnership (within the meaning of FA 2003, Sch. 15, para. 1) to which the property which subject to a land transaction is to be transferred.

Law: SI 2005/1868 Schedule

Proposed extension of SDLT disclosures

In 2008, it was announced that SDLT disclosures might be extended to cover schemes relating to residential property worth in excess of £1m.

A consultation document was published in April 2009 but at the time of writing no legislation had been published.

Rules applying since 1 August 2006 – income tax, corporation tax and capital gains tax

63.12.3 Hallmarks of avoidance

The disclosure regime was widened with effect from 1 August 2006 to cover, potentially, any scheme for the avoidance of income tax, corporation tax or capital gains tax. However, to prevent routine advice from being subject to a disclosure requirement, the regulations require that the scheme must fall within one or more 'descriptions'. These descriptions are discussed below.

Where a scheme is implemented by a taxpayer without a promoter, there is a general rule that a disclosure is necessary only if the taxpayer is a company or a partnership or a person otherwise charged to income tax in respect of trading or property income. Furthermore, the taxpayer must be a small or medium-sized enterprise (defined in accordance with the EC Recommendation of 6 May 2003).

This means that the business must have:

- fewer than 250 employees; and
- either:
    (a) a balance sheet total of EUR43m or less;
    (b) turnover of EUR50m or less; or
    (c) both.

⚠ **Warning!**

Care must be taken because the test is similar to but different from that determining the filing requirements of companies.

(1) The number of employees may not equal 250.

(2) The tests based on financial results are alternatives – they may not be used instead of the headcount test.

(3) The financial tests are necessarily dependent on exchange rates.

(4) The test is applied using the results of the 'latest approved accounting period' – therefore, one does not have to predict the current year's figures.

(5) If a company breaches the limits for one year, it will automatically cease to be a small or medium-sized company until publication of a subsequent

year's results showing that the thresholds were not exceeded. In other words there is no let-out if a business temporarily exceeds the limits.

⚠ Warning!

The hallmarks are due to be revised with effect from a date late in 2010. The proposals as announced in the 2010 Budget include (in summary):

- a minor simplification of the confidentiality hallmarks;
- revisions to the hallmark concerning tax-based fees for services;
- removal of the off-market terms hallmark;
- extension of the losses hallmark so as to include losses for corporation tax purposes;
- reintroduction of a hallmark relating to employment-remuneration strategies;
- a new hallmark focusing on schemes that convert income into capital;
- a new hallmark focusing on offshore planning.

Law: SI 2006/1543 reg. 3, 4

General hallmarks

63.12.4 Confidentiality – when a promoter is involved

Confidentiality from other promoters

A scheme must be disclosed if:

- it involves a promoter;
- any element of the arrangements (including the way in which they are structured) gives rise to an expected tax advantage; and
- it might be reasonably be expected that a promoter would wish the way in which that element secures the tax advantage to be kept confidential from other promoters.

This expected confidentiality must:

- last from the date of the first transaction forming part of the arrangements; and
- continue to the due date for a return reporting the scheme.

Example 63.8

Richards Limited enters into an arrangement set up by its accountants on 12 December 2006 which was intended to give rise to a tax advantage on the same date. Richards Limited prepares its accounts to 31 December each year.

If the scheme is notifiable, Richards Limited would be required to make a return under s. 313 by 31 December 2007.

Therefore, any reasonable expectation for confidentiality lasting until 31 December 2007 would make the scheme notifiable.

> **Planning point**
>
> It might be possible to circumvent the confidentiality rule. Suppose the promoter made it an explicit condition that the confidentiality requirement lasts until, say, a week before the filing date of the return.
>
> Arguably, with such an explicit requirement, it could be said that it can no longer be 'reasonably ... expected that a promoter would wish the way in which that element secures the tax advantage to be kept confidential' for the entire period ending with the due date for a return reporting the scheme.

Confidentiality from HMRC

A scheme must also be disclosed if:

- it involves a promoter;
- any element of the arrangements (including the way in which they are structured) gives rise to an expected tax advantage;
- it might be reasonably be expected that a promoter would wish the way in which that element secures the tax advantage to be kept confidential from HMRC; and
- a reason for doing so would be to facilitate repeated or continued use of the same or substantially the same element.

In such a case, this expected confidentiality must exist at some time between:

- the date of the first transaction forming part of the arrangements; and
- the due date for a return reporting the scheme.

Confidentiality from HMRC – where promoter protected by legal professional privilege

A different test applies in cases where the promoter is protected by legal professional privilege. In that case, the user of the arrangement must actually want the tax-advantage element to be kept confidential from HMRC.

It is possible that this test is self-defeating (because it contradicts the rule that the legal professional privilege exemption is disapplied – see **59.10**) but it is probable that the Courts will interpret it purposively.

Law: SI 2006/1543 reg. 6

63.12.5 Confidentiality – when no promoter is involved

A scheme must be disclosed if:

- it does not involve a promoter;
- the intended user of the arrangements is a large business;
- any element of the arrangements (including the way in which they are structured) gives rise to an expected tax advantage;
- the user of the arrangement must actually want the tax-advantage element to be kept confidential from HMRC; and

- a reason for doing so would be to facilitate repeated or continued use of the same or substantially the same element.

In such a case, this expected confidentiality must exist at some time between:

- the date of the first transaction forming part of the arrangements; and
- the due date for a return reporting the scheme.

Law: SI 2006/1543 reg. 7

63.12.6 Premium fees

A scheme must be disclosed if it is such that a premium fee might reasonably be expected by a promoter (or a person connected with the promoter).

> ⚠ **Warning!**
>
> It does not matter whether or not the promoter of the scheme itself is entitled to a premium fee. What is important is that the same arrangements or arrangements that are substantially similar *might* command a premium fee.
>
> Additionally, the expectation of a premium fee must be considered without regard to the disclosure requirements.

> ⚠ **Warning!**
>
> A scheme is notifiable even if there is no promoter involved – for example, it is developed in house. However, this exception applies only if the tax advantage will be obtained by an individual or a small or medium-sized business.

For these purposes, a 'premium fee' is one which is chargeable by virtue of the arrangements (including the way that they are structured) which is:

- to a significant extent attributable to the tax advantage; or
- to any extent contingent upon the obtaining of that tax advantage.

Law: SI 2006/1543 reg. 8

63.12.7 Off market terms

Schemes are notifiable if:

- the tax advantage expected to be obtained arises (more than incidentally) due to the inclusion of one or more financial products;
- a promoter or a person connected with the promoter becomes party to one or more of these financial products; and
- the price of the financial product (or products) differs significantly from that which might reasonably be expected to apply in the open market if compared

with a product that is (or products that are) the same as (or substantially similar to) the product or products in question.

> **Planning point**
>
> Arguably, this third bullet can never be truly satisfied because it is highly unlikely that any two products which are substantially similar will have significantly different prices in the open market.
>
> However, it is probable that a Court will strive to interpret this provision purposefully.

For these purposes, a 'financial product' is:

- a loan;
- a derivative contract which either:

    (a) is within the scope of FA 2002, Sch. 26;

    (b) would be within the scope of FA 2002, Sch. 26 but for FA 2002, Sch. 26, para. 4; (It should be noted that para. 4 excludes contracts whose underlying subject matter is land, chattels (other than commodities), intangible fixed assets, shares, rights under a unit trust scheme and assets representing loan relationships.); or

    (c) would be within either of the above two headings if it were the contract of a company.

- an agreement for the sale and repurchase of securities as described by ICTA 1988, s. 730A(1)(a) to (c) (ICTA 1988, s. 730A(1)(a) to (c) considers the sale and repurchase of securities at different prices where the original owner re-acquires the securities by exercising an option.);
- a stock lending agreement within the meaning of Taxation of Chargeable Gains Act 1992 (TCGA 1992), s. 263B(1); (TCGA 1992, s. 263B deals with transfers of securities (otherwise than by sale) where there is a requirement imposed on the transferee to transfer the securities back to the transferor (also otherwise than by sale).)
- a share; or
- another contract which:

    (a) either alone or in combination with one or more other contracts (which may be of the type listed above) has substantially the effect of a loan (or advance or deposit of money); and

    (b) consequently falls to be accounted as a loan, deposit or other financial obligation (under GAAP) or would do so if the entity were subject to the Companies Act 1985. However, finance leases are excluded.

However, a scheme is not notifiable if the only financial product involved is one which satisfies the conditions for an ISA.

Law: SI 2006/1543 reg. 9

63.12.8 Standardised tax products

This description is designed to catch heavily marketed schemes which are rolled out to a large number of taxpayers. However, as can be seen, its scope is far wider.

This description considers schemes by applying three overlapping tests. First, it considers whether an arrangement is a 'product'. Then it considers whether an arrangement is a 'tax product'. Finally, it considers whether an arrangement is standardised.

Arrangements are a 'product' if:

- they have standardised or substantially standardised documentation:
    (a) where the purpose of the documentation is to enable the implementation of the arrangements by the client; and
    (b) the form of the documentation is determined by the promoter and not tailored (at least materially) to reflect the client's circumstances.
- a client must enter into a specific transaction or series of transactions; and
- the transaction (or series) is standardised or substantially standardised in form.

Arrangements are a tax product if an informed observer (who has studied the arrangements) would reasonably conclude that *main* purpose of the arrangements would be to enable a client to obtain a tax advantage.

Arrangements are standardised if a promoter makes them available for implementation by three or more people in total.

> ⚠ **Warning!**
>
> It should be noted that most basic tax mitigation exercises could fall under this heading provided that they are offered to three or more clients.

Law: SI 2006/1543 reg. 10

Exceptions

Certain arrangements are however specifically excepted from being notifiable as standardised tax products. These are:

- arrangements involving solely of one or more leases of plant or machinery (these are dealt with under a separate description below);
- enterprise investment schemes;
- arrangements using venture capital trusts;

- arrangements qualifying under the corporate venture scheme;
- arrangements qualifying for community investment tax relief;
- ISAs;
- approved SIPs;
- approved share option schemes;
- approved company share option plan schemes;
- the grant of one or more qualifying EMI options (plus reasonably necessary associated steps);
- registered pension schemes, relevant non-UK pension schemes or exempt overseas pension schemes; or
- schemes for the periodical payment of personal injury damages (to which ITTOIA 2005, s. 731 applies).

Law: SI 2006/1543 reg. 11

Transitional rule

A scheme is also not notifiable if it was the same or substantially the same as a scheme first made available for implementation before 1 August 2006.

> **Planning point**
>
> In the original draft of the 2006 regulations, it was stated that this transitional rule applied only if the previous implementation was *by the same promoter*. This would have put new practitioners at a slight disadvantage and it this additional requirement was deleted when the final version of the regulations was published.

Specific types of scheme

63.12.9 Introduction

In addition to the five general hallmarks, three specific types of scheme have been prescribed as notifiable.

63.12.10 Loss creation schemes

The first of these considers schemes that create losses. However, the promoter must expect more than one individual to implement the same or substantially the same arrangement.

> **Planning point**
>
> Schemes that generate losses for companies or trusts are not covered by this notification requirement.

There is an objective test that the main benefit expected to accrue to some or all of the individuals who participate in the arrangements is that losses will arise which would be used by the individuals to offset against their income or capital gains.

> ⚠ **Warning!**
>
> It is standard practice for taxpayers who have realised substantial gains to consider ways of mitigating the resulting tax liability. A common approach is for assets standing at a loss to be disposed of. In many cases the asset would have been disposed of eventually, but the existence of taxable gains has acted as a catalyst.
>
> This rather straightforward form of tax planning however is notifiable under this regulation provided that it is expected to be used by more than one individual.

Law: SI 2006/1543 reg. 12

63.12.11 Leasing arrangements

The second specific type of scheme considers schemes involving the lease of plant or machinery. However, so as to limit its scope to larger businesses, there must be either:

- a single item of leased plant or machinery worth at least £10m; or
- a total value of leased plant or machinery under the arrangements of at least £25m.

> **Planning point**
>
> Some equipment can often be considered as made up of separate identifiable components. Where these components are each subject to a separate lease, it can be possible for the £10m threshold to be overcome – provided, of course, that no single component is worth £10m or more.

In addition, there must be either a promoter in relation to the scheme or the tax advantage must be intended to be obtained by a large business (which is not an individual).

Furthermore, there must be an element of 'unacceptability' in the eyes of HMRC. These are considered as the additional conditions in reg. 15. These conditions (only one of which must be met) are:

- one or more of the leases must involve at least one party who is entitled to a plant and machinery allowance in respect of the expenditure and at least one party (other than a guarantor) outside the charge to corporation tax;
- the arrangements include provision that removes from the lessor the risk of sustaining a loss if payments due under the lease are not made and these arrangements are in the form of money or a money debt (as defined in ITEPA 2003, s. 702(6)); and
- the arrangements include or consist of a sale and finance leaseback (within the meaning of CAA 2001, s. 221) or a lease and finance lease back (within the meaning of CAA 2001, s. 228F(5)) subject to the exceptions below.

Law: SI 2006/1543 reg. 13–17

Relaxation for some sale or lease and finance leaseback arrangements

A scheme which includes a sale and finance leaseback or a lease and finance leaseback is not notifiable under this rule if the plant or machinery is (or the promoter expects it to become) a fixture leased with the relevant land (as defined in the fixtures legislation (see CAA 2001, s. 173(2)).

⚠ Warning!

However, this exception does not apply (and so the scheme will be notifiable again) if the plant or machinery is used for storage or production. Storage or production is widely defined.

⚠ Warning!

This exception similarly does not apply (and so the scheme will be notifiable again) if the arrangements are designed in such a way that:

- the qualifying expenditure on the fixture amounts to *more than* half of the aggregate value of the assets subject to the lease; and
- the rent payable under the lease is directly or indirectly dependent on the availability of plant and machinery allowances in respect of any plant or machinery comprised in the lease.

In addition, sale and finance leaseback arrangements (as opposed to lease and finance leasebacks) are not notifiable if:

- the assets are or will be unused and not second hand when they are acquired or created; and
- the time between the acquisition or creation of the asset and the sale will be four months or less.

63.12.12 Obtaining additional annual investment allowance

FA 2008 has introduced a measure that permits businesses to write off the first £50,000 expenditure on plant and machinery in any year. It was suggested that the list of specific hallmarks will be increased so as to prevent abuse of the rules. However, as yet, none has been published.

63.12.13 Pension charge forestalling

FA 2009 introduced measures that would see the top rate of income tax rise to 50 per cent from 6 April 2010 and a reduction of the value of personal allowances from 6 April 2011. The latter measure would mean that many taxpayers would have a marginal tax rate of 60 per cent (before National Insurance Contributions). So as to ensure that these tax rises are not circumvented by taxpayers increasing their own pension provision, FA 2009 introduced measures that would limit the tax relief (effectively by introducing a new tax charge) on increased contributions.

From 23 April 2009, a third hallmark was introduced requiring the notification of schemes that would involve a person to accrue pension scheme benefits, where the main benefit of those arrangements is that either:

- the person would not be subject to the special annual allowance charge; or
- the person incurs the special annual allowance charge at an amount lower than would otherwise be the case.

Law: SI 2006/1543 reg. 18

In cases where the relevant date was before 1 September, notification of the scheme was required by 31 October 2009.

Law: SI 2009/2033 reg. 3

Rules applying since 1 May 2007 – National Insurance Contributions

63.12.14 NICs schemes

From 1 May 2007, disclosure is required of any scheme or proposal that would create an NICs advantage. The NICs rules follow the first five hallmarks specified above.

Law: SI 2007/785

64 Enterprise Investment Scheme

64.1 Introduction and overview

64.1.1 Relief available under the EIS scheme

The enterprise investment scheme (EIS) is intended to encourage new equity investment in trading companies by providing tax incentives to investors.

The scheme offers three separate forms of tax relief for investors, all with overlapping features:

- income tax relief;
- a chance to defer capital gains tax liabilities; and
- a chance to make capital gains on the EIS shares themselves free of any tax liability.

> **Planning point**
>
> This combination of tax-saving opportunities makes the relief an attractive option for the right investor, though the high-risk nature of EIS investments makes them unsuitable for many individuals.

> ⚠ **Warning!**
>
> The EIS rules are complex, especially in the way that the different types of relief are presented separately but with interlocking definitions. This chapter provides an outline of many of the key issues to consider. It is not, however, a comprehensive and definitive guide to all aspects of the relief.

64.1.2 Background and history of the relief

EIS replaced the business expansion scheme, but with several key differences.

> **Planning point**
>
> EIS extends to non-resident companies and non-resident individuals. Currently, any company which carries on a qualifying activity wholly or mainly in the UK can issue shares under the EIS; there is no requirement for the company to be incorporated here. Additionally, any investor with a UK tax liability qualifies for EIS relief regardless of whether he is UK-resident.
>
> The government announced in the June 2010 emergency budget that the Finance Bill planned for autumn 2010 will contain certain amendments to the venture capital schemes. For shares issued on or after the commencement date of the

Enterprise Investment Scheme

new legislation, the requirement that a company must carry on a qualifying activity wholly or mainly in the UK will be amended so that the company issuing the shares will simply be required to have a 'permanent establishment' in the UK.

⚠ Warning!

The government announced in the June 2010 emergency budget that the Finance Bill planned for autumn 2010 will contain certain amendments to the venture capital schemes. Legislation will be included, from a date to be set, to the effect that shares in a company will be excluded from qualifying for EIS if it is reasonable to assume that the company would be treated as an 'enterprise in difficulty' for the purposes of the European Commission's Rescue and Restructuring guidelines.

Following the introduction of the EIS, criticisms were levelled against schemes where the degree of risk was not considered sufficiently high. In particular, those projects which provided a substantially guaranteed return, or which carried on property-based trades, were the targets of a review of the scheme announced in the July 1997 Budget. Legislation followed in the Finance Act 1998 which had the effect of targeting relief more effectively towards the provision of venture capital for trading companies.

Planning point

An investor who becomes a paid director may qualify for relief provided, broadly, that he is not 'connected with' the company or its trade prior to his first acquisition of eligible shares. This is to attract investment from 'business angels' (individuals with business experience and funds to invest) who provide management skills in addition to new capital.

Additionally, relief may be available if an issuing company acquires a company, or the trade of a company, previously controlled by a group of persons which included the director concerned.

Other guidance: www.hmrc.gov.uk/eis

64.1.3 Recent changes

Several important pieces of recent legislation have introduced changes to the EIS rules. The changes are summarised in the following paragraphs.

Income Tax Act 2007

The enactment of ITA 2007 was part of the tax law rewrite process. The intention was not to change the underlying way in which the rules operate but rather the terminology in which those rules are expressed.

Introduction and Overview 64.1.3

The main effects on EIS have been twofold. First, the statutory references that previously applied are in principle replaced with new provisions in ITA 2007. However, the new rules apply only for shares issued from 6 April 2007. The earlier rules, found in ICTA 1988, therefore continue to apply for EIS shares issued before that date. In the *Law* lines at the end of numbered paragraphs of this chapter, both references have therefore been shown.

Finance Act 2007

This Act, by contrast, introduced some substantive changes, including the following:

- To raise money under the EIS scheme, a company must have fewer than the equivalent of 50 full-time employees at the time the relevant shares are issued (ITA 2007, s. 186A).
- The total amount of relevant investments made in the issuing company in the year ending with the date the relevant shares are issued must not exceed £2m (ITA 2007, s. 173A).
- The rules relating to the transfer of trades involving the exploitation of relevant intangible assets were broadly aligned, from 6 April 2007, with those relating to other qualifying trades (ICTA 1988, s. 297).
- Groups of companies have had greater flexibility since 6 April 2007 as to which group company carries on the qualifying trade: that trade may be carried on by the EIS company itself, its direct 90 per cent subsidiary or a 100 per cent subsidiary of that subsidiary. The trade may also be carried on by a 90 per cent subsidiary of the EIS company's direct 100 per cent subsidiary (ITA 2007, s. 190).
- The period in which a fund manager has to invest 90 per cent of funds raised by an EIS approved investment fund was extended (for funds closed from 7 October 2006) from 6 months to 12 months from the date that the fund closes (ITA 2007, s. 251(1)(c)).

Finance Act 2008

This Act introduced the following changes:

- As a result of the controversial changes made from April 2008 to personal allowances, and the abolition of the starting rate of tax, the concept of the 20 per cent 'EIS rate' is introduced to replace the former use of the term 'savings rate'.
- Changes to ensure that the new 'entrepreneurs' relief' is available in appropriate circumstances in relation to EIS shares.
- An increase to £500,000 in the maximum amount for which an individual can claim tax relief for EIS investments in the year. This increase applies from 6 April 2008.
- The list of excluded activities for EIS purposes is expanded to include shipbuilding, coal extraction and production, and steel production.
- The time limit for making an assessment to withdraw or reduce EIS relief is

subject to a technical amendment but remains broadly at six years from the end of the relevant tax year in most circumstances.

Finance Act 2009

The time limit for employing invested money (i.e. broadly 80 per cent within 12 months of the share issue or commencement of trading (if later), and the balance within a further 12 months), has been relaxed, so that all money raised by the issue of shares must be wholly employed in a qualifying activity within two years of the EIS share issue, or (if later) within two years of the qualifying activity commencing.

The link to other shares of the same class issued at the same time as qualifying shares has also been removed, so there is now no restriction on the use of money raised by non-EIS shares. The provisions preventing the capital gains tax share-for-share exchange rules from applying when all deferral relief has been recovered has also been removed.

Finally, the carry-back period for EIS relief has been extended, and investors may carry back the full amount subscribed for shares (subject to the EIS qualifying limit), with effect from the tax year 2009–10.

Proposed changes to legislation with effect from 6 April 2010

The government announced in the June 2010 emergency budget that the Finance Bill planned for autumn 2010 will contain certain amendments to the venture capital schemes. For shares issued on or after the commencement date of the new legislation, the requirement that a company must carry on a qualifying activity wholly or mainly in the UK will be amended so that the company issuing the shares will simply be required to have a 'permanent establishment' in the UK.

The government also announced in the June 2010 emergency budget that the Finance Bill planned for autumn 2010 will contain legislation, operative from a date to be set, to the effect that shares in a company will be excluded from qualifying for EIS if it is reasonable to assume that the company would be treated as an 'enterprise in difficulty' for the purposes of the European Commission's Rescue and Restructuring guidelines.

64.1.4 Periods A, B and C

The revised rules as contained in ITA 2007 use the concept of Periods A, B and C to replace some of the more descriptive terminology of the predecessor legislation.

Period A begins with the date on which the company is incorporated or (if later) the date two years before the date on which the shares were issued, and ends immediately before the 'termination date' relating to the shares.

Period B begins with the date on which the shares were issued, and ends immediately before the 'termination date' relating to the shares.

Period C begins 12 months before the shares are issued, and ends immediately before the 'termination date' relating to the shares.

Termination date

The termination date relating to the shares normally means the third anniversary of the issue date. However, if the money raised was used for a qualifying business activity within ITA 2007, s. 179(2) (broadly any qualifying activity except one of research and development), and if neither the issuing company nor any of its qualifying 90 per cent subsidiaries had begun to carry on the trade in question on the issue date, then the termination date is the third anniversary of the date on which the company or subsidiary begins to carry on that trade.

Law: ITA 2007, s. 159, 256

64.2 Income tax relief

64.2.1 Overview of income tax relief

Outline of relief

> **Planning point**
>
> An investor obtains income tax relief for EIS investments at the EIS rate (a new concept from April 2008: formerly the savings rate). The EIS rate is set at 20 per cent and relief (which must be claimed) is given by way of an income tax reduction.

Thus, for example, in 2009–10, a taxpayer obtains income tax relief for EIS investments by claiming to reduce his income tax liability by 20 per cent of any amounts subscribed for qualifying shares. This reduction in a taxpayer's income tax liability takes place before other personal reliefs.

> ⚠ **Warning!**
>
> The income tax reduction is limited to the lower of:
> - 20 per cent of the eligible subscription; and
> - the amount which reduces the investor's tax liability to nil.

> **Example 64.1**
>
> Geoff has taxable income (after personal allowances) of £40,000 in 2008–09. In November 2008, he invests £35,000 in shares qualifying for EIS relief. Geoff's income tax liability is:
>
> | | |
> |---|---:|
> | £34,800 @ 20% | £6,960 |
> | £5,200 @ 40% | £2,080 |
> | £40,000 | £9,040 |
> | Less: tax relief for EIS subscription (£35,000 @ 20%) | (£7,000) |
> | Income tax liability | £2,040 |

> **Example 64.2**
>
> Assume that in the previous example Geoff invests £200,000 in EIS shares. The maximum reduction from his income tax liability in respect of the EIS investment is now the lower of:
>
> - 20 per cent of the amount of the subscription: £40,000 (£200,000 at 20%); and
> - the amount that reduces his tax liability to £Nil – i.e. £9,040.
>
> The relief for the year is thus £9,040.
>
> The excess of £30,960 (£40,000–£9,040) remains unrelieved.

Law: ITA 2007, s. 158

64.2.2 Claiming income tax relief

To obtain EIS relief, an investor must submit a claim. In general, an investor cannot make a claim unless and until a qualifying trade has been carried on for four months. However, a claim can be made if the company concerned is wound up, or dissolved without winding up before the end of the four-month period. The dissolution or winding up must take place for bona fide commercial reasons and not as part of a scheme or arrangement in which one of the main purposes is to avoid tax.

An investor can make a claim in respect of shares issued to raise money for either research and development or oil exploration as soon as that activity has been carried on for four months.

A company must furnish the Revenue officer with a statement to the effect that all conditions for relief are satisfied, excepting only those relating to the claimant. This must be done within two years of the end of the tax year in which the shares were issued or, if later, within two years of the end of the tax year in which the above four-month period ended. For this purpose, any part of a share issue carried back for relief in the previous year is not deemed to have been issued in the previous year.

Once the Revenue officer has the above statement, he will authorise the company to issue a certificate certifying that the conditions for relief, so far as applying to the company and the trade, are satisfied in relation to those shares. A claim for relief can only be made if the claimant has received such a certificate from the company.

An investor must claim EIS relief no later than the fifth anniversary of the 31 January following the tax year in which the company issued the shares.

Interest on repayments of tax which arise as a result of an EIS claim are dealt with under the normal rules applicable for all self assessment claims.

Law: ITA 2007, s. 202,205

64.2.3 Conditions for relief

General conditions

For an individual to qualify for relief, a number of requirements must be satisfied, some relating to the individual's connection with the company and some to the subscription itself.

Relief is only available where an individual subscribes for shares in a qualifying company wholly in cash. The shares ('the relevant shares') must be issued in order to raise money for a qualifying business (either a qualifying trade, research and development or oil exploration).

To qualify for relief under the scheme, minimum and maximum subscription requirements must be satisfied.

Law: ITA 2007, s. 157

Minimum and maximum subscription

Relief is only available if an individual subscribes an amount exceeding £500 in the tax year for shares in the company concerned, including amounts carried back to the previous year (see below).

> **Planning point**
>
> In practice, many individuals tend to invest through the medium of an approved investment fund and, where this is the case, the minimum level of £500 does not apply.

Enterprise Investment Scheme

The maximum allowable subscription is £500,000 per year from 6 April 2008 (£400,000 prior to this date).

It is not possible to carry forward unused relief, but there is a carry-back facility.

Carry back of relief

> **Planning point**
>
> Prior to 2009–10 and subject to the overall annual limit of £500,000 (from 6 April 2008; £400,000 prior to then), an individual could claim relief in one tax year (say, 2008–09) for one-half of any amount invested in qualifying shares before 6 October in the following year (i.e. before 6 October 2009). The maximum amount that an investor could request to carry back in this way was £50,000. Finance Act 2009 extended the carry-back period so that for 2009–10 onwards, investors may carry back the full amount subscribed for shares (subject to the EIS qualifying limit). The amount of the subscription carried back is treated as though it related to a share issue made in the previous tax year.

Law: ITA 2007, s. 157ff; FA 2009, Sch. 55

Attribution of relief to shares

If, in any tax year, an individual claims EIS relief in respect of two share issues, the total relief obtained is attributable to each share issue in proportion to the amounts subscribed.

If there is subsequently an issue of 'corresponding bonus shares' (i.e. bonus shares which are issued in respect of the shares in the original issue and carry the same rights, and are of the same class as the shares in the original issue), the total EIS relief obtained on the original issue is apportioned between the original holding and the new shares. The bonus shares are treated as though they were acquired at the time of the original issue.

Relief is not apportioned to bonus issues of shares or securities which would not have been eligible for EIS relief themselves. Any reduction of relief is attributed to any bonus shares issued in respect of the original shares, provided they are of the same class and carry the same rights.

Law: ITA 2007, s. 201

64.2.4 Individuals qualifying for relief

Individuals, trustees, investment funds

An individual who subscribes on his own behalf for eligible shares, and who satisfies the conditions detailed below, qualifies for EIS relief. It is not necessary for the individual to be resident in the UK.

Trustees can make a subscription on behalf of two or more individuals if they hold the shares issued on trust for the individuals absolutely. Although the trustees subscribe for the shares, the individuals concerned own the shares beneficially and are treated as having subscribed for the shares as individuals. The total amount subscribed is divided by the number of beneficiaries and allocated to the individuals concerned accordingly.

Shares may also be subscribed via a nominee or approved investment fund. The actions of the nominee are treated as those of the individual on whose behalf the nominee is acting. Where the subscription for EIS shares is made via an approved investment fund, the minimum £500 subscription requirement does not apply. Relief is only available at the time when the fund subscribed for eligible shares, although, in certain circumstances, this may be advanced to the date when the fund is able to make subscriptions. Broadly, the fund managers must, within 12 months of the date after which the fund can accept no more investments, have subscribed for eligible shares representing not less than 90 per cent of the individual's investment in the fund.

Law: ITA 2007, s. 250ff

Connected persons: directors

> ⚠ **Warning!**
>
> Subject to one important exception (see below), an investor does not qualify for EIS relief if he is 'connected with' the issuing company at any time during the period that starts from two years before the share issue and ends with the 'termination date relating to the shares' (see **64.1.4**).

Under the EIS scheme an individual is connected with a company if he, or an associate of his:

- is an employee of, or of a partner of, the company or any subsidiary;
- is a partner of the company or any subsidiary;
- is a 'paid' director of (see below), or of a company that is a partner of, the company or any subsidiary; or
- owns or can acquire more than 30 per cent of the company or any subsidiary.

Enterprise Investment Scheme

The term 'subsidiary' includes all companies that are 51 per cent subsidiaries at any time in Period A (see **64.1.4**).

Law: ITA 2007, s. 159, 163ff, 256

Meaning of 'paid director'

An individual is connected with the company as a paid director only if he (or an associate, or a partnership of which he or an associate is a member) receives, or is entitled to receive, any payment during the period beginning two years prior to the share issue and ending three years after the issue.

Direct and indirect payments made by the issuing company, or any 'related person', are payments for this purpose. A 'related person' is any company of which the individual, or an associate, is a director and which is either a 51 per cent subsidiary of the issuing company at some time during the individual relevant period (see above), or a partner of the issuing company or of any such subsidiary. A person connected with any of these companies or with the issuing company is also a related person.

However, certain payments must be disregarded when deciding whether a director is paid, whether as director or as employee, as follows:

- payment or reimbursement of travel or other expenses incurred wholly, exclusively and necessarily in the performance of the director's duties;
- a reasonable commercial rate of interest on money lent to the issuing company or a related person;
- dividends or other distributions which do not exceed a normal return on the investment;
- payment for the supply of goods, which does not exceed their market value;
- a reasonable commercial rent paid in respect of a property occupied by the issuing company or a related person; and
- reasonable and necessary remuneration for services rendered to the issuing company or a related person in the course of the individual's trade or profession, provided the remuneration is taken into account in computing for tax purposes the profits of that trade or profession (or would be if it fell within a Case I or II basis period). This does not extend to secretarial or managerial services, or to services of a kind provided by the person to whom they were rendered.

Law: ITA 2007, s. 167ff

Circumstances in which a paid director may qualify for EIS relief

An individual connected with a company only because either he, or an associate, is a 'paid' director may obtain EIS relief in one important circumstance. Relief is available provided that the subscriber was not at any time prior to the share issue, either connected with the company, or an employee of any person who carried on the trade subsequently carried on by the issuing company.

> **Planning point**
>
> These rules are intended to allow a 'business angel' to take an active part in the management of a company as a paid director without losing entitlement to relief. The director concerned must not receive remuneration in excess of an amount that is reasonable for the services performed.

> ⚠ **Warning!**
>
> To obtain relief, the director must never have been involved in carrying on any part of the issuing company's, or a subsidiary's, trade. Such involvement may have been as a sole trader, partner, director or employee. If this condition is fulfilled in respect of one share issue, relief is available on all issues made within the next three years.

Law: ITA 2007, s. 169

Connected persons: persons interested in capital, etc. of company

An individual owns more than 30 per cent of a company if he directly or indirectly possesses, or is entitled to acquire, more than 30 per cent of:

- the ordinary issued share capital;
- the aggregate of the loan capital and issued share capital;
- the voting power of the company; or
- the assets available for distribution to equity holders in a winding up, or in any other circumstances.

The loan capital referred to above does not include a normal business bank overdraft but it does include a debt incurred by the company in respect of any of the following:

- money borrowed or capital assets acquired;
- a right to receive income created in its favour; and
- consideration whose value to the company at the time the debt was incurred was substantially less than the aggregate of the debt and any premium on it.

An individual is entitled to acquire anything that he is, or will be, entitled to acquire at a future date. The rights and powers of the individual's associates are attributed to him for this purpose.

To identify equity holders and the percentage of assets to which they are entitled, CTA 2010, s. 158, 166 apply. References in s. 166 to the first company are taken to be references to the equity holder, and references to a winding up are taken to include any other circumstances where the company's assets are available for distribution to equity holders.

An individual is not connected with a company by reason of holding (or an associate holding) subscriber shares when:

- the company has no shares in issue other than subscriber shares; and
- the company has not begun carry on business, or to make any preparations to carry on business.

This addresses the situation where holders of subscriber shares on formation of the company may temporarily fall foul of the 30 per cent ownership test before the holding is diluted by issue of further shares.

Law: CTA 2010, s. 158, 166; ITA 2007, s. 170

Loan-linked investments

An investor is unable to obtain EIS relief in respect of shares if, at any time during the relevant period he, or an associate of his, takes out a loan which is linked to the shares. A linked loan is one that would not have been made, or would not have been made on the same terms, if the individual had not subscribed for the shares.

> ⚠ **Warning!**
>
> The purpose of this rule is to restrict EIS relief to those investors who genuinely lay out capital for at least three years. Relief is denied where the individual, or an associate of his, receives a loan which would not have been made, or would not have been made on the same terms, had the investor not subscribed, or planned to subscribe, for the shares.

When applying this rule in practice, HMRC are primarily concerned with the motive of the lender in making the loan, rather than the reasons why the borrower applied for it. The crucial test is whether the lender would have made the loan on the same terms had the eligible shares not been involved. In determining whether this is the case, HMRC will have regard to:

- the qualifying conditions which the borrower must satisfy;
- whether any incentives or benefits were offered to the borrower;
- the time allowed for repayment;
- the timing of interest payments;
- the amount of repayment and interest charged; and
- the nature of the security involved.

For example, a loan would be linked with the investment if it was made on a specified security which included eligible shares for which the borrower had subscribed or was intending to subscribe. By contrast, HMRC will not seek to deny relief where the investor, for example, obtains a bank loan for the purpose of buying eligible shares if that loan would have been made on similar terms to another borrower intending to use it for a different purpose.

The HMRC approach is set out more fully in Statement of Practice SP 6/98.

Law: ITA 2007, s. 164

Other guidance: Statement of Practice SP 6/98

Pre-arranged exits from EIS

> ⚠ **Warning!**
>
> Relief is denied where, at the time of an investment, certain exit arrangements are in place which guarantee the investor a way of disposing of the shares at the end of the qualifying period, effectively turning the whole investment into a low-risk venture.

Broadly, relief will be denied where the terms of the issue include, or there already exist at the time of issue, arrangements for repurchasing or exchanging the shares, ceasing the trade, disposing of assets of the company or otherwise providing some form of protection or guarantee for the investor. More specifically, an individual is not eligible for relief on shares if the terms of the issue include, or there already exist at the time of issue, arrangements facilitating:

- the later repurchase, exchange or other disposal of the shares, or of other shares in or securities of the same company;
- the cessation of any trade carried on, or to be carried on, by the company or a person connected with the company;
- the disposal of, or of a substantial amount of, the assets of the company or of a person connected with the company; and
- partial or complete protection for investors, by way of insurance, indemnity, guarantee or otherwise, against what would otherwise be the risks of investing in the company's shares.

Relief is still available for arrangements of the following kind, however:

- arrangements for an exchange of shares of the kind envisaged by ITA 2007, s. 145, where a company with EIS shares becomes a wholly-owned subsidiary of a new company in return for shares in the new company. In such cases, EIS relief is preserved and carried forward into the new shares;
- arrangements applicable only on the winding up of a company, unless the winding up is itself part of the arrangements, or is not for bona fide commercial reasons; and
- insurances, indemnities, guarantees, etc. which merely provide protection for

the company or any of its EIS-qualifying trading subsidiaries against the normal commercial risks associated with carrying on its business.

'Arrangements' are defined as including any scheme, agreement or understanding, whether or not legally enforceable.

> ⚠ **Warning!**
> Where tax relief is withdrawn because of the existence of such exit arrangements, interest runs from the date on which relief was granted, or – if relief was given effect by virtue of PAYE regulations – 5 April in that tax year.

Where relief is claimed, but an inspector has reason to believe that it may not be due because of the existence of exit arrangements, he may by serving at least 60 days' notice require the claimant, the company or any person connected with the company to provide him with information about any such arrangements.

Law: ITA 2007, s. 145, 177, 239(1)

64.2.5 Conditions to be satisfied by the company

Introduction

Before it issues shares qualifying for EIS relief, a company must satisfy a number of conditions. For a claim for relief to be allowed, a certificate must be issued by the company (in such form as HM Revenue & Customs (HMRC) may direct) stating that these conditions are satisfied in relation to the shares.

A specialised HMRC centre provides a centralised service for companies using EIS, VCT, CVS and EMI schemes. All enquiries about whether a small company meets the requirements of any of these schemes should be directed to:

Small Company Enterprise Centre
CRI
Ty Glas
Llanishen
Cardiff CF14 5ZG
Tel: 029 2032 7400
Fax: 029 2032 7398
Email: *enterprise.centre@ir.gsi.gov.uk*

The conditions applying to companies are detailed and complex and are touched on in the following pages.

Law: ITA 2007, s. 180

Other guidance: *www.hmrc.gov.uk/eis/part2/2-1.htm*

Requirements to be met at the beginning of Period B

The company must meet certain conditions relating to unquoted status at the beginning of Period B (see **64.1.4**).

The conditions relating to unquoted status are that:

- the EIS company is unquoted; and
- that no arrangements exist for it to either:
    (a) cease to be an unquoted company; or
    (b) for it to become a subsidiary of a company which is itself subject to arrangements that would lead to it ceasing to be unquoted.

'Arrangements' includes any scheme, agreement or understanding, whether or not legally enforceable.

A company is 'unquoted' if none of its shares, stocks, debenture or other securities are marketed to the general public. Where any of a company's shares, debentures, etc. are listed on a recognised stock exchange (including an HMRC designated, non-UK exchange) or dealt in outside the UK by a means designated by HMRC, they are deemed to be marketed to the general public.

Securities on the Alternative Investment Market (AIM) are treated as unquoted. The company will not lose its unquoted status if its shares are listed on an unrecognised exchange which then becomes recognised after the EIS shares are issued.

Law: ITA 2007, s. 159(3), 184, 257(1)

Other guidance: Revenue press release, 20 February 1995

Requirements to be met throughout the relevant period

Further key conditions to be met throughout Period B are as follows:

- the company must be either:
    (a) a company that exists only for the purpose of carrying on one or more qualifying trades (apart from purposes incapable of having any significant effect on the extent of its activities); or
    (b) the parent company of a trading group.
- the company must not normally be a subsidiary of another company, or otherwise be under the control of another company. An exception is made in certain circumstances where it becomes a wholly-owned subsidiary of a new holding company after the shares have been issued;
- any subsidiary of the company must be a 'qualifying subsidiary', and the company must not control any company which is not a qualifying subsidiary; and

Enterprise Investment Scheme

- the company must not have a 'property managing subsidiary' at any time during the company's relevant period unless it is a 'qualifying 90% subsidiary'.

For these purposes, a company is the parent company of a trading group if it has one or more subsidiaries, as long as non-qualifying activities (investment activities and non-qualifying trades) do not form a substantial part (interpreted to mean more than 20 per cent) of the business of the group taken as a whole.

Since 6 April 2007, groups of companies have had greater flexibility as to which group company carries on the qualifying trade: that trade may now be carried on by the EIS company itself, its direct 90 per cent subsidiary or a 100 per cent subsidiary of that subsidiary. The trade may also be carried on by a 90 per cent subsidiary of the EIS company's direct 100 per cent subsidiary.

Law: ITA 2007, s. 181, s. 190

Qualifying trades

A qualifying trade must be conducted on a commercial basis with a view to the realisation of profits throughout the period of three years following the share issue or, if later, following the commencement of the trade. The trade must not, at any time during that period, consist of one or more of the following activities if it forms, or they form together, a substantial part of the trade. The following list applies to shares issued from 6 April 2008:

- dealing in land, in commodities or futures or in shares, securities or other financial instruments;
- dealing in goods otherwise than in the course of an ordinary trade of wholesale or retail distribution;
- banking, insurance, money-lending, debt-factoring, hire-purchase financing or other financial activities;
- leasing (including letting ships on charter or other assets on hire) or receiving royalties or licence fees;
- providing legal or accountancy services;
- property development;
- farming or market gardening;
- holding, managing or occupying woodlands, any other forestry activities or timber production;
- shipbuilding;
- coal production (including the extraction of coal);
- steel production;
- operating or managing hotels or comparable establishments or managing property used as an hotel or comparable establishment;
- operating or managing nursing homes or residential care homes, or managing property used as a nursing home or residential care home; or
- providing services or facilities for any trade carried on by another person (other than a company of which the company providing the services or facilities is the

subsidiary) which consists to any substantial extent of activities within any of the bulleted points above and in which a controlling interest is held by a person who also has a controlling interest in the trade carried on by the company.

The list of excluded activities for EIS purposes is expanded to include shipbuilding, coal extraction and production, and steel production.

> **Planning point**
>
> The exclusions for hotels and comparable establishments, and nursing and residential care homes, do not apply unless the person carrying on the activity has an estate or interest in the hotel or home, or is in occupation of it.

The term 'property development' is defined as the development of land by a company which has, or has at any time had, an interest in the land, with the sole or main object of realising a gain from the disposal of an interest in the land when it is developed. An 'interest in land', for these purposes, is widely defined and would include, for example, an option to purchase land conditional on the granting of planning permission, or the interest of the purchaser under a contract for a sub-sale. An interest in land does not include the interest of a secured creditor such as a mortgagee.

The restrictions relating to coal, steel and shipbuilding apply from 6 April 2008, but with no effect in relation to shares issued before that date.

Law: ITA 2007, s. 181, 189, 192ff

Other guidance: Revenue Interpretation in *Tax Bulletin*, Issue 54, August 2001

Restriction on the amount of capital raised under the EIS

The total amount of relevant investments made in the issuing company in the year ending with the date the relevant shares are issued is restricted to £2m.

In addition to the restriction on the amount raised, a further rule is that the issuing company's relevant assets must not exceed £7m immediately before the issue of the eligible shares, or £8m immediately afterwards.

'Relevant assets' are the gross assets of the company. Where the company has subsidiaries, the test is applied to the sum of the gross assets of the group. The value of rights against another member of the group, or of shares or securities of another member, are ignored. For these purposes, the group comprises the issuing company and its qualifying subsidiaries.

Law: ITA 2007, s. 173A, s. 186

Other guidance: www.hmrc.gov.uk/eis/chapter2/eis-chapter2_2.htm

Restriction on the number of employees

If the issuing company is a single company, there must be no more than 50 full-time employees at the time the relevant shares are issued. Where there are part-time employees then a just and reasonable proportion of their time is taken into account for this purpose.

Where the company issuing the EIS shares is a parent company then the number of its own employees and those of any qualifying subsidiaries must be added together and the total must not exceed 50.

Directors are included but students on vocational training are excluded. Employees are not counted whilst they are on maternity or paternity leave.

Law: ITA 2007, s. 186A

Shares

A further condition of relief is that the relevant shares must comply with the following conditions throughout Period B (see **64.1.4**):

- they must be new ordinary shares which, for the three years following the issue, must not carry preferential rights to dividends or assets or any present or future right to redemption. These requirements mean that preference shares, debentures and loan stock cannot qualify for relief, but deferred shares may; and
- they must be subscribed for (and issued) for bona fide commercial reasons and not as part of a scheme or arrangement one of the main purposes of which is to avoid tax.

Law: ITA 2007, s. 173

Requirements as to use of money raised

Using the money raised: time limit

Prior to 22 April 2009, the legislation specified that eighty per cent of the money raised from an EIS share issue must be used within 12 months of the share issue (or within 12 months of the commencement of trading if later). The remaining 20 per cent of the monies raised had to be used within the later of 24 months of the share issue or the commencement of trading. However, Finance Act 2009 relaxed this time limit, so that all money raised by the issue of shares must be wholly employed in a qualifying activity within two years of the EIS share issue, or (if later) within two years of the qualifying activity commencing. The use to which the monies raised must be put, within the specified time limit, is a 'qualifying business activity'.

These conditions are not treated as failed if some of the funds are applied for a non-qualifying purpose provided the amount so used is 'not significant'. No guidance is given regarding the meaning of 'not significant', but in other contexts a proportion may be regarded as 'significant' once it exceeds five per cent. In the absence of detailed guidance, this level could probably be argued as being the measure of a significant amount.

In *Forthright (Wales) Ltd v HMIT*, the company was formed to take over an existing business (FMS) which provided management services to an accountancy firm. The moneys obtained on the issue of shares (nearly £300,000) were used to settle liabilities taken over from FMS and to pay dividends to its shareholders, some of whom were employees of the company who had agreed to be remunerated by way of dividend. It was held that the payments of FMS's liabilities and dividends to investors (as opposed to employees) using money raised by the share issue did not employ the money wholly for the purposes of the (otherwise) qualifying trade. The dividends paid to employees who had agreed to be paid through dividends rather than wages were found to be made for the purposes of the trade. The payments of the former trader's liabilities and significant dividends (30 per cent of the total) to non-employee investors were not made for the purposes of the company's trade and so the claim for EIS relief failed (at the commissioners and High Court).

Law: FA 2009, Sch. 55; ICTA 1988, s. 289; ITA 2007, s. 175

Other guidance: Forthright (Wales) Ltd v Davies (HMIT) [2004] BTC 298

Qualifying business activity

A 'qualifying business activity' is:

1. An existing qualifying trade carried on by either the issuing company or any qualifying subsidiary. At any time during the three years following the share issue when this trade is carried on, it must be carried on 'wholly or mainly in the United Kingdom' (see below).

2. A qualifying trade that the issuing company, or any qualifying subsidiary, is preparing to carry on. At any time in the three years following the commencement of the trade when this trade is carried on, it must be carried on wholly or mainly in the UK. The trade must commence within two years of the issue.

3. Research and development intended to result in the derivation of a qualifying trade that will be carried on by the company or any qualifying subsidiary. One of these companies must either already be carrying on the research and development on the date of the share issue, or it must start to do so immediately thereafter. At any time in the three years following the share issue when the research and development or the qualifying trade derived from it is carried on, it must be carried on wholly or mainly in the UK.

Enterprise Investment Scheme

HMRC guidance on what is understood by 'wholly or mainly in the United Kingdom' includes the following:

> 'In considering whether the requirement is satisfied, the Inland Revenue will take into account the totality of the activities of the trade. For example, they will consider where the capital assets of the trade are held, where any purchasing, processing, manufacturing and selling is done, and where the company's employees and other agents are engaged in its trading operations. For trades involving the provision of services, the location of the activities giving rise to the services and the location where they are delivered will both be relevant.'

> ⚠ **Warning!**
>
> The government announced in the June 2010 emergency budget that the Finance Bill planned for autumn 2010 will contain certain amendments to the venture capital schemes. For shares issued on or after the commencement date of the new legislation, the requirement that a company must carry on a qualifying activity wholly or mainly in the UK will be amended so that the company issuing the shares will simply be required to have a 'permanent establishment' in the UK.

Law: ITA 2007, s. 179

Other guidance: Revenue *Tax Bulletin*, Issue 22, April 1996, p. 305; Statement of Practice SP 3/2000

When shares are issued

The question of when shares were issued was considered, in connection with the BES, in *National Westminster Bank v CIR; Barclays Bank plc v IR Commrs*. Both banks offered loans in connection with two business expansion schemes. The House of Lords held that the shares were issued on the date on which they were entered into the companies' registers, not on the earlier date on which they were allotted to investors.

Other guidance: National Westminster Bank v CIR; Barclays Bank plc v IR Commrs [1994] BTC 236

64.2.6 Withdrawal of relief

Disposal of shares

A withdrawal of relief occurs if, within three years of the share issue (five years for shares issued prior to 6 April 2004), an investor makes a non-arm's length disposal of EIS shares or acquires an option that entitles him to dispose of the shares. Furthermore, relief is unavailable if either event occurs within the two years before issue.

Relief is also withdrawn if an investor makes an arm's-length disposal during the above periods. In this case, if the investor obtained full income tax relief on the acquisition of the shares, the relief withdrawn is equal to the amount or value of the consideration received for the disposal multiplied by the lower rate of tax applicable in the year for which relief was obtained. If the income tax relief obtained on the acquisition of the shares was restricted, the relief withdrawn is restricted by the same proportion. This means that if the sale proceeds exceed the issue price of shares, the relief is withdrawn in full, but that, if the proceeds are less than the issue price, only partial withdrawal occurs.

> **Example 64.3**
>
> In April 2007, Sue invests £100,000 in 80,000 EIS shares. She obtains income tax relief of £10,000 for the investment. In March 2010 she sells the shares for £90,000.
>
> Although Sue's investment was eligible for income tax relief of £20,000 (£100,000 at 20%) she obtained relief of only £10,000. The amount of the relief withdrawn is thus £9,000 (20% × £90,000 × £10,000/£20,000).

A disposal for the above purpose includes the grant an option that binds the investor to sell the shares.

Law: ITA 2007, s. 209

Matching of shares

Care is needed as special matching rules apply for EIS purposes. The first-in-first-out ('FIFO') principle applies for shares of the same class issued on different days.

Where shares of the same class are acquired on the same day, disposals are matched in the following order.

(1) With shares on which there is neither CGT deferral nor income tax relief under the EIS scheme.

(2) With shares on which there is CGT deferral, but not income tax relief.

(3) With shares on which there is income tax relief, but not CGT deferral.

(4) With shares on which there is both CGT deferral and income tax relief.

Particular rules apply in the case of husband and wife transfers, CGT reorganisations and share options.

> **Planning point**
>
> Where, however, an individual has acquired shares of the same class as a result of different transactions on the same day, and some of the shares have been

> acquired through an employee share scheme, the individual can elect for an alternative ordering rule to apply for matching disposals with acquisitions where there is a part-disposal of a holding of shares.

Law: ITA 2007, s. 246

Pre-arranged exits

As discussed at **64.2.4** above, relief is not due where a pre-arranged exit route exists.

Investor receives value

Where an investor receives value from the company (or from anyone connected with the company) that is more than just an insignificant amount, some or all of the EIS obtained may be withdrawn.

There is a 'period of restriction', which is the period beginning one year before the eligible shares are issued and ending on the 'termination date' (generally three years from the shares' issue date if the company is already trading or three years from the commencement of trading, if that is later).

Value is received from a company if it repays, redeems or repurchases any share capital, etc. or makes any payment for giving up rights over shares, etc. The repayment to the individual of a debt (or paying an individual for giving up rights in a debt) may also count unless the debt was incurred after the issue of eligible shares. Other transactions between the company issuing the eligible shares and the individual claiming relief that may constitute receiving value include:

- the release or waiver of a loan made to the individual by the company;
- discharging any of an individual's liabilities to any third party;
- making a loan to the individual (except one that is repaid in full by the date of the share issue);
- transferring assets to the individual for no consideration (or at less than market value) or acquiring assets from the individual at greater than market value;
- providing any benefit or facility for the individual; and
- except for genuine reimbursements or payment of genuine trade debts the provision of any other payment.

> ### Planning point
>
> An individual does not suffer a withdrawal merely on the ground that he received reasonable remuneration for his services as director or employee.

⚠ Warning!

An investor's EIS relief may also be withdrawn if any other member (other than another person who has received EIS relief) receives a capital repayment during the specified period.

Law: ITA 2007, s. 213ff

Insignificant amount

There is a statutory definition of what is meant by an 'insignificant' amount of value:

- £1,000 or less; or
- if greater than £1,000, an amount that is 'insignificant in relation to the amount subscribed by the individual'.

Thus, £1,000 is an effective lower limit on the amount of value that may be returned without the withdrawal of relief, but as to values above this, it depends on the amount originally subscribed.

⚠ Warning!

There is an exception to this minimum value rule: where there are 'arrangements in existence' at any time during the period beginning one year prior to the issue date and ending with the issue date for any value to be returned to the individual then no amount can be regarded as insignificant.

Law: ITA 2007, s. 213ff

Acquisition of share capital by new company

An EIS company may become a wholly-owned subsidiary without losing income tax relief for its investors.

A precondition for this is that either the EIS company, or the new company, must apply to HMRC for clearance that the arrangements are for bona fide commercial reasons and that there is no scheme whose main purpose is the avoidance of CGT or corporation tax. The application must be in writing, and contain details of the operations to be carried out. HMRC may, within 30 days, require further particulars to be delivered. There is a 30-day deadline for submission of information requested by HMRC.

The holding company (Newco), whose only issued share capital must consist of subscriber shares, must acquire all the shares of the EIS company. All the consideration for the shares of the EIS company must be in the form of shares in Newco. Where there are different descriptions of shares in Newco, consideration must be in the form of shares in the EIS company which are of a 'corresponding description'. This means shares that would be in the same class and carry the same rights were they to be in the same company. Shares in Newco must be issued in respect of and in proportion to holdings of shares in the EIS company.

Provided all the above conditions are satisfied, the disposal and acquisition of shares involved in the exchange is ignored, and any relief attaching to the old shares is attributed to the new shares. This is reinforced by providing that, where an individual subscribed for the old shares attracting relief, the new shares are treated as standing exactly in the shoes of the old. This is so even if the old shares were acquired on an inter-spouse transfer.

The new company inherits the actions and responsibilities of the EIS company in respect of certifying issues of eligible shares, and notifying circumstances in which relief is withdrawn, as well as receiving notice from the inspector that relief should be withdrawn. Similarly, the new company may pursue an appeal against such a notice from the inspector which was given to the EIS company.

The provisions of ITA 2007, s. 139 prohibiting an EIS company being a subsidiary, etc. are specifically disapplied.

Except in relation to the phrases 'eligible shares' and 'subscriber shares', the expression 'shares' encompasses securities.

Law: TCGA 1992, s. 138(2); ITA 2007, s. 247ff

Replacement capital

EIS relief is withdrawn in respect of all of the shares held by an investor in the company concerned, if at any time in Period A (see **64.1.4**) the company or any qualifying subsidiary:

- begins to carry on, as the whole or part of its trade, a trade previously carried on by another person; or
- acquires all, or most, of the assets previously used for the purposes of a trade by another person;

and at sometime during that period, the investor either, himself, or as one of a group of persons:

- owned more than 50 per cent of both the previous trade and the trade carried on by the issuing company; or
- controlled both the company that previously carried on the trade and the issuing company.

The ownership of the trades and control of the companies as mentioned above do not have to occur simultaneously.

Relief is also withdrawn if at any time during Period A, the company acquires all of the issued share capital of another company and at some time during that period the investor himself, or as one of a group of persons, controlled both companies. This applies whether or not both companies were controlled at the same time.

Law: ITA 2007, s. 232ff

64.2.7 Interaction with the corporate venturing scheme

A company may have corporate shareholders who invested under the corporate venturing scheme as well as individual shareholders who invested under EIS. If the corporate venturing scheme relief is withdrawn or reduced due to a repayment of share value to another member, the EIS income tax relief can continue without reduction. If the repayment made to the shareholder is insignificant and thus disregarded for the purpose of CVS investment relief, the repayment is also disregarded for EIS income tax relief.

Similarly, EIS deferral relief continues when a repayment of share value is made to another member which causes CVS investment relief to be withdrawn or reduced.

Law: ITA 2007, s. 231

64.3 CGT reinvestment relief

64.3.1 Outline of relief

> **Planning point**
>
> EIS reinvestment relief offers the chance to postpone (rather than to exempt) a capital gains tax liability. It has effect by deeming part or all of a gain to accrue not at the date of the disposal but at some later date on the occurrence of a 'chargeable event'.

An earlier form of reinvestment relief was abolished and the decision was taken that the amended relief should be grafted onto the already complex EIS provisions.

Relief under these provisions is available where:

- an individual realises a chargeable gain on the disposal of any asset, or a gain is deemed to accrue in certain circumstances (including a deemed gain arising under these EIS deferral rules);
- the individual makes a qualifying investment;
- eligible shares are issued to him at a 'qualifying time';
- the company is a 'qualifying company';

Enterprise Investment Scheme

- the company has applied the funds raised for the purposes of a 'qualifying business activity' within a prescribed period; and
- the individual is resident and ordinarily resident in the UK both at the time the gain arises and at the time of the making of the qualifying investment.

Relief is only available to individuals and certain trustees. As might be expected, there are detailed anti-avoidance provisions.

Qualifying time

The issue of eligible shares to an individual take place at a qualifying time if it occurs at any time within the period beginning one year before and ending three years after the date on which the gain accrues, ('the accrual time'). This may be extended by HMRC, at their discretion. HMRC policy on this is to extend the time limits where the claimant can show that he or she:

- had a firm intention to comply with the time limits, but
- was prevented by some fact or circumstance beyond his or her control from complying; and
- acted as soon as he or she reasonably could after ceasing to be so prevented.

HMRC go on to make the following observations in this respect (the wording referring to Venture Capital Trusts but the same principles being applied to EIS shares):

> 'It is a question of fact and degree and each case is considered on its own merits. Examples of circumstances outside the claimant's control might include death or serious illness of a vital party at a crucial time, unsettled disputes or litigation or unexpected delay in receipt of disposal consideration.
>
> A mere change of intention at a late stage or a shortage of funds arising out of the application of the disposal consideration to some purpose other than the subscription for VCT shares will not normally be regarded as circumstances beyond the claimant's control. In particular, where a claimant chooses to defer applying for shares until late in the statutory reinvestment period any subsequent issue of shares outside that period will not normally be regarded as a circumstance beyond the claimant's control justifying an extension to the time limit.
>
> No decision on a possible extension of the time limits can be made until the disposal has taken place, the VCT shares have been issued and all other conditions of relief are satisfied.'

Law: TCGA 1992, Sch. 5B

Other guidance: VCM 38030, 68060

64.3.2 Manner and amount of relief

> ⚠️ **Warning!**
> EIS deferral relief is a hold-over relief, not a roll-over relief. In other words, the gain is simply held in suspense until the happening of a chargeable event. The consideration for the disposal of the original asset and for the acquisition of the relevant shares is not reduced as a consequence of relief.

When the relevant shares are sold, the gain on those shares will be calculated on normal rules and will be chargeable (subject to possible further exemption as discussed at **64.4** below) in addition to any deferred gain which is deemed to accrue.

The deferred gain is the chargeable gain which would, in the absence of a claim, arise on the original disposal. It is therefore the gain after any of the following reliefs:

- business asset roll-over relief;
- incorporation relief;
- business asset gift relief; and
- (formerly) taper relief.

Where gains are deferred from 6 April 2008 as a result of an investment in qualifying EIS shares, entrepreneurs' relief is similarly claimable in determining the amount of gains to be deferred.

Transitional rules allow entrepreneurs' relief to be claimed where gains that were deferred before 6 April 2008 because of an EIS investment become chargeable on or after that date. Relief is given if the disposal that gave rise to the deferred gain would have qualified for relief if the rules had been in force at the time of that earlier disposal.

Where a claim for relief is made an amount of qualifying expenditure is set against the gain concerned. A corresponding part of the gain is then treated as not having accrued on the date it would otherwise have accrued, but as accruing on the occurrence of a chargeable event in relation to the eligible shares. That part of the gain is deferred until the chargeable event occurs.

The amount of the deferred gain is determined by the claimant specifying the amount of the qualifying expenditure to be set against the gain, the only limitations being:

- the available qualifying expenditure is that part of the total expenditure on the relevant shares remaining after previous claims; and
- the claim cannot exceed the amount of the gain remaining after previous claims

under these provisions and claims for the relief that used to be available for investment in Venture Capital Trusts.

> ⚠ **Warning!**
>
> The capital gains tax rate(s) on a gain subject to certain deferral reliefs such as under the enterprise investment scheme, are those applicable when the deferral ends and the gain becomes liable to tax. Hence pre-23 June 2010, gains (i.e. before the introduction of the 28 per cent CGT rate) which are deferred until 23 June 2010 or later will be liable to CGT at the 18 per cent or 28 per cent rates.

Law: TCGA 1992, Sch. 5B, para. 1(1)(b), para. 2; FA 2008, Sch. 3, para. 8

64.3.3 Claims

The procedure for making claims is as follows.

Company statement

The company must furnish the inspector with a statement to the effect that it satisfies the conditions applicable to itself and to its trading activities. That statement must contain such information as the Board of HM Revenue & Customs reasonably require and a declaration that the statement is correct to the best of the company's knowledge and belief.

This statement must be submitted not later than:

- two years from the end of the year of assessment in which the shares were issued; or
- two years and four months from the date the company commenced to trade (or began to carry on research and development or oil exploration),

whichever is the later.

Certificate

HMRC will then authorise the company to issue a certificate to the individual, certifying that the conditions for EIS deferral relief as regards the company and its activities are satisfied in relation to the shares. A company which issues certificates without authority, or has issued a certificate or furnished a statement fraudulently or negligently, will be liable to a penalty of up to £3,000.

The claim

> ⚠ **Warning!**
> A claim cannot be made unless the individual has received a certificate from the company.

The claim must then be made:

- not earlier than four months after the company commenced trading (or research and development or oil exploration, as appropriate); and
- not later than five years after the 31st January next following the year of assessment in which the eligible shares were issued.

> ⚠ **Warning!**
> However, in view of the requirement that the money raised by the share issue 'is employed' for the purposes of a qualifying business activity, a valid claim cannot be submitted until the money has been so applied.

Law: ITA 2007, s. 202

64.3.4 Qualifying investments

A qualifying investment is one where:

- eligible shares are subscribed by an individual and those shares are issued to the subscriber at a 'qualifying time' (and if the chargeable gain that is to be deferred accrued after the qualifying time, then the shares must still be held when the chargeable gain accrues);
- the subscription for the 'eligible shares' is wholly in cash;
- the subscribed eligible shares are fully paid up;
- the only other shares of the company that the subscriber may have received on the same day as the subscribed eligible shares are bonus shares;
- the company is a 'qualifying company' in relation to the eligible shares;
- the subscription and the issue of the eligible shares are for bona fide commercial reasons and not as part of arrangements which have, as one of their main purposes, the purpose of avoiding tax;
- at no time in the relevant period is the 'relevant qualifying trade', any 'relevant preparation work' and any 'relevant research and development' (see below) carried on by a person other than the qualifying company or a qualifying 90 per cent subsidiary of that company; and
- all the shares are issued to raise money for the purpose of a 'qualifying business activity'.

Enterprise Investment Scheme

> ⚠ **Warning!**
>
> With regard to the condition of subscribed eligible shares having to be fully paid up, shares are not fully paid up if there is any undertaking to pay cash to any person at a future date for the acquisition of these shares.

With regard to the condition that only the qualifying company or the qualifying 90 per cent subsidiary carries on the relevant qualifying trade, etc. during the relevant period, the following definitions are given.

1. The 'relevant period' is basically the period beginning with the issue of the eligible shares and ending immediately before the 'termination date' – the termination date is the later of:

    (a) the third anniversary of the share issue; or
    (b) the third anniversary of the start of the qualifying trade (see below) by the qualifying company or any of its qualifying 90 per cent subsidiaries.

2. The 'relevant qualifying trade' is the qualifying trade that is the subject of the 'qualifying business activity' referred to above.

3. 'Relevant preparation work' is preparation work which is:

    (a) the subject of the 'qualifying business activity' referred to above; and
    (b) for carrying on a qualifying trade that:

    (i) on the date of the issue of the shares, is intended to be carried on wholly or mainly in the UK by the qualifying company or any of its qualifying 90 per cent subsidiaries; and
    (ii) is begun to be carried on wholly or mainly in the UK by the qualifying company or any of its 90 per cent subsidiaries within two years after the date of the issue of the shares (but see 'warning' below for proposed changes regarding this rule).

4. 'Relevant research and development' is:

    (a) research and development that is:
    (b) the subject of the 'qualifying business activity' referred to above; and

    (i) carried on wholly or mainly in the UK by the qualifying company or any of its 90 per cent subsidiaries at the time of, or immediately after, the issue of the shares; and
    (ii) intended to bring about a qualifying trade which will be carried on wholly or mainly in the UK by the qualifying company or any of its 90 per cent subsidiaries (but see 'warning' below for proposed changes regarding this rule); or

5. Any other preparations for the carrying on of the qualifying trade which is the subject of the qualifying business activity referred above.

CGT Reinvestment Relief 64.3.7

> ⚠ **Warning!**
>
> The government announced in the June 2010 emergency budget that the Finance Bill planned for autumn 2010 will contain certain amendments to the venture capital schemes. For shares issued on or after the commencement date of the new legislation, the requirement that a company must carry on a qualifying activity wholly or mainly in the UK will be amended so that the company issuing the shares will simply be required to have a 'permanent establishment' in the UK.

Law: TCGA 1992, Sch. 5B, para. 1

64.3.5 Eligible shares

The concept of 'eligible shares' is the same for these purposes as for EIS income tax relief – see **64.2.5**.

> ⚠ **Warning!**
>
> Shares are excluded from being eligible shares, if:
>
> - the funds raised by the share issue are not applied or not wholly applied for the purposes of the qualifying business activity by the end of a prescribed period;
> - arrangements exist for a 'pre-arranged exit';
> - options are granted over the shares;
> - value is received from the company by the individual or by certain other persons; and
> - an 'investment-linked loan' is made to the individual.

See **64.2.4** for further discussion of some of these concepts.

Law: TCGA 1992, Sch. 5B, para. 19(1)

64.3.6 Qualifying companies

A company is a qualifying company for EIS reinvestment relief purposes if it meets the requirements of ITA 2007, Pt. 5, Ch. 4, discussed in detail at **64.2.5** above.

Law: TCGA 1992, Sch. 5B, para. 19(1)

64.3.7 Chargeable events

Overview

As indicated above, the gain against which relief is given is only deferred until the happening of a 'chargeable event' in relation to the relevant shares acquired by the making of the qualifying investment. There are three categories of events which are chargeable:

- disposals of the relevant shares;
- emigration; and
- where the conditions for relief are subsequently breached.

The gain accruing on the occasion of a chargeable event is to be treated as accruing to:

- the person who makes the disposal;
- the person who becomes neither resident nor ordinarily resident in the UK; or
- the person holding the shares at the time they cease to be 'eligible shares',

as the case may be.

> ⚠ **Warning!**
>
> In addition, anti-avoidance legislation prescribes that shares will lose their status as eligible shares (and therefore breach the conditions for relief and in turn give rise to a chargeable event) where:
>
> - an option is granted over the relevant shares;
> - value is received from the company by the individual or another person; or
> - the individual receives an 'investment-linked loan'.

Death is not a chargeable event, as assets held on death are not deemed to have been disposed of by the deceased on his or her death. Where, after the death of the individual concerned, an event occurs which would otherwise be a chargeable event, it is to be disregarded for these purposes.

Where a chargeable event first occurs in relation to any relevant shares, a chargeable gain is treated as accruing on the occurrence of that chargeable event. The amount of the chargeable gain accruing is equal to so much of the deferred gain as is attributable to the shares in relation to which the chargeable event occurs.

The deferred gain, which is the amount of the original gain against which expenditure has been set, less any amount previously brought into charge, is to be attributed to each of the relevant shares held by the investor (and his or her spouse or civil partner, where they have acquired the shares as a result of a transfer between spouses or civil partners) immediately prior to the chargeable event. The amount of the deferred gain becoming chargeable is to be the amount which is attributable to the shares giving rise to the chargeable event.

Where, by the time the chargeable event occurs, the relevant shares are represented by other assets (e.g. as the result of a reorganisation of the company concerned), the deferred gain is to be apportioned between those assets on a 'just and reasonable' basis.

CGT Reinvestment Relief 64.3.7

> **Planning point**
>
> The gain arising on a chargeable event may itself be deferred if a further qualifying investment is made within a qualifying time. However, that further investment cannot be in the same or a 'relevant' company.

Law: TCGA 1992, s. 62(1)(a), Sch. 5B, paras. 3, 4, 5

Disposals

A chargeable event occurs where the individual, or the spouse or civil partner of the individual (if that individual has acquired the relevant shares by means of an transfer between spouses or civil partners) disposes of the relevant shares.

Inter-spouse transfers, and transfers between civil partners, are not themselves regarded as a chargeable event.

Law: TCGA 1992, Sch. 5B, para. 3

Emigration

A chargeable event occurs where the individual or spouse (if the spouse has acquired the relevant shares by means of an inter-spouse transfer) becomes not resident and not ordinarily resident in the UK within three years from the issue of the shares, whilst still holding the relevant shares. Once more, these rules now apply for civil partners as they do for spouses.

However, a chargeable event will not arise if:

- the reason for the person becoming non-resident in the UK is that the person works in an employment or office in which all the duties are performed outside the UK; and
- the person again becomes resident or ordinarily resident in the UK before:
    (a) the period of three years from the time that the person became non-resident; and
    (b) disposing of any of the relevant shares.

It is likely that a chargeable event does arise in respect of shares held by one spouse (whether held as a result of that spouse's acquisition of the shares through purchase or inter-spouse transfer) where that spouse's non-residence is a consequence of the other spouse's employment abroad.

> **Example 64.4**
>
> A husband transfers shares to his wife and they both become non-resident due to his employment abroad. It is likely that the chargeable event occurs when the wife becomes non-resident even though she still holds the shares on their return

> to the UK within three years from becoming non-resident. This is because the wife's non-residence is a consequence of her husband's employment abroad and not of her own employment.

> ⚠ **Warning!**
>
> Where an individual becomes non-resident in the UK as a consequence of that individual's employment or office abroad, it is necessary to wait to see whether or not this will cause the relief to fail. Hence, the position will remain uncertain for three years from the date of non-residence as the outcome will depend on whether the return to UK residence occurs before the three-year time limit. However, HMRC should be advised of the situation in the tax return covering the period before non-residency occurs.

Hence, where an individual or spouse or civil partner emigrates and there is the possibility that the exception for working abroad will apply, it is likely that HMRC will not seek to raise a clawback assessment at that time but will wait (up to three years) until such time as a chargeable event is known to have occurred.

Law: TCGA 1992, Sch. 5B, para. 3

Breach of conditions

A chargeable event occurs where there is a breach of the conditions necessary for deferral relief which results in the relevant shares losing their status as 'eligible shares'. The reason for the loss of that status will determine the time when the shares cease to be eligible shares.

64.3.8 Reorganisations and reconstructions

Reorganisations

Where an individual holds ordinary shares in a company, some of which fall into two or more of the following categories:

- shares to which both EIS deferral relief and income tax relief is attributable;
- shares to which only EIS deferral relief is attributable; or
- shares to which no EIS deferral relief is attributable,

and a reorganisation within TCGA 1992, s. 126 takes place, then each category of share is to be treated as a separate holding of original shares and identified with a separate new holding.

Where there is a rights issue within TCGA 1992, s. 126(2)(a) and deferral relief has been claimed in respect of the expenditure on the original holding, or is claimed on the cost of taking up the rights issue, the two holdings are not to be regarded as a single holding.

Law: TCGA 1992, Sch. 5B, para. 7

Reconstructions

Normally, share-for-share exchanges are not treated as a disposal of the old shares for taxation purposes. But where EIS deferral relief was attributable to the old shares, the rules in TCGA 1992, Sch. 5B prevent the share for share rules from applying, to ensure that the exchange is a chargeable event bringing the deferred gain back into charge.

However, this means that there is a disposal of the old shares for tax purposes, so that, in addition to the deferred gain being brought back into charge, a taxable gain can arise in relation to the old shares. As a result of the changes made by paragraph 1, on the occasion of a share for share exchange qualifying under TCGA 1992, s. 135 and 136, any deferral relief given will be brought back into charge as before but no gain or loss will be brought into charge in respect of the disposal of the shares that form the subject of the exchange.

Finance Act 2009 amended TGCA 1992, Sch. 5B so it can no longer disapply TCGA 1992, s. 135 and 136 generally but can only disapply those sections for the purposes of the application of paragraphs 3 and 4 of Schedule 5B (which provide for the deferred gain under EIS to be brought back into charge).

Law: TCGA 1992, Sch. 5B, para. 8, 9; FA 2009, s. 27 and Sch. 55

64.3.9 Anti-avoidance

There are numerous anti-avoidance rules, the detail of which should be checked in any given scenario. Most of these anti-avoidance rules have qualifications to ensure that they do not bite in inappropriate circumstances. In brief, the rules may be summarised as follows.

Reinvestment in same or a relevant company

> ⚠ **Warning!**
> Provisions exist to prevent the exploitation of deferral relief by 'bed & breakfasting' shares in a qualifying company, or in a member of the same group. Where shares are issued by a qualifying company, an individual is not regarded as making a qualifying investment if the disposal against which deferral relief is claimed is of shares in or other securities of the qualifying company. The prohibition also extends to shares in any company which is a member of the

Enterprise Investment Scheme

> same group of companies as the qualifying company, either at the time of the disposal, or when the shares were issued.

In addition, it is not possible to have two bites of the same cherry; once there has been a disposal of relevant shares in a company it is not possible to make a second qualifying investment into the same company, or a company in the same group.

Law: TCGA 1992, Sch. 5B, para. 10

Pre-arranged exits

Where an individual subscribes for shares, those shares will not be 'eligible shares' if the 'relevant arrangements' under which the shares are issued to the individual and any arrangements made before, but in relation to, that issue, include arrangements:

- with a view to the subsequent repurchase, exchange or other disposal of those shares, or any other shares or securities in the same company;
- with a view to the cessation of any trade carried on by the company or a person connected with it, or with a view to the disposal of, or a substantial amount of, the assets of that company or person; or
- the main purpose, or one of the main purposes, of which is to provide partial or complete risk protection for investors, such protection being provided by means of insurance, indemnity, guarantee or otherwise.

Law: TCGA 1992, Sch. 5B, para. 11

Put and call options

Attempts to provide a guaranteed return on the investment by the use of options will either prevent relief from being due or, if already granted, will lead to a chargeable event.

If an individual subscribes for eligible shares and, during the 'relevant period', grants a 'put' option, or is granted a 'call' option, the shares will not be 'eligible shares'.

Law: TCGA 1992, Sch. 5B, para. 12

Value received by individual or by a third party

Shares will not be regarded as 'eligible shares' if the individual or the individual's spouse or civil partner (having acquired shares by means of a transfer between spouses or civil partners) 'receives any value from the company' during the 'period of restriction', which commences one year before the shares are issued and ends on the third anniversary of that issue.

Relief may also be lost where an unconnected third party receives value from the company.

Complex rules determine what is meant by receiving value from the company for these purposes. The case of *Blackburn & Anor* determined that a taxpayer was entitled to EIS deferral relief in respect of certain shares issued to him by a qualifying company. Payments to the company in advance of the issue of shares were to be treated as capital contributions and not loan arrangements which would be caught by the 'value received' provisions.

Law: TCGA 1992, Sch. 5B, para. 14, 19

Other guidance: Blackburn & Anor v R & C Commrs [2008] BTC 158

Investment-linked loans

Shares will not be eligible shares where an investment-linked loan is made to an individual or an associate at any time in the period beginning two years before the issue of the shares (or the date of the company's incorporation, if later) and ending five years after the issue. Where the loan is made before the share issue, the shares are regarded as never having been eligible shares and where the loan is made after the share issue, they are treated as ceasing to be eligible shares at the date of the making of the loan.

Law: TCGA 1992, Sch. 5B, para. 15

64.4 Tax-free sale of EIS shares

64.4.1 Exemption from CGT

A gain is to be exempt from capital gains tax where:

- the gain arises on the disposal of relevant shares in respect of which an amount of EIS income tax relief is still attributable; and
- the disposal occurs more than three years after either the date of the issue or, if later, the date of the commencement of the trade.

See **64.2.6** above (*Matching of shares*) for details of the share identification rules applying for EIS purposes.

> ⚠ **Warning!**
> Where EIS income tax relief has not been given in respect of the full amount of the qualifying investment, only part of any subsequent gain on the relevant shares will be exempt. That part is to be calculated by applying the fraction A/B, where:
>
> A = reduction in income tax liability as a result of the relief actually given; and

Enterprise Investment Scheme

> B = tax at the basic rate for that year on the amount subscribed for the relevant shares.

However, this restriction is not to apply where full relief could not be given solely because the individual did not have sufficient income tax liability to absorb that relief.

> **Example 64.5**
>
> Imogen invests £100,000 in shares qualifying for EIS relief. Her income tax liability for the tax year in which she made the investment is £10,000. Therefore, the income tax relief is £10,000 (i.e. the lower of £20,000 (20% × £100,000) and £10,000 (the amount which reduces her income tax liability to nil).
>
> After the end of the relevant period, she sells the shares, realising a gain of £40,000. The full gain is exempt, because her income tax relief was reduced only by virtue of her income tax liability being insufficient to utilise the full measure of relief.

Law: TCGA 1992, s. 150A

64.4.2 Withdrawal of income tax relief

The withdrawal of EIS income tax relief is discussed in detail above. In broad terms, EIS income tax relief is withdrawn where, during a nominated period, the investor receives value from the issuing company or from its 51 per cent subsidiary or if value is received by a third party.

Where the whole of the gain would otherwise be exempt, the gain is restricted by deducting an amount equal to the gain as multiplied by the fraction:

> income tax relief withdrawn / income tax relief attributable to the shares

Thus, where the income tax relief is withdrawn in full, the whole gain becomes chargeable.

> **Example 64.6**
>
> Ralph invests £100,000 in shares qualifying for EIS income tax relief of £20,000. About six months later, the company repurchases some of its own shares, and Ralph receives £15,000 and that amount of income tax relief is withdrawn. Ralph sells the remaining shares after the end of the relevant period, realising a gain of £12,000.

> As Ralph has received value from the company, the exempt gain is reduced to £9,000 (£12,000 − ((£15,000/£20,000) × £12,000)), so leaving £3,000 chargeable.

Where the exempt proportion has already been reduced, because full income tax relief was not available at the time of the investment, the exempt gain is further reduced by a fraction equal to the amount of income tax relief withdrawn because of the value received (numerator) divided by the amount of the income tax relief given in respect of the shares (denominator). If the income tax relief is withdrawn in full as a result of value having been received, the whole gain will be chargeable, the exempt proportion being reduced to nil.

Example 64.7

> Holly subscribes £50,000 for eligible shares. However, she is only entitled to income tax relief of £5,000, rather than the full relief of £10,000. She receives value from the company of £3,000. Subsequently, she sells the shares after the end of the relevant period and realises a gain of £8,000.
>
> As full income tax relief was not available, not all of the gain was exempt. The exempt gain is initially calculated as £4,000 (£8,000 × £5,000/£10,000). As value is received from the company, the exempt gain is further reduced to £2,500 (£4,000 − (£3,000/£5,000) × £4,000)).

Where income tax relief has been withdrawn on more than one occasion as a result of value received by the company, the numerator in the fraction (i.e. the relief withdrawn) is the aggregate of the amounts of relief withdrawn in this manner.

Any relief withdrawn as a result of value being received from the company is not taken into account in determining the denominator of the reducing fraction, i.e. the denominator is the value of relief given before any withdrawal or restriction of relief as a result of value given.

In determining whether relief is available and the amount of the relief, the EIS legislation in ICTA 1988 applies (see above). 'Eligible shares', for the purpose of restricting the capital gains tax exemption, have the same meaning as for that legislation.

There may be a reduction or withdrawal of EIS relief following a rights issue. The amount of this reduction or withdrawal is deductible in calculating any allowable loss or chargeable gain arising on the subsequent disposal of shares or debentures allotted under the rights issue. Conversely, the allowable deductions available on the disposal of the original shares are reduced by the same amount. The relief withdrawn is apportioned as between the original shares and, as between the rights shares and/or debentures, in a way which is just and reasonable.

Law: TCGA 1992, s. 150B

64.4.3 Allowable losses

Despite the exemption for gains, an allowable loss may arise on the disposal of EIS shares. However, any income tax relief given, which is not withdrawn on the disposal, reduces the cost allowable in calculating the loss.

> **Example 64.8**
>
> Ann invests £100,000 in shares qualifying for EIS relief and obtains tax relief of £20,000 (£100,000 × 20%) in respect of the investment. After the end of the relevant period, Ann sells the shares for £65,000.
>
> No withdrawal of EIS relief occurs on the disposal of the shares, but the allowable loss arising for capital gains tax purposes is £15,000 (£65,000 − (£100,000 − £20,000)).

> **Planning point**
>
> In situations where a loss accrues, the EIS provisions override the general rule that a loss arising on the disposal of an asset is not an allowable loss where a gain, had it arisen on the disposal of that asset, would not have been a chargeable gain. The disapplication of this rule for EIS purposes allows the taxpayer (provided the other conditions for relief are satisfied) to enjoy the benefit of an allowable loss, even though a gain, had it arisen, would not have been a chargeable gain.

Setting losses against income

Relief for an allowable loss arising on a disposal of shares to which EIS income tax relief is attributable is available in the normal way. Alternatively, an investor may claim for the loss to be set against his statutory total income in either the year of the loss or the preceding year.

As usual, the latter relief is available only if the loss arises on an arm's-length disposal for full consideration, on a negligible value claim, or on a distribution in the course of dissolving or winding up a company.

Furthermore, relief is unavailable for a loss which arises as a result of TCGA 1992, s. 137 (i.e. on a reconstruction or amalgamation not effected for bona fide commercial reasons).

A loss relieved against income cannot also be claimed for capital gains tax purposes, and any necessary capital gains tax adjustment will be made accordingly.

Law: TCGA 1992, s. 150A; ITA 2007, s. 131ff

65 Farming in the UK

65.1 Overview

65.1.1 Taxation of trading income

Profits from trading in the UK are chargeable to income tax or corporation tax.

All farming and market gardening in the UK, and any occupation of land in the UK where the land is managed on a commercial basis with a view to realising profits, is treated as trading and is chargeable to income or corporation tax accordingly.

While both farming and market gardening are trades, they are separate and distinct ones.

'Farm land' means 'land in the UK wholly or mainly occupied for the purposes of husbandry' and 'farming' is to be construed accordingly. Unless otherwise stated, 'husbandry' includes arable, dairy farming and livestock breeding.

Short rotation coppice ('a perennial crop of tree species planted at high density, the stems of which are harvested above ground level at intervals of less than ten years') is regarded for tax purposes as farming rather than forestry. Consequently, the land on which it is undertaken is regarded as farmland or agricultural land and not commercial woodland.

However, 'farming' has different meanings in different contexts for tax purposes. For example, for the purposes of restricting certain loss reliefs which would otherwise be available to farmers or market gardeners 'farming' and 'market gardening' are interpreted as above, but with the difference that activities carried on outside the UK are included.

'Farm land' excludes 'market garden land'. 'Market garden land' means 'land in the UK occupied as a nursery or garden for the sale of produce (other than land used for the growth of hops) and "market gardening" is construed accordingly.'

> **Planning point**
>
> Anyone whose house has a garden attached may be a market gardener. However, in order to counter the use of a small garden as a mere device for tax avoidance, the rule which HMRC apply in practice is that only if commercial purposes predominate will the garden be regarded as a market garden. However, this rule is unlikely to be rigidly applied where the taxpayer sells fruit or

> vegetables as part of a wider business. For example, a farm shop on farm premises which sells farm produce is unlikely to be treated as a separate trade even if, in order to keep the shop worker busy, the taxpayer brings in goods from outside for resale.

All farming which is carried on by a sole trader, persons in partnership or body of persons is treated as one trade. Accordingly, profits derived from more than one farm must be aggregated into a single chargeable source of income where the taxpayer operates more than one farm at the same time, whether the farms are in the same or in different parts of the country. Nor would it be relevant if the two farms were managed as separate economic units with separate sets of accounts. The 'one trade' principle is, however, restricted to farming upon land in the UK. Income from farming outside the UK is chargeable as income from foreign possessions. It has been held that travelling expenses incurred by the taxpayer on a visit to Australia to investigate the possibility of buying a farm there and emigrating were not deductible as expenditure wholly and exclusively laid out for the purposes of the taxpayer's farming trade in the UK (*Sargent v Eayrs* (1972) 48 TC 573).

Where a farmer ceases to operate one farm and starts to operate another he is not normally treated as having ceased to carry on one trade and as having begun to carry on a new trade. Thus the commencement and cessation rules do not, in general, apply.

However, where there has been a substantial lapse of time between the cessation of operations on one farm and the commencement of operations on another, HM Revenue & Customs (HMRC) are likely to treat the taxpayer as having ceased to carry on one trade and as having begun to carry on a new one. What amounts to a significant lapse of time is a question of fact to be decided in the light of all the circumstances of a particular case.

If a particular activity does not fall within the definition of 'farming' and 'market gardening', it may still be treated as being some other trade or part of some other trade. The taxpayer should take particular care to avoid the activity being regarded as casual or occasional. If the activity is treated as such, profits derived from it are charged to income tax under different rules (formerly Case VI of Schedule D) which are far less favourable for income tax purposes than the trading income rules (formerly Case I of Schedule D).

65.1.2 Overview of other tax considerations

The main areas with special legislation relating to farmers are concerned with income tax or, as the case may be, corporation tax.

Special rules for farmers are not totally confined to these two taxes, however. Inheritance tax, for example, has its own rules for agricultural property relief. The capital gains tax legislation makes specific reference to milk and potato quota, and there are numerous decided cases in relation to such topics as private residence relief for farmhouses, agricultural tenancies and so on.

65.2 One trade

All farming is treated as the carrying on of a trade, and all farming carried on in the UK by the same person or partnership is treated as one trade.

> **Planning point**
>
> This is particularly useful in relation to the carry forward of losses as it is possible, for instance, for the same person to give up farming in one area and recommence elsewhere, and carry forward any unabsorbed losses against future profits from the new farm. Where there is a gap between the sale of one farm and the purchase of another, it may still be possible to treat it as a continuing business (and therefore, for example, to carry forward unused losses).

The HMRC guidance makes the following observation in this respect:

> 'Where there is an interval between the discontinuance at one farm and commencement at another, the farming should be treated as discontinued and a new trade as having commenced only where the facts support the conclusion that there was a permanent discontinuance of the original trade.'

> **⚠ Warning!**
>
> It is understood that HMRC will generally accept that there is no cessation where the gap is not more than 12 months and where is a genuine intention to continue to carry on farming. However, this is no more than a rule of thumb and where the amounts at stake are significant great care will be needed.

The ability to carry forward losses from one farm to another was the subject of the decision in *Bispham v Eardiston Farming Co (1919) Ltd*. In that case, unrelieved losses of one farm sold were allowed against another farm's subsequent profits. The point is particularly relevant in a company situation where there is a change in ownership, as CTA 2010, Pt. 14, Ch. 2 might otherwise restrict the carry-forward of losses. Such a challenge is less easy for the HMRC in the case of a farming company, as all farming is specifically deemed to be one trade.

> **Planning point**
>
> Where there is a change in the persons carrying on a business, extra care is needed to ensure that maximum loss relief is obtained as early as possible. For example, where a business is transferred from a sole trader to a partnership, any trading losses of the sole trader are available to carry forward only against the trader's share of the partnership's subsequent profits. If, therefore, the sole trader has very substantial trading losses brought forward, it is wise to draft the partnership agreement carefully so that initially, if possible, the former sole trader receives the greater part of any profits arising.

The position regarding unused capital allowances depends upon whether or not the business is deemed to be continuing. If the business continues, unused capital allowances are carried forward and deducted from future profits of the business. If there is a cessation, all unused capital allowances lapse, except for those applicable to the continuing partners and attributable to the part of the year before the change.

Where there is a succession between connected persons, the rules permit an election, with a two-year time limit, to persons chargeable to UK tax on the profits of the trade. The trade is not deemed to be continuing, but the successors can take over the plant and machinery at tax written-down value. However, there is an extended definition of 'connected persons' to include partnerships.

Law: CAA 2001, s. 266; ITTOIA 2005, s. 9, 10

Other guidance: Bispham v Eardiston Farming Co (1919) Ltd (1962) 40 TC 322

65.3 Losses

65.3.1 Generally

Trading losses may generally be set against other income (of an individual or company). Where an individual has incurred a trading loss, any excess that cannot be relieved against income may be set against capital gains of the same or following year.

A number of provisions may, however, restrict the ability to offset farming losses against other taxable income, as discussed below.

Law: ITA 2007, PartPt. 4, Chapter Ch. 2

65.3.2 Hobby farming

There is a restriction on the set-off of losses (including capital allowances) against general income or total profits where there have been five years of continuous losses by the same person. To determine whether there are five successive years of losses, the loss is computed on normal business tax principles but *without* regard to capital allowances.

> ⚠ **Warning!**
>
> In giving income tax relief for losses, it is normally possible to use the loss incurred in the accounting period ending in the year of assessment to establish whether there has been a loss or a profit. For hobby farming purposes, however, it is necessary to apportion profits and losses on a fiscal year basis. The farmer must, therefore, make a profit in one of the five years of assessment preceding that for which a loss relief claim is made.

> ⚠ **Warning!**
>
> It follows from this that a single year of profit may not be sufficient to prevent five successive tax years of loss.

> ### Example 65.1
>
> | | |
> |---|---|
> | 31 December 2001 | Profit £1,000 |
> | 31 December 2002 | Loss £9,000 |
> | 31 December 2003 | Loss £20,000 |
> | 31 December 2004 | Loss £22,000 |
> | 31 December 2005 | Loss £18,000 |
> | 31 December 2006 | Profit £2,000 |
> | 31 December 2007 | Loss £18,000 |
>
> Using these figures it appears that the rules will not bite for 2006–07. However, on a tax year basis there will be losses in both 2005/–06 and 2006/–07 (of £13,000 and £3,000 respectively), as well as in earlier and subsequent years.

Special rules apply at the start of a farming business, and HMRC confirm in this respect that:

> 'The year of commencement is not counted for this purpose so, in the case of a new business which makes losses consistently, the loss of the seventh year of assessment is the first to be caught.'

Anti-avoidance provisions prevent husband-and-wife partnerships being formed or dissolved in order to recommence another cycle of five years' losses. Generally, where at least one person is involved in carrying on a trade both before and after a deemed discontinuance, the discontinuance is ignored in reckoning whether there have been five years' losses.

There is a 'let-out' from these provisions if the farmer can prove that no competent farmer could have made a profit in the sixth year if he or she had undertaken the farming at the beginning of the five years concerned. HMRC also make a concession concerning the rearing of certain forms of livestock – for instance, deer farming, stud farming or other long-term breeding projects.

> **Planning point**
>
> As the losses are based on the ordinary adjusted loss, it is best where possible to minimise revenue expenditure (such as repairs) in the fifth year. Equally, where there is a choice of structuring interest as an expense, or as a deduction from total income, the latter course should be taken as this will not then enter into the calculation of the loss. Thus, if a partnership wishes to buy more land, the partners should borrow and inject their personal borrowings into the partnership as capital or interest free loans, in order to purchase the land as partnership property. The interest is then a charge against their total incomes. HMRC do not operate any concession where the high cost of borrowing is the cause of the loss.

Where losses are restricted under these provisions, they are carried forward and are available to set against future farming profits.

Law: ITA 2007, s. 67

Other guidance: BIM 75625

65.3.3 Farming not conducted on a commercial basis

Further restrictions apply where a trade is not conducted on a commercial basis and with a view to the realisation of profits. HMRC do not take a hard line on the interpretation of this section, quoting the comments of the Chancellor of the day when the legislation was being debated in 1960:

> 'We are after the extreme cases in which expenditure very greatly exceeds income or any possible income which can ever be made and in which, however long the period, no degree of profitability can ever be reached.'

Specifically, and in relation to farming, HMRC go on to say that:

> 'The small farmer and the farmer farming marginal land who are genuinely trying to make a living from their farms in difficult circumstances are not caught.
>
> Nor does the Section be used [sic] to deny relief to a farmer who incurs temporary losses while establishing an enterprise, for instance by building up a production herd or bringing land back into fertility, provided the enterprise in which he or she is engaged is likely in due course to become an economic undertaking.'

Planning point

Subject to these points, it may be necessary to distinguish between an activity that merely helps to offset expenditure and one that has a genuine prospect of generating profits.

Where HMRC contend that a trade is not continued on a commercial basis, this also poses a threat to any relief claimed by an individual under rules applying to losses incurred in the early years of a trade. Where an individual carries on a trade and sustains a loss in the first year of assessment or in any of the next three years, he or she may claim to carry back the losses to the period before that trade was commenced. However, the legislation denies this relief where the trade is not conducted on a commercial basis and: 'in such a way that profits ... could reasonably be expected to be realised in [the period in which the loss arose] or within a reasonable time thereafter'.

A HMRC officer may mount a challenge under any or all of these provisions.

Law: ITA 2007, s. 66, 74 (individuals) and; CTA 2010, s. 37 (companies)

Other guidance: Brown v Richardson (1997) Sp C 129; BIM 75615

65.4 Stocks

All animals for farming are treated as trading stock for tax purposes unless the 'herd basis' applies (see **61.5** below). This means that the animals should each theoretically be valued at the lower of cost or net realisable value. In March 1993 the Inland Revenue published Business Economic Note 19 *Farming – stock valuation for income tax purposes*. This note, which remains valid and is now reproduced in full at BIM 55410, represents the definitive official view on the valuation of farming stocks and reference should be made to it in any cases of doubt or difficulty.

The note is divided into the following sections.

1. Introduction.
2. General principles.
3. Livestock, growing and harvested crops.
4. Co-operatives.
5. Grants and subsidies – effect on stock valuations.
6. Consumables.
7. Deemed cost valuation.

Law: ITTOIA 2005, s. 30(1); CTA 2009, s. 50(1)

65.5 Herd basis

65.5.1 General principles

It is possible to elect for the 'herd basis' to apply, as an alternative to the usual trading stock basis (see above), in respect of production herds – such as a dairy herd or a ewe flock – kept only for the sale of milk, wool, eggs, young animals or other produce. The herd basis cannot apply to animals kept for only a short time, such as steers for fattening or a 'flying flock' of ewes.

> **Planning point**
>
> A herd basis election is useful in times of high inflation and where numbers in the herd or flock are stable. By contrast, such an election is not much use where the numbers in the initial herd are likely to be increased. Where numbers are likely to fluctuate, averaging may be a more appropriate strategy to adopt.

An election has to be made to adopt the herd basis, and normally it should be made within 12 months following 31 January after the relevant tax year in which the farmer first keeps the production herd of the class in question. The election, once made by the farmer, is irrevocable.

> **Planning point**
>
> As the election has to be made by the farmer, a fresh election has to be made on a change of partners or on an incorporation of the farming business. If an election has not been made previously, such a change would provide a fresh opportunity to make one.

> **Planning point**
>
> It is also possible to make an election if a farmer's production herd, or a substantial part of it (normally 20 per cent or more), has had to be slaughtered compulsorily on account of disease. In this case the election should be made within two years of the end of the year of assessment that is based on the accounts for the year in which the compensation is receivable.

> **Planning point**
>
> Similarly, if farmers cease to keep a production herd of the class in question for a period of at least five years, they may make an election in respect of such herds after the end of that period, if they reacquire such a herd.

Generally, the effect of making an election is that, if the whole herd is sold without being replaced or if a substantial part of it is sold (normally 20 per cent or more), any profit on the sale is free of all tax (as profits from the animals are also exempt from capital gains tax because the animals are wasting assets). If the numbers in the herd increase within five years of such a substantial reduction, a proportion of the previously 'tax free' profit is brought back into account.

Any profit on a lesser reduction of the herd is brought into account as income, whilst replacements (provided that they are not home-bred) are written off to the profit and loss account as the cost of rearing new home-bred animals will already have been deducted as part of the expense of labour, foodstuffs, etc. Any extra cost due to any improvement element in the replacement animal is not deducted. Immature animals are generally not treated as part of the herd, with a few exceptions, such as hill sheep.

> **⚠ Warning!**
>
> It is clear from the above that, where an election is made and numbers in the herd are likely to fluctuate, accurate records of herd transactions must be kept.

Note that making an election for the herd basis to apply, other than on first keeping a herd, does not mean that the animals are appropriated from stock at market value. If that were the case, the farmer would lose the benefit of the election. Rather, the animals are treated as never having been part of the stock in the period in question, and are thus removed at their book value from stock for tax purposes, with no income or corporation tax charge resulting from this change.

Generally, the legislation is unclear as to whether, where there are sales and replacements spanning the end of an accounting period, the sale proceeds have to be brought in and taxed when received and relief only given for the replacement when incurred, or whether some other basis may be adopted.

> **Planning point**
>
> In practice, provided that the replacement occurs within 12 months, HMRC have allowed the sale proceeds to be carried forward to be credited against the cost of replacement. There seems to be no particular time limit for replacement, provided that there is a clear intention to replace the animal. An attempt to ignore this practice by one officer has been rejected by the commissioners. In some cases, farmers have not replaced animals for several years. This is especially likely to occur with pedigree herds, where replacements are found from home-bred stock. However, the position is far from clear and a cautious approach should be adopted.

Note that in a share farming arrangement, each part-owner has to elect for the herd basis to apply for the election to be valid.

Following representations, HMRC reconsidered their interpretation of the herd basis legislation. In *Tax Bulletin* Issue 64 (April 2003) (article superseded by HMRC *Business Income Manual* at para. BIM 55550), the Revenue stated that it is no longer considered necessary or appropriate to compute the profit on a minor disposal from the herd, without replacement, using what the Revenue had previously described as the 'herd basis cost' (which consisted of the initial cost of the herd and the cost of any improvement or increase in herd size). Such costs were not and still are not deductible in the farm trading account. When an animal replaced another of the same quality, it took on the 'herd basis cost' of its predecessor.

HMRC consider a disposal amounting to less than 20 per cent of the herd to be minor. Profits on these disposals are taxable. In the past this profit was computed by reference to 'herd basis cost'. In older established herds the original animals would have been replaced, perhaps several times, and this brought into charge a profit largely due to inflation. On the newer HMRC view, where a farmer sells without replacement a small part of the herd, HMRC accept that the profit should be computed by reference to the actual cost of the animal or animals disposed of. The fact that an animal taken from the herd replaced an earlier one is no longer relevant.

The following example illustrates the practical effect.

Example 65.2

Jim has been a dairy farmer since 1950. He started his herd with an initial purchase of 60 cows costing £100 each. Over the years he has maintained his herd by regularly replacing his stock with animals of the same quality.

In 2010, at the age of 70, he decided to sell ten of his most recently purchased cattle without replacement. The sale proceeds were £5,500 in total. As this disposal amounted to less than 20 per cent of the herd the profit needs to be included in the trading account of the farm. The 'herd basis cost' of these animals would have been £100 each, but they actually cost him £450 each.

Using the 'herd basis cost' the profit would have been:

£5,500 − (10 × £100) = £4,500.

Using actual cost the profit becomes:

£5,500 − (10 × £450) = £1,000.

In a situation where the farmer's records are simply so bad that this identification is not possible, HMRC will accept that the cost of the animals removed be computed by reference to the BEN 19 formula applied to the sale

> price. In this case it would work out at £3,300 (60 per cent of £5,500). The chargeable profit would then be £2,200.

Law: ITTOIA 2005, s. 118(1)–(5); CTA 2009, s. 116

65.5.2 Partnership changes and the herd basis

Following the introduction of the current year basis the Inland Revenue published Revenue Interpretation 173 in June 1997. The text is reproduced below.

> 'Partnership changes and the herd basis
>
> Schedule D, Case I – *Partnership changes and the herd basis* – TA 1988 s. 113, Sch. 5
>
> [The Revenue] explained in *Tax Bulletin* Issue 3 (May 1992) that a fresh herd basis election is required after a change in the membership of a partnership if herd basis treatment is to continue. [They] have been asked whether the changes to TA 1988 s 113 introduced as part of the preparation for self-assessment remove this requirement.
>
> TA 1988 Sch 5 (the herd basis) applies to "animals kept by a farmer". It is clear from paragraphs 2(3), [and] 5 that in this context, where the farming is carried on in partnership, the partnership is the farmer. Moreover, a partnership before a change in its membership is not the same partnership as that after the change. An election applies to all production herds of the class concerned kept "by the farmer making the election".
>
> Under the new Self Assessment rules, TA 1988 s 113(2) disapplies s 113(1) so that a change in the membership of a partnership does not trigger a cessation and recommencement of the trade. But this does not alter the fact that the farmer carrying on the trade before the change is not the same as the farmer after the change. So the herd is no longer kept by the farmer making the election. It follows that a fresh herd basis election by the new farmer is still required after a partnership change, if the new partnership wants the herd basis to apply. Thus there is no change from the view of the law set out [by the Revenue] in the May 1992 article.
>
> There is no special form for making a herd basis election, nor is there a requirement that the election be signed by the farmer. Where it is clear from material submitted to the Revenue within the time limit that a farmer has applied the herd basis, then [the Revenue] would regard an election as having been made. For example, the Help Sheet IR 224 which assists farmers in completing the self-employed pages of their returns, suggests that the additional information space on the return is used to record an analysis of herds on the herd basis and details of any adjustments. If this information is provided [the Revenue] would not need a separate election. But if the new partnership wants the herd basis to apply and this is not obvious from the return or other information routinely submitted, a written election stating the class of herd should be made.'

65.6 Averaging of fluctuating profits

65.6.1 Introduction

Farming and market gardening profits often fluctuate substantially from year to year, partly as a result of the vagaries of international trade and partly as a result of the weather. Consequently, a farmer, etc. could suffer a severe tax charge in one particularly successful year because of the higher rate of income tax, whilst he may not enjoy any substantial relief in a subsequent, less successful year, unless there were provision to the contrary in the legislation.

Special legislation therefore allows farmers and market gardeners (and, incidentally, creative artists) to 'average' their farming profits in any two consecutive tax years, provided that the profits in either year do not exceed a specified proportion of the profits for the other year. The profits are the profits as adjusted for tax purposes (and therefore after any capital allowances) but before any deduction for losses.

'Farming' for this purpose includes the intensive rearing of livestock or fish on a commercial basis for the production of food for human consumption. The HMRC view is that a prerequisite for a claim is the occupation of farmland so that relief is not due for agricultural contractors. Relief will also be denied where 'the trade includes substantial non-farming activities such as haulage or a caravan site as well as farming'.

The relief does not apply to profits subject to corporation tax.

Law: ITTOIA 2005, s. 221

Other guidance: BIM 73110

65.6.2 Calculation of relief

Averaging can be claimed if the profits for either of the two years do not exceed 70 per cent of the profits of the other year or are nil. A loss is treated as a nil profit for this purpose. There is a marginal relief where the profits of one year exceed 70 per cent of the other but are less than 75 per cent. If the profits for any two years ('years one and two') have been revised under an averaging claim, it is the revised figure for year two that is then used in any averaging claim for years two and three, and so on for any subsequent claims.

> **Planning point**
>
> It follows that profit averaging can be a continuous process. For example, the second year of a pair may be the first year of a subsequent pair and so on. On

Averaging of Fluctuating Profits 65.6.2

taking a view over a three-year period it may be best not to average the first year with the second year, even if a claim were possible, but rather to average the second year with the third year. Many combinations and permutations are possible.

Planning point

Consideration should also be given to the effect of profit averaging on the cash flow of the farming business. It may be best from a pure tax point of view over a three-year period not to claim average profits for the first and second years. However, a tax benefit may be outweighed by the cash flow benefit resulting from a claim to average profits for the first two years. The claim may result in lower tax payable for the earliest two years (at a cost of higher tax due in the third year), thus producing cash which may be urgently required in the business.

⚠ Warning!

Care should be taken where the claimant has paid retirement annuity premiums up to the maximum allowable amount in any year and later on an averaging claim is made in respect of the relevant year. In such a case it may well be that excess premiums will have been paid, and there appears to be no provision for this eventuality in the relevant legislation. This is not an issue with excessive personal pension plan premiums paid which must be refunded to the payer.

Full averaging

If the claimant's profits for either year do not exceed 70 per cent of his profits for the other year, or are nil, his profits for each such tax year are to be adjusted to the average of his profits for the two years taken together.

Example 65.3

Full averaging

Archer, a farmer, has assessable farming profits of £28,000 in 2009–10 and assessable profits of £13,800 in 2010–11. Since his profits in 2010–11 do not exceed 70 per cent of his profits in 2009–10, he may claim full averaging. If he does so, the result will be that his profits in each year are to be added together and his averaged profits for each year will become one-half of £28,000 plus one-half of £13,800, i.e. £20,900 in each year.

Restricted averaging

If the claimant's profits for either year exceed 70 per cent but are less than 75 per cent of his profits for the other year, his profits for each year are to be adjusted by adding to the profits that are lower and deducting from those that are higher an amount equal to three times the difference between them, less 75 per cent of those that are higher. This can be expressed as:

$$(D \times 3) - (P \times 0.75)$$

where:

D is the difference between the profits for the two years; and

P is the higher figure of relevant profits.

> ### Example 65.4
>
> **Restricted averaging**
>
> Pesh raises fish on an intensive basis for human consumption. His profits are £40,000 in 2009–10 and £56,000 in 2010–11. The lower profit figure lies between 70 and 75 per cent of the upper figure so he may claim restricted averaging. If he does so, the adjustment figure will be calculated as:
>
> $(16,000 \times 3) - (56,000 \times 0.75) = 48,000 - 42,000 = £6,000$.
>
> His adjusted profit figures will therefore be £46,000 for 2009/10 and £50,000 for 2010/–11.

Losses

Any loss which the claimant suffers in a particular tax year is treated as neither a gain nor a loss in that year for averaging purposes. However, any rights to loss relief which the claimant may have are still preserved.

> ### Example 65.5
>
> **Losses**
>
> Frank, a farmer, makes up his accounts to March 31. In the year to March 31 2009 there is an adjusted loss of £20,000 and in the year to March 31 2010 there is an adjusted profit of £40,000.
>
> Frank's position as regards profit averaging is as follows:
>
> | | |
> |---|---|
> | 2008/09 assessable profits | Nil |
> | 2009/10 assessable profits | £40,000 |
>
> These profits may be averaged to give assessable profits of £20,000 for each tax year. However, the £20,000 loss can be relieved in 2008–09 in the normal way.

Law: ITTOIA 2005, s. 223

65.6.3 Claims

An averaging claim must be made on or before the first anniversary of the normal self-assessment filing date for the second of the tax years to which the claim relates. However, where the profits for either of the two years which are the subject of the averaging claim are adjusted (under ITTOIA 2005, s. 224), any further averaging claim will not be out of time as long as it is made on or before the first anniversary of the normal self-assessment filing date for the tax year in which the adjustment for the other reason is made.

No claim is possible in respect of the year in which a trade commences or is discontinued. This includes a year where a partnership change is treated as a discontinuance. A claim does not affect relief for losses.

Averaging can create profits against which losses can be set, and time limits for loss claims are, therefore, extended to the end of the period during which the averaging claim must be made.

A stand-alone averaging claim cannot be made. The claim must be made on the tax return for the second year. Therefore a claim to reduce the payments on account in respect of the second year's liability (where profits are falling) cannot be validly made. The date of submission of the tax return claiming the relief is treated as the date of payment of the credit arising as a result of a claim for overpaid tax for earlier years. Interest runs from the due date of the payments on account until the date of the submission of the tax return. The moral is to prepare the client's accounts and submit the self assessment return as soon as possible.

> ⚠ **Warning!**
>
> Once a claim has been made for two consecutive years, it cannot be made for any years preceding those years. The effect on pension relief (for example) needs to be considered in all cases.

> **Planning point**
>
> In a partnership, each individual partner can decide whether or not to make a claim.

The computation of income for tax credits purposes ignores the income tax averaging of farming profits. For example the farming profits for 2009–10 may have been £75,000 and for 2010–11 £13,000. An averaging election will result in 2010–11 taxable income of £44,000, but income for that year for tax credit purposes will still be just £13,000.

Where a person claims to average his profits in respect of any tax year, any claim by him for relief for that year under any other income tax provisions:

- may be made before the end of the period in which the claim for profit averaging has to be made; and
- if already made, may be revoked or amended before the end of such period.

> **Planning point**
>
> A profit averaging claim may therefore enable the claimant also to claim some other relief which might otherwise have been missed and now be out of time.

Law: ITTOIA 2005, s. 222, 223, 224, 225

65.6.4 Tax and financial planning

In considering whether or not to elect to average profits, certain tax planning and financial aspects must be taken into account.

Profit averaging can be a continuous process. For example, the second year of a pair may be the first year of a subsequent pair and so on. On taking a view over a three-year period it may be best not to average the first year with the second year, even if a claim were possible, but rather to average the second year with the third year. Many combinations and permutations are possible.

Consideration should also be given to the effect of profit averaging on the cash flow of the farming business. It may be best from a pure tax point of view over a three-year period not to claim to average profits for the first and second years. However, a tax benefit may be outweighed by the cash flow benefit resulting from a claim to average profits for the first two years. The claim may result in lower tax payable for the earliest two years (at a cost of higher tax due in the third year), thus producing cash which may be urgently required in the business.

A profit averaging claim may enable the claimant also to claim some other relief which might otherwise have been missed and now be out of time.

65.7 Capital allowances

Farmers and market gardeners are entitled in certain circumstances, to capital allowances in the same way as are any other traders. It is, however, appropriate to mention here the system of capital allowances in so far as it applies particularly to farmers and market gardeners.

The two main types of allowance which will be considered here are those in connection with the provision of:

- machinery and plant; and
- agricultural buildings and improvements.

The treatment of agricultural buildings allowances is covered in detail in **Chapter 9**.

Some of the main problems in this area concern dairy houses or purpose-built structures for intensive rearing of livestock, where the equipment element is so integrated with the rest of the structure that the building works can be regarded almost as no more than cladding for the plant and machinery, and thus the whole structure should qualify as plant. HMRC resist this approach except in the case of mobile poultry houses, pig units or similar items.

Machinery and plant

Capital allowances may be available to farmers and market gardeners as for other traders and in particular for machinery and plant. The words 'machinery' and 'plant' are not defined, and so bear their ordinary meanings. It is generally clear which items comprise a farmer's or market gardener's machinery and plant. The following items normally qualify as such: tractors, distributors, harvesters, grain dryers, grain silos, effluent treatment plants, and text, reference and other books used in the business.

Even though some of the above items are structures they normally qualify for the relief because they perform a function, as compared with barns, cattle sheds, implement sheds and so on, which would not normally qualify since the latter are merely structures in which functions are performed.

Law: Schofield v R & H Hall Ltd (1974) 49 TC 538; *Munby v Furlong* (1977) 50 TC 491

Horses and other animals

The Court of Appeal has held that living creatures could be 'plant', and that in the particular business in question, horses (and carts) were the most material part of the plant, since they were:

> 'the materials or instruments which the employer must use for the purpose of carrying on his business, and without which he could not carry it on at all.'

However, the case was not concerned with tax legislation.

By way of contrast, in *Earl of Derby v Aylmer* (1915) 6 TC 665 the High Court held that the horse in question, which was kept for breeding, was not plant for capital allowance purposes even though it was used for production, because its diminution in value resulted, not from wear and tear, but merely from its

Farming in the UK

approaching the end of its life. The facts of the case were that Lord Derby claimed capital allowances on two valuable stallions which served both his own and other owners' mares. Rowlatt J held that the taxpayer was not entitled to capital allowances on the horses. The judgment is, however, of little help in deciding whether or not stallions may qualify as plant, because:

- *Yarmouth v France* (above) was not considered; and
- it is no longer necessary to show diminution of value by reason of wear and tear in order to be entitled to a capital allowance.

In *IR Commrs v Scottish & Newcastle Breweries Ltd* [1982] BTC 187 Lord Wilberforce took it for granted that a horse could be 'plant' for tax purposes. Indeed, a horse can, under certain circumstances, amount to 'plant' for tax purposes (see below). Although *Yarmouth v France* (above) was, on the narrow point, a workmen's compensation case, if Lindley LJ had to decide the point now, after uttering his dictum in *Yarmouth v France* he would have had to have held that a horse could be plant. His dictum expressly referred to chattels, whether 'dead or alive'. The words 'dead or alive' could hardly be relevant if animals could not conceivably qualify as 'plant'.

The Revenue have expressed their view on this point as follows (Farm Tax and Finance, Vol. 2, No. 1, 14 January 1984, at p. 6):

> 'In order to qualify for capital allowances a trader needs to show that he has incurred capital expenditure on the provision of plant ... Where there has been expenditure on a work horse and the practice has not been to write the cost off in computing profits such expenditure may be treated as capital expenditure on plant for these purposes and a capital allowance claimed. Expenditure on horses kept or bred for sale would not however qualify for a capital allowance.'

Law: Yarmouth v France (1887) 19 QBD 647

Planning point

Also, whilst Land Rovers qualify for writing down allowances without restriction, note that a Range Rover is regarded as a private car.

65.8 Revenue receipts and payments

65.8.1 Introduction

There are a number of special points concerning revenue receipts and payments.

65.8.2 Compulsory slaughter

Special treatment applies where compensation is paid under certain specified schemes for compulsorily slaughtered stock for which a herd basis election cannot be made. The profits arising, being the excess of the compensation over the book value of the animal (or over cost in the case of animals bred or purchased during the current year) can be taken out of the accounts for the current year and spread over the next three years in equal amounts.

There is a right of election for the herd basis where a substantial part (normally 20 per cent or more) of a production herd is compulsorily slaughtered. In such a case, this spreading relief cannot be claimed for the mature animals in the herd, even if the farmer chooses not to elect for the herd basis thereafter. The relief normally, therefore, applies only to young stock and followers, flying flocks and animals kept for fattening, and to mature animals where less than one-fifth of the herd is slaughtered.

Other guidance: BIM 55185; ESC B11

65.8.3 Set-aside

Land set-aside payments are treated as trading income under the normal principles of taxation for such receipts, to the extent that the payments are made for keeping land out of production for a period of five years on a 'care and maintenance' basis, and thus compensate for lost trading income.

Where the land is treated as continuing to be farmed, roll-over and hold-over reliefs will be available without restriction. If the set-aside period represents an interruption in the trade which then resumes, there is a restriction to such relief by reference to the period of non-trading use. If the trade does not resume, roll-over and hold-over reliefs should not be completely lost but, as confirmed in the Court of Appeal decision, this does not apply to roll-over and hold-over reliefs where proportionate relief continues.

Other guidance: Richart v Lyons & Co Ltd [1989] BTC 337

65.8.4 Drainage

Net expenditure incurred, after crediting any grants receivable, in order to restore efficient draining or on re-draining (the land having become waterlogged), are admitted as revenue expenditure, provided that it excludes:

- any substantial element of improvement; and
- the capital element (where the current owner is known to have acquired the land at a depressed price because of its swampy condition).

Other guidance: BIM 55270; SP 5/81

65.8.5 Other receipts and expenses

The HMRC *Business Income* manual contains extensive guidance on issues of particular relevance to farmers, including the following headings in relation to receipts and expenses.

- Farming grants and subsidies: general.
- Farming: tax treatment of grants and subsidies: general principles.
- Farming: timing of recognition of grants and subsidies.
- Farming: particular grants which may cause doubt or difficulty.
- Farming: grants to outgoing farmers under Agriculture Act 1967.
- Farming: sales via marketing co-operatives.
- Farming: compensation received for compulsory slaughter of animals.
- Farming: spreading relief following compulsory slaughter computation.
- Farming: method of allowing spreading relief.
- Farming: insurance compensation: compulsory slaughter of animals.
- Farming: receipts from sales of turf.
- Farming: receipts from sales of timber, etc.
- Farming: Christmas trees.
- Farming: receipts for grants of easements or wayleaves.
- Farming: receipts from licence given to treasure seekers.
- Farming: payments for protection of field monuments.
- Farming: compensation for land, etc. acquired by public bodies.
- Farming: compensation for notice to quit given by a landlord.
- Farming: tenant right.
- Farming: expenses of farmhouse.
- Farming: farmhouse rent.
- Farming: farm cottages.
- Farming: cost of reclaiming scrubland formerly under cultivation.
- Farming: land drainage expenditure: SP5 81.
- Farming: orchards.
- Farming: subscriptions to NFU and agricultural and breed societies.
- Farming: tenant right.
- Farming: professional fees for valuation of tenant right.

Other guidance: BIM 55150ff

65.8.6 Employee accommodation

HMRC will not seek to tax the provision of free board and lodging for lower-paid agricultural employees, even if off the farm, provided that, in the latter case, the employer has a contract with a third party for its provision, and that payments under the contract are made direct to the third party.

> **Planning point**
>
> Strictly, because under the Agricultural Wages Acts workers are entitled to take a higher wage on which they would be taxed and to pay their own board and lodging, they are taxable on the value of the board and lodging supplied (under the principles laid down in *Heaton v Bell* (1969) 46 TC 211). However, provided that workers are not directors or higher-paid, and that their contract of employment provides for a net cash wage with free board and lodging, they are not taxed on such free board and lodging.

> **⚠ Warning!**
>
> Where agricultural workers are entitled to a gross cash wage, they are assessable on the gross amount, even if their contract of employment provides for their employer to deduct a sum to pay for board and lodging.

Other guidance: EIM 50011

65.9 Partnerships and joint ventures

65.9.1 Partnerships

If a partnership is to be set up from a certain time, it is necessary to ensure that the facts support the existence of the partnership from that time, irrespective of what any partnership agreement says. This point was emphasised in the farming case of *Dickenson v Gross* and in the cases of *Waddington v O'Callaghan* and *Saywell v Pope*. It is thus not possible to make a partnership retrospective.

Similarly, a partnership agreement of itself is not conclusive evidence of a partnership if it conflicts with the realities of the situation, e.g. where the children are not really acting as partners but are employees.

Other guidance: *Dickenson v Gross* (1927) 11 TC 614; *Waddington v O'Callaghan* (1931) 16 TC 187; *Saywell v Pope* (1979) 53 TC 40

65.9.2 Joint ventures

There are numerous forms of joint ventures in farming. Usually one party supplies the land as capital, and the other supplies the rest of the fixed and working capital and manages the farming operations on the land.

> ⚠ **Warning!**
>
> Such arrangements are usually entered into to ensure that the landowner continues to trade for tax purposes – particularly where there are unabsorbed losses – and also to avoid the grant of a tenancy. However, the letting of land on a 364-day grazing licence for grass keep might not be regarded as trading. Also, any arrangement under which the profit share of the landowner is guaranteed, whatever the outcome of the venture, might also not be treated as a trading activity.

> **Planning point**
>
> The share of the landowner should, therefore, fluctuate, so that a claim to loss relief can be sustained.

65.9.3 Share farming

HMRC accept that both parties to a share farming agreement (where two parties jointly farm the same land) may be considered to be carrying on farming. Landowners in an agreement based upon the CLA model may be regarded as trading provided they take an active part in the share farming venture, at least to the extent of concerning themselves with details of farming policy and exercising their right to enter on to their land for some material purpose, even if only for inspection and policy making.

HMRC are on the lookout for agreements that purport to be share farming but that do not in fact come within the meaning of that term:

> 'For an agreement to be share farming it is essential that each party has their own business, albeit that the two businesses are very closely linked. The landowner must take an active part in the trading venture, at least to the extent of concerning himself with the details of some material aspect, if only limited to inspection and policy making.'

Where a new share farming agreement does not amount to a partnership landowners should, for tax purposes, continue to carry on any existing farming trade, so that any unabsorbed losses are available to set off against their share of any profits. From the agreed proportion of the outputs of the venture there is deducted the agreed inputs, in order to arrive at the profit assessable on the landowner only.

> ⚠ **Warning!**
>
> Stocks sometimes cause complications in share farming arrangements. If they are transferred from one party to the other when mature, 60 per cent or 75 per cent of their market value is accepted as cost in the normal way for home-bred

> animals. However, if there are joint interests in the animals, each party must account for a proportionate share of 'cost' in the profit and loss account. Such joint ownership, if the joint venturers also share in the ultimate results for the year, can be construed as a partnership, with consequential 'one assessment' implications.

> ### Planning point
>
> Instead, therefore, shares of inputs and outputs should be different, so that one joint venturer can make a loss and the other a profit.

Companies sometimes enter into joint-farming ventures with individuals or other companies. A company, even if it is a partner, is assessed separately on its share of profits, etc. as if it were carrying on the trade on its own (under the special rules for partnerships involving companies). It appears therefore that, where it has sustained losses in the past in its farming trade, these can be set against future profits from the joint venture.

Law: CTA 2009, s. 1259, 1260

Other guidance: BIM 55080

65.9.4 Pension funds

Institutions, in particular pension funds, have invested in agricultural land. Typically, the pension fund owns the land and the farmer is the fund's own subsidiary or a third party in partnership with such a subsidiary. The pension fund can then receive its share of profits in the form of rents which can be geared partly to profits.

> ### Planning point
>
> These rents are exempt from tax in its own hands, unlike trading income. Provided that the rents paid do not exceed the highest possible tender rent, they should be deductible by the subsidiary or the third party, on the authority of the case of *Union Cold Storage Co Ltd v Adamson*. As the pension fund will not want normally to grant an agricultural tenancy to a third party, its own trading subsidiary usually shares occupation of the land in partnership with the outside operator. Consequently, any expenditure generating tax allowances should be incurred in the trading company rather than in the pension fund, which receives only exempt income.

Other guidance: Union Cold Storage Co Ltd v Adamson (1931) 16 TC 293

65.10 Capital gains tax

65.10.1 Hold-over relief

All land that qualifies for IHT agricultural property relief, whether at the 100 per cent or 50 per cent, continues to qualify for hold-over relief where, for instance, it is given by a parent to a child. HMRC have confirmed that even if the land has development value which does not qualify for agricultural relief for inheritance tax purposes, hold-over relief still applies.

Other guidance: CG 66962

65.10.2 Roll-over relief

Improvements

Roll-over relief is often especially useful for farmers. In this connection, improvements to land and buildings are accepted by HMRC as 'new assets'. Such improvements can include, for example, drainage channels and other building work that cannot rank as 'fixed plant', e.g. sprinkler systems. In addition, if a tenant farmer purchases the freehold reversion, that is also accepted as a new asset.

> ⚠ *Warning!*
>
> However, if a farmer has to sell part of the land to which the freehold relates, for example, in order to meet the cost of the freehold, the sale proceeds of that part cannot be rolled over against the cost of the freehold. In that situation, the proceeds would derive from the same asset as the 'replacement' asset, and thus there would be no new asset. The farmer can only roll over the sale proceeds of other land already owned against such an acquisition (see ESC D22).

Land overseas

There is no territorial limitation to roll-over relief (subject to restrictions in connection with dual-resident companies). Farmers who remain UK-resident can sell a farm in the UK and roll over the gain into the acquisition of a farm, say in the USA, provided that where the UK trading operations cease, they carry on the new trade successively. This means, in practice, not more than three years from the cessation of the old trade – the same period as that normally allowed for purchasing new assets.

Cottages

Agricultural cottages should qualify as eligible assets, provided that they can be said to be used in the farm business. This means that they must be in the representative occupation of a farm worker. Following the case of *Anderton v Lamb*, it is not clear whether a house occupied by a business partner, other than the farmhouse, would qualify. However, if such a house were partnership property and restricted as to occupation to someone engaged in agriculture, it might rank as a business asset for roll-over relief.

Other guidance: *Anderton v Lamb* (1980) 55 TC 1

Joint ownership

Land that is in joint ownership often has to be partitioned to enable, say, two brothers to farm separately. A partition is also accepted as qualifying for roll-over relief. Provided that there is equality of exchange, full relief is given for the gain, with restriction on relief where there is a partial gift or where the land includes or becomes a dwelling-house. This concession is extended to include exchanges of joint interests in milk and potato quota, where these accompany exchanging joint interests in land to which the quota is attached.

Other guidance: ESC D26

65.10.3 Part-disposals

The proceeds on small part-disposals can be deducted from the cost rather than be assessed. This can help farmers who have to sell land to repay borrowings. However, for the relief to apply, the value of the land being disposed of cannot exceed one-fifth of the whole. There is also a monetary limit of £20,000. If the transferor makes any other disposals of land in the same year of assessment, the relief does not apply if the total value of the consideration for all disposals exceeds £20,000.

> ### *Planning point*
>
> Where land has been held for a long time and has a relatively low base cost compared with its market value, it may be to the owner's benefit to use the part-disposal, or a 'just and reasonable' formula, to calculate the gain (see below).

In general, it is not necessary to apply the strict part-disposal formula where part of an estate is disposed of. Instead, HMRC accept that the part disposed of can be treated as a separate asset and any just or reasonable method of apportioning part of the total cost of it is accepted, for instance, by reference to the value of that part at acquisition. Similar treatment applies where an election is made for market value as at 6 April 1965 to be treated as cost. The cost identified is then deducted from the total cost for future part disposals. Consistency should, in general, be the rule and, once the taxpayer has opted for this basis, it should be adhered to. This basis means that it is possible to choose whether to elect for 6 April 1965 value on each disposal, unlike the situation where the normal part-disposal formula is used.

Presumably, in the absence of an election under TCGA 1992, s. 120(5) for all relevant disposals to be based on the value of the asset at 31 March 1982, this practice has to be adapted to allow either original cost or the market value at 31 March 1982 to apply on each disposal, whichever is the more favourable.

Law: TCGA 1992, s. 242

65.10.4 Tenancies

It was held in *Henderson v Karmel's Executors* that, even where land is let to a company controlled by the owner of the land, the freehold should still be valued for capital gains tax purposes having regard to the tenancy, i.e. without vacant possession. In that case, the existence of the tenancy depressed the value at 6 April 1965.

However, unlike a tenancy in favour of an individual, a tenancy granted to a company can effectively be assigned by the transfer of shares in the company. Hence, both for capital gains tax and inheritance tax purposes, HMRC may argue that a company tenancy has a value in assessing the value of the company's shares.

The Capital Taxes Office have successfully argued in a case before the Scottish Lands Tribunal (*Executors of George A Baird v CIR*) that a share in a tenancy formed by a Scottish partnership had a very substantial value for capital transfer tax purposes on death because it was transferred on death to the wife and son of the deceased.

A similar decision was given by the Lands Tribunal on 31 July 1991 in the case of *Executors of the Honourable Myra Alice Lady Fox (Deceased)* where a share in a partnership tenancy was held to have a significant value for capital transfer tax purposes (45 per cent of vacant possession premium), although it had to be valued separately from the reversion, and not as a single unit of property with the reversion as HMRC contended.

A sum paid to a tenant to give up a tenancy, insofar as it is statutory compensation for disturbance is free of capital gains tax, following the case of *Davis v Powell*. It had been accepted by HMRC, before that case, that payments under the 1968 Act were free of capital gains tax, but the case established that a payment under the 1948 Act was not derived from an asset and was thus free of capital gains tax.

Where there is no notice to quit, or where there is a negotiated payment to induce the tenant to surrender the lease, HMRC argue that no part of the compensation is free of tax, on the basis that the payment is derived from the lease.

Capital Gains Tax 65.10.5

All such payments should be deductible by the landlord as enhancement expenditure in computing capital gains tax liability.

Other guidance: *Davis v Powell* (1976) 51 TC 492; *Henderson v Karmel's Executors* [1984] 58 TC 201

65.10.5 Quotas

Milk

Roll-over relief is available where there is a disposal or an acquisition of a milk quota. Quota and land are separate assets for capital gains tax purposes.

Reductions in milk quotas have resulted in the selling of existing quotas on the sale of the herds with which they are associated. This is often achieved by the seller granting to the buyer temporary grazing rights over the land to which the quota attaches. A lump sum is paid for the benefit of the quota. Under a separate agreement, the seller agrees to cooperate with the buyer in securing the identification of the quota with land belonging to the buyer, following the transfer of the cattle to his or her land. In some cases, the quota is 'leased' to a neighbour.

It seems that a sale of the quota is a chargeable occasion for capital gains tax purposes, whilst leasing the quota would generate receipts assessable to income tax. There are provisions in the regulations for a straightforward transfer of the quota on a change of occupation of the farm. If no part of the sale price of the farm is allocated to the quota, it is arguable that HMRC cannot apportion a notional value for tax purposes to the quota.

HMRC published an article in *Tax Bulletin* 6 (February 1993) following the non-tax case of *Faulks v Faulks*. The view expressed is that the case did not affect the treatment of milk quota for CGT purposes.

The HMRC view was subsequently upheld by the Special Commissioners in *Cottle v Coldicott*.

Other guidance: *Faulks v Faulks* [1992] 15 EG 15; *Cottle v Coldicott* (1995) Sp C 40

Potatoes

The removal of control over the acreage for growing potatoes means that potato quota has become worthless. Where there was a base cost for CGT purposes, a negligible value claim will often have been appropriate.

66 HMRC Enquiries

66.1 Introduction

The Inland Revenue and Customs and Excise were merged in April 2005 to form a new department, HM Revenue & Customs (HMRC). At the same time, a new independent prosecutions office – the Revenue & Customs Prosecutions Office (RCPO) – was set up to prosecute HMRC cases in England and Wales.

66.1.1 Powers of HMRC

After the creation of HMRC, a major review was announced, involving wide consultation, of the powers, deterrents and safeguards that will underpin the new revenue department.

The consultation process led to:

(1) HMRC piloting some of their ideas for 'interventions' that they thought would provide options for making enquiries that would be proportionate and less costly. The pilot, aimed at testing the effectiveness of the interventions, started in July 2006 and ended in October 2006. HMRC issued a report on the pilots setting out the lessons learned. Some of the approaches tested are now used when carrying out compliance checks using their information and inspection powers (see 8. and 9. below, **66.2.6** and **66.2.7**);

(2) a new penalty regime for incorrect returns applying to all the main taxes, Income Tax (IT), Corporation Tax (CT), Capital Gains Tax (CGT), Value Added Tax (VAT), Construction Industry Scheme (CIS), employers' PAYE (Pay As You Earn) and National Insurance Contributions (NICs) enacted by *Finance Act* 2007, replacing entirely the existing penalty regime with effect from 1 April 2009. The first penalties under the new regime are chargeable in respect of inaccuracies in returns or documents for return periods starting on or after 1 April 2008 where the due date for filing is on or after 1 April 2009 (see **66.9.5**);

(3) the introduction of a new enquiry window by *Finance Act* 2007, altering the period during which HMRC can start to enquire into a tax return (see **66.3**);

(4) the inclusion of provisions in the *Finance Act* 2007 to apply the provisions of the *Police and Criminal Evidence Act* 1984 (PACE) to all criminal investigations carried out by HMRC, whether they relate to ex-HM Customs and Excise or ex-Inland Revenue matters;

(5) the inclusion in *Finance Act* 2008 of a provision to extend the new penalty regime for penalties for incorrect returns to other taxes and duties that HMRC administer. This includes all excise duties, environmental taxes, inheritance tax, insurance premium tax, stamp duties and petroleum revenue

tax. The extended penalty regime applies with effect from 1 April 2010. The new regime replaces entirely the existing penalty regime;

(6) the introduction by *Finance Act* 2008 of a new penalty regime for failure to notify. The new regime applies to IT, CT, CGT, class 2 and 4 NICs, VAT, excise duties, environmental taxes and insurance premium tax. The new regime replaces entirely the existing penalty regime for failure to notify. It applies to failures that occur after 1 April 2010;

(7) the introduction by *Finance Act* 2008 of a new statutory record keeping requirement, empowering HMRC to specify the records to be kept by particular types of business. They will also issue additional non-statutory guidance on the types of records they will expect businesses to maintain to satisfy the statutory requirements. (see **66.1.2** and **66.5**);

(8) the introduction by *Finance Act* 2008 of new information and inspection powers to support compliance checks and the statutory record keeping requirement (also introduced by *Finance Act* 2008). The new information powers replace TMA 1970, s. 19A and s. 20 powers and can be used at any time to demand information or documents reasonably required to check a person's tax position – their use is not restricted to carrying out an enquiry into a return. The new inspection powers give HMRC the power to enter businesses premises at any time to inspect the statutory records, the business premises and business assets. In effect, HMRC can start enquiring into a person's tax position at any time, pre- or post-return. The new information and inspection powers apply from 1 April 2009 (see **66.1.2**, **66.4**, and **66.5**);.

(9) changes to the time limits for assessments and claims made by *Finance Act* 2008 (see **66.8**).

(10) the introduction by *Finance Act* 2009 of a new penalty regime for failing to meet obligations to file returns or pay tax on time.

Where an enquiry was started before 1 April 2009, HMRC can use only the new information powers contained in *Finance Act* 2008, Sch. 36 after that date. They must not, however, use the new powers to obtain information that they wanted previously but were unable to obtain using the old s. 19A powers.

Example 66.1

HMRC wanted information from a third party in the course of an enquiry started in January 2008 but they were unable to obtain it as they could require only the production of documents, not information, under TMA 1970, s. 20(3). The investigation is still ongoing at 1 April 2009 but HMRC is not permitted to use their powers under *Finance Act* 2008, Sch. 36 to revisit the matter and demand the information from the third party.

Example 66.2

In the course of an enquiry that was started in January 2008, HMRC issued an information notice under TMA 1970, s. 19A for some of the business records.

> The enquiry is still ongoing at 1 April 2009 and at some time after that date HMRC decide they need to see some more of the records. The records form part of the person's statutory records so, under the new powers contained in *Finance Act* 2008, Sch. 36 they have the power to visit the business premises to inspect the statutory records that are on those premises at the time of the visit. They can also issue an information notice, against which there is no appeal as it relates only to the statutory records.

> ⚠ **Warning!**
> A refusal to provide information which is relevant to the enquiry should not be used as a delaying tactic. HMRC can impose a penalty for failing to comply and it will be further reflected in the amount of the final penalty charged in respect of the inaccuracies found in the return.

Law: *Finance Act* 2007, s. 82, 96, 97 and Sch. 24; *Finance Act* 2008, s. 122 and Sch. 40, s. 123 and Sch. 41, s. 115 and Sch. 37, s. 113 and Sch. 36, s. 118 and Sch. 39

Other guidance: The leaflet HMRC powers and your rights, can be read on the HMRC website at *www.hmrc.gov.uk/about/powers_rights.htm*

HMRC have produced a series of factsheets explaining what will happen during a compliance check, what powers they have and what rights the taxpayer has. These can be found on the HMRC website at: *www.hmrc.gov.uk/compliance/factsheets.htm*.

66.1.2 Statutory framework for investigations

The introduction of self assessment (SA) was accompanied by some major changes in the way HM Revenue and Customs (HMRC) carry out enquiries into a person's tax affairs. For the first time, a statutory framework was provided governing the opening, working and closing of an enquiry.

The framework for making a formal enquiry will continue to exist but *Finance Act* 2008 contains provisions that:

- enable HMRC to use their new information and inspection powers and the discovery provisions to make enquiries at any time, without being restricted by the enquiry window;
- extend the first and third party information powers so that they can be used at any time if HMRC suspect that tax may not have been assessed, not just when enquiring into a return; and
- enable HMRC to specify the records that must be kept and give them the power to inspect business premises, records and assets whenever they wish.

The main statutory provisions governing enquiries are as follows:

Statutory provision	Individuals TMA 1970 section:	Partnerships TMA 1970 section:	Companies FA 1998, Sch. 18 paragraph:	Individuals, Partnerships and Companies FA 2008 Sch. 36 paragraphs:
Opening the enquiry	9A	12AC	24(1)	
Obtaining information and inspecting businesses				1 to 92
Closing the enquiry	28A(1)	28B(1)	32(1)	
Application to close	28A(4)	28B(5)	33(1)	
Records to be kept	12B	12B	21	

Broadly, the effect of these provisions is that:

- if the enquiry window is open (see **66.3.2**), HMRC must notify the taxpayer in writing of their intention to enquire into a tax return;
- the notice must be issued within the statutory time limit;
- enquiries can be made at HMRC's discretion – no reason has to be given;
- business premises, assets and records can be inspected at any time it is reasonably required to check a person's tax position;
- certain information and records must be provided on demand;
- HMRC can issue an information notice for the production of information or documents reasonably required for checking a person's tax position;
- a formal closure notice must be sent by HMRC setting out their conclusions and amendments; and
- taxpayers can apply to the Tribunal for a closure notice if they think an enquiry should be terminated.

Example 66.3

Having started an investigation into the affairs of a limited company by issuing a notice under FA 1998, Sch. 18, para. 24(1), the inspector has demonstrated that the company's business records are unreliable. The directors have been asked to provide copies of their private bank account statements. HMRC no longer need to issue enquiry notices under TMA 1970, s. 9A to each of the directors to obtain this information. Under the provisions of FA 2008, Sch. 36, if the

> directors fail to provide the information voluntarily, HMRC can, with the approval of the Tribunal, issue third party information notices to obtain it.

> **Planning point**
>
> When preparing work schedules, firms should factor in the inevitability of some enquiry work. A decision should be made on which enquiries will be dealt with in-house and which by a specialist. If insurance is to be arranged to cover the cost of an enquiry, research into the most suitable policy should be undertaken. Firms should also decide in advance their response to each stage of the enquiry, for example.
>
> (1) When to meet with the client for an initial discussion and authorisation for the fees for the additional work that will be required to deal with the enquiry.
>
> (2) Whether a new engagement letter is required to cover the work on the enquiry.
>
> (3) Whether an early disclosure of irregularities is appropriate.
>
> (4) Whether to seek the client's agreement to the preparation of a full review to be sent to HMRC.
>
> (5) The circumstances when it would be appropriate to apply to the Tribunal for a formal closure notice.

66.1.3 Process now, check later

The statutory provisions which underpin self assessment introduced a 'process now, check later' regime. There are clear, enforceable rules for making returns and paying the tax due. These rules enable the returns to be processed routinely on receipt and the tax to be collected without the need for an assessment to be raised by HMRC.

The routine acceptance and processing of the return is subject, however, to the return being selected later for enquiry. HMRC have only a limited period in which to issue a written enquiry notice. This period, the *enquiry window*, was amended by the *Finance Act* 2007 (see **66.3.2**).

In addition to carrying out a formal enquiry, HMRC can carry out a compliance check at any time, either before or after a return has been submitted (see **66.1.6**).

> **Planning point**
>
> Tax Offices are instructed to ensure that no one firm suffers a disproportionate number of enquiry cases each year. Any accountancy firm that feels that they

HMRC Enquiries

> receive more than their fair share of enquiries should raise the matter with the Area Director.

Law: TMA 1970, s. 9, 9A, 12AA, and 12AC; FA 1998, Sch. 18, para. 7 and 24(1)

66.1.4 No reason to be given

Before the introduction of self assessment, the old TMA 1970, s. 29 required that the officer be dissatisfied with a return before starting an enquiry. Under the SA provisions HMRC have an absolute right to make enquiries into a return and do not have to demonstrate grounds for dissatisfaction with it. Indeed, HMRC instructions to staff are clear that no reason should be given.

This change has two effects.

(1) HMRC can – and they do – select cases for enquiry at random. Their reason for doing this is that it provides them with a control against which to measure the success of their selections by way of risk assessment.

(2) The practitioner can no longer challenge HMRC at the outset to justify their concerns about a return to ensure that they are valid. This has removed an important protection from the taxpayer, who can now be subjected to a lengthy, harrowing and expensive investigation on the flimsiest of evidence or indeed no evidence at all.

An enquiry into a tax return can be:

- an aspect enquiry, where only certain aspects of the return are enquired into – for example whether or not an item is correctly classified as revenue expenditure and so appropriate for inclusion in the profit and loss account; or
- a full enquiry, where a full in-depth investigation will be carried out into the whole return (any enquiry selected at random will be carried out as a full enquiry).

Initially HMRC did not intend to indicate in the opening letter whether the enquiry into a tax return was random, aspect or full. After representations from the accountancy bodies, however, they agreed that their opening letter would make it clear if the enquiry was an aspect enquiry.

> **Planning point**
>
> Although no reason for the enquiry will be given, the terms of the opening letter from HMRC will make it clear whether the enquiry is a full enquiry or an aspect enquiry (see **66.3.5** below). This enables practitioners to plan their response. Although an aspect enquiry can be extended to become a full enquiry, the inspector should be asked to justify any change of tack. The practitioner should be alert to the possibility of an aspect enquiry sliding into a full enquiry without any justification other than the inspector's curiosity or inability to see when it is

> time to close the enquiry. Consideration should be given in appropriate cases to seeking a closure notice.

Law: TMA 1970, s. 9A, 12AC; FA 1998, Sch. 18, para. 24

66.1.5 Demand for information

There is a statutory requirement to maintain and retain the records needed to complete a tax return. If HMRC make a compliance check (including an enquiry), the records that a person is required by statute to maintain (their '*statutory records*') can be inspected by HMRC using their inspection powers under FA 2008, provided the inspection is reasonably required for the purpose of checking a person's tax position.

In addition, when carrying out a compliance check (including an enquiry) HMRC can use their information powers under FA 2008 to request any information that is reasonably required to check the person's tax position.

HMRC now give greater emphasis to the examination of business records. Staff are trained in the techniques of records examination and can call on accountancy support staff to assist them.

> ⚠ *Warning!*
> Practitioners can expect in the opening letter, which encloses a copy of the enquiry notice sent to the client, the routine request for all the client's business records. This request has to be complied with.

66.1.6 Compliance checks

A compliance check is a check into a person's tax position. A check can be carried out either before or after a return has been submitted. The legislation under which compliance checks are carried out came into force on 1 April 2009. HMRC have produced a series of factsheets explaining what will happen during a compliance check, what powers they have and what rights the taxpayer has. These can be found on the HMRC website at: *www.hmrc.gov.uk/compliance/factsheets.htm*.

Legislative framework

The new powers to carry out compliance checks apply in the same way to Income Tax, Capital Gains Tax, Corporation Tax, PAYE and NICs, Construction Industry Scheme and VAT. The new legislative framework, which is contained in *Finance Act* 2008, provides for:

- inspection powers – Sch. 36;
- information powers – Sch. 36;
- record keeping – Sch. 37;
- time limits for assessments and claims – Sch. 39; and
- the power to access and inspect computers – s. 114.

What is a compliance check?

HMRC carry out compliance checks to make sure that taxpayers are complying with their obligations, paying the right amount of tax at the right time and claiming the correct reliefs and allowances. They may do this, as they do at present, by asking for information and documents or by arranging a meeting or visit.

While they have always been able to request a visit to the business premises or ask for an interview, they now have the power to visit business premises to inspect them, the business assets and the statutory records. The position continues to be that HMRC cannot insist on interviewing taxpayers.

A compliance check can be carried out either before or after a tax return has been submitted. Although HMRC had the power to carry out pre-return checks for the purposes of PAYE and VAT before the introduction of the new powers in *Finance Act* 2008, they had no such powers relating to Income Tax, Capital Gains Tax and Corporation Tax.

A compliance check should be carried out only where a risk has been identified in relation to the taxpayer's tax affairs or where the taxpayer is included in HMRC's programme of random selection for enquiry. The taxpayer should always be made aware when the compliance check has started. A check is completed once the risk has been investigated and, if appropriate, any additional tax, interest and penalty has been charged. Once the check has been completed the taxpayer must be made aware of this.

Transitional matters

After 1 April 2009 HMRC officers must only use the new information and inspection powers included in *Finance Act* 2009, even if they are continuing an enquiry that started before that date. The old provisions were repealed when the new powers were introduced so they cannot, and must not, be used.

If, however, an officer has used the previous powers to obtain information by issuing a TMA 1970, s. 19A notice, and the information has not been provided, the powers to enforce the notice remain in place. For example, if a s. 19A notice was issued on 25 March 2009, giving a thirty day time limit for producing the required information, and the taxpayer fails to comply with the notice, the officer can assess a fixed penalty and settle any appeal against it under TMA 1970, s. 54.

Introduction 66.1.6

If a compliance check starts after 1 April 2009, the only information and inspection powers available to the officer are those contained in Sch. 36. Officers are warned against using the powers in Sch. 36 to request information or documents that they would like to have requested before 1 April 2009 but were unable to obtain under the old powers.

Pre-return checks

The new compliance checking powers enable HMRC to carry out examinations of contemporary business records to check that they are adequate and comply with the statutory record keeping requirements. Any errors can be discussed and corrected to avoid the submission of an incorrect tax return. Where an examination shows that there is the likelihood of something being dealt with incorrectly, the officer will be able to offer advice on the correct treatment before the tax return is submitted.

HMRC envisage that pre-return checks will be carried out:

- to assist with clearance applications, and where a pre- or post-transaction ruling has been requested;
- if a trader regularly makes a voluntary disclosure of errors after submitting a VAT return;
- to check on activities suspected to be within the hidden economy;
- where a previous check has shown that the business record-keeping was poor and a follow-up visit is needed to check that the position has improved – this will always be necessary where a penalty for poor record keeping has been suspended;
- to check that the way information is kept on computer is adequate to ensure that a correct return can be made;
- to find out about tax planning and avoidance schemes; and
- if fraud is suspected.

As with any other compliance check, a risk must have been identified before a pre-return check can be carried out unless the taxpayer has asked for a check.

Errors found

The way in which any errors found in the course of a pre-return check will be dealt with depends on whether or not the errors affect a return that has already been filed. If they do not, the officer will simply offer guidance on how to correct the error to avoid submitting an incorrect return or on paying the correct amount of tax for the period covered by the check.

If a pre-return check shows that a taxpayer has made an error that has led to them paying too much tax, they can:

- amend their tax return if the enquiry window is still open; or

- make an error or mistake claim for earlier years if claims for those years are still in date.

If the check leads the officer to suspect that tax has not been assessed, or has been under-assessed, or that excessive reliefs have been given, then:

- if the enquiry window is still open, an enquiry will be started; or
- if the enquiry window is closed, an assessment will be made for the chargeable period, provided the time limits for assessment permit it.

If the officer can raise an assessment then the information powers contained in *Finance Act* 2009, Sch. 36 can be used to obtain the information needed to decide on the quantum of the assessment.

Compliance checks and the enquiry window

The officer will always have to consider whether or not it is appropriate to open a formal enquiry before starting a compliance check.

If the compliance check is to be made into VAT or PAYE/CIS, the officer will not need to open an enquiry before making the check, even if the taxpayer's Income Tax or Corporation Tax position is to be checked at the same time.

If the aim of the compliance check is to review records relating to the taxpayer's Income Tax or Corporation Tax position, and the risk is within an open enquiry window, the officer must issue an enquiry notice if one has not been issued already.

If the officer has identified a risk for a period for which an enquiry window has closed and either the risk is unlikely to affect other years or the risk can't be identified by checking the current period or a period for which the enquiry window is still open, consideration will have to be given as to whether a discovery assessment can be made. An example would be the situation where a capital gain had not been assessed.

Information and inspection powers

The framework for compliance checks is supported by the new information and inspection powers contained in Sch. 36 (see **66.4**).

The inspection powers give HMRC the power to visit business premises and check assets and records. They can use this power before a return has been received. While any visit will normally be by prior arrangement, HMRC have the power to make unannounced visits.

Provided they are reasonably required for the purpose of checking a tax position, the new powers give HMRC the power to require taxpayers or third parties to provide information and produce documents.

Safeguards

There are safeguards for the taxpayer provided as part of the new framework for compliance checks which are intended to ensure that:

- the powers are used reasonably and proportionately;
- it is clear to the taxpayer when a check starts and ends;
- no visits can be made to private residences without invitation; and
- unannounced visits must be authorised.

Law: FA 2008, Sch. 36, Sch. 37 and Sch. 39, and s. 114

Other guidance: HMRC factsheets for compliance checks can be found on the HMRC website at *www.hmrc.gov.uk/compliance/factsheets.htm*

66.1.7 Stages of an enquiry

When seeking to agree a timetable for working an enquiry (the *Faster Working* initiative), the Revenue identified the various stages of an enquiry. It will help practitioners to know what these stages are so that they can monitor the progress of an enquiry. It also helps to identify when an enquiry has stalled and the reasons for it so that the process can be restarted and progressed to a satisfactory conclusion or a closure notice can be sought (see **66.9.1**).

The stages are as follows.

1. Selection (whether by risk assessment or at random).
2. A detailed review of the return and other information held, including the taxpayer's compliance history.
3. Identification of the information needed to check the return.
4. Opening letter with copy of enquiry notice to practitioner.
5. Obtaining information needed to check the return.
6. Examination of the information.
7. Drawing conclusions and identifying the further information needed.
8. Settlement and issue of completion notice.

> **Planning point**
>
> Although the *Faster Working* initiative was dropped and no timetable for working an enquiry was agreed between HMRC and accountancy bodies, HMRC will seek to impose very short time scales for providing information. This is for their own benefit to enable them to meet their internal targets. It should not be allowed to interfere with the client's right to be treated fairly. Practitioners should resist excessive pressure for a quick response where this prejudices the likelihood of determining the correct amount of the tax due.

> ⚠ **Warning!**
>
> If a practitioner considers that unrealistic deadlines are being set, the inspector should be reminded that HMRC's own internal instructions at *Enquiry Manual* EM1811 say that realistic timetables should be agreed for action by an agent.

Other guidance: Inland Revenue *Tax Bulletin*, Special Edition 2

66.2 Selection for enquiry

66.2.1 Introduction

Although the practitioner plays no part in the selection process, it is helpful to understand how the process works and what will lead to a client being selected for enquiry. Knowing why a client may be selected for enquiry enables the practitioner to provide with their tax returns the additional information or explanations which can prevent an unnecessary enquiry.

If a client is investigated, knowing the relative importance of the areas of possible concern to HMRC will help the practitioner to keep the enquiry focused. It also makes it possible to recognise when the most important matters have been dealt with so that the officer can be invited to close the enquiry.

> ***Planning point***
>
> If the practitioner judges that all substantial matters have been resolved and the officer is pursuing only trivial matters, an application for a closure notice can be considered (see **66.9.1** below).

> ⚠ **Warning!**
>
> The practitioner should check that the additional information provided with the client's tax returns has been made available to the investigating inspector when the case was selected for enquiry (see **66.3.7**).

Law: TMA 1970, s. 28A, 28B; FA 1998, Sch. 18, para. 33

66.2.2 Random selection

The legislation relating to SA enquiries allows HMRC to select cases at random. Their reasons for doing so are:

- so that no one will think that their evasion will remain undetected;

- to monitor the level of non-compliance; and
- to check on the effectiveness of their selection process and to help them to refine their risk assessment strategy.

In the HMRC *Tax Bulletin*, Special Edition 2, August 1997 it was stated that in the case of a random selection of a non-business taxpayer with less complex affairs they would only go beyond a request for the records used to complete the return, for example to request private financial records, if they

> '... expect to be able to satisfy the Commissioners that the request is reasonable in the particular circumstances of the case.'

However, in a talk to the Chartered Institute of Taxation in June 1995 the Revenue said that they:

> '... do not expect Commissioners to uphold appeals (against s. 19A notices requiring the provision of information etc.) made on the basis that we cannot reasonably require information if we have no grounds for thinking the return is incorrect.'

It is suggested that the Tribunal (previously the commissioners) would, in fact, find that a request for further information from a non-business taxpayer with less complex affairs was unreasonable if HMRC had no grounds for thinking the return is incorrect. For information to be reasonably required the Tribunal will take into account whether the cost and the work involved in providing it is in proportion to the tax at risk. If no tax can be shown to be at risk, the Tribunal will have to consider whether HMRC can justify imposing the burden of providing the information simply to enable them to provide themselves with statistics about the general level of compliance and the effectiveness of their compliance strategy.

As a result of the changes introduced by *Finance Act* 2008, information can be demanded if it is reasonably required for the purpose of checking a person's tax position (not tax return). What is said above about the need for HMRC to have grounds for suspecting that a person's tax return was incorrect before imposing a burdensome requirement to provide information could reasonably be extended to checking a person's tax position.

Planning point

The practitioner has an important role to play in ensuring that the undertakings given by HMRC with regard to random enquiries are honoured. They have given assurances that:

- they will not pursue an enquiry if the risk is trivial; and
- in the case of a non-business taxpayer with less complex affairs they will normally request only those records which were used to complete the return.

Law: TMA 1970, s. 9A, 12AC; FA 1998, Sch. 18, para. 24

Other guidance: Inland Revenue *Tax Bulletin*, Special Edition 2, August 1997

66.2.3 Selection by risk assessment

The introduction of the 'process now, check later' regime and a more centralised computer selection process has enabled HMRC to improve its selection procedures to target more worthwhile cases where greater amounts of tax are at risk. Risk assessment is constantly refined, using the results of enquiries which have been concluded to confirm the importance or otherwise of particular risk factors. Risk factors include:

- being the type of business where evasion is thought or has been shown to be widespread;
- poor trading results, particularly if it is a cash business;
- inadequate drawings from the business;
- unexplained capital accretions;
- a poor compliance history;
- third party information held by HMRC.

The automated risk assessment process is only the first step. The results are passed to the investigating officer so that a critical review of all the information held on file can then be made before a final decision is made on whether to select the case for enquiry.

As part of the review of their powers, HMRC piloted ideas for 'interventions' intended to provide options for investigations that are more proportionate to the risk that has been identified and can be undertaken at less cost to taxpayers and HMRC (see **66.1.1** above and **66.2.6** below). The new power given to HMRC by *Finance Act* 2008 to inspect business records, premises and assets will be incorporated into the risk assessment process so that a business that is found on inspection to have poor records is likely to be selected for enquiry.

Planning point

Where selection has been by way of risk assessment, practitioners will find it more difficult to convince HMRC that a client's return is complete and correct. Success in doing so will depend on:

- detailed research;
- a carefully argued case; and
- determination in the face of stubborn resistance from the officer.

⚠ Warning!

While the aim of risk assessment is to select the most worthwhile cases for investigation, experience has shown that large numbers of three line accounts information cases for businesses with a turnover of less than £15,000 are also selected.

66.2.4 Risk assessment

Finance Act 2008 allows HMRC to stipulate what records particular types of business should maintain (see **66.5**). It also allows them to inspect those records, the business premises and business assets. If the inspection reveals that the records are inadequate, or that they do not reflect the economic reality of the business operations, the tax at risk will be taken into account when deciding whether to check the person's tax position.

The HMRC computer holds various core risk rules which are used in the risk assessment of every case. Local compliance managers can specify additional criteria for producing the monthly list of cases for enquiry, for example all taxi businesses with a fuel-takings ratio below a certain level. The core risk rules include the following.

Type of business

Various types of business are considered to pose a significant risk of evasion. The majority have in common the fact that they are cash businesses, making it easier to divert takings.

HMRC provide their investigators with Business Economics Notes (BENs) explaining the background to the way particular trades operate. They explain how to approach an enquiry and what irregularities to look out for in each type of business covered. They draw attention to the possibility of small amounts of cash being received even in a business which is almost entirely non-cash (for example swearing fees received by a solicitor). Although the amounts themselves are trivial, their omission from the accounts will be used to justify a more in-depth enquiry. Material which HMRC consider to be of a sensitive nature is removed from the BENs before publication. Practitioners will find more comprehensive material for a greater number of trade sectors in CCH *Business Focus*.

As well as targeting cash businesses, HMRC also target businesses where it is known to be the practice that employees (usually low-paid) have their wages supplemented by cash payments. Examples are nursing home staff, children's nursery staff, coach drivers, cleaning staff, etc. The risk factor is classified as high because payment of cash wages requires the understatement of takings and the wages themselves escape PAYE tax and NICs. Furthermore, because of the element of collusion needed, these cases are likely to be considered for prosecution.

> **Planning point**
>
> Practitioners who explain to their clients the importance of strict control over cash handling will give them a greatly improved chance of surviving an enquiry. The process of handling cash from the moment it is received until the moment it is banked or spent should be discussed with the client and a comprehensive

> recording system put in place. Without this, it will be impossible to show that cash has not been misappropriated, especially if the officer considers the results of a business economics exercise to be unsatisfactory.

Other guidance: CCH *Business Focus*

Poor trading results

The gross profit rate is used as an indicator of the possible diversion of takings. The formula to calculate the gross profit rate (GPR) is:

$$\text{GPR} = \frac{\text{Gross profit}}{\text{sales}} \times 100$$

Clients will often be more familiar with their mark-up rate (MUR) than with their gross profit rate and may confuse the two. It is important that, at the outset, the practitioner ensures that the client understands the difference to avoid misunderstanding. It will often be useful to be able to convert a mark-up rate to a gross profit rate and vice versa. The formulae for converting one to the other are:

$$\text{GPR} = \frac{\text{MUR}}{100 + \text{MUR}} \times 100$$

$$\text{MUR} = \frac{\text{GPR}}{100 - \text{GPR}} \times 100$$

> ### Example 66.4
>
> A 50% MUR converts to a 33$^1/_3$% GPR:
>
> $$\text{GPR } 33^1/_3 \% = \frac{\text{MUR } 50}{100 + \text{MUR } 50} \times 100$$

> ### Example 66.5
>
> A 33$^1/_3$ % GPR converts to 50 % MUR:
>
> $$\text{MUR } 50 \% = \frac{\text{GPR } 33^1/_3}{100 - \text{GPR } 33^1/_3} \times 100$$

The gross profit rate will be examined from three points of view.

(1) How it compares with the norm for this type of business?

(2) How it compares with other similar businesses in the area?

(3) How it compares with the gross profit rate shown by earlier accounts for this business?

To assist the client, the practitioner should obtain information on the gross profit norm for the trade. Steps should be taken to establish and record the reasons why the results are less good than might be expected. This exercise will benefit the client from a purely commercial point of view and may suggest ways of improving profitability. If steps are taken to improve profitability, a note should be kept of what these were and their effect in case the resulting fluctuation in the trading results is itself the cause of selection.

When considering the results it is helpful to review:

- the buying terms from suppliers and whether they could be improved by negotiation or changing supplier;
- stock handling and storage, including wastage, breakages and pilfering; and
- selling prices, including any discounting policy, in the context of a break-even calculation and their effectiveness.

When comparing the results with those of similar businesses in the same locality, care should be taken to ensure that the comparison is valid. Rarely will two businesses be so similar that there will be no differences to account for variations in results. The practitioner should look for differences between the terms of supply and sale of stock, the goods sold and the product mix and the other factors which affect the business ratios. A refusal by the officer to say what businesses have been used for the purposes of comparison will weaken HMRC's case as it makes it impossible to justify the comparison without this information. Any such refusal should be drawn out if the case progresses to a hearing before the Tribunal.

As well as comparing the gross profit rate achieved with the norm and with that achieved by other similar businesses in the area, the officer will also compare it with the results achieved by the business itself in earlier years. Once again, this can be a useful commercial exercise, encouraging the client to identify what has led to good results in the past and the reasons for less good performance.

Reasons for fluctuations in the gross profit rate from year-to-year should be identified. These might include:

- changed terms of supply;
- greater or smaller stock losses; or
- increases or decreases in prices, giving discounts, 'happy hours', etc.

When the return is submitted, fully supported explanations of why the results appear poor when compared with the norm or why the gross profit rate has fluctuated from year-to-year will help to avoid unnecessary selection for enquiry.

Planning point

The practitioner should keep a year-by-year summary of trading results for each client and explore with the client the reasons for any substantial fluctuations. The white space on the tax return should be used to explain the reasons for apparent anomalies to avoid unnecessary selection for enquiry.

To assist with the review of the trading results, as well as talking to the client, the practitioner should refer to as much independent evidence as possible. CCH *Business Focus* will provide background information on various trades, together with guidance on the likely results and the factors that may affect them.

Other guidance: CCH *Business Focus*

Inadequate drawings

Apparently inadequate drawings taken from the business is another of the core risk rules. The drawings will be judged against:

- what might be expected to be a minimum given the client's personal circumstances; and
- the level of drawings comparing one year with another.

This is another area which practitioners can explore with their clients so that information can be provided with the return which avoids unnecessary selection for enquiry.

If drawings appear to be particularly low in absolute terms it can be helpful to explain the likelihood of selection to the client and to provide a detailed personal and private expenditure questionnaire for completion. This will demonstrate whether or not the drawings figure is inherently unlikely and provide the opportunity to discuss this aspect with the client before submission of the return.

The reasons for fluctuations in drawings between years, or the failure to keep up with inflation, should also be established. Providing this information with the return will, if it is a full and credible explanation, avoid selection.

When reviewing drawings, the adequacy of private use adjustments should be considered. Where private use or own consumption is likely, it should be established whether any adjustment has been made and, if so, whether it is visible to HMRC. If no adjustment is needed or if an adjustment has been made by debiting drawings, it is important that HMRC are made aware of this. It will also assist if the method of calculating private adjustments is shown and it is demonstrated that they take into account changing personal and family circumstances.

Finally, it should be borne in mind that HMRC will compare the level of drawings with the wages paid to the highest paid employee of the business, expecting the former to exceed the latter. If the wages paid to the highest-paid employee exceed the drawings of the proprietor, there will often be very good reasons for this. Failing to make it clear in the return why this is, however, may lead to an enquiry.

Example 66.6

The inspector has made a review of the actual drawings compared with the drawings projections based on applying the Retail Price Index (RPI) to the drawings taken in the year ended 31 December 2010. As the drawings have not kept pace with inflation and there is nothing on file to explain the reduced level of drawings an enquiry notice was issued. The review showed:

y/e 31 December	2010	2011	2012	2013	2014	2015
RPI (illustrative)	170.3	173.4	176.2	181.3	186.7	192.0
Actual drawings	18,000	18,300	18,600	16,000	16,500	17,000
RPI projections from 2010		18,328	18,624	19,163	19,733	20,294
Discrepancies		28	24	3,163	3,233	3,294

At interview it emerged that the client's eldest child had been at university during 2010, 2011 and 2012 and that the client had provided assistance towards fees and living costs of £3,000, £3,050 and £3,100 respectively. After taking this into account, the amended review, with the projections based on £15,000 'other drawings' in 2010 compared with 'other drawings' in subsequent years, showed:

y/e 31 December	2010	2011	2012	2013	2014	2015
RPI (illustrative)	170.3	173.4	176.2	181.3	186.7	192.0
Total drawings	18,000	18,300	18,600	16,000	16,500	17,000
University costs	3,000	3,050	3,100			
Other drawings	15,000	15,250	15,500	16,000	16,500	17,000
RPI projections from 2010		15,273	15,520	15,969	16,445	16,911
Discrepancies		23	20	-31	-55	-89

This showed that the drawings had, in fact, been unusually consistent and in line with inflation so that the inspector's concerns were answered. If the fluctuating drawings were the sole reason why the client was selected for investigation, the investigation could have been avoided if an explanation had been provided for the drop in the level of drawings.

Planning point

The practitioner needs to know as much as possible about a client's personal circumstances and to consider the ongoing pattern of drawings in this context. To do this, the practitioner needs to:

HMRC Enquiries

- keep a permanent note of the client's personal circumstances and any changes to them; and
- keep an ongoing record of drawings, showing how they are made up.

If the level or pattern of drawings is likely to be a cause for concern it may avoid unnecessary selection for enquiry if explanations for any unexpected pattern are provided in the white space on the tax return.

Unexplained capital accretions

If a return indicates substantial unexplained capital, either by a large, sudden increase in investment income or by showing capital introduced into the business, it will almost certainly lead to an enquiry.

Planning point

Information should always be provided with the return to explain the immediate source of the capital invested or introduced, with a note of its immediate source and how it was held previously.

Poor compliance

A poor compliance record includes:

- returns sent in late;
- tax paid late;
- PAYE returns sent in late;
- late payment of PAYE tax and NICs;
- incorrect returns;
- a failure to comply with the statutory record keeping requirements or to maintain the records recommended by HMRC for the particular type of business.

If there are difficulties in submitting a return on time, provisional figures can be used provided they are reasonable and the reason for them is explained. Difficulties in paying tax due should be discussed with the Collector as soon as possible and before any collection proceedings are started.

A serious failure to comply with the statutory record keeping requirements will inevitably lead to an enquiry at some time in the future so that HMRC can check whether the records have been improved and are being properly maintained. These requirements will not be so strictly interpreted, however, that estimates can no longer be used when completing a return.

Planning point

Clients should be made aware that a casual approach to compliance with their obligations under the Taxes Acts, or improving their cashflow at HMRC's expense, can incur more expense than the immediate charges to interest and penalties.

⚠ Warning!

Practitioners should ensure that delays in their office are never the cause of a client being selected for enquiry because of a poor compliance record.

Law: TMA 1970, s. 12B; FA 1998, Sch. 18, para. 21

Other guidance: Inland Revenue *Tax Bulletin*, Special Edition 2, August 1997 and Issue 57, April 2002

Third party information

One of the most common reasons for selection for enquiry is information held by HMRC which was obtained from a third party. This information may come from:

- HMRC using their information powers, for example to obtain details of licences issued by local authorities;
- information provided by other tax offices, often as a result of another enquiry;
- disgruntled ex-employees, ex-spouses, trading partners, etc.; or
- members of the public.

The officer is not usually reticent about letting the client and the practitioner know that HMRC are holding information which has been obtained through official channels. Difficulties arise, however, when the information comes from informers. Under the SA regime, the reason for selection will not be given, making it difficult to challenge information which may be incorrect either due to malice or simply to a mistake. Furthermore, HMRC will not reveal the source of the information provided by informers.

Even if the information provided by an informer turns out to be incorrect, HMRC's internal instructions are that a full enquiry should still be carried out but that it will normally be appropriate to reduce the amount of information requested.

Planning point

If the officer will not disclose what information is held by HMRC or if it is discredited but the enquiry continues, the practitioner may wish to consider making an application for a closure notice (see **66.9.1** below).

> ⚠ **Warning!**
> Whenever additional information or explanations are provided with the tax return, the practitioner should check that the information provided has been made available to the investigating inspector at the time when the case is selected for investigation (see **66.3.7**).

66.2.5 Critical review

Once the automated selection process has been made by reference to the risk rules, the case is passed to the officer who will carry out the enquiry so that a critical review of all the information available can be made. The purpose is twofold:

(a) to check that a full enquiry is appropriate; and
(b) if it is, to:

 (i) summarise and interpret the available information;
 (ii) identify the further information needed; and
 (iii) decide how best to obtain the further information.

> **Planning point**
> As soon as practitioners receive a copy of the enquiry notice, it would be a useful exercise to mirror the officer's critical review to put themselves on equal terms with the officer and to prepare themselves for any meetings between the client and the officer.

Overview

The practitioner's plan for carrying out his or her own critical review should include the following:

- a summary of all the information held on file, including any information held in correspondence files;
- a tabular summary of the figures from the last six years' accounts with the years across the top and the headings on the left;
- background reading about the business and the trade sector in which it operates;
- preparation of a business model;
- an appraisal of the business ratios shown by the accounts;
- a review of the business records, identifying any weaknesses; and
- a year-by-year tabular summary of the last six tax returns and the drawings shown by the accounts.

Background reading

The background reading will help to understand how the trade operates and what activities are likely to be found. This will indicate what records might be expected and may also reveal that there are certain records which a trader is legally required to maintain, for example, an animal movements book.

Thinking about the way the trade operates may also help to identify the non-financial records which must be kept for the smooth running of the business and which will usually supplement and explain the financial records when preparing the business model.

When researching the trade operating practices, practitioners should take particular note of any indications of what business ratios might be expected, the factors which will affect those ratios and whether there are likely to be minor sources of cash income which might be omitted from the records.

> **Planning point**
>
> CCH *Business Focus* provides background information on operating practices, likely activities and the records, including any non-financial records, that can be expected to be kept to run the business.

Other guidance: CCH *Business Focus*

Business model

It will help if at an early stage the client understands what a business model is and that the officer can substitute the results of a business model in place of the results shown by the accounts without having to 'prove' that the accounts are not correct.

It is suggested that a very approximate business model is prepared by the client and the practitioner together. Using the client's broad estimates of the product mix of the business, the costs and sales of each product group and estimates for wastage, etc. an approximation of the gross profit rate which might be achieved can be calculated.

It is likely that when the results shown by the accounts are compared with the results of the above exercise and with the norm for the trade, the client will appreciate the need for, and authorise the expense of, a more detailed mark-up exercise.

The more detailed exercise should be based on an analysis of the purchase invoices for at least one month. If this is not representative a longer period, or two separate months at different times of the year, should be used. While the invoice analysis work is being carried out, the client could keep a record of actual wastage, etc. at the present time to refine the mark-up exercise.

> **Planning point**
>
> HMRC are likely, at some stage, to send someone to visit the business premises covertly. It is as well for the practitioner to be familiar with the premises, both to ensure that HMRC have no greater knowledge of the case and to identify ways in which losses and inefficiencies which might affect the business model could arise.

Reviewing the accounts summary

The tabular summary of the figures from the accounts for a six-year period will help the practitioner to identify and understand the reason for the questions which the officer is likely to raise. It may also provide some answers which the officer has overlooked.

1. The level of turnover should be considered against movements in the Retail Price Index and any available index for the performance of the particular trade sector concerned. Unexpected fluctuations may highlight changes in the trade which also help to explain fluctuating margins.

2. If the accounts show no debtors, the practitioner should consider whether this is normal or if they have been overlooked, for example a newsagent's unpaid newspaper accounts. If there are debtors in the balance sheet, the debtor days can be compared with the norm for the business sector.

3. The figure of stock may indicate that there has been no stock take and that the estimate has been made without due care. In *Pooley v R & C Commrs* (2006) Sp C 525 the absence of proper records of stock and the failure to make proper valuations for opening and closing stock was found to indicate a careless approach to the preparation of the taxpayer's tax return amounting to negligent conduct. If the stock level is below what is the norm for the trade the officer will seek an explanation for this and may seek an uplift, with the consequent increase in profits.

4. Creditor days should be compared with the norm. If the liabilities are such that the current ratio shows the business to be illiquid, the practitioner may want to consider if any borrowings are secured against personal assets and if this impacts on the review of drawings and private assets (see below).

5. If cash appears to be an estimate each year, the lack of cash control and of a regular cash reconciliation will be of concern to the officer.

6. Large fluctuations in the profit and loss entries should be explained and may themselves give an indication of changes in the business which account for any unexpected business ratios or fluctuations in results.

Example 66.7

Accounts summary

y/e 31 December	2010	2011	2012	2013	2014	2015
RPI (illustrative)	170.3	173.4	176.2	181.3	186.7	192
Turnover	185,068	201,562	350,000	387,927	438,260	440,831
RPI projection from 2010		188,368	191,409	196,950	202,816	208,573
Cost of goods sold	128,002	139,361	280,068	310,879	354,608	358,080
GP	57,068	62,201	69,932	77,048	83,652	82,751
GPR %	31%	31%	20%	20%	19%	19%
Wages	30,000	31,564	80,184	82,604	85,062	87,474
Repairs	2,345	546	25,489	3,204	685	1,894
Professional fees	1,200	1,354	7,853	1,400	1,450	1,500
Stock	9,000	9,000	9,000	9,000	9,000	9,000
Trade debtors	20,354	22,257	40,385	43,761	50,568	51,065
Cash	200	200	200	200	200	200
Trade creditors	19,692	20,440	43,287	48,828	54,555	55,198
Drawings	18,000	18,328	18,624	19,163	19,733	20,294

The fall in the GPR from 31 per cent to 19 per cent will be of immediate concern to the inspector who may conclude that the business grew well ahead of expectations, with turnover double what might have been expected by 2015, so that the taxpayer started to siphon off some of the takings. Debtors and creditors have been consistent, and at reasonable levels, but cash and stock appear to be estimates, the same figures being used every year. Drawings have increased in line with inflation but do not reflect the increased prosperity of the business, so may have been supplemented with undisclosed takings. The nature of the large debits for repairs and professional fees will need to be explored as it seems likely that they are capital expenditure.

The real explanation for the increased turnover and reduced GPR is that the business has started a wholesale activity and the margins for that side of the business are lower, thus reducing the overall GPR. More staff were taken on in 2012 to help with the wholesale activity. The expenditure on repairs and professional fees was indeed capital expenditure incurred to enlarge the premises for the new business activity. Cash has remained at the same level because this is the float which is retained each day, the balance being banked using a night-safe facility. Stock, however, has not been properly taken and the same figure has been used each year.

The full explanation for the fall in the GPR could have been given when the reduction occurred. Keeping a tabular record of the accounts figures would have alerted the practitioner to the need to explore the nature of the repairs and professional fees and the unlikelihood of the stock figure provided by the client. This would have enabled remedial action to be taken and, together with the explanation for the change in the nature of the business, avoided the client's selection for investigation.

Planning point

CCH *Business Focus* provides guidance on performance, results and norms for different trade sectors.

Other guidance: CCH *Business Focus*

Records

Knowledge of the operating practices and the activities of the business obtained from the background reading and talking to the client to prepare the business model will enable the practitioner to form a view on how comprehensive and accurate the business records are. This has become a very important aspect since the new record keeping requirements included in *Finance Act* 2008 and HMRC's new power to inspect them at any time.

Private side

As with the accounts figures, the drawings should be listed in tabular form, year by year, so that the pattern which emerges can be seen and considered in the context of the client's family circumstances.

Explanations should be sought if the drawings appear to increase or decrease substantially in real terms (i.e. after adjusting for inflation) comparing one year with another.

Summarising the tax returns in tabular form will also help to show any increases or decreases in investments. Any substantial changes should be noted as these will be investigated by the officer. For increases in investments, the client should be asked for details of the immediate source of the money and where it was held previously. If the investments decrease, it is equally important to establish where the proceeds went; HMRC will wish to know that they have not been invested in an income producing asset, the income from which has been omitted from the return.

Planning point

Practitioners may encounter resistance from clients when they ask about the private side because the client often cannot understand how it is relevant and does not, in any case, think it is anyone else's business. A simple explanation of the connection that the officer will make between suppressed takings and low drawings and/or unexplained increases in investments will help to gain the client's cooperation. It can also be explained that the HMRC information powers

> mean that the officer can demand the production of capital statements if it is considered necessary.

66.2.6 Small business letters

HMRC have instituted a policy of sending letters to a number of business people with guidance on completing the self-employment pages of the Tax Return. HMRC hopes that the guidance will help to avoid common errors that might:

- lead to understatements of business profit;
- affect a significant number of Returns;
- present a real risk of tax loss to the Exchequer; and
- increase the burden of tax for other taxpayers.

Where HMRC have been notified that an agent is acting, they will send a copy of the letter to the agent. The letters will be sent to some small businesses with turnover up to £150,000.

The difference between guidance letters and enquiries

HMRC carry out enquiries to check for, and if necessary put right, any errors, mistakes or omissions. The small business letters are not enquiries. They are to provide taxpayers and their agents with the opportunity to consider the next tax return so as to minimise the risk of enquiry.

Selecting individuals to receive a letter

HMRC select people to receive a letter by certain pre-identified criteria based on the Standard Accounts Information that they capture from the tax return. They identify features that commonly suggest inaccuracies in tax returns over one or more years.

It should be noted that features that suggest possible inaccuracies include departures from expected patterns. If it is considered that features of a particular business result in an unusual pattern, it is strongly advised that the reasons for this are flagged up in the notes space on the tax return. Although HMRC have in the past failed to capture and take note of the information provided in the notes spaces of the return, they have promised to improve their performance in this respect.

The sending of a letter is not an indication that something is known to be wrong with a person's tax returns and no decision to begin an enquiry should be taken solely because an individual was among those who received a small business letter. Before any case is selected for full enquiry, the local office should undertake an individual review.

In response to practitioners' concerns about HMRC contacting the client direct, HMRC have stated that their research into the outcome of completed enquiries suggests that significant numbers of expense claims are incorrect, even when an agent is acting. They do not consider it appropriate, therefore, that they should exclude represented taxpayers from direct contact where they consider that they have genuine reasons for considering that there may be errors or oversights.

Before completing the next tax return

The letters include a telephone number for making direct contact to discuss the next tax return with someone from the local compliance team. The officer will provide some general information about the criteria used in selecting people to receive a letter, but will not be able to direct the enquirer towards a specific tax return box as requiring attention. This is in accordance with current policy that HMRC does not disclose its risk assessment processes. The officer will only be able to help with questions or uncertainties about allowable deductions, about record keeping, or about where and how to access leaflets or technical guidance published by HMRC.

HMRC recommends that if a client receives a letter, the practitioner should take the opportunity to consider the business pages of the tax return with them, exploring:

- whether records are adequate;
- the accuracy of any estimated figures;
- whether business expense claims are technically correct;
- whether private use adjustments have been properly made; and
- whether all income is included.

66.2.7 Interventions to assure compliance

As part of the process of modernising their approach to compliance, between July and October 2006 HMRC trialled six interventions to assure compliance. These were:

- Self audit – taxpayers within specific risk groups were pointed to areas where HMRC thought there was a risk that they might have made an incorrect declaration and asked to confirm their declaration was correct or to correct it.
- Short risk review – taxpayers within trade, professional or behaviour groups that commonly make errors in their returns were sent a letter explaining what the common errors were and asking them to check their return and either confirm it was correct or correct it.
- Real time health check – taxpayers were invited to review generic risk areas on their returns before they were submitted and correct any errors this revealed.
- Real time records review – a review to check the adequacy of the business records before the tax return was submitted.
- Telephone contact – taxpayers for whom HMRC held third party information indicating that they should have included property income on their returns but hadn't were telephoned to discuss the matter and decide whether the return needed to be amended.
- Correction challenge – this was used where HMRC held third party information

(usually notifications of bank interest received) and had confidence in its level of accuracy and which could be clearly and easily communicated to the taxpayer.

Conclusions

Although HMRC concluded that most of the interventions were unsuitable for use in investigations, they have included in *Finance Act* 2008 legislation to enforce Real time records reviews for direct tax purposes so that they have similar powers of inspection for direct taxes as for VAT and PAYE.

Selection for intervention were made using HMRC's risk assessment procedures. Of concern to practitioners will be the low number of selections where an adjustment was found to be needed, even where HMRC were absolutely confident of the basis for their risk assessment because they held third party information in which they placed absolute confidence.

The report, which provides a useful indication of many of the risk areas identified by HMRC for selecting enquiry cases, can be read at *www.hmrc.gov.uk/new-interventions/evaluation-report.pdf*.

66.3 Opening the enquiry

66.3.1 Introduction

The changes brought in by *Finance Act* 2008 mean that, in practice, HMRC can start to check a person's tax position at any time. They have the power to inspect business records, premises and assets at any reasonable time if such an inspection is reasonably required for checking a person's tax position. If this, or anything else, leads them to suspect that tax may not have been assessed, they can demand whatever further information they need to check a person's tax position.

As a result of the changes made by *Finance Act* 2008:

- if they have issued an enquiry notice while the enquiry window is open, HMRC can issue a taxpayer notice demanding any information they consider necessary for checking the person's tax position; and
- if the enquiry window is closed, they can issue a taxpayer notice if they **suspect** that tax may not have been assessed – they do not, as at present, have to make a discovery first.

It will be noted that in neither case is the demand for information limited to checking that a particular tax return is correct. The only restriction is that the information must be reasonably required for checking a person's tax position.

The enquiry window will continue to apply if HMRC want to start an enquiry on receipt of a tax return and have the right to issue a taxpayer notice without having to suspect that tax has not been assessed. However, they can start to make enquiries after the enquiry window has closed, and issue a taxpayer notice requiring that information be provided, if they suspect that tax has not been assessed.

Law: TMA 1970, s. 9A, 12AC; FA 1998, Sch. 18, para. 24 as amended by FA 2007, s. 96; FA 2008, s. 113 and Sch. 36.

66.3.2 The enquiry window for individuals, partnerships and trustees

Returns for years 2007–08 onwards

Practitioners have expressed concern that by submitting clients' returns early they are leaving them exposed to the risk of enquiry for longer. In response to their suggestion that the enquiry window be linked to the date the return is submitted, and to encourage early submission of returns, the enquiry window was amended by *Finance Act* 2007.

Under the amended provisions, where an individual, a partnership or a trustee files a return for 2007–08 onwards on or before the filing deadline, the enquiry period runs for 12 months starting from the date the return is filed. There is no change in the provisions relating to returns submitted after the filing date.

Returns for years up to and including 2006–07

In the normal case, an enquiry notice must be issued within 12 months of the filing date for the return which is to be enquired into. If the return is submitted before the filing date, HMRC still have from the date of the submission until 12 months after the normal filing date to commence an enquiry.

If a return is delivered after the filing date, HMRC have until the first anniversary of the quarter date next following the date of delivery to commence an enquiry. The quarter days are 31 January, 30 April, 31 July and 31 October. The same time limit applies if an amendment to the return is made after the filing date.

Example 66.8

1. 2005/06 return made 31 January 2007; enquiry can be made up to 31 January 2008.

2. 2005/06 return made 30 June 2006; enquiry can be made up to 31 January 2008.

3. 2005/06 return made 30 June 2007; enquiry can be made up to 31 July 2008; i.e. the anniversary of the first quarter day after 30 June 2007.

> 4. 2005/06 return made 30 June 2006 and amendment made 30 November 2006; enquiry on both the return and the amendment can be made up to 31 January 2008.
>
> 5. 2005/06 return made 30 November 2006 and amendment made 31 August 2007; enquiry can be made on the return up to 31 January 2008 and on the amendment up to 31 October 2008, i.e. the anniversary of the first quarter day after 31 August 2007.
>
> 6. 2005/06 return made 31 May 2007 and amendment made 31 October 2007; enquiry can be made on the return up to 31 July 2008 (i.e. the anniversary of the first quarter day after 31 May 2007) and on the amendment up to 31 January 2009 (i.e. the anniversary of the first quarter day after 31 October 2007).

The wording of TMA 1970, s. 9A and 12AC was amended by FA 2001 with effect from 11 May 2001 in relation to returns:

- whether made before or after 11 May 2001; and
- whether relating to periods before or after 11 May 2001,

to make it clear that enquiry notices could be sent up to 31 January. The effect of the legislation as originally enacted was to limit the enquiry period to 30 January next following the filing date.

It should be noted that, although HMRC accept that a return filed on 1 February or found in the tax office post box by 7.30 am on 2 February will not incur a penalty for late submission, the period during which an enquiry notice can be issued is extended to 30 April of the following year.

It has been suggested that delaying submission of a return until the very end of the enquiry window reduces the chance of selection for enquiry. However, HMRC assured the House of Commons Treasury Committee (Eighth Report HC 681) that returns filed early were not more likely to be selected. Indeed, the reverse is the case; as HMRC's risk analysis shows that a greater number of inaccuracies are found in the returns of late filers, the risk score reflects this.

Law: TMA 1970, s. 9A and 12AC; FA 2007, s. 96

66.3.3 The enquiry window for companies

Accounting periods ending after 31 March 2008

Finance Act 2007 amends FA 1998, Sch. 18, para. 24 as it relates to company tax returns for accounting periods ending after 31 March 2008. For most companies, where a return is delivered to HMRC on or before the filing deadline, the time allowed for an officer of HMRC to give notice of their intention to enquire into that return will be 12 months from the date on which the return was delivered to HMRC.

For groups of companies, other than small groups, the enquiry window will remain the same as before and will continue to be 12 months from the filing date.

There is no change in the provisions relating to late returns or amendments.

Law: FA 2007, s. 96

Accounting periods ending up to and including 31 March 2008

A company's filing date is normally 12 months after the end of the period for which the return is made. This is extended to 30 months from the beginning of the period of account if the accounting period exceeds 18 months. The enquiry window for accounting periods up to and including 31 March 2008 runs for 12 months from the filing date. The company's tax return and self-assessment normally become final and conclusive if no enquiry is raised during the enquiry window.

Example 66.9

A Ltd's return and accounts for the 12 months ended 31 December 2005 are filed on 1 August 2006 (i.e. before its filing date of 31 December 2006). A notice of enquiry into the return can be given at any time up to 31 December 2007.

Example 66.10

B Ltd's return and accounts for the 12 months ended 31 December 2005 are filed on 8 June 2007 (i.e. after its filing date of 31 December 2006). A notice of enquiry can be given at any time up to 31 July 2008.

Amendments

A company can amend its return at any time up to 12 months from the filing date. Notice of enquiry into the amended return can be given at any time up to the quarter day next (see above) following the first anniversary of the date on which the amendment was made.

It should be noted that if the notice of enquiry is given at a time when it is not possible to give notice of enquiry into the original return, the enquiry is normally limited to matters relating to the amendment. However, HMRC reserve the right to enquire into the whole of the amended return if they consider that the amendment has a fundamental impact.

Example 66.11

A Ltd's return and accounts for the 12 months ended 31 December 2005 are filed on 1 August 2006 and it amends the return on 30 September 2006 (i.e. before its filing date of 31 December 2006). A notice of enquiry into the return can be given at any time up to 31 December 2007 into the whole of the return, as amended.

Example 66.12

B Ltd's return and accounts for the year ended 31 December 2005 are filed on 1 August 2006 and B Ltd amends the return on 1 August 2007. The time-limit for enquiry into the original return expires on 31 December 2007, but notice of enquiry into the amendment may be given at any time up to 31 October 2008.

Law: FA 1998, Sch. 18, para. 24(1)

66.3.4 Appeals

The statute gives HMRC an absolute right to make an enquiry into a return. No reason has to be given and none will be given. There are no grounds, therefore, on which an appeal can be made against an enquiry notice.

⚠ Warning!

There is no right of appeal against an enquiry notice.

66.3.5 Validity of the enquiry notice

An enquiry notice has to be:

- in writing;
- delivered to the taxpayer; and
- delivered before the time limit expires.

Although the notice must be sent to the taxpayer, HMRC have agreed that if the taxpayer has an agent acting on his or her behalf, a copy of the notice will always be sent to the agent.

To be valid, the taxpayer must receive the enquiry notice by midnight on the last date of the period during which it can be issued. For years when the enquiry window starts on the filing date, if the filing date is 31 January and the return is filed on time, a notice to enquire must be received by midnight on 31 January of the following year. For years when the enquiry window starts when the return is filed, a notice to enquire must be received by midnight on the anniversary of the day the return was filed.

In the Special Commissioners case *Wing Hung Lai v Bale* the Special Commissioner decided that the date of receipt in the ordinary course of second class post, which is used for issuing notices, is the fourth working day after posting. Depending on the number of working days, therefore, the last date for posting a valid notice would be:

- 27 January for years when the enquiry window starts on the filing date; or
- four working days before the anniversary of the day the return was filed for years when the enquiry window starts from when the return is filed.

Notwithstanding the general presumption that a notice will be delivered on the fourth working day after posting (*Wing Hung Lai v Bale*), if it can be proved that it was delivered later, then that later date is to be taken as the date of delivery (*Holly and Laurel v HMIT*).

> **Planning point**
>
> In the general run of continuing cases the validity of the enquiry notice is unlikely to be important because, if the time limit has expired, HMRC will issue an enquiry notice in the following year and reopen the earlier year(s) by way of discovery. It may be important, however, if the matter into which HMRC wished to enquire were a one-off charge to capital gains tax.

Law: TMA 1970, s. 9A, 12AC, Sch. 1A, para. 5; FA 1998, Sch. 18, para. 24; FA 2007, s. 96; *Wing Hung Lai v Bale* (1999) Sp C 203 and *Holly and Laurel v HMIT* (1999) Sp C 225

66.3.6 Only one enquiry per return

The statutory provisions governing self assessment permit only one enquiry per return. Once the enquiry period has expired or an enquiry has been concluded with a closure notice, the only way to open another enquiry into the same return is by way of the discovery provisions (but see **66.3.1** for the position after *Finance Act 2008*).

> **Planning point**
>
> Practitioners need to be clear on what is and what is not an enquiry to be able to protect their clients from a series of enquiries on the same return.

Law: TMA 1970, s. 9A, 12AC; FA 1998, Sch. 18, para. 24

Not an enquiry

The SA legislation permits HMRC to make corrections to a taxpayer's return. These must be no more than the correction of obvious mistakes such as arithmetical errors. HMRC have said that they may make a phone call to check that their proposed correction is itself correct. An HMRC correction is not an enquiry.

From 1 April 2010, HMRC will be able to correct a return, taking into account other information it holds and believes to be correct, even if the error or omission is not obvious from simply examining the return.

As a safeguard against inappropriate use of the extended correction power, the taxpayer can reject the correction. If, following rejection, HMRC still believes a correction is necessary, it can give notice of intention to enquire into the return. The taxpayer then has access to the closure and appeal safeguards provided by the enquiry procedures.

Taxpayers are also permitted to make corrections to their returns. HMRC action to give effect to a taxpayer's correction is not an enquiry, even if HMRC charge interest and a penalty, because the correction was necessary due to the taxpayer's fraudulent or negligent actions.

Charging interest and penalties on late returns or due to a failure to notify is not an enquiry in itself. Only if HMRC decide that the failure is sufficient to warrant an enquiry into the return as a whole and issues an enquiry notice will it become an enquiry.

An enquiry

An enquiry has clearly been opened when an enquiry notice is issued by HMRC. An enquiry may be a full enquiry, where the whole return is subjected to a detailed scrutiny, or it may be an aspect enquiry where only one or several particular matters are the subject of enquiry. An example of an aspect enquiry is where the officer asks for more information about a large debit for repairs in the profit and loss account to confirm that it is revenue and not capital expenditure.

> ⚠ **Warning!**
>
> Practitioners should be alert to the officer making informal enquiries to determine whether or not to start a full enquiry. Any questions asked by the officer that are not related to a correction and which are intended to check that a return is correct and complete are an enquiry and should be preceded by the issue of an enquiry notice.

66.3.7 Opening letter

As a result of the wider powers given to HMRC by the SA legislation, the opening letter at the start of an enquiry no longer has to be as circumspect as in pre-SA enquiries. Because HMRC have an absolute right to enquire into a return without giving any reason, the opening letter will simply state the officer's intention to make some enquiries into the return and enclose the Code of Practice relating to enquiries.

HMRC have undertaken to make it clear whether the enquiry is an aspect or full enquiry (random enquiries are always full enquiries). Normally this is clear in any event because of the nature of the information requested and because the letter is accompanied by the short, rather than the full, code of practice. In the case of a full enquiry, the opening letter will also request the business and other records used to prepare the return and explanations from the practitioner of the work done on the records to produce the accounts (see **66.5** below for the records that can be demanded).

For enquiries and demands for information before 1 April 2009, practitioners could resist a request to see the client's private records when such a request was made in the opening letter unless the officer could justify the need to see them. HMRC instructions made it clear that private records should only be requested if:

- they had been used to complete the return; or
- it could be shown that they are necessary to check that the return is complete and correct.

After the changes made by *Finance Act* 2008, which introduced information powers for checking a person's tax position rather than to check if a tax return is correct, the test that must be applied from 1 April 2009 is whether the request to see private records is reasonable in the circumstances. HMRC accept that non-business bank details should not be requested in the opening letter as a matter of course. For examples of when HMRC consider that it might be appropriate for them to request non-business account details, see **66.4.2**.

The working papers of the practitioner which HMRC are entitled to demand (see **66.4** below) should not be routinely demanded in the opening letter. The officer is, however, justified in asking for information on the work done by the practitioner, including details of:

- any estimates included in the accounts;
- any computed or balancing figures required to make the accounts balance;
- accountancy adjustments;
- the basis of valuing stock or work in progress; and
- how the figure of drawings is made up.

Since the opening letter is intended to be neutral, making no assumptions as to the accuracy or completeness of the return, it would also be inappropriate for the officer to seek an interview in the opening letter.

The opening letter of the enquiry will be the informal request for information preceding a formal demand under HMRC's information powers contained in FA 2008, Sch. 36. It will state the date by which the information should be produced. Officers are encouraged to agree a time limit for response (normally 30 days as a minimum) but they are instructed to be flexible, especially if, for example:

- the taxpayer is known to be abroad, or to be incapacitated in circumstances which will prevent compliance within 30 days;
- a final figure has been requested to replace a provisional one included in the return, and it clearly cannot be supplied within 30 days; or
- the request is made to an agent in January close to the filing date when it is known that the agent's workload will be especially heavy.

After receiving a copy of the enquiry notice, the practitioner should check that the inspector has all the information provided with the return, particularly information intended to explain any apparent anomalies. This is important because it has come to light that HMRC do not have in place procedures for reliably capturing additional information provided with the return, even if it is entered in the boxes for additional information provided on the return itself. If the information has not been provided already, the practitioner should carry out a critical review of the client's affairs to mirror the officer's (see **66.2.5**). At the meeting with the client, the client should be asked to confirm whether or not any further disclosure should be made to HMRC.

> *Planning point*
>
> A full disclosure at the outset of any irregularities will earn maximum reduction of any penalty which might ultimately become due. Any disclosure at this stage would have to be in general terms if further work is required to quantify actual figures. Such a general disclosure will, however, be sufficient to earn maximum reduction provided it is followed up by a complete disclosure without undue delay.

Other guidance: Codes of Practice COP 11 *Enquiries into tax returns by local Tax Offices* and COP14 *Corporation tax: Self Assessment Enquiries*

66.3.8 Discovery

The provisions relating to discovery assessments were amended with the introduction of self assessment. The amended provisions now permit discovery assessments to be made only in the circumstances described in the provisions. Broadly, these are where there is a loss of tax brought about carelessly or deliberately (previously where there was a loss of tax due to fraudulent or negligent conduct) or where it is not possible to use the SA enquiry powers because the time limit for starting an enquiry has expired or a completion notice has been issued.

Law: TMA 1970, s. 29, 30B; FA 1998, Sch. 18, para. 41; FA 2008, s. 118 and Sch. 39, para. 3

When discovery assessments can be made

For self-assessment years, a discovery assessment can be made if the following conditions are satisfied.

1. There must have been a loss of tax because:
   (a) profits or gains were not assessed;
   (b) insufficient tax was assessed; or
   (c) excessive reliefs were given.
2. The assessment must be made either:
   (a) because the loss of tax was brought about carelessly or deliberately (prior to *Finance Act* 2008, where there was a loss of tax due to fraudulent or negligent conduct) by the taxpayer or someone acting on his or her behalf; or
   (b) because the right to enquire into a self-assessment return has passed or a completion notice in respect of an enquiry has been issued and the officer could not have been reasonably expected, on the basis of the information made available before that time, to be aware of the loss of tax.

Law: TMA 1970, s. 29; FA 2008, Sch. 39, para. 3

Deliberately or carelessly

There is no definition of 'deliberately' in the Taxes Act as there was not for fraudulent conduct. It is expected that for the purposes of interpreting the *Finance Act* 2008 provisions the courts will interpret deliberately in much the same way as fraudulently. In general law, a representation is fraudulent if, at the time it was made, it was known to be false or if it was made recklessly, without any regard for whether or not it was true.

Fraud requires a positive act; the mere omission to fulfil some obligation imposed by the Taxes Acts can never amount to fraudulent conduct.

It is also expected that 'carelessly' will be interpreted by the courts in the same way as they interpreted negligently. Negligent conduct is the failure to do what a normally reasonable and prudent person would do. In the context of tax, this would include doing all those things which are necessary for satisfying the obligations imposed by the Taxes Acts completely, correctly and within the statutory time limits. A failure in this regard which led to the submission of an incorrect return would lead to the imposition of a financial penalty for neglect.

Information 'made available'

The question of when and whether information has been made available so that the officer could have been reasonably expected on the basis of it to be aware of the loss of tax is dealt with in s. 29(6). This states that information is made available when it is:

- contained in the taxpayer's return for the relevant year, or in any accounts, statements or documents accompanying it;
- contained in a claim or in any accounts, statements or documents accompanying it;
- contained in any accounts, documents or particulars provided for the purpose of an enquiry into the return; or
- information whose existence and relevance could reasonably be expected to be inferred from the above or was notified in writing to the officer.

The HMRC view on discovery assessments has been set out in the various Revenue *Tax Bulletins* and the practitioner will find useful guidance in them. It should be noted that HMRC will not accept that information was made available if it was included in material so voluminous that the officer could not reasonably have been aware of it or its relevance to a particular point. It is HMRC's view that, where the material provided is voluminous, the onus is on the taxpayer to draw attention to any important information that is relevant to the liability to tax.

Law: TMA 1970, s. 29(6); FA 2008, Sch. 39, para. 3

Other guidance: Tax Bulletin, Issues 23, June 1996, 50, December 2000 and 54, August 2001

Achieving finality under self assessment

The decision in *Langham (HMIT) v Veltema* meant that, where a self-assessment depends on a valuation, HMRC can raise a discovery assessment if they successfully dispute the accuracy of that valuation. It was held that, even though the inspector was informed that a valuation had been used when making the self-assessment, he could not have known at the time that the valuation was wrong. Nor was it incumbent on him to make enquiries on receipt of the tax return to establish that it was wrong. He could not, therefore, have been reasonably expected, on the basis of the information made available at the time, to be aware of the loss of tax. The provisions of TMA 1970, s. 29(5) were satisfied so that the officer could make a discovery assessment.

This decision led to uncertainty for taxpayers as to whether the risk of a Revenue enquiry disappeared at the end of the enquiry period. Guidance was therefore developed by HMRC in consultation with representative bodies to help taxpayers achieve finality for most practical purposes. This guidance is as follows.

Valuations

Most taxpayers who use a valuation in completing their tax return and state in the Additional Information space at the end of the Return that:

- a valuation has been used,
- by whom it has been carried out; and
- that it was carried out by a named independent and suitably qualified valuer if that was the case, on the appropriate basis

will be able, for all practical purposes, to rely on protection from a later discovery assessment, provided those statements are true.

Exceptional items in accounts

Most taxpayers will be able to gain finality with exceptional items in accounts. An example might be a deduction in the accounts under Repairs. If an entry in the Additional Information space points out that a programme of work has been carried out that included repairs, improvements and new building work and that the total cost has been allocated to revenue and capital on a particular basis, the inspector should not enquire after the closure of the enquiry period unless he becomes aware that the statement was patently untrue or unreasonable.

Rejecting HMRC guidance

Taxpayers who adopt a different view of the law from that published as HMRC's view can protect against a discovery assessment after the enquiry period. The Return would have to indicate that a different view had been adopted by entering in the Additional Information space comments to the effect that they have not followed HMRC guidance on the issue or that no adjustment has been made to take account of it.

> **Planning point**
>
> Since the decision in *Langham v Veltema*, HMRC have given guidance on when information is 'made available' and have stated that taxpayers can be assured of finality if they use the white space on the return to:
>
> - give the name of the independent, suitably qualified valuer (if that is the case) who made any valuation included in the return and confirm that the appropriate basis was used;
> - give full details of any exceptional items in the accounts, what was involved and the reasons for the treatment of the items in the accounts; or
> - indicate that a different view of the law from that published as the HMRC view had been adopted;
>
> provided that the information and explanations are true and reasonable.

Law: TMA 1970, s. 29(6); *Langham v Veltema* [2004] BTC 156

Other guidance: The HMRC statement of practice SP 01/06, *Self Assessment: Finality and Discovery*, setting out their interpretation and practice with regard to discovery after *Langham v Veltema* can be read on the HMRC website at / www.hmrc.gov.uk/practitioners/sp01-06.pdf

When discovery assessments cannot be made

The amendments to s. 29 for SA years make it clear that there are two situations where a discovery assessment cannot be made.

No assessment can be made when an officer has a change of mind on the information provided. This is different from the pre-SA position where the courts had held that a change of mind by a later inspector, or even the same inspector, was sufficient for there to be a discovery for the purposes of the old s. 29 (*Williams v Grundy Trustees*).

The other situation where the Act prohibits the making of a discovery assessment is where the loss of tax arose due to an error or mistake concerning the basis on which the tax liability was calculated and that basis was the generally prevailing practice at the time the return was made.

Law: *Williams v Grundy Trustees* (1933) 18 TC 271

Time limits for assessment

Finance Act 2008 altered the period from five years to four for making assessments to recover a loss of tax brought about by carelessness. The 20 year period remains but it applies only to assessments to recover a loss of tax brought about deliberately or by a failure to notify liability or comply with the obligation to provide information about avoidance schemes.

Prior to the changes made by *Finance Act* 2008:

- unless there was fraudulent or negligent conduct on the part of the taxpayer or someone acting on the taxpayer's behalf, a discovery assessment had to be made within five years of the statutory filing date for the tax year. This applied even if the return was issued late; and
- if there was fraudulent or negligent conduct, the time limit for making a discovery assessment was 20 years after 31 January following the end of the tax year.

Law: TMA 1970, s. 34, 36; FA 1998, Sch. 18, para. 46, *Finance Act* 2008, s. 119 and Sch. 39, para. 7 and 9

Pre-SA years

There is a substantial body of case law interpreting the meaning of discovery as originally enacted in s. 29 and how it applies for pre-SA years. These decisions established that the inspector made a discovery when he 'found out' that tax had not been assessed and it included a change of opinion on the same facts.

This very broad interpretation of discovery was later restricted by the decisions in *Cenlon Finance Co Ltd v Ellwood* and *Scorer v Olin Energy Systems Ltd*. As a result of these decisions, the Revenue issued *Statement of Practice* SP 8/91 which explained the law and how they would apply it. This summarised the main principles as follows:

> 'Two main principles are relevant in considering whether a discovery assessment may be made in any particular circumstances.
>
> First, the Inland Revenue does not go back on a specific agreement made by an inspector on a particular point and raise a discovery assessment in respect of that point, whether or not the inspector correctly took account of current law and practice in entering into that agreement.
>
> Second, in circumstances where it cannot be said that the particular point was the subject of a specific agreement, the Revenue regards itself as bound by the inspector's acceptance of a computation if the view of the point implicit in the computation was a tenable one.
>
> But the Revenue does not regard itself as bound by any agreement made, or considered to be made, or any decision taken by an inspector, if any of the information supplied on which that agreement or decision was founded was misleading.'

> **Planning point**
>
> When an enquiry includes pre-SA years, the practitioner should take the above into account when deciding if HMRC have the right to raise discovery assessments for those years.

Law: *Cenlon Finance Co Ltd v Ellwood* (1962) 40 TC 176 and *Scorer v Olin Energy Systems Ltd* (1985) 58 TC 592

66.4 Information and inspection powers

66.4.1 Introduction

HMRC have a formidable array of powers to require the provision of information to help them with their enquiries. These have become more extensive over the years and the introduction of self assessment brought additional information powers with it.

New information powers are contained in *Finance Act* 2008. They apply across all taxes and replace in their entirety all the existing information powers.

Information and Inspection Powers 66.4.2

Both TMA 1970, s. 19A and s. 20 were repealed by *Finance Act* 2008, along with the other information powers. The new information and inspection powers contained in *Finance Act* 2008, Sch. 36 include:

- the requirement to make available information and documents that are legally required to be maintained, including business records;
- giving HMRC access to business assets and premises;
- the requirement for those whose tax position is being checked (first parties) to produce supplementary information and documents; and
- the requirement for third parties to produce existing information about named taxpayers.

The new information powers included in schedule 36 replace the old information powers that were contained in:

- TMA 1970, s. 19A – written information powers for SA enquiries;
- TMA 1970, s. 20 – written information powers (for direct taxes only);
- TMA 1970, Sch. 1A, para. 6 – written information power for enquiries into a claim;
- TMA 1970, Sch. 1A, para. 6 – written information power for CTSA enquiries;
- FA 1998, Sch. 18, para. 27–29 – VAT power to look at records and information power;
- VATA 1994, Sch. 11, para. 7 – the power to look at PAYE records;
- SI 2003/2682, reg. 97 – the power to look at National Insurance contributions records; and
- SI 2001/1004, Sch. 4, para. 26 – the power to look at Construction Industry Scheme records.

> ⚠ **Warning!**
>
> After 1 April 2009 only the information and inspection powers in FA 2008, Sch. 36 can be used. And they must not be used to obtain information the officer would have liked to have had before 1 April but was unable to obtain under the old provisions.

66.4.2 Information powers

When they carry out an enquiry or a compliance check, HMRC can use their powers under FA 2008, Sch. 36 to issue a formal notice to a taxpayer (a taxpayer notice) requiring them to provide information and documents reasonably required to check their tax position. These will usually be requested informally in the first instance but a formal notice will be issued if the taxpayer:

- refuses to comply with an informal request; or
- fails to provide all the information and documents requested informally by the specified date.

If the taxpayer needs more time to provide the information than that specified by the informal request they should immediately, or as soon as this is realised, contact the officer to agree a realistic time scale. Delay in contacting the officer will lead to complications and possibly the imposition of a penalty for delay. It should be noted, however, that if the officer does not consider that there is a good reason for requesting extra time a formal notice will be issued as soon as the time limit in the informal request has expired.

The notice can ask only for information and documents reasonably required for checking the taxpayer's tax position. There is no right of appeal against a notice requiring the provision of statutory records. However, there is a right of appeal against a notice requiring the provision of supplementary information and documents if the taxpayer does not agree that they are reasonably required.

Supplementary information could include such things as:

- appointment books, booking diaries, room occupancy records etc.;
- estimates books;
- till rolls; or
- evidence to support a stated position which HMRC suspect does not exist.

⚠ Warning!

The officer can issue as many information notices as necessary throughout the course of an enquiry. However, an informal request for the information must be made in each case.

Private records

HMRC can use their information powers to request private records, including bank and building society statements, paying-in slips and details of property or other assets. The information or documents requested must, however, be reasonably required for checking the taxpayer's tax position. HMRC consider that reasonable equates to 'fair and sensible in the circumstances'. Whether a request is reasonable is, therefore, dependent on the circumstances in each case.

The opening letter of a compliance review or enquiry will normally include a request for the business records to be sent to HMRC. Any request in the opening letter for private records should be resisted, unless it is clear that the records are clearly inadequate – for example if the accounts for a business are not based on sound and well kept records and include unvouched or unverified sums.

HMRC accept that simply depositing in a private account correctly and contemporaneously recorded drawings from a business is not sufficient grounds for asking to see the private records for that account.

HMRC also accept that it would be inappropriate to ask to see private records where unvouched or unverified items relate only to minor matters – for example, the business proportion of household expense when the home is used for business purposes, laundry bills etc.

As private records do not form part of the statutory records they are supplementary information. There is therefore a right of appeal against a notice requiring them. The onus will be on the officer to satisfy the Tribunal that the information is reasonably required.

Matters which HMRC have indicated that they consider would make it reasonable to request sight of private records include where:

- payments from an account into the business (for example capital introduced) are unverified and treated as non-taxable;
- it is reasonable to suppose that the taxpayer's records are incomplete;
- it is reasonable to suppose that undeclared income or gains have been credited to the account;
- the officer has doubts or questions about the taxpayer's means;
- it is reasonable to suppose that the return was based on the 'private' bank account documents; or
- taxable receipts or expenditure are unvouched or estimated and it is reasonable to expect that this expenditure should have been vouched or recorded.

When requesting private records, HMRC acknowledge the need to take account of:

- the cost – for example the cost of obtaining duplicate bank statements; and
- the taxpayer's right to privacy – the officer must be able to demonstrate that seeing the private records is an effective way of checking the person's liability to tax and that it will cause the minimum necessary intrusion into their private lives.

Planning point

Clients should be advised to operate a separate business bank account so that they cannot be required to immediately produce their private records at the start of an enquiry.

Restrictions on taxpayer notices

A taxpayer notice cannot require the taxpayer to provide for inspection:

- documents not in the taxpayer's possession or power;
- documents relating to a pending appeal;
- journalistic material;
- personal records or information from them (as defined in s. 13 of the *Police and Criminal Evidence Act* 1984);

- documents more than six years old at the date of the notice, unless approved by an Authorised Officer; or
- privileged information or the privileged part of a document.

Normally a statutory auditor cannot be required to produce their audit papers or a tax adviser their advice papers.

Complying with notice

The officer should carefully consider how much time is needed to comply but they will not necessarily know all the circumstances. If the time-limit they set is too short, it is important to contact them immediately, or as soon as it becomes clear that more time is needed, to agree a longer time. If the officer refuses to accept that more time is needed an appeal can be made to the Tribunal on the grounds that the officer allowed insufficient time.

If the information cannot be obtained or documents do not exist, the officer can set aside the relevant part of the notice. They may, however:

- charge a penalty for failing to keep records; or
- take the record keeping failure into account when determining the amount of the penalty for any inaccuracy in a return.

HMRC will not accept that a legal or professional adviser's duty of confidentiality towards their client is sufficient reason for not complying with a taxpayer notice addressed to themselves for the purpose of checking their own tax position. They have given assurances that information obtained:

- will remain confidential within HMRC, unless the law provides for it to be shared; and
- will not be used to enquire into the affairs of others.

So, for example, they will not use information about a patient's expensive private medical treatment, obtained in the course of checking a doctor's tax position, to start an enquiry, or as part of an enquiry, into the patient's tax affairs.

In view of the sensitivities, the officer will normally issue a formal notice at the start so that the professional can point to this as their justification for providing otherwise confidential information. They will also be particularly careful to ensure that the notice cannot be challenged under *Human Rights Act* 1998, s. 8 for not being proportionate. Any request must be for information or documents that are relevant to the compliance check and the least intrusive way of resolving any doubts or queries.

Medical records

The information powers in FA 2008, Sch. 36 cannot be used to obtain medical records. Where the records mix both medical and financial information, HMRC take the view that they can be requested but that a request for patient's records (or other records containing patient information) should only be made if:

- there is reason to believe that fees have been omitted from the return because the records;
- examination shows weaknesses that may have led to an understatement of fees it has been established that the patient record cards are prime income records; and
- that the patient record cards are the most effective way of working out the true amount of liability.

A medical record is:

- any record which contains information relating to the physical or mental health or condition of an individual; and
- has been made by or on behalf of a medical professional in connection with the care of that individual.

Legal professional privilege

Common law, the *Data Protection Act* 1998, *Human Rights Act* 1998, s. 8 and FA 2008, Sch. 36, para. 23 give protection to legally privileged documents. HMRC cannot obtain any documents in respect of which the legal professional is entitled to legal professional privilege.

If the legal professional asserts that the documents requested are protected by their client's legal privilege, HMRC will quote the part of the judgment in the case of *R v Special Commissioners and another ex-parte Morgan Grenfell & Co Ltd* [2002] BTC 223 where, Lord Hoffman, when commenting on the case of *R v IR Commrs, ex parte Taylor (No. 2)* [1990] BTC 281, said:

> 'In consequence, I do not think that the disclosure of the documents by Mr Taylor [the solicitor] in confidence for the limited purpose of determining his own tax liability infringed any LPP vested in his clients. If I am wrong about this and technically it did, then I think that to that limited extent the statute can be construed as having authorised it.'

> ⚠ **Warning!**
> If the time limit set for providing information is not sufficient, the officer should be contacted immediately to agree a revised deadline.

Failure to comply

If the taxpayer fails to comply with a taxpayer notice HMRC may impose an initial penalty of £300 and a daily penalty of up to £60 until it is complied with.

Before doing so, the officer should try to contact the taxpayer to find out why the notice has not been complied with and, if necessary, agree more time. They should also explain that a penalty will be charged if they do not comply with the notice.

HMRC Enquiries

No penalty should be imposed while the appeal period is still open or if an appeal has been made against the notice and the appeal is still open.

Tribunal approval

Although most taxpayer notices will be issued without the approval of the Tribunal, HMRC will seek their approval where:

- the tax at risk is large, the time-limit for making an assessment is close and an appeal may mean that the tax cannot be quantified and assessed;
- the taxpayer has a history of making appeals to delay matters and then withdrawing them at the last minute;
- there is a history of refusing to provide information;
- the officer wishes to protect their information from being disclosed at an appeal hearing on the notice – for example where they hold information from an informer or a third party; and
- they have reason to believe that documents may be destroyed and it is necessary to consider criminal proceedings.

There is no appeal against a taxpayer notice that has been approved by the Tribunal.

If HMRC want to inspect documents and business premises at the same time, they can ask the Tribunal for their approval for both the inspection visit and the taxpayer notice.

> ⚠ **Warning!**
>
> The inspector can issue as many information notices as necessary throughout the course of an enquiry. However, an informal request for the information must be made in each case.

Law: FA 2008, Sch. 36

Other guidance: Codes of Practice COP 11 *Enquiries into tax returns by local Tax Offices* and COP14 *Corporation tax: Self Assessment Enquiries*.

66.4.3   Inspection Powers

Finance Act 2008, Sch. 36 contains powers that enable HMRC to inspect business premises, business assets and statutory records ('statutory records' are defined in FA 2008, Sch. 36, para. 60). Such inspections form an important part of carrying out compliance checks.

The powers must be used reasonably and proportionately and can only be used to inspect business premises, not premises that are used wholly for residential

Information and Inspection Powers 66.4.3

purposes. However, the premises must be used wholly for residential purposes to be exempt from the powers. If they are used only partly for business purposes then they are subject to HMRC's inspection powers.

There are safeguards built into the legislation intended to ensure that the use of the powers is reasonable and proportionate. And HMRC must take care not to breach a taxpayer's right to privacy under the Human Rights Act.

When visits will be made

As in the past, compliance checks for PAYE/NICs and VAT will normally be carried out by visiting the business premises.

Most compliance checks for small and medium size businesses will continue to be carried out by asking for documents and information to be sent to an HMRC office. Generally, visits to business premises will be made only if it is convenient for the officer and the taxpayer to see the business records there, or if it is necessary to:

- inspect the business assets, for example to check the stock held;
- detect people operating in the black economy;
- detect people operating in the black economy; and
- to carry out credibility checks.

Before an inspection visit is made, the risk should have been identified and a note made of why it is best addressed by way of a visit instead of calling for documents and information. The timing of the visit should be reasonable and the officer must be able to show that the compliance check is reasonable and proportionate so that the conditions of s. 8(2) of the *Human Rights Act* 1998 are satisfied.

A taxpayer should tell the officer if there is a good reason why the officer should not visit their business premises. This might be due to lack of space, disruption caused to the operation of the business or the adverse affect on customers. The officer may then arrange to see the business records at an HMRC office or the premises of the practitioner.

Officers are reminded that:

> 'Managers are ultimately responsible for ensuring that visits are reasonably required and proportionate to the risk and that inspection powers are used in a way that minimises disruption and interference with taxpayers' right to privacy.'

Types of visit

Visits can be announced or unannounced.

Announced visits will usually be by prior arrangement, following an informal request asking for information and an inspection of the business records and premises. If the taxpayer refuses an informal request for a visit, the officer can arrange a visit by issuing a formal notice.

If the nature of the risk requires it, HMRC may carry out an unannounced visit, without giving any notice of the intended visit. No unannounced visit should be carried out unless it has been approved by an Authorised Officer.

If the officer believes that their inspection may be obstructed they can, with the approval of an Authorised Officer, apply to the Tribunal for their approval to a visit. If this is given, the taxpayer can be penalised for obstructing the officer carrying out the inspection.

Visits arranged or with notice
When an announced visit is arranged the taxpayer will be notified of the date and time of the visit, the name of the visiting officer and the records that are to be inspected. They will also be sent the Fact Sheet on visits explaining their rights and responsibilities.

As the only documents that can be inspected using the inspection powers in FA 2008, Sch. 36 are those that are held on the business premises, the officer may issue a notice requiring that other necessary documents are produced at the premises at the time of the visit. It is likely that if the visit is arranged by way of a formal notice rather than by agreement, the officer will also issue a notice requiring that the records should be produced at the business premises.

Although a visit arranged by agreement might, with the taxpayer's agreement, be made with less than seven days notice, if it has not been possible to reach agreement on the time of the visit, the officer must give at least seven days notice.

Unannounced visits
Unannounced visits will be used to tackle the black economy and where serious fraud is suspected. HMRC will consider making an unannounced visit where:

- appointments have been repeatedly missed;
- there is a risk that the business may have been established to facilitate fraudulent tax repayments;
- they are expected to provide evidence of:
    - a failure to register for VAT or operate PAYE;
    - suppression of cash takings;
    - trading in a second, off book activity; and
    - missing trader VAT and Labour Provider fraud cases.

An Authorised Officer must approve an unannounced visit and, for it to be reasonable and proportionate, they should only give their approval if it is the only way of establishing the correct tax position.

Where it is anticipated that the inspection will be obstructed, HMRC will seek approval for the visit from the Tribunal so that the taxpayer can be penalised for any obstruction.

As with announced visits, unannounced visits must be made at a reasonable time and the occupier of the premises must be given written notice of the inspection, together with the Fact Sheet on unannounced visits. The officer will then explain the reason for the visit and how they intend to carry it out.

If the taxpayer is present the officer must advise them of their right to ask their agent to be present but need not delay the start of the inspection to await their arrival.

> **Planning point**
>
> Clients should be advised that if an officer makes an unannounced visit they should ask to see the Tribunal's authorisation for the visit. If there the Tribunal's authorisation has not been obtained, the client does not have to allow access to the premises. It will be sufficient to agree a more convenient date and time for the officer to call back.

Visits authorised by Tribunal

With the approval of an Authorised Officer, the officer can apply to the Tribunal for their approval of a visit to the business premises.

The object of seeking the Tribunal's approval is to deter non-compliance. A penalty can be imposed on a taxpayer who obstructs a visit that has been approved by the Tribunal.

At the same time as seeking the Tribunal's approval for the inspection visit, the officer will also seek approval for a taxpayer notice to make the records available at the premises if they are required there for inspection. By obtaining the Tribunal's approval, the officer ensures that no appeal can be made against any of the requirements in the notice.

> **⚠ Warning!**
>
> There is no appeal against a Tribunal authorised visit and a penalty can be charged for obstructing it.

Private residences

HMRC do not have the power to inspect premises that are used wholly as a private residence unless invited to do so by the taxpayer. If the premises are used partly for business and partly as a private residence, HMRC can inspect the parts used for the business.

It is the view of HMRC that they can inspect a private residence if:

- the business is run from the home;
- business assets are stored at the home;

- business records are kept at the home; or
- a home is registered as the principal place of business for VAT.

HMRC accept that storing records at home because there is nowhere else to keep them is not sufficient to allow them to inspect the private residence unless invited to do so.

> **Example 66.13**
>
> A dental surgery is run from the dentist's home. The officer can inspect the offices and waiting rooms and any consulting rooms that are not in use. The inspection cannot be extended into any areas that are used solely as a private residence.

> **Planning point**
>
> Practitioners can help to strengthen their clients' position in the event of an enquiry (or, after the changes made by *Finance Act* 2008, a records inspection) by advising on the maintenance of adequate business records. This advice will also ensure that clients are not penalised for failing to comply with the record-keeping obligations imposed by the *Taxes Management Act* 1970.

For examples of when HMRC consider it is and is not suitable to inspect private premises see *www.hmrc.gov.uk/manuals/ch1manual/CH255020.htm*.

The visit

At the start of the visit the officer will give the taxpayer a copy of the Fact Sheet on visits and explain what will happen during the visit. They may indicate that they would like to discuss the records with the person who keeps them. They can only do this with the agreement of the taxpayer.

The taxpayer has the right to refuse to allow the officer to enter the premises. However, unless the taxpayer agrees to a visit at a later date, the officer will consider asking the Tribunal for approval for the inspection. If the Tribunal has approved the inspection, the taxpayer can be penalised for obstructing the visit unless there is a reasonable excuse such as illness or unavoidable delay. The penalty for obstructing an inspection that has been approved by the Tribunal is £300 plus a daily penalty of up to £60.

The taxpayer has the right to refuse to allow the officer to enter the premises. However, unless the taxpayer agrees to a visit at a later date, the officer will consider asking the Tribunal for approval for the inspection. If the Tribunal has approved the inspection, the taxpayer can be penalised for obstructing the visit unless there is a reasonable excuse, such as illness or unavoidable delay. The penalty for obstructing an inspection that has been approved by the Tribunal is £300 plus a daily penalty of up to £60.

Inspecting things means nothing more than looking at them. It does not include opening boxes and searching in them. Nor does it include walking unaccompanied around the premises, which requires the taxpayer's agreement. The officer should not mark the records that are inspected in any way, even to indicate that they have been checked. Goods or assets can, however, be marked to show that they have been inspected, although the officer must not damage them when doing so.

The officer can record the information obtained in the course of the inspection and can take copies of the documents inspected or make extracts from them, if necessary by removing them from the premises. If a written receipt for any documents removed is not offered, the taxpayer can request one.

Documents removed by an officer should not be retained longer than necessary. If any are lost or damaged the taxpayer is entitled to compensation.

Law: FA 2008, Sch. 36

Other guidance: HMRC Compliance Checks factsheets, including factsheets about pre-arranged and unannounced visits, are available on the HMRC website at www.hmrc.gov.uk/compliance/factsheets.htm

66.4.4 Other information powers

In addition to the information powers explained above which are commonly used to obtain information in the course of an enquiry, there are other, less commonly used powers, including:

- s. 20A notices (where a tax practitioner has been convicted of a tax offence or had a s. 99 penalty imposed for assisting in the preparation or delivery of information, documents or returns, knowing them to be false);
- s. 20C powers (entry and search with a warrant); and
- s. 20BA notices (where serious fraud is suspected).

66.5 Records

66.5.1 Introduction

The examination of business records has always been an important aspect of HMRC enquiries but under self assessment even greater emphasis will be given to it. The training on records examination has been extended and accountancy support is available to local offices if they wish to call on it.

For a successful enquiry, HMRC will always hope to show that:

- the records are deficient;
- the business ratios are suspect; and
- the drawings are inadequate.

Of the three, the most important is to show that there are deficiencies in the records which have led to omissions from the accounts.

> ⚠ **Warning!**
>
> HMRC have an absolute right to inspect statutory records, as defined by FA 2008, Sch. 36, para. 60.

> **Planning point**
>
> As with all other aspects of an enquiry, it is important that the practitioner is aware of HMRC's approach to records examination so that there are no unwelcome surprises. However, this is also one area where the practitioner can take truly effective preventative action.
>
> Practitioners can help to strengthen their clients' position in the event of an enquiry (or, after the changes made by *Finance Act* 2008, a records inspection) by advising on the maintenance of adequate business records. This advice will also ensure that clients are not penalised for failing to comply with the record-keeping obligations imposed by the *Taxes Management Act* 1970.

66.5.2 Obligation to keep records

With the introduction of self assessment, a statutory obligation was imposed on taxpayers to maintain records to enable them to complete their tax returns. The records which have to be kept are described in the relevant sections. *Finance Act* 2008 introduced additional statutory record keeping requirements which will be monitored by inspections, underpinned by the new inspection powers (see **66.4.3**). This paragraph explains the basic position before the additional requirements introduced by *Finance Act* 2008.

For business taxpayers, including those letting property, the legislation states that a record must be kept of:

- receipts and expenses;
- sales and purchases; and
- all supporting documentation for the above.

For non-business taxpayers the records which must be kept are not specified. They must, however, be sufficient to enable a complete and correct return to be made.

HMRC have issued guidance on the records which should be kept in leaflet SA/BK4.

Taxpayers are advised to keep invoices for all purchases and expenses. Clearly it is advisable to do so and a failure in this respect will amount to a failure for TMA 1970, s. 12B purposes. Practitioners should, however, resist the incorrect assertion by officers that a lack of documentary evidence to support an expense means that the expense cannot be claimed as a deduction in computing profits. The standard of proof required to establish that an expense was incurred is the civil standard of the balance of probability. So, for example, occupation of business premises for the purposes of the trade would be sufficient to justify a claim to deduct the rent paid for them even if some of the receipts for rent had been mislaid.

> **Planning point**
>
> Provided there is sufficient circumstantial evidence to support a claim for an expense, the lack of documentary evidence will not prevent a deduction being given for it.

Law: TMA 1970, s. 12B; FA 1998, Sch. 18, para. 21

Other guidance: HMRC leaflets SA/BK4 *Self Assessment. A general guide to keeping records* and CTSA/BK4, *A general guide to Corporation Tax Self Assessment*

Period of retention

Non-business taxpayers must retain their records for one year from the fixed filing date. For business taxpayers, the general rule is that the records must be retained for five years from the fixed filing date. However, this is extended if:

- an enquiry is still open at the date when the records could be disposed of: in that case they must be retained until the enquiry is completed;
- no enquiry has been opened but the return was filed late: in that case they must be retained until the last date to start an enquiry has passed or, if later, the date any such enquiry is completed; or
- a return is issued more than five years after the fixed filing date: in that case, the records in existence at the time must be kept until the latest date for starting an enquiry or, if later, the date any such enquiry is completed.

Penalties

The Act provides for a penalty of up to £3,000 for a failure to comply with the requirements of s. 12B. In a *Tax Bulletin*, Special Edition, HMRC made it clear that penalties would only be charged in the more serious cases, for example:

- where records were deliberately destroyed to obstruct an enquiry; or
- there was a history of serious record-keeping failures.

On the first occasion that HMRC becomes aware of a failure to keep proper records, and it cannot be proved that there was a deliberate destruction of records, they will issue a written warning to the taxpayer (with a copy to the practitioner). The warning will state that the failure makes the taxpayer liable to a penalty but that none will be charged on this occasion. The practitioner should leave the client in no doubt about the seriousness of the position however. The letter is the first step in establishing a history of serious record keeping failures. If there is a second failure, consideration will be given to making a penalty determination. If a determination is made, it will be done immediately, rather than at the end of the enquiry. Even if no penalty is charged under this provision, the second failure will be reflected in an increased penalty at the end of the enquiry.

The *Tax Bulletin* also made it clear that a full enquiry will routinely involve an examination of the business records and that the abatement of any penalty which becomes chargeable will depend on whether records have been maintained and preserved.

> ⚠ **Warning!**
> HMRC will normally issue a warning when an enquiry shows that the records are inadequate. If in the course of a subsequent inspection visit or enquiry it is found that nothing has been done to improve the records, consideration will be given to charging a penalty under s. 12B because there would then be a history of record keeping failures.

Other guidance HMRC *Tax Bulletin*, Special Edition 2, August 1997

Advice to clients

If in the normal course of preparing the annual accounts it becomes clear to the practitioner that there are deficiencies in the records maintained by a client, it should be made clear to the client what was wrong and how it can be put right so that the records can be improved for the future. The client's attention should be drawn to the obligation to maintain and retain full and accurate records of business income and expenditure. It may also be appropriate to draw the client's attention to the penalties that can be charged for failure to keep and preserve correct and complete records.

If the inspector becomes aware in the course of an enquiry that the client's records are poor, he is instructed to draw attention to this and give advice on how to improve the record keeping system. Where, however, the client is represented by a reputable accountant, the inspector will merely point out the errors and shortcomings and leave it to the accountant to explain in detail to the client what steps need to be taken to improve things. In that case, the practitioner should make it a priority to arrange to meet with the client to provide the necessary guidance.

To be able to advise clients on the appropriate records to keep for their business, the practitioner will first of all have to have a full understanding of the business. The officer will have a similar aim when starting an enquiry so as to know what records should be expected. The practitioner should establish:

- what goods or services are provided;
- who are the suppliers and what are their terms;
- who are the customers and what terms are they given;

- what is the pattern of trade, weekly and annually;
- what is the normal pattern of stock holding;
- how any wastage is incurred;
- the role of each person who works in the business; and
- how employees are remunerated and if with bonuses how these are calculated.

Once the business is fully understood, advice can be given on how to keep records which accurately record all aspects of the business.

> **Planning point**
>
> CCH *Business Focus* helps practitioners to gain a full understanding of various types of business and provides background information on operating practices, likely activities and the records, including any non-financial records, that can be expected to be kept to run the business.

Other guidance: CCH *Business Focus*

66.5.3 Additional requirements introduced by the Finance Act 2008

Prior to the new provisions relating to record keeping contained in FA 2008, Sch. 37, the records that had to be kept for tax purposes differed across taxes:

- for IT, CGT and CT taxpayers had to keep whatever records were required to make a correct and complete return or claim;
- for PAYE and NIC employers had to maintain and produce for inspection the records specified by the legislation; and
- for VAT taxable persons had to keep business and accounting records. Further guidance provided more detail about the nature of the records to be kept and some records were required to be kept by law.

Finance Act 2008 includes provisions for aligning the record keeping obligations for IT, CGT, CT and VAT. Their approach is to:

- include in primary legislation the basic record keeping requirement for tax purposes;
- extend the basic requirement with more detailed requirements in secondary legislation. Where the taxpayer is operating the VAT system or applying PAYE or NICs, the record keeping requirements will be more specific; and
- extend the statutory provisions with non-statutory guidance on what is likely to meet the basic requirement. The non-statutory guidance would be tailored to business, non-business, capital gains and so on.

The view of HMRC is that this will allow taxpayers to decide what records they need to keep based on their own particular circumstances, subject to the need to comply with any special rules. While there will be specific requirements when discharging an obligation on behalf of the government, such as operating VAT or PAYE, where the taxpayer is discharging their own obligation to keep the records needed to make a complete and correct return, they will have more discretion. HMRC will, however, provide non-statutory guidance and it will, no doubt, be difficult to justify the use of the supposed discretion if their guidance is not followed.

There will continue to be a financial penalty for not keeping the records required by statute. This will apply to all taxes. HMRC will be able to suspend the penalty in the same way they can under the new penalty regime for incorrect returns introduced by *Finance Act* 2007 (see **66.9.5**).

Finance Act 2008 also contains:

- provisions for extending to direct tax the current VAT-only facility to request a shortening of the time limit for retaining records; and
- provisions for taxpayers to keep their records on computer or in other formats and for HMRC to have access to them.

HMRC have published guidance on record keeping giving examples of the sorts of records they expect taxpayers to keep for income tax, capital gains tax, corporation tax, PAYE and VAT. The guidance deals separately with:

- non-business taxpayers;
- business taxpayers;
- employers and contractors; and
- VAT registered businesses.

It appears likely that HMRC will use their powers to make secondary legislation to extend the statutory record keeping requirement to cover such things as:

- diaries/appointment books;
- year planners;
- copies of quotations given to customers; or
- work sheets used to prepare invoices.

These are not required under the provisions of TMA 1970, s. 12B and require secondary legislation under *Finance Act* 2008 before they are a statutory requirement. So far, no secondary legislation has been passed.

Penalties and appeals

Various matters are still under review by HMRC as part of their review of their powers, including the position with regard to penalties and appeals. The matters still under consideration include:

- the penalty for not keeping adequate records;
- what is covered by the defence of reasonable excuse;
- the suspension of penalties; and
- appeals against penalties.

> **Planning point**
>
> There is going to be a large number of SME clients who will find the record keeping requirements very onerous. Practitioners may wish to consider offering their services to carry out a review of existing records, to advise on what is required to make good any deficiencies and possibly consider offering a bookkeeping service for clients that meet the requirements of the new provisions. Once clients are fully aware of the new provisions, it is likely that they will wish to engage someone to deal with the day to day record keeping, in the same way as many do already for VAT, so that they can get on with running their business.

Law: Finance Act 2008, Sch. 37

Other guidance: Guidance on record keeping can be found on the HMRC website at *www.hmrc.gov.uk/record-keeping/index.htm*

66.5.4 HMRC approach to records examination

The officer will be seeking to establish to what extent the records are robust and reliable. Even a single omission from the records will be sufficient to discredit the records not only for the enquiry year but for earlier years too (*Rosette Franks (King Street) Ltd v Dick (HMIT)*).

Poor records will not always justify replacing the profits shown by the accounts with the officer's estimate, however, as shown by the case of *Marsden (t/a Seddon Investments) v Eadie (HMIT)*. The explanations for the various discrepancies were accepted by the Special Commissioner who found that the records were in an innocent muddle.

As a first step, the officer will ask what work was done by the practitioner to produce the accounts. The questions will be directed to establish what records were made available and what estimated, computed or balancing figures were required to make the accounts balance. If this initial enquiry shows the records to be worthless a request to see the taxpayer's private records will be made immediately.

When the officer has examined the records, further information will be sought, preferable at an interview. This will include:

- what underlying records were kept which were written up into the accounting records;
- what non-financial records are kept for the efficient running of the business;
- who keeps the records and when are they written up;
- what supporting documentation is available;
- how are debtors and creditors controlled;
- what stock records exist;
- whether all expenses are supported by invoices;
- whether drawings, including goods for own consumption, are recorded; and

- how cash is controlled from the moment it is received until it is either spent or banked and whether the cash balance is regularly reconciled.

Having obtained a general overview of the records, their robustness and likely accuracy, the officer will then consider specific items in the accounts to assess whether the records are accurate.

> **Planning point**
>
> The practitioner should carry out a review of the records, and the work done on them to produce the accounts, to identify any apparent weaknesses before they are sent to HMRC. The client should be given the opportunity to comment on the apparent shortcomings to establish their effect on the accuracy of the accounts. For example, the same figure of cash in hand every year may not indicate that it is an estimate but that a cash float is maintained. This review will enable the practitioner to provide a full explanation where appropriate and so answer any doubts the officer might otherwise have had about the reliability of the records.

Law: Rosette Franks (King Street) Ltd v Dick (HMIT) (1955) 36 TC 100 and Marsden (t/a Seddon Investments) v Eadie (HMIT) (1999) Sp C 217

Sales

In many types of business there is scope for receiving small amounts of ancillary income. The officer will be aware of this from reading the *Business Economics Note* produced by HMRC. These small amounts of ancillary income are often received in cash and may be omitted from the records.

It may be possible to relate a major purchase with a particular job to check whether the income from the work done appears in the records. For example, a load of slates purchased by a builder should tie up with income from a job which includes roofing work.

Numbered invoices will be checked to see if any are missing from the sequence and to check that the correct figure of debtors is included in the accounts. The officer will be aware if it is the type of trade where small amounts of debtors might have been omitted (for example a newsagent's delivery accounts) and what the norm is for debtor days for the particular trade sector.

Many businesses will have non-financial records for the efficient running of the business, such as bookings sheets, appointments diaries and so on, or because they are required to by law, for example an animal movements book, a scrap dealer's police record book, etc. The officer will compare these with the financial records to pinpoint any discrepancies.

> **Planning point**
>
> Practitioners should review with their clients:
>
> - what non-financial records they maintain (particularly those they are required to keep by law); and
> - who receives any ancillary income and how this is recorded.
>
> CCH *Business Focus* can help practitioners with this by identifying likely sources of ancillary income for a particular type of business. It will also provide guidance on the non-financial records that can be expected in each type of business.

Other guidance: CCH *Business Focus*

Purchases

HMRC have realised that, as people have become aware of the checks made on the gross profit rate shown by accounts, some have realised that suppressing purchases made in cash enables an amount of sales to be omitted from the records without adversely affecting the gross profit rate. The officer will look for unusual breaks or changes in the pattern of purchases to identify the possibility of there being omitted cash purchases and sales. HMRC may hold evidence of purchases made in cash obtained from investigating the supplier and will be particularly interested to see if these appear in the records.

Invoices and till receipts from suppliers generally have codes printed on them. These may sometimes be used to discredit the records by demonstrating that the item purchased was:

- unrelated to the disclosed business and was sold in a separate, undisclosed business;
- a capital item incorrectly included in the records as a revenue expense; or
- nothing to do with the business at all but was for private use.

The officer may also take into account the norm for creditor days for the type of business when assessing the accuracy of the record of purchases.

Patterns

One of the reasons the officer will have asked about the pattern of trading is to be able to check the pattern of purchases and sales to see if it reflects the busier days or periods.

If patterns are broken close to the accounting date, the officer will be looking for entries in the records which show the artificial transfer of profits to the following year or, if the taxpayer has one, a different business with a different accounting date.

> **Planning point**
>
> As well as looking at the gross profit rate, the pattern of purchases should be considered in the light of what is known about the nature of the client's trade.

Expenses

Large items of expenditure will always be checked against the original invoice to ensure that the entry in the records is correct. If the original invoice has been mislaid, it is likely that the officer will want to see the returned cheque.

A review of the cheque book stubs will be made, comparing each with the corresponding entry in the business records. It is not unusual to find that the description on the stub shows that the expense was private not business as shown in the records.

While small items of cash expenditure which are unvouched are likely to be accepted as described in the records if they are of the type for which a receipt is not normally provided, larger unvouched items are likely to be treated as cash drawings by the officer.

In the type of business where it is common to employ casual labour or to supplement low wages with additional cash payments, the officer will be looking out for this. The only source of the additional, undisclosed wages would be omitted takings. While one will balance the other, so having no effect on profit, discovering additional cash wages paid from undisclosed takings:

- shows the records to be inadequate; and
- leads to additional PAYE liabilities.

Despite the statutory requirement to keep records, it is not always wrong to include some degree of estimation in accounts figures. HMRC's view on this is set out in a *Tax Bulletin*, Special Edition.

> ⚠ **Warning!**
>
> Practitioners should never allow clients to give themselves the benefit of the doubt in deciding whether to record expenditure as business or private. Claiming a deduction for an item of expenditure which is clearly not allowable is fraudulent or negligent conduct. A practitioner who makes such a misallocation will be guilty of fraudulent or negligent conduct on behalf of the client.

Other guidance: HMRC *Tax Bulletin*, Special Edition 2, August 1997

Stock and work in progress

When requesting the records in the opening letter, the officer will, if appropriate, ask for the records on which the figures of stock and work in progress have been based. The level of stock shown by the stock take will be considered against:

- the norm for the type of trade;
- the regularity of deliveries and the day on which the accounting date falls;
- the available space for storing stock; and
- the possibility that stock is held elsewhere.

Certain trades lend themselves to a more detailed method of checking stock levels. For a farm, for example, it might be possible to create a livestock grid, reconciling opening stock with purchases, sales, births, deaths and the closing stock.

> **Planning point**
>
> As part of educating clients in what is required to avoid unnecessary selection for enquiry, practitioners should encourage them to prepare a detailed stock take at each year end that can be justified if challenged. A broad, unsubstantiated estimate will justify further investigation by the officer.

> **⚠ Warning!**
>
> When valuing work in progress, accountants and other professionals will be expected to have followed the guidance on income recognition set out in UITF 40.

Other guidance: HMRC *Tax Bulletin*, December 1998, and ICAEW UITF 40

Cash

HMRC are aware that most accountants treat the records from which the accounts for a small businesses are prepared as incomplete. This will generally mean that the practitioner has to make adjustments in the course of preparing the accounts, normally making a net addition to sales or drawings to balance the cash account. Adjustments to other figures may also be required, together with estimates to cover minor unrecorded items.

The inspector will not wish to recreate the cash account that was prepared as a preliminary to drawing up the accounts and will ask to see the one prepared by the practitioner. As well as showing how the balance on the account was treated, it will also show how the practitioner drew up the account.

If the figure of cash in the balancing sheet has to be estimated, this will be seen as completely discrediting the records. Tight cash control is seen as essential if the records are to be reliable.

The officer will look at the way cash is handled and recorded from when it is received until it is banked or spent looking for possibilities that it could be misappropriated. Failure to reconcile cash regularly and frequently or a long delay in writing up the records would lead to the conclusion that the records are neither robust nor reliable.

HMRC Enquiries

In a worthwhile case, the officer will prepare a cash flow test to check that there was never 'minus' cash.

Example 66.14

The taxpayer tells the officer that he keeps a cash float of £50 and provides a cashflow test that he has prepared for a two week period and brought to the meeting. This shows:

		£
Opening cash		50
Takings		2,438
Total		2,488

	£	
Banked	2,106	
Wages	70	
Drawings	100	
Cash expenses	162	2,438
Closing cash		50

The officer retains the business records and prepares a more detailed cashflow test, breaking the period into two separate weeks. This shows:

		£
Opening cash		50
Takings	Monday	176
	Tuesday	180
	Wednesday	99
	Thursday	215
	Friday	248
	Saturday	293
	Total	1,261

	£	
Banked	1,106	
Wages	35	
Drawings	50	
Cash expenses	105	1,296
Closing cash		-35

		£
Opening cash		-35
Takings	Monday	178
	Tuesday	182
	Wednesday	100

	Thursday	218
	Friday	253
	Saturday	296
	Total	1,192
	£	
Banked	1,000	
Wages	35	
Drawings	50	
Cash expenses	57	1,142
Closing cash		50

The officer's test shows minus cash at the end of week 1, which is of course impossible. In worthwhile cases, the officer will prepare a cashflow test on a day by day basis to check that the cash was available to cover bankings and expenditure as and when it occurred.

Drawings

If drawings were not recorded, HMRC would expect the practitioner to have questioned the client closely about the level of cash drawings to arrive at a reasonable estimate for inclusion in the cash account and not to have simply taken drawings to be the balance on the cash account. The basis for any estimate will be examined closely by HMRC. If drawings are simply the balance on the cash account, the inspector will want to discuss the level of drawings in detail with the client.

Where cash drawings are not recorded or there is a large deficiency on the cash account, it will be taken by HMRC to demonstrate that the records are incomplete and are likely to be unreliable. If the practitioner maintains that the records contained only minor imperfections, the inspector may decide to prepare a cashflow test for a short period to see if in fact the adjustment needed for the year is less than the adjustment needed for the shorter period chosen for the test.

Private records

Guidance on when HMRC can request private bank account details is at **66.4.2** above.

The private records most commonly sought are copies of statements for bank and building society accounts. To obtain the private records of a spouse, partner or minor child of the taxpayer, the officer must not act in breach of the *Human Rights Act* 1998, s. 8. To comply with this, the officer must:

- be acting within the law;
- show that the request is necessary, proportionate and the minimum necessary to check the accuracy of the return; and
- demonstrate that it is in the economic interests of the country.

When reviewing private account details, the officer will consider:

- the pattern of deposits and the source of the money;
- the pattern of withdrawals and the destination of the money;
- whether drawings by cheque or bank transfer appear in the private accounts disclosed or if there remain undisclosed accounts;
- whether a gap in deposits to the business account coincides with unexplained deposits in private accounts; and
- how private expenditure was financed if there is a gap in the regular withdrawals from a private account.

The review of the private records will be carried out as part of the review of drawings to consider their adequacy to fund private expenditure and to account for savings in private bank, etc. accounts. In a worthwhile case, the officer may prepare a private cash flow test and/or a detailed means test for the year in question or a part of it.

> **Planning point**
>
> The practitioner should refer an officer who persists in making unreasonable demands to see a client's private records to the HMRC *Enquiry* Manual instructions at EM 2220 and 2221.

Law: FA 2008, Sch. 36

Other guidance: Further guidance on how the Human Rights Act affects requests for private records can be found at HMRC *Enquiry* Manual EM 1350ff.

66.5.5 Enquiries into accounting matters

HMRC published an article in *Working Together*, Issue 13, concerning the use made of HMRC accountants and their approach to determining the correctness of accounting policies. The article indicated the following areas in which HMRC Accountants have found particular problems.

Post Balance Sheet Events

Insufficient or no attention paid to adjusting post balance sheet events (SSAP 17 paragraph 22) e.g.:

(1) Stock obsolescence provisions, which in fact value the stock at below net realisable values actually achieved.

(2) Specific bad debt provisions where debts are recovered in full.

(3) Provisions for claims against an entity that were settled for less in the post balance sheet period. For example, £1m claim was settled for £400,000 in the post balance sheet period.

Stock and Work in Progress

(1) Stock provisions not supported by the facts.

(2) Long-term contracts not identified and accounted for as such (SSAP 9 paragraph 22).

(3) Stock and work in progress valued at net realisable value on the theoretical basis that it would have to be sold as an emergency sale in its current condition, rather than being sold in the normal course of business. (SSAP 9 Appendix 1 paragraphs 19 and 20).

(4) Work completed before the year end but invoiced afterwards not being correctly accounted for (FRS 18 paragraph 26).

Provisions

(1) Provision incorrectly made for recurring periodic expenditure on assets owned by the entity (FRS 12 paragraph 19 and example 11);

(2) Excessive provisions made for onerous leases, in particular where no account is taken of expected rental income or surrender or sale of the lease (FRS 12 paragraph 73);

(3) Provisions made where the facts show that there is no real likelihood of having to pay, for example where the creditor company has already been wound up and the liquidator has decided not to pursue the debt (FRS 12 paragraph 23); and

(4) Provisions made to smooth profits (FRS 12 paragraph 14).

Practitioners can also expect the HMRC accountants to keep a close eye on the proper application of the guidance contained in UITF 40 in respect of income recognition and the valuation of work in progress.

Other guidance: Working Together, Issue 13 on the HMRC website at www.hmrc.gov.uk/workingtogether/publications/wt_13.htm

Computerised records

Many businesses now have some or all of their records on computer and these can be subject to HMRC examination in the same way as paper records.

Section 114 of the *Finance Act* 2008 ensures that where access to a document can be obtained under other provisions of the Taxes Acts, that access extends to documents held on computer. It allows HMRC:

- the same access to records held on computer as would be allowed if the records were held on paper; and
- to inspect, make extracts from or copies of, or remove any document.

It should be noted that s. 114 does not extend HMRC's powers in relation to computer records beyond those records they would already be entitled to inspect, if they were on paper.

HMRC Enquiries

As part of the examination of computerised business records clients can expect to be asked about their computer hardware so that the inspector can establish:

- what equipment there is;
- whether it is owned or leased;
- where it is kept – at the business premises or at home;
- who operates it;
- if it is used for anything other than accounts work and if so what;
- when it was purchased or installed;
- what experience the operator has; and
- who, if anyone, provides expert assistance when needed.

Similarly the inspector will want to find out about the software used for accounts preparation to know what to expect and what to look out for. The information sought will include:

- the software package and name of the manufacturer;
- when the current package was first used;
- if it is the first year of use the action that was taken to ensure that the accounts are prepared on the same basis as before;
- details of the previous system; and
- details of the parts of the package that are used and the records that are kept on the computer.

The inspector will also ask for the person who operates the accounting system to explain how it actually works, in the same way as a bookkeeper would be asked how a sale is recorded in a paper based system.

If some of the records are not held on computer, the inspector will want to see these as well. These might include, for example:

- bank statements;
- cheque book stubs;
- the cash book and petty cash book if either is maintained manually; and
- any employee records kept on paper.

Inspectors are aware that many computerised accounting systems have management information reporting functions included in them. These systems will show business trends and commercial ratios and so would be of interest to the inspector as part of any records examination.

If it is claimed that accounting records or other data has been destroyed the inspector will ask about:

- security backups or copies;
- the cause of the loss; and
- the attempts that were made to recover the records.

HMRC inspectors use IDEA as their main tool for examining business records. It contains a history file of all the work done when examining a set of records. It is recommended that practitioners request a copy of the history file so that they have their own record of the work done on a set of records by the inspector. Inspectors are advised to provide a copy of the history file if requested.

66.6 Interviews

66.6.1 No legal right to interview

HMRC cannot insist that the taxpayer attends an interview (or 'meeting' as they prefer to call it). There was no change in this respect with the introduction of self assessment nor as a result of the changes made to HMRC's inspection and information powers by *Finance Act* 2008.

HMRC policy is to encourage investigators to interview as early as possible once an enquiry has started and officers will bring a great deal of pressure to bear on the practitioner and the client to try to force the issue. They will frequently threaten to restrict the reduction of the penalty for disclosure when calculating any penalty charge which may become due if the taxpayer refuses to attend an interview.

HMRC's stated reason for wanting to interview the taxpayer is that it reduces delay in dealing with the enquiry. The true purpose is to try to catch the taxpayer out in lies and inconsistencies, which they consider to be an easier task at an interview than in correspondence.

To allay the taxpayer's concerns about attending an interview, HMRC changed all references to it in their literature and training to call it a 'meeting'. The officer's training is to open the interview with a very low key approach, chatting pleasantly about inconsequential matters until the taxpayer has relaxed and become talkative.

But inside the velvet glove is a very hard iron fist. HMRC training in interview techniques reminds the officer that:

> 'your thorough preparation for the interview, probably at greater depth than the accountant, almost certainly at a greater depth than the taxpayer'

and:

> 'your appreciation that few accountants and solicitors are really experienced in enquiry work'

should instil a sufficient degree of self-confidence for the officer to feel that:

> 'You are in charge of the meeting. You must remain in charge and this must be implicit in all your dealings with the taxpayer and the accountant. You must run the interview and the enquiry.'

The practitioner must be prepared for the officer to attempt to prevent any intervention. HMRC training tells officers that:

> 'At interview you need the taxpayer's story, not the accountant's version. Do not let the accountant answer for the taxpayer, so acting as a filter, allowing only innocuous information to reach you.'

The client should expect open questions and prolonged silences:

'Silence may encourage him/her to answer your points.'

It should be clear from this that agreeing to an interview will not be accepting an invitation to a cosy chat at a 'meeting' but to a very detailed and persistent interrogation.

It may be that a client is so nervous about being interviewed that the whole exercise would be counter-productive and a waste of time. Rather than advancing the enquiry it would delay it as the confusion caused by the nervous, ill-judged responses is sorted out. In such a case, the practitioner should explain why an interview is not considered to be worthwhile.

It may be that the practitioner agrees that an interview would be the best way to progress the enquiry quickly and effectively. In that case, it is important that the preparation for the interview, including the client's preparation, is as thorough as the officer's so that it is a meeting between equals. The preparation should be based on the critical review (see **66.2.5** above) which will form the basis for the officer's preparation.

While accepting that the officer will want to hear only from the taxpayer, the practitioner must be prepared to intervene to prevent any misunderstanding and to prevent the officer from harrying the client into giving answers which are unresearched or mere guesses. It should be firmly pointed out to the officer that a reliable answer will be provided as soon as the matter has been properly researched; the practitioner should then insist that the questioning moves on. Should the officer become aggressive or unreasonable, the practitioner should terminate the meeting and write a letter of complaint to the officer's superior.

The client must be prepared to answer specific questions and then say no more. It should be remembered that silence will be used as a tactic and the client should not fall into the trap of filling it. Anything said casually at interview will be used by HMRC if it suits their case and it will be very difficult to convince the officer that something said at interview, no matter how casually, was either incorrect or not the whole story.

> ### Planning point
>
> If the officer makes any threats to try to force an interview, he or she should be reminded that this is hardly the neutral approach which they are instructed to adopt until omissions from the return have been established and to talk of a penalty demonstrates a degree of prejudice, with regard to the honesty of the taxpayer, which gives rise to serious concern about the officer's impartiality.

66.6.2 Agenda

The officer's interview agenda will normally include:

- the business – the history and nature of the business, details of how it operates, terms of supply and the duties of all who work in it;
- the records – what records are kept, who keeps them and when are they written up, with particular regard to cash control;
- the business model – the product mix, pricing policy, wastage and pilferage;
- private expenditure – whether by cash or by cheque, bank, etc. accounts operated, investments and other assets, family circumstances and lifestyle;
- technical adjustments – if any have been identified; and
- agreeing further action.

> **Planning point**
>
> As part of the preparation for the interview, the practitioner and the client should be aware of the matters likely to be covered. The practitioner should ask for a copy of the officer's agenda. It is unlikely to be detailed but the practitioner should be able to flesh it out from the results of the critical review (see **66.2.5** above).

66.6.3 Notes of the meeting

The officer will make notes during the meeting and will send two copies to the practitioner after the meeting. The officer will ask for one of the copies of the notes to be signed and returned. There is no obligation to do so and the practitioner may wish to do no more than comment on any obvious inaccuracies without accepting that the rest of the notes are complete and correct.

> **Planning point**
>
> The practitioner should take notes during the meeting to be able to compare his or her record with the detailed notes which the officer will send after the meeting.

66.7 Business economics

66.7.1 Introduction

Business economics plays a very important role in selecting (see **66.2.4** above) and working HMRC enquiries. A business economics exercise will be prepared in almost all local tax office enquiries. These may be referred to as mark-up exercises or business models.

The essence of a business economics exercise is to find a relationship between the expenses incurred in the business and takings so that the takings can be re-computed from the expenses. This is considered by HMRC to provide a reliable basis for re-computing profits because:

- it is thought likely that all the expenses will have been recorded because a deduction can be claimed for them; and
- there are industry norms which can be used as a check on the results of the exercise.

A business economics exercise may provide the best, or indeed the only, way of re-computing profits once it has been shown that the records are unreliable. However, neither HMRC nor practitioners should forget that they will not provide an accurate or reliable result. They are only ever the least bad option. In the *Farthings Steak House* case the Special Commissioner said:

> '... in my judgement business economics exercises alone can rarely justify the sort of attack mounted by the Inland Revenue in these appeals.'

This demonstrates why so much importance is given to the examination of business records by HMRC (see **66.5** above) and why it is so crucial to their success in an enquiry to show that the records are unreliable. In *Coy v Kime (HMIT)*, the court accepted that the profits should be re-computed by way of a business economics exercise, supported by a means test, once it had been shown that the records were inadequate.

HMRC intend to use their new power to visit business premises, introduced by *Finance Act* 2008, to compare the business records with what they actually find in the course of their visit to check that the records reflect the economic reality of the business. The information found in the course of such visits will also feed into the business economics exercise used to recalculate the takings.

Law: Scott (t/a Farthings Steak House) v McDonald (HMIT) (1996) Sp C 91 and Coy v Kime (HMIT) [1987] BTC 66

66.7.2 Construction of a business economics exercise

To be able to construct a business economics exercise the aim generally is to find an expense which is directly related to takings so that the amount of the expenditure incurred is a reliable indicator of the level of takings. The proposition only has to be stated to demonstrate its inherent over-simplification of the complex interaction between income and expenditure found in any business.

For a manufacturing or retail business, the direct cost will be the cost of stock, adjusted for opening and closing stock to get at the cost of goods sold. As an important first step, the true level of stock on hand should be established. Estimates of its value which have been made without sufficient regard to the facts can have a dramatic effect on the business economics exercise.

Once the cost of goods sold has been correctly established, the figure must be adjusted to exclude the cost of items not actually sold, including:

- wastage;
- theft;
- private use; or
- discounts, etc.

Since it is unlikely that there will be any record of the effect of these, it will be appreciated that their necessary introduction into the calculation inevitably further increases the unreliability of the exercise.

Example 66.15

	£
Opening stock	5,950
Purchases	268,325
	274,275
Closing stock	6,305
Cost of goods sold	267,970
Adjustment for wastage, theft, etc.	8,300
	259,670
Goods sold marked up at 185 per cent	
Re-computed takings	740,060
Takings shown by the accounts	729,495
Omitted takings	10,565

When making this comparison, care should be taken to ensure that:

- all calculations, including the calculation of the mark-up rate, are made either net of VAT or VAT-inclusive; and
- the takings shown by the accounts include any adjustment made either in the accounts or the tax computation for goods taken for own consumption.

Different types of business require different approaches to preparing a business economics exercise. In *Coy v Kime* (referred to above) the court approved the use of an exercise based on a fuel:takings ratio for re-computing the takings of a taxi driver. A business based on the provision of services (a plumber) was considered by the court in *Brittain v Gibbs (HMIT)* when an exercise using the hourly rate charged by the proprietor was accepted as the basis for re-computing takings.

Example 66.16

Fuel:takings ratio

A trial period of one week for a taxi driver show that the cost of fuel, including regular daily private motoring (home to work), is £67. Takings for the week are £677. The total cost of fuel shown in the accounts was £3,284 and no adjustment was made for private motoring. The cab was used for holidays and fuel for this exceptional motoring was estimated at £100.

	£
Fare income & tips for trial week	677
Fuel costs (fare carrying & regular private mileage)	67
Fuel:takings ratio	1:10
Cost of fuel for year	3,284
Less cost of fuel for exceptional private motoring in the year	100
Cost of fuel net of cost of exceptional private motoring	3,184
Recomputed takings at 1:10	31,840
Takings shown by accounts	28,354
Omitted takings	3,486

Example 66.17

Service trade

A plumber, with no employees, charges £7.50 per hour for all work. He works a seven-hour day, five days per week. When he supplies materials, he marks them up to the customer at 10% on cost. During the year under review he took four weeks holiday and he was not off work through illness.

	£	£
£7.50 p.h. × 7 hours × 5 days × 48 weeks =		12,600
Cost of goods sold:		
Opening stock	150	
Purchases	10,460	
Total	10,610	
Closing stock	210	
Total	10,400	
Marked up at 10%		11,440
Total income		24,040
Sales per accounts		23,980
Difference		60

The difference is too small to be significant and the computation would be taken to support the results shown by the accounts.

Planning point

It is more effective for the practitioner to prepare a business economics exercise and submit it to the officer than to simply accept and comment on features of the officer's exercise.

Law: Brittain v Gibbs (HMIT) [1986] BTC 348

66.7.3 Gathering information

The more detailed and comprehensive the detail on which it is based, the more accurate the business economics exercise will be. The broad brush approach used by the officer will always produce a larger figure of omitted takings. It is left to the practitioner and the client (on whom rests the onus of disproving the officer's figures in any appeal proceedings) to do the detailed research needed to arrive at a more accurate result.

Covert observation

Before the merger of the Inland Revenue and Customs & Excise, Customs had routinely used covert observation of business premises to gather information before challenging the accuracy of a trader's VAT returns. Since the merger HMRC have published their Regulation of Investigatory Powers Manual, which gives guidance to their staff on the procedures to be followed when carrying out covert investigations. It explains that directed surveillance includes:

- any activity which involves watching people or their activities;
- observation of or a covert visit to business premises, if it involves monitoring any of the following: the operation of the business, its working practices, the number of staff or customers, the comings and goings or other activities of individuals (such as directors, staff or customers) even if that is not the primary objective of the visit;
- test meals or test purchases; and
- covert surveillance work undertaken to establish the residence of or to locate a taxpayer, for example in order to serve a statutory demand.

It is clear that covert surveillance will now be used by HMRC as a matter of course to gather information to assess the business economics and results shown by a trader's accounts before starting a tax enquiry.

The courts approved the use of information gathered through covert surveillance in the case of *Hossain v C & E Commrs Chancery Division*, 30 July 2004. In that case, the assessments under appeal were based on observations made by Customs' officers of the number of individuals said to have been seen to dine at the taxpayer's restaurant. Customs concluded from those observations that the taxpayer must have substantially under-declared her takings for the purposes of accounting for output tax throughout the periods assessed.

The taxpayer appealed to the VAT tribunal arguing that the assessments were totally arbitrary and disproportionate. She complained that the Customs' officers had misunderstood Indian culture by assuming that every observed customer had ordered and paid for a meal whereas many dishes were shared. Further, the officers had been over-zealous and conducted their observations with an inaccurate table plan of the restaurant which rendered their observations invalid.

On the question of whether the assessments were raised using best judgement, Hart J (dismissing the appeal) said that the procedure adopted by the tribunal in assessing the capacity of the restaurant did not exhibit any bias, or involve any unfairness to the taxpayer.

The practitioner should consider carefully the results of any covert surveillance. In the *Hossain* case, the tribunal reduced the original assessments because of errors made by Customs in counting the number of tables and in assuming that everyone who sat at a table had in fact eaten a meal.

The practitioner's approach

The officer's approach to preparing a business economics exercise will use broad assumptions which will generally favour HMRC's case. The practitioner's first step in producing a more accurate exercise is to formulate a methodical approach to identify and gather the information required. An approach might be based on the following steps.

1. Make a detailed review of the accounts as recommended as part of the critical review (see **66.2** above). The results should be considered critically looking for inconsistencies within each set of accounts and between years.

2. Carry out as much research as possible into the trade sector with particular regard to operating practices, the norms for business ratios and the factors which will affect margins.

3. Meet the client to get as much information about the business including terms on which stock is purchased and sold, the pricing policy and factors affecting margins, including wastage, theft and discount, etc. given.

4. Prepare a business economics exercise based on one representative month's purchase invoices and discuss the results with the client. This may result in the period being extended to make it more representative.

> **Planning point**
>
> The client's close involvement in, and understanding of, the preparation of the business economics exercise will produce a better result than can be achieved by either the officer or the practitioner alone and will also result in a readier acceptance of the outcome.

Law: Hossain v C & E Commrs [2004] BTC 5,767

66.7.4 Reviewing a business economics exercise

When reviewing a business economics exercise prepared by HMRC, the practitioner should make sure that the principles are sound and the arithmetic is correct. It will be found that insufficient consideration is often given to the following matters.

Representative

It is usual to make a detailed review of a short period and to then extrapolate from this to the whole year. The practitioner should discuss with the client whether the period taken is representative. In the VAT Tribunal case of *Yip*, Customs Officers were criticised for basing their figures on a sample period which was so small as to be worthless.

Particular regard needs to be had to whether the selected period is representative if the trade is seasonal or if there have been major changes in the nature or conduct of the trade during the year.

Law: Yip [1993] BVC 1,531

Cost of goods sold

Care should be taken to make sure that the cost of goods sold includes only those items which were actually sold. When the Customs & Excise computation in the case of *Hawksworth* was corrected for this, their case collapsed because the revised calculation showed that the accounts and VAT returns were correct.

An adjustment to the cost of goods sold is often forgotten, where as a separate matter, non-allowable items have been identified in purchases and a note made to add them back in the tax computation. These items should also be excluded from the cost of goods sold.

Law: Hawksworth (1988) 2 BVC 1,421

Goods for own consumption

The re-computation of takings by applying the calculated mark-up rate to the cost of goods sold results in the inclusion of any goods taken for own consumption in the re-computed figure at their full market value. The re-computed takings should, therefore, be compared with the takings shown by the accounts, adjusted for any own goods adjustment already made.

Where the own goods adjustment is correctly made at cost instead of market value (e.g. meals in a hotel, restaurant, etc.), the re-computation should be checked to ensure that the market value of such goods is not being taxed.

Wastage

HMRC often tries to impose what they consider to be a 'reasonable' figure for wastage. They must be guided away from the general and made to take account of the actual circumstances of the particular case. In the VAT Tribunal case of *James A Gordon & Sons Ltd*, the Tribunal Chairman said:

'We are satisfied on the evidence that this was not an efficiently run business and that the profit margins were excessively low ... To hold that there was an evasion of value added tax would be to impose a tax on inefficiency.'

Law: *James A Gordon & Sons Ltd* (1988) 3 BVC 1,383

Discounts

It would be rare for there to be a record in any business to show the effect on margins of giving discounts. This can, however, make a substantial difference to the gross profit rates achieved. If discounts are given to particular customers, it may be possible to calculate the effect of the discounts from the customer records.

If discounts are given at a certain time, for example during a 'Happy Hour' it may be necessary to keep a record for a trial period to be able to estimate the likely effect on margins.

Theft

As with wastage, HMRC will often try to dictate what is a 'reasonable' level of theft without any reference to the facts of the particular case. This should be resisted. In the VAT Tribunal case of *Mumford*, the £50 per week allowance for theft proposed by Customs & Excise was rejected by the Tribunal. They found that, on the actual facts of the case, losses due to theft exceeded not only the Customs & Excise estimate but also the national norm for newsagents (2 per cent) and was at a level of 2.5 per cent, or about £85 per week.

Law: *Mumford* (1987) 3 BVC 1,307

Earlier years

When any omissions have been agreed for the current year they will be related back to earlier years to establish the likely level of omissions in those years. If the basis for extrapolating back to earlier years is to apply the revised gross profit rate, the practitioner should be alert to the possibilities of differences between years which will have affected margins (see **66.8.3**).

66.8 Re-opening earlier years

66.8.1 Legal basis for re-opening earlier years

Until the changes introduced by *Finance Act* 2008, the time limit for making assessments to recover a loss of tax due to fraudulent or negligent conduct was 20 years after 31 January next following the year of assessment to which it related. Instead of categorising a loss of tax due to fraudulent or negligent conduct as a single offence for the purpose of assessment time limits, the new provisions deal separately with:

- a loss of tax brought about carelessly; and
- a loss of tax brought about deliberately.

The time limit for making an assessment to recover a loss of tax brought about carelessly will be not more than four years after the end of the year of assessment to which it relates. The time limit for making an assessment to recover a loss of tax brought about deliberately will be not more than 20 years after the end of the year of assessment to which it relates.

The new provisions reduce the normal time limit for raising an assessment, which would apply where the loss of tax was due to a mistake, from not later than five years after the 31 January next following the year of assessment to which it relates to not more than four years after the end of the year of assessment to which it relates. This reduces the ordinary time limit of six years to four years.

Once HMRC can establish that there are omitted profits in the year under enquiry, they are entitled to raise assessments for earlier years, based on the presumption of continuity, and the onus of proof remains with the taxpayer to show that the assessments are excessive:

> '... once the inspector comes to the conclusion that (the taxpayer) has additional income beyond that which he has so far declared to the inspector, then the usual presumption of continuity will apply. The situation will be presumed to go on until there is some change in the situation, the onus of proof of which is clearly on the taxpayer. (*Jonas v Bamford (HMIT)*)'

Despite the legal authority to reopen earlier years provided by *Jonas v Bamford*, HMRC recognise that the more distant the year, the less reliable is the evidence on which any re-computation of profits is based. Also, their policy is to use their resources to pursue worthwhile cases. Although they do not publish their guidelines to officers on reopening earlier years, it would appear that it is on the lines of the following:

Omissions in enquiry year	Basis of settlement
Below £1,000	Current year addition, no interest or penalty
£1,000 to £2,000	In-date years, no interest or penalty
Above £2,000	All years (to maximum 20) plus interest and penalty

The guidance to officers is to be applied with discretion. There will be situations where it is deemed appropriate to penalise smaller omissions with the addition of interest and penalties. When scaling back to earlier years, even if there was a large addition in the enquiry year, earlier years will no longer be reopened once the scaled back addition falls below £1,000.

The presumption of continuity established in Jonas v Bamford can be rebutted by the facts of the case. A special commissioner decided in *Gaughan v R & C Commrs* that, in computing the amount of the profits of the taxpayer for one tax year under Sch. D, Case I, income had been understated and expenditure overstated on his tax return. However, in respect of the two previous years, HMRC had not discharged the burden of proving that income which ought to have been assessed to income tax had not been assessed as a result of negligent conduct on the part of the taxpayer or a person acting on his behalf.

> ### Planning point
>
> Careful consideration should be given to whether there are factors that relate only to the enquiry year and not the earlier years that make it possible to rebut the presumption of continuity of the omissions from the client's tax returns.
>
> Part of HMRC's practical approach is to recognise that a lack of means may be a factor to take into account when deciding whether to reopen earlier years and, if so, how many. If means are likely to be a factor when agreeing a settlement, the earlier the practitioner makes the officer aware of this the less time will be wasted arguing over figures that have no practical importance.

Law: Jonas v Bamford (HMIT) (1973) 51 TC 1; Gaughan v R & C Commrs (2006) Sp C 575

66.8.2 Negotiation

In the great majority of cases it is in everybody's interests that a negotiated settlement is reached. It may be that the evidence for some or all of the omissions is incontrovertible, for example a second set of books may show the true income and expenditure of the business. Clearly, there is no room for negotiation on this and it would be counterproductive to expend time and goodwill on anything other than ensuring that the evidence is correctly interpreted.

Normally, however, such firm evidence of omissions will not be available and the way the omissions established in the enquiry year are to be scaled back, and in what amounts, is open to negotiation.

Omissions scaled back

The officer may propose scaling back the omissions in the enquiry year by applying the Retail Price Index. It may be possible to show that there were exceptional circumstances arising in the enquiry year which should be factored out before the omissions are scaled back. It may also be possible to show that different circumstances in the earlier years should also be taken into account. Things to take into account include:

- the enquiry year was a particularly good year for the business so that there was more scope for extracting cash from it;
- exceptional personal circumstances in the enquiry year required additional cash;
- there may have been a particularly bad year or years prior to the enquiry year when circumstances made it impossible to extract cash; and
- particularly in the early years, all available resources might have been used to build up the business.

Example 66.18

The business started in January 2011. The omitted profits for the year ended 31 December 2015, the enquiry year, have been agreed at £4,600. The inspector has proposed additions to profits of:

y/e 31/12	2011	2012	2013	2014	2015
RPI (illustrative)	173.4	176.2	181.3	186.7	192.0
Agreed omissions					4,600
Proposed additions (£)	4,154	4,221	4,344	4,473	

The inspector accepted that there was no scope for extracting funds from the business in the first two years and that thereafter the extractions grew; say at the rate of one third and then two thirds of the level taken in 2015. This gave omissions of:

	2011	2012	2013	2014	2015
RPI (illustrative)	173.4	176.2	181.3	186.7	192.0
Agreed omissions					4,600
Proposed additions (£)	0	0	1,448	2,982	

Adjustment to gross profit rate

One of the core risk rules for selection for enquiry is a fluctuating gross profit rate (GPR). The HMRC assumption is that a business which:

- sells the same things;
- on the same terms;
- having acquired them on the same terms;

will make approximately the same GPR year-on-year.

The variations in terms of supply and sale and changes in product mix alone make HMRC's assumption problematic. In addition, there will be changes in competition, wastage, theft, etc. to take into account.

Planning point

Before raising these matters in negotiation, as much research as possible should be carried out to provide whatever circumstantial evidence there is to support the client's argument. As with all negotiating points, the practitioner should quantify the effect of each argument to give a basis for discussion.

Private expenditure

Another alternative for providing a basis for scaling back the enquiry year omissions to earlier years is to add the omitted takings to drawings and then increase the drawings to a similar level, adjusted for inflation, in the earlier years.

If this method is adopted, the practitioner may be able to negotiate reductions to take account of:

- changing family circumstances;
- the increased expenditure in the enquiry year being due to exceptional private expenditure; and
- exceptional capital expenditure/investments made in the enquiry year.

Example 66.19

The agreed omitted profits, based on additional drawings, for the year ended 31 December 2015 are £2,050. The inspector proposed additional profits of:

	2010	2011	2012	2013	2014	2015
RPI (illustrative)	170.3	173.4	176.2	181.3	186.7	192.0
Agreed omissions						2,050
Proposed additions (£)	1,818	1,851	1,881	1,936	1,993	

The inspector accepts that the drawings requirement was greater in 2013 to 2015 because of the additional expense arising from a child, who was previously at state school, going to university. The extra cost is estimated as £1,000 in each year so it is agreed that the additions for the earlier years be reduced by £1,000:

	2010	2011	2012	2013	2014	2015
RPI (illustrative)	170.3	173.4	176.2	181.3	186.7	192.0
Agreed omissions						2,050
Proposed additions (£)	1,818	1,851	1,881	1,936	1,993	
Reduction	1,000	1,000	1,000	0	0	0
Revised additions	818	851	881	1,936	1,993	2,050

In view of the level to which the additions have been reduced by 2010, the inspector does not propose re-opening years prior to that.

> **Planning point**
>
> Practitioners may find it difficult to start negotiations, fearing that to do so will be taken as an admission of weaknesses in the client's case. It is recommended that the practitioner adopts the same approach as the officer, setting out the client's 'best case' position and then offering to discuss a compromise on a completely 'without prejudice' basis. This leaves it open to both sides to return to their original positions should compromise be impossible and recourse to a Tribunal hearing becomes necessary.

66.8.3 Additional reliefs

Reopening earlier years may give rise to the possibility of claiming further reliefs for:

Claiming further reliefs

- farmers' averaging;
- wages paid to a spouse; and
- pension contributions.

Professional fees

Professional fees relating to an enquiry will not normally be allowable unless:

- there are no adjustments to profits; or
- there is an adjustment in the enquiry year only, with no addition for interest and penalties arising out of fraudulent or negligent conduct.

Other guidance: HMRC *Tax Bulletin*, Issue 37, August 1997

66.8.4 VAT

When negotiating a settlement the practitioner should take account of the VAT that should have been charged on any additional takings and ensure that the tax settlement is based on additional takings that are net of VAT. If VAT should have been charged, there will, of course, be an additional VAT liability that must be paid by the business. This additional VAT may be an allowable deduction for IT or CT purposes.

An additional liability to VAT may arise because:

- registration for VAT was made late and no VAT was charged on sales in the period before registration;
- part of the business outputs has been wrongly treated as exempt from VAT or zero-rated; or

- despite being registered for VAT, VAT has not been charged on some sales, either deliberately or due to a misunderstanding.

Provided the additional VAT liability has been met by the business (because no VAT was charged on the output when it originally arose and a further charge on the original customer cannot be made) then that VAT is an allowable deduction.

Additional VAT not allowable

When additional VAT is payable because the business has under-declared turnover to HMRC, but has charged VAT on that under-declared turnover, no deduction will be allowed. The business has collected the VAT but simply failed to pay it to HMRC at the appropriate time.

Where additional VAT liability arises because input tax on non-business expenditure has been claimed, the VAT will not generally be allowable as a deduction.

VAT penalties and interest

Penalties and interest payable as a result of HMRC VAT investigations are not allowable deductions in computing profits or losses for tax purposes.

66.9 Completion of enquiry

66.9.1 Closure notices

Unless a contract settlement is concluded between the taxpayer and HMRC, a closure notice will be issued. HMRC have issued a revised leaflet IR160 stating that in the case of a contract settlement:

> 'We will not seek to take advantage of the fact that ... a completion notice has not been given.'

The closure notice will state the conclusions reached as a result of the enquiry and the adjustments required to the SA return. Where appropriate, an amended self assessment will be issued. The Act provides for an appeal to be made against the closure notice within 30 days.

As well as at the conclusion of an enquiry other than by way of a contract settlement, the officer will also consider issuing a closure notice if:

- the taxpayer refuses to cooperate and the formal information powers have been exhausted; or
- information has been provided (by the taxpayer or a third party) which enables the amount to be included in the self assessment to be determined and the taxpayer has ceased to cooperate.

Law: TMA 1970, s. 28A, 28B; FA 1998, Sch. 18, para. 32

Other guidance: HMRC leaflet IR160

Application for a closure notice

A new right was given to taxpayers with the introduction of self assessment enabling them to apply to the Tribunal for a closure notice.

Unusually, the onus of proof is on HMRC to show that they have reasonable grounds for continuing their enquiries. If they cannot satisfy the Tribunal in this respect, the Tribunal will issue a direction to HMRC that they must issue a closure notice.

The special commissioner in the case of *Jade Palace Ltd v R & C Commrs*, [2006] Sp C 540, held that HMRC had not shown reasonable grounds for not giving a closure notice. He held that, once an application for closure was made, it was for HMRC to show reasonable grounds for not giving a closure notice within a specified period. Those grounds should take account of:

- proportionality; and
- the burden on the taxpayer.

The issue on such application was not simply whether a closure notice should be directed, but whether it should be directed within a specified period.

The period necessary would vary with the circumstances and complexity of the case and the length of the enquiry. The longer the period of the enquiry, the greater the burden on HMRC to show reasonable grounds. It was for the tribunal giving a direction to specify the period. It was not necessary for the company making the application to specify the period in the application, although that might help to focus the application.

In the circumstances of this particular case, the special commissioner found that HMRC had not shown reasonable grounds for not giving a closure notice within a specified period. Provided the matter was given proper priority, four months was adequate. Further the enquiry into 2003–04 should also be closed within four months. The taxpayer's business was not large or complex. It consisted of a single restaurant and takeaway receiving part of its takings in credit cards. The enquiries must have involved substantial accountancy costs. By the time the closure notice took effect over two years would have elapsed from the opening of the 2002–03 enquiry.

An application is to be heard in the same way as an appeal, giving the taxpayer the right to be present and to be heard. There is no limit to the number of applications for a closure notice that can be made.

> **Planning point**
>
> Practitioners should always draw to the attention of the Tribunal the fact that the onus of showing that they should not issue a closure notice rests (unusually) on the officer. Although it is not for the practitioner to show why a closure notice should be issued, it is clearly advantageous to present the client's case for having satisfied all HMRC's legitimate concerns.

Law: TMA 1970, s. 28A(4) (for individuals), s. 28B(5) (for partnerships); FA 1998, Sch. 18, para. 33(1) (for companies); *Jade Palace Ltd v R & C Commrs*, [2006] Sp C 540

Uses of an application for a notice

An application for a closure notice cannot be used to:

- prevent HMRC from opening an enquiry; or
- avoid the need to provide information required by a taxpayer notice under the new information powers set out in *Finance Act* 2008.

It does, however, give the taxpayer a practical remedy for dealing with several situations where previously there was none. It can be used to:

- curb HMRC delays by forcing the officer to say what is required or to close the enquiry;
- counter vindictiveness of the type found in *Farthings Steak House*;
- bring to an end an unreasonable enquiry.

It is not unusual for an enquiry to be pursued beyond the point at which the practitioner considers it reasonable. This is sometimes because the practitioner has unreasonable expectations of what HMRC should accept without any supporting evidence. It is sometimes the case, however, that the officer is reluctant to have a 'nil' settlement recorded against him or her.

If the practitioner feels that an objective review of the case will demonstrate that the officer has no reasonable grounds for continuing with the enquiries, an application for a closure notice should be made. The hearing should be treated as a contentious hearing and at least a day allowed for the proceedings so that the client's case can be put as fully and as forcefully as possible.

HMRC have made it clear that, if the taxpayer succeeds in an application for a closure notice, the notice they issue will be in figures which they consider to be correct and they will amend the self assessment accordingly. It has yet to be seen if HMRC will use this ploy to thwart the decision of the Tribunal and, if they do, whether they will succeed. The appeal against the amended self assessment will be heard by the same Tribunal which directed that the closure notice be issued because there were no reasonable grounds for continuing the enquiry. They are unlikely to be sympathetic towards an attempt to circumvent the consequences of their earlier decision.

> **Planning point**
>
> If the amendment to the self assessment simply reflects the officer's case, it would be reasonable to draw to the attention of the Tribunal this attempt by HMRC to circumvent the intention of their decision to grant a closure notice.

Law: Scott (t/a Farthings Steak House) v McDonald (1996) Sp C 91

66.9.2 Interest

The way in which interest is charged on unpaid tax was changed substantially with the introduction of self assessment. The major changes are as follows:

- TMA 1970, s. 88, which charged interest on tax lost due to the default of the taxpayer, was repealed;
- all interest is now chargeable under TMA 1970, s. 86;
- the reason for the loss of tax is irrelevant for the purposes of s. 86;
- interest is chargeable from the self-assessment due date until the date of actual payment;
- an increase in profits increases the interim payments which should have been made and interest is chargeable on the increased amount due;
- there is no statutory power to mitigate interest (although HMRC can use their general powers under their collection and management responsibility to mitigate interest in certain circumstances, for example delay on the part of HMRC); and
- there is no right of appeal against a charge to interest.

Law: TMA 1970, s. 86

66.9.3 Penalties for incorrect returns for returns for periods commencing before 1 April 2008

A new penalty regime was introduced by *Finance Act* 2007 for returns for periods commencing on or after 1 April 2008 (see **66.9.5**). The old penalty regime continues to apply for returns for periods commencing before 1 April 2008. This commentary and the commentary on mitigation in **66.9.4** below describes the penalty regime as it applies to returns for periods commencing before 1 April 2008.

An incorrect return is a return which self assesses the amount of tax in a figure which is not that finally found to be due. Not every incorrect return leads to a penalty being charged however. If the error is innocent, as opposed to being as a result of fraudulent or negligent conduct, there will be no penalty. None of these terms is defined but if an incorrect return is made other than as a result of fraudulent or negligent conduct, it will be incorrect as a result of innocent error.

Conduct is fraudulent if a person:

- did not believe a statement to be true; or
- was reckless as to whether or not a statement was true.

A person will be guilty of negligent conduct for failing to do what a prudent and reasonable person would have been expected to do. This would include:

- keeping proper records to enable a correct return to be made;
- complying within statutory time limits with the obligations imposed by the Taxes Acts; and
- seeking advice, either from a tax practitioner or HMRC, on matters of difficulty.

HMRC consider that negligent conduct may be found and penalised in both full and aspect enquiries. When confirming this, they said that they have always considered penalties in cases ranging from serious fraud down to a minor degree of negligence. As negligence includes carelessness or a lack of reasonable care it can encompass basic errors in a tax return which might be subject to an aspect rather than a full enquiry.

Negligent conduct does not, however, include making an incorrect return in the following circumstances.

(1) Valuations – an honestly made valuation used in the preparation of a return which is successfully challenged by HMRC.

(2) Provisional figures – provided the provisional figures are clearly noted as such in the return, the reason for their use is stated and the date by which the firm figures will be provided is given.

(3) Third party information – if information provided by a third party (for example a bank interest certificate) is later shown to be wrong.

(4) HMRC advice – if guidance sought from HMRC and acted on by the taxpayer when completing the return later proves to be incorrect.

Law: TMA 1970, s. 95, 95A; FA 1998, Sch. 18, para. 20

66.9.4 Mitigation of the penalty for periods commencing before 1 April 2008

The categorisation of certain tax penalties as a criminal charge for the purposes of art. 6 of the European Convention on Human Rights (*King v Walden*) has led HMRC to issue revised guidance to its staff on what can be said about the mitigation of penalties. HMRC's aim is to avoid accusations of inviting taxpayers to incriminate themselves and offering them a financial inducement to do so. The guidance is intended to strike a balance between making it clear that taxpayers are not obliged to incriminate themselves while drawing attention to the potential to reduce penalties by making a disclosure and cooperating fully with HMRC in their enquiries.

Penalties will be mitigated from a maximum amount of 100 per cent of the additional tax to take account of:

- disclosure;
- cooperation; or
- size and gravity.

Law: King v Walden [2001] BTC 170

Other guidance: www.hmrc.gov.uk/specialist/humanrights.pdf

Disclosure

A disclosure of irregularities does not have to be detailed and quantified to qualify for mitigation. A disclosure in general terms which identifies all the areas of irregularity and indicates the approximate amounts involved will suffice.

The normal maximum mitigation for disclosure is 20 per cent but this can be increased to 30 per cent for a spontaneous voluntary disclosure when the taxpayer had no reason to suspect that the default would be discovered.

To earn the 20 per cent mitigation, the taxpayer must make an immediate full disclosure when first challenged. At the other extreme, the person who continues to deny any irregularity until the conclusion of the enquiry will earn no mitigation. There are various degrees of disclosure falling within these extremes and the level of mitigation is a matter for negotiation between the practitioner and the officer.

Cooperation

The mitigation for cooperation, which can be up to 40 per cent, is given to reward the taxpayer's willing cooperation to enable the errors on the return to be corrected. The factors taken into account in assessing the amount of mitigation include the speed of response when providing information and whether there has been any deliberate obstruction of HMRC's enquiries.

A threat to reduce the mitigation for cooperation for a failure to attend an interview is one of the ways in which HMRC will try to force a meeting even though they have no legal right to insist that a meeting takes place. If the taxpayer has good reason for not agreeing to be interviewed, this pressure should be resisted (see **66.6.1** above).

The following gives some idea of the level of mitigation which might be expected.

(1) Complete and willing cooperation – 40 per cent.

(2) Complete and willing cooperation but with occasional delays – 30 per cent to 40 per cent.

(3) Complete and willing cooperation but with some longer delays – 20 per cent to 30 per cent.

(4) Complete and willing cooperation with some longer delays leading to the issue of a s. 19A notice – 10 per cent to 20 per cent.

(5) Long delays but no deliberate obstruction – 5 per cent to 10 per cent.

(6) Deliberate obstruction – 0 per cent.

> **Planning point**
>
> A failure to provide information without the need for a s. 19A notice (now, a FA 2008, Sch. 36 taxpayer notice) would be viewed as obstructive. If the practitioner cannot provide information in the time given by the officer, going back with a sensible revised timetable will avoid a s. 19A or Sch. 36 notice, thus helping to obtain the maximum mitigation for cooperation.

> **⚠ Warning!**
>
> Mitigation for cooperation is the one aspect of the penalty charge that the practitioner can influence. Practitioners should do everything they can to avoid the charge that they have failed to maximise the mitigation for cooperation, or indeed jeopardised any mitigation, through delays in their office.

Size and gravity

The mitigation for size and gravity cannot be affected by the taxpayer's response to HMRC's enquiries. It depends entirely on:

- the amount of tax at risk; and
- the seriousness of the offence.

Thus, a settlement involving a very large amount of tax lost due to the taxpayer's fraudulent conduct over a long period will earn less mitigation than the case of a small amount of the tax lost due to negligent conduct over a short period.

Maximum mitigation would be earned where the omissions were less than the limit for reopening earlier years (see **66.8.1** above) and there was no more than negligent conduct on the part of the taxpayer.

The Special Compliance Office (SCO), which deals with the most serious cases involving fraud, will normally allow mitigation for size and gravity of 15 per cent, so it would not be expected that a local office enquiry would lead to mitigation of less than this.

> ### Example 66.20
>
> A trader who has been in business for 20 years sends in a return which is selected for full enquiry. He admits that he has been omitting takings from the records and cooperates fully to establish the amount of the omissions.
>
> All information is provided promptly and it is established that there have been omissions in all years reaching a maximum of £1,500 in the current year.
>
> | | | % |
> |---|---|---|
> | | | 100 |
> | Disclosure: Confessed on challenge | 20 | |
> | cooperation: Excellent | 40 | |
> | Size and gravity: The offence was deliberate and, depending on the circumstances, might be fraud. It has continued for 20 years. Although the omissions never became very large, the total omissions over 20 years were substantial | 15 | 75 |
> | Penalty loading: | | 25 |

> ### Example 66.21
>
> A trader who has been in business for six years sends in a return which is selected for full enquiry. He denies any irregularities and gives only grudging cooperation. There are some long delays and a s. 19A notice was required to obtain some information.
>
> Omissions of £9,000 are established, but he continues to deny that there could possibly have been any at all, despite irrefutable evidence to the contrary. Rather than appear before the Tribunal, he agrees to make an offer in settlement.
>
> | | | % |
> |---|---|---|
> | | | 100 |
> | Disclosure: Denials in the face of irrefutable evidence | 0 | |
> | cooperation: Poor but just falling short of deliberate obstruction | 10 | |
> | Size and gravity: Omissions are large in all years and on such a scale that he must have known about them. The offence would almost certainly have been committed deliberately | 15 | 25 |
> | Penalty loading: | | 75 |

66.9.5 New penalty regime for returns for periods commencing on or after 1 April 2008

Changes to the penalty regime were enacted by *Finance Act* 2007. The changes took effect in respect of any return for a period commencing on or after 1 April 2008 that is completed on or after 1 April 2009. An outline of the changes is provided below.

Introduction

As part of the process of unifying and modernising its powers, HMRC issued various consultation papers. The last one dealing with penalties for incorrect returns was issued in December 2006. The paper concerned itself exclusively with the question of the penalties that are appropriate for deliberate understatements of direct or indirect taxes. It set out in detail the expected shape of the new penalty structure and included illustrative draft clauses to implement it. The draft clauses have now been included in *Finance Act* 2007 in the form proposed in the consultation paper.

The new penalty regime will result in a substantial increase in the level of penalties for deliberate understatements of tax. It will also place a much greater responsibility and financial burden on the taxpayer to be proactive in providing a disclosure report.

The new regime reflects the view of HMRC that penalties should be higher because over the years they have tended to decrease as the levels of abatement given have increased. The way in which the proposed new approach will produce higher penalties is by fixing a statutory maximum and minimum amount for the penalty to be charged for different 'behaviours'.

The new regime

The main elements of the new penalty regime are that:

- it will be a single regime applying to incorrect returns for both direct and indirect taxes;
- there will be statutory penalties provided for each of three different 'behaviours';
- reduction of the penalty will be allowed but only for disclosure, the amount of the reduction depending on the 'quality' of the disclosure;
- reduction of the penalty will never reduce the penalty below a statutory minimum;
- the statutory minimum is lower for an unprompted disclosure than for a prompted disclosure;
- HMRC will have the power to suspend penalties; and
- they will also have discretion to reduce penalties below the statutory minimum

if, exceptionally, the penalty was deemed to be disproportionate or otherwise inappropriate.

Behaviours

Different statutory penalties will be set for each of three different behaviours with different degrees of culpability applying to each. The culpable behaviours are:

- making careless inaccuracies;
- making deliberate understatements that are not concealed; and
- making deliberate understatements with concealment.

Mistake

As under the old penalty regime, where a taxpayer makes a genuine mistake there will be no penalty provided the taxpayer had taken reasonable care to complete the return correctly and the mistake was notified to HMRC without unreasonable delay.

In what appears to be an attempt to reduce the need for argument over what constitutes a genuine mistake, HMRC have set out in some detail what they consider would be covered, such as:

- an innocent error after taking reasonable care;
- a reasonable view of the law that proves to be wrong or is not pursued;
- an action or omission that does not form part of a pattern of behaviour and is untypical of the taxpayer concerned; or
- the adoption of a treatment for tax purposes that is clearly disclosed to HMRC in a return or accounts, even if subsequently changed by agreement or determination of a tribunal.

Examples provided by HMRC of what would be treated as making a mistake despite taking reasonable care include:

- an arithmetical error, but not so big as to produce an odd result that ought to have been questioned;
- misclassifying an unusual item of income or expenditure, not big enough to prompt the need for professional advice;
- misinterpreting legislation or regulations in respect of an unusual item, not big enough to prompt the need for professional advice;
- a mistake made by an assistant or employee, but not so big (relative to overall liability) as to be easily picked up by a quality check;
- omitting a small (relative to overall liability) item from a return which is otherwise correct;
- a reasonable judgement is made (after advice where appropriate) where the legislation requires this: for example, a valuation, and the basis on which the valuation is made is disclosed;
- a reasonable view of the law is adopted after giving it careful consideration or taking advice where appropriate, even if this differs from HMRC guidance; and

- trying to get HMRC advice but finding none was available in a form accessible to the taxpayer or not being able to find it or understand it or it subsequently proved to be wrong or out of date.

Careless inaccuracies

The new penalty regime lays down a maximum statutory penalty of 30 per cent of the revenue lost for understatements due to a failure to take reasonable care. The maximum reduction in the penalty for a disclosure that was completely unprompted could reduce this to a statutory minimum penalty of nil.

The minimum statutory penalty for a prompted disclosure of an understatement due to a failure to take reasonable care would be 15 per cent of the revenue lost.

'Reasonable care' is used in place of 'negligent conduct' because it is felt that taxpayers will find it easier to understand what it means. However, it can be expected that the existing law relating to negligent conduct or negligence will be applied to decide if someone has used reasonable care.

HMRC have indicated how they will interpret reasonable care. They say that:

- 'reasonable' means reasonable in regard to the circumstances of which the actor, called on to act reasonably, knows or ought to know; and
- 'reasonable' is a relative term: it must be interpreted in the light of all the circumstances prevailing.

To decide whether someone has taken reasonable care, HMRC will therefore look at their pattern of behaviour as well as the particular instance. As a result, a history of failures would make it more likely that an incorrect return will be treated as being due to a failure to take reasonable care. HMRC consider that a failure to take reasonable care would include:

- a breach of a duty existing at the time when the duty should have been performed;
- not doing something that the person knew or should have known ought to be done and which the person concerned had the power to do;
- the absence of such care, skill and diligence as it was the duty and capacity of the person to bring to the work;
- omitting to do something a reasonable person would do and the person concerned could do, or doing something a reasonable person would not do; or
- negligence, importing some neglect of duty in relation to facts or to interpretation of the law, provided the capacity to perform the duty is present.

Once again, to limit argument over what constitutes a failure to take reasonable care, HMRC have given examples of what they think would be covered, including:

- omitting items from a return (too many, or too large relative to overall liability, to suggest that they are simply mistakes);

Completion of Enquiry 66.9.5

- failing to notify a new source of income in time, where the person could reasonably be expected to have known liability arose;
- failing to bring to HMRC's attention a mistake or misinterpretation which is identified by the taxpayer, whether made by HMRC or the taxpayer, and which is significant in relation to overall liability;
- making arithmetical errors (too many, or too large, relative to the overall liability, to suggest they are simply isolated mistakes);
- misclassifying items of income or expenditure without giving the matter adequate consideration or, if the amounts and complexity warrant it, taking professional advice;
- keeping books and records that are incomplete in some respects;
- not having appropriate accounting systems in place, including to ensure items captured in the correct return period (failure over a sustained period may however be an indication of deliberate understatement);
- omitting occasional items of income or gains;
- having insufficient quality control and not checking the work of others;
- applying PAYE wrongly occasionally or to an unusual item without checking on the correct treatment; and
- failing to check a return is consistent with underlying records.

Deliberate understatement but not concealed

The maximum statutory penalty for deliberate understatements without concealment will be 70 per cent of the lost revenue. The penalty for an unprompted disclosure can be reduced to no less than 20 per cent of the lost revenue and for a prompted disclosure the statutory minimum penalty will be 35 per cent of the lost revenue.

HMRC interpret a deliberate understatement to be:

- deliberately not doing something that ought to be done; or
- deliberately getting something wrong.

and the examples they give of this behaviour include:

- not disclosing a new source of income over a sustained period, where the taxpayer could reasonably be expected to know that it should be disclosed;
- systematically paying wages without operating PAYE or NIC;
- not keeping books and records at all, or keeping them so imperfectly as to suggest more than lack of attention;
- not recording all sales, especially where there is a pattern to the under-recording, in circumstances that appear to rule out genuine misunderstanding;
- including personal expenditure in business expenditure, or inflating expenditure, in circumstances that appear to rule out genuine misunderstanding;
- making obviously inadequate adjustments for 'own goods', or private motoring, where the figures are significant;
- misclassifying items of income or expenditure in circumstances that seem to preclude error;

- omitting significant amounts of income in relation to overall liability from a return, or from more than one return (relative to overall liability);
- adopting inappropriate accounting treatment in circumstances that appear to rule out genuine misunderstanding, including putting items in the wrong return period, and not disclosing it on the accounts;
- describing transactions inaccurately or in a way likely to mislead; and
- deliberately misinterpreting the law with a view to understatement.

Deliberate understatement with concealment

The maximum penalty for deliberate understatement with concealment will be 100 per cent of the lost revenue. Where the disclosure is unprompted, the minimum statutory penalty will be 30 per cent of the lost revenue. The minimum statutory penalty for a prompted disclosure of a deliberate understatement with concealment will be 50 per cent of the tax lost.

HMRC interpret deliberate understatement with concealment as out and out fraud since the understatement would arise out of deliberately getting something wrong and then taking steps to systematically cover it up. The examples they give of this type of behaviour include:

- creating false invoices;
- backdating or post-dating contracts or invoices;
- creating fictitious minutes of meetings or minutes of fictitious meetings;
- destroying books, records and documents in order that they should not be available;
- deliberately misleading accountants or HMRC;
- altering invoices or other documents; and
- systematically diverting taxable receipts into undisclosed bank accounts and covering the traces.

Reduction of the penalty for disclosure only

The old penalty regime started with a maximum penalty amount of 100 per cent which was then mitigated to take account of disclosure, cooperation and size and gravity of the offence.

Under the new regime there will be no place for reduction in the penalty for size and gravity because the maximum and minimum penalties are be laid down by statute to reflect the seriousness of the offence. To obtain the maximum reduction for disclosure, the taxpayer would have to:

- admit the understatements, describe them, saying how long they have gone one for, who was involved in them or was aware of them and giving an indication of the scale of the irregularities, even if precise quantification is not possible;
- take active steps to quantify the understatements, either personally or by commissioning a report at their own expense;

- permit HMRC access to underlying records and documents to enable them to test the completeness of the disclosure; and
- be proactive, doing more than simply complying with HMRC's requests for information by identifying documents or information that may be relevant and actively producing them or commissioning others to produce them or authorising HMRC to obtain them, if unable to do so.

In measuring the reduction for the quality of the disclosure, HMRC will take into account the:

- timing;
- nature; and
- extent.

Of the three elements of disclosure, that is:

- telling;
- helping; and
- giving access.

The weighting that will be given to each of the three elements of a disclosure are:

- helping – 40 per cent;
- telling – 30 per cent; and
- giving access – 30 per cent.

Example 66.22

After an initial denial, a person admitted that their return was inaccurate and provided the information needed to calculate the tax lost, but only after some short delays. The quality of the disclosure might be determined as:

	Possible reduction	Actual reduction
Telling	30%	15%
Helping	40%	30%
Giving access	30%	25%
Quality of disclosure	100%	70%

Calculating the penalty

The stages for calculating the amount of the penalty are as follows:

(1) Identify the behaviour leading to the inaccuracy and whether the disclosure was prompted or unprompted.

(2) Identify the maximum (a) and the minimum (b) penalty.

(3) Deduct the minimum penalty from the maximum penalty to work out the maximum permitted reduction for disclosure (c): $c = a - b$.

HMRC Enquiries

(4) Work out the percentage reduction for the quality of the disclosure (d).

(5) Apply the percentage reduction for the quality of the disclosure to the maximum permitted reduction for disclosure to work out the actual reduction percentage for disclosure (e): e = d × c.

(6) Deduct the actual reduction percentage from the maximum penalty percentage to work out the penalty percentage (f): f = a − e.

(7) Apply the penalty percentage to the potential lost revenue (PLR) to work out the amount of the penalty: amount of the penalty = PLR × f.

Example 66.23

A person made an unprompted disclosure of an inaccuracy that was deliberate but without concealment. The PLR is £43,000. The quality of the disclosure justifies a reduction for disclosure of 80 per cent:

(1) The failure was deliberate but without concealment and the disclosure was unprompted.

(2) The maximum penalty is 70 per cent and the minimum 20 per cent.

(3) The maximum permitted deduction for disclosure is 50 per cent (70% − 20%).

(4) The reduction for the quality of the disclosure has been determined as 75 per cent.

(5) The actual reduction percentage for disclosure is 37.5 per cent (50% × 75%).

(6) The penalty percentage is 32.5 per cent (70% − 37.5%).

(7) The penalty is £13,975 (PLR £43,000 × 32.5%).

Example 66.24

A person made a prompted disclosure of a careless inaccuracy. The PLR is £6,000. The quality of the disclosure justifies a reduction for disclosure of 60 per cent.

(1) The inaccuracy was careless and the disclosure was prompted.

(2) The maximum penalty is 30% and the minimum 15 per cent.

(3) The maximum permitted deduction for disclosure is 15 per cent (30% − 15%).

(4) The reduction for the quality of the disclosure has been determined as 60 per cent.

(5) The actual reduction percentage for disclosure is 9 per cent (15% × 60%).

(6) The penalty percentage is 21 per cent (30% − 9%).

(7) The penalty is £1,260 (PLR £6,000 × 21%).

FA 2010 changes

The *Finance Act* 2010, s. 35 and Sch. 10 amended the level of penalties that may be charged under FA 2007, Sch. 24 in cases where certain offshore income, gains or assets have not been declared to HMRC. The existing penalty levels continue to apply to domestic matters and where the offshore matter concerns a jurisdiction which automatically exchanges information with the UK. For other jurisdictions, for income tax and capital gains tax only, the penalties are increased by a factor of 1.5 or 2 depending on the tax transparency of the jurisdiction concerned.

The level of the penalty and the reductions permitted for disclosure depend on which of three categories the inaccuracy falls into. If a single inaccuracy is in more than one category it is treated as if it were separate inaccuracies, one in each relevant category according to the matters that it involves, and the potential lost revenue is calculated separately in respect of each separate inaccuracy.

The new regime will come into force on a day to be appointed by Treasury Order.

Suspension of penalties

The new regime introduces a new concept: the suspension of all or part of a penalty. The intention is that where someone is merely haphazard or careless in their approach to their tax affairs but is not essentially non-compliant, any penalty chargeable for not taking reasonable care might be suspended wholly or in part for up to two years. This approach might be applied, for example, in the case where defective accounting systems had led to the understatement.

If at the end of the period of suspension the taxpayer can demonstrate that the cause of the understatement has been corrected and the improvement maintained, the penalty would be cancelled. It is anticipated that the suspension could end sooner if:

- the conditions specified had not been met and a further incorrect return has been received, in which case the suspended penalty would become payable together with any penalty in respect of the later return; or
- HMRC is satisfied the conditions have been met in which case the suspended part of the penalty would be waived.

The onus will be on the taxpayer to demonstrate that they have met the conditions and they would be required to provide access to HMRC to check the position themselves.

It is hoped that this will be seen as a positive use of the penalty system, encouraging future compliance rather than merely punishing past failures.

Discretion

HMRC acknowledge that the statutory penalties and reductions may, on occasion, produce a result that is disproportionate or otherwise inappropriate. They have, therefore, retained discretion to further reduce penalties in special circumstances. They expect, however, that such discretion would need to be exercised only rarely.

Matters relating to companies

As with income tax, the new penalty regime will take effect in respect of any company return for a period commencing on or after 1 April 2008 completed on or after 1 April 2009. As well as the changes affecting all taxpayers there are some that will affect companies. These are aimed at:

- the avoidance of a penalty through using group relief;
- collecting penalties for deliberate understatements of company profits from an officer of the company.

Group relief

The new provisions will prevent groups of companies using group relief to avoid a penalty being charged where profits have been understated in a group company. A typical example would be where companies A, B and C form a group and:

- company A declares profits of £500,000 but has understated them by £500,000 so that a penalty should be due;
- company B has correctly declared profit of £2m;
- company C, has losses of £1m, and had surrendered £500,000 to Company A and £500,000 to Company B. The surrender is amended to surrender the full loss of £1m to Company A. Company B will pay tax on additional £500,000 but Company A now has no liability on which a penalty can be charged.

Had companies A, B and C been divisions of one company, it would have declared a profit of £1.5m which would have been increased to £2m and a penalty would be calculated using the £500,000 understatement. The old penalty regime gives a group an advantage over a single company competitor.

Under the new regime, groups will still be allowed to reallocate group relief as they wish but the penalty will be calculated before group relief is set off against any understated profit.

Penalties for company officers

The new penalty regime will align the company penalty position for direct taxes with the existing VAT provision. This allows for part or all of a company penalty to be charged on an officer of the company (for example, a director or company secretary) if VAT has been evaded partly or wholly due to the dishonest conduct of that officer. Under the new regime, a penalty can be charged on the officer of the company where any taxes, direct or indirect, have been lost due to the officer's dishonest conduct.

This change is aimed at preventing the avoidance of a penalty by owner-managed companies putting their company into liquidation and then restarting as a new entity – phoenixism.

Burden of proof

The new regime alters the burden of proof in any penalty proceedings. Under the old regime, if a penalty could not be agreed, HMRC was required to commence formal penalty proceedings before a penalty can be imposed. Under the new regime, HMRC can impose a penalty if they think the taxpayer has become liable to it and can fix the penalty in whatever amount they think fit. The taxpayer would have to appeal against the decision and in any appeal proceedings the onus would now be on the taxpayer to show why a penalty should not be charged or why the amount is too much.

Law: FA 2007, s. 97

66.9.6 Penalties and the Human Rights Act

Penalties charged under the *Taxes Management Act* 1970 can be categorised as criminal or civil for the purposes of the *Human Rights Act* 1998 (HRA). The taxpayer will have the protection of the HRA if a penalty is categorised as criminal but not if it is categorised as civil. The scope of criminality in this context is wider than might generally be thought to be the case and may encompass penalties not categorised as criminal by the State. For example, a penalty may be treated as criminal if the amount effectively makes it criminal in nature.

Art. 6 of the ECHR

The HRA incorporates into domestic law the rights contained in the European Convention on Human Rights (ECHR). art. 6 of the Convention guarantees the right to a fair hearing to determine any criminal charge against a person by providing that everyone has a right to:

- a fair and public hearing within a reasonable time; and
- representation at the hearing (free if necessary).

It is implicit that people facing a criminal charge also have a right to remain silent and not to incriminate themselves.

Civil or criminal?

The European Court of Human Rights (ECHR) decided in the case of *Georgiou (t/a Marios Chippery) v United Kingdom*, Application 40042/98 that whether or not penalty proceedings amounted to a 'criminal charge' for the purposes of art. 6 depended on:

- the classification of the proceedings in domestic law;

- the nature of the offence; and
- the nature and degree of the severity of the penalty that could be imposed.

In the special commissioners' case of *Sharkey v De Croos* (HMIT) (2005) Sp C 460, the taxpayer appealed against a fixed penalty imposed under TMA 1970, s. 97AA(1)(a) for a failure to produce documents and information specified in a TMA 1970, s. 19A notice, claiming that it breached his rights under the HRA. When considering each of the points made by the ECHR, the commissioner concluded that:

- in the case of fixed penalties, domestic law categorised them as civil;
- the nature of the offence was regulatory – there was no imputation of dishonesty and the penalty (which was pecuniary) was in no sense severe; and
- the possibility of the imposition of a daily penalty in future under s. 97AA(1)(b) could not affect the classification of the fixed penalty under s. 97AA(1)(a).

In any event, as far as the last point was concerned, the commissioner did not consider that a penalty under s. 97AA(1)(b) would itself be criminal. Even though it could be much heavier than a penalty under s. 97AA(1)(a), it was not sufficiently severe to make it criminal within the terms of art. 6.

It followed from this that the imposition of a small fixed penalty did not amount to a 'criminal charge' so that none of the rights provided under art. 6 applied.

In the special commissioners case of *Auntie's Café Ltd v R & C Commrs*, the taxpayer company appealed against two fixed penalties, each of £1000, imposed on it for being late in filing its Corporation Tax returns for its accounting periods ended 30 June 2000 and June 2001. The company accepted that the tax legislation prescribed fixed penalties of £1000 for the late filing of the two returns and no claim was made that it had a reasonable excuse for the late filing of the returns. It argued, however, that the penalties breached its rights under art. 1 of the First Protocol to the European Convention on Human Rights (the ECHR) because:

- fixed penalties were more onerous for small companies with modest assets than for large profitable companies and, in particular, they had a disproportionate impact if the company had no liability to tax, thus breaching the requirement that the penalties should be proportionate;
- the fixed penalty was excessive as compensation for the loss to HMRC since there was no loss as the company had no liability to tax; and
- it was unfair that companies that were struck off would escape paying a penalty while those that were not struck off would have to pay penalties for late filings etc.

In deciding that the company's rights under the ECHR were not breached, the special commissioner considered that HMRC had shown that the fixed penalties were correctly charged under the law and that they were proportionate, saying:

'I consider that it is not enough, as the Appellant suggests, merely to suggest that a fixed penalty impacts more adversely on a taxpayer with fewer assets than on one with more assets. The factors that must be balanced are whether the deprivation of property is justified because it is effected under legislation that is in the public interest and that is required for the collection of taxation and penalties. In my judgment HMRC has amply demonstrated that some form of modest fixed penalties are a sensible and required feature of the taxation system; the penalties are extremely modest; there are several safeguards to deal with postal delays, and reasonable excuse; and the penalties only rise from figures of £100 and £200 (which for companies one might describe as derisory) to still very modest figures of £500 and £1000 for companies which can fairly be described as 'persistent offenders.'

Criminal penalties

Based on the criteria for identifying criminal penalties set out in the *Georgiou* case, it would appear that all tax-geared penalties will be treated as criminal, even if HMRC have indicated at the outset that the maximum penalty is likely to be mitigated. In the *De Croos* case, HMRC accepted that, following *King v Walden* [2001] BTC 170, tax-geared penalties under TMA 1970, s. 95 are criminal.

It is possible too that certain fixed penalties will fall into the category of criminal if they are intended to punish the offender rather than to be compensatory. For example, a limited company can be penalised up to £1,000 under FA 1998, Sch. 18, para. 17(3) for late submission of corporation tax returns even though it may have had no liability to corporation tax for any of the relevant accounting periods.

When there is the possibility that a tax-geared penalty will be charged, HMRC staff will take steps to avoid breaching the taxpayer's rights under the HRA. They will make it clear to taxpayers that they do not have any obligation to incriminate themselves, while at the same time drawing to their attention the fact that by making a disclosure and cooperating with the enquiry they may be able to reduce any penalty finally charged. They will also issue a leaflet explaining the availability of Criminal Defence Service funding.

HMRC have instructed staff that, at the stage when it appears that penalties are likely to be considered, they should explain to taxpayers that:

- a penalty may be due;
- they do not have to cooperate with the enquiry; but
- their full disclosure and cooperation will be taken into account in arriving at the amount of any penalty.

At this point the Revenue officer will hand the taxpayer the penalty leaflet IR160 and a Public Funding leaflet explaining when assistance towards the legal costs of contesting a penalty charge may be due. This states that:

'In practice, funding is most likely to be available where you are seeking to contest a penalty which is substantial either in terms of its amount or impact, and which has been imposed beyond your assessed liability.'

Law: *Human Rights Act* 1998, *European Convention on Human Rights*, art. 6, *Georgiou (t/a Marios Chippery) v United Kingdom*, ECHR Application 40042/98, *Sharkey v De Croos* (HMIT) (2005) Sp C 460, *King v Walden* [2001] BTC 170, *Auntie's Café Ltd v R & C Commrs* [2007] Sp C 588

Other guidance: Inland Revenue *Tax Bulletin*, Issue 61, Penalty leaflet IR160 and Public Funding leaflet

66.9.7 Deceased persons

HMRC's internal instructions tell inspectors that they can impose a penalty on the personal representatives of a deceased taxpayer (see *Enquiry Manual*, EM 1375). The instructions acknowledge, however, that there may be some doubt over whether the imposition of such a penalty would be prohibited by art. 6 of the Human Rights Act 1998. Inspectors are advised, when reaching a settlement with the personal representatives, that they should prepare a side letter accepting that the penalty will be refunded together with interest if HMRC subsequently accepts that the penalty cannot be charged because of art. 6.

Although the internal instructions have not yet been amended, it would appear that HMRC now accept that art. 6 does prevent them from charging a penalty on tax owed by a deceased taxpayer. In March 2007 HMRC issued booklet DS101 providing guidance on making a disclosure to the Offshore Disclosure Facility. In the section dealing with specialist questions and answers, in response to the question asking whether an executor or administrator should make a disclosure in respect of an overseas bank account held by a deceased person, HMRC's response is:

> 'Yes. The executor or administrator is responsible for the estate of the deceased. Different time limits mat apply and no penalty will be payable on liabilities up to the date of death.'

This should be drawn to the attention of any inspector who seeks to apply the existing instructions in the *Enquiry Manual*.

Other guidance: HMRC *Enquiry* Manual EM 1375

66.9.8 Other matters

Before reaching a final settlement, the officer will normally ask for:

- a certificate of disclosure; and
- a statement of assets and liabilities.

There is no legal obligation to provide a certificate of disclosure but HMRC consider it reasonable to seek one to replace the certificate appended to the tax return, which has been shown to be false. A failure to provide such a certificate will lead to HMRC continuing with their enquiries.

It will be explained to the taxpayer that signing the certificate is a very serious matter and that signing a false certificate may lead to prosecution. If a certificate of disclosure is later found to be false in a material respect it will be referred to SCO.

The signed statement of assets and liabilities is required to confirm that everything has now been disclosed to HMRC in the course of the enquiry. A refusal to provide one will lead to a taxpayer notice (previously a s. 19A notice) requiring its production as one of the particulars required by the notice, although HMRC could not insist that it is certified. The submission of a false statement of assets and liabilities can itself attract a penalty, as seen in *King v Walden*.

Once the certificate of disclosure and statement of assets and liabilities have been provided, the enquiry will be concluded either by a closure notice and an amendment to the self assessment or by way of a contract settlement effected by a formal letter of offer and acceptance.

In the case of *R (on the application of R & C Commrs) v General Commissioners of Income Tax for Berkshire* [2007] EWHC 871 (Admin), it was held that, on the true construction of a contract settlement between HMRC and certain taxpayers for the payment of a sum of unpaid tax, interest and penalties, it did not preclude HMRC from raising enquiries and serving notices in respect of later years. The settlement related to periods up to July 2002 but was not agreed until May 2004. The taxpayer maintained that the settlement agreement prevented HMRC from raising enquiries for the tax year to 5 April 2003.

Law: *King v Walden (HMIT)* (1999) Sp C 235, *R (on the application of R & C Commrs) v General Commissioners of Income Tax for Berkshire* [2007] EWHC 871 (Admin)

Re-opening a settlement

Although the taxpayer has entered into a binding contract which precludes any adjustment to the terms, HMRC will in certain circumstances be prepared to re-open a settlement. These circumstances do not include general regrets about the offer made (and accepted) or claims that, for example, a lower rate of gross profit should have been adopted in the computations or the figures used for personal and private expenditure were excessive, unless the incorrect figures used were supplied by the taxpayer and could have formed the basis for a s. 33 error or mistake claim.

The most common claims for re-opening are:

- loss relief;
- relief for repayment of a loan or advance under ICTA 1988, s. 419(4);
- error or mistake claims under TMA 1970, s. 33;

- and reliefs overlooked when the computations were made.

Claims are admitted if all the requisite conditions (except for the absence of formal assessments) are satisfied and the relevant time-limits are met.

In recalculating the reduction of tax and NIC and interest and penalty, the inspector will restrict the further relief due if the settlement was sub-standard due to inadequate means. No reduction of interest charge is due in the case of a ICTA 1988, s. 419(4) refund.

66.10 Serious Fraud Investigations

66.10.1 Introduction

Prior to their merger to form HM Revenue & Customs (HMRC), the Inland Revenue and Customs & Excise had their own procedures for investigating serious fraud. The approaches differed, however, in one important respect. The Customs & Excise Civil Evasion procedures were recognised by the courts as civil proceedings. The Inland Revenue Hansard procedures, on the other hand, were held by the Court of Appeal to be criminal proceedings. Following the decision in *R v Gill*, Hansard interviews were held under caution and recorded.

66.10.2 Civil Investigation of Fraud procedure

The new Hansard approach that evolved after *R v Gill* was not considered to be satisfactory and the opportunity was taken with the formation of the new department to introduce a common Civil Investigation of Fraud procedure for HMRC for both direct and indirect tax investigations. The new procedures apply to all investigations started after 1 September 2005. The old Hansard procedures and Customs Notice 730 will continue to apply to any investigations started before that date. A new code of practice, Code of Practice 9 (2005), has been issued explaining the new procedures.

After the creation of HMRC, the Revenue's Special Compliance Office (SCO) and the Law Enforcement Investigation section of Customs have been combined in a new HMRC office, Special Civil Investigations (SCI). In the first instance, the new Civil Investigation of Fraud procedures were used only by SCI but HMRC have now formed new teams in Local Compliance and National Compliance to tackle serious fraud where the Civil Investigation of Fraud procedure is appropriate.

66.10.3 Major changes

The most significant change in the Civil Investigation of Fraud procedure will be the removal of the underlying threat of prosecution, which was an integral part of the old Hansard investigation carried out by SCO. Where HMRC decides to investigate using the new Civil Investigation of Fraud procedure, the taxpayer will be told at the outset that HMRC will not seek a prosecution for the tax fraud that is the subject of the investigation.

As a result of making the proceedings entirely civil, SCI interviews will not be held under caution and nor will they be tape-recorded, as has been the case with SCO interviews since *R v Gill*.

Finally, there will be a single meeting to discuss both direct and indirect tax matters. Pending the outcome of the ongoing review of HMRC powers, the powers relating to direct and indirect taxes remain separate and distinct. The meeting will therefore have to be structured so that the taxpayer is aware of what tax is being discussed and so that each tax is dealt with separately. When the investigation is complete, the tax, interest and penalties for the different types of tax will also have to be negotiated separately.

The threat of prosecution is only lifted in respect of the tax fraud itself. Having been given the opportunity to make a complete disclosure, the taxpayer who, in the course of a civil investigation, makes materially false statements or provides materially false documents with the intention to deceive will still face the possibility of a criminal prosecution. The prosecution would, however, be in respect of the deceitful conduct, not the tax fraud being investigated.

If HMRC decides not to use the Civil Investigation of Fraud procedures, they can instead, as at present, pursue a criminal investigation with a view to prosecution where they consider it necessary or appropriate. The civil procedures are unlikely to be offered in the cases outlined in the prosecution policy statement issued by HMRC. Instead, HMRC would seek to mount a prosecution in respect of the tax fraud itself.

HMRC are satisfied that the new procedures are compliant with the Human Rights Act 1998, and in particular art. 6, which gives the right to a fair trial. They consider that the case of *Khan v C & E Commrs* [2005] EWHC 635 (Ch), endorsed the principles inherent in the new procedures.

66.10.4 New Code of Practice

The new Code of Practice 9 (2005) has been written to reflect the new civil procedure. It starts with a statement of the practice of HMRC in cases of suspected serious tax fraud.

(1) The Commissioners reserve complete discretion to pursue a criminal investigation with a view to prosecution where they consider it necessary and appropriate.

HMRC Enquiries

(2) Where a criminal investigation is not considered necessary or appropriate the Commissioners may decide to investigate using the Civil Investigation of Fraud procedure.

(3) Where the Commissioners decide to investigate using the Civil Investigation of Fraud procedure they will not seek a prosecution for the tax fraud which is the subject of that investigation. The taxpayer will be given an opportunity to make a full and complete disclosure of all irregularities in their tax affairs.

(4) However, where materially false statements are made, or materially false documents are provided with intent to deceive, in the course of a civil investigation, the Commissioners may conduct a criminal investigation with a view to a prosecution of that conduct.

(5) If the Commissioners decide to investigate using the Civil Investigation of Fraud procedure the taxpayer will be given a copy of this statement by an authorised officer.

In the same way as the previous Code of Practice, the new Code goes on to outline the steps of the enquiry, including asking the five formal questions that were asked at the start of a direct tax enquiry and the four that were asked at the start of a VAT enquiry.

> ⚠ **Warning!**
>
> Practitioners should warn their clients that they may still face prosecution if, having been given the opportunity to make a complete disclosure, they make materially false statements or provides materially false documents with the intention to deceive. They could be prosecuted for deceitful conduct (but not the tax fraud being investigated).

Law: Human Rights Act 1998, Khan v C & E Commrs [2005] EWHC 635 (Ch)

Other guidance: Code of Practice 9 (2005), read the HMRC Criminal Investigation Policy at *www.hmrc.gov.uk/prosecutions/crim-inv-policy.htm*

66.11 Money Laundering

66.11.1 Introduction

Practitioners need to be aware of the requirements of the anti-money laundering provisions of the *Proceeds of Crime Act* 2002 and the *Money Laundering Regulations* 2003. These provisions came into effect on 1 March 2004 and apply to any knowledge or suspicion of money laundering that arises after that date.

66.11.2 What is money laundering?

Money laundering is specifically defined by the legislation. It occurs when someone:

- conceals, disguises, converts, transfers or removes (from the UK) criminal property;
- enters into or is concerned in an arrangement which they know or suspect facilitates the acquisition, retention, use or control of criminal property by or on behalf of another person; or
- acquires, uses or has possession of criminal property;

and they know or suspect that the property constitutes or represents a benefit from criminal conduct.

Tax evasion is criminal conduct, and criminal property includes the proceeds of tax evasion, no matter how small the amount – there is no de minimis limit. Examples of what constitutes money laundering in the field of taxation include:

- deliberately understating profits;
- deliberately overstating expenses;
- failing to notify HMRC, once it comes to light, of an innocent or negligent error which led to a loss of tax; or
- failing to notify HMRC of an over-repayment of tax when the repayment is know to be excessive.

66.11.3 When to make a report

If, in the course of his or her profession, a practitioner suspects, or ought to have suspected that someone has been involved in money laundering a report must be made to the Serious Organised Crime Agency (SOCA) as soon as possible. The practitioner does not require evidence in support of the suspicion and nor is it necessary to be sure that a criminal offence has been committed – a report has to be made if the practitioner merely suspects money laundering.

The obligation to make a report is a personal one. It does not matter that the practitioner thinks that someone else has made a report and nor is the obligation to make a report affected by the known willingness of HMRC to seek a civil settlement in the case.

66.11.4 Tipping off

It is an offence under the legislation for the practitioner to tell someone that it is known or suspected that a report is to be, or has been made to SOCA. It is also an offence to tell anyone else if doing so will prejudice any investigation which is made as a result of SOCA receiving the report.

66.11.5 Overseas offences

Originally the legislation required that a report be made even if the acts which produced the proceeds took place in a country overseas and those acts would have been a criminal offence had they taken place in the United Kingdom.

Under amendments to the *Proceeds of Crime Act* 2002 made in 2006, a new defence to the money laundering offences in that Act was introduced. Subject to certain exceptions, the defence applies where:

- a person knows or believes on reasonable grounds that the acts which produced the proceeds took place in a particular country overseas and the acts were lawful in that country; and
- the act generating the proceeds would not be punishable in the United Kingdom by a maximum sentence of more than twelve months imprisonment.

66.11.6 Privilege

An exemption from reporting knowledge or suspicion of money laundering that came to a person in privileged circumstances was originally available only to lawyers. The legislation was amended so that, with effect from 21 February 2006, the exemption was extended to accountants, auditors and tax advisers who are members of appropriate professional bodies.

This means that knowledge or suspicion of money laundering that comes from information received when providing legal advice and acting in respect of litigation does not have to be reported to SOCA unless the services provided will be used in the furtherance of a criminal purpose.

The exemption applies only to reports of money laundering required under the *Proceeds of Crime Act* 2002; it does not apply to the reporting requirement under the *Terrorism Act* 2000.

> ⚠ **Warning!**
> The exemption is not optional; if it applies it must be used.

66.11.7 Steps required

Practitioners are require to take certain steps to comply with the money laundering regulations. They must:

- appoint a money laundering reporting officer to receive reports from colleagues and make reports to SOCA;
- train principals and staff in the requirements of the legislation so they know

how to check the identity of clients and can recognise and report money laundering;
- verify the identity of new clients; and
- establish internal procedures to detect and deter money laundering.

The CCAB guidance that has been approved by the Treasury for accountants and tax advisers can be found on the CCAB website at: *www.ccab.org.uk/PDFs/ Guidance%20Clean.pdf.*

Law: *Proceeds of Crime Act* 2002 and the *Money Laundering Regulations* 2003, Amendments to the *Proceeds of Crime Act* 2002 made in 2006

Other guidance: Detailed coverage can be read at the ICAEW website at: *www.icaew.co.uk/librarylinks/index.cfm?AUB=TB2I_28377*

Website: *www.ccab.org.uk/PDFs/Guidance%20Clean.pdf*

67 Insolvencies

67.1 Introduction

This chapter first examines the Crown's position in insolvencies and HM Revenue & Customs' policy (HMRC) on proving for penalties in insolvencies. Comprehensive coverage of the technical aspects of insolvencies is beyond the scope of this publication. However, the practitioner can find useful guidance in the HMRC Manual: *Insolvency*.

HMRC's general policy is to take bankruptcy, etc. proceedings only where all other attempts to encourage payments of tax debts have failed (*Hansard*, 10 December 1992). This is absent any wilful default by the taxpayer.

The second part of this chapter deals with companies in liquidation, administration or receivership, and the tax aspects relating to each situation.

67.1.1 Types of insolvency

There are numerous types of insolvency, each subject to certain general features. The broad types of corporate insolvency and nature of the same are summarised in the tables below:

Comparative table of insolvency procedures

	Administrative Receiver	Fixed Charge Receiver	LPA Receiver
Status	Must be IP (s. 230(2), and 388(1)(a))	Need not be IP	Need not be IP
Appointment	By charge in circumstances set out in security documentation	By charge in circumstances set out in security documentation	By charge in the limited circumstances set out in the LPA 1925

Insolvencies

	Administrative Receiver	Fixed Charge Receiver	LPA Receiver
Charges	To qualify as AR,	Chargeee will hold	As for Fixed Charge Receiver
	• Must be appointed over whole or substantially whole of company's property	• Fixed charge(s)	
	• By holders of floating charges (s. 29(2)).	• And possibly floating charge(s) also	
Agency	Agent of the company (s. 44(1)(a))	Security documentation will state agent of company	(s. 109(2) LPA) Agent of the mortgagor (company)
Liability on contracts	• Personally liable on contracts entered into in performance of functions (s. 44(1)(b)).	• Personally liability on contracts entered into in performance of functions (s. 37(1)(a))	• s. 29 includes LPA receiver in definition of receiver generally.
	• Subject to indemnity out of assets of company (s. 44(1)(c))	• Subject to indemnity out of assets of company (s. 37(1)(b))	• Therefore s. 37 applies
Liability on adopted contract of employment	• Personally liable on adopted contracts of employment to extent of qualifying liabilities only (s. 44(1)(b))	• Personally liable on adopted contracts of employment	As for fixed charge Receiver
	• Entitled to indemnity out of co's assets	• Not restricted to qualifying liabilities (s. 37(1)(a))	
	• 14 day liability free period	• Entitled to indemnity out of co. assets	
		14 day liability free period	
Powers	• Statutory powers to manage the company (schedule 1)	• Powers set out in the security documentation	• Statutory powers in LPA Limited to (s. 109(3)) demanding and recovering income and giving receipts

454

Types of insolvency 67.1.1

	Administrative Receiver	**Fixed Charge Receiver**	**LPA Receiver**
	• Debenture may limit or extend these powers	• Will normally empower receiver to take possession and sell charged assets	• No power to take possession and sell
	• s. 233 Power to demand supplies from utilities	• No such statutory powers to enforce co-operation	• No such statutory powers to enforce co-operation
	• Has statutory powers to enforce co-operation of Directions (s. 234–237)	s. 43 does NOT apply	s. 43 does NOT apply
	• s. 43 Power to apply to the court for sanction to dispose of property subject to prior charges		
Duties	• (s. 40) to pay prefs in priority to holders of floating charges	• s. 40 applies only if receiver also appointed under floating charge	• As Fix Charge Receiver
	• (s. 7(3)(d) CDDA) - to report to Secretary of State on conduct of Directors	• No duty to report	• No duty to report
	(s. 48) to report to and call meeting of unsecured creditors	s. 48 does not apply	s. 48 does not apply
	• To deal with ERA claims by employees	N/A	N/A
Receipts and Payments	(R3.32) Accounts to be delivered to Co's House within 2 months of	(s. 38) Accounts to be delivered to Co's House within 1 month of	As for fixed charge receiver
	• 12 months from appointment	• 12 months from appointment	
	• Every subsequent 12 months	• Every subsequent 6 months	
	• Ceasing to act as AR	• Ceased to act as receiver	
Publicity	(s. 39) Statement to appear on all letters invoices etc. that a Receiver appointed	As for AR	As for AR

455

Insolvencies

Receiver comparative table

Comments/ Note	Administration	Company Voluntary Arrangement (CVA)	Creditors Voluntary Liquidation (CVL)	Court Winding-up (compulsory liquidation)
Route into procedure	Out of Court:	• Members' resolution by 50% of members	• Extraordinary resolution by 75% of members	• Court Order
	• Appointment by Qualifying floating charge holder; or by directions, creditors or members.	• CVA effective when approved by 75% in debt value of creditors	• Choice of Liquidator ratified by 50% of creditors	
	• Or by Court Order			
Powers of office-holder	• Full powers to trade or sell the company business	• Powers as set out in the CVA deed		
	Overrides directors			
Office-holder Agent of the Company?	• Yes	• No	• Yes	• Yes
Duration	• Maximum 12 months; exceptionally extended to 15 months	• No set minimum or maximum; in practice up to 5 years	• As long as is necessary for Liquidator	

Types of insolvency 67.1.1

Comments/ Note	Administration	Company Voluntary Arrangement (CVA)	Creditors Voluntary Liquidation (CVL)	Court Winding-up (compulsory liquidation)
Publicity	• Announced publicly in the London Gazette. Must be stated on all invoices, correspondence etc.	• Private agreement between company and creditors. No publicity	• Resolution for winding-up must be advertised in London Gazette. • Recorded at Companies House	• Winding-up petition advertised in London Gazette. Advertised in local press and recorded at Companies House
Effect on the company	• May trade under management of Administrator • A CVA or Liquidation is then implemented	• Company trades normally, making monthly contributions to the Supervisor of the CVA • Directors unaffected	• Company ceases to trade	• Company ceases to trade
Effect on directors	• Directors cannot act without Administrator's authority	• Directors unaffected	• Directors resign • Directors can face personal liability if Court so orders on Liquidator's application	• All contacts – including director's service contracts terminated • Directors can face personal liability if Court so orders on Liquidator's application

457

Insolvencies

Comments/ Note	Administration	Company Voluntary Arrangement (CVA)	Creditors Voluntary Liquidation (CVL)	Court Winding-up (compulsory liquidation)
Repayment of debt	• Administrator must act in best interests of creditors	• Normal creditor payments stop • Creditors paid a percentage of debt	• Creditors likely to receive a nil or nominal dividend contingent upon assets available	

67.2 Measures to help businesses meet liabilities

In response to recommendations made by the Government's working group on insolvency and corporate rescue mechanisms, HMRC have formulated a package of reforms designed to help businesses in trouble. The changes include:

- creation of a single joint unit to handle all 'voluntary arrangements';
- adoption of a practice of considering voluntary arrangements in the same way as commercial creditors;
- introduction and publication of tight turn-around targets for responding to proposals;
- publication of the criteria against which proposals will be judged; and
- creation of a new forum for regular discussions between insolvency practitioners and members of the new joint unit on ways of improving mutual understanding and working practices.

The changes took effect from April 2001, or in some cases earlier.

Although not formally declared as policy, in practice HMRC are usually willing to allow a business at least one opportunity to reach an amicable, 'time to pay' agreement. As might be anticipated, such an agreement will ordinarily allow the subject business additional time for payment. Usually however, the agreement will require payment in full of the relevant liability (although the precise details of each such agreement will always be a matter for negotiation).

67.3 Crown's priority in insolvencies

67.3.1 Withdrawal of Crown preference

The provisions of the Insolvency Act 1986, which provided for the Crown's preferential treatment in respect of, amongst other things, tax deducted at source under the PAYE and construction industry schemes, ceased to have effect from 15 September 2003. This was in respect of proceedings commenced on or after that date (Enterprise Act 2002, s. 251 and the Enterprise Act 2002 (Commencement No. 4 and Transitional Provisions and Savings) Order 2003 (SI 2003/2039)).

67.3.2 Position where proceedings commenced before 15 September 2003

On the insolvency of an individual or partnership, or when a company entered receivership or liquidation, the Crown (among others) was accorded priority with respect to the payment of certain 'preferential debts' (Companies Act 1985, s. 196; Insolvency Act 1986, s. 175, 386, Sch. 6). The Crown's preferential debts included sums due from the debtor at 'the relevant date' on account of deductions which the debtor was liable to make during the previous 12 months under:

- the PAYE scheme; and
- the regime applicable to subcontractors in the construction industry.

Also included as preferential debts were VAT, insurance premium tax, landfill tax, climate change levy, aggregates levy, car tax, betting and gaming duties, beer duty, lottery duty, air passenger duty, social security and pension scheme contributions, remuneration, etc. of employees, and levies on coal and steel production.

'The relevant date', in relation to insolvent individuals, was the date when the bankruptcy order was made (or when the interim receiver was appointed). In relation to companies in receivership, 'the relevant date' was that when the receiver was appointed. In relation to companies which were being compulsorily wound up, 'the relevant date' was that when any provisional liquidator was appointed. If (as would be in the position in the vast majority of cases) no provisional liquidator was appointed, no such appointment was made, the date of the winding-up order was taken as the 'relevant date'. If a winding-up order was made immediately on the discharge of an administration order, the date when the latter order was made would be taken as the 'relevant date'. In relation to companies being voluntarily wound up, 'the relevant date' was the date when the winding-up resolution was passed by the members of the company (Insolvency Act 1986, s. 387).

Preferential debts are payable after the expenses of the bankruptcy (or winding-up of a company) but before other debts. They also include, among other items, certain debts due to HMRC (e.g. VAT referable to the six months before the relevant date plus sums on account of Class 1 and 2 National Insurance contributions which became due within the 12 months before the relevant date).

Any prerogative right that the Crown may have enjoyed in respect of priority of payment of debts not specified in the 1986 Act or predecessor legislation was impliedly abandoned in enacting that legislation which accordingly exhaustively specifies the Crown's rights: *Food Controller v Cork* [1924] AC 647; Insolvency Act 1986, s. 434(b).

If there were insufficient assets fully to cover all the preferential debts, the latter abated in equal proportions: Insolvency Act 1986, s. 175(2) and 328(1), (2).

67.4 Penalties in insolvencies

In theory, it might not be HMRC's usual practice to prove for penalties in insolvencies, since to do so would prejudice outside creditors. In practice however, (and in particular, since HMRC lost preferential creditor status) it would be an imprudent professional adviser who counselled that HMRC will not prove for penalties. The only caveat is that HMRC may, in the exercise of discretion by an individual officer, decide not to impose or prove for penalties (or at least not the full extent of penalties), in a case where there is voluntary disclosure by the relevant business. Ordinarily, HMRC will regard disclosure as having been made voluntarily whether it comes from the directors of the company or from any office-holder appointed under the Insolvency Act 1986 (e.g. a liquidator). Penalties which are eventually awarded against an insolvent person in proceedings commenced before the relevant date are provable in the bankruptcy.

The points made in the last paragraph emerge from *Re Hurren (a bankrupt)* [1982] BTC 373. There, Walton J declared (at pp. 376–377):

> '... the penalties which are here in question under s. 93 and 95 of the Taxes Management Act 1970 are liabilities, contingent, to which the debtor was at the date of the [commencement of the bankruptcy] liable and which can, if given enough information, be quantified ...
>
> ... the question then arises: What next ought to be done? Mr. Hart, for the Revenue, suggests that since the ordinary duty of the Trustee is to make an estimate under [what is now the Insolvency Act 1986, s. 322(3)] of the value of that liability because it is subject to a contingency, that is precisely what he should do, and he and the Revenue should try to agree a value for the liability which the Trustee should then admit. Of course, if the Revenue and the Trustee cannot agree, why, then, the Revenue would have to put in a proof, the proof would have to be referred to this Court, and what would happen then?
>
> [U]ndoubtedly ... the Court would say that the proper body to determine the amount in the present circumstances is undoubtedly the General Commissioners before whom the proceedings are at the moment pending ...

[Counsel] for the Bankrupt, while conceding that the penalties are recoverable in the bankruptcy, properly provable, has argued very strongly that these proceedings are quasi-criminal proceedings and they cannot really expect to be got on foot until the presumption of innocence of his client is displaced. I accept that in general, but I think that in the particular circumstances of the present case, where his client has been, not once, but twice, the subject of investigation by the Inland Revenue for failure to deal properly with his tax affairs, it must be taken with a considerable pinch of salt . . .

It seems to me, especially having regard to the fact that after what I may term the ordinary claims of the Revenue have been satisfied there may be a surplus for the Bankrupt, this is a particular case where the real battle is and should be between the Bankrupt and the Inland Revenue, and that to bring the Trustee into the matter is only complicating the issue. Because the trustee does not feel very happy about having to make up his mind as to what would be a proper compromise, and one can well see that it is going to be difficult for him, being pressed on one side by the Bankrupt, who will of course threaten to appeal any decision to which the trustee comes . . . and, on the other hand, being borne down upon by the Revenue, who will say that of course there cannot be any doubt that the maximum ought to be awarded.

It seems to me that in the present case the matter is capable of very simple and very just resolution. It seems to me that there can be no reason at all why the matter should not be compromised (because claims for penalties frequently are compromised by the Revenue, anyway) but that the compromise must be one to which not only the Trustee in Bankruptcy agrees but to which the Bankrupt also agrees – and if the Bankrupt agrees I cannot really see that the Trustee in Bankruptcy will have any grounds for holding out. So in substance it is really a question between the Bankrupt and the Revenue, with the Trustee holding a watching brief to see that neither of them makes any fatal errors, which seems to me, advised as they are on both sides, extraordinarily unlikely.

That, if it can be done, will, I think, achieve the greatest possible saving of costs all ways round; but if it is going to be done then it should be done quickly. It seems to me that it would not be right to make any order staying the proceedings for the recovery of the penalties before the Commissioners for any greater time than will enable that possibility to be explored. I will discuss with Counsel in a moment what the length of the stay should be, but I would have in mind a period of something like three months . . . '

The Court of Appeal has since held that the Revenue's practice, in investigation cases, of not making preferential claims under back duty agreements was valid. Where such an agreement is made the Revenue has a new cause of action in debt for the sums agreed under its terms, the sums owing having lost their identity as tax (*IR Commissioners v Woollen* [1992] BTC 633).

67.5 Companies in liquidation, administration or receivership

67.5.1 Introduction

The position of the liquidator of a company in relation to that company differs from that of the receiver of the assets of the company whose powers are governed by the terms of his appointment. The position of the company in receivership is therefore separately discussed at **67.5.9**. The position of companies in administration after the amending provisions of the Enterprise Act 2002, s. 248 came into force (on 15 September 2003) is considered in detail at **67.7**, but also, where relevant, in **67.5.2** and other commentary below.

67.5.2 Immediate effect of winding up or administration

Winding up

On the commencement of the winding up of a company (i.e. the date when the winding-up petition is presented if a compulsory liquidation, or the date of the members' resolution to wind up in a voluntary liquidation), its accounting period comes to an end and a new one starts and accounting periods thereafter only end on the expiration of 12 months (ICTA 1988, s. 12(7)). At the same time, the company ceases to be the beneficial owner of its assets and retains only their legal ownership (*IR Commrs v Olive Mill Ltd* (1963) 41 TC 77; *Re Oriental Inland Steam Co* (1874) 9 Ch App 557). The beneficial ownership of the assets is thereafter in suspense until the rights of the various claimants of those assets are quantified and finally determined (*Ayerst v C & K (Construction) Ltd* (1975) 50 TC 651) by the liquidator.

> **Planning point**
>
> If a parent company goes into liquidation, various reliefs applicable within its group cease to be available; if a subsidiary goes into liquidation the effect is less expansive. Certain capital gains reliefs for groups continue to be specifically permitted.

On the appointment of the liquidator, the powers of the directors of the company come to an end, but may in certain very limited circumstances (and frankly normally only in exceptional cases) be continued in so far as sanctioned by the appropriate body (*Insolvency Act* 1986, s. 91(2), 103; *Fowler v Broad's Patent Night Light Co* [1893] 1 Ch 724; *Gosling v Gaskell* [1897] AC 575 at p. 587; *Re Mawcon Ltd* [1969] 1 WLR 78 at p. 82).

> **Planning point**
>
> Where a trade ceases, an employer is not entitled to deduct emoluments paid more than nine months after the end of the year in which it ceases. This is unlikely to present a problem in cases of compulsory liquidation, but in the case of voluntary liquidations, the point needs to be watched.

Administration

Prior to the *Finance Act* 2003, the appointment of an administrator had no effect on the corporation tax position of a company other than for connected parties' loan relationships (described in the subheading below). Indeed, there was correspondence between the representatives of the profession and the Revenue as to the precise significance of administration following the introduction of the relevant insolvency legislation. In that exchange, it was confirmed that the appointment of an administrator did not impact on a company in the same way as the appointment of a liquidator. However, following changes to insolvency law made by the *Enterprise Act* 2002 (effective from 15 September 2003), because it was possible to wind up a company without full liquidation, it was decided that when those changes came into force, the effect of administration should be aligned more closely with that of liquidation.

Accordingly, from the date the provisions of the *Enterprise Act* 2002 came into force for administration procedures (i.e. 15 September 2003):

- when a company enters into administration (under *Insolvency Act* 1986, Sch. B1 or equivalents) its accounting period comes to an end and a new one starts, i.e. just like the commencement of liquidation (ICTA 1988, s. 12(7ZA)). This limits the possibility of applying pre-administration trading losses against any trading profits made during the administration. This includes any capital gains tax arising from a disposal made during the administration;
- where, at that time, the company was already in liquidation the rule that accounting periods end only after that on each 12 months' anniversary (see subheading above) no longer applies (ICTA 1988, s. 12(7)); and
- when a company ceases to be in administration (again, under the *Insolvency Act* 1986, Sch. B1 or equivalents), an accounting period comes to an end and a new one starts (ICTA 1988, s. 12(3)(da), (5B)).

Pursuant to the decision in *Re Toshoku* (below) and by way of analogy, tax generated during administration is payable as an expense of the administration i.e. ahead of other creditors and the administrators' remuneration.

In *Re FGAL Realisations Ltd Times Law Reports 2 August 2000*, the Court of Appeal confirmed that statutory liability for deductions regarding PAYE and NICs (relating to the employment of a company's employees by the company's administrators, enjoyed special priority. Those expenses were payable as an expense of the administration.

In *R & C Commrs v Holland* [2009] EWCA Civ 625 M appealed a decision that he had been guilty of misfeasance and breach of duty as a de facto director in causing the payment of unlawful dividends.

M and his wife (H) had set up a business to administer the business and tax affairs of contractors working mainly in the information technology industry. M and H held the shares in and were the directors of a trading company (Services) which held the shares in two subsidiary companies (D and S). M and H were the directors of D and S.

D and S were respectively the corporate director and company secretary of 42 trading or 'composite' companies of which the contractors were employees and shareholders. The contractors held non-voting shares and the voting shares were held by a trust company owned and controlled by M and H. The composite companies supplied the services of the contractors to third parties and enjoyed the administrative support of Services.

The purpose of the structure was that each composite company would only pay corporation tax at the small companies' rate, while the contractors received a small salary and substantial dividends. The scheme was flawed because the composite companies were treated as associated and therefore were liable to pay higher-rate corporation tax. They had made no provision for it and had paid dividends unlawfully because there were insufficient distributable reserves to permit them.

The companies went into insolvent liquidation. HMRC brought misfeasance proceedings against M and H under IA 1986, s. 212. This was on the basis that M and H were liable for the unlawful dividend payments as de facto directors of the composite companies and liable to contribute to the companies' assets accordingly. The judge upheld that case in respect of M for the period after leading counsel had advised the scheme was flawed, and ordered him to make a contribution of the amount of higher rate tax that the companies should have provided for in the relevant period.

Before the Court of Appeal, M argued that he was not a de facto director of the composite companies and so not liable under IA 1986, s. 212. M also argued that there was no breach of duty because the dividends were paid in the honest and reasonable belief that it was in the companies' interests to do so.

The Court of Appeal said that membership of the board of a corporate director would not, without more, make such member a shadow or de facto director of any company of which the corporate director was a director. There was no reason why a director of a corporate director who was doing no more than discharging his duties as such should thereby become a de facto director of the subject company.

The Court of Appeal decided that M was not a de facto director of the composite companies. The crucial issue was whether M had assumed the status and function of a company director so as to make himself responsible as if he were a de jure director, *Re Kaytech International Plc* (1999) BCC 390 CA (Civ Div) applied. A person who acted as a director of the sole corporate director of a company was not, merely by so acting, to be regarded also as a de facto director of the subject company, *Re Hydrodan (Corby) Ltd (In Liquidation)* (1994) BCC 161 Ch D considered.

The Court of Appeal said that membership of the board of a corporate director would not, without more, make such member a shadow or de facto director of any company of which the corporate director was a director. There was no reason why a director of a corporate director who was doing no more than discharging his duties as such should thereby become a de facto director of the subject company.

The Court of Appeal confirmed that (on the judge's findings) M had done nothing to become a de facto director and had done no more than perform his duties as a de jure director of the corporate director. In the result, M's appeal was allowed and the cross-appeal dismissed.

Loan relationships

A liability to corporation tax on notional 'interest' arising on loan relationships (where a company was required to bring a loan relationship credit into account in respect of a debt owed by a fellow group company in liquidation) has been held by the Court of Appeal and the House of Lords to be an expense of the liquidation.

A provision intended to relax the rules for bad debts where a company is in liquidation or administration ('liquidation etc.') and to ameliorate the effect of the above decision was subsequently introduced for accounting periods beginning on or after 1 October 2002. It provides that, where a company goes into liquidation, etc., then the assumption (in FA 1996, Sch. 9, para. 6) that all debts between connected persons will be paid in full need not be made after liquidation, etc. has commenced.

For these purposes, 'liquidation, etc.' includes:

- under UK (including Northern Ireland) law:
    (a) insolvency;
    (b) an administration order;
    (c) appointment of a provisional liquidator; or
- foreign equivalents.

Law: FA 1996, Sch. 9, para. 6A

67.5.3 Date of commencement of winding up

For the purpose of the termination and recommencement of an accounting period, where a company is being wound up under the provisions contained in the *Insolvency Act* 1986 the winding up commences on the earlier of:

- the passing of the appropriate resolution to wind up the company; and
- the presentation of the winding-up petition on which a winding-up order is made.

If the winding up takes place overseas, it commences when a similar act is done with the intention of winding it up.

Law: ICTA 1988, s. 12(7)

67.5.4 Position of liquidator and vesting of assets

On going into liquidation the property of the company normally remains vested in the company. The liquidator is the agent of the company. However, the liquidator may apply to the court for an order to be made vesting the company's assets in the liquidator (*Insolvency Act* 1986, s. 145; *Insolvency (Northern Ireland) Order* 1989 (SI 1989/2405), art. 496). Whether the company's assets are vested in the company or the liquidator, it is specifically provided that the acts of the liquidator in relation to the assets of the company are treated as the acts of the company and any transfer of assets between the liquidator and the company are disregarded.

Law: TCGA 1992, s. 8(6)

In the light of the doctrine that on going into liquidation a company ceases to be the beneficial owner of its property which it thereafter holds in 'trust' for the benefit of its creditors and contributors, this provision may appear to be unnecessary, at least so far as transfers from the company to the liquidator are concerned, the argument being that any such transfer would be from one trustee to another, who are regarded as a continuing body of persons. However, this would be to disregard the special sense in which the expressions 'trust property' and 'trust' are used in this context. In *Ayerst v C & K* after reviewing a number of authorities on the beneficial ownership of the property of a company in liquidation, Lord Diplock observed at p. 180:

> 'My Lords, it is not to be supposed that in using the expression "trust" and "trust property" in reference to the assets of a company in liquidation the distinguished Chancery judges whose judgments I have cited and those who followed them were oblivious to the fact that the statutory scheme for dealing with the assets of a company in the course of winding up its affairs differed in several respects from a trust of specific property created by the voluntary act of the settlor. Some respects in which it differed were similar to those which distinguished the administration of estates of deceased persons and of bankrupts from an ordinary trust; another peculiar

to the winding-up of a company is that the actual custody, control, realisation and distribution of the proceeds of the property which is subject to the statutory scheme are taken out of the hands of the legal owner of the property, the company, and vested in a third party, the liquidator, over whom the company has no control. His status, as was held by Romer J in *Knowles v Scott* [1891] 1 Ch 717, differs from that of a trustee "in the strict sense" for the individual creditors and members of the company who are entitled to share in the proceeds of realisation. He does not owe to them all the duties that a trustee in equity owes to his *cestui que trust*. All that was intended to be conveyed by the use of the expression "trust property" and "trust" in these and subsequent cases (of which the most recent is *Pritchard v M H (Wilmslow) Builders Ltd* [1969] 1 WLR 409 was that the effect of the statute was to give to the property of a company in liquidation that essential characteristic which distinguished trust property from other property, namely, that it could not be used or disposed of by the legal owner for his own benefit, but must be used or disposed of for the benefit of other persons.'

When the position of a company in liquidation is understood in the sense explained above it becomes clear that the commencement of a winding up does not give rise to the creation of a settlement or trust, but merely determines and qualifies the rights of the company in relation to its property. Such determination of the company's rights, being involuntary and for no consideration, does not amount to a chargeable disposal of the company's assets. This is so because there cannot be a disposal without any transfer; nor can it be said that the property rights of the company have been forfeited; they merely become crystallised.

It follows that in his dealings with third parties involving the company's assets the liquidator acts in right of the company. This accords with his position under company law (see for example *Re Duckworth* (1867) 2 Ch App 578 at p. 580 per Cairns LJ; *Re Dronfield Silkstone Coal Co* (1880) 17 Ch D 76 at p. 96; *Waterhouse v Jamieson* (1870) LR 2 HL Sc 29 at p. 37).

Law: TCGA 1992, s. 69(1)

67.5.5 Transactions by liquidator involving company assets

Where in the course of the liquidation the liquidator disposes of a company asset the company is chargeable to corporation tax on any chargeable gain made on the disposal and is entitled to relief if there is an allowable loss.

> ⚠ **Warning!**
>
> A distribution by the liquidator in respect of share capital, where he transfers an asset *in specie* to a contributor, the asset is treated as having been transferred at its market value and may give rise to a charge to corporation tax on any chargeable gain.

Insolvencies

> **Planning point**
>
> Note that no charge arises on certain distributions in the course of a demerger.

Law: ICTA 1988, s. 8(2), TCGA 1992, s. 17(1)(a), 122

67.5.6 Trading by liquidator

The liquidator of a company has limited powers to carry on the business of the company insofar as it may be necessary for the beneficial winding up of the company. The company is chargeable to corporation tax on any profits made from the carrying on of its business in this way in the course of its winding up.

The House of Lords has clarified this area in a lengthy and important judgement, namely *Kahn v IR Commrs* [2002] BTC 69 ('Toshoku').

In *Toshoku*, the House of Lords confirmed that corporation tax chargeable on a company's post-liquidation profits, (including income that it had not received but which the taxing provisions required it to bring into the computation of those profits), was a necessary disbursement payable out of the assets of the company. The House of Lords also said that such payments were to be treated as an expense of the winding-up and in priority to the debts proved in the winding-up (pursuant to *Insolvency Act* 1986, s. 115).

In *Toshoku*, the liquidators appealed from the decision of the Court of Appeal by which it allowed an appeal by the Revenue and held that the liquidators, as the joint liquidators of Toshoku Finance UK Plc ('the company'), were obliged to account for corporation tax upon interest receivable by the company out of its assets in priority to all other claims, as an expense of the winding up.

The liquidators contended in *Toshoku* that, for expenses to be treated as liquidation expenses within r. 4.218(1), not only did they have to fall within one of the paragraphs contained in that rule but they also had to satisfy the 'liquidation expenses' principle as expounded by Nicholls LJ in *re Atlantic Computer Systems plc* (1992) Ch 505, 520. The 'liquidation expenses' principle was that they had to be expenses incurred as the result of a step that had been taken with a view to, or for the purposes of, obtaining a benefit for the estate. The liquidators further contended that, because they had neither received nor taken any steps to recover the interest in question, it was therefore unfair that the creditors would have to bear the burden of corporation tax on fictitious credits.

Law: Insolvency Act 1986, s. 165(3) and 167(1)(a), ICTA 1988, s. 8(2), 74(1)(a)

67.5.7 Basis and periods of assessment

The profits made by a company in the course of liquidation are calculated for each accounting period and assessed to corporation tax in the same way as the profits of a company not in liquidation.

The accounting period in which a company goes into liquidation comes to an end on the commencement of the winding up and a new accounting period begins on that date. Thereafter an accounting period of the company comes to an end and a new one begins on each anniversary of the date on which the winding up commenced until the completion of the winding up at which time the accounting period then current comes to an end.

However, for administrative ease the liquidator and the inspector may agree a date on which the winding up is likely to be completed. The accounting period of the company then comes to an end on the agreed date even if the winding up is not yet complete. Subsequent accounting periods of the company end on the anniversary of the agreed date until the final accounting period which ends on the completion of the winding up.

For the equivalent provisions for the administration procedures introduced by the *Enterprise Act* 2002 with effect from 15 September 2003, see **63.7**.

Law: ICTA 1988, s. 8(2), 12(7), 342(5), (6)

67.5.8 Rates and fractions for corporation tax

Because the rates of corporation tax and the fraction of chargeable gains to be included in a company's profits for a financial year are sometimes fixed after the end of that financial year it is necessary to have special rules to determine the rate of tax and fractions to be applied where a company's winding up is completed in a financial year before the passing of the Finance Act relating to that year.

Normally the rates and fractions fixed for the financial year immediately before that in which the liquidation is completed ('penultimate year'), are applied to the financial year in which the winding up is completed ('final year'). However, if the rates and fractions have been fixed for the final year by a Finance Act or a budget resolution (i.e. a resolution of the House of Commons) those rates and fractions are applied. If the rate or fraction that has been so fixed is proposed to be changed by a budget resolution, the altered rate or fractions are used.

Where the winding up has commenced before the final year the rates and fractions that are applicable to its profits in the penultimate year are the latest fixed by a Finance Act or Budget resolution.

If before the company was in liquidation it was assessed to corporation tax on the basis of rates and fractions that had not yet been finally fixed for that financial year

(ICTA 1988, s. 8(4)), and the interaction of these winding-up provisions with such previous assessments result in an overpayment or underpayment of tax under the assessment an adjustment can be made by discharge or repayment of tax or by a further assessment as may be necessary.

For the equivalent provisions for the administration procedures introduced by the *Enterprise Act* 2002 with effect from 15 September 2003, see **63.7**.

Law: ICTA 1988, s. 342

67.5.9 Consequences of Liquidation for group relief purposes

As noted above, if a company goes into liquidation, it loses beneficial ownership of its assets. This includes beneficial ownership of any shares it previously owned. The implications of this are serious.

This can be seen if one imagines four companies A, B, C and D. Assume company A directly owns the shares of both company B and company C. Also assume that B directly owns the shares of company D. B goes into liquidation.

In these circumstances, the group relationship between D and all of the other companies in the group is broken. This means that group relief cannot be surrendered to or from D. However, the group relief relationship is preserved as between the other companies.

However, if it is A that goes into liquidation, the only group relief relationship which is preserved is that between B and D.

67.5.10 Consequences of liquidation for directors personally

It is trite to point out that as and when a company becomes insolvent – whether by virtue if its notional balance sheet or upon a cash-flow basis – the officers of the company owe fiduciary duties primarily to the creditors of the company. This is as oppose to the shareholders of the company. The rationale is that it is the creditors who will suffer the financial pain from the company's insolvency, and accordingly, the business of the company should (from the date of the notional insolvency) be conducted for the benefit of the creditors.

This analysis should be considered in the light of the *Companies Act* 2006 (2006 Act), which codified certain common law and equitable duties of directors. In summary, the seven general duties under the CA 2006 are:

- to act within powers;

- to promote the success of the company;
- to exercise independent judgment;
- to exercise reasonable care, skill and diligence;
- to avoid conflicts of interest;
- not to accept benefits from third parties; and
- to declare an interest in a proposed transaction or arrangement.

The first four duties came into force on 1 October 2007. The last three duties came into force on 1 October 2008. On the relevant date, the statutory duty replaced the corresponding common law or equitable duty.

However, the 2006 Act duties must be interpreted and applied in the same way as those common law rules and equitable principles, and regard must be had to those rules and principles in applying them (CA 2006, s. 170(4)). Further, the codification is not exhaustive, and directors will still have certain duties under common law and equity. The previous law on directors' duties will therefore remain highly relevant. Rules and equitable principles will continue to be relevant.

While the 2006 Act provides that the general duties are based on, and have effect in place of, certain common law rules and equitable principles (CA 2006, s. 170(3)), it also provides that:

- the general duties should be interpreted and applied in the same way as the common law rules and equitable principles, and regard should be had to the corresponding common law rules and equitable principles when interpreting and applying the statutory duties (CA 2006, s. 170(4)). Accordingly courts will need to interpret and apply the general duties in a way that reflects the rules that they replace and will need to take account of future developments in the law of trusts and agency;
- the civil consequences of breach (or threatened breach) of the statutory duties are the same as would apply if the corresponding common law rule or equitable principle applied;
- further, the codification is not exhaustive. The statutory duties do not cover all the duties that a director may owe to the company, such as:
  - the duty to consider or act in the interests of creditors, which is expressly preserved by CA 2006, s. 172(3) (and stated to apply in times of threatened insolvency); and
  - the duty of confidentiality owed by a director to the company, although it would appear that the duty of confidentiality will now be subordinate to the general duties.

In practice, the duties may become blurred. IA 1986, s. 214 deals with the position where a director is guilty of wrongful trading; in such event a director can be held personally liable to contribute to the deficiency to creditors. This where the directors knew (or should reasonably have concluded) that the company had no reasonable prospect of avoiding insolvent liquidation, and they failed to take every step thereafter to minimize the loss to creditors.

In a tax context, the practical issues arising from insolvency and wrongful trading are illustrated by a case involving a company which had largely been incorporated to take advantage of certain concessions to the film industry. This was the decision in *Re Nine Miles Down UK Ltd* [2009] EWHC 3510 (Ch), where an application for summary judgment in a claim for wrongful trading was refused. This was because it could not be said that the relevant director knew that the company was likely to go into insolvent liquidation at the time he entered into a contract containing significant financial liabilities.

In *Nine Miles Down*, the liquidator (S) of a film company (C) had issued proceedings for wrongdoing against C's director (H). C had acquired the rights to make a film, and in 2006 started making arrangements to produce it in Namibia. However, C had no funding of its own and so relied upon a group of companies (X) to arrange financial backing and funding which would qualify for low-budget film tax relief under the *Finance (No. 2) Act* 1997, s. 48.

C informally arranged for production services to be provided by a South African company (O) from mid-February 2006. This was in order to allow principle photography to begin in time to claim the tax relief. On March 24 2006, C entered into a formal production services agreement with O under which it agreed to pay a production services fee. A substantial part of that fee became due immediately.

The court had to determine whether, when entering into the agreement with O on March 24, 2006, H knew or ought to have concluded that there was no reasonable prospect that C would avoid going into insolvent liquidation.

S argued that by March 24, 2006, H knew that C had:

- no assets;
- no secure finance in place;
- not signed a leading actor; and
- needed to begin principle photography in order to receive the necessary s. 48 funding.

S thus argued that H knew (or ought to have known) that C would be unable to produce the film and therefore would be unable to pay its debts (i.e. that C was thus insolvent).

The Court decided that:

- H accepted that C had no funds of its own and that there was no evidence that it ever had a legally enforceable agreement with X; and
- H knew C needed s. 48 funding and that the principal actor had not been signed.

However, the Court thought H had strong grounds for vigorously disputing the contention that by March 24, 2006 he knew or ought to have known there was no reasonable prospect that C would avoid going into insolvent liquidation. This was because:

- it was unusual in the film industry for a film company to begin its activities with sufficient funds of its own; production often proceeded on the basis of verbal arrangements both with actors and organisations providing finance and production facilities.
- O had provided production services from mid-February 2006 and X had paid money to O, in each case without any contractual obligation to do so.
- despite the lack of legal commitment, C had the full support of X for finance. H knew that X wanted the film to be made, as supported by the payment made by X to O: there would have been no purpose or value in making that payment if X did not intend to continue to support the project and see it through to completion if reasonably possible.
- a second company had indeed gone on to make the film and was financed by X.
- H's co-director (W) had been in daily contact with the principal actor. Email communications between H and W did not hint at the difficulties W had experienced in trying to secure the actor's attendance at the shoot. It was not possible to resolve on a summary judgment application precisely what had occurred; nor was it possible to ascertain the state of mind of all the participants in those communications. However, the court was not in a position to reject H's clear evidence that he understood that he had an agreement in principle with the actor and that it was not until March 30, 2006 that he knew the actor would not attend the film shoot.
- the court was in a position to reject H's evidence that on March 24, 2006 he believed the project had the full backing of X and that principle photography could begin on the scheduled date. Accordingly, it could not be said that H knew or ought to have known on March 24, 2006 that there was no reasonable prospect that C would avoid going into insolvent liquidation.

In short, the Court refused to give summary judgment because it considered that H had a realistic prospect of success which was more than merely arguable. This test was accepted pursuant to the decision in *Pegasus Management Holdings SCA v Ernst & Young (A Firm)* (2008) EWHC 2720 (Ch), (2009) PNLR 11.

Another common scenario was considered in *Ebsworth* [2009] TC 00152 where a family company had been liquidated, and shares in a second company transferred, for genuine commercial reasons. The Court decided that HMRC had failed to identify an alternative structure. Accordingly, there was no basis for saying that the taxpayer had obtained a tax advantage for the purpose of ICTA 1988, s. 709.

In *Ebsworth*, E appealed against a notice issued by HMRC under ICTA 1988, s. 703. E and his wife were the sole shareholders of a company (X), which comprised two distinct divisions. The first, and more profitable, division relied upon a US multinational company (W) for business.

E and his wife separated. Shortly afterwards W terminated the relationship with X in consideration of a balloon payment. E's wife wanted to withdraw her investment from X but could not do so until the balloon payment had been received.

A second company was incorporated, in which E and his wife were the shareholders. E's wife later transferred her shareholding in the second company to E as a gift. X's second division, which had no connection to W, was purchased by the second company. X was liquidated following the balloon payment and capital distributions were made to E and his wife.

E argued that:

- a liquidation was the appropriate way to bring the enterprise with his wife to an end;
- there was no alternative course against which the tax consequences of the liquidation could be judged;
- the creation of the second company and the transfer of shares were not necessary for the liquidation of X;
- X's second division was valueless and could simply have been discontinued; and
- all of the transactions were carried out for genuine commercial reasons.

Liquidation was the simple and commercially logical way of achieving the objective of E and his wife separating. In particular, the structure of the transaction suited the wife's requirement for a clean break. That finding was not affected by E having taken tax advice; the mere taking of tax advice did not automatically equate to tax avoidance, pursuant to the decision in *IR Commrs v Brebner* (1967) 2 AC 18 (HL).

The parties had accepted that X fell within ICTA 1988, s. 704D. This was because formation of the second company and the gift of shares in it from the wife to E were transactions in securities. It was therefore necessary to consider whether there was a tax advantage in consequence of the transaction in securities either alone or with the liquidation of X.

E had received capital in the liquidation which was taxable at a lower rate than a dividend would have been. However, in order for a finding of a tax advantage to be made there had to be some form of comparison. The tribunal thought that HMRC had failed to identify such an alternative structure.

HMRC had suggested that a buyback of own shares could have been undertaken. However, HMRC had not shown how this was to be funded nor that tax clearance would have been given. HMRC had also suggested that the liquidation of X could not have gone ahead unless the second company had been formed. That was not the case.

X could have been liquidated and the second division distributed in specie. X had undergone a normal liquidation and not one of the type described in *IIR Commrs v Joiner* (1975) 50 TC 449.

If one applied a 'but for' test to the issue and transfer of shares in the second company (and to the suggested tax advantage from X's liquidation), there was no obvious causal connection. Accordingly, any alleged tax advantage – assuming there was one – was not 'in consequence' of the issue or transfer of shares in the second company.

The court accepted that X's second division, which had been acquired by the second company, was not a valuable asset. It had been sold for the value of the stock with a nominal amount for goodwill and other intangibles. E had sought to continue that element of the business merely to avoid redundancies.

The tribunal was satisfied that the predominant motive of the transactions in *Ebsworth* was to bring the business and personal ties between E and his wife to an end. Consequently, the escape clause in s. 703 applied because the transactions were genuine and/or were carried out in the ordinary course of making or managing investments. None of the transactions had as their main object, or one of their main objects, the obtaining of tax advantages.

As against the scenario in *Ebsworth*, the situation in *Megtian Ltd (in administration) v R & C Commrs* [2010] BVC 314 was more complicated, but illustrates the Court taking a robust attitude where fraud was suspected. In *Megtian*, the Court decided that the VAT and duties tribunal had not erred in law in upholding a decision to disallow input tax claims. This was on the ground that the transactions to which the claims related were connected with the fraudulent evasion of VAT, (of which the taxpayer was – or ought to have been – aware).

In *Megtian*, M had appealed against a decision disallowing its claims for input tax credit. HMRC disallowed the claims for input tax credit on the basis that the transactions to which the claims related, of which there were 15 in each of two relevant accounting periods, were connected with missing trader intra-community fraud of which M was, or ought to have been, aware. Some 27 of the transactions in respect of which M was refused input tax credit were alleged by HMRC, and found by the VAT and duties tribunal, to have been part of 'dirty chains'. This meant chains of transactions involving a fraudulent evasion of VAT payable by virtue of a transaction forming part of the chain.

Three transactions were found to have been part of 'clean chains' used to conceal fraud in other dirty chains. Those three transactions were referred to as 'contra-trading' transactions.

The tribunal found that the clean chains were connected with tax fraud committed by means of related dirty chains. The tribunal also found that M knew or ought to have known that those three transactions, together with the other 27, were connected with fraud. M argued that the tribunal had made errors of law in its conduct of its fact-finding task and that it had made findings which were contrary to the evidence.

The Court confirmed that M had to identify specific errors of law in the fact-finding process and could not simply attack the correctness of the tribunal's evidential conclusions.

M argued that the tribunal's finding that there had been a fraudulent evasion of tax by three named parties to relevant dirty chains was contrary to the evidence. This was because in each case, the admitted default had been precipitated by HMRC's decision to accelerate the due date for the defaulter's next VAT return.

However, the primary facts relied upon by the tribunal for its inferences of fraud in relation to each of those three companies were amply sufficient reasonably to found such an inference. A suggestion that the inference was against the weight of the evidence disclosed no error of law on the part of the tribunal.

M also alleged that the tribunal's findings of dishonest knowledge in respect of two 'contra-traders' were contrary to the evidence. Again however, the Court held that primary facts found by the tribunal relevant to the contra-traders' knowledge were sufficient to permit the tribunal to make a finding of dishonest knowledge.

The Court said that the tribunal had not erred in law in failing properly to identify the fraud with which M knew or ought to have known its transactions were connected in the contra-trading cases. It had been held that in a case of alleged contra-trading, HMRC had to show that the person in M's position knew (or ought to have known) of the dishonest failure to account for VAT by a defaulter or missing trader in the dirty chain. Alternatively, HMRC had to show a dishonest cover-up of that fraud by the contra-trader, or both.

This was pursuant to the decision in *R & C Commrs v Livewired Telecom Ltd* [2009] BVC 172 . However, *Livewire* was addressing the question of what had to be demonstrated against an honest broker who was not a dishonest co-conspirator in the tax fraud.

In *Megtian*, the tribunal's conclusion had been M knew that the transactions on which it based its claim were connected with fraud. The Court held that participation in a transaction which the broker knew was connected with a tax fraud was a dishonest participation in that fraud.

Furthermore, the Court said that *Livewire* did not lay down as a matter of law that in every contra-trading case one or other of the alternative frauds had to be identified as being that which the broker knew (or ought to have known) about. In many, if not most, cases of contra-trading the clean chain and the dirty chain were likely to be part of a single overall scheme to defraud.

In *Megtian*, the Court felt there was sufficient evidence to justify a rational, reasonable conclusion that M knew that the transactions upon which it based its input tax claim were connected with a tax fraud. Accordingly, it followed, that even if M claimed not to have known about the fraud, then it should have known of that connection.

67.5.11 Receiverships

There are a variety of circumstances in which a receiver may be appointed to realise all or part of a company's assets and in some cases also to run the company's business. The appointment of a receiver and manager of a company does not result in the cessation of the company's trade which continues to be carried on by the company (*IR Commrs v Thompson* (1936) 20 TC 422). It follows that the company continues to be charged to corporation tax on its profits.

Usually a receiver appointed otherwise than by the court is an agent of the company and has power to deal on its behalf by the terms of the instrument under which he is appointed (*Gosling v Gaskell* [1896] 1 QB 669; *Lawson v Hosemaster Machine Co Ltd* (1966) 43 TC 337). The debenture under which the receiver is appointed will ordinarily provide him with an indemnity from the assets of the subject company.

A receiver appointed by the court is an officer of the court and not an agent of the company. He is in the same position as a trustee or executor carrying on a business and has a right of indemnity out of the available assets of the company (*Burt, Boulton & Hayward v Bull* [1895] 1 QB 276; *Re Glasdir Copper Mines* [1906] 1 Ch 365; *Boehm v Goodall* [1911] 1 Ch 155).

A receiver appointed over mortgaged land is an agent of the mortgagor (*Law of Property Act* 1925, s. 109(2)). As above however, a properly drafted legal charge (under which the receiver is appointed) will ordinarily provide him with an indemnity from the assets of the subject company.

67.6 Insolvency Act 1986 (prior to 15 September 2003): related problems

67.6.1 Introduction

Aspects of the *Insolvency Act* 1986 where the tax consequences needed either clarification or concessions were identified by the Institute of Taxation and Insolvency Practitioners Association in a joint memorandum of 1 June 1990. It claimed that many of the consequences affecting companies needed urgent attention. Since then, the *Enterprise Act* 2002 has made changes (which came into force on 15 September 2003) to the administration procedure for companies.

For commentary on administration for periods under the new procedure, see **67.7**. The commentary and extracts in this paragraph relate to periods before the new procedure applies.

67.6.2 Administration orders

A number of uncertainties regarding the tax consequences of the making of an administration order do not help to achieve the legislation's aim of rescuing ailing companies. The Institute of Taxation and Insolvency Practitioners Association sought confirmation that:

- tax liabilities arising from the administrator's transactions will be treated as the company's and will rank *pari passu* with other unsecured creditor's claims in a subsequent insolvency, or voluntary arrangements under Pt. I of the 1986 Act;
- an accounting period does not end on the making of an administration order, as this can have a material bearing on the company's ability to set off trading losses, for example, against chargeable gains; and
- there is no reason why the beneficial ownership tests of the various group relationships of a parent company should be disturbed on the making of an administration order, as the availability of group relief may have a material bearing on the tax liabilities of a company in administration.

67.6.3 Debts released in voluntary arrangements

The success of voluntary arrangements was being jeopardised by uncertainty as to their tax consequences for both debtor companies and creditors, the memorandum claimed.

The problem has been alleviated, to some extent by the definition of a 'relevant arrangement or compromise' (ICTA 1988, s. 74(2), which ensures an effective deduction for a debt which is released as part of a formal voluntary arrangement with creditors under the *Insolvency Act* 1986, or the *Insolvency (Northern Ireland) Order* 1989, or a compromise or arrangement which has taken effect under the *Companies Act* 1985, s. 425, or the *Companies (Northern Ireland) Order* 1986, art. 418.

A deduction is permitted in respect of a debt or part of a debt released by the creditor as part of a voluntary arrangement or compromise, provided that the release was wholly and exclusively for the purposes of the creditor's trade, profession or vocation. Where a debt for which a deduction has been allowed is subsequently released, and the release would normally be treated as a trade receipt, the release is not to be so treated where it takes place as part of a voluntary arrangement or compromise (ICTA 1988, s. 94(1)). Similarly, a post-cessation receipt, which arises from the release after cessation of a debt previously allowed as a deduction, is excluded from the charge to tax under Sch. D Case VI where the release was in pursuance of a voluntary arrangement or compromise (ICTA 1988, s. 103(4)(b)).

67.6.4 Interest payments

For the purpose of ICTA 1988, s. 349 (deductibility of tax from annual interest), there is considerable difficulty in determining the character of interest paid in respect of creditors' claims in a member's voluntary liquidation or in a bankruptcy (*Insolvency Act* 1986, s. 189 and 328(4)). The prudent thing to do is for an insolvency practitioner to deduct interest at source (i.e. before payment to creditors) for any payment over £25. The insolvency practitioner should then account separately to HMRC for the relevant interest.

Other problems relating to interest and charges on income are raised, together with issues concerning the liquidation of non-resident UK companies and foreign companies.

Concern about the unfamiliarity of local tax offices with the 1986 insolvency legislation, and the lack of guidance from Head Office, led the Institute of Chartered Accountants in England and Wales (ICAEW) to submit to the Revenue a memorandum on 28 June 1990 which set out areas which, in relation to companies, required clarification or concessions by the Revenue in relation to the practical problems created by the procedures.

The ICAEW memorandum has now been published by the Institute as Technical Release 799 and incorporates the Revenue response. Its full text is as follows (it should be borne in mind that not all of the legislation referred to in the release may still be in force and may have been superseded since its publication):

'INTRODUCTION

1. The Insolvency Act 1986, together with the related Insolvency Rules, has introduced two new insolvency procedures and both modified and consolidated existing insolvency law. While the basic principles of receivership and liquidation are largely unchanged, the major features of the new law include the Administration and Voluntary Arrangement procedures. During 1987 and 1988, in England and Wales, there were 330 Administration Orders, 70 Corporate Voluntary Arrangements and 1,200 Voluntary Arrangements for Individuals. However, the tax consequences of these new procedures remain unclear and this causes considerable difficulty in practice. No guidance appears to have been laid down by Inland Revenue to local districts or Enforcement Office on how to deal with the new procedures and there is general unfamiliarity in tax offices with the new Insolvency law.

Insolvencies

2. This Memorandum sets out a number of aspects of the Insolvency Act 1986 concerning companies where the tax consequences need to be clarified or where we believe concessions should be made. Some of these matters have been mentioned to the Department of Trade and Industry who have expressed concern informally that the interests of creditors (which the DTI is seeking to protect) might be prejudiced by the tax side effects of the new insolvency legislation. It will be necessary for the Department of Trade and Industry and Inland Revenue to agree their approach and it may be that the proper forum for an agreed approach would be Regulations and Notes for Guidance of Insolvency Practitioners in a form similar to the regulations which were issued under the provisions of Rule 224 of the Companies Winding-up Rules 1949 for the guidance of Liquidators appointed in a Court winding-up, and for Trustees in Bankruptcy. (The last regulations under these provisions were issued on 1 October 1977, and are no longer applicable for insolvency procedures commencing after 29 December 1986.)

Inland Revenue response:

(a) The Inland Revenue deal with every Administration Order and Voluntary Arrangement proposal on its own individual merits, taking into account all known features of the case. When deciding how to vote, the Revenue give consideration to, amongst other things, the way in which the taxpayer has attended to his tax obligations, the level of uncertainty over assets and liabilities and whether a voluntary arrangement is the appropriate course for the Revenue to approve as a creditor. The Revenue are also very much aware of the interests of other parties and of the purpose of the voluntary arrangement procedure.

(b) Both the Inland Revenue's Enforcement Office and its Collector's Offices have instructions on how to deal with matters within their own areas of responsibility. But because every case is different, rather than adhering to strict guidelines, these instructions provide for the exercise of judgement upon the facts and background of each particular case. There have been no Inland Revenue Press Releases or Statements of Practice dealing with any aspects of the new insolvency legislation.

(c) The Revenue are presently liaising with the Department of Trade and Industry over revised Regulations and Notes for Guidance of Insolvency Practitioners on the lines of those issued in 1977.

DETAILED COMMENTS

Administrators

Introduction

3. The Administrator procedure is an entirely new concept within the framework of insolvency legislation in Great Britain. The purposes for which an Administration Order may be made are set out in the Act as follows:

(i) the survival of the company, and the whole or any part of its undertaking, as a going concern;
(ii) the approval of a Voluntary Arrangement;
(iii) the sanctioning of a compromise or arrangement under Section 425 of the Companies Act 1985;
(iv) a more advantageous realisation of the company's assets than would be effected on a winding up.

4. The new procedure provides an immediate suspension of payments and court protection ahead of any scheme to compromise debts.

5. Once an Administration Order has been made, the Administrator is required to formulate his proposals as to how the purposes specified in the court order may be achieved. Until such time as the order is discharged he is responsible for managing the company's affairs through his power of agency.

6. It is clear from both the Act and the tenor of the parliamentary debate that preceded it, that the overall purpose intended for the Administrator is company rescue. There are, however, a number of uncertainties as regards the taxation consequences of the making of an Administration Order which do not help in achieving that objective, and which are causing difficulty in practice in ascertaining what the outcome for creditors will be. The following are the matters which require clarification.

Liability to tax

7. The Administrator acts throughout as agent of the company and without incurring personal liability. On his release he is specifically "discharged from all liability both in respect of acts or omissions of his in the Administration and otherwise in relation to his conduct as Administrator". (Section 20(2) Insolvency Act 1986). It remains to be confirmed that it is the Revenue's view that tax liabilities arising as a consequence of the Administrator's transactions will be treated as liabilities of the company and not the Administrator personally, and will rank *pari passu* with the claims of other unsecured creditors in a subsequent insolvency process.

Inland Revenue response:

(a) In most circumstances tax remains the company's liability.
(b) However, notwithstanding this, the administrator can discharge the liability of the company under:
   (i) his general powers in S14(1) Insolvency Act 1986;
   (ii) his specific power 13 in Schedule 1 of that Act.
(c) Moreover, he is liable to account for PAYE/NIC deductions. As agent of the company (Section 14(5)) he pays emoluments to its employees. He thereby

becomes an employer within the 1973 PAYE regulations (Reg. 2; also Regulation 3 SI 1973 No 334) and thus liable to deduct the appropriate tax.
(d) Although, under Section 20(2), the administrator is discharged from liability arising post his release and from liability outstanding at the date of his release, if a winding up order is made he may be liable under Section 212(1)(b) in respect of the period for which he was, effectively, the employer.

Consequences of the appointment of an Administrator

8. There is no apparent reason why an accounting period of a Company should end for the purposes of corporation tax on the making of an Administration Order. As this can have a material bearing on the ability of the company to set-off trading losses against chargeable gains, it would be helpful to have the position confirmed generally.

9. Whereas the beneficial ownership tests of the various group relationships of a parent company are no longer satisfied (apart from the capital gains group) after the commencement of liquidation, there is no apparent reason why such relationships should be disturbed on the making of an Administration Order. As the availability of group relief may have a material bearing on the tax liabilities of a company in Administration it would be helpful for the position to be confirmed.

Inland Revenue response:

Accounting period

(a) Section 12 ICTA 1988 sets out the circumstances in which an accounting period ends. These include the commencement of a liquidation (*s. 12(7)*); the cesser of a trade (*s. 12(3)(c)*).
(b) It is considered that neither the filing of an administration order petition, nor the making of an administration order, would bring about the end of an accounting period.

Beneficial ownership tests

(c) Whilst the Revenue would not normally regard an Administration Order itself as affecting the beneficial ownership tests of the various group relationships of a parent company, it is possible that proposals by the administrator which are approved under Section 24, Insolvency Act 1986, might well do so.
(d) Arrangements by the administrator for the sale of the shares in subsidiaries, even if they did not have the effect that the company subject to the Order lost beneficial ownership of the shares in the subsidiaries, would by virtue of Section 410(1)(b) and Section 240(11), ICTA 1988, respectively cut off entitlement to group relief and to set-off by the subsidiaries of surrendered advance corporation tax.

VOLUNTARY ARRANGEMENTS

10. A Voluntary Arrangement is based upon a "proposal to the company and to its creditors for a composition in satisfaction of its debts or a scheme of arrangement of its affairs". (Section 1 Insolvency Act 1986). The proposal must provide for a licensed insolvency practitioner to supervise its implementation.

11. The success of Voluntary Arrangements is being jeopardized by uncertainty as to the tax consequences of them for the debtor company and for creditors. The

following matters have a material bearing on the outcome of Voluntary Arrangements and require urgent clarification if the procedure is to succeed.

12. It is not clear whether a composition in satisfaction of debts under a Voluntary Arrangement would lead to those debts being treated as "released" for the purposes of Section 94 ICTA 1988 (or Section 103(4) ICTA 1988 where trade has ceased). Under the section, if the debts in question had given rise to a deduction in computing trading profits of the debtor company, the amount released would be treated as a taxable receipt arising in the period in which the release is effected. Where losses are not available to shelter such a receipt, the consequence would be to create further liabilities for the debtor company, which the Arrangements would then have to take into account. The amended Arrangements could then give rise to further charge to taxation under those provisions, and so on.

13. Such a charge to tax would not have arisen if the debtor company had gone into insolvent liquidation, and government policy should not be to seek to achieve a windfall gain for the Exchequer at the expense of creditors in these circumstances.

14. If a charge to tax does arise, it remains to be confirmed what is the status of any such tax liability in the Voluntary Arrangement. In particular, it is not certain whether the Board of Inland Revenue regard Rule 1.28(b) and Rule 5.2(b), The Insolvency Rules 1986 as prescriptive of the Supervisor's duties as regards taxation. These Rules allow there to be incurred for the purposes of the Voluntary Arrangements such fees, costs, charges and expenses which are sanctioned by the terms of the Arrangement, or would be payable:

(i)   for individuals, in the debtor's bankruptcy;
(ii) for companies, in an administration or winding-up.

15. There is a further difficulty for creditors who wish to obtain a bad debt deduction for corporation tax purposes in respect of the debtor company. Whereas no such deduction would be available in respect of any amount of the indebtedness which is repaid, there is uncertainty as to whether the amount of the debt which is "satisfied" by the Voluntary Arrangement remains eligible for relief.

16. Such relief could be available to the creditor on the balance of his claim if the debtor company went into insolvent liquidation, and if the net outcome under the Voluntary Arrangement is not as good for the creditor as it would be under insolvent liquidation, the creditor will not accept the proposals.

Inland Revenue response:

Tax treatment of debts

(i)   The debtor

    (a)   The taxation treatment of debts which have been released is dealt with by Section 94 ICTA 1988 (formerly S. 136 ICTA 1970). This provides that where, in computing for tax purposes the profits or gains of a trade, profession or vocation, a deduction has been allowed for any debt incurred for the purposes of the trade etc., then if the whole or any part of the debt is later released the amount released is to be treated as a receipt of the trade etc. arising in the period in which the release is effected.

    (b)   Section 94, ICTA 1988, originated in Finance Act 1960, Section 36, the aim of which was to rectify an anomaly whereby a trader incurred a debt, obtained a tax deduction for the amount of the debt, and subsequently got his creditor to release him from all or part of the debt. The Courts had held that the amount released could not be taxed even though the trader had obtained a deduction for the debt. The legislation in what is now Section 94 therefore imposes a charge in these circumstances.

(c) It is a feature of the legislation that it only applies where a debt is formally released by the creditor. Thus the mere failure to pay or even the bankruptcy or liquidation of the debtor will not give rise to a charge under Section 94.

(d) There is a release where there is a formal arrangement with creditors. The position is similar where there is a scheme approved by the Court, notwithstanding that there were some creditors who did not want to agree but were obliged to do so because the necessary majority agreed. A compromise in satisfaction of debt under a voluntary arrangement would therefore give rise to a "release" which would be treated as a taxable receipt of the debtor by virtue of Section 94.

(ii) The creditor

(e) The creditor will not be entitled to relief in respect of any part of a debt which is to be paid to him under the terms of an arrangement. But the release of a debt (or part of a debt) by virtue of a voluntary arrangement may not necessarily entitle the creditor to a deduction. In particular, a deduction may only be allowed by virtue of Section 74(j) for bad debts proved to be such and doubtful debts to the extent that they are respectively estimated to be bad. A release in excess of an amount arrived at on that basis is unlikely to be an allowable deduction.

(f) Inspectors will usually need to consider all the facts of a particular case before deciding whether a deduction is due in respect of any part of a debt which has been released.

Status of tax liability (S. 94 ICTA 1988)

(g) Both Rules 1.28(b) (company voluntary arrangements) and 5.28 (individual voluntary arrangements) provide what "fees, costs, charges and expenses" may be incurred for the purpose of a voluntary arrangement. Apart from those sanctioned by the voluntary arrangement itself, those permitted are defined as those which either would be payable, or would correspond to those which would be payable, (1) in an administration or winding up (companies) or (2) in the debtor's bankruptcy (individuals) – see Rule 1.28(1)(b)(ii) and Rule 5.28(b)(ii). The relevant Rules for this purpose are Rules 4.218 and 6.224 – Order of Payment of Costs etc. out of estate. The only relevant provision in Rule 4.218 is at Rule 4.218(1)(b) "expenses incurred or disbursements made by the Official Receiver or under his authority, including those incurred or made in carrying on the business of the company". Clearly the release of a debt by a creditor giving rise to a taxable receipt under Section 94 cannot be within Rule 4.218(1)(b). The same applies to the corresponding Rule for individuals at Rule 6.224(1)(b) which is in similar terms. The Section 94 tax liability, therefore, is outside the ambit of the Insolvency Rules.

INTEREST PAYMENTS UNDER SECTION 189 INSOLVENCY ACT 1986

Introduction

17. Section 189 Insolvency Act 1986 provides for payment of interest on the claims of creditors who prove in the winding-up in respect of the period since the company went into liquidation. Interest up to the date of insolvency is included in the creditor's claim for which proof is lodged. Payment of post-insolvency interest can only occur if there is a surplus after all creditors claims are met in full (including claims for pre-insolvency interest).

18. If the contract with the creditor specified a rate of interest, that rate would be payable in respect of the post-insolvency period, provided that the rate is greater than the statutory rate applicable to judgement debts, which is currently 15%.

Deduction of tax and charges on income

19. There is considerable difficulty in determining what is the correct character of this interest payment for the purposes of Section 349 ICTA 1988. Individual practitioners have been advised that the Revenue regards interest paid under Section 189 Insolvency Act 1986 as short interest and therefore that deduction of tax is not required. Where, however, interest payments would otherwise qualify as a charge on income, treating the payment as short interest will deny the opportunity for relief in the paying company. We recommend that in cases where interest payments made before liquidation would have qualified as a charge on income, the same treatment should prevail after commencement of liquidation.

20. Practical difficulties arise in obtaining relief for charges on income paid in liquidations. Where such interest payments are made out of the income of earlier periods, no relief will be available against the taxable income of the earlier period. We believe that concessionary relief from the strict application of Section 338 ICTA 1988 should be allowed in these circumstances, so that relief may be obtained.

Inland Revenue response:

(a) In normal circumstances interest paid under Section 189, Insolvency Act 1986, is not considered to be annual interest. There would, therefore, be no obligation or right for the payer to deduct tax.

(b) However, it is possible for the interest to constitute annual interest. This is on the basis that the period for which the interest is payable is known at the time it is paid, i.e. the period from the date of liquidation to the final date interest can run is ascertainable. Therefore, if interest is payable for less than a year it is short interest, but if it is payable for one year or more it is annual interest.

(c) Interest is allowable as a charge if it meets the conditions of Section 338, ICTA 1988. It appears, however, that your paragraph 20 on obtaining relief for charges goes wider than the Section 189 interest matters dealt with in the rest of this Section. Charges on income, so far as paid out of the company's profits brought into charge to corporation tax, are allowed only as deductions from the profits for the period in which they are paid. It is not clear from paragraph 20 the grounds on which you feel that there should be a departure from the statutory basis.

Disclaimer

It is likely, in practice, that a group company which is in potential receipt of interest under Section 189 IA 1986 will wish to disclaim its entitlement. Otherwise the situation could arise in a group of companies that taxable income is generated without corresponding opportunity for a tax deduction by way of group relief. It would be helpful if the Inland Revenue would accept that such a disclaimer is effective for tax purposes, and may be made at any time before the liquidator makes payment to the creditor. Such a disclaimer would not operate to turn income into capital, but rather would prevent turning capital into income.

Inland Revenue response:

The charge to tax under Case III Schedule D is on the income arising. Income arises when it is paid or made available. Therefore, provided that the interest is not paid or made available there would *prima facie* be no Case III charge.

The interaction of Insolvency Act 1986 and Taxes Management Act 1970

22. It has been confirmed to individual practitioners by the Inland Revenue that where tax liabilities are claimable in a liquidation, then interest under Section 189 Insolvency Act 1986 will only arise from whichever is the later of the date of commencement of the liquidation or the reckonable date for interest under Taxes Management Act 1970. It would be of assistance if this position could be confirmed generally.

Inland Revenue response:

(a) Interest under the Taxes Management Act 1970 will not accrue beyond the date of commencement of the liquidation (Compulsory/Members Voluntary Liquidation). Interest under Section 189, Insolvency Act 1986, may arise on tax debts claimed in the liquidation, and in addition on interest under the Taxes Management Act 1970.

(b) Where tax is claimable in a liquidation, interest under Section 189, Insolvency Act 1986, may arise from either the date of the liquidation or the reckonable date for interest under the Taxes Management Act 1970, whichever is the later.

(c) Interest under Section 189, Insolvency Act 1986, may arise from the relevant date (as in (b) above) to the date of payment of the liability, no matter what the method of payment.

(d) The Revenue's view would remain the same for assessments made after the liquidation date. For post-liquidation accounting periods, interest under Section 189, Insolvency Act 1986, would not be applicable.

LIQUIDATION OF NON-RESIDENT UK COMPANIES

Introduction

23. With the coming into law of the Insolvency Act 1986, only a UK licensed insolvency practitioner (or the Official Receiver) can now be appointed as liquidator of a UK incorporated company (Section 230, IA 1986).

24. In the past, the appointment as Liquidator over UK incorporated but non UK tax resident companies was usually taken by locally resident individuals rather than UK practitioners. A company officer or employee was frequently involved where the company was solvent. As this procedure is no longer available, it is necessary to

consider whether the appointment of a UK resident Liquidator serves to transfer the place of residence of the company to the UK and subject it to possible charge to UK corporation tax. This matter will be of increasing significance in the transitional period up to 15 March 1993 provided by FA 1988 as regards the residence status of UK incorporated companies which were not UK resident for tax purposes on 15 March 1988.

The present position

25. Under existing case law the generally accepted test of company residence is that enunciated by Lord Loreburn at the beginning of this century in *De Beers Consolidated Mines v Howe* (5 TC 198) as follows:

> "A company resides, for the purposes of income tax, where its real business is carried on; and the real business is carried on where the central management and control actually abides."

26. It has been pointed out by the Board of Inland Revenue in its 6/83, that "nothing which has happened since has in any way altered this basic principle: under current UK case law a company is regarded as resident for tax purposes where central management and control is to be found".

27. It is noteworthy that this proposition moves away from Lord Loreburn's original formulation that the place of residence of a company is where its real business is carried on; he applied the test of central management and control to identify the place where "real business" is carried on.

28. In the context of the winding-up of the company, this difference is important. Under the revised formulation it is hard to see that central management and control is exercised by anyone other than the Liquidator. Under the original formulation, however, it would be hard to find evidence of "real business". Indeed, the Revenue generally argue that a company in liquidation which has ceased to trade has no business and that its activities are directed solely to the realisation of its assets.

The future position as we would like to see it

29. The licensing provisions were introduced by the government primarily to protect creditors. It would be paradoxical if by their operation a windfall gain accrues to the Inland Revenue to the detriment of creditors generally.

30. In previous correspondence with the Inland Revenue on the Finance Bill 1988 when this subject was raised, the Inland Revenue's view was given that the problem of becoming UK resident can be avoided as "it would ... be possible for companies to rearrange their affairs in ways other than liquidation, such as by shifting assets to a company incorporated elsewhere leaving behind only a shell". Where companies are insolvent, however, such steps would not be available and we believe the position should be re-examined with a view to confirming generally that the appointment of a UK liquidator to an insolvent company which was non-UK resident will not transfer its residence to the UK.

31. If the Board feel unable to extend such confirmation to solvent companies as well, it would nonetheless be helpful to have a general statement of the position that has been confirmed on occasion to individual insolvency practitioners, that management and control would remain abroad where a UK resident liquidator carries out his duties abroad in relation to that company, or in the case of a private company

whose shareholders are the directors and the liquidator acts in accordance with the wishes of the non-resident shareholders.

Inland Revenue response:

The test of residence

(a) The 6/83 should not be read as implying that, as a general rule, the Revenue have moved in any way from the test enunciated by Lord Loreburn. A company is regarded as resident for tax purposes where central management and control is to be found because that, according to Lord Loreburn, is where the real business is carried on. (The Statement of Practice has now been superseded by Statement 1/90 but the relevant paragraph is unchanged.)

(b) The word "business" may have different connotations according to the context in which it is used. The Revenue does not consider that a company normally ceases to have a residence under Lord Loreburn's test on going into liquidation.

Application of the test

(c) In law, the liquidator has management and control of the company's affairs. It is therefore not possible to confirm that a company, whether solvent or insolvent, which has hitherto been non-resident, will not become resident in the United Kingdom on the appointment of a UK resident liquidator.

(d) However, the exercise of central management and control is a question of fact. If it is exercised abroad by the liquidator or if the liquidator acts in accordance with the wishes of non-resident shareholders so that management and control is not in fact in the UK, the company will not become resident here.

Liquidation of foreign companies

32. Foreign companies which have been carrying on business in Great Britain may be wound up under the Insolvency Act 1986, so that UK creditors including the Inland Revenue may have the protection of a local licensed insolvency practitioner dealing with the assets for their benefit.

33. UK practitioners are, however, wary of such appointments as the effect of Section 108(2) Taxes Management Act 1970 may be to make them personally liable in respect of the company's UK tax liability. Such liability is apparently not limited to the funds in the liquidation estate.

34. A similar difficulty arises from UK practitioners who are asked to conduct the liquidation of foreign companies under foreign law, if their appointment was to make the foreign company UK resident for tax purposes.

35. There is no statement of the Board of Inland Revenue's policy on the application to a liquidator of Section 108(2) TMA 1970, and it would be of assistance if the Board would make clear the circumstances in which the provision would be invoked, if at all.

36. Liquidators wish to compete freely in the international market for their specialist skills, and they are at present disadvantaged by uncertainty of their position to the detriment of the UK economy.

Inland Revenue response:

The Revenue has, as you say, no stated policy with regard to the application of Section 108(2), TMA, to liquidators of foreign companies. Where a foreign company owes tax it is the Revenue practice to proceed against the company itself, invoking the procedure in Pt. V, IA 1986, for winding up unregistered companies.

Other matters

37. Included in the matters which were dealt with in the former Regulations and Notes for guidance of Liquidators in Compulsory Liquidation, and for guidance of Trustees in Bankruptcy, were:

(i) regulations detailing how the Inland Revenue will forego excessive claims for taxation. (These provided relief where time limits had been missed);
(ii) regulations setting out the conditions which will apply where before the date of the winding-up order a Collector of Taxes has levied a distress against goods.

38. The requirement for agreed practice in such matters remains, and it should be extended to cover all insolvency procedures of the Insolvency Act 1986.

39. There should also be published those concessions which have been agreed with the insolvency profession in the past, including such matters as the Revenue's policy not to seek to recover notional ACT chargeable under Section 419 ICTA 1988 in respect of loans to participators when the lending company was already insolvent or where the participator is adjudged bankrupt.

40. There are also numerous detailed procedural matters which should be included and these should be the subject of discussion with the Inland Revenue. It is noteworthy that unlike HM Customs & Excise, the Inland Revenue does not centralise the conduct of cases involving insolvency procedures nor are there clearly identified technical or policy specialists with whom the insolvency profession can have regular discussions about matters of concern to them, not all of which have been detailed in this memorandum. We would welcome such liaison arrangements, and would be pleased to cooperate in them.'

67.7 Administration under post-14 September 2003 Insolvency Act 1986 procedures

The *Enterprise Act* 2002 made changes to the *Insolvency Act* 1986 administration procedure (effective from 15 September 2003). This led to a change in the tax position of companies in insolvent administration for periods when the revised procedure came into effect.

First of all, the commencement of administration will cause one accounting period to end and another to begin. For further commentary on the impact on accounting periods of the company under administration, see **67.6.2**.

The *Finance Act* 2003 introduced new legislation to apply similar tax provisions to companies in the course of a revised insolvent administration as those already applying to companies in liquidation. Thus:

- except where the rates, fractions, etc. are already known for the financial year (the 'final year') in which the last accounting period before application for dissolution ends, the corporation tax rates, limits and fractions for the financial year immediately before that final year (the 'penultimate year') will apply. This enables the corporation tax liability to be agreed before the company is dissolved and its assets disposed of;
- where the company entered into administration before the final year, the same application of rates, etc. described in the previous bullet applies to the penultimate year as well, except that the possible substitution of the final year rates (where known) is extraneous;
- the provisions of ICTA 1988, s. 342(7)–(9) relating to liquidations apply to administration (see **67.5.7**). So, if:
    (a) the final year rates and fractions fixed by a Finance Act or a Budget resolution are proposed to be changed by a budget resolution, the altered rates or fractions are used,
    (b) dissolution has commenced before the final year, the penultimate financial year rates and fractions are the latest ones fixed by a Finance Act or Budget resolution;
- the company was assessed to corporation tax before administration on the basis of rates and fractions that had not yet been finally fixed for that financial year (ICTA 1988, s. 8(4)), and the interaction of the administration provisions with those assessments result in an overpayment or underpayment of tax, an adjustment can be made by discharge or repayment of tax or by a further assessment;
- assessments to corporation tax may be made before the end of the appropriate accounting period;
- when making a self assessment, the administrator may assume when the application for dissolution is to be made and, if that assumption proves to be incorrect, the assumed date still applies to mark the end of one accounting period and the start of another (and a further assumption may be made as to the date of the application), and
- repayment interest (within ICTA 1998, s. 826) under £2,000 will be exempt from tax.

Law: ICTA 1998, s. 342A

Planning point

Holders of floating charges created after 15 September 2003 can no longer assert the entire charge against the ordinary unsecured creditors. A percentage of the company's net assets subject to a floating charge must be ring-fenced by the liquidator, administrator or receiver (but not CVA supervisors), and made available for the satisfaction of the unsecured debts. Due to the abolition of the Crown preference, HMRC now hold an unsecured debt, which may be satisfied in full or part from the ring-fenced fund.

> Where the company's net property does not exceed £10,000, 50 per cent of the company's net property will be set aside. Where the company's net property exceeds £10,000, 50 per cent of the first £10,000; and 20 per cent of the property exceeding £10,000 will be set aside for the unsecured creditors, including the Crown.

Law: Insolvency Act 1986, s. 176A(2); *Insolvency Act 1986 (Prescribed Part) Order* 2003 (SI 2003/2097), art. 1

The Court of Appeal has confirmed that statutory liabilities in respect of PAYE and National Insurance Contributions, (which arose when administrators allowed a company to carry on trading), were accorded priority status under s. 19(5) and s. 19(6) of the *Insolvency Act* 1986.

This was the effect of the decision in *Inland Revenue Commissioners v (1) Peter Lawrence (2) Colin Wiseman sub nom in the matter of FJL Realisations Ltd* (2000) CA (Civ Div) 10/07/2000 LTL 10/07/2000 EXTEMPORE: (2001) BCC 663: (2001) 1 BCLC 204: (2001) ICR 42: Times, August 2, 2000.

The decision in FJL followed an appeal by the administrators of F against an order of the court. By that order, the words 'sums payable in respect ... of liabilities incurred ... under contracts ...' in IA 1986, s. 19(5) and s. 19(6) were held to include sums payable to HMRC which had been deducted or were deductible under the PAYE scheme (pursuant to ICTA 1988, s. 203(1) and statutory powers relating to Class 1 National Insurance Contributions (NIC) pursuant to SSCBA 1992, s. 6 and Sch. 1, and Social Security (Contributions) Regulations 1979 as amended).

The sums at issue were those amounts deducted from any money paid or payable to employees – such amounts were priority payments under IA 1986, s.19(5) and s.19(6) (or would have enjoyed such priority if they had not already been paid).

The issue was whether PAYE and NICs deducted but owing to HMRC were accorded priority status by virtue of IA 1986, s.19(5) and s.19(6).

The Court of Appeal decided that, in considering IA 1986, s. 19(6), it was artificial and wrong to split the contractual liability into two parts and to treat only the liability to pay a net sum to the employee as the contractual liability. The liability of the administrators was to pay the full salary.

This was not limited to an amount net of PAYE and NICs. Accordingly, the judge had reached the right conclusion for the reasons he gave. Accordingly, the statutory liabilities in respect of PAYE and National Insurance Contributions, did have priority status ahead of the general body of unsecured creditors. This is obviously significant in terms of the fact that the bulk of debts owed to HMRC are not preferential. In *Re HPJ UK LTD (In administration)* Ch D (Birmingham) 26/03/07 2007 BCC 244, the court confirmed that IA 1986, Sch. B1 para. 65 was sufficiently flexible to enable administrators to make a distribution in respect of a compromised claim with HMRC, which was not pari passu with the other claims.

In *HPJ*, the administrators of H had applied for permission to make a distribution to creditors. The administrators had agreed the proposed distribution with HMRC. The administrators sought to make an interim distribution.

HMRC had raised assessments for £7.2m of corporation tax which H had not paid, and it had an undisputed claim for arrears of PAYE, National Insurance contributions, corporation tax and VAT amounting to £1.2m. The administrators agreed to pay HMRC £2.25m in full and final settlement of its claims, which would allow it to pay unsecured creditors between 62p and 81p in the pound. The administrators also sought leave to make an interim distribution to creditors (other than HMRC) of 60p in the pound.

The Court confirmed that IA 1986, para. 65, Sch. B1 was sufficiently flexible to enable administrators to make a distribution in respect of the compromised claim with HMRC. This was despite the fact that the proposed distribution was not pari passu with the other claims.

The key considerations regarding the interim distribution were the attainment of the objectives of the administration and what was in the interests of the creditors as a whole. It was clear that no body of creditors would be disadvantaged by the proposed interim distribution, GHE Realisations Ltd (formerly Gatehouse Estates Ltd), Re (2005) EWHC 2400 (Ch), (2006) 1 WLR 287 considered. Accordingly, the Court sanctioned the proposed distribution.

67.8 Administration – consequences for group relief

As already indicated, the appointment of an Administrator (either by the Court or out of Court) does not divest a company of beneficial ownership of its assets. Accordingly, subsidiary companies will be entitled to relief from their corporation tax liabilities if they accept a surrender of their parent's trading losses.

HMRC has confirmed this position – at least by implication in ICAEW Technical Release 799 above, at paragraph 9(c) and (d).

However, there is a counter-argument argument which is understood to have been raised by HMRC. This is that ICTA 1988, s. 410(1)(b)(i) of applies because no one has control of a company in administration. Accordingly, HMRC have argued that there is no person who controls both the parent in administration and its subsidiaries.

It is suggested that the ICTA 1988, s. 410 argument is potentially flawed. This is not least because the Administrator has, by virtue of the *Insolvency Act* 1986, all the powers (and more) which could be exercised by the directors of the company.

HMRC has also acknowledged that an administration order breaks the group relationship above the company in administration. This will have the effect of denying any upward relief to a parent company (or a company linked to the company through the parent).

HMRC's argument in relation to upward relief is that, with regard to the group above the company, 'arrangements' exist within ICTA 1988, s. 410(1)(b)(ii) of to deny relief. Section 410(1)(b)(ii) requires there to be a person (or persons together) controlling, or capable of obtaining control of, either one of the companies but not both.

At shareholder level, control of the company is lost as a result of an administrator being appointed. This is because the shareholders can no longer regulate the conduct of the company's affairs.

Again, HMRC's argument has been contested. This is upon the basis that ICTA 1988, s. 410 is an anti-avoidance provision and should be read in that light. If this is accepted, s. 410 is really designed to prevent highly artificial arrangements allowing losses to be used outside the economic group in which they are incurred. There is no intention to catch administration in this section; administration being a tool for corporate rescue and rehabilitation, rather than any tax avoidance device.

HMRC's stance is strong because it is based on a literal interpretation of section 410. The alternative argument relies on a purposive interpretation that it cannot have been an intended consequence of the legislation to exclude administration. Such a purposive construction is rarely accepted by the Court. It may thus be dangerous to rely on this sort of argument.

The effect of this can be profound. The effects of these arguments are far-reaching, not only for companies in administration but, possibly, also for other insolvency procedures, for example, liquidation.

67.9 Hive down – how a resurrection really feels

A hive down may be undertaken for a number of reasons, which may be tax driven or commercial.

When a company is insolvent or in financial difficulties, ironically, one of its most valuable assets may be the very losses that placed it in financial difficulties in the first place. Those losses may be valuable to its solvent parent or sister companies in connection with surrenders of group relief.

Insolvencies

In addition, one possibility in a corporate insolvency may be for an insolvent company to sell its assets and business.

In these circumstances, there may be significant losses, which may be of financial value. Subject to complex anti-tax avoidance legislation, such losses could be useful to a potential buyer to use as it rebuilds the business. It is thus worth bearing in mind how such losses can be protected and repackaged to make the business more valuable to such a buyer.

In the case of a hive down, a company may merely be in financial difficulties and the directors may choose a course of action to avoid any of the above becoming necessary.

Loss relief in corporate insolvency: general

In addition to the tax issues that arise in connection with a hive down of a company's business and assets and the issues surrounding the surrender of losses, there are a number of other general tax points that need to be considered in connection with a corporate insolvency. These include the following:

- upon cessation of trade, an insolvent company is only eligible for relief for post-cessation losses against post-cessation receipts (ICTA 1988, s. 105), replaced from 1 April 2009, with effect for accounting periods ending on or after that date, by CTA 2009, s. 196. For this reason, the carried-forward trading losses may not be set against chargeable gains arising after the cessation of the trade.
- loss relief under ICTA 1988, s. 393A is available upon the cessation of a company's trade. This allows trading losses in the 12 months preceding the termination of the trade to be set against trading profits and chargeable gains of the accounting periods in the three 12-month periods immediately preceding the accounting period in which those losses were incurred.
- for companies that have not ceased their trade, as a temporary measure only and subject to limits, the 2008 Pre-Budget Report announced that businesses will be able to carry back trading losses against the profits of the three preceding years and obtain a repayment of tax. For corporation tax purposes, the rule will apply to losses for accounting periods ending in the period 24 November 2008 to 23 November 2010 (FA 2009, s. 23 and Sch. 6).
- Depending on what is going to happen to the company (in particular, if there is to be a hive down), it will often be useful to carry on the company's trade for as long as possible so as to take the maximum possible benefit of loss relief.

Sale by way of hive down

The decision to structure the purchase on the basis of acquiring the shares in a hive down company may be taken for tax reasons or, if it suits a buyer for other reasons, such as corporate structuring within its own group in the case of a larger, more complex transaction.

A potential tax advantage of hiving down is that the tax benefit of trading losses is transferred from the insolvent parent company to the hive down company. This is pursuant to ICTA 1988 s. 343. Such losses may be carried forward.

However, the tax effects must be examined carefully before taking a decision to insist on a hive down. This is because restrictive anti-avoidance legislation can make it difficult to preserve and obtain the benefit of trading losses carried forward. In addition, the amount of transferable losses will be limited to the extent that liabilities are left in the insolvent parent company.

The use of hive down companies has become rarer following the introduction of this restriction limiting the amount of historical trading losses that can be utilised. In all cases, specialist tax advice should be obtained by the buyer to ensure that there are no other adverse consequences from structuring a sale in this way. For example, such advice should preclude the possibility of the hive down company being secondarily liable for tax for which the hive down company's group is primarily liable.

If the buyer is satisfied that trading losses can be preserved and utilised, or that a hive down is advantageous for other reasons, then the insolvency practitioner should be approached to secure his agreement to structuring the sale on a hive down basis.

A hive down may be effected most often via administration, not least due to the stigma and terminal consequences of liquidation.

If the sale is structured on this basis, it will be documented by a hive down agreement between:

- the insolvent parent company;
- the insolvent parent company's new subsidiary; and
- the insolvency practitioner.

There will also be a subsequent share sale agreement between:

- the insolvent parent company;
- the insolvency practitioner;
- the subsidiary company; and
- the buyer.

Although the buyer is not a party to the hive down agreement, the agreement will, (unless the insolvency practitioner has already hived down the business following his appointment), usually be negotiated by lawyers acting for both the buyer and the insolvency practitioner. This is because it will dictate the terms on which the hive down subsidiary acquires the business and assets.

Restrictions on the tax effectiveness of hive downs are now contained in ICTA 1988, s. 343(4). As a result, the principal reasons for a hive down in insolvency now relate to the preservation and/or realisation of the business itself or parent.

Insolvencies

Utilisation of trading losses by the buyer will be part of this process but will be subject to the anti-avoidance legislation contained in ICTA 1988, s. 768–769, which provides that there must be no major change in the nature of conduct of the trade by the buyer.

The benefits of a hive down, other than tax, include all of the following:

- the administrator can choose to hive down the part of the trade that is profitable, or valuable assets that are worth transferring, and keep back the rest;
- if the trade is transferred, carried-forward capital allowances and trading losses will be available for use against future profits for Newco's tax purposes;
- despite the restrictions in s. 343(4) of ICTA 1988, a hive down is the only means of transferring the whole of a trade to a company so that the losses and allowances of that trade will be available. A hive down must happen before any agreement for the onward sale of Newco if the tax losses are to be utilised. It will be too late after the agreement for sale is signed since the beneficial interest in Newco's shares will normally pass to the buyer;
- Newco will be a 'clean company'. In other words, it will not have Parent's debts or disadvantageous credit standing.
- it should be easier to establish the profitability of the trade of Newco;
- trading may continue without interruption even if Parent is wound up; and
- Newco will be a new customer and, therefore, it can obtain gas, electricity and telecommunications services without the personal guarantee required under s. 233 of the *Insolvency Act* 1986.

Method of hive down

Newco will usually be a newly-formed, off-the-shelf company or a dormant subsidiary of Parent. The assets to be transferred to it usually include:

- plant;
- machinery;
- office furniture;
- equipment;
- motor vehicles;
- stock and work-in-progress;
- goodwill (including the right to Parent's trading name as successor to that business); and
- the benefit of trading contracts.

On an insolvency hive down, the following are (initially, at least) left in Parent:

- interest in land;
- trademarks;
- patents;
- licences;
- copyright;
- design rights;
- cash; and

- book debts.

These are left behind because there is usually no advantage in incurring expenses in transferring land (for example, stamp duty land tax (SDLT)) and intellectual property rights in an initial hive down. This is when it is not necessarily clear that Newco will be able to trade successfully or that a buyer will be found for it. Indeed, there is often a disadvantage in doing so.

Additionally, if land or other assets that stand at an accrued but uncrystallised gain are transferred to Newco and then Newco leaves Parent's group, then Newco may be subject to the *Taxation of Chargeable Gains Act* 1992 (TCGA), s. 179. This creates a degrouping charge or similar charges on the transferred assets if they were transferred in the preceding six years).

By contrast, a direct sale of the property to Newco, or even the buyer, after Newco has been sold to the buyer means that the chargeable gains tax liability will be an unsecured claim in the liquidation of Parent. The advantage of this is that Parent may have trading or capital losses from that accounting period or brought-forward capital losses to shelter such gains.

Preservation of losses: s. 343 of ICTA 1988

The application of ICTA 1988, s. 343 is fundamental to the tax success of a hive down. If this provision applies, tax losses and capital allowances will continue to be available as if there had been no change in the ownership of the trade. However, the anti-avoidance provisions of s. 768–769 of ICTA 1988 should be noted in this regard.

For tax purposes, s. 343 of ICTA 1988 will only apply if the parent company has beneficial ownership of the shares in the hive down company immediately before, and for long enough after, the hive down. It follows that if Parent is in liquidation, s. 343 cannot apply.

Ideally, the period that Parent should own the shares of Newco after the hive down should be at least one week. Where, at the time the business and assets are transferred to the hive down company, there is an agreement for the sale of the shares in the hive down company to a buyer, the insolvent parent will no longer have a beneficial interest in the shares of the hive down company and the trading losses will not be transferred.

Although a shorter period of ownership is not necessarily fatal to the application of s. 343 of ICTA 1988, the Parent should be able to show that the trade is actively carried on while it owns the shares of Newco, which will be easier if it holds the shares for more than a minimal length of time.

One way of dealing with these problems is for an option agreement (taking the place of the share sale agreement) to be entered into at the same time as the hive down agreement. In the case *J Sainsbury v O'Connor* [1991] BTC 181, it was held that a seller will not lose beneficial ownership of an asset even if it is subject to 'cross options'.

This means that, notwithstanding the option, the business is carried on for a few days by the hive down company, during which time, the buyer has no beneficial interest in the shares of the hive down company. The option agreement is made between the insolvent company, the insolvency practitioner, the hive down company and the buyer and, as well as containing an option, embodies the terms that would otherwise be contained in the share sale agreement referred to above.

Under the option agreement, the buyer (for a nominal consideration) grants to the insolvent company the option to sell the shares in the hive down company to the buyer. There is a cut-off date before which the option must be exercised (usually, a date falling a few days after the date on which the hive down agreement is entered into), after which it will lapse. In other words, the option is a put option, exercisable by the insolvency practitioner on behalf of the insolvent parent company.

In theory, therefore, the buyer, by granting such an option, bears the risk of non-exercise by the insolvency practitioner. However, in practice, this is a remote contingency since non-exercise would probably deprive the insolvency practitioner of his only (or most likely) buyer. A buyer contemplating the use of an option agreement in the circumstances outlined above should always take specialist tax advice before doing so.

Details

Strangely, the predecessor of ICTA 1988, s. 343 started life in the early part of the twentieth century as an anti-avoidance provision. However, it has now transformed into a helpful device for use in corporate insolvencies.

ICTA 1988, s. 343 applies where:

- there is a transfer of a trade between two companies; and
- on the transfer, or at any time within two years after it, the trade, or a 75 per cent interest in the trade, belongs to the same persons to whom it belonged at some time within the year of the transfer.

The concept of 'belonging' is explained in detail in s. 344 of ICTA 1988 and, in essence, a trade is treated as belonging to those who are ultimately entitled to the profits of that trade. This means that in the case of a subsidiary, the trade belongs to its parent's shareholders.

The trade must not, within the 'specified period', be carried on by a company that is not within the charge to UK tax in respect of the trade, such as a non-resident company not carrying on a trade through a UK branch or agency (ICTA 1988, s. 343(1)(b)). If part of a trade is transferred, there are apportionment provisions in s. 343(8) and (10).

If s. 343 applies, there is no cessation of trade as far as loss relief is concerned (see above). Subject to the limitations of s. 343(4), Newco effectively inherits all of the losses incurred in the trade by Parent. These may be carried forward indefinitely under s. 393(1) of ICTA 1988 as if the trade had always been carried on by Newco.

ICTA 1988, s. 343(2) also provides that no capital allowances balancing charges are to be made on Parent and no balancing allowances to be given to it either. It also provides that the capital allowances computations for Newco are to be made as if it were a single company that carried on the trade throughout. However, Parent is precluded from making a claim for loss relief on the cessation of its trade under s. 393A(2A) of ICTA 1988 by virtue of s. 343(4A).

Anti-avoidance: s. 343(4) of ICTA 1988

Section 343(4) of ICTA 1988 limits the application of s. 343 in cases where Parent has insufficient assets to cover its liabilities. The losses available for relief are reduced by the amount by which Parent has 'relevant liabilities' (as defined in s. 344(6) and (8)-(10) of ICTA 1988) that exceed the open market value of its 'relevant assets'. In both cases, this is ascertained just before the hive down takes place.

The term 'relevant assets' is defined in s. 344(5) as:

- assets vested in Parent immediately before the hive down and that were not transferred to Newco, together with any consideration given by Newco for the hive down; and
- excluding liabilities assumed by Newco on Parent's behalf.

The term 'relevant liabilities' is defined as meaning liabilities outstanding and vested in Parent immediately before the hive down and that were not transferred to Newco. They do not include liabilities representing Parent's:

- share per capital (unless it results from the conversion of relevant liabilities within the year before the hive down);
- share premium account (unless it results from the conversion of relevant liabilities within the year before the hive down);
- reserves (unless it results from the conversion of relevant liabilities within the year before the hive down); and
- loan stock (unless it results from the conversion of relevant liabilities within the year before the hive down or is loan stock where the loan stockholder was carrying on the trade of lending money when the liability was incurred).

Pricing structure

The consideration payable in a hive down can present problems to the parties. There are three possible ways of structuring the price for a hive down so that it is fixed:

1 **Transfer the assets in exchange for shares in Newco.** Parent transfers the relevant assets to Newco in consideration of an allotment of shares in Newco.

Even though it may seem that there is no need to allocate a consideration for those shares, the return of allotments needs to be filed with the Registrar of Companies. It is unlikely that relief from stamp duty will be available under s. 42 of the *Finance Act* 1930 because a buyer already exists so the consideration must be known. Stamp Office adjudication may be required, which can result in delays. This course is, therefore, fairly infrequently used.

2 **Transfer the assets in exchange for cash left outstanding as an inter-group loan.** Parent transfers the assets to Newco for a stated consideration that is left outstanding upon inter-company account.

The problem here is establishing the value of the consideration. If market value is used, this will prejudice negotiations with the buyer of Newco. However, if book value is used and it exceeds market value, Newco can start life already insolvent, so defeating the point of the exercise. Moreover, if Parent is in administration and Newco is sold for greater than the amount subscribed for the shares, a chargeable gain will arise.

3 **Transfer in exchange for a consideration to be certified at a later date.** When structuring the hive down, it is important that when Newco is sold, it is sold in such a way as does not generate a profit or loss for Parent (unless there are sufficient losses available to shelter the gain).

One way of doing this is by providing in the hive down contract for the consideration to be certified either by an independent valuer. The purchase price is then left outstanding on inter-company loan as above. When Newco is sold to the buyer, a supplementary agreement is made between Parent and Newco in which the requirement for the valuer's certificate is varied and replaced by inserting a figure for the price. This figure will equate to the price at which the hive down assets have been valued, or a certificate is issued at the appropriate price.

The buyer then agrees to acquire the inter-company loan such that, on completion, Parent receives a sum effectively equal to the purchase price for the assets sold. The price paid by the buyer will equal the net value of Newco after taking account of the inter-company loan.

There is, of course, the prospect of a degrouping charge under TCGA 1992, s. 179, and the buyer will, normally, expect to be indemnified against it or that the price will be reduced.

There are difficulties with the first two options described above so the third option is, generally, preferred in practice.

Further pricing point

The receiver or administrator will also, generally, enter into another agreement with the buyer for the sale of any indebtedness owed by Newco. The buyer may discharge the indebtedness of Newco or procure that Newco does so itself.

If the former approach is adopted, the buyer will not pay stamp duty on the debt transfer provided it comes within the loan capital exemption of s. 79 of *Finance Act* 1986.

The consideration for the shares will not be increased by the debt under s. 57 of *Stamp Act* 1891 since they will not be conveyed in consideration of a debt. However, there is a base cost issue because the buyer will want to maximise his base cost for the Newco shares. To the extent that some of the monies paid by the buyer are attributable to the redemption of debt, the base cost of the shares is less than it would have been had all of those monies been attributable to the acquisition of the shares.

If, on the other hand, the transfer is subject to the debt and the buyer procures payment, stamp duty will be payable but the 'relevant asset', for s. 343 of ICTA 1988 purposes of Parent, will be increased. Given the balancing exercise between maximising losses available for carry forward and the stamp duty saving (at 0.5 per cent of the consideration), this is often the favoured course.

Anti-avoidance: ICTA 1988, s. 768 to 769

Sections 768 to 769 of ICTA 1988 disallow the carry forward of losses if either:

- within the period of three years, there is both a change in the ownership of a company and (either earlier or later in that period, or at the same time) a major change in the nature or conduct of a trade carried on by the company; or
- at any time after the scale of the activities in a trade carried on by a company has become small or negligible and before any considerable revival of the trade, there is a change in the ownership of the company.

These provisions can create considerable uncertainty in connection with a hive down. It is often the case that the buyer will make his offer on the basis that there is a genuine risk that the losses may not be available. In this sense, the losses may be seen as an additional, almost unexpected benefit of the hive down.

Degrouping charges

On a hive down, consideration will need to be given to whether any of the assets hived down would give rise to a degrouping charge on the sale of Newco. This will happen if a sale of the asset for market value, at the time of the hive down, would have given rise to a chargeable gain. If this is the case, the asset could be excluded from the hive down and sold directly so that the charge arises in Parent, where there may be losses to shelter it, rather than in Newco itself.

However, excluding assets from the hive down may have adverse implications on the availability of the historic losses to Newco, the availability of relief from stamp duty on the hive down and the treatment of the transfer as a transfer of a going concern for VAT purposes.

Alternatively, Newco and Parent could enter into an election so that the degrouping charge is treated as arising in Parent (TCGA 1992, s. 179A). However, the buyer should note that Newco would be secondarily liable for the degrouping charge in the event it is not sheltered or discharged by Parent.

Capital assets

A potential problem with a hive down is that if any capital assets were transferred into Newco that have appreciated in value while under the ownership of the seller group, there will be a deemed disposal of those assets when Newco is sold to the buyer. This assumes that Newco is transferred to the buyer within six years of the transfer of the relevant assets (TCGA 1992, s. 179). This is a so-called 'degrouping' tax charge.

Since 1 April 2002, the degrouping rules have been relaxed (TCGA 1992, s. 179A–179B), allowing:

- companies to elect to treat a degrouping charge as arising to another group member (so capital losses of other group members can be used to offset the gain); and
- a roll-over of the gains arising into qualifying assets acquired by the transferee company or others in its group.

As this degrouping tax charge would arise in Newco and effectively be borne by the buyer of Newco, the buyer may seek an indemnity from the seller or seek the inclusion of a clause in the asset purchase agreement under which the seller must elect to reallocate the degrouping charge.

Alternatively, the seller could sell on assets which such charges might arise directly to the buyer rather than via Newco. This should be possible for most assets except goodwill, which must naturally follow the trade. Another alternative would be for there to be a hive out of all assets not being sold, with the seller selling the shares in the transferor company.

Intangible assets

Other degrouping charges that might be triggered by a hive down include the degrouping charge that applies to certain group transfers of intangible assets under the UK corporation tax regime.

The degrouping charge for intangible assets is fundamentally the same as that contained in the capital gains equivalent in TCGA 1992, s. 179. However, the intangibles degrouping charge arises immediately before the transferee leaves the group. The timing of the change is, therefore, different from, and later than, the capital gains equivalent.

Loan relationships and derivative contracts

Under the loan relationship code and the derivative contract rules, it is possible to transfer loan relationships or derivative contracts between group members without incurring a tax charge.

Following a transfer, the transferee company takes over the historic position of the transferor company.

The *Finance (No.2) Act* 2005 introduced further degrouping charges that may apply on intra-group transfers of loan relationships and derivative contracts (FA 1996, Sch. 9, para. 12A, replaced from 1 April 2009, with effect for accounting periods ending on or after that date, by CTA 2009, s. 344–346 and FA 2002, Sch. 26, para. 30A, replaced from 1 April 2009, with effect for accounting periods ending on or after that date, by CTA 2009, s. 630–632). Such degrouping charges ensure that profits arising on such intra-group transfers do not escape the charge to tax.

The added provisions apply after 15 March 2005. In order for there to be a degrouping charge, there must be an intra-group transaction within six years of the transferee company leaving the group. If the transferee company leaves within six years, that company is deemed to have assigned and re-acquired the asset or liability for a fair value immediately before it ceased to be a member of the group. However, this rule only applies if one of two conditions is satisfied:

(1) Following the deemed disposal and re-acquisition, there is a credit to be brought into account by the transferee.

(2) If the loan relationship in question is a creditor relationship, the company has a hedging relationship between a derivative contract and the creditor relationship and, in consequence of FA 2002, Sch. 26, para. 30A(2)(a) (replaced from 1 April 2009, with effect for accounting periods ending on or after that date, by CTA 2009, s. 631(2)(a) and (b)), a credit falls to be brought into account by the transferee.

Value added tax

There is a potential VAT charge on the transfer of assets from the seller to a buyer unless the sale is a transfer of a business as a going concern or both companies selling and buying are in the same VAT group. There is also a potential VAT charge where assets are acquired as a transfer of a going concern from a third party outside the VAT group by a member of a partially-exempt VAT group.

VAT groups

Two or more companies can be registered as a group for VAT purposes if one controls the other(s) or some person (not necessarily a company itself) controls all of them, and each company either is resident in the UK for VAT purposes or has an established place of business in the UK.

The test of control is that which applies in CA 1985, s. 736 so that one company is a subsidiary of another if the second company satisfies any of the following:

- it holds a majority of the voting rights in the first company;
- it is a member of the first company and has the right to appoint or remove a majority of the first company's board of directors; and
- it is a member of the first company and controls alone, pursuant to an agreement with other shareholders or members, a majority of the voting rights in the first company.

Transfers of a going concern

In order to ensure that the sale of assets is treated as a sale of a business as a going concern such that no VAT is chargeable, a number of conditions must be fulfilled, including:

- the assets must be intended to be used (and actually used) for carrying on an economic activity, which may or may not be the same economic activity as that carried on by the seller;
- if the seller is a taxable person Newco (as buyer) must already be, or by virtue of the transfer become, a taxable person (that is, registered, or liable to be registered, for VAT);
- there must not be a significant break in trading and Newco must intend to operate the business and not simply immediately liquidate the activity or sell the stock. This is, in any event, necessary to ensure that trading losses are transferred; and
- where there is a transfer of part of a business, it must be capable of separate operation.

Special VAT rules apply when land and property is transferred to Newco as part of the transfer of a business. Additionally, if the transferee is part of a partly-exempt VAT group, the representative member will, normally, have to account for VAT on the self-supply of other assets of the seller that were less than three years old at the time of the transfer. The buyer should be aware that if any of the assets transferred are subject to the VAT capital goods scheme, as defined in the *VAT Regulations* 1995 (SI 1995/2518), it will acquire responsibility for any adjustment of input tax for the remaining part of the adjustment period.

HMRC regards successive transfers, that is, those involving a sale to a hive down company that does not carry on the business, as not being transfers as a going concern. For example, if the seller transfers the business into a hive down company and, immediately following the sale of the hive down company, the business is then transferred to a member of the buyer's group, HMRC may argue that there has not been a transfer of a going concern.

Stamp taxes

A disadvantage of a hive down is that there may be an additional stamp duty or SDLT charge payable by the hive down company. Following the changes to stamp duty and the introduction of stamp duty land tax in 2003, a hive down is unlikely to give any stamp duty or SDLT saving.

Indeed, if any real property interests are included in the assets transferred, there will be a double cost: SDLT on the hive down of the property and stamp duty on the resultant increase in the value of the shares in Newco. This can be avoided by excluding real property interests from the hive down. However, this can have other tax consequences, which must be considered.

Stamp duty

The rate of stamp duty on the transfer of stock, marketable securities and certain interests in partnerships is 0.5 per cent. These are the only assets that may be subject to stamp duty on transfer.

Stamp duty group relief, for a hive down of such assets, may be available to the transferee for such transfers between 75 per cent group companies (FA 1930, s. 42).

However, this relief is not available in certain circumstances, including where the transfer forms part of arrangements under which the transferee (Newco) is being sold or transferred to a third party or controlled by a third party, or the consideration (or any part) is to be provided or received by a person other than a group company (FA 1930, s. 42(2) and FA 1967, s. 27).

Stamp duty land tax

SDLT is a tax on land transactions and the transfer of certain partnership interests. Intra-group transactions are exempt from the SDLT charge. The rules provide that companies are in the same group if one is the 75 per cent subsidiary of the other or both are 75 per cent subsidiaries of a third company (FA 2003, Sch. 7).

Similarly to stamp duty group relief, SDLT relief is not available where, at the effective date of the transaction, either:

- there are arrangements under which, at that or some later time, a person has (or could obtain), or any persons together have (or could obtain), control of the buyer but not of the seller; or
- there are arrangements under which the consideration (or any part of it) is to be provided or received by a person other than the group company, or the seller and buyer are to cease to be members of the same group by reason of the buyer ceasing to be a 75 per cent subsidiary of the seller or a third party.

There is a real chance that provisions excluding SDLT relief could apply in the context of a hive down and, in particular:

- SDLT group relief will, generally, be withdrawn where, within three years of the effective date of the transaction, the buyer ceases to be a member of the same group as the seller. These rules broadly mirror the claw-back provisions under existing stamp duty law (as amended by the FA 2003) but go further in

an important respect: under the SDLT regime, claw back also applies if degrouping occurs after the three-year period if there are arrangements for degrouping within that three year period.
- The *Finance (No.2) Act* 2005 has extended the situations in which group relief can be withdrawn to where there has been a chain of sales within a period of three years, each of which has been free from SDLT because of group relief, reconstruction relief or acquisition relief. Where the final group buyer claims group relief and, within three years, there is a change of control of that company, group relief is withdrawn if the final buyer ceases to be in the same group as the company that first sold the property in the preceding three years. However, with effect for land transactions that have an effective date on or after 13 March 2008, this withdrawal does not apply where there is a change of control because a loan creditor obtains (or ceases to have) control of the buyer and the other persons who controlled the buyer before the change continue to do so.

Previously, group relief was not withdrawn where the group's relationship was broken because the seller left the group by reason of a transaction relating either to shares in the seller or to shares in another group company. This was unless the transaction related to a company that is not above the seller in the chain of ownership (FA 2003, Sch. 7, para. 4, as amended by F(No.2)A 2005, Sch. 10).

However, legislation has been included in s. 96 of the *Finance Act* 2008 extending the scope of the claw back. This legislation applies if the seller leaves the group and there is a subsequent change in the control of the buyer within a period of three years of the property having been transferred. The legislation allows HMRC to link these two events and treat the buyer as having left the group first so that it can claw back group relief previously claimed by the buyer.

However, this withdrawal does not to apply where there is a change of control because a loan creditor obtains (or ceases to have) control of the buyer and the other persons who controlled the buyer before the change continue to do so. This legislation has effect where the relevant land transaction has an effective date on or after 13 March 2008.

Before FA 2008 extension of claw back applied, it may have been preferable instead to 'hive out' all assets not intended to be sold and for the seller than to sell the transferor company. However, from an SDLT perspective, *Finance Act* 2008 change means that this is no longer attractive from an SDLT perspective.

In practice, a hive out is used less frequently than a hive down (even without regard to the FA 2008 change to SDLT claw back: see above) because of the relative complexity of transferring out the retained businesses compared with transferring out a target business.

If a hive out route is to be used, the seller can take advantage of ICTA 1988, s. 343 to transfer to Newco part of the trading losses of the transferor company before the disposal of the transferor, which now holds only the target business.

Other tax points

If there is a worthless capital asset, it may be worth making a negligible value claim under TCGA 1992, s. 24 (which deems there to be a disposal of an asset if it becomes of negligible value and the taxpayer's inspector of taxes is satisfied that this the case), either before or after any necessary group transfer or joint election under TCGA 1992, s. 171A to ensure that the gains and losses are realised in the same company.

In the context of a hive down, it is necessary to be aware of the provisions of ICTA 1988, s. 703–709 (superseded by Ch. 1 of Pt. 13 of ITA 2007 for income tax, but not corporation tax, purposes for periods from 2007–2008). These anti-avoidance measures apply to the combined effect of a transaction and the liquidation of a company. In *IR Commrs v Joiner* (1975) 50 TC 449, it was held that a liquidation agreement (as usually found in a reconstruction involving a liquidation) will be a 'transaction in securities'.

In addition, the writing off of debts can have a tax impact. If the debt is not a loan relationship debt (that is, it is a trade debt) and it is treated as bad and then released, a taxable receipt arises in the debtor's hands under ICTA 1988, s. 94 unless the exception for a statutory insolvency arrangement applies or, with effect for releases on or after 22 April 2009, the release is between connected parties (see FA 2009, s. 42).

For loan relationships, there is a mirroring rule for relevant arrangements or compromises, or, in certain circumstances, where an amortised cost basis of accounting is used. In these cases, no credit in respect of the write-off need be brought into account (FA 1996, Sch. 9, para. 5(3), replaced from 1 April 2009, with effect for accounting periods ending on or after that date, by CTA 2009, s. 322).

68 Interest Relief

68.1 Introduction

68.1.1 Generally

Income tax relief (at various effective rates) is available for an interest payment if it relates to one of the specified categories of loan, below.

Relief is not granted in the following circumstances:

- where interest is paid on an overdraft or under credit card arrangements;
- where interest is paid at a rate greater than a reasonable commercial rate (in which case the excess is ineligible for relief);
- where the main benefit of the arrangement is the reduction of tax; or
- where relief is sought by a company within the charge to corporation tax.

Interest paid as a revenue rather than capital item on money borrowed wholly and exclusively for the purposes of a trade, profession or vocation is not subject to the foregoing restrictions. There are provisions intended to prevent any double deductions for interest.

68.1.2 Categories of qualifying loan

Interest relief is available on loans applied for the following purposes:

- to purchase machinery and plant;
- in acquiring an interest in a close company;
- in acquiring an interest in a co-operative;
- in acquiring shares in an employee-controlled company;
- in acquiring an interest in a partnership;
- to pay inheritance tax; or
- to purchase a life annuity where the borrower is 65 years old or more.

> ⚠ **Warning!**
> The giving of credit to a purchaser under any sale is treated as the making of a loan to defray money applied by him in making the purchase.

Interest Relief

> ⚠️ **Warning!**
>
> No relief is available where the business being carried on by the close company (**68.3**), employee-controlled company (**68.5**), or partnership (**68.6**) is the occupation of woodlands managed on a commercial basis with a view to profits. Where that occupation is only part of the company or partnership's business, only that part of the interest which on a just and reasonable basis can be attributed to that occupation is denied relief. The attribution has to be made having regard to all relevant circumstances and, in particular, the extent of the other part of the business

Where only part of a loan satisfies the conditions for interest relief, only a proportion of the interest will be eligible for relief. That proportion is one which is equal to the proportion of the loan fulfilling those conditions at the time the money is applied.

> **Planning point**
>
> Full interest relief is generally available on a joint loan to a husband and wife, or between civil partners, where only one of them satisfies the qualifying conditions as respects investment in a close company or partnership and that spouse, or civil partner, makes the payments or they are made out of a joint account.

68.1.3 Form of relief

Relief generally takes the form of a deduction from or offset against total income in respect of the interest paid. However, if relief is not available at source, relief for interest on a loan to purchase a life annuity is given by way of a reduction in the income tax otherwise payable, though the rate of relief in this case remains the basic rate; an effective order of offset of reliefs is provided. Any necessary apportionment of the interest where a loan is used the purpose of purchasing such annuity and for other qualifying purposes is made on a specified basis.

Where an individual would obtain relief in respect of interest on a loan but the loan is on preferential terms and is obtained by reason of his employment, no taxable benefit ultimately arises (the benefit is effectively offset by relief for the deemed interest).

68.1.4 Indirect recoveries of capital

If at any time after the application of the proceeds of the loan, the borrower has recovered capital from the close company, employee-controlled company, co-operative or partnership (but does not use it in repayment of the loan) he is treated as repaying the loan (in whole or in part) so that the interest eligible for relief, and payable for any period after capital is recovered, is reduced by an amount equal to the interest on the capital recovered.

The borrower is treated as having recovered capital if he receives consideration for the sale, exchange or assignment of his ordinary shares in the close company or of his shares in the co-operative or of his interest in the partnership. Capital is deemed to have been recovered if the company, etc. repays the loan or the partnership returns capital to the borrower. HM Revenue & Customs' view (HMRC) is that the conversion of loan stock into ordinary shares is an assignment of the loan stock to the company (in exchange for shares), so that relief ceases.

68.1.5 Claim for relief

As a general rule, a claim must be made for interest relief. The person making the claim must supply the inspector with a written statement from the lender which contains the following information:

- the date when the debt was incurred;
- the amount of the debt when incurred;
- the interest paid in the tax year for which the claim is made; and
- the name and address of the debtor.

Local authorities and building societies (or companies carrying out similar business) are excluded from this requirement. HMRC forms can be used but are not required.

> *Planning point*
>
> Interest payments on qualifying borrowings could be planned to fall within a tax year with the highest marginal rate of tax.

Law: ITA 2007, s. 23, 383

68.2 Interest on loan to buy machinery or plant

Relief is available where:

- an individual who is a member of a partnership pays interest on a loan which is used for capital expenditure on the provision of plant or machinery used by that partnership in carrying on a trade, profession or a property business;
- for the period of account in which the interest is paid, the partnership is entitled to capital allowances (or liable to a balancing charge) under CAA 2001, s. 264 in respect of that capital expenditure; and

Interest Relief

- the interest is due and payable not later than three years from the end of the period of account in which the loan was made.

The general conditions that:

- the loan must be made on the occasion of the expenditure being incurred on the qualifying purpose or within a reasonable time either before or after that expenditure; and
- the monies raised by the loan must not have been used for any other purpose prior to the expenditure for the qualifying purpose,

are not applicable to relief under this heading.

Where the machinery or plant is used only partly for the trade, etc. carried on by the partnership, only that part of the total interest which it is just and reasonable to attribute to the use in the trade, is eligible for relief. Regard must be paid to all the relevant circumstances and, in particular, to the extent of the use for the other purposes.

The predecessor legislation, former ICTA 1988, s. 359(1), suggested that relief for interest paid in a period of account was dependent upon the partnership being entitled to a capital allowance for that period. Thus if a 100 per cent first year allowance was given on the asset being brought into use, no allowance would be due in subsequent periods even though the asset may still be in use. A similar situation would arise where the whole of the capital expenditure has been relieved by allowances given in earlier periods. To avoid this interpretation, the partnership is treated as being entitled to a capital allowance for a period of account if it was so entitled in a previous period and no disposal value has yet been required to be brought into account in respect of that plant or machinery.

The predecessor legislation also only referred to the partnership carrying on a trade, profession or vocation. The Tax Law Rewrite team considered that a partnership could not actually carry on a vocation and so that term was not retained in the Income Tax Act 2007. A more significant change was the confirmation that relief would be available where the partnership carried on a property business. There are arguments for and against saying that property businesses were always a permitted partnership activity (for the detailed arguments see the Explanatory Notes to the *Income Tax Act* 2007, Annex 1, Change 68). In view of that uncertainty it is now specifically provided that the permitted partnership activities are the carrying on of a trade, profession or an ordinary property business.

Planning point

Where the machinery or plant is used partly for the trade carried on by the partnership and partly by the partners for their own purposes, then only the interest which it is just and reasonable to attribute to the purposes of the trade is

> eligible for relief. Regard must be had to all the relevant circumstances and, in particular, to the extent of the use for the other purposes.

Similarly, the holder of an office or employment is entitled to relief where he is entitled under to a capital allowance, or is liable to a balancing charge (or would be so entitled or liable but for some contribution made by the employer), for any tax year in respect of machinery or plant belonging to him and in use for the purposes of the office or employment, and he pays interest in that year on a loan to defray money applied as capital expenditure on the provision of that machinery or plant. However, interest falling due and payable more than three years after the end of the tax year in which the debt was incurred is not eligible for relief.

> **Planning point**
>
> Where the machinery or plant is used partly for the office or employment and partly for other purposes then only the interest which it is just and reasonable to attribute to the purposes of the office or employment is eligible for relief. Regard must be had to the relevant circumstances and in particular, to the extent of the use for the other purposes. Where part only of a debt fulfils the conditions described above for interest on the debt to be eligible for relief, such a proportion of the interest will be treated as eligible as is equal to the proportion of the debt fulfilling those conditions at the time of the application of the money in question.

Law: ITA 2007, s. 388

68.3 Interest on loan to invest in a close company

68.3.1 General

Interest paid on a loan made to an individual may be eligible for income tax relief if the money is borrowed:

- to acquire ordinary shares of a qualifying 'close company';
- in making a loan to a qualifying close company where the loan is used wholly and exclusively for the business of the company or of any associated qualifying close company; or
- in satisfying an earlier loan which would have qualified for interest relief.

A close company is a qualifying close company if it falls within one of the types of company excluded from being a close investment-holding company.

Relief will generally be denied unless either of the conditions set out below is satisfied. However, the following points should be noted:

- HMRC are willing to allow relief for interest, following a reorganisation involving an exchange of shares after the loan proceeds are applied, provided the conditions for relief would have been met had the loan been a new loan taken out to invest in the new business entity; and
- relief has been allowed where taxpayers borrowed money to buy shares in a close company formed to put into effect a management buy-out, even though the company had not started trading when the loans were taken out: the High Court said that if a loan was made and shares subscribed to enable a company to acquire a business, it could be said that the company existed for the purpose of carrying on that business and that the acquisition of the business was the means by which that purpose was to be achieved and not an end in itself (*Lord (HMIT) v Tustain [1993] BTC 447*).

Investors with a 'material interest'

The company must be a qualifying close company at the time the interest is paid and the borrower must have a material interest in the company. Basically, an individual has a material interest if he, alone or with any associate(s), owns beneficially or is able to control more than five per cent of the ordinary share capital of the company or would be entitled to more than five per cent of the assets on a winding up, etc. (for accounting periods beginning before 1 April 1989: five per cent of the apportionable income). As well as holding a material interest, the claimant must also show that he has not recovered any capital from the company apart from any amount taken into account in reducing the interest eligible for relief. If the company exists wholly or mainly to hold investments or other property, the borrower must not use property held by the company as a residence unless he has spent the majority of his time in the management or conduct of the company's business or that of an associated company.

Note that the definition of 'associate' for the purpose of establishing a material interest prevents the personal shares of other trust beneficiaries being aggregated with those of the participator. The effect is that close company interest relief is not available where a material interest has been artificially created by a token trust holding.

Investors managing the company

At the time the interest is paid the company must be a qualifying close company and the borrower must hold shares of the company. Up to the date of the interest payment, the borrower must have worked for the majority of his time in the management or conduct of the company or of an associated company. He must also show that he has not recovered any capital up to the time interest is paid apart from any amount taken into account in reducing the interest eligible for relief.

Relief in respect of shares acquired is denied if the acquirer or his spouse claims EIS relief in respect of them. Relief continues to be denied whatever relief is claimed under the new EIS (which combines the old EIS relief with reinvestment relief for CGT).

Law: ITA 2007, s. 392, 409(1)–(2), 410

Other guidance: SP 3/78, *Close companies: income tax relief for interest on loans applied in acquiring an interest in a close company*

68.3.2 Acquiring an interest in a close company

Interest paid is eligible for relief, if it is interest on a loan to an individual to defray money applied:

- in acquiring any part of the ordinary share capital of a close company complying with CTA 2010, s. 34(1);
- in lending to such a close company money which is used wholly and exclusively for the purposes of the business of the company or of any associated company of it which is a close company satisfying any of those conditions; or
- in paying off another loan interest on which would have been eligible for relief had the loan not been paid off (on the assumption, if the loan was free of interest, that it carried interest).

The relief is unavailable if the person who acquires the shares, or that person's spouse, claims relief under the enterprise investment scheme (see **Chapter 64**) in respect of shares acquired up to 5 April 1998 or, in relation to shares acquired after that date, claims relief under TCGA 1992, Sch. 5B.

In addition, the close company must satisfy one of two sets of conditions.

Law: ITA 2007, s. 392

First set of qualifying conditions

When the interest is paid the individual must have a 'material interest' (see below) in the company ('the relevant company'), which must continue, throughout the accounting period, to exist wholly or mainly for any one or more of the following purposes (CTA 2010, s. 34(2)):

- to carry on a trade or trades on a commercial basis;
- to invest in land or estates or interests in land, the land being, or intended to be, let to persons other than a person either 'connected with' the company or who is the spouse or civil partner of an individual connected with it or a 'relative' (brother, sister, ancestor or lineal descendant), or spouse or civil partner of a relative, of such an individual or such an individual's spouse or civil partner;

- to hold securities of, or make loans to, one or more companies each of which is a 'qualifying company' (see below) or a company which is under the control of the relevant company, or of a company which has control of the relevant company, and which itself wholly or mainly exists to hold securities of, or make loans to, one or more qualifying companies;
- to coordinate the administration of two or more qualifying companies;
- of a trade or trades carried on a commercial basis by one or more qualifying companies or a company which has control of the relevant company;
- of the making, by one or more qualifying companies or by a company which has control of the relevant company, of investments as mentioned in the second bullet point above. A company is a 'qualifying company' if it:

    (a) is under the control of the relevant company or of a company which has control of the relevant company; and
    (b) exists wholly or mainly for at least one of purposes the first two bullet points above (CTA 2010, s. 34(6)).

Material interest

A person has a material interest in a company for the purpose of the conditions set out above if he, either on his own or with one or more 'associates', or if any associate of his with or without such other associates:

- is the beneficial owner of, or able, directly or through the medium of other companies, or by any other indirect means to control, more than five per cent of the ordinary share capital of the company; or
- possesses, or is entitled to acquire, such rights as would, in the event of the winding up of the company or in any other circumstances, give an entitlement to receive more than five per cent of the assets which would then be available for distribution among the participators.

For the purposes of ascertaining whether an individual has a material interest, 'associate' means.

(1) A relative or partner of the individual.

(2) The trustees of any settlement in relation to which the individual (or one of his relatives) was the settler.

(3) The trustees of a settlement, or personal representatives of a deceased person, where the property subject to trusts (in which the individual has an interest) includes shares or obligations of the company. However, this does not apply to the trustees of an approved profit sharing scheme in relation to shares held by them in accordance with the scheme, and not yet appropriated to an individual, or to the rights exercisable by them.

In relation to loans made before 14 November 1986, an individual's associates include any person interested in a trust which holds shares or obligations of a company in which the individual himself has an interest. However, the personal shares of other trust beneficiaries are dissociated from those of the individual and his relatives and partners in determining whether he has a material interest. 'Relative', for these purposes, means the participator's husband or wife, parent or remoter forebear, child or remoter issue, or brother or sister.

In relation to a loan made after 26 July 1989, or for shares acquired under employee share ownership plans, or enterprise management incentives where the individual has an interest in shares or obligations of the company as beneficiary of an 'employee benefit trust', the trustees are not regarded as associates of his by reason only of that interest unless, at any time after that date:

- the individual, either on his own or with an associate(s); or
- any associate of his, with or without such associates,

has been beneficial owner of, or able (directly or through the medium of other companies or by any other indirect means) to control more than five per cent of the ordinary share capital of the company.

An 'employee benefit trust' is a trust:

- under which all or most of a company's employees are eligible to benefit; and
- none of whose property has been disposed of after 26 July 1989 (whether by sale, loan or otherwise) except in the ordinary cause of its management or qualifying disposals within ITEPA 2003, s. 551.

Second set of qualifying conditions

(1) At the time when the interest is paid, the company continues to comply with CTA 2010, s. 34(2) (see above) and the individual holds any part of the ordinary share capital of the company.

(2) In the period from the application of the proceeds of the loan to the payment of the interest the individual has worked for the greater part of his time in the actual management or conduct of the company (see below) or of an associated company of the company.

(3) He shows that in the period from the application of the proceeds of the loan to the payment of the interest he has not recovered any capital from the company apart from any amount taken into account in reducing the interest eligible for relief under ITA 2007, s. 393.

'Greater part of his time' is interpreted by HMRC as meaning more than one-half the normal working day throughout the period in question, apart from normal holidays.

Company ceasing to be close

Provided the company was a close company at the time when the loan was applied, relief on interest will continue to be available if the company thereafter ceases to be close, provided the other conditions for relief are satisfied (SP 3/78).

Reorganisations

Relief may continue to be available where the close company is the subject of a take-over.

Under the provisions relating to investment in close companies, employee-controlled companies, co-operatives and partnerships, the conditions imposed would normally mean that relief will be lost when certain business reorganisations take place, e.g.:

- the incorporation of a partnership (because the individual will no longer be a partner); and
- where a company is taken over by means of a share exchange (because the individual will no longer hold the shares he acquired with the loan, or will not hold shares in the company to which he lent the proceeds of the loan).

Relief is, however, preserved where:

- the original loan qualified for relief under the above provisions;
- the company (close or employee-controlled), partnership or co-operative is the subject of a transaction whereby the individual acquires shares in, or lends money to another company or co-operative; and
- had the original loan been made at the time of this transaction and applied for the purchase of the shares acquired or the money lent under the transaction, it would have qualified under one of the provisions relating to close companies, employee-controlled companies or co-operatives.

Where these conditions are satisfied, the original loan is treated as having been used for the purchase of the 'new' shares or lending money to the 'new' company or co-operative.

The predecessor legislation did not contain any provisions for the continuation of relief in such circumstances but ESC A43 provided for relief in similar terms and has therefore now been given statutory effect.

Law: ITA 2007, s. 410(1), (2)

68.4 Interest on loan to invest in a co-operative

68.4.1 General

A co-operative is a common ownership enterprise or a co-operative enterprise as defined in the *Industrial Common Ownership Act* 1976, s. 2.

An individual is entitled to relief on interest on a loan used:

- in acquiring shares in a body which is a 'co-operative';

- in lending money to a co-operative which is used wholly and exclusively for the purposes of the business of that co-operative or one of its subsidiaries; or
- in repaying another loan which itself was used for either of those purposes.

The following conditions must also be satisfied:

- when the interest is paid, the body concerned continues to be a co-operative;
- in the period from the use of the loan to the payment of the interest, the individual has worked for the greater part of his time as an employee of the co-operative or one of its subsidiaries; and
- he has not recovered any capital from the co-operative, apart from any amount taken into account in reducing the interest eligible for relief.

The predecessor legislation, former ICTA 1988, s. 361, contained a further requirement that the loan must have been taken out after 10 March 1981; this has not been repeated in the *Income Tax Act* 2007. In the unlikely event that there are loans still in existence which were taken out before that date, they will, assuming all other conditions are satisfied, now qualify for relief with effect from 6 April 2007.

Law: ITA 2007, s. 401

68.5 Interest on loan to invest in an employee-controlled company

68.5.1 General

Interest may be eligible for income tax relief if it is paid on a loan made to an individual to acquire ordinary shares in an employee-controlled company or to pay off another loan which would have qualified for interest relief.

Conditions for relief

Relief will only be given if the following conditions are satisfied.

(1) The company must be (from the date on which the shares are acquired to the date on which interest is paid):

    (a) an unquoted company resident only in the UK; and

    (b) a trading company or the holding company of a trading company.

(2) The shares must be acquired before, or not later than 12 months after, the date on which the company first becomes an employee-controlled company.

(3) During the tax year in which the interest is paid, the company must either:

    (a) first become an employee-controlled company; or

    (b) be employee-controlled throughout a period of at least nine months.

(4) The individual must be a full-time employee of the company from the date of

buying the shares to the date on which the interest is paid. Relief will continue to be given for interest paid up to 12 months after the taxpayer has ceased to be a full-time employee.

(5) The taxpayer must not have recovered any capital from the company unless that amount is treated as a repayment of the loan in whole or in part.

What is an employee-controlled company?

A company is an employee-controlled company at any time when at least 50 per cent:

- of the issued ordinary share capital of the company; and
- of the voting power in the company,

is beneficially owned by persons who are full-time employees of the company.

Where an individual owns beneficially more than ten per cent of the issued ordinary share capital or controls more than ten per cent of the voting power in the company, the excess over ten per cent is not regarded as being owned by a full-time employee.

Law: ITA 2007, s. 397

68.5.2 Loan applied in investing in employee-controlled company

Interest paid is eligible for relief under ITA 2007, s. 397 if it is interest on a loan to an individual to defray money applied:

- in acquiring any part of the ordinary share capital of an employee-controlled company; or
- in paying off another loan, interest on which would have been eligible for relief had the loan not been paid off (on the assumption, if the loan was free of interest, that it carried interest).

The following conditions must also be satisfied in order for the interest to be eligible for relief.

(1) Throughout the period from the date the shares are acquired to the date on which the interest is paid, the company is:

    (a) an unquoted company resident in the UK and not resident elsewhere; and

    (b) a trading company or the holding company of a trading group.

(2) During the tax year in which the interest is paid, the company either:

    (a) becomes an employee-controlled company for the first time; or

    (b) is such a company throughout a period of at least nine months.

Interest on Loan to Invest in an Employee-Controlled Company 68.5.2

(3) Either; if at that date he has ceased to be such an employee, ending with whichever is the later of:

  (a) the individual is a full-time employee of the company, throughout the period beginning with the date on which the proceeds of the loan is used to acquire the shares to the date on which the interest is paid; or

  (b) he ceased to be an employee not more than 12 months before the interest payment date, but was a full-time employee throughout the period from the use of the loan to the date of cessation.

(4) He has not recovered any capital from the company, apart from any amount taken into account, in reducing the interest eligible for relief.

> **Warning!**
> Where, however, the business carried on by the company is the occupation of woodlands on a commercial basis, relief is denied.

A company is employee-controlled at any time when more than 50 per cent of the issued ordinary share capital of the company and of the voting power in the company is beneficially owned by persons who are full-time employees of the company.

Where an individual owns beneficially more than ten per cent of the issued ordinary capital of, or voting power in, a company, the excess will be treated as being owned by an individual who is not a full-time employee of the company.

Definitions

A 'full-time employee' in relation to a company means a person who works for the greater part of his time as an employee or director of the company or of a 51 per cent subsidiary of the company.

A 'holding' company means a company whose business (disregarding any trade carried on by it) consists wholly or mainly of the holding of shares or securities of one or more companies which are its 75 per cent subsidiaries.

A 'trading company' means a company whose business consists wholly or mainly of the carrying on of a trade or trades.

A 'trading group' means a group the business of whose members, taken together, consists wholly or mainly of the carrying on of a trade or trades, and for this purpose 'group' means a company which has one or more 75 per cent subsidiaries, together with those subsidiaries. An 'unquoted company' means a company none of whose shares are listed in the Official List of the Stock Exchange.

Law: ITA 2007, s. 396

68.6 Interest on loan to invest in partnership

68.6.1 General

Interest is eligible for relief if it is interest on a loan to an individual used:

- to purchase a share in a partnership;
- to contribute money to a partnership by way of capital or premium, or by way of loan, where it is used wholly for the purposes of the trade or profession carried on by the partnership; or
- in paying off another loan used for any of these purposes.

The predecessor legislation, former ICTA 1988, s. 362, required the money lent to the partnership to be used for the purposes of its 'trade, profession or vocation'. The reference to a 'vocation' was omitted when the legislation was re-written for the Income Tax Act 2007 because it was felt that it was actually impossible for a partnership to carry on a vocation. Where, however, the business carried on by the partnership is the occupation of woodlands on a commercial basis, relief is denied. Another restriction applies where the money is invested in a film partnership, where only 40 per cent of the eligible interest qualifies for relief.

The following conditions must also be satisfied:

(1) throughout the period from the use of the loan until the interest was paid, the individual has been a member of the partnership (including a 'sleeping partner' but not a limited partner or as a member of an investment limited liability partnership (defined as one whose business, for any accounting period, is mainly the making of investments from which it derives the greater part of its income (ITA 2007, s. 399(6)). Retirement as a partner will therefore terminate any right to relief for subsequent payments of interest (HMRC Manuals Relief Instructions RE432); and

(2) in that period he has not recovered any capital from the partnership, apart from any amount taken into account, in reducing the interest eligible for relief.

Interest may also be eligible for relief if a loan is used by a partner to buy land occupied by the partnership.

Law: ITA 2007, s. 398

68.6.2 Partners eligibility

Salaried partners

In SP A33 (11 June 1970) the Revenue acknowledged that the predecessor legislation extended 'to salaried partners in a professional firm who are allowed independence of action in handling the affairs of clients and generally so to act that they will be indistinguishable from general partners in their relations with clients'.

That Statement has been incorporated into ITA 2007 because an individual who is not a partner, is treated as a partner for these purposes if:

- the partnership carries on a profession (as opposed to a trade);
- the individual is employed in a senior capacity; and
- is allowed to act independently in dealing with clients and to act generally as a partner in relation to those clients.

Scottish partnerships

The Partnership Act 1890 applies in England, Wales and Scotland, but a few provisions specifically apply in Scotland but not in England; in particular, by s. 4(2), in Scotland a partnership is a legal person distinct from the partners of whom it is composed. This can cause some difficulties in determining who has paid and who is entitled to relief.

In the case of *Major (HMIT) v Brodie*, [1999] BTC 141 Mr and Mrs Brodie were partners in a trading partnership known as the 'Skeldon partnership' which, as a Scottish partnership, was a separate legal entity and was itself a partner in the 'Murdoch partnership' along with a Mr Murdoch. Mr and Mrs Brodie took out a loan and introduced the capital into the Skeldon partnership, which then in turn applied it for the purposes of a farming trade carried on by the Murdoch partnership. HMRC sought to deny interest relief under the predecessor legislation, former ICTA 1988, s. 362, on the grounds that the monies had not been applied for the purposes of the trade carried on by the Skeldon partnership. The Court held that a trade carried on by a partnership was carried on by the members of that partnership and by each of them. Thus, in its capacity as a partner in the Murdoch partnership, the Skeldon partnership was carrying on the farming trade of the Murdoch partnership and the funds had therefore been used for the purposes of a trade carried on by the Skeldon partnership. Although this concerned Scottish partnerships, the High Court considered that the same result would arise in the case of partnerships in England and Wales.

Relief following incorporation or reconstruction

Relief will continue to be available if the partnership is dissolved if the individual becomes a member (or a salaried partner) of a new partnership formed to carry on the whole or part of the undertaking of the old partnership and interest payable on the loan up to the dissolution qualified for relief. In such a case, the old and new partnerships are to be treated as if they were the same.

The conversion of a partnership into a limited liability partnership is not regarded by HMRC as a recovery of capital and therefore relief is not withdrawn in those circumstances (HMRC Manuals *Relief Instructions* RE433).

Relief also continues to be available following incorporation. In both these scenarios the predecessor legislation did not strictly provide for a continuation of

Interest Relief

relief. However this anomaly was remedied by former concession, ESC A43 (now enacted by ITA 2007, s. 409(1)–(2) and 410(2), the final paragraph of which provided for continuation of relief in these circumstances, provided 'the conditions for relief would have been met if the loan had been a new loan taken out by that person to invest in the new business entity. The rules restricting or withdrawing relief where the borrower recovers any capital from the business continue to apply in the normal way.'

Return of partnership capital

Capital contributed by a partner may appear in the balance sheet as a credit item separate from his current or drawings account or there may be a single account for both capital and drawings. Where separate accounts are maintained, repayments of capital will usually be apparent. HMRC will normally contend that a reduction in the credit balance on the current or drawings account amounts to a constructive repayment of capital, even though the account moves temporarily into debit. Where there is only a single account, drawings should be treated as coming primarily from profits (including past profits and capital profits) credited to it, and to that extent as not being a return of capital.

Example 68.1

C, on becoming a partner in A, B and C on 1 January 2007, pays £5,000 into the firm met partly by a loan of £4,000 on which he pays interest. The £5,000 is credited to an account with the firm used also to record C's share of profits and drawings.

The balance on the account at 31 December 2006 is £7,000, the increase of £2,000 representing undrawn profits. In the year to 31 December 2009, the account is credited with £2,000, C's share of business profits, and £1,000, his share of capital profit. Drawings of £4,000 are debited, leaving a balance of £6,000.

There is no return of capital in 2009, the balance of £6,000 excludes the original capital of £5,000 and no restriction of the interest claim is, therefore, necessary.

Example 68.2

The facts are the same as in the example above, except that in the year to 31 December 2010 the account is credited with £1,000, share of business profits, and debited with drawings of £4,000, leaving a balance of £3,000.

£2,000 of the capital has, therefore, been returned (£5,000 less balance of £3,000) and C is treated as if he had repaid that amount of his £4,000 loan with a consequent restriction of relief for subsequent payments of interest.

68.6.3 Loans to invest in film partnerships

Additional conditions are imposed on relief for an investment in a partnership where:

- that partnership carries on a trade whose profits are calculated under the special rules in ITTOIA 2005, Pt. 2, Ch. 9, relating to expenditure on the production or acquisition of films or sound recordings; and
- the loan raised by the individual is 'secured on an asset or activity of another partnership' (termed the 'investment partnership', of which the individual is, or has been a member; and
- at any time of the year the proportion of the profits of the investment partnership which are liable to income tax and to which he is entitled, is less than the proportion of his contribution to that partnership's capital.

Where these conditions are satisfied, the interest on a loan to invest in a film partnership which is eligible for relief is limited to 40 per cent of that which would otherwise be eligible.

These provisions were first introduced by FA 2006, s. 75 and apply in respect of payments of interest accruing on or after 10 March 2006 (ITA 2007, Sch. 2, para. 96). They are anti-avoidance measures designed to counter arrangements which seek to shelter the income from the exploitation of the film by loan interest payments. Such arrangements would involve the whole of the individual's investment in the film partnership being funded by a loan set at such a rate of interest as will be equal to the lease rental income from the film. In order to repay the borrowings, the individual invests his own capital in the investment partnership which has a non-resident corporate partner. Capital contributed to this partnership is around 75 per cent by the corporate partner and 25 per cent by the individuals and is invested in a financial instrument which is intended to generate the individuals a capital return sufficient to pay off the loans used to invest in the film partnership. During the life of that instrument the bulk of the income arising is due to the non-resident corporate partner but the position is reversed at the maturity of the financial instrument and the bulk of the capital is received by the individuals. By this means the individuals will have had the benefit of the trading losses of the film partnership caused by the initial expenditure on the production or acquisition of the master tapes, but the subsequent income will have been sheltered by the interest payments. The losses, which would otherwise have created a tax deferral until such time as profits were generated, have therefore been turned into an exemption.

A loan is 'secured on an asset or activity of another partnership' if there is an arrangement:

- whereby an asset of that partnership may be used or relied upon, wholly or partly to guarantee repayment of any part of the loan; or

Interest Relief

- under which any part of the loan is expected to be repaid out of the assets or income of that partnership, whether directly or indirectly.

'Partnership's capital' is interpreted in accordance with generally accepted accounting practice and any amounts lent by the partners or persons connected with them (ITA 2007, s. 400(3)). Connected persons for these purposes are:

- the individual's spouse or civil partner;
- the individual's relatives (i.e. siblings, ancestors or lineal descendants; ITA 2007, s. 994(1));
- the spouses or civil partners of the individual's relatives;
- the relatives of the individual's spouse or civil partner; and
- the spouses or civil partners of relatives of the individual's spouse or civil partner.

In determining at any point the amount of capital contributed to the investment partnership by the individual or those connected with him, the following are to be taken into account:

- any amount paid to acquire the interest in that partnership held at that point in time;
- any amount made available to another person (and, presumably, used by that person to acquire an interest in that partnership) so far as he has an interest in that partnership at that time;
- any amount the individual has lent to the partnership;
- any amount he has made available to another person which that person has lent to the partnership and which has not been repaid; and
- any other amounts prescribed by regulations made by HMRC.

Law: ITA 2007, s. 400

68.7 Interest on loan to pay inheritance tax

68.7.1 General

Relief is available to the personal representatives of a deceased person against the income arising in the estate for interest on a loan which is used:

- to pay inheritance tax and associated interest which they are obliged to pay under IHTA 1984, s. 226(2) (A document provided by a Revenue & Customs officer is to be taken to be sufficient evidence of these amounts; or
- in repaying an earlier loan which was used for that purpose.

Relief is only given so far as the interest is paid in respect of a period ending within one year from the making of the loan.

Where, for the year in which the interest is paid, there is insufficient income in the estate to enable full relief to be given, the unused relief may be carried back against income of the preceding tax years, later ones taking precedence over earlier ones. If this fails to exhaust the unused relief, it will instead be carried forwards against income of subsequent years in order.

The predecessor legislation, former ICTA 1988, s. 364, referred to payment of the capital transfer tax or inheritance tax which was payable before the grant of representation or confirmation on the delivery of the personal representatives' account and attributable to the value of personal property to which the deceased was beneficially entitled immediately before his death and which vests in the personal representatives or would vest in them if the property were situated in the UK. This derives from the time of estate duty and concepts which are no longer of relevance to inheritance tax; capital transfer tax, of course, is no longer chargeable. ITA 2007 achieves the same effect as s. 364 by a simple reference to the tax due under IHTA 1984, s. 226(2).

Law: ITA 2007, s. 430–405

68.8 Interest on loan to purchase life annuity

68.8.1 General

This is a relief which only applies to loans which were taken out before 9 March 1999 by individuals who were already over the age of 65. As a result, it is of limited application and the number of individuals affected will diminish every year. These provisions were not rewritten into the *Income Tax Act* 2007 and therefore are one of the few remaining provisions of ICTA 1988 which continue in force for income tax purposes.

Relief is given by means of a reduction in the claimant's tax liability at Step 6 of the calculation and the reduction is 23 per cent of the eligible interest paid in the tax year.

Relief is due in respect of interest on a loan in respect of which the following conditions are satisfied.

(1) The loan was made before 9 March 1999.

(2) The loan was made as part of a scheme under which not less than nine-tenths of the proceeds of the loan were applied to the purchase of an annuity by the person to whom the loan was made.

(3) The annuity is for the life of the borrower or for the joint lives of the borrower or one or more other persons ('the annuitants').

(4) At the time the loan was made, the borrower, or each of the annuitants, had attained the age of 65 years.

(5) The loan was secured on land in the UK or the Republic of Ireland and the borrower or one of the annuitants owned an interest in that land.

(6) If the loan was made after 26 March 1974, the borrower or each of the annuitants used the land on which it was secured as his only or main residence immediately before 9 March 1999.

Interest is only eligible if it is payable by the borrower or by one of the annuitants.

The conditions for relief allow someone over 65 with a life annuity 'home income plan' to leave their home without losing interest relief on the loan used to buy the annuity. Relief continues to be available for interest payments, where:

- a person leaves his main residence on which a loan; and
- within 12 months of leaving the property intends to dispose of it, and takes steps to actually do so.

The interest payments continue to attract relief for a period of 12 months from the date on which the property was vacated (or such longer time as the Commissioners for HMRC may allow), or the date on which the property was disposed of, if sooner.

In the case of a loan made after 26 March 1974, interest is only eligible for relief to the extent that the amount on which it is payable does not exceed £30,000 (the 'qualifying maximum'). Where the interest is payable by two or more persons, the interest payable by each of them is so eligible for relief on a proportion of the total eligible interest.

Where tax reductions are due under more than one provision of the Income Tax Acts for the same year, a specific order of priority is prescribed (ITA 2007, s. 27, 28).

A specific rule applies to loans which were used partly to purchase a life annuity and partly for some other qualifying purpose within ITA 2007, s. 383 attracting relief as a deduction from total income. In this situation, the interest is apportioned between on the basis of the proportions of the total amounts borrowed which were applied for the different purposes.

> **Planning point**
>
> An elderly person's investments may be producing poor returns and tying up large amounts of capital. An annuity from a competitive insurance company can often produce an equivalent return (and can be guaranteed for, say, five years at modest extra cost) by investing only part of the available funds because part of the annuity is tax free capital. This leaves the balance free to use or even give away. This can be particularly effective, perhaps in conjunction with single premium bonds, in protecting entitlement to age allowances.

Law: ICTA 1988, s. 365, 370; FA 1999, 39, 40; FA 2000, s. 83

68.9 Interest and other costs of borrowing

68.9.1 General

Interest paid on loans to, or overdrafts of, a business is generally deductible as a 'business expense', under general principles, provided the interest is paid wholly and exclusively for the purposes of the business and at a reasonable rate of interest; in the case of companies, the interest must be 'short' rather than 'annual' (see below) or, broadly, be payable on an advance from a bank. There are certain additional requirements for income tax purposes in relation to payments to non-residents. No deduction is allowed if the sole or main benefit to the payer from the transaction is a tax advantage.

It is not necessary for the loan to fall within one of the categories in respect of which an individual is permitted to deduct interest from total income, but interest which receives relief under those provisions may not also be deducted against business profits so as to give double relief.

No deduction is due if the loan effectively funds a proprietor's overdrawn current/capital account. In considering whether this is the case, accumulated realised profits must be distinguished from anticipated profits. A revaluation of business assets is therefore disregarded and the disallowance of the interest in point cannot be avoided by crediting the revaluation surplus to an overdrawn account.

Where a property development company charges disallowable interest to work in progress in accordance with 'correct' accounting practice, the interest need not be disallowed in the tax computation until it is effectively charged in the profits and loss account; conversely interest so charged is not allowable until it is similarly charged.

Incidental costs of business borrowings

Incidental costs of obtaining loan finance, such as fees, commissions, advertising and printing, are also specifically deductible in most cases. Such costs of taking out a life assurance policy as a precondition of receiving a loan would be included but the cost of the policy itself, i.e. the premiums, would, in the Revenue's view be excluded. The deduction for incidental costs is given at the same time as any other deduction in computing profits for income tax purposes.

Yearly (annual) interest

The interest on loans capable of lasting longer than one year (whether or not they do in fact do so) is yearly interest and deciding whether interest is in fact 'yearly interest', regard is had to the loan agreement and the intention of the parties. A loan repayable on demand has been held to be an investment on which yearly interest was paid. Interest on an informal loan replacing an overdraft by a parent company to its subsidiary has also been held to be yearly interest.

Law: ITTOIA 2005, s. 52, 58, 362(1)–(2); CTA 2009, s. 131; *Minsham Properties Ltd v Price (HMIT)* [1990] BTC 528; *Cairns v MacDiarmid (HMIT)* [1983] BTC 188; *Corinthian Securities Ltd v Cato* (1969) 46 TC 93

Other guidance: HMRC *Business Income Manual* para. BIM 45650 and BIM 45815

68.9.2 Costs of loan finance

The incidental costs of obtaining loan finance are deductible. This applies to costs of obtaining a loan in respect of which the interest is itself allowable, or by means of an issue of loan stock the interest on which is allowable.

A loan or loan stock which carries a right of conversion into, or a right to the acquisition of, shares or other such securities is disqualified if the right is exercisable within three years of the date when the loan is obtained or the stock issued. This three-year rule is relaxed if the right of conversion is not actually exercised within the three-year period. If the right of conversion is only exercised for part of the loan or security within the three-year period, the relief for the costs of the balance is obtainable.

'Incidental costs of obtaining finance' means expenditure on fees, commissions, advertising, printing and other incidental matters, wholly and exclusively incurred for the purpose of obtaining the finance, of providing security for it, or of repaying it. Stamp duty is not included. Expenditure on abortive applications is allowed if the expenditure would have qualified had the finance been obtained.

Income tax relief is not given under these rules for expenditure as a result of, or for obtaining protection against, fluctuations in currency exchange rates. Similarly, relief is not given for the cost of repaying a loan or loan stock so far as attributable to its being repayable at a premium or to its having been obtained or issued at a discount.

The legislation does not specify the timing of a deduction for incidental costs of finance. The HMRC view, at BIM 45820, is that the timing is determined by normal principles and that:

> 'where incidental costs have been spread or deferred in accounts, and those accounts have been correctly prepared under applicable accounting standards, it is not permissible to make an adjustment in the [business tax] computation to deduct all the costs in the year the loan finance is obtained'

Interest paid to non-residents

Special restrictions apply to interest paid to persons not resident in the UK. First, such payments are only allowable as a business deduction to the extent that the rate is a reasonable commercial one. Second, deduction is permitted for income tax only if either:

(1) The payer properly accounts for income tax at source.

(2) The following conditions are satisfied:

    (a) the business, etc. is carried on by a UK resident;
    (b) liability to pay the interest was incurred exclusively for business purposes;
    (c) either the liability was incurred wholly or mainly in respect of activities outside the UK, or else the interest is payable in a currency other than sterling;
    (d) the interest is, or may be, required to be paid outside the UK; and
    (e) the interest is in fact paid outside the UK.

The conditions in (2) above cannot be applied to:

- interest paid to a partner, or in respect of a share in the partnership capital; or
- interest paid by a trading company to a person with a controlling interest (or vice versa) or between persons over whom another person has control.

Interest deductible as a result of condition (1) above is deductible gross.

68.9.3 Interest paid on business loan to fund proprietor's overdraft

Interest paid on a loan used to fund the proprietor's overdrawn current or capital account is not deductible.

Useful guidance is given at BIM 45705ff, including the following paragraphs:

> 'The only foolproof way of ascertaining how much of an overdraft or loan has funded private expenditure is to look at each individual entry. This is usually impracticable and it is necessary to use a reasonable basis as an approximation.
>
> An overdrawn capital account shown in the balance sheet is no more than an indication that a loan or overdraft is being used to fund private drawings. You must be able to demonstrate that it is private drawings which have caused the account to become overdrawn and that the overdrawn capital account has been funded by bank borrowings. You must look carefully at all of the components of the balance sheet to judge how the proprietor's drawings have been funded.
>
> These sorts of issues were considered in *Silk v Fletcher* Sp C 201 (with final figures being determined in Sp C 262). The Special Commissioner's decision in Sp C 201 contains clear reasoning about the facts in that particular case to decide whether interest was paid wholly and exclusively for the purposes of the profession.'

> **Example 68.3**
>
> The following example is extracted from the HMRC *Business Income Manual*, para. BIM 45715.
>
> Mr A sets up a new shop called 'British Weather' selling rainwear. He introduces £50,000 capital and borrows £50,000 from the bank. After a good initial period of trading his business is disrupted by continual roadworks in the area followed by an area regeneration project. The business makes trading losses totalling £30,000 in the first two years. At the end of year two he has taken total drawings of £20,000 out of the business so his capital account is nil (capital introduced £50,000 less losses £30,000 less drawings £20,000). He sees signs of improvement to the business so borrows a further £50,000 from the bank. In year three he takes out drawings of £10,000 and the business makes a trading loss of £5,000, so his capital account is overdrawn by £15,000 at the end of the year. The restriction of the deduction for interest is based on the drawings of £10,000 and not on the total amount of the overdrawn capital account.

Other guidance: Silk v Fletcher (HMIT) (2000) Sp C 262

68.10 Finance lease rental payments

HMRC have issued a statement of practice (SP 3/91) on the way they treat rentals payable by lessees under finance leases entered into after 11 April 1991. The statement deals with the situation where Statement of Standard Accounting Practice (SSAP) No. 21 has been applied and also where SSAP 21 has not been applied. Its main thrust is to require an appropriate spreading of rental payments for tax purposes in accordance with the accruals concept. However, the statement also refers to the practice – in cases where SSAP 21 is applied – of allowing the depreciation charged in the accounts to be treated as the measure of the deductible 'capital' element of rental payments.

SSAP 21 distinguishes between two categories of leases: finance leases and operating leases. The difference between the two depends on whether most of the risks and rewards associated with ownership of the asset rest with the lessor or the lessee. Under a finance lease they rest with the lessee; under an operating lease with the lessor.

An operating lease (defined by SSAP 21 as any lease which is not a finance lease) is essentially a hire contract which involves the lessee paying rental for the use of the asset for a period of time normally substantially less than its useful economic life. Such expenditure would normally be deductible as business expenditure for tax purposes in full in the period to which it relates, subject to a restriction in the case of 'expensive' cars. Assets under operating leases should not be capitalised in the balance sheet. Capital allowances are not available for the lessee (though they may be for the lessor).

A finance lease usually involves payment by the lessee to the lessor of the full cost of the asset together with a finance charge. It is defined by SSAP 21 as a lease which transfers substantially all the risks and rewards of ownership to the lessee. A lease is presumed to come within this category if, at its inception, the present value of the minimum lease payments, including any initial payment, amounts to substantially all (this is taken to mean 90 per cent or more) of the fair value of the asset.

Under SSAP 21 a finance lease should be capitalised in the balance sheet (recognising the quasi-ownership of the asset) at the present value of the minimum lease payments (usually the fair value of the asset will do) and a corresponding creditor set up. Rentals payable are then apportioned between the finance charge, charged to profit and loss account, and the 'capital' repayment which reduces the outstanding balance sheet liability. The asset should be depreciated over the shorter of the lease term and its useful life. The lease term includes any secondary term (which usually depends on the exercise of an option by the lessee) where it is reasonably certain, at the start of the lease, that this will take place.

Planning point

Although capitalised in the lessee's balance sheet, assets under a finance lease do not attract capital allowances for the lessee. Any entitlement to capital allowances for qualifying expenditure rests with the lessor. The lessee fails the basic test – as under an operating lease – that the asset should belong to him (CAA 2001, s. 11). Payments made by the lessee under the lease have been, and continue to be, treated as revenue expenditure for the use of the asset. As such they are deductible in computing business profits. The finance charge element of lease payments passes through the profit and loss account and so presents no particular difficulty in terms of the business tax computation. However, the 'capital' repayment element is merely a balance sheet movement and thus a profits adjustment needs to be made for tax purposes. Again, a restriction applies in the case of 'expensive' cars. Depreciation, strictly, must be added back in the tax computation.

For finance leases under SSAP 21, SP 3/91 is of interest in that it states the Revenue's views on the spreading of deductions (and thus affects leases where rental payments are not spread evenly), and it permits properly computed commercial depreciation to be used as the measure of the deductible 'capital' repayment element of lease payments.

The accruals concept is to be applied to determine the deductibility of rental payments under finance leases which are not subject to SSAP 21; there is no entitlement as such to deduct the rentals simply by reference to the due dates of payment (for example, under a heavily front-loaded lease contract).

Indeed, the practice enjoined by SSAP 21, to the extent that it requires spreading of rental payments over the life of the lease, was upheld by the Court of Appeal in *Gallagher v Jones (HMIT)* [1993] BTC 310; *Threlfall v Jones (HMIT)* [1993] BTC 310 in the context of just such a heavily front-loaded lease contract. The court rejected the finding of Harman J that commercial accountancy practice required revenue expenditure to be allowed in the accounting period in which it was incurred.

Following *Gallagher v Jones (HMIT)*; *Threlfall v Jones (HMIT)* (above), and the issue by the Accounting Standards Board of FRS 5, *Reporting the Substance of Transactions*, HMRC published a lengthy article in *Tax Bulletin*, February 1995, cited in the 1996 revision of the text of SP 3/91 set out above. Under FRS 5, which provides for the substance of transactions within its scope to be reflected in accounts rather than their legal form, certain operating leases as understood by SSAP 21 are nonetheless treated as though they were finance leases, and HMRC apply SP 3/91 and the *Tax Bulletin* article to those leases also. The article also sets out the HMRC's approach to particular situations, a summary of which appears below.

(1) In certain leasing arrangements, amounts are paid by the lessee before the primary period, or during the primary period but while the asset is still being constructed or manufactured. Payments in the pre-primary period will usually consist of only a finance charge, but payments in the primary period may involve a further element being the balance of the full rentals due under the lease. Where the finance charge paid in the pre-primary period is capitalised, it will form part of the cost of the rights to be written off under SSAP 21 and the tax deduction will normally follow the accounts treatment when that write-off is made. Where the finance charge element is charged against commercial profits in the period in which it is incurred, and that treatment is in accordance with generally accepted accountancy practice, the treatment may be followed for tax. The further element, being the balance of rentals due under the lease, will, under SSAP 21, be set against the obligation outstanding, but no further tax deduction will be made (over and above the finance charge element) until the asset comes into use. The amount of that deduction in any period will normally be the depreciation charge calculated by reference to the shorter of the lease term (including any secondary or later periods) or the asset's useful life. HMRC regard an asset as coming into use when the rights in it start to be depreciated in the accounts drawn up under SSAP 21.

(2) Where there is likely to be a rebate to the lessee at the end of the lease, it should be taken into account in calculating at the inception of the lease the total rentals to be allocated to periods of account in accordance with SP 3/91. In other words, the total rentals deduction (leaving aside the finance charge element) should reflect the estimated reduction in value of the asset over the expected duration of the lease or expected useful life of the asset if that is shorter. The article adds that SSAP 21 accounting should normally achieve

that result without further adjustment, unless the lease term is significantly shorter than the useful life of the asset, and the asset is wholly written off over the lease term, in which case the deduction for rentals may need to be restricted in the tax computations for each period over which the asset is written off.

(3) If, during the term of a lease, there is a change in the rate at which a leased asset is depreciated and the revised view of the life of the asset can be justified, then the allocation of the rentals from the year of change should reflect the revision.

(4) In the same way, where a lease which has previously been regarded as an operating lease is subsequently treated in accordance with FRS 5 as if it were a finance lease, the prior year adjustment needed to make the transition will be taken into account for tax as a revenue item for the current period of account.

(5) Where a sale followed by a leaseback results in a profit because the capital value attributed to the asset for the purposes of the lease exceeds the book value up to the sale, the asset could under SSAP 21 be treated as sold and the profit amortised over the lease term, but under FRS 5 the asset must stay in the vendor's balance sheet at its book value and the sale proceeds be shown as a creditor. Under the first method, the finance and depreciation charges under SSAP 21 could be accepted for tax as a means of spreading rental payments in the same way as they would have been if the asset had been finance-leased from new. Under the second method, the sale and leaseback of the asset will be recognised. The non-finance charge element of the rentals will be represented by a deduction equal to the depreciation which would have been debited in the profit and loss account had the lease been dealt with under the first method, but the rate of depreciation applied in the accounts will normally indicate the rate to be applied in this computation.

(6) Where there are multiple assets under a single lease, HMRC will accept that in applying the approach in SP 3/91 the rentals may be apportioned on a systematic and reasonable basis to the various assets.

(7) Where long-life assets are leased, and (exceptionally) regulatory requirements prevent the rights in them from being depreciated in the lessee's accounts drawn up under SSAP 21, HMRC will (in those circumstances only) accept that allocation of the rentals to periods of account may proceed by reference to the depreciation which would reasonably have been charged in the absence of this requirement.

Where finance leases are of assets (such as buildings) which are not likely to lose value at all over the life of the lease, and the rights in the leased asset are not depreciated in the lessee's accounts, then only the finance charge element in the rentals is deductible over the period of the lease unless the rebate turns out to be less than the total non-finance charge element, in which case the difference will be deductible on termination. Where the lease of a non-depreciating building also includes depreciating fixtures, the two elements may be dealt with separately and relief obtained for the fixtures which depreciate.

(8) Where a finance lease contains provisions for a rebate or other adjustment by reference to the value of the asset at the end of the term, such sums are in essence adjustments of past revenue outgoings and should be taken into account in computing trading profits for the period in which they are recognised in the lessee's accounts. Where necessary, the sum paid or received on termination must be adjusted for tax so as to ensure that over the life of the lease, deductions are made for the aggregate rentals paid, net of any rebate but including any supplemental rental. Any exit charge on early termination of the lease would normally be capital, unless it wholly or partly represented an adjustment of past rentals, or was calculated by discounting future rentals and by taking into account the value of the asset on the premature termination.

69 Lloyd's Underwriters

69.1 Introduction

The Lloyd's insurance market started over 300 years ago in a coffee house. Lloyd's was incorporated by the Lloyd's Act 1871, becoming the Society and Corporation of Lloyd's. The activities of the Society and Corporation of Lloyd's are governed by the Lloyd's Acts 1981 to 1982 and the Insurance Companies Act 1982. Its principal role is the management of the affairs of the Lloyd's insurance market, the advancement and protection of Lloyd's members and the collection, publication and diffusion of intelligence and information.

The Lloyd's insurance market is unique, allowing individuals, and more recently corporations, to participate in the business of insurance through the syndicate mechanism. Lloyd's underwriters must be members of the Society and Corporation of Lloyd's and, generally, brokers must be approved by the society if they are to place business with Lloyd's underwriters on behalf of their clients.

A syndicate is the basic business unit at Lloyd's. Groups of members get together to form syndicates to do business. The syndicate members receive a share of trading profits, as well as a slice of the income and gains derived from invested premiums, in return for bearing a share of the insurance risks undertaken by the syndicate. A syndicate is not a separate legal entity and the syndicate members do not form a partnership. This has several implications; first, a name is regarded as carrying on business on his own account and second, because syndicate members are not in partnership, a name is only liable for his share of syndicate debts and losses. However, a name has unlimited liability for his share of the risks.

69.2 Syndicate accounts

69.2.1 Introduction

Syndicates' accounts are prepared annually on a calendar-year basis. Each year of trading is known as an 'underwriting account'. For example, the 2008 underwriting account runs from 1 January 2008 to 31 December 2008. At the end of the underwriting account, the books are kept open for a further two years so that claims can be settled and quantified. This period is known as the 'running off period'. At the end of this period, the account will normally be closed and any outstanding claims reinsured with the next account. For example, the 2010 account will close on 31 December 2012.

Where claims are too large or the extent of the claim too uncertain to allow the account to be reinsured with the next account, the account is left open and is known as a 'run-off account'. It will remain open until such time as all outstanding claims are settled or it becomes possible to reinsure into a subsequent account.

Once an account has been closed, the profits of the account are distributed amongst those participating in the account. It is the responsibility of the managing agent to maintain the syndicate accounting records and organise for the preparation and audit of the accounts.

To enable Lloyd's to be compared more favourably with its peers, a move to annual GAAP accounting applies from 2005. Syndicates must prepare existing three-year accounts and annual accounts from this year, although the normal distribution basis after three years continues.

Law: FA 1993, s. 176

69.2.2 Membership

No unlimited liability members have been allowed to join after 1 January 2003 but existing names may continue indefinitely or convert to one of the forms of limited liability membership.

There used to be a number of conditions, both personal and financial, that had to be satisfied before an individual could become a member of Lloyd's but most of these requirements have now been changed. Whilst Lloyd's will only wish to admit suitable candidates, the onus has now been mainly transferred to members' agents under the principle of 'know your client'. Entrance fees for new candidates and conversion fees for existing members still apply at various levels and these fees are not deductible for tax purposes.

There is a minimum requirement to lodge suitable Funds at Lloyd's of at least £350,000. Similarly, from 2002, the ratios of required Funds at Lloyd's compared with the overall premium income being written have been standardised between names and limited liability members so that a minimum of 40 per cent of the overall premium limit must be provided, subject to any risk-weighting by reference to the specific syndicates with which the member is involved. Thus, for members writing premium income of, say, £600,000, the overall minimum of £350,000 comes into play whereas, for members with premium income of, say, £1m, the minimum Funds at Lloyd's requirement would be £400,000 subject to any higher limit required under the risk-weighting assessment of the syndicates involved.

> **Planning points**
>
> Entrance fees for new candidates and conversion fees for existing members are payable, but such fees are not deductible for tax purposes.
>
> The present minimum requirement to lodge suitable Funds at Lloyd's is £350,000.

69.2.3 Funds at Lloyd's

'Funds at Lloyd's' are those funds held in trust at Lloyd's to support each member's underwriting activities. These funds comprise the Lloyd's deposit (see below) together with any personal or additional reserve funds established via the members' agent. Any special reserve fund assets could not be taken into account for this purpose up to 1999, but can now represent ten per cent of the overall premium limit which, together with the deposit and other reserves, make up the total funds at Lloyd's requirement of 40 per cent.

Names are required to maintain their funds at Lloyd's at all times and have to satisfy an annual solvency test. A name who fails the solvency requirements must provide additional funds before the start of the next underwriting year or have his underwriting limits reduced or perhaps be suspended from underwriting altogether. All assets held as funds at Lloyd's must be in the form of readily realisable assets or be provided by way of a letter of credit or bank guarantee.

The security provided by way of a name's funds at Lloyd's is in addition to the amount held by the managing agent in premium trust funds.

69.2.4 Lloyd's deposit

The Lloyd's deposit is a deposit held subject to the terms of the Lloyd's Deposit Trust Deed, must consist of readily realisable assets and must be maintained at a minimum level of £35,000 from 2002. Where a name is not resident in the UK, additional deposits may be required in certain circumstances. The Lloyd's deposit is a fund of last resort from the point of view of meeting losses, any special reserve or personal reserve funds being used first.

69.2.5 Overall premium limit

There is now no maximum on a name's overall premium limit which determines the amount of business which he may underwrite, but the limit must be supported by at least 40 per cent of readily realisable assets being held within the funds at Lloyd's. Thus, for a name who wishes to maintain an overall premium limit of, say,

£3m, there would have to be readily realisable assets held within his funds at Lloyd's of at least £1.2m.

69.2.6 Members' Agents Pooling Arrangement

A Members' Agents Pooling Arrangement ('MAPA') is an administrative arrangement under which a member's agent pools underwriting capacity and the participating members share rateably in participations across a spread of syndicates. The Lloyd's members effectively pool their rights to participate in various syndicates. Those syndicate rights are chargeable assets for capital gains tax purposes. The position is complicated in that changes in syndicate rights within the MAPA and changes in the members participating in the MAPA are all potential occasions of charge to capital gains tax for all of the participating members.

Law: FA 1999, s. 82

69.2.7 Annual subscription

A name is required to pay an annual subscription to Lloyd's which is allowable for tax purposes. After the first year of membership, the underwriting agent usually pays the fee on the name's behalf and deducts it from any profits to which he is entitled. The first subscription is usually paid by the name to the agent who passes it on to the committee. An underwriting agent is an individual, firm or company which has complied with the requirements of the Lloyd's Committee for carrying on an Underwriting Agency at Lloyd's. There are now only three registered members' agents operating within Lloyd's.

> **Planning point**
>
> The annual Lloyd's subscription is allowable for tax purposes.

69.2.8 Membership — first three years and after

A name does not receive any distribution of profits from the syndicate during the first three calendar years in which he is a member. Every underwriting account (syndicate trading account) remains open for not less than three years during which time the agent handles premiums for members and deals with any claims and pays any administrative charges. He then invests those premiums, but the name only has an interest in the capital gains which are made from the investment of his deposit and the income from it.

The amounts deposited with Lloyd's provide the first fund to meet claims which exceed premiums received. There is no disposal for capital gains tax or inheritance tax purposes when the securities are transferred into the name of Lloyd's. The Corporation of Lloyd's or the syndicate managers hold the name's investments as bare trustees. The name must agree to the selling and reinvestment of such investments. If any disposal of these investments is subject to capital gains tax, it is the responsibility of the name to return it on his personal tax return.

Once a name has been a member for three years, he receives a set of accounts which include the results of the first year of underwriting. They detail the profits and losses made by the syndicate in that year and the amount apportioned to the name which is then transferred into his own account. Thereafter, the name is entitled to a share of the profits and must bear a share of the losses made each year by the syndicates of which he is a member.

69.3 Taxation of Lloyd's underwriters

69.3.1 Introduction

The Finance Act 1994 introduced far-reaching changes to the basis of assessment for underwriting profits. The revised basis, which took effect for the 1994 and subsequent accounts, enables the self assessment provisions to be applied without the need for complex modification. The revised rules basis also brought the treatment of individual underwriters into line with that introduced for corporate underwriters.

For 1994 and subsequent accounts, profits are assessed in the tax year corresponding to that in which the results are declared and distributed For example, the 2006 account closes on 31 December 2008 and the results are declared in 2009. As the underwriting year 2009, the year in which the results are declared, corresponds to the tax year 2009–10, the profits of the 2006 account are assessed in 2009–10. This basis of assessment is known as the 'distribution year basis'.

Law: FA 1993, s. 172(1), as amended by FA 1994, Sch. 21, para. 2

69.3.2 Underwriting income and gains

An underwriter will receive income and gains from various sources, comprising some or all of the following:

- underwriting profits;
- syndicate investment income;
- interest and dividends from investments from the name's ancillary trust funds, Lloyd's deposit and personal reserve funds (but not the special reserve fund);
- income charges under the accrued income scheme;

- capital appreciation in respect of investments acquired with the syndicate's premium income;
- capital gains arising on the disposal of investments from the name's ancillary trust funds, Lloyd's deposit, other personal reserve funds (but not the special reserve fund) and syndicate capacity;
- income, gains and withdrawals from the name's special reserve fund;
- stop loss recoveries; and
- compensation receipts.

69.3.3 Trading income

As a result of the simplifications introduced by the Finance Act 1993, assessable Lloyd's trading income comprises two elements:

- syndicate-related income; and
- other income.

The first category includes pure underwriting profits and premiums trust fund income and gains (including the annual appreciation/depreciation of trust fund assets).

'Other income' covers income from ancillary trust funds, Lloyd's deposit and any personal reserve funds but not income arising from assets held in the new-style special reserve funds.

Since 6 April 1993, Lloyd's trading income has been regarded as earned income for all names, wherever resident.

External names, in addition to working names, have always been liable to Class 2 and 4 National Insurance contributions. However, the liability for external names was only enforced from 5 January 1997 in the case of Class 2 NIC and from 1997–98 in the case of Class 4 NIC on profits and gains chargeable to income tax.

> **Planning points**
>
> A name can apply for small earnings exception from Class 2 NICs if expected self-employed earnings will be below the annual exemption limit.
>
> It may be appropriate to claim deferment of Class 4 contributions where the name is paying Class 1 or Class 4 NIC in respect of other earnings.

Law: FA 1993, s. 180

Other guidance: Lloyd's market bulletin, 10 April 1997

69.3.4 Allowable deductions

Apart from the expenses normally deductible from income from self-employment, there are a number of special items applicable to Lloyd's underwriters. A cash basis applies so that, generally, expenses paid in a calendar year are deductible in the tax year in which the calendar year ends.

Expenses incurred by the managing agent of the syndicate on behalf of the name are allowed in the corresponding underwriting year in which the results are declared. Therefore, expenses incurred in the year ended 31 December 2007 will be allowed in arriving at the 2007 account profit which is taxable in the 2010–11 year of assessment.

Relief for accountancy fees is given on a cash basis. The expenses deductible are those actually paid in the underwriting year. Thus, for example, accountancy fees paid in the calendar year 2009 are allowable as a trading deduction in 2009–10.

Where a name holds an estate protection plan, the premiums paid in a calendar year are allowable in the tax year in which the calendar year ends.

The subscription to the Association of Lloyd's Members (ALM) and the cost of the Lloyd's underwriting syndicates (Blue Book) are allowable on a cash basis, as are any additional expenses.

Where a name takes out insurance against losses in his underwriting business, known as a stop loss policy, the premiums paid are allowable – on a cash basis – as a deduction in computing his trading profit.

Quota share contract premiums are premiums paid by a name to induce another person to take over his liabilities. Deductions are given on a cash basis. Relief for reinsurance premiums has been available since 1987.

Litigation fees and subscriptions to action groups are generally allowable.

Relief for payments of interest depends on the purpose for which the money is borrowed.

Interest on money borrowed to fund underwriting losses is allowable on a cash basis.

Law: FA 1993, s. 172(1) (a) and (c)

69.4 Treatment of losses

In recent years, Lloyd's has suffered heavily and many names suffered losses in the 1998/2001 accounts. Given this climate, it is increasingly important that losses are utilised efficiently. Any loss suffered must first be set against a withdrawal from the name's special reserve fund. Any withdrawal from a name's special reserve fund is treated as a trading receipt which will reduce or eliminate the loss. Withdrawals from the special reserve fund are made gross.

A name is treated as carrying on the business of underwriting and, thus, any loss is regarded as a trading loss. The provisions for relieving trading losses generally apply, with some modification, to any loss remaining after set-off against any withdrawal from the name's special reserve fund. Thus, a name may relieve an underwriting loss in one or more of the following ways:

- set-off against general income;
- under the provisions for losses incurred in the early years of a trade;
- against future underwriting income;
- under the terminal loss relief provisions; or
- against chargeable gains.

In common with other taxpayers, Lloyd's underwriters were affected by the changes to the trading loss provisions as a result of the introduction of self assessment.

Losses for a tax year are those declared in the corresponding underwriting year. For example, a loss which arises in the 2006 account would be a loss for the tax year 2009–10. The results of this account are declared in 2009–10 (the 2009 underwriting year), which corresponds to the tax year 2009–10. This basis allows the self-assessment provision to be applied to Lloyd's underwriters without the need for complex modification.

The business of underwriting is treated as a trade and consequently a name is entitled to take advantage of the provisions for relieving losses made in the early years of trade. Where a name sustains a loss in the first tax year in which he carries on the trade of underwriting, or any of the next three tax years, he can claim for relief against income of the three tax years preceding the tax year in which the loss was sustained. In relieving the loss, income for an earlier year is taken before income of a later year.

A name may also carry forward underwriting losses for set-off against future underwriting income. The loss may be carried forward indefinitely, provided the name continues to underwrite. For this purpose, income from his trade as a Lloyd's underwriter includes income from a name's ancillary funds, Lloyd's deposit and personal reserve funds. A claim is needed to establish the loss. Relief under this provision is normally only claimed once all other options have been considered.

Where a name ceases to carry on his underwriting business, either as a result of death or resignation, he can claim relief for the loss of his final underwriting account (provided he is not in run-off syndicates) against his underwriting profits of the preceding three tax years. For this purpose, underwriting profits include trading profits (after deducting losses brought forward), income from a name's ancillary funds, Lloyd's deposit and personal reserve funds. Relief is given against Lloyd's income of the preceding tax year and, once those profits are reduced to nil, to the year before that. Any unused balance of loss is then given against Lloyd's income of the year before that.

Example 69.1

Richard commenced underwriting in 1997. He suffers a loss for the 2006 account of £20,000. He has no special reserve fund, nor any personal fund income or expenses. He has other income of £135,000 in 2008–09 and £150,000 in 2009–10.

The distribution year basis of assessment applies. The results for the 2006 account are declared in the underwriting year 2009, which corresponds to the tax year 2009–10.

Richard can either set the loss against his income of 2009–10 or against his income of 2008–09. He must make a claim by 31 January 2012.

Special rules apply to determine a name's last underwriting year for the purposes of a terminal loss relief claim under ITA 2007, s. 89, and consequently the normal rules for determining the date of cessation contained in FA 1993, s. 179 are not in point.

A name is able to claim relief for underwriting losses against his chargeable gains of the year in which the loss is made and the preceding year. The relief, which operates as an extension of relief for set-off against general income (ITA 2007, s. 64) is only available for so much of the loss that cannot be relieved against the claimant's other income for the year of the loss and has not already been relieved against income of a previous year.

A name cannot claim relief against chargeable gains arising for a tax year which commenced after he ceased to trade as an underwriter.

Law: ITA 2007, s. 64, 71, 89

69.5 Chargeable gains

Underwriters will receive income and gains from various sources. The main sources of capital gains and losses are:

- capital gains arising on disposals of investments for the name's Lloyd's deposit, old-style special reserve fund (if any) and other personal reserve funds;
- for 1993 and earlier accounts, unrealised gains and losses arising from the annual revaluation of syndicate funds at 31 December each year;
- for 1993 and earlier accounts, realised gains on disposals of assets from a name's premiums trust fund; and
- the disposal of syndicate rights in Lloyd's syndicates.

Planning point

Disposal of a syndicate chargeable asset will generate a gain or loss. However, such gains/losses are assessed to income tax rather than capital gains tax.

Law: FA 1993, s. 171(1), (2), 172(1)(b), 176, 184(1)

Non-syndicate gains and losses – 1992–93 and subsequent tax years

A name may be liable to capital gains tax (CGT) on gains arising from the disposal of assets from an ancillary trust fund of his. Broadly, an ancillary trust fund is any trust fund required or authorised by the rules of Lloyd's or required by a member's agent or the managing agent of any syndicate in which the name participates; it does not include a premiums trust fund or his (new-style) special reserve fund, if any. The Lloyd's deposit and personal reserve funds are ancillary trust funds for this purpose.

A name is treated for CGT purposes as absolutely entitled against the trustees to assets forming part of an ancillary trust fund of his. Gains and losses arising from disposals of assets in ancillary trust funds remain within the CGT regime, and are computed in accordance with the normal CGT rules.

Any pooling election for quoted securities does not extend to assets held in an underwriter's ancillary trust funds or special reserve funds.

Gains and losses on ancillary trust funds will be amalgamated with non-Lloyd's gains for the purpose of computing a name's CGT liability for a particular year.

Example 69.2

Annabel's tax return shows the following gains and losses for 2006–2007:

	£
Lloyd's deposit – net gain	12,952
Personal reserve fund – net loss	(6,895)
Non-Lloyd's gains	10,978

Annabel has capital losses brought forward from 2005–06 of £4,566. She is liable for CGT at the marginal rate of 40 per cent.

Her capital gains tax computation for 2006–07 is as follows:

	£	£
Non-Lloyd's gains		10,978
Funds at Lloyd's Lloyd's deposit Personal reserve fund	12,952	(6,895)
		6,057
Net gains		17,035
Less: annual exemption		(8,800)
		8,230
Less: losses brought forward from 2005–06		(4,566)
Chargeable gains		3,660
Capital gains tax at 40%		1,467.60

Law: FA 1993, s. 176; 184

69.5.1 Syndicate gains and losses – 1994 and subsequent accounts

Premiums received by a member or by managing agents on behalf of a member are placed in premiums trust funds and are available for payment of reinsurance premiums, claims and other syndicate expenses. Each member has three funds:

- a sterling fund;
- a US dollar fund (known as the 'Lloyd's American trust fund'); and
- a Canadian dollar fund (known as the 'Lloyd's Canadian trust fund').

A name is regarded as absolutely entitled as against the trustees to the syndicate assets held in the premiums trust funds.

Unrealised gains and losses

All investments held in the premiums trust funds are revalued annually on 31 December.

From the 1994 account onwards, the annual appreciation is chargeable to income tax, as for syndicate profits and losses. Although this simplifies the taxation of underwriting syndicates, the name loses the benefit of the indexation allowance, where available.

Realised gains

Actual disposal of syndicate chargeable assets will generate gains and losses.

However, for 1994 and subsequent accounts any gains/losses arising from disposals of syndicate assets are assessed to income tax under ITTOIA 2005 rather than CGT, 'profits' so charged including gains.

For any tax year, a name's syndicate gains and losses will be his share of the syndicate gains or losses allocated to the corresponding underwriting account. The syndicate accountants report each member's share of syndicate gains and losses on their taxation advice slip. The apportionment is based on the contribution made to that year's portfolio by each of the open years: for example, the realised gains or losses arising from disposals during the calendar year 2009 will be apportioned to the 2007 account, the 2008 account and 2009 account. The method of apportioning gains in this way is in accordance with the 'Riesco formula'. Any gains or losses arising in respect of a run-off account are allocated to the underwriting account closed at the end of that year: for example, gains in 2007 in respect of a 1995 run-off account will be credited to the 2007 account.

69.6 Lloyd's estates

In general, income received prior to death cannot have post-death income tax consequences. However, in the case of Lloyd's estates there is an interesting provision under which pre-death losses carried forward by the deceased can be set by the personal representatives against post-death Lloyd's income which would otherwise be assessable on them. This means that the personal representatives are treated as if they were continuing the deceased's business. Once the Lloyd's affairs have subsequently been wound up and the deposit released from the Corporation at Lloyd's, the release of any net income by the personal representatives (as part of the Lloyd's assets) to the person or persons entitled under the will or intestacy will carry no further income tax implications for the beneficiaries.

> *Planning point*
>
> Personal representatives can carry forward pre-death losses of the deceased and set them against post-death Lloyd's income which would otherwise be assessable on them.

Law: Lloyd's Underwriters (Tax) Regulations 1995 (SI 1995/351), reg. 12)

69.7 Payment of tax

69.7.1 Introduction

Formerly, members' agents were responsible for deducting basic rate tax from all syndicate profits collected on behalf of their names (after deducting losses for the year), making a return to the Revenue and paying this tax on behalf of names. Since the 1994 account, all such profits have been distributed gross to names who now have full responsibility for returning their trading result. Consequently, members' agents do not now need to make returns direct to HMRC in connection with syndicate results. Managing agents continue to be responsible for making returns to HMRC for each syndicate result for which they are responsible and these returns are considered below.

69.7.2 Returns by managing agents

The managing agent is required to make a return of the syndicate profit or loss for the tax year in question. For 1997–8 and subsequent years the submission date is the later of 1 September in the tax year or three months from the date on which the notice is served. If the managing agent fails to make the return within the prescribed time limit, he may be liable to a penalty at the rate of £50 per day for each 50 (or odd part thereof) members of the syndicate for as long as the failure continues. The maximum penalty for fraudulently or negligently delivering an incorrect return is £3,000 multiplied by the number of members in the syndicate.

Once the HMRC officer is satisfied that the return shows the correct profit or loss, he will issue a determination.

The managing agent is also required to supply HMRC with an apportionment schedule showing what part of the profit or loss belongs to each member of the syndicate.

In addition, the managing agent is required to make returns of any payments of interest on gilt-edged securities made gross to premiums trust funds and of tax for which he is accountable.

Since 1992/93, the member's agent is not required to deduct and pay over basic rate tax, which is wholly due by names.

69.7.3 HMRC's determination: returns by managing agent

The profit or loss is determined in accordance with the return delivered to HMRC, if they are satisfied that it affords correct and complete information. If HMRC are not so satisfied, or if no return has been made, the HMRC officer is required to determine the syndicate profit or loss to the best of his judgment. If, after making his determination, he later discovers that this determination understates profits or overstates losses, he may vary the original determination. Notice of any determination must be served on the managing agent, and must state the time for appealing. After the notice of determination has been served, it may not be altered, otherwise than in accordance with the express provisions of the Taxes Acts.

69.7.4 Appeals against HMRC's determination

The agent may appeal by written notice given to the inspector within 30 days of the date of the HMRC notice.

Although rare following the introduction of the distribution basis of assessment and the self assessment tax regime which allows more time for agreement, nevertheless, where the agent has appealed, and a name has been assessed and has appealed against that assessment, TMA 1970, s. 55 (recovery of tax not postponed) applies subject to the following modifications.

(1) References to notices of assessment are construed as references to notices of determination.

(2) References to the appellant believing himself to be overcharged to tax are references to his believing that the determination overstates the syndicate profits or understates the losses.

(3) References to a determination of the amount of tax to be postponed are construed as references to a direction that syndicate profits were reduced or losses increased as specified in the direction.

(4) Amendments are made to TMA 1970, s. 55 which in essence prevent tax becoming payable pending the appeal, or upon the determination of the appeal. (Time for payment of tax by the name will be on the determination of his appeal against the assessment.)

69.7.5 Apportionments of profits

The HMRC officer may require from the agent a return apportioning profits or losses stated in the determination in its final form between the names, and may require this information by notice in writing specifying a period of not less than 30 days within which the apportionment is to be delivered. The penalty for failure to comply with the notice is set at £5 per day for each 50 members, or part thereof.

69.7.6 Variation of determination

The determination of a syndicate profit or loss for a year of assessment is conclusive for the purpose of determining the liability of names in respect of the syndicate's performance for that year. The assessment giving effect to the change in the determination must be made within a year of that change, and the rules concerning the right of appeal against the assessment and postponement of tax pending the appeal have effect as if references in TMA 1970, s. 31, 55 to the date of notices of assessment were references to the date of change of the determination. The effect of this is chiefly that a notice of appeal and a request to postpone payment of tax must be given within 30 days of the variation or modification of the determination.

Law: FA 1993, s. 182(1), Sch. 19; Lloyd's Underwriters (Gilt-edged Securities) (Periodic Accounting for Tax on Interest) Regulations 1995 (SI 1995/3225), as amended by SI 1996/1014 and SI 1996/1182)

70 Money Laundering Reporting

70.1 General

Accountants are required to adhere to two pieces of anti-money laundering legislation which have a very significant impact on how they deal with clients and on their business practices generally – the Proceeds of Crime Act 2002 (PCA 2002,) and the Money Laundering Regulations 2007 (SI 2007/2157) (which replaced the Money Laundering Regulations 2003 from 15 December 2007), which impose a statutory requirement for systems and procedures. The Terrorism Act 2000 (as amended by the Anti-terrorism Crime and Security Act 2001) (TA 2000) is also important. The money laundering requirements introduced major changes to accountants' responsibilities and imposed potential criminal liability for all accountants working in the UK, but particularly for accountants working in practising firms and any other relevant business (see below).

Broadly, money laundering is the process by which the proceeds of crime are converted into assets which appear to have a legitimate origin and which can then be retained by the criminal or recycled to fund further criminal activity. Guidance on what constitutes money laundering, and how it can be reported, is given below, together with further guidance on requirements for those employed in relevant business.

> ⚠ **Warning!**
> It is extremely important to consult your professional body for specific guidance in all the areas dealt with below. Failure to do so would contravene the regulations and would harm any possible defence.

Law: PCA 2002; *Money Laundering Regulations* 2007 (SI 2007/2157)

Other guidance: HMRC guidance: *www.hmrc.gov.uk/news/new-mlr-guid.htm*

70.2 Requirements

In summary, accountancy firms are required to:
- appoint a money laundering reporting officer (MLRO) to receive reports of suspicions of money laundering from colleagues and to report these to the Serious Organised Crime Agency (SOCA) (formerly the NCIS (National Criminal Intelligence Service));

- train relevant principals and employees who come in contact with clients' funds on the requirements of the legislation, including how to recognise and deal with money laundering, how to report to the MLRO, and how to properly identify clients;
- verify the identity of new clients and keep records of the evidence obtained in identification; and
- establish appropriate internal procedures to forestall and prevent money laundering.

These obligations apply to sole practitioners with employees. Sole practitioners without employees have slightly different legal requirements, because they do not have to appoint an MLRO, but in all other respects are subject to these rules.

The 2007 Regulations (Regulation 26) require all businesses to be supervised by an appropriate anti-money laundering supervisory body. There are a number of supervisory bodies, including the financial services authority (FSA), HMRC, and a number of professional bodies which are listed in the 2007 Regulations. Businesses that are supervised by HMRC must apply to be registered. Accountancy service providers (ASPs) where the business is not supervised by a designated professional body (such as the institute of Chartered Accountants of England and Wales or the institute of certified book keepers (ICBK)) fall into this category. For many businesses acting as external accountants and/or auditors, tax advisers or insolvency practitioners, the supervisory authority will be the professional body to which they belong.

These firms should follow the guidance published by the consultative committee of accountancy bodies (CCAB) (*www.ccab.org.uk*).

> ### Planning point
>
> Firms should develop their own checklist documentation to help ensure that they identify what actions are required and allocate responsibility for their completion. Items might include:
>
> Has the firm appointed an individual to act as MLRO?
>
> Has the role, responsibility and authority of the MLRO been agreed and confirmed in writing by all principals within the firm?
>
> Has the MLRO been provided with adequate resources to fulfil his responsibilities?
>
> Have all personnel within the firm been informed of the identity, role and authority of the MLRO?
>
> Has the firm considered appointing a deputy for the MLRO to provide cover during periods of absence?
>
> Have suitable internal procedures been introduced to:

- identify the persons (human or corporate) whose identity should be confirmed to satisfy requirements concerning new clients?
- establish what forms of confirmation of identity will be acceptable to it?
- confirm the identity of all new clients of the firm being requested?
- establish a record of the evidence of identity seen in respect of all relevant persons (human and corporate)?
- establish a system of storage for such records of identity subject to appropriate retention policies?

Have the anti-money laundering training needs of all personnel (partners and all staff chargeable and non-chargeable) been assessed?

Have all personnel (partners and all staff chargeable and non-chargeable) been provided with initial training?

Have plans to meet the assessed training needs of all personnel (partners and all staff chargeable and non-chargeable) been prepared and agreed?

Have contracts of employment, partnership deeds, shareholder agreements, etc. been updated to include the requirement to comply fully with the firm's anti-money laundering procedures?

Has the firm introduced suitable internal procedures to ensure that all suspicions of money laundering activities are reported to the MLRO?

Has the firm established suitable reporting procedures to ensure that all suspicious activities encountered by the firm's personnel are promptly and properly reported to the Serious Organised Crime Agency (SOCA) (formerly the National Criminal Intelligence Service (NCIS))?

70.3 Key concepts

Accountants should take note of the following key concepts and definitions with a view to how the relevant authorities will interpret them.

1. Criminal property (as defined in PCA 2002, s. 340(2)), includes money, real property, personal property, heritable property, moveable property, and intangible property. Property is considered criminal property if:

    '(a) it constitutes a person's benefit from criminal conduct or it represents such a benefit (in whole or part and whether directly or indirectly); and

    (b) the alleged offender knows or suspects that it constitutes or represents such a benefit.'

2. Criminal conduct (PCA 2002, s. 340(1)) is any conduct which constitutes an offence in any part of the UK. Note that the location of the offence is not relevant. Even if the activity is not an offence in the jurisdiction in which it was committed, in the UK it will still be considered criminal conduct. Note also that these definitions mean that the rules now apply to the laundering of an offender's own proceeds of crime as well as those of someone else.

3. Knowledge or suspicion – the regulations and PCA 2002 refer to both knowledge and reasonable grounds for suspicion. The effect of this is to remove the option for an individual to ignore what might otherwise be construed as evidence, as to have a suspicion requires the same action as to have actual knowledge. Individuals are expected to apply logic and common sense and should look to professional bodies for guidance. Indeed, to be able to demonstrate that guidance has been sought and followed can be a defence.

The following will therefore be considered an offence:

- failing to act on actual knowledge;
- deliberately closing one's mind to the obvious;
- deliberately refraining from making inquiries or seeking knowledge that one might prefer not to be burdened with; and
- failure to act upon knowledge of circumstances which would indicate the facts to any honest and reasonable person.

There is no relevant definition of suspicion in existing legislation. Case law and other sources indicate that suspicion can be considered as being more than speculation but falling short of proof or knowledge. Suspicion is personal and subjective but will generally be built on some objective foundation and so there should be some degree of consistency in how a firm's MLRO treats possible instances of suspicion.

Law: PCA 2002, s. 340

70.4 Offences

70.4.1 Generally

The combined effect of the definitions in PCA 2002, s. 340, is to create three principal money laundering offences, presented in s. 327–329. Because of the definition of criminal property at s. 340, all three principal money laundering offences now apply to the laundering of an offender's own proceeds of crime as well as those of someone else.

1. *Concealings, etc.* (PCA 2002, s. 327): an offence is committed where a person concealed, disguised, converted, transferred or removed from the jurisdiction criminal property. It is a defence if an authorised disclosure is made (under s. 338) as soon as possible after the transaction has taken place, or if the disclosure is made before the act has taken place and the discloser has obtained the appropriate consent, or there was a reasonable excuse for not making such a disclosure. Such offences do not distinguish between the proceeds of drug trafficking and the proceeds of other crimes.

2. *Arrangements* (PCA 2002, s. 328): the prosecuting authority establishes that a person entered into or became concerned in an arrangement which he knew or

suspected would make it easier for another person to acquire, retain, use or control criminal property and that the person concerned also knew or suspected that the property constituted or represented benefit from criminal conduct. The same defences apply as for concealings above.

3. *Acquisition, use and possession* (PCA 2002, s. 329): a person commits an offence if he acquires criminal property, uses criminal property, or has possession of criminal property. Again, this offence is only committed where a person knows or suspects that the property which is acquired constitutes or represents his own or another's benefit from criminal conduct. The same defences apply as for the other offences listed above. Furthermore, persons such as tradesmen, who are paid for ordinary consumable goods and services in money that comes from crime are not under any obligation to question the source of the money.

4. *Tipping off, etc.* (PCA 2002, s. 333): it is an offence to make a disclosure likely to prejudice a money laundering investigation being undertaken or which may be undertaken by law enforcement authorities. It is a defence if the person did not know or suspect that the disclosure was likely to prejudice the investigation. The legislation also refers to the notion of 'consent' which is where a MLRO carries out or allows a prohibited act if an authorised disclosure is made and specifies that consent decisions must be made within 7 working days.

Law: PCA 2002, s. 327–329, 333

70.4.2 Tax-related offences

The proceeds or monetary advantage arising from tax offences are treated no differently from the proceeds of theft, drug trafficking or other criminal conduct. This includes tax offences committed abroad if the action would have been an offence were it to have taken place in the United Kingdom. There is no requirement for there to be any consequential effect on the United Kingdom's tax system.

Tax evasion offences will include both the under-declaring of income and the over-claiming of expenses. For direct tax, common criminal offences generally involve some criminal intent or dishonesty. However, for indirect tax s. 167(3) of the Customs and Excise Management Act 1979 provides that a wide range of innocent or accidental errors are criminal offences even though they are, in practice, generally dealt with under the civil penalty regime. That is not relevant for making reports under the Act.

Law: CEMA 1979, s. 167

70.4.3 Serious Organised Crime and Police Act 2005

The Serious Organised Crime and Police Act 2005 received Royal Assent on 7 April 2005. Broadly, this Act made various amendments to the money laundering rules in POCA 2002. The main amendments affecting firms are as follows:

- A limited defence has been introduced to the money laundering offence and disclosure rules. This applies if there are reasonable grounds for believing that criminal conduct occurred outside the UK, if that conduct was lawful in the foreign country or territory when it occurred. This amendment is designed to provide some defence against certain administrative offences (e.g. breaches of health and safety regulations) or regulatory offences.
- From 1 July 2005 the rules allow banks (and other deposit takers) to continue operating the accounts of money laundering suspects in respect of ongoing small value transactions (e.g. 'lifestyle' payments such as mortgage repayments or heating and lighting bills) without obtaining prior consent from NCIS in each case. A money laundering offence is not committed if the transaction is below a 'threshold amount' of £250, or such higher amount as may be authorised (POCA 2002, s. 339A). However, there is still a requirement to report knowledge or suspicion of money laundering (e.g. initially when the account is opened, or when the suspicion first arises), irrespective of the amounts involved.
- The requirement to make a money laundering report (normally a 'Limited Intelligence Value' report) has been removed from 1 July 2005, where the identity of the suspect and whereabouts of the property are unknown, if there is no information to help identify the offender or the whereabouts of the criminal proceeds. Previously, the auditor would have been required to submit a report to NCIS, even though it contained no information of practical value to law enforcement.
- It is an offence to make a report to NCIS other than in the prescribed form and manner, unless there is a reasonable excuse for failing to do so.

Law: SOCPA 2005, s. 102–107

Other guidance: Standard NCIS disclosure form: *www.ncis.gov.uk/disclosure.asp*

70.5 Failure to disclose

The money laundering regulations impose a negligence test with the effect that an offence is committed where a person has reasonable grounds for knowing or suspecting that another party is engaged in money laundering, even if they did not actually know or suspect. The duty to report applies to those persons who receive information in the course of relevant business.

The offence is committed if the 'required disclosure' is not made. The 'required disclosure' is defined as being a disclosure to a MLRO, or to a person authorised by the Serious Organised Crime Agency (SOCA). This reflects the policy that disclosures in the regulated sector should be made directly to SOCA, rather than through a constable or a customs officer. It gives those in the regulated sector the choice of either disclosing direct to SOCA, which might be appropriate for sole practitioners, or disclosing to the MLRO who will operate as a filter for disclosures to SOCA.

It is an offence for MLROs who receive reports under s. 330 (the failure to disclose offence) which cause them to know or suspect or gives reasonable grounds for knowledge or suspicion, that money laundering is taking place, to fail to disclose that report as soon as practicable after the information comes to them.

It is a defence for a person who has a reasonable excuse for not disclosing the information and also for a lawyer, where the information came to him in privileged circumstances. There is also a defence for staff who have not had adequate training concerning the identification of transactions which may be indicative of money laundering. In order to use this defence successfully, the defendant would have to show that he did not actually know or suspect that another person was engaged in money laundering and that, in his case, his employer had not complied with requirements to provide employees with such training as is specified by the regulations.

The rules acknowledge the importance of guidance issued by relevant professional bodies and provide that the court must take any guidance issued by such a body into account when determining whether an offence has been committed. It is therefore strongly recommended that practitioners look to their professional body for guidance.

70.6 Internal reporting procedures

70.6.1 Generally

The 2007 regulations implement the EC Third Money Laundering Directive in the UK and reflect the recommendations of the international financial action task force (FATF), which was set up to tackle money laundering on a worldwide basis. In particular, the customer due diligence obligations under the 2007 regulations are designed to make it more difficult for businesses in the regulated sector to be used by criminals for money laundering or terrorist financing.

The 2007 Regulations specify that businesses that are supervised by HMRC must apply to be registered. ASPs where the business is not supervised by a designated professional body (such as the institute of chartered accountants of England and Wales (ICAEW) or the ICBK fall into this category. ASPs were required to register from 1 April 2008 and by 1 July 2008 at the latest. The cost of registration from 1 June 2009 is £120 per premises.

Firms involved in relevant business are required to maintain internal reporting procedures which facilitate the following:

- a firm must appoint an individual to receive disclosures of knowledge or suspicion of money laundering activity from its employees or representatives;
- where a firm's employee or representative obtains information on, or has suspicion of, money-laundering, that person is required 'as soon as is practicable after the information or other matter comes to him' to disclose it to the firm's nominated officer;
- in the event of such disclosure, the nominated officer must evaluate the employee's information or suspicions in order to determine whether or not it provides reasonable grounds to suspect money laundering; and
- if the nominated officer does indeed suspect money laundering, the relevant information or evidence must be disclosed to SOCA (or a person authorised by SOCA).

Obviously, the requirement to appoint a nominated officer does not apply to sole traders. Furthermore, the requirement to disclose to a nominated officer or SOCA does not apply in situations where such information comes to a professional legal adviser in privileged circumstances, i.e. in the course of providing legal advice to a client or in connection with legal proceedings, unless such information is passed with the intention of 'furthering a criminal purpose'

Law: Money Laundering Regulations 2007 (SI 2007/2157)

70.6.2 When to report

In considering whether to report your suspicions to SOCA, the following two questions must be addressed:

- has a crime been committed?
- have proceeds been derived from that crime?

If these two tests are met then reporting is mandatory and it is an offence not to do so.

70.6.3 Is it a crime?

Accountants are expected to have a sufficient understanding of tax and company law to enable them accurately to identify what constitutes a crime. Also, as indicated above, those involved in relevant business are expected to apply common sense with regard to criminal activities such as drug crime, theft and other serious offences. Accountants are not required to seek legal advice on the criminality or otherwise of clients' activities since the existence of suspicion alone requires the report to be made.

70.6.4 What are proceeds?

Proceeds of crime relate to any pecuniary benefit gained through a criminal act. This interpretation might range from the proceeds of drug trafficking in one extreme to a firm saving costs by cutting corners on, for example, failing to adhere to health and safety regulations. Any resulting saving from not following the law can therefore be interpreted as proceeds of crime.

This creates particular problems for auditors who are required by SAS 120 Law and Regulations to gain an understanding of the laws and regulations applying to the client's business.

Reports should be made to:

- the Serious Organised Crime Agency (SOCA);
- the police; and
- HM Revenue & Customs.

HM Revenue & Customs are not a report taking body for money laundering purposes. For the majority of money laundering offences only a report to SOCA is sufficient. It is therefore good practice to make all reports to SOCA.

As indicated above, PCA 2002, s. 336 provides for some suspicious transactions to proceed with the consent of the authorities. The following procedures exist:

- the authority to whom the report is made may give consent for a transaction to proceed if, for example, they believe that to do so might help to trace the source or destination of the proceeds and may therefore lead to the detection of further or related criminal activity;
- if a report is made to the authorities and no response specifically refusing consent is received within seven days, the person may proceed with the transaction; and
- where a report is made and consent has been refused, a 31-day moratorium period comes into effect. Transactions may not proceed during this period. However, after this period has expired if no restraint order has been issued then the transaction may proceed. This therefore gives the authorities 31 days to make a decision as to whether or not to take action on the report.

Law: PCA 2002, s. 336

70.6.5 What to look for

There are three phases which together describe the process of money laundering.

1. *Placement* – where the funds first enter the banking system or business.

2. *Layering* – the carrying out of multiple transactions with the intention to confuse the trail. Often during this process the transactions appear to have no economic purpose. Accountants are often asked to assist with this stage of the process.

3. *Integration and repatriation* – where the funds are brought back into the legitimate economy. They will appear to have arisen legally from earned funds.

The following methods are often used to facilitate money laundering:

- *mingling* – where legitimate and illicit funds are mixed to confuse the trail;
- the *creation or adoption of corporate structures* where the commercial or financial enterprise is used as a disguise; and
- *trusts* – used in the same way as corporate structures above.

70.6.6 Commonly used techniques

The following is a summary of the techniques used.

1. Cash and retail banking sector – the launderer will use cash deposit and basic banking services together with electronic transfers. They prefer to use private and specialist banks. The mechanisms used are deposit structuring, connected accounts, collection accounts, pass book-operated accounts, payable-through accounts, bank drafts, loanback arrangements.

2. Money service business – this technique seeks to exploit bureaux de change and other money service operators. It facilitates the conversion of funds to other currencies.

3. Investment banking and securities – launderers will normally use the wholesale market and therefore the transactions will be large. Bearer shares are popular vehicles.

4. Insurance and personal investment products – financial products will be bought for cash and then surrendered early in order to obtain a refund. In the past, general insurance was a popular method as this was not regulated under the previous money laundering regulations (MLR 1993).

5. Trading companies and business activities – cash-based businesses provide the best cover for money laundering. This allows the funds to be easily placed within the banking sector. This then allows for real or fictitious suppliers to be paid. Common activities will include import/export as this allows for the movement of funds between jurisdictions. It might also include the purchase of real estate.

6. Lawyers, accountants and other intermediaries – lawyers and accountants will be used as gatekeepers to set up the corporate structures or trusts. Launderers will likely use nominee shareholders, directors and trustees. They might also

use the client account as a method of laundering the funds which may be used to purchase personal investment products.

7. Non-financial sector services – casinos, bookmakers, real estate agents, gold and other precious metals dealers, and high value goods dealers are all frequently used to process cash transactions.

Other activities which might be indicative of money laundering activity include:

- shops, restaurants and bars where cash is placed in an open till drawer, and sales are not rung up;
- construction and building services where the suppliers request payment in cash and are reluctant to provide an invoice;
- businesses which offer a discount for cash and are reluctant to accept credit cards or cheques;
- traders who want to complete transactions in car parks or other unusual places;
- electrical goods and mobile phones for sale at substantially less than normal retail selling price from shops, market stalls and pubs;
- businesses which do not number their sales invoices and request that payment is made to someone other than the business; and
- advertisements in local newspapers and shops offering goods or services VAT free.

70.7 The training requirement

The Regulations require that every person or firm involved in relevant business in the United Kingdom must take appropriate measures to ensure that relevant employees are made aware of the provisions and effect of the Regulations, Pt. 7 of PCA 2002 and s. 18 and 21A of TA 2000 and consequently training must be provided on how to recognise and deal with transactions which may be related to money laundering.

The object of such training is to enable firms to establish a culture of compliance with the money laundering rules and it should result in the creation of adequate internal reporting procedures. It is strongly recommended that firms document all training undertaken to enable them to demonstrate their compliance as this will possibly provide a defence where an employee is deemed to have committed an offence.

Guidance on the level and type of training to be undertaken should be sought from the appropriate professional body. The content of training courses is not dealt with in the legislation. Generally speaking, the level of training provided to individuals should be appropriate to their role and seniority within the firm. Apart from knowledge of the main money laundering offences, relevant individuals are not required to have a detailed knowledge of what constitutes a criminal offence beyond that knowledge which could reasonably be expected of a person of their position and seniority involved in their line of business. As noted above, however, auditors who are bound by SAS 120 will be expected to gain an understanding of the laws and regulations applying to the client's business.

Training need not necessarily be performed in-house, although for many medium-sized and larger firms this would provide the opportunity to have the training tailored to the firm's particular needs. Attendance by individuals at conferences, seminars and training courses run by external organizations, or participation in computer-based training courses, may be taken to represent an effective method of fulfilling their training requirement.

> ### Planning point
>
> As money laundering is an ongoing issue the MLRO should not stop at the completion of the initial training.
>
> Firms should amend their induction documentation to ensure that all new staff are properly trained and then at least on an annual basis the MLRO should consider whether additional training should be given to all principals and staff.

> ### Planning point
>
> As well as setting up the necessary procedures the MLRO will need to ensure that steps are taken to confirm that those procedures are being complied with. It would be appropriate to undertake an annual compliance review to enable this confirmation to take place.
>
> This review will not only focus on whether the necessary training, etc. has taken place but should involve a review of a sample of files to ensure that:
>
> - identification has been asked for and received when necessary;
> - reports have been made when necessary; and
> - where a report has been made there is no evidence of tipping off.

71 National Insurance Contributions

71.1 Introduction

Social security in general represents the largest single class of government expenditure each year, but only around one-half of social security expenditure is financed by National Insurance Contributions (NICs); the remainder is funded from general tax revenues. Broadly, the aim of the UK's National Insurance scheme is to protect individuals who fall upon hard times. However, its resemblance to commercially-based insurance is limited, in that it only involves in part the payment of compulsory and voluntary contributions by people with some link to the UK (e.g. residence, presence, or habitual residence in the UK) in return for certain state benefits.

Whilst the National Insurance Fund is a notionally separate entity within the government accounts, it only ever contains enough money at any point to pay out benefits derived from it for between two and four months. In the main, the National Insurance system is a system of cross-generational transfer, in that contributions of the current working population are used mainly to pay current state pensions, the balance being used to fund other current benefits.

The National Insurance Contributions Office (NICO), an Executive Office of Her Majesty's Revenue & Customs (HMRC), currently exercises almost all the functions connected with the contributions side of the National Insurance system.

71.2 Liability to NICs

71.2.1 Charge to NICs

Liability to NICs depends on the class of contributor into which the individual falls, i.e. whether an individual is employed or self-employed. In most cases this will be obvious, but at the margin it is a question of law and is not determined merely from a job description or contract. Those paying contributions are further identified as being:

- employed earners;
- employers and other persons paying earnings;
- self-employed earners; and
- others paying voluntarily in order to provide or make up benefit entitlement.

An 'earner' may be employed or self-employed, since the term must be construed according to the definition of earnings, which includes any 'remuneration or profit derived from an employment'. The term 'employment' includes any trade, business, profession, office or vocation, so contributions are potentially due in connection with any income derived from working, be it as an employee or as a self-employed person.

In order to establish whether a liability to NICs arises and, if so, to calculate that liability, it is first necessary to be able to determine the group or category into which an earner falls.

71.2.2 Classes of contributions

Liability to NICs depends on the class into which the individual falls. The classes are as follows:

- Class 1: earnings-related, primary contributions being payable by employed earners and secondary contributions being payable by employers and others paying earnings;
- Class 1A: contributions payable annually by secondary contributors only, based on the cash equivalent value of taxable benefits in kind;
- Class 1B: contributions paid by employers on the extension of PAYE settlement agreement principles to NICs;
- Class 2: flat rate, payable by self-employed earners;
- Class 3: flat rate, voluntary contributions; and
- Class 4: earnings-related, payable by self-employed earners.

71.2.3 Employed earners

The distinction between employment under a contract of service and employment in an office can be important for NIC purposes. For example, some company directors receive fees as emoluments of the office but at the same time they are employees under a contract of service with an associated company, and since special rules apply to the calculation of the contribution liabilities of company directors (see **71.4.6**), it is important to know the true source of the individual's income. Class 1 contributions are levied on the earnings of 'employed earners'. This includes persons gainfully employed in Great Britain either under a contract of service, or in an office with emoluments chargeable to income tax under the provisions of the Income Tax (Earnings and Pensions) Act (ITEPA) 2003.

> **Planning point**
>
> The definition of 'contract of service', which is central to the distinction between employed and self-employed earners, is defined as 'any contract of service or apprenticeship whether written or oral and whether expressed or implied.' This definition is equivalent to that used in employment protection law for the term 'contract of employment'. However, there are a number of

situations in which a person is deemed by NIC regulations to fall into a category other than that into which he would normally fall, but it is generally the case that a person who falls to be treated as an employee for the purposes of NICs will equally be treated as an employee for the purposes of employment protection law, income tax law, and VAT law. The general discussion on employed or self-employed for income tax purposes (see **Chapter 34** above) is therefore also relevant to NICs.

Some employees will be categorised as 'deemed employed earners'.

Example 71.1

Examples of deemed employed earners include.

(1) Office cleaners, or those working in a similar capacity in any premises other than those used as a private dwelling-house.

(2) Telephone kiosk cleaners, excluding those working in premises used as a private dwelling-house.

(3) Employment by a spouse for the purposes of the spouse's employment (which includes self-employment).

(4) Lecturers, teachers, instructors or similar in an educational establishment by a person providing education. The deemed employee must give the instruction in the presence of the persons to whom the instruction is given, and the earnings must be paid by or on behalf of the person providing the education. The rule does not apply where the lecturer, etc. has agreed in advance that he will not give instruction on more than three days in three consecutive months or the instruction is given as public lectures.

(5) Ministers of religion, not being employed under a contract of service or in an office within the provisions of ITEPA 2003. This rule is not applicable to ministers whose remuneration is not wholly or mainly stipend or salary, which means that, e.g. a Roman Catholic priest is not an employed earner because his stipend is minimal.

(6) Employment via the agency of a third party. An employment is deemed to be employed earner's employment if the person concerned renders, or is obliged to render personal service and is subject to supervision, direction or control, or to the right of supervision, etc. as to the manner of the rendering of such service and he is supplied by or through some third person. Furthermore, for this rule to apply, the earnings paid must be paid by or through, or on the basis of accounts submitted by, the third person or in accordance with arrangements made with him, or payments other than to the person employed must be made by way of fees, commission, etc. which relate to the continued employment in that employment of the person in question. This rule specifically includes the possibility of a partnership supplying the services of one of its members, in which case the member concerned would be treated as an employed earner in relation to that employment. The deeming rule is expressed not to operate in respect of

> homeworkers or outworkers supplied through a third party, nor does it extend to persons employed as actors, singers, musicians or other entertainers, or as fashion, photographic or artists' models.

71.2.4 Self-employed earners

A self-employed earner is any person who is gainfully employed in Great Britain other than in employed earner's employment. There are a series of tests used to differentiate between employed and self-employed earners. This does not, of course, mean that a particular individual may not be simultaneously employed and self-employed. However, what is clear is that a self-employed individual can only be self-employed once. As an independent contractor, he may provide his services to numerous customers and the services provided need not be the same in each case. The only requirement of contribution law is that he be gainfully employed in Great Britain.

> ### Planning point
>
> Although the charge to Class 2 contributions arises on a weekly basis in respect of any self-employed earner (see **71.7.1**), it is insufficient to test the status of any particular individual on the basis of one week's activity or lack of activity. Inevitably, there are certain situations in which the motive and opportunity for gain are difficult to determine. Although an individual may not have a motive of gain in entering into an arrangement to provide services, nevertheless, where actual gain arises, he will be gainfully employed and will fall to be treated as a self-employed earner. Equally, someone in a business may be a partner simply because he has made an investment but takes no part in the managing, or working in the business. He therefore has a motive of gain but is not in fact employed in performing services. Such a sleeping partner falls outside the definition of a self-employed earner.

71.2.5 Deemed non-employment

Several types of employment are disregarded for NIC purposes. These include:

- employment by a close member of the family in a private dwelling house other than for the purposes of that family member's business;
- any employment by a spouse otherwise than for the purposes of the spouse's employment;
- any employment as a self-employed earner (including examiners, etc. deemed to be so) where the earner is not ordinarily employed in such employment or employments. In practice this is mainly taken to apply to those in an employed earner's employment who earn less than £800 per year from part-time self-employment but the limit has not been set by regulation, has remained unchanged since 1981–82 and as such is potentially open to challenge;

- employment for the purposes of any statutory election as a returning officer, etc. or any person employed by him;
- employment by visiting military forces, either as a member of those forces or as a civilian employee, except for civilians who are ordinarily resident in the UK; and
- employment as a member of any duly designated international headquarters or defence organisation, other than in the case of serving members of HM Forces or civilians ordinarily resident in the UK who are not members of the organisation's retirement scheme.

71.2.6 Personal service companies

In a bid to remove opportunities for the avoidance of Class 1 National Insurance Contributions (NICs) by the use of intermediaries, such as service companies or partnerships, in circumstances where the worker would otherwise be an employee of the client, or the income would be the income from an office held by the worker, provisions were introduced that conferred wide ranging powers to make regulations to treat all money received by the intermediary in respect of a certain engagement, less certain deductions, as paid to the worker in a form subject to Class 1 NICs. The rules, which are generally known as 'IR 35', came into force on 6 April 2000 and provide that where:

- an individual ('the worker') personally performs, or has an obligation personally to perform, services for the purposes of a business carried on by another person ('the client');
- the performance of those services by the workers is referable to arrangements involving a third party, rather than referable to a contract between the client and the worker; and
- the circumstances are such that, were the services to be performed by the worker under a contract between him and the client, he would be regarded as employed in the employed earner's employment by the client,

then the relevant payments and benefits are treated as earnings paid to the worker in respect of the employed earner's employment. These rules apply irrespective of whether the client is a person with whom the worker holds any office or employment.

Planning point

The effect of coming within the IR35 legislation is that the worker is treated as being employed by the intermediary in the employed earner's employed employment. He is deemed to have received a payment of his 'attributable earnings' (as calculated in accordance with the regulations) from the intermediary on 5 April in the tax year concerned. The worker's attributable earnings are aggregated with any other earnings paid to or for the benefit of him or her by the intermediary in the year concerned. The amount of earnings-related contributions is determined on the aggregate amount according to normal rules.

National Insurance Contributions

> The intermediary is to be treated for those purposes as the secondary contributor.

Regulations (SI 2003/2079) were brought into force with effect from 1 September 2003, which removed the requirement that a worker performs services for the purposes of a business, thereby extending the scope of the principal regulations (SI 2000/727) to all workers providing services through an intermediary.

With regards to domestic workers, such as nannies or butlers, Finance Act 2003 introduced changes to the intermediate legislation designed to close an avoidance device whereby such workers, who would otherwise be directly employed by the person to whom they provide their services, operate instead through an intermediary, such as a company. It should be noted that the operative date for the changes are different for income tax and NIC purposes. For NIC purposes, the changes apply to income received by the intermediary for services provided on or after 8 August 2003. This means that a separate deemed payment calculation for the year ending 5 April 2004 is required for income tax and NIC purposes.

> *Warning!*
>
> In June 2010 the new coalition government formed the Office of Tax Simplification, which has been tasked with reviewing the IR35 rules as a priority.

Law: Cable & Wireless PLC v Muscat [2006] EWCA Civ 220

71.2.7 Decisions on employment status

Where there is any confusion over the class of NICs into which an individual falls, a decision may be obtained from the National Insurance Contributions Office (NICO). Such a decision will be binding in respect of both income tax and NICs, provided all relevant facts are disclosed. It is possible to appeal against a decision regarding status.

Where HMRC rule that an individual who has previously been treated as self-employed should be recategorised as an employed earner, any Class 2 NICs which the contributor has paid erroneously as a result of the change of status from self-employed to employed earner are reallocated as employee (primary) Class 1 contributions. Any balance of employee contributions due and any arrears of employer (secondary) contributions are generally requested from the employer. If the erroneous Class 2 contributions amount to more than the employee Class 1 contributions due the excess is refundable. HMRC refund Class 4 contributions overpaid as a result of a change of status. Any Class 2 contributions paid in error may be reallocated as employee Class 1 contributions, but this is at the discretion of HMRC.

> **Planning point**
>
> Where recategorisation has taken place and the individual concerned has thereby been transferred into the category of self-employed earner after having paid Class 1 contributions, it is usual practice to treat the recategorisation as having effect only from the date of the relevant decision. This effectively prevents any repayment claim in respect of Class 1 contributions paid, despite the fact that the individual has been found to have been self-employed during the period in question. However, the choice to make the change only prospectively rather than retrospectively may be challenged on those very grounds, and the question may even be taken as far as a decision by the Secretary of State under the procedure for the determination of questions.

Where an individual's status changes from employed to self-employed but Class 1, Class 1A or Class 1B NICs continue to be paid on the basis that the individual is an employed earner, adjustments to NICs are made not for the preceding six years, but only for the tax year in which the error came to light and the preceding year. This means that for all earlier periods the individual's contributions and contributory benefits position, and entitlement to statutory sick pay and statutory maternity pay, are unaffected by the change in status. Conversely, employers will receive no refund of secondary contributions paid in error in earlier years.

71.3 Earnings

71.3.1 Definition of 'earnings'

For NIC purposes, 'earnings' include any remuneration or profit derived from an employment. 'Employment' includes any trade, business, profession, office or vocation, subject to a proviso that regulations may make exceptions to this definition in appropriate circumstances. While the term is in principle all-embracing, regulations made under the Social Security Contributions and Benefits Act 1992 make numerous amendments to the definition in specified circumstances with the result that the rules for employed and self-employed earners are very different.

When seeking to establish earnings for NIC purposes, it is necessary to consider the rewards paid for services under a contract of employment. The meaning of the term 'remuneration' was considered in a 1974 employment law case concerning redundancy pay. Although not directly relevant to NIC, the comments of Sir John Donaldson are of persuasive authority in a NIC context. In that case, 'remuneration' was held to include any wage or salary, but to exclude any benefit in kind or amount paid by someone other than the employer. Additionally, expenses paid to the employee should be considered, with any payment which was a profit to the employee rather than reimbursement of an expense being included as remuneration.

Since dividends are derived from the ownership of shares in a company rather than employment, they are not earnings for NIC purposes. If a company declares a dividend to director-shareholders which is illegal (for example, because there are insufficient distributable profits) or outside the terms of its Articles of Association, it may be officially argued that the payment must be derived from the employment and is therefore earnings. The validity of this argument is questionable. A similar situation arises in respect of directors' current account balances. Since interest credited to a director on any balance standing to his credit in the company's books is derived from the lending of money rather than from the employment, such income will be free of NIC liability.

71.3.2 Calculating earnings

Subject to certain exceptions, the amount of a person's earnings for Class 1 contribution purposes is calculated on the basis of gross earnings from the employment or employments concerned. Payments must be derived from employment before they attract a Class 1 liability and this means that not all payments will automatically be treated as earnings. Unless the NIC law dictates specifically how a particular type of payment is to be treated, it is necessary to examine the nature of the payment and ascertain whether it fits the criterion stated. Furthermore, it is important to note that the judicial definition offers two alternatives, bringing into earnings not only payments received by an employee in return for his acting as an employee, but also payments in return for his being an employee. While the first part of this definition covers the common sense view of an employee being rewarded for services rendered or to be rendered, the second covers the less obvious position of employees who receive payments from their employer unrelated to the services they perform but which they would not have received had they not been employees.

Example 71.2

Earnings include the following items:
- wages, salaries, fees, overtime pay, bonuses, commission, etc.;
- holiday pay (see **71.3.11**);
- inducement payments;
- contractual maternity pay; and
- statutory sick pay, statutory maternity pay, statutory paternity pay and statutory adoption pay.

71.3.3 Timing of payment

In general where, in any tax week, earnings are paid to or for the benefit of an earner in respect of any one employment of his which is employed earner's employment, a primary and secondary Class 1 contribution will be payable. The most frequent problems with timing arise from payment in advance. The key factor to be considered is the unreserved entitlement to a payment. Where an employer takes on an employee on the basis that his salary will be paid monthly in arrears, but at the end of the first week lends the employee part of his first month's salary to tide him over until the first payroll run, no payment of earnings takes place, as the payment made is a loan. Until the employee has an unreserved entitlement to the first month's salary, the money in his hands is owed to the employer. Until it becomes his own money at the end of the month, it cannot be earnings for contribution purposes. The position is the same in principle, but quite different in effect, if it is agreed between the employer and employee that salary will regularly be paid in advance. Such advance payments will generally be treated as normal pay and NICs will be deductible in the normal way.

71.3.4 Directors

Special rules identify the earnings of company directors. Any payment made by a company to, or for the benefit of, any of its directors is treated as earnings if it is paid on account of or by way of an advance. A company director is not usually entitled to remuneration until it has been voted to him by the members of the company. Such voting may, of course, take place in advance, or the director may be given a service contract which sets out a basis for his regular remuneration. This would mean that any amounts paid to him under normal circumstances would be earnings for NIC purposes. However, where a company director draws cash from his business without the benefit of an agreed service contract or the advance voting of fees, he will effectively take a loan, albeit technically unauthorised, until such time as the members vote his remuneration. For these purposes, directors include shadow directors, though a person is not to be treated as such by reason only that the directors act on advice given by him in his professional capacity.

> ### *Planning point*
>
> It should be noted that no Class 1 liability arises on overdrawn accounts unless payments which caused the account to become overdrawn were made in anticipation of earnings. A liability would still arise:
>
> - where payments are made on which PAYE tax has been assessed;
> - where an agreement between the employer and the employee is in force providing for the payments to be made in anticipation of remuneration becoming due; or

> where shareholders have agreed that the director can make withdrawals from the account in anticipation of the voting of fees or remuneration.

71.3.5 Settling pecuniary liability

Where an employee incurs a personal liability to a supplier of goods or services, his liability to that supplier is usually measured in terms of money. For NIC purposes, as with income tax, if the employer pays the amount due by the employee to the creditor, the employer is effectively doing no more than giving the employee cash with which he settles his debt. Where an employer contracts with a provider of goods and services, there is no Class 1 NIC liability (although a Class 1A liability may arise). However, if the contract is between the employee and the provider, a Class 1 NIC liability arises if the payment is made direct to the provider or payment is made or reimbursed direct to the employee.

> **Example 71.3**
>
> In a typical small family company, the directors may routinely settle personal bills with a company cheque and charge the amount in question to a current or loan account. This should not present any difficulty if the account is in credit (i.e. the director has previously lent amounts to the company and has not at that point withdrawn them), but a liability to Class 1 contributions may well arise if the account is, or by virtue of the payment becomes, overdrawn.

71.3.6 Readily convertible assets

Payments in the form of readily convertible assets must be included in gross pay for NIC purposes. A 'readily convertible asset' is one which:

- is capable of being sold on a recognised investment exchange or London Bullion market (e.g. stocks, shares and other financial instruments, gold bullion, other precious metals, etc.);
- is a right over a money debt (e.g. trade debts assigned by an employer to an employee);
- is subject to a fiscal warehousing regime, such as a bonded warehouse;
- gives rise to a right to enable an employee to obtain money (e.g. an interest in a trust which comes to an end shortly after being assigned to an employee, resulting in an automatic right to cash);
- is subject to trading arrangements, either at the time that the asset is provided or that come into existence shortly afterwards as a result of an arrangement or understanding (e.g. jewellery that can be sold either at the time of its provision or shortly afterwards in consequence of an arrangement or understanding existing at the time the jewellery was provided); and
- is already owned by the employee and whose value is enhanced by the

employer (e.g. the payment by the employer of an additional premium to an employee's life assurance policy, thereby greatly increasing its value).

The value that is included in gross pay is the 'best estimate' at the time the payment is paid or treated as paid. The payment is added to other payments made in the relevant earnings period and NIC worked out on the total in the normal way. The NIC liability arises at the same time as income tax is due under PAYE.

71.3.7 Share options

Since 6 April 1999 NI has been payable by both employer and employee on the gains arising when share options granted after 5 April 1999 are exercised outside a HMRC-approved scheme (or are cancelled or assigned) and where the shares or the options are readily convertible into cash. Prior to this time, NICs were payable when share options were granted, but only if the options were granted at a discount and any charge was limited to the amount of this discount.

Employees may now bear the employer's NIC on share option gains. Any employer's NIC paid by employees qualifies for relief against the share option. This may be achieved in one of two ways:

- the employer and employee agree that the employee bears some or all of the secondary NIC, the legal liability remaining with the employer and the employer recovering the sum from the employee; or
- the employer and employee jointly elect for some or all of the secondary NIC liability to be transferred to the employee, the employee assuming legal liability for NIC so transferred.

Law: SSCBA 1992, Sch. 1, para. 3A, 3B

71.3.8 Shares subject to forfeiture

Many companies offer their employees shares in the company they work for as part of their earnings. These shares often form part of a long-term investment plan (LTIP) and unconditional ownership of the shares is based on the employee satisfying relevant conditions (e.g. meeting performance targets). If the shares are readily convertible assets and are not issued via a HMRC-approved scheme:

- there will normally be no NIC liability when shares subject to forfeiture are first awarded, but
- there will be a liability based on the market value of the shares at the time when the risk of forfeiture is lifted, or, if sooner, when the shares are sold, less any consideration previously paid.

There will also be an NIC liability if the shares can still be subject to risk of forfeiture more than five years after they are first awarded. This is intended to stop

NIC liability being postponed indefinitely but as most LTIPs run for five years or less, few employees will actually pay NICs when the shares are first awarded.

71.3.9 Convertible shares

Convertible shares are shares of a certain class which can subsequently convert into another class, for example, some have different voting or dividend rights. An employer may grant one class of share, which can then be converted to a more valuable class. If such shares are not issued via a Revenue-approved scheme and are readily convertible assets, a NIC liability will arise on the gain from the conversion. Generally, the gain is the market value of the converted share less any consideration previously paid, and any NICs paid when the shares were first awarded.

> *Planning point*
>
> Income tax relief may be available for employees who agree to meet some or all of their employer's secondary NI liability arising from restricted or convertible employment-related securities.

Law: FA 2004, s. 85 and Sch. 16

71.3.10 Employment tribunal awards

Where an NIC liability arises in respect of protective awards, an order for reinstatement or re-engagement or an order for continuation of employment required by an employment tribunal, the NIC liability should be based on the gross amount of the award, not the net amount payable. If the tribunal decides that an employee was unfairly dismissed and the employer is ordered to re-employ the employee and pay arrears of pay, the award is liable to NIC. For NIC purposes, the payment of arrears is treated separately from other payments made at the same time. Where payment is made in a lump sum, the earnings period is the period covered by the award. If payment is made in instalments, the instalments must be added together and the NIC liability computed on the total amount. Again, the earnings period is the period of the award.

> *Planning point*
>
> Where an employment tribunal orders that employment continues while a complaint of unfair dismissal is dealt with, the award attracts NICs. The earnings period is the period for which each payment (which must be made under the order) relates, or a week, if longer.

The tribunal may order the employer to pay wages for a certain time if it decides that the employer has broken some rules when making the employee redundant. This is known as a protective award, and is liable to NICs. Such payments are treated separately from other payments. The earnings period is the longer of the protected period, the part of the protected period to which the payment relates or a week.

71.3.11 Holiday pay

Special rules apply for working out the NIC liability on certain types of holiday pay.

As regards a scheme where a group of employees contribute to a central, independently managed holiday pay fund, the amount spent on special stamps or credits used in the scheme and the holiday pay itself, whether paid directly through the fund or by the employer, is excluded from gross pay for NIC purposes. However, any holiday pay that comes from the employer rather than the scheme funds is included in gross pay for NIC purposes. Schemes of this nature are common in the construction industry.

> *Planning point*
>
> Where holiday pay is paid from an amount voluntarily set aside from the employee's pay during the year to be paid at certain times (e.g. Christmas or a summer holiday), the amount set aside should be included in gross pay at the time that it is set aside. Holiday pay may also be paid under a holiday credit scheme under which money is set aside each pay day to be paid in a lump sum when the employee takes his or her holiday. If the employee can have the money at any time, the sum set aside must be included in gross pay for NIC purposes at the time that it is set aside. If the employee can only have the money at the time that the holiday is taken, it is included in gross pay at the time when payment is actually made.

71.3.12 Non-cash vouchers

Since April 1999, the computation of an employed earner's earnings for Class 1 NIC purposes includes payment made by non-cash vouchers, unless the vouchers are of a type specifically excluded by the legislation. The value of the voucher is the cost to the employer of providing that voucher.

The following types of vouchers are specifically exempt:
- transport vouchers provided for the employee of a passenger transport undertaking under arrangements in operation on 25 March 1982 where the employee is earning less than £8,500 a year;

- vouchers for leave travel facilities for members of the armed forces;
- vouchers for sporting and recreational facilities (subject to the same conditions applying for income tax exemption);
- vouchers for long service awards, provided that the cost of providing the voucher does not exceed £20 for each year of service and there has been no similar award in the previous ten years;
- vouchers for social functions organised for employees, provided that the cost of providing vouchers does not exceed £150 per head and the function is open to employees generally;
- vouchers for travel between home and work provided to a person with a severe and permanent disability who is unable to travel on public transport;
- childcare vouchers;
- meal vouchers for meals provided on the employer's premises or in a canteen where meals are provided for staff generally;
- luncheon vouchers to a maximum of 15 pence per day and £1.05 per week;
- a voucher provided by a donor who is not the employer and is unconnected with allowing the employee to obtain goods, provided that the total of this and other vouchers provided by the donor does not exceed £150 per year and the voucher is not given in recognition of past or future services; and
- the provision of a non-cash voucher in respect of the private use of a car where such provision attracts a Class 1A liability.

71.3.13 Retirement benefit schemes

No NIC liability arises in respect of an employer's contribution to a HMRC-registered retirement benefit scheme. Generally, no NIC liability arises if there is no liability to income tax. However, contributions to a funded unapproved retirement benefits scheme (FURBS) attract NICs. Where there is a separate trust for each employee, the full amount paid into the FURBS on behalf of the employee must be included in gross pay for NIC purposes.

In the event that there is a single trust fund, but each employee has a distinct and separate benefit share, the amount paid to secure the employee's separate benefit share should be included in gross pay. However, if there is a single trust fund and at the time payments into the fund are made, the trustees have no indication of the benefit to be received by each employee, the amount of the payment must be apportioned equally between the employees who are members of the scheme, the sum apportioned in this way being included in each employee's gross pay for NIC purposes.

71.3.14 Personal incidental expenses

No Class 1 NIC liability arises where an employer pays for personal incidental expenses relating to a qualifying absence up to a maximum of £5 per night for stays within the UK and £10 per night for overnight stays outside the UK. The NIC exemption mirrors that available for income tax purposes. Sums paid in excess of the tax free limits must be included in gross pay.

71.3.15 Prize incentive schemes

A prize incentive scheme is one where employees receive prizes or awards from either the employer or a third party. The awards may be made in cash or may be in the form of holidays, goods, vouchers, etc. The extent to which an NIC liability exists depends on the nature of the award. However, where the award is in a non-cash form, it should be noted that although a Class 1 liability may not arise, from 6 April 2000 there may be a liability to Class 1A. Where the award is made by way of a non-cash voucher, the rules described at **71.3.12** are in point.

71.3.16 Redundancy payments

No liability arises in respect of redundancy payments. The regulations do not specify that it covers only statutory redundancy pay. Since redundancy payments are really little more than compensation for the loss of rights in the employment, it would seem that any amount paid in excess of the statutory entitlement would also fall to be excluded from earnings. Before a payment is officially accepted as a redundancy payment, the following conditions must be met:

- the employee's contract has been terminated;
- the termination has occurred because of redundancy; and
- the payment is not being made for any reason other than redundancy.

For the redundancy to be officially regarded as a genuine redundancy, it must have arisen either because the employer ceased, or intends to cease, carrying on the business for the purpose of which, or the place in which, the employee was employed, or the requirements of the business have changed such that the employee's job is no longer needed (see **Chapter 44**).

71.3.17 Relocation payments

Changes were made from 6 April 1998 to the NIC treatment of the payment of relocation expenses and allowances to or for employees who have to move residence as a result of being relocated in the UK. Before that date NICs were not collected on relocation allowances, but now may be if they do not qualify for income tax relief.

For employees who started work at a new location after 5 April 1998, all relocation allowances paid which qualify for income tax relief are excluded from gross pay, even if they exceed the £8,000 cap for tax. For NIC purposes there is no time limit within which the payment of qualifying allowances must start being paid.

Relocation allowances which are taxed through PAYE settlement agreements continue to be excluded from NIC liability for 1998–99, as thereafter the NIC treatment of items included in such agreements has been aligned with the tax treatment.

71.3.18 Round sum allowances

An employer who pays a round sum allowance to an employee and who can identify specific and distinct business expenses can exclude these from gross pay for NIC purposes. If the employer cannot identify the business expense, the whole allowance is included in gross pay, regardless of whether an expense is actually incurred.

71.3.19 Travel and subsistence

The changes to the income tax rules on employee travel and subsistence which apply from 6 April 1998 are also applicable to NICs from the same date. Broadly, reasonable travel and subsistence allowances paid to employees for business journeys are excluded from 'earnings' for NIC purposes.

Site-based employees

Before 6 April 1998, amounts paid by employers towards the costs of travel and/or subsistence of employees with no permanent workplace who worked for a short period at one place before moving on to another, were treated as 'earnings' attracting NICs. From that date reasonable costs are excluded from gross pay.

Triangular travel

Where an employee with a normal, permanent place of work travels directly from his home to another temporary place of work, after 5 April 1998 reasonable travel and subsistence expenses paid by the employer can be excluded in calculating gross pay for NIC purposes.

Home-to-work travel

The basic rule is that any reimbursement by an employer of home-to-work travel expenses to an employee is a payment of earnings for Class 1 purposes, though the rule is qualified in a number of respects.

Unexpected call-outs

If an employee is recalled to work unexpectedly (e.g. in the evening) reimbursement of the travelling expenses incurred is only a payment of earnings if the employee's conditions of service or employment require him to be on call.

Disabled employees

If the reimbursed employee is a disabled employee or trainee within the terms of the Disabled Persons (Employment) Act 1944, s. 15, or is a severely disabled person who cannot use public transport, travelling costs are NIC free.

Temporary postings away from a permanent workplace

If an employee is temporarily sent to work somewhere other than his usual place of work for a period expected from the outset to be 24 months or less, the employer may pay travelling expenses free of contribution liability. If the absence lasts longer than 24 months, contributions should be paid once payments have been made for more than two years. If the posting is expected from the outset to last more than two years, all payments are liable to contributions from the start.

Employer-provided transport

If the employer contracts for transport to be provided, the payment-in-kind rules exclude the payments made from earnings. However, from 6 April 2000, a Class 1A liability may arise.

Payments to employees travelling abroad

Where employers pay the travelling expenses of employees travelling between the UK and an overseas employment, or mariners who work outside UK territorial waters, the payments may be excluded from earnings if those expenses are not taxable for income tax purposes.

Late-night transport home

Late-night taxi, etc. fares home which are reimbursed rather than paid direct to the taxi company may be excluded from earnings.

Disruption of public transport

If public transport is disrupted by a strike or other industrial action, and employers reimburse employees with the cost of taxi or other fares or overnight accommodation near the place of work, such reimbursements are excluded from earnings.

Allowances for carrying passengers and equipment

Allowances paid to cover the additional expense of carrying passengers and/or equipment specifically related to the employment are excluded from gross pay.

Car parking costs and fines

Car parking costs may be excluded from earnings either entirely, if the employer contracts directly with the provider of the parking space, or at least in part if the employer reimburses parking fees incurred for business purposes. A record should be kept of individual items of expenditure. Parking fines paid for employees are stated specifically to constitute earnings to be included in gross pay.

Employers paying insurance

Where road fund licence, insurance premium, car servicing and AA/RAC, etc. membership are paid directly by the employer in respect of a vehicle which he owns, the payment-in-kind rule would normally operate to exclude payments from earnings for Class 1 purposes (although a Class 1A liability may arise). However, where the employer pays for these items in respect of the employee's own vehicle, the payments for these items must be included in the gross pay.

71.3.20 PILON

Pay in lieu of notice (PILON) is regarded as a compensation payment made to an employee whose contract is terminated (i.e. breached) early or without notice. Golden handshakes, etc. are no more than colloquial terms applied to any mixture of payments covering the termination of an employment, including redundancy, compensation and *ex gratia* elements. Since such payments derive from the termination of the employment rather than from the employee's acting as or being an employee, they could in principle be outside the definition of earnings. However, some contracts of employment make specific provision for such payments to be made. Where it is known from the commencement of an employment relationship that compensation will be paid to the employee in the event of breach by the employer, the contingent right to such compensation may form part of the consideration given by the employer as his half of the employment bargain. It is therefore quite clearly a payment of earnings when made and the normal NIC charges will apply.

71.4 Class 1 NICs

71.4.1 Charge

Class 1 contributions, which are earnings-related and based on an employed earner's employment (see **71.3.1**), are payable in two parts:

- primary contributions, payable by employed earners; and
- secondary contributions, payable by the employers of employed earners or, in certain circumstances, other persons paying earnings.

The structure of Class 1 NICs was radically reformed from April 1999, with the introduction of a secondary earnings threshold, aligned to the personal allowance for tax purposes, below which no secondary contributions are payable. This was followed in April 2000 with the introduction of a primary threshold, which is aligned with the personal allowance from 2001.

> **Warning!**
>
> A primary Class 1 liability arises where, in any tax week, earnings are paid to, or for the benefit of, an earner in respect of any one employment of his which is employed earner's employment; and:
>
> - he is over the age of 16; and
> - the amount paid exceeds the primary threshold (£110 per week in 2009–10 and 2010–11) for Class 1 contributions (or the prescribed equivalent in the case of earners paid otherwise than weekly).
>
> A secondary Class 1 contribution is payable if the amount paid exceeds the secondary threshold.

71.4.2 Primary contributions

From 6 April 2003, primary contributions at the rate of eleven per cent are payable on earnings between the primary threshold and the upper earnings limit (UEL). A national zero-rate of contribution is payable on earnings that equal or exceed the lower earnings limit (LEL) but that do not reach the primary threshold. This is to preserve benefit entitlement for employees earning in excess of the LEL.

Employees contracting out of SERPS effectively pay a lower primary rate as a result of the contracting-out rebate.

In addition, from 6 April 2003, an additional one per cent Class 1 NIC contribution was introduced on earnings above the UEL. The NIC system has historically worked on annual maximum amounts so that employees did not pay more than the overall contribution limit based on the UEL. The new legislation introduced mimics this principle, but allows for a charge of one per cent on all earnings, without limit. Maximum NICs payable annually are therefore calculated with respect to a certain amount of earnings rather than an absolute maximum.

71.4.3 Secondary contributions

Since 6 April 1999, employers of employees whose weekly earnings do not exceed the current 'earnings threshold' pay no (secondary) Class 1 NICs. Above that threshold, from 6 April 2003 they pay NICs at 12.8 per cent (if the employee is not contracted out). There is no upper earnings limit for secondary Class 1 purposes.

Example 71.4

With bonuses and commissions, Keith is paid £1,000 in a tax week in 2011–11. He pays £82.30 ((11% × (£844 – £110)) + (1% × (£1,000 – £844)) and his employer pays £113.92 (12.8% × (£1,000 – £110)).

71.4.4 Contracting out

A person who contributes at the standard rate to the NI scheme will eventually (assuming certain conditions are met) receive from the state both a basic and an additional pension. Class 1 contributions (including 'notional' contributions payable from 6 April 2000 on earnings at the LEL) buy the right to the basic pension and all other contributory benefits, while contributions on earnings above the LEL and below the UEL buy the additional pension, also known as S2P (the state second pension) – previously, SERPS (the state earnings-related pension scheme).

Planning point

It is possible to contract out of S2P/SERPS and instead join an approved occupational pension scheme that will provide the equivalent of the S2P/SERPS pension on retirement. Alternatively an individual may take out an appropriate personal pension policy with a life assurance company to provide similar benefits. Since an individual who contracts out of S2P/SERPS will effectively relieve the state of the responsibility of funding the additional pension, the Class 1 contribution rates on band earnings are reduced.

The rates so reduced are known as the contracted-out rates and the reduction is known as the contracted-out rebate. It is accounted for in one of two ways. In occupational schemes, both employer and employee are allowed to deduct the rebate from the contributions paid to HMRC each month, thus enabling them to pay the amount saved directly into the occupational scheme. Holders of personal pensions and their employers continue to pay the full not-contracted-out rate of contribution, receiving the rebate directly into their policy by means of a payment from NICO once year-end returns have been processed.

Where an employee joins a Contracted-Out Salary Related (COSR) pension scheme, a rebate is given on earnings from the LEL to the UEL. This is given by reducing the primary contributions deducted from pay by 1.6 per cent (except where the employee has a deferment certificate and pays only the 1 per cent additional primary rate), and the secondary contributions due by the employer by 3.7 per cent for 2009–10 and 2010–11. The 5.3 per cent rebate may be more than the contributions actually due, if earnings are low. In that case, the rebate may be recovered by the employer from other NIC or PAYE deductions as a subsidy towards the costs of private pension contributions. The rebate is fixed, irrespective of the age of the contributor, as all investment risk is borne by the sponsoring employer.

The rebate applies only to band earnings, since contributions on earnings up to the LEL count towards only the basic state retirement pension. Employers' contributions on earnings below the LEL and above the UEL are therefore due at the full rate.

> **Planning point**
>
> Employers pay secondary contributions only on the earnings above the secondary (or employer's) threshold. However, the NI rebate is still available in respect of all earnings between the LEL and the UEL, including those between the LEL and the secondary threshold on which no employer's NICs are payable. Employers operating contracted-out schemes can reduce their overall NIC liability to reflect the rebate applicable to the employer's contributions on earnings above the LEL and up to and including the secondary threshold.

> **Planning point**
>
> The introduction of the primary threshold from 6 April 2000 introduced a further complication. As noted above, from April 1999, employees do not pay primary Class 1 contributions until their earnings reach the primary threshold. However, the employee's NI rebate remains payable in respect of earnings between the LEL and the UEL, including those above the LEL and up to and including the primary threshold. In the first instance, the rebate reduces total NICs payable by the employee. However, if the NIC payable by the employee is reduced to nil, the excess rebate is available for the employer to offset against his overall NIC bill.

71.4.5 Earnings period

An 'earnings period' is a period to which earnings paid to or for the benefit of an employed earner are deemed to relate, irrespective of the period over which they were earned. Class 1 liability is calculated on the basis of the earnings paid in the earnings period and the limits applicable to that earnings period. No person may have more than one earnings period in respect of a single employment.

The majority of employees are paid a wage or salary at regular intervals of a week or a month. Where only a single regular payment pattern exists, except in the case of company directors in respect of whom special rules apply (see **71.4.6**), the earnings period equates with the pay interval, provided the interval is seven days or more (i.e. an employee who receives a weekly wage will have a weekly earnings period). The regular intervals need not be exactly equal, so payment on the last working day of each calendar month will satisfy this test, despite the fact that some months contain five weeks.

Where an employee (again, other than a company director) has more than one regular pay interval, special rules apply to identify the single earnings period on which liability is based. The earnings period is the shorter or shortest of those intervals, unless that interval is less than seven days. An employee in receipt of monthly salary, quarterly commission and annual bonus would therefore normally have a monthly earnings period, unless a written direction to the contrary is made by NICO.

An earnings period cannot be less than seven days in length and, if there is more than one such interval of less than seven days, the earnings period is set at a week. The same rule applies if there is more than one regular pay interval, one or more of which is less than seven days.

> ### Planning point
>
> The year contains either 365 or 366 days, which is not exactly divisible by seven. It is possible for an employee to be paid 53 lots of weekly wages in a single year if the first pay day falls on 6 or 7 April. Week 53 is treated as a full week, even though this may mean the employee enjoys a total NIC-free band of 53 × £110 (in 2010–11), which is more than the annual limit. The same principle applies to employees paid on a four-weekly cycle, who may receive 56 weeks' pay in a single calendar year. Although this also means that contributions are paid for 56 weeks in one year, no refund of the excess over 53 weeks is possible (unless the employee has another job or is also self-employed in the same year).

If the regular payment interval is other than a week or month, the regular interval becomes the earnings period. The exact percentage method of calculation must also be used.

There are special rules for certain employment rights payments. Official guidance sets out the earnings period rules in a number of unusual circumstances. NICO may sometimes direct that a particular earnings period should be used.

Bonuses and commissions

Bonuses, commissions and such like are treated as part of the total pay at the time they are paid. If extra payments are made at a regular interval shorter than that for basic pay, the shorter period becomes the earnings period, but NICO can direct that the longer or longest interval be used if the greater part of earnings is paid at that interval, even if the structure of pay intervals was not intended as a method of avoiding contributions. If a second one-off payment is made after the normal rules have been applied to a first payment, the two payments must be aggregated within the earnings period to calculate the contribution rate. The deductions working sheet must be amended.

Employment rights payments

Payments made by employers to employees (other than directors) under the Employment Rights Act 1996, where the payments represent earnings, may have their own earnings period and are not in that case added to other payments of earnings made at the same time. These payments include:

- guarantee payments paid for weeks when there is no work – the normal earnings period rule applies;
- medical suspension payments paid for weeks when an employee is suspended on medical grounds – the normal earnings period rule applies;
- awards of arrears in cases of orders for reinstatement or re-engagement – the earnings period is the period for which arrears have to be paid under the order made by the industrial tribunal, or a week if longer;
- pay due following an order for the continuation of employment – the earnings period is the period covered by the order, or a week if longer; and
- pay due following a protective award – the earnings period is the longest of the protected periods stated in the award, the part of the protected period the sum is paid for, or a week.

Official directions

Manipulation of the earnings period rules by employers may lead to an official direction that a different earnings period should be used. Further, where the incidence of earnings-related contributions is avoided or reduced by means of irregular or unequal payments, counteracting directions may be given. However, any direction given may not be retrospective.

Changes in normal pay days

Where a payment is not made on the usual day, it is treated as falling in the earnings period in which the usual day falls, unless that day falls in another tax year, in which case it is treated as made on the last day of the regular interval at which it is treated as paid in the same tax year. Thus a payment of salary always made on the last Friday in the month attracts a monthly earnings period. If the payment is exceptionally made on Thursday (e.g. before Good Friday), the change of pay day is irrelevant. If two weeks' wages are paid together because an employee will be away on the next pay day, two earnings periods of a week are used. If the second of those weeks falls in the next tax year the earlier year's rates are used for that week but it is not aggregated with the payment in the last earnings period of the old year.

Two payments received in an earnings period

If an employee receives two payments in an earnings period because for example, the pay day is changed permanently or there is a change in week-in-hand arrangements, each payment has its own earnings period based on the regular interval.

Employer changes the earnings period

Where an employer changes the earnings period, the treatment depends on whether the new interval is shorter or longer:

- shorter interval (e.g. monthly paid becomes weekly paid) – contributions are worked out on payments made after the change completely separately using the new earnings period, even if the two earnings periods overlap; or
- longer interval (e.g. weekly paid becomes monthly paid) – contributions are worked out as above, unless payment has already been made at the old short interval in the first longer period, in which case all earnings are aggregated in the new period and the total contributions adjusted to take account of those already deducted.

Such a change from weekly to monthly pay often involves entry into a contracted-out occupational pension scheme. All payments made in the new earnings period are charged at the contracted-out rate.

71.4.6 Directors

For ordinary employees, the earnings period is usually set by a person's regular pay interval or intervals (see **71.4.5**). Company directors are generally in a position to decide when and how they receive a payment of earnings, which potentially gives them the ability to avoid primary Class 1 contribution liability by astute use of the earnings period rules. For this reason, a director's earnings period is a tax year, even if he is paid, say, monthly or leaves during the year.

The only exception to the above rule is where a director is first appointed during the course of a tax year. In such an event the earnings period is the period from the date of appointment to the end of the tax year, measured in weeks. The calculation of the earnings period includes the tax week of appointment, plus all remaining complete weeks in the tax year (i.e. week 53 is ignored for this purpose). This is known as the *pro rata* earnings period.

> **Example 71.5**
>
> Chris is appointed to the board of Teachers Ltd in week 44 of the tax year. The primary threshold and upper earnings limit are calculated by multiplying the weekly values by 9, because the earnings period starts with the week of appointment.

> In 2010–11, Chris will pay NIC at the main rate of 11 per cent on his director's earnings between £990 (9 × £110) and £7,596 (9 × £844) and at the additional 1 per cent rate on all earnings above £7,596 paid up to 5 April.

Payments on account

Companies can save time and money by calculating directors' NICs in a similar way to other employees. Instead of paying very high levels of NICs on a short-term basis, directors who are paid regularly (e.g. directors who have contracts of service with their companies) can spread their contributions evenly throughout the tax year. The earnings period remains an annual earnings period, but contributions are made on account throughout the tax year.

Payments made in unusual circumstances

There are special earnings period rules where payments are made to directors in unusual circumstances:

- payments under the Employment Rights Act 1996 – add any payments to other earnings from the company in the tax year of payment; or
- payment to director for the period before appointment (i.e. for work as an employee) – use the earnings period which applies when the earnings are paid (i.e. the annual or *pro rata* period).

Payment after resignation in respect of office previously held (even if the person is still an employee):

- the same year – use annual or *pro rata* earnings period for the year, adding payments to other earnings already paid; or
- later tax year – separate from other earnings in the year, apply a separate annual earnings period and limits.

Directors include shadow directors, though a person is not to be treated as such by reason only that the directors act on advice given by him in his professional capacity.

Law: Social Security (Contributions) Regulations 2001 (SI 2001/1004), reg. 2(1)

Other guidance: HMRC leaflet CA44

71.4.7 Aggregation of earnings

If an employee or director concurrently has more than one employment, it is a fundamental principle that contributions must be calculated separately for each.

However, regulations contain aggregation provisions which lead in prescribed circumstances to different earnings being added together before contribution liabilities are calculated. The situations envisaged by the regulations are where earnings are paid in respect of different employments:

- under the same employer;
- with employers carrying on business in association (see below);
- with employers of whom only one is deemed by regulation to be the secondary contributor; or
- with employers of whom none is the secondary contributor because some other person is deemed by regulation to be the secondary contributor.

The main exception to these rules applies where it is not reasonably practicable to aggregate the earnings.

Employers are associated (see above) if they are carrying on business in association, which involves sharing profits or losses, or to a large extent sharing resources such as accommodation, equipment, personnel and customers, such that their fortunes are to some extent interdependent. Mere constitutional links between two companies (e.g. a parent/subsidiary relationship) are irrelevant for this purpose unless the companies also fulfil the above criteria.

If an employee receives two or more salaries or wages which are not aggregated he may be eligible for deferment of contributions in one or more jobs.

If all the employments of an earner are contracted-out, the normal aggregation rules as set out above apply. If, on the other hand, the employments under consideration are mixed, i.e. not-contracted-out and contracted-out, the earnings must be kept separate for the purposes of calculating liability. In the case of mixed employments, the procedure that is to be followed depends on whether or not the employee has an appropriate personal pension arrangement. Further refinements apply where the earnings relate to employments with mixed occupational pension schemes, where some may be salary-related and others money purchase.

> **Planning point**
>
> The basic rule is that contributions are calculated by adding all earnings together and establishing the earnings limits for the common or shortest earnings period to establish whether contributions are due. Priority is given to the earnings period for the contracted-out earnings, but the procedure depends on the value of the contracted-out earnings. Detail guidance is given in HMRC's booklet CWG2 (*Employer's further guide to PAYE and NICs*) and in CWG1 (*Employer's quick guide to PAYE and NICs*).

71.4.8 Class 1 calculation methods

There are two methods of calculating Class 1 liabilities, the exact percentage method and the tables method. Either may be used, but only one may be used in any single tax year in respect of any single employee, unless NICO expressly permits a change. Permission is not required for a change resulting from a switch from a manual to a computerised payroll or vice versa.

Exact percentage method

The exact percentage method is the more accurate and is generally used by payroll software. It is provided that contributions are to be calculated separately at the appropriate rate and rounded to the nearest penny. This method must be used in certain specified circumstances, e.g. where earnings from two employments are aggregated and one of those employments is contracted-out while the other is not.

Tables method

The alternative method is the tables method, which relies on ready reckoner tables in booklets prepared and distributed by NICO each time rates change.

> **Example 71.6**
>
> The employee contributions due on weekly earnings of £107.01 are, on the exact basis, £0.22. Table A gives £0.27, because it is based on earnings of £107.50.

The contribution tables are divided into sections identified by letter. NICO generally refers to these letters in order to identify the category of Class 1 contribution payable by an earner and his employer.

Table A, which appears in Booklet CA38 and covers not-contracted-out full rate contributions, is used for:

- all male employees aged 16 to 64 and in not-contracted-out employment;
- all female employees aged 16 to 59 who are in not-contracted-out employment and paying standard rate employee's NICs; and
- any employee with an appropriate personal pension or appropriate personal stakeholder pension.

Table B, which appears in CA41 and covers not-contracted-out reduced rate contributions, is used for married women and widows who are:

- aged under 60 in not-contracted-out employment; and
- who are entitled to pay employee's contributions at the reduced rate.

The employer must have a valid certificate of election (CA4139 or CF383) or a valid certificate of reduced liability (CF380A) in respect of these women.

Table C, which appears in CA41 and covers employees over pensionable age or whose liabilities are deferred, is used for:

- men aged 65 and over and women aged 60 and over for whom a valid certificate CA41410 or CF384 is held;
- employees who are in not-contracted-out employment for whom a form CA2700 is held allowing them to defer paying employee's contributions; and
- employees in COSR schemes or the salary-related part of a contracted-out mixed benefit scheme for whom a form CA2700 is held authorising deferment of employee's contributions.

Table D, which appears in CA39 and covers contracted-out full rate contributions in respect of COSR schemes, is used for:

- all male employees aged 16 to 64 in a COSR scheme or the salary-related part of a contracted-out mixed benefit scheme; and
- all female employees aged 16 to 59 who are in a COSR scheme or the salary-related part of a contracted-out mixed benefit scheme and paying standard rate employee's contributions.

Table E, which appears in CA39 and covers contracted-out reduced rate contributions in respect of COSR schemes, is used for married women and widows:

- aged under 60 and in a COSR scheme or the salary-related part of a contracted-out mixed benefits scheme; and
- who are entitled to pay employee's contributions at the reduced rate.

A valid certificate of election (form CA4139 or CF383) or a valid certificate of reduced liability (form CF380A) must be held in respect of such women.

Table F, which appears in CA43 and covers contracted-out full rate contributions in respect of COMP schemes, is used for:

- all male employees aged 16 to 64 in a COMP scheme or contracted-out money purchase stakeholder pension scheme, or the money purchase part of a contracted-out mixed benefits scheme; and
- all female employees aged 16 to 59 who are in a COMP scheme or contracted-out money purchase stakeholder pension scheme, or the money purchase part of a contracted-out mixed benefits scheme and who are paying standard rate employee's contributions.

Table G, which appears in CA43 and covers contracted-out reduced rate contributions for COMP schemes, is used for married women and widows:

- aged under 60 in a COMP scheme or contracted-out money purchase stakeholder pension scheme, or the money purchase part of a contracted-out mixed benefits scheme; and
- who are entitled to pay employee's contributions at the reduced rate.

A valid certificate of election (form CA4139 or CF383) or a valid certificate of reduced liability (form CF380A) must be held in respect of such women.

Table J, which appears in CA38, is used for all employees who are not in contracted-out employment, for whom a form CA2700 is held allowing them to defer payment of employee contributions at the full main percentage rate.

Table L, which appears in CA39, is used for employees in a COSR scheme or the salary-related part of a contracted-out mixed benefit scheme for whom a valid form CA2700 is held authorising deferment of the employee's contributions at the full main percentage rate.

Table S, which appears in CA43, is used for employees in COMP schemes or contracted-out money purchase stakeholder pension schemes, or the money purchase part of contracted-out mixed benefit schemes and for whom form CA2700 is held authorising deferment of employee's contributions.

The letter X signifies that no contributions have been collected, for example because earnings are below the LEL or because the employee has a certificate of coverage under a foreign social security scheme.

71.4.9 Married women: reduced rate elections

Prior to 12 May 1977, married women and widows were able to elect to pay reduced Class 1 contributions. Similarly, if self-employed they could elect to pay no Class 2 contributions (although Class 4 contributions remained payable).

Married women and widows who had reduced liability on 12 May 1977 can keep it unless:

- in the case of married women, the marriage ends in divorce or is annulled;
- the marriage ends because the woman is widowed and she does not qualify for widow's benefits;
- widow's benefit ends, other than on remarriage; or
- there has been no liability to pay NICs for two consecutive tax years after 5 April 1978 and the woman was not self-employed in those tax years.

Alternatively, a woman may decide to give up the right to reduced rate liability since, while reduced rate contributions are payable, the woman has no right to:

- retirement pension or other contributory benefits in respect of reduced Class 1 contributions;
- home protection responsibilities;
- pay voluntary contributions; and
- credits (except in the case of widows with reduced liability).

Employers should only deduct reduced rate contributions if the woman holds a certificate of election (form CA4139 or CF383).

Law: Social Security (Contributions) Regulations 2001 (SI 2001/1004), reg. 126–139; *Whittaker v R & C Commrs* (2006) Sp C 528; *Gutteridge v HMRC* (2006) Sp C 534

71.5 Class 1A NICs

71.5.1 Charge

Class 1A contributions were introduced with effect from 6 April 1991, the charge originally applying only where an income tax benefit arises (or, but for allowable deductions, would arise) on a director or P11D employee in respect of private use of an employer-provided car and, where appropriate, fuel. However, from 6 April 2000, the Class 1A charge is widened to include most taxable benefits in kind (unless specifically exempted from the charge by the regulations). The liability for Class 1A contributions arises only in respect of the secondary contributor (i.e. the employer); there are no primary (employee) Class 1A contributions. The charge, based on the cash equivalent value of the benefit as calculated for tax purposes, is charged at the main secondary contributor rate.

The Class 1A contribution is based on tax years and is payable once annually after the end of the relevant tax year, on the basis of the cash equivalent value of the benefits as calculated for P11D purposes.

71.5.2 Liability

Class 1A contributions are payable only by secondary contributors (usually employers) and are based on the cash equivalent of benefits-in-kind. The liability from 6 April 2000 applies in respect of benefits provided:

- to directors and other persons in controlling positions irrespective of the level of their earnings, unless the director does not have a material interest in the company and he or she is a full-time working director and the company is a charity or non-profit making concern; and
- to employees and directors excluded above earning at the rate of at least £8,500 per annum, including expenses and benefits.

No Class 1A liability arises in respect of benefits and expenses provided to employees earning at a rate of less than £8,500 per annum, even if a P9D is required for tax purposes. Similarly, no Class 1A liability arises if any benefit arising for tax purposes is offset by a corresponding deduction: for example, if the benefit was provided for use by the employee wholly, exclusively and necessarily in the performance of the duties of his employment or in the course of qualifying business travel.

> **Example 71.7**
>
> A person may have two or more concurrent but independent employments: e.g. working four days per week for company C and one day per week for company D. If both C and D make available a company car and pay earnings, both have a Class 1A liability if the employee is a P11D employee. However, if C were to pay earnings but not provide a company car, while D paid no earnings whatsoever but made available a company car for private use, neither would have a Class 1A liability, provided it could be shown that the car was not made available by D by reason of the employment with C, and that the payment of salary by C was unconnected with the employment by D. However, it should be noted that a payment of £1 of earnings by D would make D liable to Class 1A contributions.

> **Planning point**
>
> The key questions in identifying the person liable to pay the Class 1A contribution are as follows.
>
> (1) To which job does the provision of the car relate?
> (2) Who uses the car?
> (3) Who made the last payment of earnings to that person in the tax year in question?
> (4) Who was liable to pay the secondary Class 1 contribution on those earnings (or who would have been liable had they exceeded the primary threshold)?

Where a person holds two or more employments and is provided with one car by virtue of both employments, whether under the same employer or different employers, the Class 1A charge is shared equally between the employers involved. It is irrelevant that the employee may cover 10,000 business miles on behalf of the first employer and only 5,000 on behalf of the second.

A shared car can be:

(a) a car made available for concurrent use by two or more employees by reason of their employment and available for use by both; or
(b) a car which is made available for private use to one employee by reason of two or more employed earners' employments with the same or different employers.

For (a) above a Class 1A NIC liability arises in respect of each employee. For (b) above each employment attracts a Class 1A NIC liability. If the two employments are with the same employer, the calculation will need to take into account any differences in the employee's conditions of employment in the separate employments.

There is no tax charge on the benefit of a car if it is a pooled car used only for business purposes. Similarly, there is no liability to Class 1A NICs for that car or for fuel supplied for that car. There may however, be a liability for Class 1 NICs if a lump sum or mileage allowance is paid.

Fuel provided for private purposes

Where in any tax year fuel is provided for private use by a director or P11D employee, for Class 1A purposes, the amount of any cash equivalent taxable on the employee is added to the cash equivalent of the benefit of the car. The contribution is calculated by applying the Class 1A percentage for the year of provision of the benefit to the total of the two figures).

If the full cost of private fuel is reimbursed by the employee, no Class 1A NICs are payable.

If the employer simply pays a round sum allowance which bears no relation to the actual expense incurred by the employee, the allowance should be included in gross pay and subjected to Class 1 contributions in the same way as a payment of wages or salary. In such a case, the employer does not provide free fuel for private motoring: the employee purchases the fuel personally out of net income. There is, accordingly, no liability to Class 1A contributions in respect of that employee.

Similarly, there is no question of a Class 1A liability arising in respect of fuel provided for private motoring in an employee's own car or in a van, lorry, etc. irrespective of the owner of the vehicle.

71.5.3 Calculating the charge

Class 1A NICs are payable at a single rate applied to the cash equivalent of the benefit as calculated for income tax purposes. The single rate applicable is known as the Class 1A percentage and is equal to the main secondary contributor rate for Class 1 purposes.

No reduction of the rate applies where the employment is contracted-out, or a reduced rate of Class 1 contribution applies for some other reason (e.g. where a married woman or widow pays at the reduced rate, or where the foreign-going rebate applies to a mariner's earnings).

71.6 Class 1B NICs

71.6.1 Charge

PAYE settlement agreements (PSAs) allow employers to account for any tax liability in respect of their employees on payments that are minor or irregular, or that are shared benefits on which it would be impractical to determine individual liability, in one lump sum. From 6 April 1999, the principle was extended to NICs through a new contribution class: Class 1B. Where an employer has a PSA with HMRC, he will be liable to Class 1B contributions (at the secondary rate) on the amount of the emoluments in the agreement that are chargeable to Class 1 or Class 1A contributions, together with the total amount of income tax payable under the agreement.

71.6.2 Calculating the charge

Class 1B contributions are calculated on the value of the items included with the PAYE settlement agreement (PSA) that would otherwise have attracted a liability for Class 1 or Class 1A NICs and the total tax payable under the PSA. The Class 1B contributions due are at the secondary rate.

> *Example 71.8*
>
> Blur Ltd rewards its top salesman, Tony, by allowing him to use the company villa and reimbursing his travel costs. The taxable benefit for the use of the villa is agreed to be £800 and the tickets cost £400. Tony is a 40 per cent taxpayer and already pays maximum Class 1 contributions at the main primary rate.
>
> In the absence of a PSA, Tony's benefit of £1,200 would be reported on his P11D. Tony would pay tax of £480. The benefit of the villa would be subject to Class 1A contributions, but the reimbursement of the ticket costs would be within Class 1 and should be dealt with through payroll.
>
> Blur enters into a PSA before any of the transactions take place (see below for the significance of this point) and accounts for tax of £800 (40% × £1,200 × 100 ÷ 60) on 19 October following the end of the tax year. Class 1B contributions are due on £2,000, i.e., the chargeable emoluments of £1,200 and the income tax of £800.
>
> Blur could have simply given Tony enough cash to ensure he could (after tax and NIC) rent the villa. As Tony is a 40 per cent taxpayer, he would already have paid maximum primary NICs at the main rate, so only 1 per cent extra would be due. Blur would therefore have had to give him £2,033.90 gross. Blur's secondary Class 1 liability would have been on £2,033.90.

71.7 Class 2 NICs

71.7.1 Charge

Class 2 contributions are payable at a flat weekly rate by every 'self-employed earner' over the age of 16 and under state retirement age for any week during which he or she is such an earner. The weekly flat rate for 2009–10 and 2010–11 is £2.40. Special rates apply to share fishermen and volunteer development workers.

A self-employed person who does not earn any income in any particular week (e.g. due to holidays) does not thereby cease to be self-employed, but a person who is not ordinarily self-employed will have no Class 2 liability provided his earnings from self-employment do not exceed an annual amount.

71.7.2 Calculating the charge

Since Class 2 contributions are payable at a flat weekly rate no calculations need to be performed in arriving at the value of a contribution. The level of total earnings in a tax year is used to determine whether a Class 2 contribution need be paid in respect of each week of self-employment in that particular year, since self-employed earners with small earnings may claim exception from liability in certain circumstances.

A week is treated as falling wholly within the year in which it begins. In the past, if payment of Class 2 contributions was made at regular weekly intervals, it was possible in some years that 53 weekly contributions would be paid, since each year consists of 52 weeks and one or, in leap years, two days. If a year has 53 contribution weeks, this will be reflected in the quarterly bills.

> **Planning point**
>
> A Class 2 contribution paid will count towards the benefit entitlement of the individual concerned, but the benefits covered do not include contribution-based jobseeker's allowance or the earnings-related component of the state pension scheme.

71.7.3 Residence

No person is liable or entitled to pay contributions of any class unless he fulfils prescribed conditions of residence or presence in Great Britain. Before a person may become liable to pay Class 2 contributions in respect of any particular week, he must be ordinarily resident in the UK or, if he is not so ordinarily resident, he must have been resident in the UK for at least 26 out of the preceding 52 contribution weeks. Before entitlement to pay a Class 2 contribution can arise for a self-employed earner, the earner in question must have been present in the UK in the week in respect of which the contribution is to be paid.

Law: SSCBA 1992, s. 11(1)

71.7.4 Incapacity exemption

Automatic exception from Class 2 liability is granted to a self-employed earner for a week where certain conditions are fulfilled, though he may, if he wishes, pay the contribution, subject to certain restrictions. Exception is mandatory in respect of a contribution week where the earner is:

- in receipt of sickness benefit, invalidity benefit or incapacity benefit in respect of the whole week;
- incapable of work throughout the whole week;
- in receipt of maternity allowance;
- detained in legal custody or imprisoned during the whole week; or
- in receipt of unemployability supplement or invalid care allowance.

Those provisions which refer to a whole contribution week mean a week which excludes Sunday or some other day which is excluded on religious grounds from the working week.

Law: SI 2001/1004, reg. 43

71.7.5 Small earnings exception

A self-employed person may, on application and subject to conditions, be excepted from an otherwise unavoidable Class 2 liability for any period in which his earnings from self-employment are (or are treated as being) less than a specified amount (£5,715 for 2010–11 (remaining unchanged from 2009–10)).

If NICO approves the application, it issues a certificate of exception, CF17, which states the period of coverage, normally a tax year, or a period ending on 5 April if application is not made before the start of a tax year. The earner must produce the certificate to any official on request.

If any of the conditions for the granting of exception is not, or ceases to be, fulfilled (e.g. the earner ceases to be a self-employed earner), the certificate becomes invalid at that time and the earner must notify NICO of the fact, which is achieved by completing a declaration on the certificate and returning it to NICO. Similarly, the earner must notify NICO in writing (in practice also by completing a declaration on the certificate itself) if he wishes the certificate to be cancelled for whatever reason and the certificate ceases to have effect from a date specified by NICO.

National Insurance Contributions

Certificates may be renewed if the conditions of issue are still fulfilled and, indeed, NICO prompts any earner in possession of a certificate to apply for renewal shortly before the old certificate expires. Certificates can cover three years from issue.

> ### *Planning point*
>
> The granting of exception and the consequent non-payment of contributions may prejudice the earner's future benefit entitlement, which depends on the individual's contribution record. Individuals should be advised to keep a close eye on contributions and likely future benefit entitlements.

The key criterion for the availability of exception is the level of earnings. Earnings, in the context of the self-employed earner, means net earnings from employment as a self-employed earner, which is officially interpreted as meaning profits calculated according to normal commercial accountancy principles such as would be shown in a profit and loss account, time-apportioned to the relevant tax year. Total net earnings are to be arrived at by deducting from income business expenses incurred in the course of the self-employed activity, e.g. rent and rates, insurance, employees' wages, printing and stationery, repairs and postage. Furthermore, official guidance states that the earner should make an allowance for depreciation of equipment such as a vehicle, if it is used for the business, and any stock taken for the earner's own use is to be taken into account as income. However, the guidance makes it clear that no deduction is available in respect of income tax or Class 2 or Class 4 contribution liabilities. Earnings from all sources as a self-employed earner must be aggregated in arriving at a total to compare with the exception limit.

In looking at the likely level of earnings, NICO usually accepts the evidence of an income tax assessment, or the accounts for a period not yet agreed with the Revenue, or if neither is available, any evidence which the earner has to support his application, such as a record of business receipts and expenditure for the year.

Earnings which suffer Class 1 contributions, but are included in business profits (e.g. for sub-postmasters) may be excluded from the calculation of profit for the purposes of the small earnings exception.

> ### *Planning point*
>
> Claims for retrospection may be made, in writing and with supporting evidence. Any application for exception must be made between 6 April following the end of the tax year and the following 31 December. As earnings are officially defined as profits as shown in the accounts for the year in question and expects those profits to be calculated on an actual basis (i.e. time-apportioned if the accounting year does not end on 5 April), many self-employed earners whose accounting year ends other than on 5 April find it impossible to make an application for a certificate. It is understood that local offices have been

instructed to accept any reasonable evidence of profits in the period from the accounting year end to the following 5 April.

Planning point

A retrospective claim may involve the contributor repaying benefits already claimed on the basis of those contributions. The repayment automatically excepts the earner from liability for the period covered by the repayment if the earner is not already excepted, and NICO must issue the appropriate certificate to that effect.

Law: SSCBA 1992, s. 11(4); SI 2001/1004, regs. 44(4)–(6), 45(2), 46

71.7.6 Married women and widows

There is no separate rate or type of Class 2 contributions payable by married women or widows. However, where such earners are entitled by virtue of a reduced rate election made before 12 May 1977 not to participate in the NIC scheme, it is currently possible for them to elect not to pay Class 2 contributions.

Law: SI 2001/1004, reg. 127(1)(b)

71.8 Class 3 NICs

71.8.1 Charge

Class 3 contributions are voluntary contributions. A person is never liable to pay Class 3 contributions, but he may be entitled to pay, to protect entitlement to widows' benefits and the basic retirement pension. In certain limited cases involving overseas employment, voluntary Class 2 contributions may be paid as an alternative to Class 3 in order to protect entitlement to incapacity benefit and maternity allowance on the employee's return to the UK. Class 3 contributions are flat-rate contributions. The weekly flat rate for Class 3 contributions for 2010–11 is £12.05 (remaining unchanged from 2009–10).

71.8.2 Eligibility

Class 3 contributions may be made by men between the ages of 16 and 65 years and by women between the ages of 16 and 60 years who satisfy the following conditions in respect of any tax year:

- the person is resident in the UK throughout the year;

National Insurance Contributions

- the person has arrived in the UK during the year and has been or is liable to pay Class 1 or Class 2 contributions in respect of an earlier period during that year;
- the person has arrived in the UK during the year and was either ordinarily resident in the UK throughout the year or became ordinarily resident during the course of it; or
- the person not being ordinarily resident in the UK has arrived during the year or the previous year and has been continuously present in the UK for 26 complete contribution weeks, entitlement where the arrival has been in the previous year arising only in respect of the next year.

> **Warning!**
>
> No Class 3 contributions may be paid in respect of a contribution year if the individual has in any case satisfied certain contribution conditions by reference to Class 1 or Class 2.

Married women and widows with certificates of reduced liability following an election before 12 May 1977 (or under transitional provisions) cannot pay Class 3 contributions.

71.9 Class 4 NICs

71.9.1 Charge

Class 4 contributions are profit-related and are payable by self-employed earners in addition to any Class 2 contribution liability. The Class 4 contribution liability arises in respect of tax years and is based on the earner's annual profits or gains immediately derived from the carrying on or exercise of one or more trades, professions or vocations, being profits or gains chargeable to tax under ITTOIA 2005 for the year of assessment corresponding to the tax year. Class 4 contributions do not count towards benefit entitlement but are nevertheless income of the National Insurance Fund used for the payment of benefits.

Law: SSCBA 1992, s. 15(1)

71.9.2 Exceptions

The following categories of person may, on application, be excepted from Class 4 contributions:

- men aged 65 or over and women aged 60 or over at the beginning of the tax year (including people whose sixtieth/sixty-fifth birthday falls on 6 April). However, a person reaching 65/60 during the tax year is liable for Class 4 contributions up to the following 5 April;

- those who are non-resident in the UK for tax purposes during the tax year;
- in some cases, a trustee, executor or administrator;
- a sleeping partner (i.e. someone who supplies capital and takes a share of the profits but takes no active part in running the trade); and
- a diver or diving supervisor working in connection with exploration or exploitation activities on the UK continental shelf or in the UK territorial waters and whose earnings are taxed under ITTOIA 2005 (such divers pay Class 1 contributions).

Planning point

It should be noted that exception is not automatic and must be applied for. The certificate should be requested before the start of the year to which it relates, but NICO may accept a later application.

71.9.3 Earnings

The profits to which the specified percentage rate for Class 4 NICs is applied are closely related to the taxable profits.

The 'earnings' for Class 4 contributions purposes are defined as the profits or gains immediately derived from the carrying on of one or more trades, professions or vocations, being profits or gains chargeable to income tax under ITTOIA 2005. Furthermore, the charge is based on the full amount of such profits or gains, subject to deductions for allowances for capital expenditure (whether given by way of deduction from trading profits or by discharge or repayment of tax) available in respect of the activities of the trade, profession or vocation and to additions for any balancing charges arising. There is some relief for losses (see **71.9.4**).

The term 'immediately derived' means that a contributor will not be liable to pay Class 4 contributions on profits or gains in the earning of which he was not personally involved. This covers the position of a sleeping partner, who is in reality no more than an investor in the business, supplying capital but taking no active part in the running of the business. Payment of a share of profits to a retired partner who provides no services, and the income of non-working Names at Lloyd's should also be covered by this rule.

Planning point

The basis of assessment adopted for income tax automatically applies for Class 4 contribution purposes. It is also possible that the profits liable to Class 4 contributions will be affected by the use of the rule which allows farmers to average their year-on-year profits or by a change of accounting date, which

National Insurance Contributions

> allows HMRC to adjust the profits chargeable to income tax for more than one year.

Income from the commercial letting of furnished holiday accommodation is not normally brought into charge to Class 4 contributions unless the owner runs it as a trading business falling within the rules governing ITTOIA 2005.

> ### Planning point
>
> Although, in principle, Class 4 contributions are levied on the taxable profits or gains from a trade, etc. it is important to distinguish those rules which apply for tax purposes but do not apply for Class 4 contribution purposes. The following are not deductible for Class 4 purposes:
>
> - any personal allowance;
> - deductions for personal pension premiums or retirement annuity premiums, etc.;
> - interest paid in any tax year which falls under ITA 2007, s. 383;
> - where a business charge exceeds available income in a year and an assessment has been raised on the person who paid the charge to collect the tax which he deducted at source in making the payment, such that the surplus is carried forward against the profits of a later year from the same trade as if it were a trading loss (though relief may be given differently);
> - relief for excess interest payments laid out wholly and exclusively for the purposes of a trade, etc. by means of treating the excess as a loss available for carry-forward or carry-back under the terminal loss provisions (though relief may be given differently); and
> - concessionary relief for self-employed doctors and dentists to qualify for relief in respect of contributions to the NHS superannuation scheme, does not extend to Class 4 contributions, a Special Commissioner has held.

Partnerships present potential difficulties in the context of Class 4 contributions and specific provision is made in respect of the earnings of partners. Where a trade or profession is carried on by two or more persons jointly, the liability of any one of them in respect of Class 4 contributions is based on his share of the profits or gains of that trade or profession (bearing in mind that such profits must be immediately derived from that trade or profession) together with his share of the profits or gains of any other trade, etc. which he carries on.

Law: ITA 2007, s. 383; SSCBA 1992, s. 15(1), (3A), (4), 16(3) and Sch. 2, para. 4; *Pegler v Abell* (1972) 48 TC 564; *Stekel v Ellice* [1973] 1 All ER 465

71.9.4 Loss relief

For the purposes of calculating the amount of profits or gains in respect of which Class 4 contributions are payable, relief is available under, and in the manner provided by, a number of provisions of the Taxes Acts, including the extension of offset to capital allowances:

- the set-off of trading losses against general income (though relief is restricted for Class 4 contribution liability to losses arising from activities the profits or gains of which would be brought into computation for the purposes of Class 4 contributions);
- the carry-forward of losses from trading not utilised under the aforementioned rules against future profits from the same trade; and
- terminal loss relief.

The rules of Class 4 loss relief are extended beyond certain of the restrictions imposed by income tax law. Where losses are carried forward for income tax purposes, they reduce profits from the same trade in a later period, thereby automatically reducing Class 4 profits in that same period. Similarly, where the terminal loss provisions apply, the relief is restricted for income tax purposes to a reduction in taxable profits from the same trade, which has retrospective effect on the assessment for the tax year affected and, again, automatically reduces the Class 4 profits for that year.

Example 71.9

Where a trading loss is relieved by a claim to set it off against income other than that derived from a trade, for income tax purposes, the trading profits of other years would be unaffected and there would, in the absence of special provision, be no reduction in Class 4 contribution liabilities. Where a person claims and is allowed relief in respect of a loss in any relevant trade, profession or vocation against total income, rather than against the profits of the same trade, the deduction granted is to be treated as far as possible as reducing the profits or gains for that year of any relevant trade, profession or vocation.

Any excess of loss in that year is carried forward to reduce the first available profits or gains for later years, again from any relevant trade, etc. irrespective of whether a claim for a current year loss exists in those years.

Whether a trading loss is time-apportioned to tax years on the statutory basis or is claimed in full in the year in which the period-end falls on the concessionary basis, any amount which is set against non-trading income must be separately identified and claimed against other trading income in the same or a later year for Class 4 contribution purposes.

Law: SSCBA 1992, Sch. 2, para. 3

71.9.5 Interest and annuity payments

Profits for Class 4 contribution purposes may be reduced by certain payments of interest for which income tax relief is, or can be, given. The deduction is available in the year in which payment is made to the extent that such interest has been paid and incurred wholly or exclusively for the purposes of any relevant trade, profession or vocation. Where the profits or gains of the tax year of payment are insufficient to allow relief in full, the payments are carried forward and deducted from, or set off against, the first available profits or gains of any subsequent year:

- it is irrelevant that the payment of interest may not be deductible for income tax purposes in that later year. The fact that the interest was incurred in respect of a relevant trade, profession or vocation is sufficient to create a deduction, which is carried forward until it has been fully utilised against profits;
- the deduction need not be given against the later income from the same trade, profession or vocation, since the Act refers to deduction from the profits or gains of any relevant trade, etc.; and
- relief is not lost if the trade in which the loss arose ceases, provided there are earnings at some later point from some relevant trade, etc. since relief is carried forward without limit until it can be deducted.

Relief is also granted on the same basis as that applied to interest in respect of annuities (e.g. to retired partners) and other annual payments made under deduction of tax and wholly or exclusively for the purposes of the business.

71.9.6 Calculating the charge

The calculation of liability to Class 4 contributions is based on limits and rates amended annually by statutory instrument, applied to a profit figure based closely, but not exactly, on that arrived at by applying the rules of income tax. Contributions are payable at a prescribed rate on so much of the relevant profits or gains as exceeds a specified lower annual limit.

Contributions are payable on earnings between the lower and upper limits and, from 2003–04, there is an extra one per cent contribution on profits above the upper limit. Both the lower and upper limits for Class 4 purposes apply on an annual basis and are not time-apportioned if the trade is not carried on for a full year.

Where NICO is satisfied that there is doubt as to the extent, if any, of an earner's liability to pay Class 4 contributions for a particular tax year (e.g. because of Class 1 liabilities) a certificate of deferment may be issued which defers the collection of the Class 4 liability until a later date.

An examiner, moderator, invigilator, etc. (employed other than through the agency of another) who would normally be an employed earner is treated as a self-employed earner. Such a person is liable to pay a 'special Class 4 contribution' where, in any tax year:

- he has earnings (disregarding the amount) which would otherwise be Class 1 earnings;

- the earnings are taxable (but not necessarily taxed) under the charge on employment income provisions of ITEPA 2003; and
- his total earnings exceed a lower annual limit (which is in practice usually set at the same level as the limit for ordinary Class 4 purposes).

The special contribution is calculated using the same basis as ordinary Class 4 contributions applied to the earnings calculated as if they were Class 1 earnings and rounded down to the nearest pound.

For 2010–11 the applicable rate is 8 per cent between £5,715 and £43,875 (remaining unchanged from 2009–10). Above the upper limit, the rate is 1 per cent.

71.10 Interaction of NIC classes and annual maxima

71.10.1 Need for NIC interaction rules

An individual can be liable to pay contributions in any year of Class 1, 2 and 4, e.g. because he has a job and also a part-time self-employed activity. He may also make voluntary contributions if necessary to make the year a qualifying year for benefit purposes. The rate of payment of each contribution is calculated initially without reference to any other class payable.

71.10.2 Annual maximum amounts

Historically, the National Insurance system has worked on annual maximum amounts so that no employee ever paid more than the overall contribution limit based on the UEL. The new legislation, which came into force on 6 April 2003, mimics this principle, but also provides for a charge of one per cent on all earnings without limit. The maximum contributions payable is now therefore a maximum with respect to a certain amount of earnings rather than an absolute maximum.

From 6 April 2003, the maximum amount anyone is liable to pay in Class 1 contributions is equal to 53 weeks' full contributions at the main rate of 11 per cent, plus one per cent on all earnings above this sum. However, where multiple jobs are held a primary threshold (£110 per week for 2010–11) will apply to each.

An employee with a job paying £875 in 2010–11 will bear NIC at 11 per cent only up to £844 per week, and would pay one per cent on £31 per week. If the employee has a further job, he would be liable to one per cent on those earnings in excess of the threshold of £110. However, the following scenario is much more likely.

Example 71.10

Lisa has two jobs in which she earns £450 per week and £600 per week respectively. Class 1 NICs calculated for 2010–11 are as follows:

Job 1: weekly rate £37.40. Total in 52 weeks £1,944.80.

Job 2: weekly rate £53.90. Total in 52 weeks £2,802.80.

Total contributions borne in year: £4,747.60.

The amounts paid will prompt a refund after the year end as follows:

Maximum amount of Class 1 NICs payable: at the full rate 53 weeks at £844 minus £110 is £4,279.22 on earnings of £38,902.

Job 1: £450 − £110 × 52 = £17,680.

Job 2: £600 − £110 × 52 = £25,480.

Total = £43,160.

Less earnings at full rate (as above) = (£38,902).

Amount on which one per cent is due = £4,258.

Total NIC liability = £42.58 + £4,279.22 = £4,321.80.

The balance over and above this sum is refunded. No credit can be given during 2010–11 for this overpayment. However, after the tax year ends a refund of £425.80 may be claimed.

71.10.3 Class 1 deferment

Employees with more than one employment, who anticipate earning in excess of the UEL in one, or in a number of employments, may apply to NICO for deferment of some of their contributions liability. Where permission is obtained, the employee will pay a reduced main employee rate of one per cent on all earnings from the earnings threshold to the UEL and the additional employee rate of one per cent on all earnings above the UEL in the deferred employments.

Where deferment is obtained, form CA2700 will be sent to the employers concerned authorising them to deduct primary NICs at a rate of one per cent on all earnings above the earnings threshold. Employer's contributions will remain payable at the full standard rate.

Where there is a choice, standard rate employee Class 1 contribution liability will always be deferred, rather than contracted-out liability.

Any application for deferment should be made before the beginning of the tax year for which it is sought. An application form for deferment (CA72A (CF379)) is contained within Revenue leaflet CA72: *Deferring payment.*

Any employee Class 1 contributions which should have been paid but which, as a result of deferment, have not been paid, will be collected by direct assessment of the employed earner.

71.10.4 Repayment

Where an individual has overpaid contributions, the order of repayment is as follows.

1   Class 4, both ordinary and special.

2   Primary Class 1 at married women's rate.

3   Class 2.

4   Primary Class 1 at standard not-contracted-out rate.

5   Primary Class 1 at contracted-out rate.

However, this order is changed if the contributor concerned has a contracted-out personal pension plan or stakeholder personal pension plan: the order of the fourth and fifth items is reversed.

71.11 Administration

71.11.1 Class 1 returns

An employer must keep a P11 deductions working sheet (or computer equivalent) for each employee and record on it various information about the employee and the payments made. At the end of the tax year, the employer must submit forms P14 for all employees, summarised on P35, on or before 19 May, together with any outstanding remittance of PAYE and contributions. Special rules apply to employers of mariners, who are subject to unusual rules on earnings periods and apportionment of earnings.

Employers are actively encouraged to submit year-end returns electronically and in fact, from 2011 electronic filing will be compulsory for all employers.

Even if the employer uses HMRC's electronic filing facility, he must still produce and give to his employee a paper copy of the P14, known as P60, if the employee is in his employment on the last day of the year.

The contents of the P14/P60 in relation to contributions (which must be issued for contribution purposes even if not required under the PAYE regulations) for the year in question are specified in regulations.

> **Planning point**
>
> Where an employer is outside the jurisdiction, or exempt from compliance with UK law by virtue of any treaty or convention (e.g. the Vienna Convention on diplomatic relations), an employee who is still liable to primary contributions is required to prepare his own deductions working sheets and year-end returns and pay the deductions to the Accounts Office at the same time as he pays any tax deductions under a direct payment PAYE scheme. Remittances are in practice made quarterly. He faces broadly the same time limits and possibility of enforcement action and penalties for non-payment as any employer.

71.11.2 Class 1A information requirements

From 2000–01, the Class 1A charge was widened to include most taxable benefits in kind. In consequence, the employer will need to know the cash equivalent value of benefits provided, as calculated for income tax purposes and returned on forms P11D, to enable him to calculate the Class 1A liability. The revised P11D applying from 2000–01 includes Class 1A indicators and coloured boxes to make it easier to identify those figures required for the Class 1A return.

From 2000–01, the P11D(b) is the statutory Class 1A return. It is due to HMRC no later than 6 July after the end of the tax year. The form contains boxes for the calculation of Class 1A NICs due and any adjustments which may be necessary to the total benefits figure shown as liable to Class 1A on the P11D.

As far as company cars are concerned, there is an onus of proof on the employer, as the contribution is his liability.

71.11.3 Class 1B information requirements

To calculate the amount of Class 1B contributions due in respect of a PAYE settlement agreement (PSA), records will need to be kept of:

- the overall cost of providing the benefits in question;
- the number of employees who received them;
- an indication of what rate of tax they pay;
- an indication which benefits and expenses give rise to a Class 1 or Class 1A liability; and
- the total tax payable under the PSA.

71.11.4 Class 2 information requirements

Every person liable to pay a Class 2 contribution, or not liable but entitled and intending to do so, who has not made special direct debit arrangements with NICO or been granted a certificate of exception, must notify NICO of the commencement or cessation of his liability or entitlement to pay a contribution (see the HMRC website at *www.hmrc.gov.uk/selfemployed/iwtregister-as-self-employed.htm* for details on how and when to register for tax and NICs). There is also a requirement that every person liable to pay a Class 2 contribution or paying voluntarily must immediately notify NICO in writing of any change of address.

> ### Planning point
> Persons who have not previously notified NICO of their self-employment should complete and return to NICO CWF1, found at the back of booklet CWL1: *Starting your own business?*

71.11.5 Class 3

Since Class 3 contributions are voluntary contributions, there are no reporting requirements.

71.11.6 Class 4 information requirements

Income tax information reporting requirements apply to anyone who is liable for Class 4 contributions.

71.11.7 Payment and collection of NICs

Class 1 payment and collection

The secondary contributor (usually the employer), as well as being liable for his own contributions, is liable in the first instance for the employee's primary contributions, on behalf of and to the exclusion of the earner. Any primary contributions paid by the secondary contributor are deemed to have been paid by the earner. However, the secondary contributor may recover the primary contributions by deduction from the earnings paid to the employed earner and in no other way, subject to conditions laid down by regulations.

Where earnings are subject to the aggregation rules, the secondary contributor may deduct primary contributions from any part or parts of those earnings.

When an employer makes an error in good faith which results in the under-deduction of primary contributions when earnings are paid, he is given a limited right to recoup that under-deduction from later payments of earnings within the same tax year. The maximum supplementary amount which may be deducted in each later period is an amount equal to the primary contributions otherwise due in respect of that later payment of earnings. Correction of past errors may not cross tax year-ends.

The secondary contributor is to pay, account for and recover Class 1 contributions in the same way as he pays, accounts for and recovers income tax deducted from emoluments under PAYE.

Remittances of contributions, net of SSP and SMP recoveries, are generally made each month at the same time as any PAYE is remitted to the collector (i.e. within 14 days of the end of the tax period). Small employers can remit quarterly on or before 19 July, 19 October, 19 January and 19 April in respect of deductions in the quarter ended on the preceding fifth of the month. To qualify for this system, employers' average monthly remittances in the current year in respect of total deductions of PAYE, NICs and tax under the construction industry tax deduction scheme have to be less than £1,500 for periods beginning after 6 April 2000. Quarterly payment may be chosen where the employer has reasonable grounds for believing that the £1,500 per month condition is met, or in the case of an employee who receives a fixed salary or wage, where the inspector of taxes has issued a week one or month one PAYE code.

Payment by cheque is treated as made on the day on which the cheque is received by the collector.

Class 1A payment and collection

From 2000–01 and subsequent tax years, Class 1A contributions are payable by the secondary contributor to his or her PAYE reference at the Accounts Office by 19 July following the end of the tax year. Where payment is made other than by direct debit, a special Class 1A payslip should be used.

Class 2 payment and collection

Direct debit and quarterly billing are, in general, the only approved methods of paying Class 2 contributions. A third method of payment officially sanctioned by social security law is the deduction of contributions at source from certain state benefits at the time of payment.

Direct debit mandate is a payment system which is officially encouraged. Relevant guidance and an application form are provided in Booklets CA04 and CWL1. Payments under this arrangement will normally be made by debit to the contributor's bank or building society account on the second Friday in every month covering each of the contribution weeks in the preceding tax month. This may cover four or five weeks' contributions (the exact number is based on the number of Sundays in the preceding tax month), or less if the earner is incapable of work throughout a particular week and NICO is made aware of the fact (e.g. by the making of a claim to incapacity benefit).

Where Class 2 contributions are not payable as above, the contributor should receive within 14 days of the end of the 'contribution quarter' a written notice setting out the number of weeks of liability in that quarter (as reduced for any weeks when benefit was claimed or the liability did not otherwise arise, e.g. where self-employment commenced or ceased), the weekly rate and the formal date of notification. He must then pay the amount due for the quarter within 28 days of the formal date of notification. If the notice is not received, or is lost, defaced or destroyed, or the amount of the notice is disputed, NICO may issue or reissue the notice, giving a new date of notification. The notice must include a bank giro credit form in order that payment may be made at a bank or Post Office. The term 'contribution quarter' means one of the four periods of not less than 13 contribution weeks commencing on the first day of the first, fourteenth, twenty-seventh or fortieth contribution week in any year.

Deduction of contributions at source from certain state benefits is sometimes possible. The benefits in point include war disablement pension.

Class 3 payment and collection

Since Class 3 contributions are voluntary contributions, there are less strict requirements for payment. The options are the quarterly bill or monthly direct debit (as with Class 2 contributions), or single annual cheque.

Payment of Class 3 contributions is normally due on or before 5 April following the tax year in which the deficiency occurred, though six years may be allowed.

Class 4 payment and collection

Most Class 4 contributions are self-assessed in the same way as tax and collected by HMRC, together with income tax. Subject to specific exceptions, provisions as to assessment, collection, repayment, recovery and penalties apply as they do to income tax under ITEPA 2003.

Appeals

The appeals system applicable to income tax assessments now also extends to Class 4 contributions assessments, though the provisions of income tax law have no effect on determinations of questions arising in relation to certificates of exception or deferment, or in relation to special Class 4 contributions.

Partnership assessments

Where two or more persons are carrying on business in partnership, the assessment to both tax and NICs will usually be made as a joint assessment in the name of the partnership, though it is possible for each partner to be assessed separately.

Share option elections – annual return

A special annual return is required where any amount of secondary contributions is transferred by election from employer to employee in respect of share option gains or, from 1 September 2004, relevant employment income. Before 7 July (i.e. by

6 July) following the year end, the employer must report to HMRC a list of employees concerned with, for each, the amount of contributions due on the option gains or relevant employment income, the amount transferred to the employee, and the date on which payment of the liability was made to the Accounts Office. The deadline is now the same as that for all share scheme reporting for income tax purposes set by FA 2003.

The Form 42 return issued by HMRC or available from the website is the official document for reporting transactions in employment-related securities under ITEPA 2003, s. 421J. For those employers to whom the return was issued on time, the reporting deadline for 2010–11 is 6 July 2011. The form encompasses the information required by the National Insurance election reporting process, so it may be assumed that the deadline applies for these purposes as well as the ITEPA purposes for which it was introduced.

Guidance on form 42 procedures are available on the HMRC website at *www.hmrc.gov.uk/manuals/ersmmanual/ERSM140100.htm*.

Law: Social Security (Contributions) Regulations (SI 2001/1004), Sch. 4, para. 23

71.11.8 Enforcement, etc.

When a person fails to pay a contribution which he or she is liable to pay, and is found guilty of a criminal offence, such a person shall be liable, on conviction on indictment, to imprisonment for a term not exceeding seven years or a fine, or both, or a summary conviction to a fine not exceeding the statutory maximum.

The collector of taxes, whose responsibilities include the collection of Class 1 contributions, may visit the employer's premises to inspect the records, in order to establish whether an underpayment has occurred. If the collector is not satisfied that the employer has paid the correct contributions due, he may notify the employer of his best estimate of the liability and request a return in respect thereof, to be made within 14 days. In certain circumstances, the contributions so specified will be certified as the amount of the true liability.

The collector's certificate thus issued is sufficient evidence of non-payment of contributions (or, from 6 April 1999, of interest on or penalties in respect of contributions), until the contrary is proven, in any court proceedings. Any document which purports to be such a certificate of non-payment is deemed to be such, until it is proven otherwise.

No time limit is placed on the period covered by the certificate which the collector issues, except that it covers the years or income tax months or quarters covered by the inspection.

Where a secondary contributor claims that a contribution has been paid but is unable to produce evidence of the fact, a statutory declaration by the officer dealing with the case to the effect that no record of the contribution has been found will be admissible in evidence in criminal proceedings against the secondary contributor, provided it has been served on the person charged with the offence at least seven full days before any hearing or trial of the offence. The declaration must be served in the same way as a summons or citation. However, the accused may give notice to the court, not less than three days before the due date of the hearing, requiring the person who made the declaration to attend the hearing. In such a case, the statutory declaration may not be admitted in evidence.

In most cases, if earnings have not been subjected to contribution liability, they have also escaped PAYE deduction. It is therefore specifically provided that proceedings may be (but need not be) brought for the recovery of the total amount of contributions and tax.

Criminal proceedings for non-payment of contributions (see above) may be brought at any time within three months from the date on which evidence sufficient to justify them comes to the attention of the Secretary of State (i.e. the collector, or NICO), or within 12 months of the commission of the offence, whichever is later.

An employer compliance officer or any other person authorised to do so may conduct proceedings before a magistrates' court for such an offence. He need not be legally qualified.

Where a company commits an offence of failure to pay a contribution, NICO may also proceed against any director, manager, secretary or other similar officer of the company if the offence has been committed with his consent or connivance, or is attributable to his neglect. The fact that a person is not formally a director is irrelevant if he is a member of a company that is managed by its members.

Such an offending director may have his personal assets frozen by High Court order until a confiscation order is paid.

Where a company fails to pay contributions (or interest or penalties in respect of contributions) within the prescribed time, due to the fraud or neglect of a director, manager or secretary, etc. a 'personal liability notice' may be served on the culpable person, requiring him to pay some or all of the contributions, etc. Where there is more than one culpable person, the amount between them may be apportioned in the proportion which each person's culpability bears to that of all the culpable persons taken as a whole. In assessing such individual culpability, regard may be had both to the gravity of the person's fraud or neglect, and to the consequences of it. Any amount paid will be deducted from the company's liability.

These measures are intended to deal with 'phoenix directors'.

There is a right of appeal against the issue or contents of a personal liability notice, but only on the ground that:

- the failure to pay the contributions due was not attributable to any fraud or neglect on the part of the individual concerned;
- the individual was not a director, manager or secretary, etc. of the company at the time of the alleged fraud or neglect; or
- the opinion formed by the Secretary of State as to the degree of culpability of the individual was unreasonable.

Enforcement of Class 2

Conviction on such a charge of failing to pay a contribution which remains unpaid at the time of the conviction leads to a liability to pay to the Secretary of State a sum equal to the amount of the contribution which the contributor failed to pay. The amount so due is recoverable as a penalty but counts as a Class 2 contribution if that is indeed what it represents.

Failure to pay a Class 2 contribution rarely leads to court proceedings, especially if arrears of contributions are paid by the contributor. A ministerial statement on 24 February 1978 disclosed that what is now the National Insurance Contributions Office waives arrears, by unpublished concession, in various cases (col. 836). The examples mentioned are where the contributor would have been entitled to small earnings exception for the year in question had it been claimed and where the contributor's financial circumstances would make recovery impracticable. The statement disclosed also that this practice extends to many thousands of cases each year.

> ### Planning point
>
> Where Class 2 contributions are paid late, they may have to be paid at a higher rate and they may not count for benefit purposes. Where a contribution is paid in the year in which the liability arises or in the next year, the rate is that which applied on the normal due date. If payment is more than 12 months after the end of the year in which the contribution week in question fell, it must be paid at the highest of all rates which have applied in any of the years between the year of liability and the year of payment. In limited circumstances, another rate may apply.

71.11.9 Penalties

Where NICs remain unpaid at the time when a person is convicted of the offence of failing to pay them, the defendant is liable to pay a sum of the same amount as the unpaid contributions to NICO. The sum payable is mandatory, non-mitigable and, although recoverable as a penalty, is treated as contributions of the appropriate class.

The penalty provisions for Class 1 and Class 1A contributions are based on the income tax model.

The penalty provisions for late returns of Class 1A contributions cannot apply until a return (as opposed to a payment) is in fact required, which is not until 19 May, 58 weeks after the end of the year in which the benefit was provided.

The penalty regime for Class 4 contributions is that for income tax.

71.11.10 Interest on underpaid/overdue NICs

Interest is chargeable on Class 1 (and Class 1A) contributions not paid by the due date. The rate of interest is the same as for late-paid income tax or repayment supplement and is non-deductible in the employer's tax computation. For Class 1, the reckonable date for interest is 19 April following the end of the year in which the earnings are paid (i.e. as for PAYE). For Class 1A, the reckonable date is now 19 July after the tax year.

Such interest may also be charged on Class 4 contributions collected by assessment. The statutory provisions relating to the final and conclusive nature of an assessment are extended to the Class 4 contribution liability and the Class 4 assessment may only be adjusted in accordance with the rules for income tax assessments, subject to an extension to allow relief for annuities, interest and other annual payments.

Where Class 1 or Class 1A NICs are repaid after the 'relevant date', repayment supplement is now payable. The relevant date is:

- for NICs overpaid more than 12 months after the end of the year in respect of which the payment was made, the last day of the year in which they were paid; or
- for any other case, the last day of the year after the year in respect of which the NICs in question were paid.

Interest may be remitted in cases of official error or omission, where the employer or his agent did not cause or materially contribute to the error or omission. Instead of running from the normal relevant date, interest does not begin to run until 14 days after the official error is rectified and the employer is advised of the rectification.

If a dispute over Class 1 contribution liability arises which leads to a question being put to the Secretary of State or a referral to the High Court (or Court of Session in Scotland), it is provided that the interest is still chargeable (on the amount ultimately due) but not actually payable until the question has been formally and finally determined. However, it does not run for the period from the date the question is put to the Secretary of State or the referral to the court is made until 14 days after the final determination of the question.

71.11.11 Avoidance and the NIC Act 2006

The National Insurance Contributions Act 2006 received Royal Assent on 30 March 2006 and came into force on that day.

The Act contains measures which aim to ensure that all employers and employees pay the correct amount of tax and National Insurance contributions. It takes forward the announcement made on 2 December 2004 that where HMRC became aware of tax and NICs avoidance schemes, the Government would legislate to close them down, where necessary, from that date.

The Act is not intended to have effect on employers and employees who organise their affairs properly. In particular, genuine employee share schemes and share option plans will not be affected.

The Act provides the power to make regulations in respect of NICs on backdated anti-avoidance tax changes that take effect on or after 2 December 2004. These tax avoidance payments may be outside the scope of existing NICs legislation. The power will allow for NICs liability to be applied on these avoidance payments going back to 2 December 2004, if necessary.

The Act also allows for consequential changes for the purposes of contributions, contributory benefit and statutory payments where appropriate. Where a NICs liability is backdated, to mirror the start date of anti-avoidance tax measures, any additional earnings on which primary NICs are due up to the Upper Earnings Limit will be allowed to count for the purposes of contributory benefit and statutory payments.

The Act also allows for the extension of the avoidance disclosure rules that previously applied to tax to NICs. It will prevent the use of NIC elections and agreements over securities in avoidance schemes that have been targeted by any backdated NICs regulations so that employers cannot pass on the secondary NICs liability that they have tried to avoid to their employees.

72 Property Income

72.1 Introduction to property income

72.1.1 Sources of property income

Income may be derived from property in a number of ways. These include rent and other receipts from let property, income from holiday lettings or rent received from a lodger. Where property is let, it may be let furnished or unfurnished. The amount of income that may be derived from property letting can vary considerably, ranging from a property rental business with numerous properties to the individual who lets out his or her spare room to a lodger. Income from let property is taxed for income tax purposes in accordance with the property income provisions of the Income Tax (Trading and Other Income Act) 2005. The legislation covers furnished and unfurnished lettings, furnished holiday lettings, and the rent a room scheme.

In the main, thehe rules apply only to income derived from properties in the UK. Income from property situated outside the UK is described for tax purposes as overseas property income and is taxed as foreign income. However, the computation rules are broadly the same as those apply to a UK property rental business. The exception to this is furnished holiday lettings in the EEA which benefit from the same treated as furnished holiday lettings in the UK. However, at the time of writing, the tax rules on furnished holiday lettings were under review.

This chapter focuses on the property income rules as they apply for income tax purposes in relation to:

- unfurnished lettings;
- furnished lettings; and
- holiday lettings.

It also examines the provisions of the rent a room scheme and the compliance obligations associated with income from property.

The rental business of a company or other taxpayer liable to corporation tax is called a Schedule A business. Consideration of Schedule A businesses is outside the scope of this chapter.

Law: ITTOIA 2005, Pt. 3

72.1.2 HMRC guidance

Guidance on income from property is available from a variety of sources including HMRC's Property Income Manual, which is available on the HMRC website at *www.hmrc.gov.uk/manuals/pimmanual/index.htm*.

Guidance on completing the land and property pages of the self-assessment tax return is available in accompanying notes, SA105, *Notes on Land and Property* (available on the HMRC website at *www.hmrc.gov.uk/worksheets/sa105-notes.pdf*.

72.2 Basic principles

72.2.1 Concept of a property rental business

Profits from land and property in the UK are treated as arising from a business. The profits from the rental business are computed using the same principles as for other trades with the crucial difference that the taxpayer is not treated as actually trading. This is an important distinction as it means that some of the reliefs that are available to traders are not available to those with a property rental business. The exception to this is in the case of furnished holiday lettings, which are treated as if they are a trade for certain purposes (see **72.8**ff).

A property rental business is carried on if a person (or body or persons) own or have an interest in land or property in the UK and they enter into transactions that produce rents or other receipts that are liable to income tax (or corporation tax in the case of a company).

A rental business may be carried on by an individual, partners in a partnership, trustees, personal representatives, trustees in bankruptcy and non-resident companies that are subject to income tax on their income from property. A person is still regarded as carrying on a property rental business if that person engages an agent to handle the business for them. The person is treated as carrying on the property rental business through the agent.

72.2.2 Concept of a single rental business

Generally, all sources of income from land and property in the UK are treated as deriving from the same single rental business. It does not matter how many properties are involved. For tax purposes, the income and expenditure is regarded as being part of the same rental business. This has some advantages. In addition to simplifying the administrative burden, it also means that expenses incurred in connection with one property can be deducted from income derived from another property.

The concept of a single rental business only applies where the activities are carried on by the same person acting in the same legal capacity. Where a person owns property in different capacities, a consolidated approach is only taken in relation to properties owned in the same capacity. For example, if a person owns property in his own right and also has a share in a property owned by a partnership as partner in that partnership, the property owned in the person's own right would comprise one rental business and that owned as a member of the partnership would compromise a different rental business.

Although rental income from all properties owned by the same person in the same legal capacity is treated as forming a single rental business, special rules apply in relation to:

- furnished holiday lettings;
- receipts from letting a room in the taxpayer's house within the rent-a-room scheme;
- properties not let on commercial terms;
- activities from properties outside UK;
- agricultural land;
- jointly-owned property and partnerships; and
- trusts and trustees.

Planning point

There is no need, for tax purposes, to work out the profit for individual properties as all income from property in the UK is treated as comprising a single rental business. This also means that expenses in relation to one property can effectively be relieved against income from another.

72.2.3 Basis period

Property income is assessed to tax on a tax year basis. The profits that are assessed are those for the tax year, i.e. the year to 5 April coinciding with the tax year. For example, the profits assessed for 2010–11 are those for the year to 5 April 2011.

For this reason, it is usual for those with a property business to draw up accounts to 5 April each year as this simplifies matters from a tax perspective.

If accounts are not drawn up to 5 April, it is necessary to apportion profits and losses to the tax year. The apportionment is done on a daily basis.

Example 72.1

Accounts are drawn up to 31 December each year.

Property Income

> The basis period for 2010–11 is the year to 5 April 2011.
>
> To find the profit or loss for this basis period, it is necessary to take 270/365 of the profits (or loss) for the year to 31 December 2010 and 95/365 of the profit (or loss) for the year to 31 December 2011.
>
> Thus, if the accounts to the year to 31 December 2010 show a profit of £20,000 and the accounts for the year to 31 December 2011 show a profit of £30,000, the amount assessed for 2010–11 is £22,603 (being (270/365 x £20,000) + (95/365 x £30,000)).

Where the accounts are not drawn up to 5 April, the taxpayer may not have all the figures available to work out the tax in time, particularly if the accounts are drawn up to January or February. In this situation tax should be paid on the best estimate of the time-apportioned profits for the tax year. This is less than ideal because it may result in tax being underpaid triggering an interest charge.

Where possible, those with a property income business should adopt a 5 April year end as this provides the maximum time to compute the tax liability accurately and also simplifies the calculation.

Accounts should be prepared on an earnings basis. However, HMRC will accept accounts prepared on a cash basis where total gross receipts for the year (i.e. before deduction of expenses) are not more than £15,000, the cash basis is used consistently and the basis is reasonable and does not differ substantially from the strict earning basis. However, HMRC may insist that the strict earnings basis is used if there are unusual features.

In the event that the property from which the income is derived belongs to a partnership that is carrying out a trade or profession, the basis period will not necessarily be the tax year. It will depend on the type of partnership and the partner's personal circumstances. Where the letting income is ancillary to the trading income the same basis period is used for the rental income as that for the trading income. Thus, if accounts are prepared to 31 December, the basis period for 2010–11 for trading purposes is, on a current year basis, 31 December 2010. This is mirrored for rental income purposes. The rental income for 2010–11 is assessed on the profits for the year to 31 December 2010 rather than those for the year to 5 April 2011.

However, where the partnership runs an investment business that does not amount to a trade, the basis period is the tax year.

Planning point

Where possible accounts should be prepared to 5 April this year as this simplifies matters from a tax perspective and minimises the risk of the figures not being available in time, resulting in an interest charge on tax underpaid.

Other guidance: Property Income Manual PIM 1101

72.2.4 Commencement of a property rental business

The rental business usually commences when the first letting begins. Any expenditure incurred before the first property is let can be relived under the pre-trading provisions.

As all let properties are treated as comprising a single property rental business, any expenses incurred in purchasing further properties to let out will be incurred for business purposes and as such will be expenses of the letting business. The pre-trading expenses rules only apply before the first property is let. Once a letting is in place, the business has commenced.

Pre-trading expenditure is allowable to the extent that it incurred in the period of seven years before the start of the business, is not otherwise allowable and would have been deductible had it been incurred after the business started. The expenditure is treated as incurred on the day that the business commenced.

As with other expenses, a distinction is drawn between revenue and capital items. Capital expenditure to improve a property prior to letting is not relievable as pre-trading expenditure.

The first basis period starts from the commencement of the first letting, not the start of the tax year in which the business commences.

Planning point

Expenses are usually incurred prior to the first letting. These can be relieved under the pre-trading provisions providing that the expenses would have been deductible had they been incurred once letting had commenced.

Law: ITTOIA 2005, s. 57 (as applied by ITTOIA 2005, s. 272)

Property Income

72.2.5 Cessation of a property rental business

A rental business usually ceases when the last property is disposed of or starts to be used for another purpose (e.g. owner-occupation). If the letting ceases and recommences, it is a question of fact whether a new business has started or the old one recommenced. As a guide, HMRC will treat the existing business as continuing if the gap between the two is less than three years.

The rules on post-cessation receipts and expenses apply to rental businesses as they apply to trading concerns.

72.2.6 Application of trading rules

Although a property rental business is not treated as a trade, the trading rules are adopted for the purposes of computing the profits of the property rental business.

72.2.7 Chargeable persons

The person who is normally charged to tax in respect of the profits of a rental business is the person who carries on that rental business. For income tax purposes, the tax liability falls on the person receiving or entitled to the profits. Generally, the same person will be entitled to the rental income and receiving it, but this is not always the case. For example, if the landlord uses an agent to run the rental business on his behalf, the agent will receive the income from the tenant before passing it on to the landlord, usually after deducting commission. However, it is the landlord who is entitled to the rent. The landlord is treated as carrying on the rental business through the agent and it is the landlord who is charged to tax.

In the event that the landlord lives abroad, tax may be collected from the agent.

Law: ITTOIA 2005, s. 271

72.2.8 Jointly-owned properties

Where property is jointly-owned, the tax treatment of the rental income will vary depending on whether or not the letting is carried on in partnership. In most cases, the joint letting will not amount to a partnership and each taxpayer's share of the profits is taxed as their personal rental business profits.

> *Example 72.2*
>
> Lucy and Jane jointly own two properties that they let out. Lucy's ownership share is 60 per cent and Jane's is 40 per cent.

Basic Principles 72.2.8

> For 2010–11, the profits from letting the properties amounted to £10,000. The profits are allocated £6,000 (60 per cent) to Lucy and £4,000 (40 per cent) to Jane. Each is taxed on her own share.

Although profits will normally be allocated between joint owners in accordance with their ownership share in the let property, this is not mandatory and the joint-owners can agree to share profits differently. The allocation for tax purposes will follow the actual allocation of profits agreed between the joint owners. So, for example, if in the above example Lucy and Jane had agreed to split profits equally, each would be taxed on £5,000 of profits for 2010–11.

Where the property is jointly-owned by a husband and wife or by civil partners, for tax purposes profits and losses are treated as arising to them equally, regardless of the actual ownership split. However, if both entitlement to income and the property are in unequal shares, both spouses or civil partners can ask the tax office to tax the profit split to match the actual ownership of the property; but if one partner or spouse does not agree to an actual split, a 50:50 allocation prevails.

Rental income for all properties owned in the same legal capacity are treated as single rental business. This means that any profits from jointly-owned profits are amalgamated with the profits from properties solely owned by the taxpayer in arriving at the profits for the taxpayer's rental business.

Occasionally, a taxpayer may jointly own properties that are let out as part of a partnership business. This may arise where the partnership is a trading or professional partnership that lets out some of its land and buildings. It may also arise where partnership runs an investment business comprising or including the letting of property which does not amount to a trade.

A partnership rental business is treated as a separate business from any property rental business carried on by any of the partners in their own account. This is because the property is owned in a different capacity. This means that a partner's share of profits or losses arising from the partnership rental business are not added to the profits or losses arising from profits owned in his or her own account.

> **Example 72.3**
>
> Chris owns three houses which he lets out. He is also a partner in a partnership which owns a building from which the partnership is run. The partnership lets out a floor of that building.
>
> Chris has two separate property rental businesses for tax purposes. One comprises the three houses he owns in his own account and lets out. The second comprises his share of the profits from the partnership's rental of the floor.

Property Income

Whether the letting of a jointly-owned property in itself gives rise to a partnership will depend on the facts in each case. In most instances, the fact that a jointly-owned property is let out will not be sufficient for there to be a partnership. However, if there are several joint owners who let the property jointly and provide significant additional services in return for payment, a partnership may exist. For there to be a partnership there must be more than just a jointly-owned property – there must be a business.

By contrast, if a partnership already exists, any income from property belonging to that partnership would normally be treated as part of the partnership business.

> **Planning point**
> - Where property is owned jointly by person who are not spouses or civil partners, they can choose how to allocate the income for tax purposes. It does not have to follow the actual ownership of the property.
> - Profits and losses arising in respect of property owned jointly by civil partners and spouses are treated as accruing to them equally, although they can elect for the tax treatment to follow the actual ownership share of the property.

Other guidance: Property Income Manual PIM 1030

72.3 Chargeable income

72.3.1 Income of a rental business

The definition of income for rental business purposes is wide. A UK rental income business should take into account all rents and similar receipt from the exploitation of land and property in the UK.

In most cases, the main source of receipts of property rental business will be rents from the tenants or licensees of land or property. Rental income from letting domestic or commercial property is taxable as property income regardless of whether the property is let furnished or unfurnished. In the event that the property is let furnished, any separate sums received from the tenant in respect of the use of the furniture are also taxable as receipts of the rental business.

Income from other sources may also be taxable as property income. Examples include:

- income from the grant of sporting rights, such as fishing rights and shooting permits;
- premiums and other lump sums received on the grant of certain leases;
- reverse premiums;

- income arising from letting waste be buried or stored on land;
- income from letting others use land or property, for example where a film crew pays to film inside a house;
- grants from local authorities contributing towards revenue expenses, such as repairs, which are deductible as expenses in computing the profits of the property rental business;
- rental income received through enterprise zone trust schemes;
- income from caravans and houseboats that are in single location and not moved around;
- service charges from tenants in respect of certain services that are ancillary to the occupation of the property;
- deposits and bonds from tenants; and
- insurance recoveries under policies providing for non-payment of rent.

It should be noted that income falling into any the above categories is treated as if it arose from a rental business, even if the receipt was a one-off event arising from a single transaction. The charge on property income extends to casual lettings.

72.3.2 Separate sums for use of furniture

If a property is let furnished, the tenant may pay a separate amount for the use of the furniture in addition to the rent for the use of the property itself. Such sums are treated as income of the property rental business . This treatment applies equally to payments for the use of furniture in a caravan or houseboat.

Law: ITTOIA 2005, s. 508

72.3.3 Rent-charges, ground annuals or feu duties

A rent-charge or ground annuals is a periodical sum of payable that is payable out of land and is not attributable to a tenure. A rent-charge is not rent under a lease and may be payable in respect of a freehold property. A rent-charge may be payable for a fixed number of years or in perpetuity. Such sums are taxed as property income.

It has not been possible to create new rent-charges since 21 August 1977.

Feu duties are annual sums payable in respect of grants of land in feu in Scotland. It has not been possible to create new feu duties or ground annuals since 1 November 1974. Such sums are also taxed as property income.

Any payment to discharge the rent-charge, ground annual or feu duty is a capital payment rather than a revenue payment and as such is taxable to capital gains tax in the hand of the recipient, rather than income tax.

72.3.4 Sporting rights

Property income may also take the form of income received for the grant of sporting rights, such as fishing rights and shooting rights. The income from the exploitation of such rights in generally taxed as property income because derives from the recipient exploiting an interest or right in or over land. In rarer instances, the commercial exploitation of sporting rights may amount to a trade.

Such receipts may also be included in the trading income of a farming trade, where the income derived from the exploitation of sporting rights in small.

72.3.5 Waste disposal rights

In most cases, income received from the grant of rights to dispose of waste on land is treated as property income. The amount will only be treated as a capital receipt if it represents a once and for all realisation of part of the capital value of the land.

Other guidance: Property Income Manual PIM 1052

72.3.6 Local authority grants

Grants from local authorities and similar may be taxed as property income. The following are examples of grants or contributions likely to be taxable in this way:

- contributions to the expenditure on repairs of a let property;
- insurance recoveries on policies covering the non-payment of rent; and
- refunds of rebates of rental business expenditure.

Where a grant is made to meet capital expenditure the correct treatment is to reduce the qualifying capital expenditure for capital allowance purposes rather than to tax the grant as income.

72.3.7 Deposits from tenants

Deposits paid by tenants are normally treated as receipts of the property rental business. Normal accounting procedures should be applied, with the receipt being deferred and matched with the cost of the providing the associated service or carrying out the associated repairs.

In the event that the deposit is refunded to the tenant, either partially or in full, the deposit is excluded from rental income to the extent that it is returned to the tenant.

Deposits not refunded at the end of the tenancy are included as income to the extent that they have not already been recognised as such.

72.3.8 Premiums

A distinction is drawn between a premium paid for the grant of a lease and rent due under the lease. A lease may be granted on terms that require both the payment of a premium and rent. Rent paid under the lease is taxed as property income in the usual way.

A premium is a lump sum payment that is paid on the creation of an interest in property. Under normal rules, such a payment would be a capital payment rather than a revenue payment. To prevent landlords attempting to avoid income tax by seeking premiums rather than rent, special rules apply to premiums granted in respect of leases with 50 years or less to run.

Under the anti-avoidance rules a proportion of the premium is taxed as income and a proportion is treated as capital. The shorter the lease, the greater the proportion charged as income. If the lease is for more than 50 years, the special rules do not apply and the full amount of any premium paid for the grant of a lease is taxed as capital.

The part of the premium which is taxed to income tax is calculated on a sliding scale that depends on the length of the lease. The longer the lease, the smaller the proportion of the premium that is charged to income tax as property income and the higher the proportion that is charged as capital. The amount of the premium that is taxable as income is reduced by two per cent for each complete year of the lease after the first, so that the full amount of the premium is taxable as income where the lease is less than two years, 98 per cent of the premium is taxable as income if the lease is for two years or more but less than three years, 96 per cent is chargeable as income if the lease is for three years but less than four years, and so on.

The percentage charged as income is determined by the formula:

$100 - (2\% (n - 1))$

Where n is the number of years of the lease.

The amount of the premium charged as income is treated as a receipt of the property rental business.

Example 72.4

Mike grants a lease to James for 30 years. Under the terms of the agreement, James must pay Mike a premium of £20,000 on 1 March 2011 and rent of £1,000 per month. The rent is payable on the first of each month.

As the lease is for 30 years, the proportion of the premium charged to income tax is:

Property Income

> $100 - (2\% \times 29) = 42\%$
>
> The amount of the premium charged as property income is thus £8,400.
>
> Therefore, Mike must include both rent of £2,000 (being the rent payable under the lease on 1 March 2011 and 1 April 2011) and the income proportion of the premium of £8,400 as receipts of his property rental business for 2010–11.

Normally the length of the lease will be straightforward and the length of the lease is generally taken as being equal to the term for which it was granted. However, if HMRC have reason to believe that the actual duration of the lease is different and there has been some attempt to gain a tax advantage, they may require further information in order to establish the duration of the lease and the correct income/capital split.

Where a landlord pays a premium to obtain a property that is let, the landlord may be able to obtain relief for the premium paid.

Items treated as premiums

Certain other sums that relate to leases of 50 years or less are treated in the same way as lease premiums for tax purposes. These include:

- the value added to the landlord's reversionary interest in the property because the tenant agrees to spend money on improvements when the landlord grants the lease;
- lump sums in place of rent due under the lease;
- lump sums for the surrender of the lease under the terms under which the lease is granted;
- receipts other than rent for the variation or waiver of the terms of a lease;
- receipts for the assignment of a lease that was originally granted by the landlord at an under-value;
- receipts for a freehold or a lease where the seller has a right to repurchase the property or to the grant of a lease back; and
- informal or hidden premiums.

These are designed to circumvent attempts to avoid the premium rules by providing the consideration for the premium in a different form. The premium rules apply to any payment that is in the nature of a premium, regardless of the label attached to it and whether it is covered by a written agreement between the parties. This ensures that the rules extend to informal and hidden premiums. A premium may be hidden for example by requiring the tenant to pay over the odds for the use of fixtures and fittings. The over-value would be treated as a premium and taxed accordingly.

> **Planning point**
>
> If a lease is for less more than 50 years, a proportion of any premium charged is assessed as income rather than capital. This rule aims to prevent a high premium being charged instead of rent to avoid income tax.

Law: ITTOIA 2005, Pt. 3, Ch. 4; ITTOIA 2005, s. 287, 305

72.4 Deductible expenses

72.4.1 General rule for deduction of expenses

In calculating the profits of a rental business, a taxpayer can deduct business expenses provided that the expenses are incurred wholly and exclusively for business purposes and are not of a capital nature.

The profits of a property rental business are calculated in the same way as the profits of a trade and as a result similar considerations apply to determine the deductibility of expenses.

The list of expenses potentially allowable as a deduction in computing the profits of a rental business is long. Some of the expenses more commonly incurred in a property rental business are outlined at **72.4.3ff**.

Law: ITTOIA 2005, s. 272(1)

72.4.2 Wholly and exclusively rule

The trading expenses rule that expenses must be wholly and exclusively for business purposes applies equally for the purposes of computing the profits of a property rental business.

For an expense to be deductible, the business purpose must generally be the sole purpose. Strictly speaking, any non-business or private purpose will jeopardise the deductibility of the expense as in many cases it will not be possible to distinguish the business element from the non-business element.

However, where a definite part of proportion of the expense is wholly and exclusively incurred for the purposes of the business, HMRC will allow a deduction for the business part or proportion. An example of where it may be possible to deduct the business proportion of a dual purpose expense would include the cost of heating a lighting premises used for partly domestic and partly for business purposes where part of the premises is used exclusively for business purposes.

> **Planning point**
>
> As for other businesses, expenses of the property income business must satisfy the 'wholly and exclusively' rule in order to be deductible.

72.4.3 Repairs

A repair is normally a revenue expenses that can be deducted in computing the profits of the rental business. A distinction is drawn between repairing an item (which is a revenue expense) and significantly enhancing it (which is capital expenditure). For these purposes, a repair is defined as the restoration of an asset by replacing a subsidiary part of the whole asset. Replacing a number of roof tiles blown off in a storm would be a repair, whereas replacing the whole roof to improve the property would be capital expenditure.

HMRC cite the following as examples of common repairs that are normally deductible in computing rental business profits:

- exterior and interior painting an decorating;
- stone cleaning;
- damp and rot treatment;
- mending broken windows, doors, furniture and machines such as cookers or lifts;
- re-pointing; and
- replacing roof tiles, flashing and gutters.

It may not always be clear cut as to whether there has been a repair or a capital improvement, particularly where work is done on an old asset. Repairing an old building using modern materials may create an impression of improvement. However, HMRC will accept that the expenditure is revenue in nature where any improvement only arises as a result of new materials being used, provided that these are broadly equivalent to the old materials. For example, the cost of replacing wooden beams with steel girders or the cost of replacing lead pipes with copper or plastic pipes would normally be accepted as being revenue in nature and deductible as a repair. However, if wooden beams were replaced with steel girders to enable the building to take larger machines as a result of the work, the expenditure would be regarded as being capital in nature.

In some cases, the degree of improvement is so small that it is incidental to the repair. In this situation, the whole cost would be regarded as revenue unless there were other capital indications. By contrast, any extensive alterations or extensions to the building are capital in nature and as such not deductible as repairs.

Some work may include both capital and revenue elements at the same time. The expenditure on repairs is allowable. Expenditure should be apportioned on a reasonable basis in order to determine the repair element.

In the event that a property is acquired in a dilapidated state, the cost of repairs to reinstate it will normally be allowable. It does not matter whether the repairs are carried out immediately after acquisition. However, a change of ownership, combined with additional factors, may mean that the expenditure is capital rather than revenue in nature. For example, if the property was not in a fit state for use in the business until the repairs had been carried and the repairs were undertaken immediately after the property was acquired, the expenditure would be treated as capital.

In the event that the landlord receives a grant for repairs, the repairs are covered by an insurance policy or the tenant contributes to the repair, the cost of the repair remains deductible, but any receipts received by the landlord (i.e. in the form of grants, insurance receipts or contributions from tenants) must be taken into account as income of the property rental business.

> **Planning point**
>
> A distinction is drawn between repairs and improvements. Repairs are revenue items and are deductible where as improvements generally are capital items and are not deductible. In practice, the lines can become blurred, particularly in relation to older properties where repairing the property may also improve it.

Other Guidance: Property Income Manual PIM 2020

72.4.4 Rates and council tax

Depending on the nature of the letting agreement, responsibility for water rates, council and similar expenses may fall on either the landlord or the tenant. Under some letting agreements, it is the tenant who is responsible for expenses of this nature, whereas under other agreements, responsibility falls on the landlord.

If the charges are met by the landlord, HMRC will normally allow a deduction for rates on business premises, water rates and water service charges and council tax. In the event that part of the property is let and part is occupied by the landlord, a deduction will be allowed for the proportion of the charge that relates to the let element.

A deduction for council tax will be given where this is borne by the landlord. It is more common for tenants to meet their own council tax liability.

72.4.5 Rent paid out

In the event that the landlord rents a property and lets part of that property out, the rent paid in relation to the let part will allowed as a deduction.

Similarly, if the landlord pays rent on a property, not all of which is let, but all of which is intended for letting, HMRC will accept that the rent is paid for the purposes of the rental business and a deduction will be permitted. This may arises in the case of rent paid for a house divided into flats, all of which are available for letting but only some of which are actually let out.

72.4.6 Insurance premiums

A deduction is permitted in computing the profits of the property rental business for premiums paid in respect of insurance policies that cover the following risks:

- damage to the fabric of the property;
- damage to the contents; and
- loss of rents.

A deduction is given for insurance premiums both in respect of properties that are actually let and those that are available for letting, but vacant.

The deductibility of a premium means that any recovery under the insurance policy is taxable. Recoveries in respect of damage to the property or its contents should be set against the cost of the repairs. Any recoveries in respect of lost rents are taxable as income of the property rental business.

72.4.7 Legal and professional fees

The extent to which legal and professional fees incurred in relation to the property rental business are deductible in computing the profits of the business depends on whether they are revenue or capital in nature and whether the wholly and exclusively rule is met.

No deduction is given for legal and professional fees that are capital in nature. As a general rule, the fees are capital in nature if they relate to a capital matter. Therefore, the fees associated with the purchase of a property would be capital rather than revenue and, as such, not deductible. Likewise, expenses incurred with the first letting or sub-letting of the property for more than one year are capital and non-deductible. Such expenses may include legal costs related to the during up of the lease and agent's and surveyor's fees and commissions.

If the let is less than one year, the associated legal and professional fees are allowable.

Also allowable are the legal and professional fees incurred on the renewal of a short lease (i.e. a lease that is for less than 50 years). However, any proportion of the costs that relate to the payment of a premium on the renewal of the lease are not allowable.

HMRC cite the following examples of other legal and professional costs as being allowable in the computation of the profits of a property rental business:

- costs of obtaining a valuation for insurance purposes;
- normal accountancy expenses incurred in preparing rental business accounts and agreeing tax liabilities;
- subscriptions to associations representing the interests of landlords;
- the costs of arbitration to determine the rent of a holding; and
- the cost of evicting an unsatisfactory tenant in order to re-let the property.

By contrast, the following are cited as examples of legal and professional fees that would not be allowed as a deduction:

- legal costs incurred in acquiring, or adding to, a property;
- costs in connection with negotiations under the Town and Country Planning Acts; and
- fees in pursuing debts of a capital nature, for example, the proceeds due on the sale of the property.

Expenses that are disallowed in the computation of profits on the grounds that they are capital in nature may be allowable for capital gains tax purposes in computing any gain or loss on the disposal of the property.

Other guidance: Property Income Manual PIM 2205

72.4.8 Advertising

Advertising for tenants is often a necessary part of a property rental business. A deduction is allowed for advertising costs provided that the expenditure meets the wholly and exclusively rule and is revenue in nature. Newspaper advertising is treated as a revenue expense and is deductible. However, advertising by means of a permanent sign or other permanent fixture displaying vacancies is treated as capital expenditure.

The costs incurred in advertising properties for sale is also capital in nature and is taken into account in calculating any capital gain on the sale of the property.

72.4.9 Bad and doubtful debts

Rents earned in the year are taken into account as income of the property rental business even if the rents are unpaid at the year end. However, a deduction is

Property Income

allowed for a debt that is clearly irrecoverable and a doubtful debt to the extent that it is estimated to be irrecoverable.

A deduction for bad and doubtful debts is only given if the taxpayer has taken all reasonable steps to recover the debt. The deduction is given for the tax year in which the debt becomes bad or doubtful. If the debt is later recovered, the recovery is taxed as a receipt of the rental business.

A deduction is only given for specific bad and doubtful debts and not for a general bad debt reserve. However, if the landlord has a large number of tenants and records show a stable past pattern, it may be possible to calculate with sufficient accuracy that a tenant already in arrears will never pay. HMRC may allow a deduction for a bad debt provision calculated on that basis.

Other guidance: Property Income Manual PIM 2015

72.4.10 Expenditure on common parts

Some buildings, such as blocks of flats and office blocks, may contain parts that are not let out but are used in common by the tenants, such as stairwells and landings. Expenditure on the upkeep of common parts is normally deductible in computing the profits of the rental business. However, if the landlord uses part of the property for private purposes or there is uncommercial letting, the deduction may be restricted.

72.4.11 Fees for loan finance

The costs incurred in obtaining loan finance for a property rental business are generally deductible in computing the profits of that business providing that they relate wholly and exclusively to property that is let out on a commercial basis.

Expenditure of this nature would include loan fees, commissions, guarantee fees and fees in connection with the security of a loan.

72.4.12 Energy saving items

A deduction is available for expenditure incurred between 6 April 2004 and 5 April 2019 on cavity wall insulation and loft insulation. From 7 April 2005, the deduction was extended to cover draught proofing and insulation for hot water and from 6 April 2007, it was further extended to cover floor insulation.

The provisions, known as the Landlord's Energy Saving Allowance, were introduced to encourage landlords to install cavity wall and loft insulation in let residential properties. The maximum permitted deduction is £1,500 for each dwelling.

There are a number of restrictions that apply to the relief. A landlord cannot claim a deduction in the following circumstances:

- the rent-a-room exempt amount is claimed in respect of the same property;
- the property meets the qualifying tests for furnished holiday lettings;
- the expenditure is incurred in respect of the provision of insulation or draught proofing a residence which at the time that the item was installed was in the course of its construction or is comprised in land in which the person claiming the deduction does not have an interest in or in the course of acquiring an interest or further interest in; or
- in respect of pre-trading expenditure unless the expenditure is incurred after 5 April 2004 and in the six months before the rental business started.

In the event that the landlord installs the insulation or draught proofing in a single building, only part of which is let as residential property, apportionment is necessary. A deduction is only allowed for the part of the expenditure incurred in relation to the let residential property in the building or, if less, £1,500. Any apportionment should be done on a just and reasonable basis.

If the landlord owns the building with other people, a deduction is only permitted in respect of the landlord's share of the expenditure incurred in respect of the let residential property in the building or, if less, the landlord's same share of the £1,500 maximum deduction. Again, any apportionment should be done on a just and reasonable basis.

> **Planning point**
>
> The deduction for energy saving items provides an immediate revenue deduction for capital expenditure.

Law: ITTOIA 2005, s. 312–314; FA 2007, s. 18; SI 2004/2264; SI 2005/1114; SI 2006/912 and SI 2007/831

72.4.13 Owner occupied property

The requirement that expenses satisfy the wholly and exclusively rule in order to be deductible means that expenditure on a house or a flat that is occupied by the landlord is not normally allowable. However, where a landlord runs a rental business from home, a deduction will be given for the extra business costs, such as extra heating and lighting costs, which are incurred. A deduction may also be given for a proportion of interest on a loan for the purchase or improvement of the property.

If specific parts of the property are used exclusively for the running of the business, then HMRC may permit a deduction for a proportion of the fixed expenses referable to those parts of the property. A deduction may be given in this way for the expenses attributable to any rent paid by the landlord, property insurance, repairs etc. Any split between business and private use should be done on common-sense principles. Unless a definite part is set aside to let and a tenant is actively sought, periods when the home is unoccupied are normally treated as periods of non-business use.

A time or area basis of apportionment may not always be appropriate. For example, it may be more appropriate to take a longer term view of use in apportioning the cost of a heavy repair, such as a major roof repair. For example, if a property has been used as a residential property for 20 years and partially let commercially for two, a further restriction may be needed to reflect the true business use. Likewise, if the property has been let for 20 years and partially occupied in a residential capacity for the last two years, it may be more appropriate to allow a greater deduction to properly reflect the rental use of the property.

72.4.14 Additional services

A landlord may not just rent a property to a tenant. He or she may also provide additional services. The cost of providing those services is allowable as a deduction in computing the profits of the property rental business provided that the receipts earned from the provision of the services are included as part of the rental business income. Additional services provided by the landlord may include cleaning and gardening services for example.

In rare cases, the provision of additional services may be more than an incidental element of the letting business and amount to separate trade of providing services. In this case, the costs incurred would be deductible in computing the profits of the separate trade rather than of the property rental business. However, it would be unusual for the provision of additional services to be regarded as a separate trade.

72.4.15 Rent collection

Any costs incurred in the collection of rent from tenants are allowable in computing the profits of the property rental business, provided that the wholly and exclusively rule is met.

72.4.16 Wages and salaries

The salaries and wages paid by a landlord to employees of the property rental business are deductible as an allowable expense of the business. Likewise, a deduction is given for normal pension contributions. However, no deduction is given for wages and salaries that are not paid during the tax year, unless they are paid within nine months of the end of the tax year. If payment is made after this time, the deduction is given at the time that the payment is actually made.

A deduction is not permitted for any time spent by the landlord working in their own property rental business, although a deduction is allowed for wages and salaries paid to a spouse or civil partner.

PAYE and NIC must be operated in respect of payments made to employees.

72.4.17 Travelling expenses

Travel expenses must satisfy the wholly and exclusively rule in order to be deductible. The cost of travelling between different properties solely for the purposes of the rental business is deductible in computing the profits of the business.

72.4.18 Sea walls

Special rules apply to sea walls. A sea wall is a wall or embankment that is needed to protect land or property from flooding by the sea or any tidal river.

In the absence of these special rules, capital expenditure on a sea wall would not be allowable as a deduction in computing the profits of the property rental business. However, the rules allow the expenditure to be written off against profits over a fixed 21-year period.

Law: ITTOIA 2005, s. 315

72.5 Deductibility of interest

72.5.1 General rule on deductibility of interest

For income tax purposes, interest that is payable on loans used to buy land or property that is used in a property rental business is deductible in computing the profits of that business. In the same way, interest on loans to fund repairs, improvements or alterations is also deductible.

Any interest that is payable under hire purchase agreements or on an overdraft is deductible if the asset is used for the purposes of the business.

In determining whether interest is allowable, the normal rules for deciding whether an expense is deductible (see **72.4.1**) apply. The wholly and exclusively rule must be satisfied.

If the borrowings are used wholly or partly for non-business purposes, the interest may not be allowable, or only allowable in part. It may be difficult to determine the extent to which any interest is allowable.

In the event that a property is only let for short periods during the tax year and is used for either private or non-business purposes for the rest of the time, any interest paid on a qualifying loan on the property must be split between the rental business and the private or non-business use. Likewise, if only part of the property is let and part is used privately, the interest must be apportioned to the business and non-business parts. A deduction is permitted only in relation to the business element. In both cases the apportionment should be done in such a way as to produce a fair and reasonable business deduction. Account should be taken of the proportion and length of business use.

However, if the property is empty for parts of the year, but available for letting and the landlord is genuinely trying to let the property, the interest will be deductible in full as the wholly and exclusively test is met.

Interest on a loan to buy a property is not allowed as a deduction in computing the profits of the rental business if rent-a-room relief (see **73.10**) has been claimed.

Relief for interest is given on an accruals interest rather than on the basis of interest paid, unless exceptionally a cash basis is used when computing profits.

> ### Planning point
>
> Where a property that is let out is purchased by means of a repayment mortgage, it is only the interest elements of the mortgage payments that is deductible. The repayment element is capital and cannot be deducted. Therefore any mortgage payments in relation to a repayment mortgage should be apportioned between interest and repayment to avoid over claiming. A common mistake is to deduct the full mortgage repayments in relation to a repayment mortgage. This is something HMRC are alert to.

72.5.2 Interest paid abroad

The residence status of the lender does not affect the deductibility of the interest in computing the profits of the property rental business. However, interest that is paid to a lender who is not resident in the UK over and above a commercial rate is not allowed as a deduction in the computation of profits, regardless of whether it would otherwise qualify for a deduction (for example, because the wholly and exclusively test is met). Generally, HMRC will accept that interest charged by a lender is an allowable deduction if it is paid on a arm's length loan on a normal commercial basis.

HMRC will not normally seek and adjustment when the payer and recipient are at arm's length.

Interest payable in the UK on an advance from a foreign bank carrying on a bona fide banking business in the UK through a branch is treated as if it were interest payable to a UK bank.

Where an adjustment is made because the rate exceeds a normal commercial rate, it is only the interest paid in excess of the normal commercial rate that is disallowed, not the full amount.

Other guidance: Property Income Manual PIM 2210

72.5.3 Release of equity

Relief is only given for interest to the extent that it is incurred wholly and exclusively for business purposes. If the loan is funding the business, the associated interest is deductible. However, interest is not deductible to the extent that the loan is used for non-business purposes.

Where a property is purchased as an investment and let out, it is common to release equity by re-mortaging the property to benefit from inflationary rises in value without necessitating the need to sell the property and to crystallise a capital gain.

Relief is only available for the interest to the extent that the loan is used for the purposes of the business. If the equity released by way of the re-mortgage is used for the purposes of a business, for example as a deposit on a further property which is bought to let out, the interest on the higher loan, together with interest on any loan used to purchase the second property remains deductible.

> *Example 72.5*
>
> Ben owns various properties that he let out.
>
> He purchased one property in 2004 for £160,000. In July 2010 it is revalued at £210,000. Ben re-mortages the property for £190,000. He uses the £30,000 equity released on the re-mortgage as a deposit on a further property costing £170,000, which he purchases with the £30,000 deposit and a mortgage of £140,000.
>
> Interest on the new mortgage of £180,000 on the first property and that on the mortgage of £140,000 on the second property is deductible in computing the

Property Income

profits of the rental business as both loans are fully used in funding the property rental business.

However, if a property is re-mortaged to release equity for private purposes, interest relating the any portion of the loan in excess of the value of the property was first let is not allowable as an expense of the business. The excess released for private purposes is not funding the business.

Example 72.6

Julie bought a flat in 2000 for £120,000. The flat was purchased using £20,000 of her savings and a mortgage of £100,000. The flat is let out and interest on the mortgage is allowable as an expense in computing the profits of the property rental business.

In 2010, the flat is revalued at £250,000. Julie increases the mortgage on the property to £200,000, using the equity released to partially fund a larger residential home.

Only interest attributable to the let property is eligible for relief. This is $^{120}/_{200th}$ of the interest attributable to the higher loan of £200,000 (i.e. the proportion relating to the value of the property at the time it was first rented out). The balance is attributable to private purposes and as such is not deductible.

Planning point

The basic rule is that interest is allowable on any loan to the value of the property at the time it was first let. Once the loan exceeds this (for example where a mortgage is increased to release capital once the property has gone up in value), the interest relating to the excess is not deductible.

Other guidance: Business Income Manual BIM 45690

72.5.4 Deposit provided by re-mortgage of own home

A common scenario is for an individual to buy a property to let out and fund the deposit by remortaging his or her own residence, such that the let property is funded partly by a buy-to-let mortgage and partly by the deposit provided by equity released from the remortgage of the main residence.

The interest on the buy-to-let mortgage and that part of the residential mortgage funding the deposit is allowable as a business expense. The wholly and exclusively rule is met.

> **Example 72.7**
>
> Angela purchases a property to let out for £150,000. It is funded by a buy to let mortgage of £100,000 and a £50,000 deposit provided by increasing the mortage on her own home from £150,000 to £200,000.
>
> All of the interest relating to the buy-to-let mortgage is deductible.
>
> Also deductible is ¼ of the interest relating to the mortgage on her home as this relates to the £50,000 released to fund the purchase of the let property.

> **Planning point**
>
> Interest on a mortgage on the landlord's main residence is allowable as an expense of the property income business to the extent the funds are used to fund the purchase of the let property.

72.6 Properties not let at a commercial rent

72.6.1 Deduction for expenses: properties let at less than commercial rent

The need for expenses to satisfy the wholly and exclusively rule operates to deny relief for properties that are not let at a commercial rent.

HMRC take the view that unless the landlord charges a full market rent for a property and imposes normal market lease conditions, it is unlikely that the expenses of the property are incurred wholly and exclusively for business purposes. Where a property is let at a rent that is less than the commercial rate or the property is occupied rent-free, for example by a relative, the assumption by HMRC is that the expenses are incurred for a personal or philanthropic reason (namely that of providing the occupant with a home) rather than for a business purpose. This has implications for the deductibility of those expenses.

Taking a strict approach, expenses that are not incurred wholly and exclusively for the purposes of the business are not deductible in computing the profits of that business. However, HMRC do not take that harsh a line and where a property is let at a rate that is less than the market rate they permit expenses to be deducted up to the value of the rent. This means that the expenses cannot create a loss and excess expenses cannot be carried forward to be used in later years or set against the income from other properties in the rental business. If expenses exceed the rent for a property that is uncommercially let, the result is that the property produces neither a profit nor a loss. No relief is given for the excess expenses.

Property Income

> **Planning point**
>
> If a property is let at less than commercial rent, expenses can only be deducted up to the value of the rent. Unlike a property let at a commercial rent, no relief is given for excess expenses.

Other guidance: Property Income Manual PIM 2220

72.6.2 Properties let rent-free

A distinction is drawn between properties that are let at a rate that is less than the market rate and properties that are let rent-free. If a property is let rent-free it is completely outside the property income regime. There is no income of the property as a source of rents or other receipts.

As the property is outside the property income tax regime, there is no mechanism for deducting expenses incurred in relation to it. Consequently, the expenses are not incurred for a business purpose and are not deductible.

Law: ITTOIA 2005, s. 266(1)

72.6.3 Periods of commercial and uncommercial lettings

It may be the case that a property is let commercially for part of the tax year and let at a low rent or occupied rent free for other parts of the tax year. The degree to which any expenses associated with the property are deductible in computing the profits of the rental business will depend on the particular circumstances surrounding the lettings.

For example, a property may be available for commercial lettings but the property is occupied between lettings by a friend of relative of the landlord who house sits. If the property is genuinely available for commercial letting and the landlord is actively seeking tenants during the house-sitting periods, the expenses incurred in relation to the property will be fully deductible, provided that they are incurred wholly and exclusively for business purposes. In determining whether this test is met, it is necessary to consider whether the expenses are incurred for the purposes of the rental business or whether the expenditure is for personal reasons. Although HMRC do not give firm guidelines as to what will be tolerated, they state as a guide that ordinary house sitting by a relative for, say, a month in a period of three years or more will not normally lead to a loss of relief whereas relief will be lost if the reality of the situation is that the relative is taking a month's holiday in the property.

If a property (for example, a holiday home) is made available only to relatives, friends, business associates and personal staff of the landlord, the associated expenses can only be offset up to the rent received in respect of the property. Expenses incurred in relation to such a property cannot be set against the income from commercial lettings.

If the property is let commercially some of the time and used by relatives rent-free or at low-rent the rest of the time, it is necessary to apportion the expenses on a reasonable basis between the commercial and uncommerical use. The expenses relating to the uncommercial use can only be offset up to the rent received, if any, in respect of the periods where the property is occupied on an uncommercial basis. However, those relating to the commercial let are deductible in full and, to the extent that they exceed the rent received, can be set against rent from other commercially let properties or, of still unrelieved, carried forward for offset against future income of the property rental business. By contrast, excess expenses relating to periods of uncommercial letting are lost.

When apportioning expenses, the basis of apportionment must be reasonable. HMRC will not allow high expenses that essentially arise from the non-business use of the property to be deducted from the income derived from the commercial lets simply because the expense was incurred during a period when the property was let commercially.

> ### *Planning point*
>
> The extent to which expenses are allowable where a property is let commercially some of the time and at less than commercial rent for the remainder of the tax year will depend on whether the landlord was actively seeking tenants at full rent during the uncommercial lets. If this was the case, expenses are deductible in full. If not expenses must be apportioned and are only deductible at the periods of less than full rent up to the amount of the rent.

Other guidance: Property Income Manual PIM 2220

72.7 Capital allowances

72.7.1 No deduction for capital expenditure

As noted at **72.4.1**, a deduction is only permitted for expenses to that extent that the expenses are incurred wholly and exclusively for business purposes and are not of a capital nature. No deduction is given in computing the profits of a property rental business for expenditure that is of a capital nature. Instead, the landlord may be able to claim capital allowances or, in the case of property that is let furnished, a wear and tear allowance for furniture, furnishing and fixtures (see **72.8**).

Property Income

Special rules apply to loft or cavity wall insulation, draught proofing and insulation for hot water systems (see **72.4.12**) in a residential property and for sea walls (see **72.4.17**) which enable certain costs to be relieved as a revenue expense.

Where capital allowances are available, they are deducted in working out the profits of the property rental business or added to the loss.

The annual investment allowance allows a business immediate write off for expenditure on plant and machinery up to the limit of the allowance (£100,000 for 2010–11). If the allowance is unavailable, or the landlord does not wish to claim the allowance, for example to avoid balancing charges on the disposal of the item, a writing down allowance of 20 per cent may be claimed instead.

Capital allowances are computed by reference to the basis period. For a property rental business this is the tax year.

When a landlord disposes of an item on which capital allowances have been claimed, there will normally be a balancing adjustment. Balancing charges are treated as income of the property rental business and balancing allowances are treated as expenses of the business.

In the event that a grant is received towards the cost of an item of capital expenditure, the amount of the grant is normally deducted in arriving at the amount on which capital allowances are due.

Although the purchase of a house or a flat is a capital item, no capital allowances are available on residential property (other than those available for agricultural buildings and hotels). Capital allowances are available for plant and machinery.

72.7.2 Capital allowances for plant and machinery

In the main, capital allowances available in respect of a property rental business will normally be for plant and machinery. Plant and machinery is defined as an asset that is used for carrying on the business and is not stock in trade, the business premises or part of the business premises.

Capital allowances are not given for the cost of a let residential property itself. Nor do items of furniture and household equipment provided for tenants in furnished letting qualify for plant and machinery capital allowances (but see wear and tear allowance at **72.8.2** and also the special rules for furnished holiday lettings at **72.8ff.**).

In the case of a property rental business, plant and machinery capital allowances may be available in respect of vehicles, tools used for maintenance and for office equipment used in the running of the business.

Examples of items that may qualify for plant and machinery capital allowances within a property rental business include:

- lifts;
- central heating;
- air conditioning;
- business furniture, furnishing and fixtures (but not those available to tenants in furnished residential lettings);
- computers used in the business; and
- tools used for maintenance, etc.

Immediate write off for expenditure on plant and machinery is available up to the level of the annual investment allowance (£100,000 for 2010–11). Once the allowance has been used, or if the landlord does not wish to claim the annual investment allowance, capital allowances for plant and machinery are given on a reducing balance basis at a rate of 20 per cent. Writing down allowances for cars depend on the level of the car's CO_2 emissions. The writing down allowance is 20 per cent for cars with CO_2 emissions of 160g/km or less, and 10 per cent for cars with CO_2 emissions in excess of 160g/km.

Example 72.8

Colin lets out several properties on a commercial basis. On 5 April 2010 his plant and machinery pool has a tax written down value of £10,600. During the year, he purchases a new computer for use in the business at a cost of £800. Assuming Colin has not used the annual investment allowance, he can claim a deduction against profits for 2010–11 for the full cost of the computer. If the annual investment allowance is not available or Colin does not wish to claim an immediate write off, he can instead claim a writing down allowance of 20 per cent.

Planning points

Furniture and household equipment are not eligible for plant and machinery capital allowances. Instead a deduction is given for furnished lettings to cover the cost of furniture, fixtures and fittings.

Immediate write off is available for plant and machinery to the extent that the annual investment allowance remains available. However, in certain cases, for example to avoid balancing charges at a later date, it may be preferable to claim the writing down allowance instead.

72.7.3 Restriction of allowances in respect of properties not let commercially

Plant and machinery relating to properties that are not let on a commercial basis (i.e. at a rent that is less than the market rent) must have their own pool. The allowances that are available in respect of the items is reduced on a 'just and reasonable basis' to reflect the degree of non-business use.

The restriction applies equally to assets used in properties let uncommercially and those used partly for business and partly for private purposes.

72.7.4 Other types of capital allowances

Capital allowances may also be available for industrial buildings, agricultural buildings and hotels within the confines of a property rental business.

Industrial buildings allowance is given for industrial building and agricultural buildings allowance is given for agricultural buildings. Certain types of hotel qualify for industrial buildings allowances.

As with capital allowances for plant and machinery, allowances (including balancing allowances) are deducted in computing the profits of the property rental business and balancing charges are treated as income of the business.

Detailed consideration of industrial buildings allowance and agricultural buildings allowance is outside the scope of this chapter.

72.7.5 Flats above shops

To encourage the conversion of empty spaces above offices, 100 per cent capital allowances are given for the costs of converting or renovating an empty space on the first or subsequent floors above a shop to create a flat. A condition of the allowance is that the flat must be unused or used only for storage for the 12 month prior to the start of the conversion work.

The allowance is set again rental income received from the short term letting of the flat.

> **Planning point**
>
> Converting a flat above a shop can be a worthwhile investment due to the availability of 100 per cent capital allowances for the conversion costs.

Law: CAA 2001, s. 393A

72.8 Furnished lettings

72.8.1 Treatment of furnished residential lettings

Income from furnished lettings is taxed as property income in the same way as income from property that is let unfurnished. The exception to this rule is furnished holiday lettings (see **72.8**ff to which special rules apply). As noted at **72.2.2** all of a taxpayer's sources of income from land and property in the UK are treated as deriving from the same property rental business. Thus, where a taxpayer has a number of properties, some of which are let furnished and some of which are let unfurnished, all the lets will be treated as forming part of the same property rental business.

In addition, the same computation rules apply to furnished lettings as to unfurnished lettings. However, separate rules apply in relation to the furniture, furnishings or fixtures within a let residential property.

Plant and machinery capital allowances are not available in respect of any furniture, furnishings or fixtures made available to the tenants in a furnished residential let because these items are not within the definition of plant and machinery. As they are capital items, a deduction is not permitted by way of an expense. Instead, the taxpayer can claim either a wear and tear allowance (see **72.8.2**) or a deduction for the net cost of replacing a particular item (known as the renewals basis: see **72.8.3**).

Which ever basis is chosen it should be consistently applied. The taxpayer cannot switch between the two depending which generates the best result.

It should be noted that rules only apply to furnished residential lettings. Different rules apply in respect of furnished holiday lettings. These are outlined at **72.9**.

72.8.2 Wear and tear allowance

Where a taxpayer lets a furnished residential property, a wear and tear allowance can be claimed to cover the depreciation of items of furniture, furnishings and fixture made available to the tenants. Alternatively, the taxpayer can claim a deduction for the net cost of replacing the items, but not for the original cost (see **72.8**).

The wear and tear allowance is a concessionary allowance, given by virtue of ESC B47.

The wear and tear allowance is given at the rate of 10 per cent of the net rents. In the event that a landlord has both furnished and unfurnished lettings, it is important that the allowance is calculated only on the net rents of the furnished lettings. The net rent is the rent less a deduction for charges and services that would normally be borne by the tenant but are in fact borne by the taxpayer, for example, council tax, water rates, etc.

The allowance is intended to cover the deprecation of items of furniture and suchlike in let residential property in respect of which capital allowances are not available. It does not cover the capital cost of the property itself or the cost of improvement, nor is it relevant to furnished accommodation other than residential accommodation (such as furnished office accommodation) in respect of which capital allowances may be claimed. The aim is to cover the depreciation of the type of items that the tenant or owner occupier would provide in unfurnished accommodation, such as:

- moveable furniture and furnishings such as sofas and beds;
- televisions;
- fridges and freezers;
- carpets and floor coverings;
- curtains;
- linen;
- crockery or cutlery; or
- cookers and washing machines.

The deduction is available regardless of the actual items included in the property. It is calculated by reference to the net rents rather than by reference to the cost of the items supplied. However, to qualify for the allowance, the property must genuinely be a furnished let, rather than an unfurnished let with a token item of furniture supplied.

HMRC will only regard a property as genuinely being let furnished if the property is capable of normal occupation without the tenant having to provide their own beds, chairs, tables, sofas, other furnishings, cooker, etc. If the property is unfurnished or only partially furnished, the wear and tear allowance is not available.

Example 72.9

Jack lets out a number of properties, three of which are let furnished. In 2010–11 he receives rents in respect of the properties as follows:

Property 1	£9,000
Property 2	£10,800
Property 3	£14,400

Jack meets the cost of the water rates and the tenants' council tax in relation to all three properties. For 2010–11 these total £5,000.

Jack claims a wear and tear allowance in respect of the furnished lettings.

This is calculated as follows:

Rents

(£9,000 + £10,800 + £14,400)	£34,200
Less: costs borne by landlord re council tax etc.	(£5,000)
Net rents	£29,200
Wear and tear allowance @10% of £29,200	£2,920

Jack is able to deduct a wear and tear allowance of £2,920 in calculating the profits of his property rental business for 2010–11.

If the wear and tear allowance is claimed, the taxpayer cannot make any claim for replacing the assets. However, a deduction is available for any costs of repairing them.

Planning point

The wear and tear allowance is a simple way of obtaining a deduction for the cost of furnishings and can be very worthwhile, particularly if the rent is high in relation to the cost of the furniture provided.

72.8.3 Renewals basis

Instead of claiming a wear and tear allowance, the taxpayer can instead obtain relief for the cost of replacing items of furniture, furnishings and fixtures. As far as furnished lettings are concerned, the renewals basis covers the same type of items as are covered by the wear and tear allowance, such as beds, sofas, tables and chairs, fridges and freezers, cookers, washing machines etc.

Under the renewals basis a deduction is given for the cost of replacing these items. However, no deduction is available for the original cost of purchasing them.

Example 72.10

Mary has a property which she lets out furnished. She claims relief for furniture, furnishings and fixtures on the renewals basis.

In 2010–11 she sells the old fridge for £25 and buys a replacement fridge for the property at a cost of £300. The new fridge is equivalent to the old fridge.

Mary is able to claim a deduction under the renewals basis for the cost of the new fridge, less the amount that she received for the sale of the old fridge. The deduction is therefore £275 (£300 − £25).

The renewals basis operates on a like-for-like approach. The deduction is given for replacing one item with another that is either the same or equivalent. If the new item represents an improvement or enhancement as compared to the old one, that part of the cost that represents enhancement expenditure is not deductible.

HMRC recognise that it will not always be possible to replace an item with one that is identical and a common-sense approach is adopted in determining what constitutes a reasonable modern replacement.

> **Example 72.11**
>
> Phil lets out a furnished property and claims relief for items of furniture, fixtures and fittings on the renewals basis. In 2009–10 the washing machine in the property breaks down and cannot be repaired. He replaces it with a washer-dryer that cost £550. A washing machine of an equivalent model to the old one would have cost £350.
>
> As the new item represents an enhancement over the original, the full cost of the replacement is not deductible under the renewals basis. A deduction is given under the renewals basis for £350, being the cost of replacing the washing machine with an equivalent model. The balance of the cost of the washer-dryer (£200) is not deductible as it represents enhancement expenditure rather than a replacement cost.
>
> The renewals allowance is also available for fixtures in unfurnished properties, such as boilers, which may be provided by the landlord and in respect of which plant and machinery allowances are not claimed. The wear and tear allowance is not available in respect of such items as the property is not let furnished.

> **Planning point**
>
> If rents are low and the cost of replacing items regularly exceeds ten per cent of the rent, the renewals basis will be more favourable than the wear and tear allowance. However, this is more cumbersome from an administrative viewpoint.

Other guidance: Property Income Manual PIM 3200

72.8.4 Wear and tear allowance versus renewals basis

The landlord of a residential property that is let furnished needs to decide whether to claim a deduction for the depreciation of furniture, fixture and fittings by reference to the wear and tear allowances or on the renewals basis. Once a method is chosen it must be applied consistently year on year.

In deciding which is the most beneficial, consider should be given to the amount spent on replacing items and whether this is generally more than 10 per cent of net rents. If it is, then the renewals basis will be more favourable than claiming the wear and tear allowance.

However, the wear and tear allowance offers the advantage of being easy to calculate, It is also available irrespective of whether there is any actual expenditure on furniture and suchlike during the year. The wear and tear allowance also offers relief from the outset of the furnished let, whereas relief is only available under the renewals basis once an item is replaced.

72.8.5 Fixtures integral to the business

Where the wear and tear allowance is claimed, the landlord can also claim a deduction for the net cost of repairing or renewing fixtures that are an integral part of the building. Integral fixtures are those that are not normally removed when the property is sold, such as central heating systems, bathroom suites etc.

The amount of the deduction is the net cost of repairing or renewing the fixture. This is the cost of the replacement, less any amount that is received for the old item.

No deduction is permitted for the original cost of installing the fixtures or for the extra cost of replacing the fixture with an improved or upgraded version. The original cost of installation covers both the cost of installing the assets for the first time in a new property and the cost of replacing old assets in a property that has been brought to let or that is being converted to let.

72.9 Furnished holiday lettings

72.9.1 Application of property income rules to furnished holiday lettings

Income for furnished holiday lettings in the UK are charged to income tax under the property income rules and the profits derived from furnished holiday lettings are treated as profits of the property rental business.

However, although in general, the rules apply to furnished holiday letting as they do to other lettings, from a tax perspective furnished lettings have some advantages over other types of lettings in that the landlord is treated as if he were trading for certain purpose. The advantages of this treatment are outlined at **72.9.4**.

The advantages apply to the commercial letting of furnished holiday letting. This means that the let must be on a commercial basis (see **72.9.2**) and that the accommodation in question must be qualifying holiday accommodation (see **72.8.2**).

The rules for furnished holiday letting are under review. At the time of writing, a consultation document has been published setting out proposals to amend the rules from April 2011. The revised rules will apply to furnished holiday lettings in the EEA in the same way as they apply to furnished holiday lettings in the UK. The application of the rules to furnished holiday letting elsewhere in the EEA is outlined at **72.9.7**. The proposed changes to the furnished holiday lettings rules are outlined at **72.9.8**.

Law: ITTOIA 2005, Pt. 5, Ch. 6.

> **Planning points**
>
> More favourable tax rule apply to furnished holiday lettings than to residential lettings.
>
> The rules are due to be changes from April 2011, reducing the beneficial treatment particularly with regard to relief for losses. Where possible, existing losses should be set against other income and gains whilst this treatment remains available.

72.9.2 Commercial letting of furnished holiday accommodation

Furnished holiday letting have a number of tax advantages over other types of lettings. However, these only apply to the commercial letting of furnished holiday accommodation. A letting of accommodation is commercial if it is let on a commercial basis with a view to the realisation of profits.

HMRC take a broad view of whether the property is let on a commercial basis and accept that during the close season lets may not produce a profit, although they would normally contribute to the expenses of maintaining the property. However, if the property is let to friends and relatives for little or no rent, this would not be regarded as commercially letting and would jeopardise the availability of the advantages for commercially-let furnished holiday accommodation.

Law: ITTOIA 2005, s. 323(2)

Other guidance: Property Income Manual PIM 4105

72.9.3 Furnished holiday accommodation

A letting is of 'furnished holiday accommodation' if the person who is entitled to use the accommodation is also entitled, in connection with that let, to the use of furniture and the accommodation is qualifying holiday accommodation.

Qualifying holiday accommodation is accommodation that satisfies the following conditions:

- the availability condition;
- the letting condition; and
- the pattern of availability condition.

The availability condition

The availability condition is the accommodation is available for commercial letting as holiday accommodation to the public for at least 140 days in the relevant period.

The letting condition

The letting condition is that the accommodation is commercially let as holiday accommodation to members of the public for at least 70 days in the relevant period. However, a let of more than 31 days to the same person (otherwise than for exceptional circumstances) is not treated as a let of holiday accommodation for the purposes of the letting condition.

The pattern of availability condition

The pattern of occupation condition requires that no more than 155 days fall outside periods of longer term occupation. A period of longer-term occupation is a continuous period of 31 days during which the accommodation is in the same occupation otherwise than because of circumstances that are not normal. Exceptional circumstances where a letting might exceed 31 days yet still count as a holiday let may include a holidaymaker who has an accident or falls ill and stays longer as a result.

This condition precludes properties let on a long-term basis, for example to students during term time, from qualifying as furnished holiday accommodation.

The conditions are applied by reference to the relevant period. This is normally the tax year. However, different relevant periods are used in the first and latter periods of letting. In the first year of letting the relevant period is the 12 months starting with the date of the first letting. In the final period of letting the relevant period is the 12 months ending with the date of the last letting.

A consultation document published in July 2010 (see **72.9.8**) sets out proposed changes to the rules for furnished holiday lettings from April 2011. The proposed

Property Income

changes include increasing the availability condition from 140 days in the tax year to 210 days in the tax year, and increasing the letting condition from 70 days in the tax year to 105 days in the tax year.

> **Planning point**
>
> The Government propose to make the availability condition and the letting condition more stringent from April 2011. landlords should consider taking necessary action in advance of April 2011 to ensure that their properties continue to qualify for the furnished holiday lettings treatment from April 2011, by making the properties available for holiday lets for a greater proportion of the tax year.

Law: ITTOIA 2005, s. 323(3), 324

72.9.4 Multiple units and averaging

If a landlord has a number of properties that are commercially let as furnished holiday accommodation, it is possible to use an average rate of occupancy for the units in determine whether the letting condition is met. However the availability condition and the pattern of occupation condition must both be satisfied in relation to each separate unit.

A claim for averaging for the purposes of the letting condition must be made no later than on year from 31 January following the end of the tax year.

> **Example 72.12**
>
> Flora has six holiday cottages that she lets as furnished holiday accommodation on a commercial basis. Each cottage satisfies the availability condition and the pattern of occupancy condition.
>
> The actual letting periods in respect of each cottage in 2010–11 is as follows:
>
> | Cottage | Days let in tax year |
> |---|---|
> | 1 | 85 |
> | 2 | 63 |
> | 3 | 127 |
> | 4 | 59 |
> | 5 | 74 |
> | 6 | 91 |
> | TOTAL | 499 |
>
> Without an averaging claim, the letting condition is not met in relation to cottage 2 and 4. However, the total lettings are 499 days, giving an average of 83 days, meaning that applying the averaging rule all six properties will qualify as furnished holiday lettings.

> Flora must make the averaging claim for 2010–11 by 31 January 2013.

> **Planning point**
>
> The averaging rule allows a global view to be taken of all properties in determining whether the letting condition is met. However, the availability and patter of occupation conditions must be satisfied in relation to all properties.
>
> Under Government proposals, the letting and availability conditions are to be made stricter from April 2011. Landlords should ensure that average lettings continue to meet these tests from April 2011 onwards.

Law: ITTOIA 2005, s. 326

72.9.5 Advantages of furnished holiday lettings treatment

Furnished holiday lettings have a number of advantages over other types of lettings. The main advantages are:

- entitlement to plant and machinery capital allowances on furniture, furnishings and fixtures in the let property as well as on plant and machinery used outside the property;
- losses can be set against total income and gains, rather than being restricted to offset against profits of the rental business (although under Government proposals, relief for losses is to be restricted from April 2011 (see **72.9.8**); and
- capital gains tax reliefs for traders, such as roll-over relief and business taper relief are available.

72.9.6 Separate calculation of profits and losses

In order to determine whether advantage can be taken on the beneficial tax rules for furnished holiday lettings, it is necessary to calculate the profits and losses arising from lets of qualifying holiday accommodation separately from other rental profits and losses. However, any overall profits is included within the total profit for the property rental business.

All furnished lettings by the same person are treated as one trade for the purposes of giving relief. Once a property meets the tests for qualifying holiday accommodation, all income will qualify for furnished holiday lettings treatment.

If the property is kept closed for part of the year because of lack of customers or business, there is no restriction of expenses provided that there has been no private use. If only part of the property is let as furnished holiday accommodation, receipts and expenses are apportioned on a just and reasonable basis.

One of the main advantages of a let qualifying for treatment as furnished holiday lettings in respect of the relief available for losses. The losses of the rental business can normally only be relived against profits of that business and not against general income. Furnished holidays lettings is the exception to this rule.

If the furnished holiday lettings generate a loss and the taxpayer's other lettings generate a greater profit, the loss on the furnished holiday lettings can be relieved against the other property rental profits. However the taxpayer can also make a claim to relief the furnished holiday letting loss against general income. This may be beneficial when other rental profits are not sufficient to absorb the loss and can result in loss being relieved earlier than might otherwise be possible. A loss in respect of furnished holiday lettings can also be relived against capital gains.

Any unrelieved losses can be carried forward and set against future profits of the property rental business.

The distinction between losses from furnished holiday lettings and other lettings is important and must be preserved to ensure that the losses are utilised in the most beneficial manner.

Law: FA 1991, s. 72

72.9.7 Application of furnished holiday letting rules to properties elsewhere in the UK

Since their introduction the special rules apply to furnished holiday letting have applied only in respect of properties situated in the UK. Furnished lettings of overseas properties were treated for tax purposes under the rules applying to overseas properties. However, HMRC now accept that the differing treatment of UK and properties located elsewhere in the EEA may not be compliant with European law. Consequently, they are now prepared to accept that the furnished holiday letting rules apply equally to all properties within the EEA, not just those located in the UK.

HMRC published a technical note on 22 April 2009 (Budget Day) setting out the treatment of furnished holiday lettings in the EEA. The note is available on the HMRC website at *www.hmrc.gov.uk/budget2009/furnished-hol-lets-1015.pdf*.

The furnished holiday letting rules, as set out above, apply to the letting of furnished holiday accommodation elsewhere in the EEA provided that the let is on a commercial basis and that the conditions set out at **72.9.3** are met. Where this is the case, the letting will benefit for the tax advantages set out at **72.9.4**.

The application of the furnished holiday letting rules to properties elsewhere in the EEA is not compulsory and landlords can choose whether they want this treatment to apply. However, where advantage is taken of the furnished holiday lettings rules, the property is treated as a furnished holiday letting for all purposes. If the landlord does not letting to be taxed by reference to the furnished holiday lettings rules, the overseas property business rules will apply instead.

In July 2010, HMRC published a consultation document setting out proposed changes to the tax rules as they apply to furnished holiday lettings (see **72.9.8**). The new rules, due to take effect from April 2011, will apply equally to furnished holiday lettings in the UK as they do to furnished holiday lettings in the EEA. However, under the proposals, a distinction is drawn for loss relief purposes between a UK furnished holiday lettings business and an EEA furnished holiday lettings business. Losses arising in relation to an EEA furnished holiday letting business can only be set against future profits of an EEA furnished holiday lettings business and losses of a UK furnished holiday letting business can only be set against future profits of a UK furnished holiday lettings business. Under the proposed new rules it will not be possible to offset a loss arising on a UK holiday let against the profits arising on an EEA holiday let and vice versa.

> **Planning point**
>
> Consideration should be given whether the furnished holiday letting treatment is more beneficial than the overseas property business rules in relation to furnished holiday lettings elsewhere in the EEA and claims should be made accordingly.
>
> The rules for relief of losses are to be tightened considerably from April 2011 and losses arising on EEA furnished holiday lettings should be set against income and gains prior to this date whilst the wider relief remains available.

72.9.8 Proposed changes to tax rules for furnished holiday lettings

Uncertainty has surrounded the future of the tax rules for furnished holiday lettings since the 2009 Budget when it was announced that the rules were to be repealed from April 2010. Despite being reiterated in the 2009 Pre-Budget report, the planned repeal did not happen and instead in the Emergency Budget on 22 June 2010, the Chancellor announced that the Government would consult on the changes to the furnished holiday letting rules over Summer 2010. A consultation document was published in July 2010, setting out proposed changes to the rules to apply from April 2011. Comments on the proposals are sought by 22 October 2010. The consultation is due to be followed by the publication of draft legislation with the changes being implemented in the Finance Act 2011.

The changes proposed in the document are as follows:

- the availability condition is to be changed so that the property must be available for commercial letting as furnished holiday lettings for at least 210 days in the tax year rather than 240 as at present;
- the letting condition is to be changed such that the property must actually be let as furnished holiday accommodation for a minimum of 105 days in the tax year (excluding lets of 31 days or more) rather than for 70 days as at present; and
- relief for losses is to be restricted so that losses from a qualifying UK furnished holiday lettings business can only be set against future profits from a qualifying UK furnished holiday lettings business and losses from a qualifying EEA furnished holiday lettings business can only be set against future profits from a qualifying EEA furnished holiday lettings business.

Under the proposals, furnished holiday letting in both the UK and EEA are eligible to qualifying for the special tax rules for furnished holiday lettings.

The proposals, if implemented, will severely restrict the advantages of the furnished holiday lettings treatment, particularly in relation to relief for losses. Under the current rules, losses can be set against income and gains in the same way as trade losses. However, under the proposals, it will only be possible to carry forward to set against profits from the same type (UK or EEA) furnished holiday lettings business. Where losses remain unrelieved, if possible they should be utilised under the existing loss relief provisions prior to April 2011 as the ability to relieve any losses from furnished holiday lettings will be seriously curtailed from that date.

The new rules will also make it more difficult to qualify for the furnished holiday letting tax treatment. Landlords currently not meeting the new criteria should consider increasing the letting periods prior to April 2011 so that they can continue to benefit from the more favourable furnished holiday lettings rules beyond April 2011.

72.10 Rent-a-room relief

72.10.1 Overview of the relief

The rent-a-room was introduced to encourage people to let out spare rooms in their home. It applies to income derived from the provision of furnished residential accommodation in the taxpayer's own home. It covers, for example, income obtained from taking in a lodger.

The scheme provides an income tax exemption for profits from the furnished accommodation provided in the taxpayer's only or main home where gross receipts from the letting are not more than £4,250 in the tax year. If gross receipts exceed this amount, the profits from the letting can be taxed on an alternative basis, which may produce a lower tax bill.

The scheme applies equally to people who let a room in a home that they rent as it does to people who own their own home.

> **Planning point**
>
> Rent a room relief provides tax-free income in return for letting a room in the taxpayer's home.

Law: FA 1992, s. 59 and Sch. 10.

72.10.2 Conditions for rent-a-room relief

The rent-a-room scheme applies to qualifying individuals who derive an income from providing furnished accommodation (or goods and services in connection with that accommodation) in their only or main home. The scheme covers income from lodgers. It can also be applied to the provision of bed and breakfast or guest house accommodation, which is normally assessable as trading income, provided that the house in which the business is carried on in is also the individual's only main residence and that the normal rent-a-room conditions are met.

The rent-a-room scheme applies equally to income assessable as property income or trading income, provided that the associated conditions are met. Further, it applies regardless of whether the property used to provide the accommodation is rented or owned.

The scheme also applies to caravans and houseboats, provided that this is the taxpayer's only or main residence, as well as to accommodation provided in houses and flats.

If the taxpayer has more than one home, the scheme only applies to accommodation provided in the taxpayer's only or main home. Whether a residence is the taxpayer's only or main home is a question of fact. HMRC will look critically at any claims for rent-a-room relief in respect of second or holiday homes.

The scheme only applies to the provision of residential accommodation. It does not apply to rooms let out for use as an office or a storage.

If the property is divided into separate residences, it is necessary to determine whether such a division is temporary or permanent. The relief only applies to rooms let in the taxpayer's own home, so income derived from a separate residence in the same building will not qualify. Thus if the taxpayer splits his house into two self-contained flats and lives in one and lets one out, the income from the let flat will not be covered by the rent-a-room exemption.

Property Income

The relief is only available while there is a source of income. Thus, the first basis period cannot commence until there is a letting agreement. Where a room is let throughout the tax year, the basis period is the tax year.

> **Planning point**
>
> Rent-a-room relief is available for a room let in the taxpayer's home. It does not matter whether the taxpayer owns or rents his or her home.

Other guidance: Property Income Manual PIM 400

72.10.3   Exempt amount

The exempt amount under the rent-a-room scheme is £4,250. It is reduced to £2,125 if during the tax year someone else received income from letting accommodation in the same property, for example where a home is jointly-owned. If two or more other people let accommodation in the same residence, the limit is still reduced to £2,125. This means that it is possible to obtain relief of more than £4,250 when three or more people let accommodation in the same residence which is their only or main residence.

The limit is also reduced to £2,125 if the period of letting is less than 12 months and some other person lets accommodation in the same residence at any time in a 12-month period that includes the short basis period.

The relief applies to total gross furnished letting receipts for the tax year from the taxpayer's own home. Gross receipts include not only rents but also any other payments made to the taxpayer for the provision of goods and services in connection with the letting, such as meals and laundry.

> **Example 72.13**
>
> Ben lets out a room in his home to a lodger. He provides meals. The lodger pay rent of £300 a month for the room. The rent paid covers both the provision of the accommodation and of the meals.
>
> In 2010–11, Ben receives gross receipts of £3,600 from the letting. This is less than the rent-a-room exemption limit, so rent-a-room relief is automatically given. The receipts from the letting are exempt from income tax and do not need to be taken into account in computing the profits of any property rental business.

Where gross receipts are below the limit the exemption is applied automatically. The taxpayer is treated as having no profit or no loss from the letting and cannot claim capital allowances in respect of any plant or machinery.

In certain cases it may be more beneficial to elect for rent-a-room not to apply (see **72.10.5**) in order to obtain relief for a loss that would otherwise arise.

Where gross receipts from the let exceed the exempt amount, unless an election is made otherwise, the taxpayer is taxed under the property income provisions on the profit from the letting in the normal way. However, the taxpayer can elect instead to have the income assessed on an alternative basis, which is to tax gross receipts in excess of the exemption limit of £4,250 (or £2,125 where more than one person lets accommodation in the same property in the same year). This is known as the simplified basis.

Where the taxpayer wishes the simplified basis to apply, the time limit for making the election is one year from 31 January following the end of the tax year. Thus, an election for 2009–10 must be made by 31 January 2012. The same time limits apply for withdrawing the election should the taxpayer wish to revert to the normal basis.

> **Planning point**
>
> Rent a room relief only applies automatically if the rents do not exceed the exemption limit.

Law: FA 1992, Sch. 10, para. 6; ITTOIA 2005, s. 789(4)

72.10.4 No relief for expenses

Where relief is given under the rent-a-room scheme no further relief is given in respect of expenses actually incurred in relation to the letting. This can be advantageous as it removes the need for the taxpayer to keep detailed records of expenses where receipts do not exceed the exemption limit.

However, if the expenses exceed the rents, rent-a-room may not be beneficial and it may advisable for the normal tax rules to apply.

72.10.5 Rent-a-room versus normal basis of assessment

Where gross receipts from letting a room in a individual's own house are less than the rent-a-room exemption limit, rent-a-room relief is given automatically. If the taxpayer does not wish the exemption to apply, an election must be made for the rent-a-room election not to apply.

The election must be in writing and must be made by the time limit, which is one year from 31 January following the end of the tax year. The election only applies for one year and can be withdrawn within the same time scale.

Where the taxpayer would otherwise make a loss, it will be beneficial to make an election in order to obtain relief for that loss. The loss can be set either against other rental profits in the same year or carried forward and set against future profits of the property rental income. If rent-a-room relief is given, the taxpayer is treated as making neither a loss or a gain, which means relief for any losses is lost.

> ### Example 72.14
>
> Gary lets out a room in his home to a lodger. His partner Lucy also lets out a room in the same property in the same tax year.
>
> Gary receives gross receipts from the letting of £1,800. He also incurs expenses of £2,500. He also rents out a flat which produces a rental profit of £4,000 in the same tax year.
>
> The rent-a-room exemption limit applicable to Gary is £2,125. The limit is halved because another person lets out a room in the same property in the same tax year.
>
> Gary's gross receipts from the letting are less than the exemption limit of £2,125 so in the absence of an election rent-a-room relief would be applied automatically. However, if Gary elects for the normal basis to apply, he would have a loss of £700 (£1,800 − £2,500) which could be offset against the profits from letting the flat, reducing the taxable property income to £3,300.
>
> It is more beneficial for the normal basis of assessment to apply. Gary must therefore elect for rent-a-room relief not to apply. The election must be made within the required time limit.

By contrast, where gross receipts exceed the rent-a-room relief exempt amount, the normal basis of assessment for property income applies and the profit is calculated in accordance with normal trading rules.

If desired the taxpayer can elect for the simplified calculation of profit to be used instead. This means that the assessable amount is simply the excess of the gross rents over the above amount. The election must be made in writing within one year from 31 January following the end of the tax year. Once made the election continues in force for subsequent years until withdrawn. The same time limit applies for withdrawing the election.

As, once made, the election continues to apply until withdrawn, it is necessary to review the position each year to ensure that the best result is achieved. The simplified profit calculation is desirable where it produces a smaller profit that derived from the normal method, typically where expenses are less than the exempt amount.

Example 72.15

Cathy lets out a room in her house to a lodger. She provides meals as well as accommodation. The lodger pays £450 per month inclusive of accommodation and meals. Cathy incurs expenses of £900 in connection with the provision of the let and the meals.

Gross receipts for the tax year are £5,400. As this exceeds the exempt amount of £4,250 the profit from the let would be computed on the normal basis giving rise to a taxable profit of £4,500 (£5,400 − £900).

However, if Cathy elects for the simplified calculation to apply, the profit is reduced to £1,150 (being the amount by which gross receipts of £5,400 exceed the exempt amount of £4,250). This is clearly beneficial and Cathy should elect for the simplified calculation to apply.

The position should be reviewed in subsequent years to ensure that the election remains beneficial. If expenses exceed the exempt amount, the normal basis will be more advantageous and the election should be withdrawn.

Planning point

The most appropriate tax treatment will depend on the level of rent and the associated expenses. Where the position is less than clear cut, it is necessary to do the sums and elect accordingly.

Law: ITTOIA 2005, s. 800

72.11 International issues

72.11.1 Overseas property

Rents from properties outside the UK are taxed as foreign income rather than under the property income provisions. This means that the profits and losses from overseas properties are not amalgamated with those from UK properties and overseas properties do not form part of the taxpayer's property rental business. This means that losses from overseas properties cannot be offset against profits from UK properties and vice versa.

HMRC now allow furnished holiday letting elsewhere in the EEA to benefit from the special rules that apply to furnished holiday lettings in the UK (see **72.9.7**). This will continue to be the case under the proposed new rules which are to apply to furnished holiday lettings from April 2011 (see **72.9.8**).

However, the rules for computing the profit in relation to overseas rental profits are largely the same as for UK properties and like UK properties the computation follows trading principles.

Detailed consideration of overseas property businesses is outside the scope of this chapter.

72.11.2 Non-resident landlords' scheme

The non-resident landlords' (NRL) scheme is a scheme for taxing the rental income of non-resident landlords. A non-resident landlord is a person who has UK rental income and whose usual place of abode is outside the UK. The scheme does not apply to UK rental income received by persons who are temporarily outside the UK, for periods of six months or less.

Under the rules of the scheme, letting agents of non-resident landlords must deduct tax from the landlord's UK rental income and pay the tax over to HMRC. Tax is deducted at the basic rate of income tax from rental income less deductible expenses.

For the purposes of the NRL scheme the year runs from 1 April to the following 31 March. Letting agents and tenants operating the NRL scheme must account for tax each quarter. A quarter is each three-month period ending on 30 June, 30 September, 31 December and 31 March. The tax calculation is performed each quarter.

In the event that there is no letting agent, the responsibility to deduct tax is passed to the tenant. If the tenant pays rent of more than £100 per week to a non-resident landlord, he or she must deduct tax from the rent paid to the non-resident landlord and pay it over to HMRC.

If a tenant pays rent to the non-resident landlord of £100 per week or less, the tenant does not need to deduct tax under the NRL scheme, unless instructed to by HMRC. However, letting agents must always deduct tax from rent paid to non-resident landlords, even if the rent is less than £100 per week.

Letting agents and tenants do not have to deduct tax from the rental income of a non-resident landlord if HMRC have advised in writing that the landlord is approved to receive rental income without the deduction of tax.

Approval for UK rental income to be paid gross to a non-resident landlord is not an exemption from tax. The non-resident landlord will be equally liable for UK tax and the UK rental income must be included on any tax issued by HMRC.

72.12 Compliance issues

72.12.1 Self-assessment tax return

An individual who has a UK property rental business must return details of that business in the land and property pages of the self-assessment return. The pages must be completed regardless of whether the individual has numerous properties or just one or whether the individual takes a lodger into his or her own home.

The land and property pages require separate details of furnished holiday lettings and other property lettings in the UK, reflecting the different rules that apply to each. If rent-a-room relief is to be claimed, it is only necessary to tick the box provided for this purpose

If the tax return is filed electronically, it must reach HMRC no later than 31 January following the end of the tax year to which it relates. However, if a paper return is filed, an earlier deadline of 31 October applies.

Other guidance: SA105: Guidance Notes to Completing the Land and Property Pages (see *www.hmrc.gov.uk/worksheets/sa105-notes.pdf*)

72.12.2 Payment of tax

The deadline for payment of tax (along with any other tax due under the self-assessment) is 31 January following the end of the tax year to which it relates. Under the self-assessment, payments on account (one-half of the previous year's liability) must be made on 31 January in the tax year and 31 July following the end of the tax year, with any balance due by 31 January following the end of the tax year.

Interest may be charged on tax paid late.

73 Raising Business Finance

73.1 Introduction

Most businesses need to raise money at some point. The majority of smaller businesses will borrow from a bank to help fund initial costs of premises, stock, etc. More mature businesses may find opportunities that require the injection of new funds or, very often, simply need an ongoing source of finance to bridge the time gap between the incurring of costs and the gaining of revenue. Struggling businesses may seek extra cash to tide them over a difficult period of trading and to avoid (or, in some cases, merely postpone) the need to wind the operation up.

As in other fields, the tax tail should not wag the commercial dog. The fundamental choice is between loan finance on the one hand and shared ownership of the business (be it equity finance, partnership, etc.) on the other. If loan finance is the choice, the next stage is to consider whether an overdraft facility is appropriate or whether a more formal loan is required (or, probably, some combination of the two). If equity sharing is chosen there will be all-important considerations as to the extent to which ownership and control of the business should be given up.

The tax implications will be completely different depending on which choices are made.

73.2 Borrowing money

73.2.1 Loans

Interest paid on loans to, or overdrafts of, a business is a deductible expense, provided the loan was made wholly and exclusively for business purposes. For income tax purposes, there is a specific statement that interest is of a revenue nature whatever the nature of the loan.

In the case of companies, all interest under a company's 'loan relationships', and all charges and expenses incurred by the company under or for the purposes of its loan relationships and related transactions, are brought into account as credits and debits. A 'loan relationship' exists whenever a company stands as a debtor or creditor in respect of a money debt, and that debt arises from a transaction for the lending of money. Under this regime, in the case of a debtor company, interest and other charges and expenses are recognised for tax to the extent that they arise under an authorised accounting method and 'fairly represent' interest payments, charges and expenses arising or incurred in connection with the relationship or transactions.

It is not necessary for the loan to fall within one of the categories in respect of which an individual is permitted to deduct interest from his total income, but interest which receives relief under those provisions may not also be deducted against profits so as to give double relief.

Interest payable in respect of the acquisition of an asset (e.g. a car) used by an individual partly for business and partly for private purposes is apportioned for income tax purposes.

No deduction may be claimed for notional interest that might have been obtained if money had been invested rather than spent on (for example) repairs.

Law: CTA 2009, s. 54; ITTOIA 2005, s. 29, 34(1)

Other guidance: BIM 45650ff; CTM 50300ff

73.2.2 Interest paid on business loan to fund proprietor's overdraft

Interest paid on a loan used to fund the proprietor's overdrawn current or capital account is not deductible. HMRC have set out their view of how to identify when such circumstances arise in an interpretation (*Tax Bulletin,* November 1991, p. 4) as follows:

> 'SCHEDULE D, CASES I AND II – INTEREST PAID ON BUSINESS LOAN USED TO FUND PROPRIETOR's OVERDRAWN CURRENT/CAPITAL ACCOUNT – REVALUATION OF BUSINESS ASSETS
>
> Where interest is incurred wholly and exclusively for the purposes of a business, it may normally be deducted as an expense in computing the profits or gains arising from the trade, profession or vocation. No deduction is due if the loan upon which the interest is paid is used to fund the proprietor's overdrawn current/capital account.
>
> In considering whether a proprietor has overdrawn his current/capital account, a distinction is drawn between accumulated realised profits (both capital and revenue) upon which a proprietor is free to draw, and anticipated profits. Anticipated profits have not crystallised, do not represent a cash item and may never be realised; they are therefore disregarded in considering whether a proprietor's account is overdrawn.
>
> A revaluation of business assets in advance of disposal is such an anticipation of profit and is therefore disregarded in considering whether a current/capital account is overdrawn. A disallowance of the relevant interest cannot be avoided by crediting revaluation surpluses to an overdrawn account.'

This 1991 guidance puts the stress on the possibility of crediting revaluation surpluses and warns that such surpluses may not be taken into account when working out how much interest needs to be disallowed.

> **Planning point**
>
> Depreciation, however, is also a form of revaluation and it seems correct that it too should be ignored when deciding whether (or to what extent) interest should be disallowed.

The current HMRC guidance accepts this principle:

> 'In many cases depreciation is charged in the profit and loss account and this reduces the net amount of profit credited to the capital account. A trader who provides for depreciation lowers the amounts he or she can draw from the capital account without that account going into deficit compared to a trader in otherwise identical circumstances who does not provide for depreciation. You need to adjust for accumulated depreciation in calculating a revised balance on the account.'

> **Planning point**
>
> Another point to watch is whether the capital account has become overdrawn because of accumulated losses rather than because of proprietorial drawings. Once more, HMRC accept that no restriction would be due in this case:
>
>> 'If the capital account has become overdrawn because the business has made losses then it is not appropriate to restrict the interest deduction in the accounts.'

HMRC provide the following example to illustrate this latter point:

> **Example 73.1**
>
> Mr A sets up a new shop called 'British Weather' selling rainwear. He introduces £50,000 capital and borrows £50,000 from the bank. After a good initial period of trading his business is disrupted by continual roadworks in the area followed by an area regeneration project. The business makes trading losses totalling £30,000 in the first two years.
>
> At the end of year two he has taken total drawings of £20,000 out of the business so his capital account is nil (capital introduced £50,000 less losses £30,000 less drawings £20,000). He sees signs of improvement to the business so borrows a further £50,000 from the bank. In year three he takes out drawings of £10,000 and the business makes a trading loss of £5,000, so his capital account is overdrawn by £15,000 at the end of the year. The restriction of the deduction for interest is based on the drawings of £10,000 and not on the total amount of the overdrawn capital account.

Elsewhere, HMRC confirm the following important principle:

> 'Proprietors of businesses are entitled to withdraw their capital from the business, even though substitute funding then has to be provided by interest bearing loans. This is on the basis that the purpose of the additional borrowing is to provide working

capital for the business. There will though be an interest restriction if the proprietor's capital account becomes overdrawn.'

Other guidance: BIM 45700, 45715; *Silk v Fletcher (HMIT)* (2000) Sp C 262

73.2.3 Loans for specific assets or purposes

HMRC give the following guidelines on how they interpret the application of the 'wholly and exclusively' rule to the use of loans taken out for specific purposes. These guidelines include the following wording (but this has been abbreviated):

'Separate loan for specific business asset

Where a separate loan is obtained to buy a specific business asset the interest on that loan is an allowable deduction in computing the business profits. The interest will continue to be an allowable business deduction unless:

- the asset starts to be used for private purposes,

or
- the asset is disposed of and the proceeds are not used for business purposes.

Separate loan for specific business purpose

Where a separate loan is taken out specifically to meet business expenditure of a revenue nature and continues to be used for this purpose the interest is deductible throughout the life of the loan.

Separate loan to buy a private asset

Where a separate loan is obtained to buy a specific asset which is not used for business purposes, the interest on that loan is not an allowable deduction in computing business profits.

If the asset later starts being used for business purposes then the interest becomes an allowable deduction. Where the asset starts being used wholly for business purposes, all the interest is allowable from the commencement of business use. Where the asset starts being used partly for business purposes, a reasonable apportionment should be made based on the extent of business use of the asset.'

The security provided for a loan is not relevant in determining the tax relief for that loan.

Other guidance: BIM 45675

73.2.4 Corporation tax — loan relationships

For accounting periods beginning after 31 December 2004, debits and credits made in accordance with generally accepted accounting practice (GAAP) that are recognised in determining the company's profit or loss for the period are used to calculate a company's taxable income or deductions resulting from its loan relationships. For earlier accounting periods, the debits and credits were those made under 'authorised accounting methods'. Some debits and credits are disallowed, even though they fall to be made for the purposes of the company's accounts.

Exchange gains and losses on loan relationships denominated in a foreign currency are included in the calculation of the overall profit or loss on the loan relationship.

Trading loan relationships

For any loan to which a company is a party for trading purposes:

- credits are treated as trading receipts; and
- debits are treated as deductible trading expenses.

These provisions expressly override any rule in CTA 2009, Pt. 3, Ch. 4 which would otherwise prevent the deduction of certain items, notably capital losses on borrowings.

The test of whether or not a company is party to a loan relationship for the purposes of its trade depends on whether the company is a creditor or debtor. As a debtor, it need show only that it took on the debt for the purposes of its trade: whether the loan represents a temporary facility or is part of the company's capital should be irrelevant. It should not matter whether the loan finances current or fixed assets.

Law: CTA 2009, s. 297

Non-trade loan relationships

Debits and credits on loans to which a company is not party for trading purposes are called, respectively, 'non-trading debits' and 'non-trading credits'. In any accounting period:

- net non-trading credits (i.e. the aggregate of a company's non-trading credits, less the sum of all its non-trading debits, if any) are taxed under Schedule D Case III; and
- net non-trading debits (i.e. the aggregate of a company's non-trading debits, less the sum of all its non-trading credits, if any) are relieved, as a 'non-trading deficit'.

Note that non-trading foreign exchange gains and losses are also dealt with under these loan relationship provisions, as are any profits or losses arising over the life of a contract which falls within the derivative contracts legislation to the extent that the company is a party to the contract other than for the purposes of a trade carried on by it. Such gains and losses will be treated as non-trading credits or debits for the purposes of the loan relationships legislation.

Law: CTA 2009, s. 299–301

Deduction of tax at source

> ⚠ **Warning!**
> A company is required to deduct income tax at source when it makes certain payments of yearly interest, annual payments and other like amounts.

Law: ITA 2007, s. 874, 900

73.3 Loans to individuals for business-related purposes

73.3.1 Overview

Tax relief is given in various specified circumstances where an individual takes out borrowings that are applied for business purposes.

73.3.2 Loan to buy plant and machinery

Partners

Relief on the payment of interest may be available where an individual is a member of a partnership which is entitled to a capital allowance or liable to a balancing charge for any tax year in respect of machinery or plant belonging to the individual. Any interest paid by him in the basis period for that year on a loan to defray money applied as capital expenditure on the provision of that machinery or plant is eligible for relief. However, interest falling due and payable more than three years after the end of the tax year in which the debt was incurred does not attract relief.

Where the machinery or plant is used partly for the trade carried on by the partnership and partly by the partners for their own purposes, then only the interest which it is just and reasonable to attribute to the purposes of the trade is eligible for relief. Regard must be had to all the relevant circumstances and, in particular, to the extent of the use for the other purposes.

Employees

Similarly, the holder of an office or employment is entitled to relief where he is entitled under to a capital allowance, or is liable to a balancing charge (or would be so entitled or liable but for some contribution made by the employer), for any tax year in respect of machinery or plant belonging to him and in use for the purposes of the office or employment, and he pays interest in that year on a loan to defray money applied as capital expenditure on the provision of that machinery or plant.

However, interest falling due and payable more than three years after the end of the tax year in which the debt was incurred is not eligible for relief.

Where the machinery or plant is used partly for the office or employment and partly for other purposes then only the interest which it is just and reasonable to attribute to the purposes of the office or employment is eligible for relief. Regard must be had to the relevant circumstances and in particular, to the extent of the use for the other purposes. Where only part of a debt fulfils the conditions described above for interest on the debt to be eligible for relief, such a proportion of the interest will be treated as eligible as is equal to the proportion of the debt fulfilling those conditions at the time of the application of the money in question.

> ⚠ **Warning!**
> No capital allowances are given for cars, vans, cycles or motorcycles bought personally by employees and used for the purposes of the employment.

Law: ITA 2007, s. 383, 388; CAA 2001, s. 36

73.3.3 Loan to acquire an interest in a close company

Interest paid is eligible for relief under ITA 2007, s. 383, if it is interest on a loan to an individual to defray money applied (ITA 2007, s. 392):

- in acquiring any part of the ordinary share capital of a close company that is not a close investment-holding company as defined in CTA 2010, s. 34;
- in lending to such a close company money which is used wholly and exclusively for the purposes of the business of the company or of any associated company of it which is a close company satisfying any of those conditions; or
- in paying off another loan, interest on which would have been eligible for relief under ICTA 1988, s. 353 had the loan not been paid off (on the assumption, if the loan was free of interest, that it carried interest).

The relief is unavailable if the person who acquires the shares, or that person's spouse, obtains relief under the EIS scheme (see **Chapter 64**).

In addition, the close company must satisfy one of two sets of conditions.

Law: ITA 2007, s. 383, 392

First set of qualifying conditions

When the interest is paid the individual must have a 'material interest' in the company ('the relevant company'), which must continue, throughout the accounting period, to exist wholly or mainly for any one or more of the following purposes.

1. To carry on a trade or trades on a commercial basis.
2. To invest in land or estates or interests in land, the land being, or intended to be, let to persons other than a person either connected with the company or who is the spouse of an individual connected with it or a 'relative' (brother, sister, ancestor or lineal descendant), or spouse of a relative, of such an individual or such an individual's spouse.
3. To hold securities of, or make loans to, one or more companies each of which is a 'qualifying company' (see below) or a company which is under the control of the relevant company, or of a company which has control of the relevant company, and which itself wholly or mainly exists to hold securities of, or make loans to, one or more qualifying companies.
4. To co-ordinate the administration:
   (a) of two or more qualifying companies;
   (b) of a trade or trades carried on a commercial basis by one or more qualifying companies or a company which has control of the relevant company;
   (c) of the making, by one or more qualifying companies or by a company which has control of the relevant company, of investments as mentioned in 2. above. A company is a 'qualifying company' if it:
      (i) is under the control of the relevant company or of a company which has control of the relevant company; and
      (ii) exists wholly or mainly for at least one of purposes 1. and 2. above.

Material interest

A person has a material interest in a company for the purpose of the conditions set out above if he, either on his own or with one or more 'associates', or if any associate of his with or without such other associates:

- is the beneficial owner of, or able, directly or through the medium of other companies or by any other indirect means, to control more than five per cent of the ordinary share capital of the company; or
- possesses, or is entitled to acquire, such rights as would, in the event of the winding up of the company or in any other circumstances, give an entitlement to receive more than five per cent of the assets which would then be available for distribution among the participators.

Law: ITA 2007, s. 394

Second set of qualifying conditions

1. At the time when the interest is paid, the company continues to not to be a

close investment-holding company (see above) and the individual holds any part of the ordinary share capital of the company.
2. In the period from the application of the proceeds of the loan to the payment of the interest the individual has worked for the greater part of his time in the actual management or conduct of the company (see below) or of an associated company of the company.
3. He shows that in the period from the application of the proceeds of the loan to the payment of the interest he has not recovered any capital from the company apart from any amount taken into account in reducing the interest eligible for relief under ITA 2007, s. 406(2).

Company ceasing to be close
Provided the company was a close company at the time when the loan was applied, relief on interest will continue to be available if the company thereafter ceases to be close, provided the other conditions for relief are satisfied.

Other guidance: SP 3/78

Relief following company reconstruction
Relief is withdrawn or reduced if the borrower recovers any capital from the business without using the proceeds to repay the loan. For example, this will occur if the borrower sells or exchanges his or her interest or shares in the business.

On a strict interpretation, therefore, relief ceased to be available if the shares in a close company are exchanged for shares in another as a result of a company reorganisation. This was remedied by ESC A43 and, since 6 April 2007, by ITA 2007, s. 410 provided that the original loan would have qualified for relief.

This relaxation will also apply in cases where a loan to a partnership is replaced by:
- a loan to a successor partnership;
- a share in a successor partnership;
- a loan to a successor corporate entity; or
- a share holding in a successor corporate entity.

Law: ITA 2007, s. 383, 392, 409, 410

73.3.4 Loan to acquire an interest in a co-operative

Interest is eligible for relief if it is interest on a loan to an individual to defray money applied:
- in acquiring a share or shares in a body which is a co-operative (as defined);
- in lending to any such body money which is used wholly and exclusively for the purposes of the business of that body or of a subsidiary of that body; or
- in paying off another loan, interest on which would have been eligible for relief

had it not been paid off (on the assumption, if the loan was free of interest, that it carried interest).

The conditions set out below must also be satisfied:

- the loan was made after 10 March 1981;
- when the interest is paid, the body continues to be a co-operative;
- in the period from the application of the proceeds of the loan to the payment of the interest the individual has worked for the greater part of his time as an employee of the body or of a subsidiary of the body; and
- the individual shows that in that period he has not recovered any capital from the body, apart from any amount taken into account in reducing the interest eligible for relief.

Law: ITA 2007, 401

73.3.5 Loan to invest in an employee-controlled company

Interest paid is eligible for relief if it is interest on a loan to an individual to defray money applied:

- in acquiring any part of the ordinary share capital of an employee-controlled company; or
- in paying off another loan, interest on which would have been eligible for relief had the loan not been paid off (on the assumption, if the loan was free of interest, that it carried interest).

The following conditions must also be satisfied in order for the interest to be eligible for relief.

1. The company is, throughout the period beginning with the date on which the shares are acquired and ending on the date on which the interest is paid:

    (a) an unquoted company resident in the UK and not resident elsewhere; and
    (b) a trading company or the holding company of a trading group.

2. The shares are acquired before, or not later than 12 months after, the date on which the company first becomes an employee-controlled company.

3. During the tax year in which the interest is paid, the company either:

    (a) first becomes an employee-controlled company; or
    (b) is such a company throughout a period of at least nine months.

4. The individual is a full-time employee of the company, throughout the period beginning with the date on which the proceeds of the loan are applied and ending with the date on which the interest is paid or, if at that date he has ceased to be such an employee, ending with whichever is the later of:

    (a) the date on which he ceased to be such an employee; or

(b) the date 12 months before the payment of the interest.

5. The individual shows that in the period from the application of the proceeds of the loan to the payment of the interest he has not recovered any capital from the company, apart from any amount taken into account in reducing the interest eligible for relief.

A company is employee-controlled at any time when more than 50 per cent of the issued ordinary share capital of the company and of the voting power in the company is beneficially owned by persons who are full-time employees of the company.

> ⚠ **Warning!**
>
> Where an individual owns beneficially more than ten per cent of the issued ordinary capital of, or voting power in, a company, the excess will be treated as being owned by an individual who is not a full-time employee of the company.

Law: ITA 2007, 396

73.3.6 Loan to acquire an interest in a partnership

Interest is eligible for relief if it is interest on a loan to an individual to defray money applied:

- in purchasing a share in a partnership;
- in contributing money to a partnership by way of capital or premium, or in advancing money to a partnership, where the money contributed or advanced is used wholly for the purposes of the trade, profession or vocation carried on by the partnership; or
- in paying off another loan, interest on which would have been eligible for relief under that section had the loan not been paid off (on the assumption, if the loan was free of interest, that it carried interest).

The following conditions must also be satisfied:

- throughout the period from the application of the proceeds of the loan until the interest was paid, the individual has been a member of the partnership otherwise than as a limited partner or as a member of an investment limited liability partnership; and
- the individual shows that in that period he has not recovered any capital from the partnership, apart from any amount taken into account, in reducing the interest eligible for relief.

> ⚠ **Warning!**
> Relief for interest on the loan is available only while the individual continues to be a member of the partnership. This can cause problems where a partner resigns from a partnership and is obliged to leave funds in the company for a period of months or years.

This point was clarified in an interpretation published by the Revenue in the *Tax Bulletin*, Issue 6, February 1993, p. 58, the text of which is reproduced below:

'INTEREST PAID: SECTION 362 ICTA 1988 – LOANS TO BUY INTO PARTNERSHIPS

Section 362 ICTA 1988 provides tax relief for interest paid by an individual on a loan used to acquire an interest in a partnership. The question sometimes arises as to whether tax relief on that interest continues to be available when the individual ceases to be a member of the partnership. Section 362(2)(a) makes it clear that the individual has to be a member of the partnership throughout the period from the application of the proceeds of the loan until the interest is paid. It follows that there are no circumstances in which relief can be given after the individual has ceased to be a member of the partnership. This is so even where the former partner is unable to withdraw the capital immediately upon leaving the partnership.'

Salaried partners

HMRC accepted that relief extends 'to salaried partners in a professional firm who are allowed independence of action in handling the affairs of clients and generally so to act that they will be indistinguishable from general partners in their relations with clients'. This was codified with effect from 6 April 2007.

Law: ITA 2007, 399(5)

Other guidance: SP A33

Relief following incorporation or reconstruction

Relief is available for interest on a loan to purchase an interest in a close company. However, relief would cease to be available if a partnership is incorporated into a co-operative, close company or an employee-controlled company, or there is a partnership reconstruction involving a merger or demerger.

However, this does not apply if a loan to a partnership is replaced by:

- a loan to a successor partnership;
- a share in a successor partnership;
- a loan to a successor corporate entity; or
- a share holding in a successor corporate entity.

See also **73.3.3** above.

Law: ITA 2007, 399

Other issues

Other tax planning considerations relating to partnerships are considered in depth at **Chapter 5**.

73.4 Raising finance through issuing shares

73.4.1 Introduction

The other key method of raising finance for business purposes is the sharing of ownership of the business. For an unincorporated business this will involve taking on a business partner; the partner introduces cash (or expertise or some other essential asset) and, in return, is able to share in the future income and capital growth of the business.

For a company, the process will typically involve the issue of shares.

> **Example 73.2**
>
> Henman owns all the shares in a business worth £50,000. He calculates that he would be better off in the long term if the company issues additional shares to a second shareholder. The company therefore allows Murray to subscribe for new shares with the result that Henman ends up owning 60 per cent of a company that is worth perhaps £100,000. By issuing the new shares, the company has raised additional funds which it uses for business purposes. It has not had to borrow money so its profitability is not harmed.

From the company's point of view, the transaction is straightforward. Assuming that the transaction was at arm's length then no tax complications arise. The company will be able to consider, going forward, whether to pay funds out by way of dividend or salary, as considered in depth in **Chapter 15**.

73.4.2 Tax considerations – overview

The tax issues governing and arising from share transactions are considered in depth in **Chapter 14** (*General Corporation Tax Planning*), **Chapter 20** (*Purchase by a Company of its Own Shares*) and **Chapter 21** (*Share Transactions in Private Limited Companies*). Groups are considered at **Chapter 22** and company reorganisations and takeovers at **Chapter 24**.

In practice, the problem in raising equity finance – especially for unquoted companies – is to persuade investors that the company is a sensible place to hold their funds. Investors will be concerned both about the possibility of losing their money and the question of whether the reward will be adequate to compensate for that risk. Investors will be looking for a combination of income and capital growth.

To encourage investors to step into such uncertain waters, various schemes exist that offer a measure of tax relief either at the point of investment or on realising capital gains or both. Key forms of relief for individuals are the Enterprise Investment Scheme (see **Chapter 64**) and Venture Capital Trusts (**Chapter 77**).

For companies prepared to act as investor, the Corporate Venturing Scheme is a vehicle that provides some reliefs that are equivalent to the EIS and VCT schemes for individuals. This is considered at **73.4.4** below.

73.4.3 Losses on unquoted shares

Individuals who do not subscribe for shares through the vehicle of the EIS or a VCT may still be eligible for income tax relief if suffering a loss on shares in certain trading companies.

To qualify for relief, the individual must have subscribed for ordinary shares – no relief is due if they have been bought from a third party. The shares must be in a qualifying trading company, defined for these purposes as for EIS relief.

An individual who incurs a loss on shares of the specified description can claim relief for an amount equal to that loss against income tax. Relief is given in priority to the offset of trading losses against general income and the carry-back of trading losses made in the early years of a trade. A loss relieved under these rules cannot then also be claimed for capital gains tax purposes, and any necessary capital gains tax adjustment will be made accordingly.

Law: ITA 2007, s. 131

73.4.4 Corporate venturing scheme

Introduction

The Corporate Venturing Scheme (CVS) provides a range of tax reliefs for companies which subscribe for shares in unquoted companies. The unquoted company must be carrying on, or preparing to carry on, certain types of trading activities.

Under the CVS, certain investing companies may be eligible for:

- investment relief;
- loss relief; and
- deferral relief.

The above tax reliefs are available in respect of shares issued after 31 March 2000 and before 1 April 2010, provided the necessary conditions are met.

The scheme, according to HMRC, 'is intended to encourage mutually beneficial co-operation between unconnected companies'.

Law: FA 2000, s. 63 and Sch. 15, 16

Other guidance: VCM 50310

Main conditions

Before a company can receive relief for the amount it has subscribed for new ordinary shares under the CVS, the following four conditions must be met.

Shares must be 'Relevant shares'

The shares must be fully paid up ordinary shares subscribed for in cash. There must be no undertaking to pay cash to any person at some time in the future in respect of the acquisition of those shares. They must be non-redeemable shares which do not, at least during the qualification period for the issuing company, have any present or future preferential rights to dividends or assets on a winding up.

Use of money raised

At least 80 per cent of the money raised by the issue of shares under the CVS must be employed within 12 months of the share issue, wholly for the purposes of the relevant trade of the issuing company or its 90 per cent subsidiary. The balance must be used within 24 months.

The 12 months is extended to run from the date trading commences if the issuing company or its 90 per cent subsidiary has not begun to trade at the date the shares were issued. The money may be used to prepare to carry on a trade, and the condition will not be broken if an insignificant amount is used for some other purpose. Unfortunately there is no guidance on the amount that will be considered as 'not significant'.

There are special rules if the company's activities consist of research and development for a qualifying trade. In this case, the money must be used for the research and development activities, or the resulting trade, within three years of the share issue date.

No pre-arranged exits

There must be no arrangements made in connection with the issuing of the shares to allow the subscriber to recover his investment through:

- a repurchase or exchange of the scheme shares or other shares or securities of the issuing company unless HMRC approval is gained in advance;

- a planned cessation of the trade except a winding up of the business for commercial reasons;
- a disposal of a significant proportion of the value of the assets of the company to a connected party; or
- any sort of insurance or guarantee to protect the investor from the normal commercial risks of carrying on a business.

Anti-avoidance

The standard anti-avoidance provision disapplies the tax benefits of the CVS if the shares are issued as part of a scheme or arrangement whose main purpose is the avoidance of tax.

Law: FA 2000, s. 63 and Sch. 15

Investing company

The investing company must not, at any time during a three-year qualification period relating to the relevant shares, have a material interest in the issuing company.

Throughout the qualification period, where the investing company is a single company, the investing company must exist wholly for the purpose of carrying on one or more non-financial trades (as defined); incidental purposes are disregarded. Parallel rules apply to group companies. 'Incidental purposes' are those that do not have a significant effect on the company's activities.

The relevant shares must be a chargeable asset of the investing company, immediately after they have been issued to the investing company. A chargeable asset of a company is an asset, on the disposal of which a chargeable gain for the purposes of corporation tax would arise.

The investing company must subscribe for the relevant shares for commercial reasons and not as part of a scheme or arrangements of which the main purpose, or one of the main purposes, is the avoidance of tax.

Law: FA 2000, s. 63 and Sch. 15

Issuing company

An issuing company is a qualifying issuing company in relation to relevant shares when the following requirements are satisfied:

- it is unquoted;
- it is independent;
- it is owned by individuals;
- it engages in trading activities;
- if it has subsidiaries at any time during the qualification period, they are all qualifying subsidiaries;

- it meets the requirements of property managing subsidiaries;
- it is not a member of a partnership or joint venture; and
- its gross assets do not exceed a maximum aggregate value (currently £15m before investment and £16m after investment).

There is no requirement for the issuing company to be resident in the UK. However, the profits of the issuing company must, to some extent, be chargeable to UK corporation tax.

> **Planning point**
>
> Before the issuing company issues any shares under the CVS, it may obtain an advance clearance from HMRC to confirm that the requirements of the scheme have been met.

Law: FA 2000, s. 63 and Sch. 15

Investment relief

Relief available

The relief given under the CVS is calculated as the lower of:

- 20 per cent of the amount subscribed for the relevant shares in the accounting period; and
- the amount which will reduce the investing company's corporate tax liability for the accounting period to nil.

The relief is given as a reduction in the corporation tax liability for the period rather than as a deduction in profits assessable to corporation tax. The relief thus cannot create a loss for corporation tax purposes.

The company must be entitled to make the claim and must actually claim the relief in its corporation tax self assessment return for the period, or as a separate claim after that return has been submitted. Although the company cannot apply to postpone tax charged by an assessment or determination on the basis that a claim for relief under the CVS will be made, it can reduce the tax paid by quarterly instalments in respect of the accounting period, before the claim is made.

If the investing company subscribes for shares from several different share issues with the same issuing company, the investment relief given must be apportioned between those issues. This is to allow the investment relief to be withdrawn or reduced should there be a breach of the scheme requirements concerning a certain issue of shares.

The investment relief can be withdrawn or reduced on the occasion of any of the following events:

- the investing company disposes of the relevant shares within the three-year qualification period;
- the investing company receives significant value, which is not replaced, from the issuing company with in the restricted period;
- the issuing company repays any of its share capital to any of its shareholders or pays them for giving up rights to share capital during the period of restriction; or
- the investing company grants options over the relevant shares during the qualification period.

Conditions for investment relief

In addition to the general requirements for the CVS, the following steps need to be taken to allow the investing company to claim the relief:

- the issuing company must submit a compliance statement to HMRC;
- when HMRC have given their authority the issuing company must produce a compliance certificate to send to the investing company; and
- when the investing company has received the compliance certificate and if the general requirements are still met, it is entitled to make a claim for the relief due to be given in respect of the accounting period in which the shares were issued.

Before the issuing company issues any shares under the CVS, it may wish to obtain an advance clearance from HMRC to confirm that the general requirements of the scheme and the specific requirement which apply to the issuing company have been met.

The investing company is entitled to make a claim for relief under the CVS only if it has received a compliance certificate from the issuing company in respect of the shares it subscribed for under the scheme.

Law: TMA 1970, s. 55; FA 1998, Sch. 18, para. 8(1); FA 2000, s. 63 and Sch. 15

Loss relief

If the investing company makes a loss on the disposal of relevant shares it can claim a capital loss to be set off against any capital gains it may make in the normal way. However, if it has held the relevant shares continuously since issue, and the investment relief given has not been withdrawn, it may claim loss relief to set against income. This income loss relief must be claimed within two years of end of the accounting period in which the loss was incurred and can be set against the profits of that accounting period and of any accounting periods ending in the previous 12 months. The disposal of the relevant shares must also fall under one of the acceptable circumstances discussed under 'Relief available'.

The loss can be carried back to an earlier period only if it cannot be wholly relieved in the later period. The loss relief must be deducted before any other charges on income and is given priority over any loss claimed under CTA 2010, Pt. 4, Ch. 5.

Law: FA 2000, s. 63 and Sch. 15

Deferral relief

Deferral relief is designed for companies that 'catch the CVS habit'. If an investing company makes a capital gain on the disposal of some relevant shares on which it has gained investment relief, it can reinvest the gain in relevant shares of another issuing company and defer the taxation of that gain until the second batch of shares are disposed of. The investing company can use deferral relief to dispose of relevant shares within the three-year qualification period while sheltering any gains made from tax. The investing company can also reinvest suitable chargeable gains in a serial fashion without limit.

The requirements for deferral relief are as follows:

- the original gain must arise on the disposal of CVS shares on which investment relief has not been withdrawn and which have been held by the investing company since issue, or it must be a gain that has crystallised due to the withdrawal of deferral relief;
- the new shares must be subscribed for under the CVS and the investing company must obtain investment relief for them;
- the new investment must be in a different company and a different group to the shares which generated the original gain; or
- the new shares must be held by the investing company within a period of four years beginning one year before the date on which the original gain arose. If these new shares were issued before that period the investing company must have held them since issue without withdrawal of the investment relief which they carry.

73.5 Expenses of raising finance

73.5.1 Overview

The incidental costs of corporate borrowing are relieved, for companies, in accordance with CTA 2009, s. 307(3).

For individuals, the incidental costs of obtaining loan finance are deductible under ITTOIA 2005, s. 58 (costs of obtaining a loan in respect of which the interest is itself allowable) or s. 59 (loan stock the interest on which is allowable).

A loan or loan stock which carries a right of conversion into, or a right to the acquisition of, shares or other such securities is disqualified if the right is exercisable within three years from the date when the loan is obtained or the stock issued. This three-year rule is relaxed if the right of conversion is not actually exercised within the three-year period. If the right of conversion is exercised for only part of the loan or security within the three-year period, the relief for the costs of the balance is obtainable.

'Incidental costs of obtaining finance' means expenditure on fees, commissions, advertising, printing and other incidental matters, wholly and exclusively incurred for the purpose of obtaining the finance, of providing security for it, or of repaying it. Stamp duty is not included. Expenditure on abortive applications is allowed if the expenditure would have qualified had the finance been obtained.

Income tax relief is not given for expenditure as a result of, or for obtaining protection against, fluctuations in currency exchange rates. Also, relief is not given for the cost of repaying a loan or loan stock so far as attributable to its being repayable at a premium or to its having been obtained or issued at a discount.

Planning point

The VAT input tax position in relation to the cost of financing position was previously thought to have been determined by the case *Trinity Mirror plc v C & E Commissioners*. [2003] BTC 5,516 which held that the costs associated with a share issue were not deductible.

This decision has since been shown to be incorrect following a decision by the European Court of Justice in *Kretztechnik A G v Finanzamt Linz* (Case C-465/03 [2006] BVC 66. Companies can consequently make claims for any additional input tax, subject to the three-year cap.

Law: CTA 2009, s. 307(3); ITTOIA 2005, s. 58, s. 59

73.5.2 Life insurance premiums

HMRC do not regard the rules outlined above as providing relief for premiums on a life insurance policy taken out by a self-employed person and required as a condition of obtaining loan finance:

> '"Incidental costs" are defined in [ITTOIA 2005, s. 58(2)] as "fees, commissions, advertising, printing and other incidental matters". The expenses listed are viewed as forming a class which would include any incidental costs of taking out a life insurance policy but not the cost of the policy itself, that is, the premiums.'

Other guidance: Tax Bulletin 2, February 1992

73.5.3 Permanent interest bearing shares

A building society may deduct the incidental costs of issuing permanent interest bearing shares (PIBS) in computing the profits of its business, if the dividends or interest in respect of the shares are deductible. However, relief is unavailable to the extent that the costs in question fall to be brought into account for loan relationship purposes. Nor is relief available for any sums paid in consequence of, or for obtaining protection against, losses resulting from changes in the rate of exchange between different currencies, or for the cost of repaying any shares so far as attributable to their being repayable at a premium or to their having been issued at a discount.

Law: CTA 2009, s. 131

73.5.4 Companies

As discussed above, all charges and expenses incurred by a company under or for the purposes of its loan relationships and 'related transactions' are brought into account as credits and debits, and are recognised for tax to the extent that they arise under an authorised accounting method, and 'fairly represent' interest payments, charges and expenses arising or incurred in connection with the relationship or transactions.

In order to be allowable for tax, 'charges and expenses' must be related directly to:

- bringing loan relationships into existence;
- entering into or giving effect to any 'related transactions';
- making payments under any loan relationships, or in pursuance of any related transactions; or
- taking steps to ensure the receipt of payments under any such relationships or in pursuance of any such transactions.

A 'related transaction' is any disposal or acquisition of rights or liabilities under a loan relationship, including those where such rights are transferred or extinguished by way of sale, gift, exchange, surrender, redemption or release. The term includes a part-disposal or part-acquisition.

The relief for charges and expenses on loan relationships and related transactions is extended to costs of arranging finance which the company does not immediately take on. This would cover, for instance, the expenses of setting up standby credit facilities. It would also cover abortive expenditure of the types listed above.

Law: CTA 2009, s. 105

Other guidance: CFM 5210

73.5.5 Anti-avoidance

> ⚠ **Warning!**
> No deduction is allowed if a scheme has been effected or arrangements made (either before or after the payment) such that the sole or main benefit accruing to the payer from the transaction is the tax advantage of being able to deduct the interest.

> **Example 73.3**
>
> Max inherited a property from his late parents. He decided to use the property as a source of rental income. At the same time he wants to make some substantial improvements to his own home which will require some borrowing from a bank. He therefore devises a scheme to enable him to offset the interest payments against his rental income by selling the property to a trust (where the trustees fund the purchase using the proceeds from a bank loan).
>
> Such a scheme might succeed but for the provisions in ITA 2007, Pt. 13, Ch. 7 which will preclude any relief (in this case to the trustees) if the scheme has been effected for tax avoidance purposes.

For another example of the type of scheme which this is intended to counter, see *Cairns v MacDiarmid*. This case involved payments made before the anti-avoidance legislation came into effect, but the Court of Appeal held that the scheme was so artificial, and so devoid of any purpose other than a fiscal purpose, as to disqualify it from consideration in the context of tax provisions.

Law: ITA 2007, Pt. 13, Ch. 7

Other guidance: Cairns v MacDiarmid [1983] BTC 188

74 Tax Aspects of Charities

74.1 Introduction

Charities (as defined) enjoy various tax privileges. Nevertheless, it is an oversimplification to claim – without qualification – that 'charities are exempt from tax'.

Tax considerations fall into three main categories: VAT angles (discussed in the companion CCH volume, *VAT Planning*), other tax issues for the charity itself (discussed mainly at **74.3** below) and tax issues for those seeking to benefit the charity (discussed at **74.4** below).

> ⚠ **Warning!**
> The definition of charity for tax purposes changed with effect from 6 April 2010. Care must be taken to ensure that the correct definitions are used.

74.2 Definitions and general principles

74.2.1 Definitions

Charity

The definition of charity for most tax purposes was revised by Finance Act 2010 with effect from 6 April 2010. For cases involving charities prior to 6 April 2010, the reader is referred to earlier editions of this work.

For tax purposes, a charity must be a body of persons or a trust that satisfies the following four conditions:

(1) it is established for charitable purposes only;

(2) it meets the jurisdiction condition;

(3) it meets the registration condition; and

(4) it meets the management condition.

HMRC may publish the name and address of any body of persons or trust that appears to them to meet (or to have met) the definition of charity.

Law: FA 2010, Sch. 6, para. 1, 6

Charitable purposes
This is a concept taken directly from charity law and is considered in further detail below.

Jurisdiction condition
The body of persons or trust will be a charity only if it is subject to the control of either:

- the English (and Welsh) High Court, the Court of Session in Scotland or the High Court in Northern Ireland in the exercise of the court's jurisdiction with respect to charities; or
- any other court in the exercise of a corresponding jurisdiction under the law of another member state or a territory specified in regulations.

This provision ensures that charities established in other member states of the European Union are able to qualify for the same tax advantages as their UK counterparts. Of course, prior to 2010, those advantages were technically available to such charities by virtue of EU law – although it might have been a difficult process obtaining them. The 2010 amendments ensure that the UK statute is now more compliant with European Law.

Law: FA 2010, Sch. 6, para. 2

Registration requirement
This requirement consists of two separate conditions.

In the case of charities with in the meaning of the Charities Act 1993, the charity must have complied with any requirement to be registered under section 3 of that Act. As will be noted below, not all charities are required to be so registered. However, the essential part of this condition is that the charity must have complied with its registration requirements, *if any*.

It should be noted that the Charities Act 1993 applies only to charities in England and Wales. Other charities will therefore be subject to the second condition.

In the case of charities that fall outside the Charities Act 1993 meaning, the requirement is that the charity must have complied with any requirement under the law of a territory outside England and Wales to be registered in any corresponding register.

Law: FA 2010, Sch. 6, para. 3

Management condition
This requires the managers of the charity to be fit and proper persons to be managers of the body or trust.

The managers for these purposes are those persons having general control and management of the administration of the charity.

If the management condition is not met for a period, it can nevertheless be deemed by HMRC to have been met if HMRC consider that either:

- the failure did not prejudice the charitable purposes of the charity; or
- it is nevertheless just and reasonable in all the circumstances for the condition to be treated as met.

Law: FA 2010, Sch. 6, para. 4–5

Charitable purposes

Charitable purposes – according to the previous Charities Act 1993, s. 97(1) – meant purposes which are exclusively charitable according to the law of England and Wales. These were broadly classified under the four heads of charity first adopted in the Charitable Uses Act 1601, and articulated by Lord McNaghten in *Special Commissioners v Pemsel* (1891) 3 TC 53 as:

- the relief of poverty;
- the advancement of education;
- the advancement of religion; and
- other purposes beneficial to the community, not falling under any of the preceding heads.

The Charities Act 2006 replaced these four heads with a new extended and modernised list designed to embrace all existing recognised charitable activities in the 21st century. For instance, the new definitions include explicit recognition of the advancement of human rights, and of the advancement of citizenship or community development.

The new categories are:

- prevention or relief of poverty;
- advancement of education;
- advancement of religion;
- advancement of health or saving of lives;
- advancement of citizenship or community development;
- advancement of the arts, culture, heritage or science;
- advancement of amateur sport;
- advancement of human rights, conflict resolution or reconciliation, and the promotion of racial and religious harmony, equality and diversity;
- advancement of environmental protection or improvement;
- relief of those in need by reason of youth, age, ill health, disability, financial hardship or other disadvantage;
- advancement of animal welfare;
- the promotion of the efficiency of the armed forces of the Crown; or of the police, fire and rescue services or ambulance services; and

- other currently charitable purposes.

> ⚠ **Warning!**
>
> Under the old rules, it was assumed in the cases of poverty relief, education and religion that the object was beneficial to the community and it was normally only necessary to prove that the number of people benefited was sufficient in size. Thus, trusts established in favour of poor relations, fringe religions and private tuition did not normally achieve charitable status because the number of people capable of benefiting was insufficient. In the last case, it was necessary not only to prove that the number of people was sufficient but also that the object itself was beneficial to the community.
>
> The new Charities Act now makes it a requirement that in addition to demonstrating that their activities fall within one or more of the new headings, *all* organisations seeking charitable status in future will have to pass the 'public benefit' test.

The question of what is charitable is the subject of considerable case law and it is dangerous to assume that what appears to be a trust for good works is necessarily charitable. If its objects contradict those of an existing charity it cannot also be said to be beneficial to the community. For example, the Anti-Vivisection Society is not a charity as it was established to oppose the practice employed by charitable medical research organisations of using live animals in experiments for such research. To grant charitable status also to the Society would have been contradictory to this.

> ⚠ **Warning!**
>
> This concept of benefiting the community is essential to the definition of charity and distinguishes charitable organisations from other non-profit-making ones. There are many non-profit-making organisations which fail to achieve charitable status because they cannot prove that their objects are of benefit to the community.

(1) An order of contemplative nuns, whose main activity was to pray in an enclosed environment for the souls of others, could not prove that this activity either advanced religion or was otherwise of benefit to the community.

(2) The Temperance Society could not prove that abstaining from alcohol was of benefit to the community.

(3) Political parties cannot prove that their beliefs are better for the community than those put forward by their opponents.

(4) Trade unions and clubs are established mainly for the benefit of their members rather than for that of the community.

The inclusion of non-charitable objects or activities can destroy the charitable status of an organisation. These include:

- political activities;
- commercial activities (but see **74.3.2** for exemptions); and
- other activities which enable those who are not objects of the charity to benefit under its terms.

> ⚠ **Warning!**
>
> For many charities, it is difficult not to engage in such activities – either trading to raise funds, or stirring up a political storm to focus attention on their cause. In either case, it is necessary for them to separate the activities, ensuring that the charity has no part in the trading or political activity.

Thus, for example:

- Amnesty International, which could not be classified as a charity because of its political aims, established a Prisoners of Conscience Fund which was registered as a charity to help political prisoners and their families in need; and
- similarly, most major charities have subsidiary trading companies to carry on their fundraising activities, leaving the charity to pursue the charitable objectives.

> ⚠ **Warning!**
>
> A problem arises where the charity does not separate its activities in this way but rather engages in certain non-charitable activities itself. Minor infringements may in practice be ignored but major transgressions will invite the attention of the Charity Commission and of Her Majesty's Revenue & Customs (HMRC). The former may, in extreme cases, seek to remove the charity from the register. The latter may deny the charity the tax privileges to which it would otherwise be entitled. This is explained more fully in **74.3.5**.

Law: Charities Act 2006, s. 2

Other guidance: *The Oxford Group v IR Commrs* (1949) 31 TC 221; *IR Commrs v The Christian Churches of England And Wales* (1926) 10 TC 748; *Gilmour v Coats* [1949] AC 426

74.2.2 Forms of constitution

Charities need not have any particular form of constitution but, since they are defined as 'a body of persons', it follows that an individual cannot be a charity. It is also normal for the objects of the charity to be in writing – otherwise the consent of the Charity Commission to registration cannot be obtained, nor will HMRC recognise its claims.

Charities are normally established in one of the following ways:

- charitable trust;
- company incorporated under the Companies Acts, normally limited by guarantee;
- society incorporated under the *Friendly, Industrial and Provident Societies Acts* 1965–1975;
- society incorporated by Royal Charter;
- society constituted by special Act of Parliament; and
- unincorporated association governed by a simple written instrument.

The Charities Act introduces a new corporate vehicle for charities to use in the future, the Charitable Incorporated Organisation, or CIO. Charities which are currently constituted as incorporated are effectively dual regulated because they have to make returns to the Charity Commission and to Companies' House, and have to comply with the accounting requirements of both the Companies Act 1985 and the Charities Act 1993. A CIO, whilst preserving the benefits of incorporation will have to report only to the Charity Commission.

74.2.3 Registration

The Charities Act 2006 amended the provisions in the Charities Act 1993 regarding the system of registration for charities under the supervisory control of the Charity Commission. For historical reasons, certain charities were exempted from this requirement whilst others have been excepted by order, e.g. most places of worship and universities. Most charities (approximately 180,000) are registered and those that are not must be able to prove why they are either exempt or excepted from the requirement. The register is kept by the Charity Commission at their offices which are listed below in **74.2.4**. Section 4 of the Charities Act 1993 says that:

> '... an institution shall ... be conclusively presumed to be or have been a charity at any time when it is or was on the register of charities'.'

Applications for the registration of charities should be made to the Commissioners who decide whether or not to include them on the register. Appeals can be made to the High Court against refusals to register or to contest the validity of a registration, but only by interested parties.

Following the introduction of the Charities Act 2006, smaller charities are now unable to register with the Charity Commission. However, those charities are instead able to apply to HMRC for recognition as a charity.

Other guidance: HMRC guidance on recognition of charities: *www.hmrc.gov.uk/ charities/tax/recognition.htm*

74.2.4 Charity Commission (formerly the Charity Commissioners)

The Charity Commission is not merely registrars. It is 'charged with the responsibility of overseeing the administration of charitable trusts by their trustees':

> 'the Commissioners shall ... have the general function of promoting the effective use of charitable resources by encouraging the development of better methods of administration, by giving charity trustees information or advice on any matter affecting the charity and by investigating and checking abuses.'

Many leaflets are available from the Charity Commission including several giving guidance to charity trustees, explaining their responsibilities, etc. A complete list of these leaflets can be obtained free of charge by downloading from the Charity Commission's website: *www.charity-commission.gov.uk*,

The Charity Commission prefers queries to be sent by email using the secure link at: *www.charitycommission.gov.uk/sendmailCRM.aspx*. Alternatively, by telephone on 0845 300 0218 (where advice can be given in over 150 languages) (or 0845 300 0219 for callers with hearing and/or speech impairments).

Written requests for information are actively discouraged by the Commission. However, any that are made should be sent to:

Charity Commission Direct
PO Box 1227
Liverpool L69 3UG

Law: Charities Act 2006, s. 6

74.2.5 Her Majesty's Revenue and Customs

Tax relief is the biggest single advantage conferred by charitable status. HMRC are involved in the initial registration of a charity and continue to monitor its activities by inspecting accounts and returns submitted in support of claims. If it is considered that the income of a charity is not exclusively applied for charitable purposes, tax reliefs or repayments may be withheld or restricted.

> ⚠ **Warning!**
>
> It is therefore imperative for every charity to obtain the sanction of HMRC before embarking upon any new activity of significance. It is equally important for the charity to be constantly aware of its obligation to apply its income for charitable purposes (see **74.3.4**).

Registering with HMRC

Charities in England and Wales, which have achieved registration with the Charity Commission, need to notify HMRC of the following details:

- their charity registration number;
- the full address to which all correspondence should be sent; and
- a completed authorised signatory form.

This last requirement is a form provided by HMRC.

> ⚠ **Warning!**
>
> Charity tax repayment claims will now be made only if they are signed by an official of the charity who has been authorised to sign on this form. There can be only one authorised signatory for each charity at any one time.

Notifications should be made to:

HMRC (Charities)
St John's House
Merton Road
BOOTLE
Merseyside L75 1BB

Tel: 0845 302 0 203

Charities in England and Wales that are not required to register with the Charity Commission, and charities in Northern Ireland, need to apply for charitable tax exemption and must send the following to HMRC (Charities):

- the signed and dated governing instrument;
- details of the charity's activities including any explanatory or promotional literature; and
- a note of the accounting reference date.

HMRC publications

The attitude of HMRC is generally very supportive and the body has published many booklets outlining its views and its interpretations of charity tax law. As an example, comprehensive guidance notes on the HMRC approach to many charity taxation issues can be found on the internet at *www.hmrc.gov.uk/charities/index.htm*.

Charity tax returns

Charities constituted as trusts are technically within the income tax self assessment regime. Charities constituted as companies, and other charities, fall within the corporation tax self assessment rules.

Before the introduction of self assessment, charities were not often called upon to make tax returns other than repayment claims. Charities, however constituted, now have to make a tax return of all income and gains and related expenditure if called upon to do so by the issue of a formal notice to file a return.

When required to make a return, charities will also have to complete charity supplementary pages to the tax return. These pages require detailed information about the income and expenditure of the charity, and about any investments or loans the charity has made.

The supplementary pages also contain a declaration certifying whether or not the charity has applied all income and gains for charitable purposes (see **74.3.4**) or has undertaken any non-qualifying expenditure (see **74.3.5**).

It is important to note that these charity supplementary pages to the self-assessment returns legally constitute a charity's claim to tax exemption for the period to which they relate. Where, as in the vast majority of cases, the charity claims total exemption, it need only file a 'nil' return for main tax return purposes, but a penalty will still result if the return, supplementary pages and accounts of the charity are not filed by the due date.

HMRC's stated policy was initially to issue returns to only a sample number of charities each year on a random or risk assessment basis. After some years of this system in operation, there now appears to be a policy of investigating the larger charities, and requiring filing of returns on an annual basis, in the same way as any other taxpayer.

> ⚠ **Warning!**
> Great care should be taken in completing the tax return supplementary pages, not least because they ask for information in a way that is not wholly consistent with the way a charity might prepare its accounts to comply with the various charity accounting disclosure rules.

74.2.6 The Official Custodian for charities

The Official Custodian is a corporation sole established by Parliament to hold property on behalf of charity trustees and to provide certain services for them free of charge. Where property is vested in the Official Custodian in trust for a charity, the Official Custodian exercises the same powers over the property as a custodian trustee appointed under the Public Trustee Act 1906, except that he or she has no power to charge fees.

Law: Charities Act 1993, s. 2, 21

Tax Aspects of Charities

74.2.7 Investment management

Charities have to consider the best way in which to have their investments held and managed. There are broadly three choices for trustees as follows.

1. Hold the investments in their own names or that of a trustee corporation and manage the investments themselves.
2. Appoint (if they have the power to do so) investment managers to manage the investments and to appoint custodian trustees to hold the investments on behalf of the trustees.
3. Transfer the investments to a common investment fund. Such a fund has the advantage that it is free to invest without the restrictions of the 'narrower range' imposed by the Trustee Investment Act 1961.

> ⚠ **Warning!**
>
> Whichever type of investment management is chosen, the trustees will still be responsible for ensuring that the investment policy is prudent, that the stock certificates are kept safe and that the income, including tax thereon, is received by the charity.

74.3 Tax exemptions and reliefs

74.3.1 Income tax and corporation tax

Income tax reliefs afforded to charities are contained in ITA 2007, Pt. 10.

Pt. 10 makes two type of provision. First, it provides for relief in respect of certain types of gift and payments made to charitable trusts. Secondly, it provides for certain exemptions in respect of some of the income received by a charitable trust.

Where the charity is a company, the equivalent reliefs are still located in CTA 2010, Pt. 11.

> ⚠ **Warning!**
>
> These rules do not grant a general exemption from tax on charity income but give specific exemptions, which are granted on a claim being made. For charities constituted as companies, the claim must be made within six years from the end of the accounting period to which the claim relates. Charities constituted as trusts must claim exemption before the expiry of five years from 31 January following the end of the fiscal year to which the claim relates.

⚠ Warning!

A claim is valid only if the receipt of the charity is applied only to the purposes of the charitable trust.

Exemptions

The exemptions may be summarised as follows:

- rents and profits from land;
- interest, annuities, dividends and annual payments which form part of the income of the charity – this exemption also applies to non-trade gains on intangible fixed assets;
- public revenue dividends on securities in the name of trustees where the income is applied only for the repair of any cathedral, college, church, chapel or other building used only for divine worship;
- trading profits, providing that either the trade is exercised in the course of the actual carrying out of a primary purpose of the charity, or the work in connection with the trade is mainly carried on by beneficiaries of the charity; and
- profits of specified small lotteries.

⚠ Warning!

The exemption for income from public revenue dividends offers greater exemptions for Christian places of worship than for other religions. Provided that the income is applied for the repair of the cathedral, church etc. the income will be exempt. For temples, synagogues and mosques (etc.), the building must be used *only* for divine worship. Therefore, other use can preclude relief. This is the case even if the other use otherwise benefits the community (for example, use as a blood donation centre, polling station or school).

Planning point

It is notable that the exemptions for a charity's passive income require the income to be applied for charitable purposes generally, whilst those for trading and lottery income depend on the income being applied for the purposes of the particular charity concerned.

The exemption for income from property covers furnished as well as unfurnished lettings. The exemption for interest, dividends and annual payments includes income from overseas sources.

Exemptions for trades

The trading exemption applies for profits of a trade exercised either:

- partly in the course of carrying out a primary purpose of the charity; or
- mainly by the beneficiaries of the charity.

Law: ITA 2007, s. 524–525; CTA 2010, s. 478–479

Exemptions for small trades

The narrower requirement that the profits be applied only for the purposes of the charity is ITA 2007, s. 526, which exempts the profits of small trading activities that are not within ITA 2007, s. 524 because they are neither primary purpose nor carried out by charity beneficiaries.

Any income for charity which would otherwise be assessable as trading income (or under certain other statutory provisions in ITA 2007, s. 1016) will be exempt if it is below a statutory annual gross income limit.

This limit is the greater of:

- £5,000; and
- the lesser of £50,000 and 25 per cent of the charity's total gross income.

HMRC website points out that this exemption can be expressed in tabular form, thus:

Total gross charity income	Maximum permitted trade sales
Under £20,000	£5,000
£20,000–£200,000	25% of total gross income
Over £200,000	£50,000

The above limits must be scaled down proportionately for accounting periods of less than a year.

There is also exemption if, when a charity exceeds the limit for the first time, there was a reasonable expectation at the start of the period that the limit would not have been exceeded.

This exemption will be welcome to many charities that raise modest funds by selling Christmas cards and the like.

Law: ITA 2007, s. 526, 528; CTA 2010, s. 480, 482

Directors of charities

Whilst employees of charities are assessable to tax on their earnings in the normal way, there is an exemption available in respect of lower-paid directors of charities. Where total earnings derived by a director of a charity are less than £8,500 per annum, the director is not regarded as being within the benefits-in-kind legislation that would otherwise apply.

Law: ITEPA 2003, s. 216

Interest on government securities

> **Planning points**
>
> In the case of government securities, the Bank of England will pay interest gross to charity trustees on receipt of an application accompanied by the charity registration slip issued by the Charity Commission.
>
> Interest on bank and building society deposits will be paid gross, on receipt by the bank or building society of proof of charitable status. It is important to make this clear at the outset, as tax will otherwise be deducted from such interest.

74.3.2 Trading activities

Exempt trades

To qualify for exemption from tax on business profits, a trade carried on by a charity must either be within the turnover exemption limits in ITA 2007, s. 528 (see **74.3.1** *Income tax and corporation tax*, above) or must be either:

- exercised in the course of carrying out the charity's primary purpose (e.g. the provision of education by a school or college in return for course charges; the provision of treatment by a hospital in return for payment); or
- carried out mainly by the beneficiaries of the charity (e.g. the sale of goods produced by the residents of a registered home).

> **⚠ Warning!**
>
> The distinction between a trade which is exempt and one which is not exempt is often a fine one. A cathedral bookshop selling religious books and artefacts is promoting religion but if it is mainly selling tourist souvenirs, it may be arguable that it is merely a fundraising business and therefore not exempt.

HMRC practice is to extend the exemption to trading activities which are ancillary to a main purpose trade: for example, the sale of textbooks and past exam papers by a school, or the provision of a canteen and shop selling necessary goods to patients and visitors in a hospital.

> **⚠ Warning!**
>
> Where part of the trade is not related to the primary purpose trade, and not regarded as ancillary, the whole of the exemption may be lost unless the non-qualifying part is within *de minimis* levels accepted by HMRC.

In this respect, the primary purpose trading exemption will not be lost where:

- the part of the trade which does not qualify is not large in absolute terms; and
- the non-qualifying turnover is less than ten per cent of the turnover of the whole trade.

HMRC have added further clarification of how this rule is applied in practice:

> 'A turnover for the part of the trade which is not primary purpose of £50,000 or less would be considered "not large" for the purposes of the first part of this test. So, a mixed trade with a non-primary purpose turnover of less than £50,000 and representing less than 10% of the total trade turnover would satisfy this test.'

However, see below the rules for partially exempt trades which came into effect on 22 March 2006.

Law: ITA 2007, Pt. 10; CTA 2010, Pt. 11

One-off fundraising events

Prior to 6 April 2000 small fundraising activities, such as bazaars, jumble sales and the like were exempted as not being taxable trades by virtue of Extra Statutory Concession C4. On the basis that profits were applied for charitable purposes, the concession was given where the event:

- was known to be for charity;
- did not amount to regular trading; and
- was not in competition with other traders.

HMRC tended to police this concession in a restrictive manner until, with the introduction of s. 46 Finance Act 2000, ESC C4 was amended in an attempt to align the direct tax treatment of charity fundraising events with VAT exemption for such activities.

ESC C4 was enacted as ITA 2007, s. 529 and CTA 2010, s. 483 which exempt fundraising activities from tax in terms of the VAT exemption in VATA 1994, Sch. 9, Grp. 12, providing the profits are transferred to charities or are applied for charitable purposes.

The HMRC interpretation of the VAT exemption allows for up to 15 one-off fundraising events of similar type in the same location each financial year, with small events raising less than £1,000 each allowed providing they are no more frequent than weekly.

> ⚠ **Warning!**
>
> Events where accommodation is provided for more than two nights are specifically excluded from the exemption.

> Further, the exemption does not apply in cases where it would be likely to create distortions of competition such as to place a commercial enterprise carried on by a taxable person at a disadvantage.

Law: ITA 2007, s. 529; CTA 2010, s. 483

Non-exempt trades

When a charity has carried on a trading activity which is neither within one of the statutory exemptions, nor within ITA 2007, s. 529 or CTA 2010, s. 483, the profits will be taxable. However, in calculating such profits charities will be able to deduct properly allowable general overhead expenses on a reasonable basis, and the going market rate for goods or services provided undervalue or free of charge.

Partial exemption

With effect for chargeable periods commencing on or after 22 March 2006, trades are apportioned (with expenses and receipts being apportioned on a 'reasonable' basis) if a trade is exercised only partly in the course of the actual carrying out of a primary purposes of the charity.

A further apportionment may be made (and on a similarly reasonable basis) where the work in connection with the trade is carried out partly but not mainly by beneficiaries of the charity.

Charity trading company subsidiary

More sophisticated tax planning will be needed if a charity carries on trading activities on a regular basis and these activities do not fall within either of the two exemptions or ITA 2007, s. 529 or CTA 2010, s. 483. At worst, its charitable status may be challenged by HMRC on the grounds that it is not established for charitable purposes only, in which case the charity loses all its exemptions from tax. At best, the profits of the trade will be liable to tax, but the other income of the charity will be unaffected.

The traditional response in such circumstances has always been to set up a wholly-owned charity trading company subsidiary. The profits of such a company would ordinarily be taxable but by entering into a profit-shedding covenant with the charity, the subsidiary was able to transfer its profit to the charity in a way which fell within one of the statutory exemptions referred to above. If the company did not have such a covenant, profits could also be transferred tax-effectively by Gift Aid donation or even by dividend.

The transfer of profit from a subsidiary to a charity by way of dividend or by deed of covenant is no longer wholly tax-effective, as discussed below.

First, though, it is important to ensure that the financial arrangements for providing the working capital of the company are an acceptable use of charity funds. The trustees must exercise their judgment on the wisdom of the investment in the subsidiary and ensure that any loans made by the charity to the company are on normal commercial terms.

From a strict legal point of view, the formation by a charity of a trading subsidiary can constitute non-qualifying expenditure (see **74.3.5**).

Except in the most extreme cases, the costs of forming a trading subsidiary will not normally be high enough to give any practical problems under the non-qualifying expenditure rules. The funding point is potentially more serious, but it is not one HMRC have been known to take unless the charity is used as a tax avoidance device to shelter profits of what is fundamentally a pure trading organisation. HMRC's main concern is to ensure that each charity and trading subsidiary keeps proper records and files prompt and accurate returns. In the case of *Nightingale Ltd v Price* (1995) Sp C 66, HMRC tried unsuccessfully to deny tax relief on the grounds that a group of companies headed by a charity was not set up for charitable purposes, but cloaked a commercial property group. However, the Special Commissioners were satisfied that, despite the emphasis of activity on commercial matters, the trustees were investing the funds of the charity in a positive manner in order to further the objects of the charity. The case is illustrative of how much leeway the Special Commissioners were prepared to give in applying what is now ITA 2007, s. 543 and CTA 2010, s. 483.

> **Planning point**
>
> In any event, there are nearly always significant non-tax reasons for setting up a limited liability trading subsidiary, such as risk, a charity's constitution and Charity Commission guidelines.

> **Planning point**
>
> From 1 April 2006, subsidiaries may be owned by more than one charity to qualify for Gift Aid treatment.

Deeds of Covenant and Gift Aid

Withdrawal of tax relief from Deeds of Covenant.
Tax relief was withdrawn from charitable deeds of covenant with effect from April 2000.

A deed of covenant still remains a legally-binding contract; it is only the tax relief that is no longer available.

Existing deeds of profit-shedding covenant at 1 April 2000 operated by charity trading subsidiaries are still enforceable legally, but payments under them are now dealt with under the Gift Aid scheme and gross payments should be made to the charity.

Gift Aid

Prior to 1 April 2000, a company could make a Gift Aid payment, to transfer profits to a charitable parent, but to be tax-effective the payment had to be made within the accounting period to which it related. Since this method always involved some anticipation of profits to a greater or lesser degree, it had its dangers. An inadequate payment left a residual tax liability and an excessive payment ran the danger of rendering the company insolvent. Such payments also had to be made under deduction of income tax.

The system now is far simpler. There is no requirement to deduct income tax and the charity therefore has no tax to reclaim and does not suffer a cash flow disadvantage. The company merely makes the payment and provided the company is wholly owned by the charity, it can delay making its Gift Aid payment until up to nine months from the end of the accounting period in question, thus providing time for an accurate calculation to be made of the amount needed to pay away the taxable profit.

Sponsorship

Sponsorship deals between businesses and charities may be pure trading transactions, purely philanthropic transactions or a mixture of the two. The tax effect is different in each case and needs to be examined carefully.

> ⚠ **Warning!**
>
> The consequences of failing to recognise the intrinsic commercial nature of most sponsorship deals can cost charities dear, both in terms of direct tax and particularly in terms of VAT.

For example, payment for a charity's name and logo by a commercial organisation which then promotes its support of the charity will be regarded at least as advertising income in the charity's hands, if not as the sale or licensing of a trademark or copyright. Such a deal should be routed through a trading subsidiary company which will need to be granted the right to exploit the charity's name, etc. by the charity in a formal agreement; otherwise the charity may still be vulnerable to the charge that it is trading its name.

The following guide may help to highlight the considerations:

	Sponsor	Charity
(a) Pure trading transaction, e.g. publicity in exchange for cost of theatrical performance	Tax-deductible expense	Taxable receipt, therefore route through trading company unless ancillary to the main purpose trade of the charity, in which case the charity can trade
(b) Pure gift, e.g. 4p to charity for every bar of chocolate sold	Arguably non-deductible but donation can be covered by Gift Aid (see **74.5.4**)	Non-taxable receipt
(c) Mixed transaction split between:		
(i) trading	Charge to profit and loss account	Receive in trading company
(ii) gift, e.g. price paid for publicity package double the commercial rate	Pay out of charitable funds	Receive direct in charity

Very often, a business sponsorship of a charity will require the completion of a commercial participator agreement. Detailed analysis of such an agreement often holds the key to determining the tax treatment.

Law: Charities Act 1992, s. 59

Land development

Charities are exempt from capital gains tax on their profits from property sales, provided in each case that the proceeds are or have been applied for charitable purposes.

> ⚠ **Warning!**
>
> Regard still needs to be had to other transactions in land, for example, where land is acquired with a view to selling it for a profit, possibly after obtaining planning permission. Such a transaction may be correctly regarded not as an investment but rather as an 'adventure in the nature of trade'. The profit would then be taxable as business trading income and, unless routed through the charity's trading subsidiary, would not be exempt in the charity's hands.
>
> The question of when a one-off transaction can be treated as trading is complex and has been considered in numerous tax cases. As a rule of thumb, if land (or

> any other asset) is acquired with the specific intention of adding value to it and re-selling it as early as possible at a profit then it is likely to be treated as trading; this applies even to a one-off transaction.

Alternatively, HMRC may seek to impose liability under legislation dealing with the avoidance of tax by persons concerned with land or the development of land; this is specifically excluded from the types of profit exempted by FA 2000, s. 46 (see **74.3.1** *Income tax and corporation tax*). This will be particularly in point when a charity is selling land to a property developer, and the trustees are under an obligation to secure the very best deal for their charity. Frequently, this involves the concept of 'overage' whereby a residual part of the sale price is dependent on the level of the developer's profit or sales value. Such payments are almost always caught.

Charities planning to carry out land development or sell land to a developer, should, therefore, seek professional advice before doing so.

Law: ITA 2007, Pt. 13, Ch. 3; CTA 2010, Pt. 18

74.3.3 Capital taxes

Capital gains

Charities are exempted from tax on capital gains tax provided that the gains are applied for charitable purposes.

> ⚠ **Warning!**
>
> A problem arises if and when property held on charitable trusts ceases to be subject to such trusts and the trustees are left holding a chargeable asset. This can arise, for example, where the property has been given to the charity for a limited period only after which it passes to a member of the donor's family. Not only are the trustees liable for the tax on the unrealised gains attaching to the property at the later date, but they are also liable for the tax on any gains realised during the preceding six years, to the extent that these were simply reinvested rather than applied for the purposes of the charity.

HMRC have up to three years after the end of the year of assessment in which the change from charitable to non-charitable status takes place, in which to raise these assessments.

Tax Aspects of Charities

> **Planning point**
>
> In such circumstances, trustees must ensure that they retain sufficient assets to meet the liability before transferring the property to the ultimate beneficiary.

A similar situation can arise where a charity has run its course and has no further charitable objects to which it can apply its income and gains.

> **Planning point**
>
> In this case, the trustees should apply to the Charity Commission for a scheme (under the Charities Act 1993, s. 16) to enable the charitable objects to be widened so that the property can continue to be held on charitable trusts and income and gains be applied for charitable purposes.

Law: TCGA 1992, s. 256

Inheritance tax

Charities are exempt from inheritance tax on any transfers of value made by them to the objects of their charity.

74.3.4 Application for charitable purposes only

Throughout the tax legislation relating to charities, reference is made to the tax relief or exemption applying only if the income, profit or gain is applied for charitable purposes only. Three questions arise.

(1) What constitutes an application for charitable purposes?

(2) Can income and gains be accumulated?

(3) What is the position if a small part is applied for non-charitable purposes?

The rules have been revised with effect for chargeable periods commencing on or after 22 March 2006.

What constitutes an application for charitable purposes?

The concept of 'charitable purposes' was explored at **74.2.1** above, and the tax exemptions described so far will only apply if the income or gains of a charity are applied for these purposes.

Frequently, there is a delay between the collection of funds and their application, e.g. an appeal by a museum to buy a painting. So long as the application of the funds is reasonably within view, HMRC are unlikely to question the exemption of the income or gains of the charity. If, however, there appears to be no charitable application, HMRC may challenge the claim for exemption from tax.

This was considered in a case in which the Crown contended that a payment of income by the trustees of the Helen Slater Charitable Trust Ltd to the trustees of the Slater Foundation Ltd, which was also charitable, did not constitute an application for charitable purposes since most of it had merely been accumulated in the second trust. The court found that since neither set of trustees had power over the other to direct the other's affairs there had been a proper application for charitable purposes by the trustees of the first trust, despite the fact that they were themselves acting as trustees of the second trust. In their capacity as trustees of the second trust, they received the funds as a capital receipt and were only obliged to account for the disposition of the income arising therefrom.

The *Helen Slater* decision opened up many possibilities for tax avoidance but this was subsequently reversed by legislation which provided that any payments made by one charity to another will be treated as taxable if:

- they are not made for full consideration;
- they are not otherwise chargeable to tax; and
- they are not of a description which would otherwise be eligible for tax relief.

The recipient charity can claim exemption from tax on making a claim but it will need to show that it has applied the 'income' for charitable purposes.

Planning point

Contrary to some earlier interpretations of this section, it is not necessary for the charity making the payment to deduct tax before passing the payment on to the second charity.

In general, therefore, a payment by one charity to another charity is regarded as an application for charitable purposes as far as the first charity is concerned but the second charity is still required to show that it has applied the receipt for charitable purposes. This is considered further in **74.3.5** in connection with the restriction of tax relief.

Also considered in that section is the case of a charity making payment to an overseas body for charitable purposes; in such cases, the onus lies on the charity making the payment to take reasonable steps to ensure that the money is used by the recipient for charitable purposes.

Tax Aspects of Charities

> ⚠ **Warning!**
>
> A charity making such payments recklessly could find itself liable to pay tax on part of its income in respect of such payments.

Law: IR Commrs v Helen Slater Charitable Trust Ltd (1981) 55 TC 230

Can income or gains be accumulated?

The *Helen Slater* case did not settle the underlying question of the extent to which a charity may accumulate its income before applying it for charitable purposes. In the case of *Nursing Council for Scotland v IR Commrs* (1929) 14 TC 645, Lord Sands expressed a view that income of a charity did not have to be spent immediately for some charitable purpose. He said:

> 'If the directors of a charitable trust deem it desirable that a capital sum should be accumulated for the service of the trust or that a reserve fund should be formed for the greater security of the trust, the income carried to the credit of any such account is, in my view, applied to a charitable purpose.'

In the same case, however, Lord Blackburn said:

> 'But it seems to me they do require that the income, if not actually expended on a charitable purpose during the year of assessment, must at least be appropriated to expenditure on charity in the immediate future . . . but so long as the Council merely apply the income accruing from year to year to increasing the capital sum, then even had there been a body established for charitable purposes I would have hesitated to agree that it was being applied to charitable purposes only and therefore entitled to exemption.'

In the *Helen Slater* case, Lord Justice Oliver, commenting on these two statements, said that he was disposed to favour the view expressed by Lord Sands. He said:

> 'Charitable trustees who simply leave surplus income uninvested cannot, I think, be said to have "applied" it at all and, indeed, would be in breach of trust. But if the income is reinvested by them and held, as invested, as part of the funds of the charity, I would be disposed to say that it is no less being applied for charitable purposes than it is if it is paid out in wages to the secretary.'

> **Planning point**
>
> As the case was not decided on this point, this must be regarded only as an *obiter dictum* but it would seem to indicate that the very least that is expected of charitable trustees is to make a conscious effort to invest any surplus income of a charity if it is to be said to have been applied for any purposes at all.

HMRC conceded in the *Helen Slater* case that, providing the trustees are not acting *ultra vires*, *accumulation for a specific purpose* does represent a *valid* application. The problem therefore exists only in respect of accumulations for general purposes and it may well be that a further case will be brought before the courts to decide this point. It is also possible that a future Finance Bill will address it.

What if part is applied for non-charitable purposes?

This can arise in one of two ways.

Part of the charity's income may be used to defray administrative expenses including salaries of permanent staff. Strictly speaking, these are not part of the charitable objects but indirectly they are essential to the ultimate achievement of those objects and therefore HMRC accept that they do not vitiate the charitable status. This is, however, a matter of degree: excessive administrative costs are a subjective question, and may be examined by HMRC or by the Charity Commission, or both.

The other way in which this question can arise is where a charity applies some of its funds in a way which it believes to be in accordance with its charitable objects but which crosses into some non-charitable area such as political activity.

> **Planning point**
>
> Where there are merely isolated incidences of such *ultra vires* actions, HMRC will in practice take little action but, where it is likely to continue, a charity must take steps to separate such activities entirely from the charity and run a separate non-charitable organisation for those activities not supported in any way from their general charitable income. Failure to do so will put their charitable status at risk.

74.3.5 Restriction of tax exemption

Chargeable periods commencing before 22 March 2006

Tax relief will be restricted if, in any given chargeable period of a charity:

- its relevant income and gains are at least £10,000;
- its relevant income and gains exceed the amount of its qualifying expenditure (as defined); and
- the charity incurs, or is treated as incurring, non-qualifying expenditure.

Relief will be denied for so much of the excess referred to above but only up to the amount of non-qualifying expenditure in that period.

(1) 'Relevant income and gains' means that income and those gains which would be taxable if it were not for the exempting provision of ITA 2007, Pt. 10, CTA 2010, Pt. 11 or TCGA 1992, s. 256.

(2) 'Qualifying expenditure' includes expenditure in the period for charitable purposes only and commitments for such expenditure entered into during the period.

Tax Aspects of Charities

(3) In the case of payments made to bodies outside the UK, these will only count as 'qualifying expenditure' to the extent that the charity concerned has taken such steps as may be reasonable in the circumstances to ensure that the payments will be applied for charitable purposes.

(4) 'Expenditure for charitable purposes' includes reasonable administrative and fundraising expenses.

(5) 'Non-qualifying expenditure' will include non-charitable expenses, e.g. political activities, trading expenses, excessive administrative costs.

The purpose of the section is to deny tax relief for taxable income and gains for those charities that misapply some or all of their income and gains. The way to calculate the extent to which relief is restricted is as follows.

1. Relief will be given without restriction under these provisions if:
   (a) no money has been spent in the period on non-qualifying expenditure;
   (b) total relevant income and gains do not exceed £10,000; or
   (c) qualifying expenditure is at least equal to the amount of relevant income and gains.

2. In any other case, compute the extent to which relevant income and gains (I) exceed qualifying expenditure (Q) and compare the resulting excess figure (E) with the amount of the non-qualifying expenditure (N). If:
   (a) E is greater than N then tax relief will be denied for an amount equal to N, but
   (b) in any other case, relief will be denied for an amount equal to E.

Example 74.1 'Bad' Charity

	£'000		£'000	
Income:	total		*relevant*	
Grant from another charity	200		200	
Investment income	50		50	
	250	(I)	250	
Expenditure:	total		*qualifying*	
Administration	30		10	(say)
Grants to UK charities	20		20	
Transfers to overseas bodies	150		50	(say)
	200	(Q)	80	
Surplus:				
Excess (I − Q)		(E)	170	
Non-qualifying expenditure		(N)	120	
As E is greater than N, relief is restricted by N			120	

Example 74.2 'Good' Charity

	£'000		£'000	
Income:	total		*relevant*	
Grant from another charity	200		200	
Donations	10		10	(Covenants)
Investment income	15		15	
	225	(I)	225	

	£'000		£'000	
Expenditure:	total		*qualifying*	
Care of residents	220		220	
Administration	30		30	
Trading expenses – non allowable	5		–	
	255	(Q)	250	

Surplus:
Excess (I − Q)   (E)   Nil
Non-qualifying expenditure   (N)   5
As E is less than N, relief is restricted by E   Nil

Non-qualifying expenditure includes investments or loans made during the period which are not qualifying investments or loans as defined in ITA 2007, s. 558. Broadly speaking, all conventional investments and loans which a charity can legally make are qualifying. Those which do not qualify are investments in, or loans to, the business of a connected person or arrangements whereby loans or investments are used as security for such loans to a person or persons. The position of loan funding to trading subsidiaries of charities should be noted, as mentioned above.

Where total expenditure exceeds relevant income, the excess, insofar as it represents non-qualifying expenditure, may be treated as having been incurred in earlier periods.

One of the curious ironies of this section, which is intended to combat tax avoidance, is that, whereas previously it was recognised that a charity had to apply its income and gains for charitable purposes only, it now seems that tax relief will not be lost even if part of the income is used for purposes other than charity.

Chargeable periods commencing after 21 March 2006

The FA 2006 rules remove the monetary limits.

Tax relief will be restricted if, in any given chargeable period of a charity, non-charitable expenditure is incurred – in which case the disallowance shall equal the amount of the non-charitable expenditure.

If the charity's non-charitable expenditure exceeds its total income or gains in any chargeable period, the excess is carried back to the previous chargeable period and treated as non-charitable expenditure of that earlier period.

Where there is insufficient income or gains in the earlier chargeable period, the excess may be carried back further – but expenditure may not be carried back more than six years.

> ⚠ **Warning!**
>
> Although these rules apply only with respect to non-charitable expenditure incurred after 21 March 2006, expenditure may be carried back to chargeable periods beginning on or before that date.

The charity may specify which of its income or gains are to be disallowed. HMRC may require the charity to specify this income or gains by notice. If the charity fails to respond within 30 days, HMRC shall determine which items are to be disallowed.

Law: ITA 2007, s. 543; CTA 2010, s. 483

Transactions with substantial donors

Further restrictions were introduced by Finance Act 2006 with effect in relation to transactions occurring on or after 22 March 2006.

They apply in respect of:

- the sale or letting of property by a charity to a substantial donor;
- the sale or letting of property by a substantial donor to a charity;
- the provision of services by a charity to a substantial donor;
- the provision of services by a substantial donor to a charity;
- the exchange of property between a substantial donor and a charity;
- the provision of financial assistance by a charity to a substantial donor;
- the provision of financial assistance by a substantial donor to a charity; or
- the investment by a charity in the business of a substantial donor.

Meaning of 'substantial donor'

A substantial donor is a person who, in respect of a chargeable period either:

- gives at least £25,000 during a period of 12 months which includes some or all of the chargeable period; or
- gives at least £100,000 during a period of 6 years which includes some or all of the chargeable period.

If someone is a substantial donor in respect of any chargeable period under any of those rules, that person is deemed to be a substantial donor for the following five chargeable periods.

> **Example 74.3**
>
> Sidney is a substantial donor to the X charity in 2006–07. Irrespective of the level of donations that follow, Sidney will be treated as a substantial donor for the tax years until (and including) 2011–12.
>
> If Sidney makes large donations in 2009–10, say, Sidney will further be a substantial donor until at least 2014–15.

Effect of transactions with substantial donors

Where these rules apply, any payments by a charity to a substantial donor will be treated as non-charitable expenditure.

Additionally, non-charitable expenditure will be deemed to have been incurred if a transaction with a substantial donor is less beneficial to a charity than would be expected in an arm's length transaction. Any shortfall will be treated as non-charitable expenditure.

Exceptions to the rules regarding transactions with substantial donors

Payments to substantial donors are exempt from being treated as non-charitable expenditure if the payment is in the form of remuneration for trustee services. However, this exemption applies only if the remuneration if approved by the Charity Commission (or other equivalent UK body) or a court.

Other exemptions apply if the transaction is in the course of:

- the donor's normal business, on arm's length terms and not part of any tax avoidance scheme;
- the actual carrying out of a primary purpose of the charity and not on terms more favourable to the substantial donor than those available to others.

Nor are the rules applied if the investment in the donor's business is through a Stock Exchange investment.

> ⚠ **Warning!**
>
> The Alternative Investment Market is *not* a recognised stock exchange for these purposes.

Law: ITA 2007, s. 549–557; CTA 2010, s. 502–510

74.3.6 Other tax reliefs

Business rates

Certain properties are exempt from paying non-domestic rates. These include places of religious worship, property used for the disabled and property situated in enterprise zones. Charities occupying non-exempt non-domestic premises are prima facie liable to pay non-domestic rates (also known as uniform business rates) but are entitled to a mandatory 80 per cent reduction in their liability. In addition, local authorities have the power to grant a further 20 per cent relief if they choose to do so.

> ⚠ **Warning!**
>
> As charities frequently carry on trading activities through subsidiary companies which covenant their profits to the charity, they may arrange for their subsidiary company to be the occupier of the non-domestic premises, typically a shop, and thus make the company liable to business rates. The company is not itself eligible for relief as it is not itself a charity, although by concession many local authorities will grant it relief.

> **Planning point**
>
> Care should therefore be taken to ensure that premises which are used predominantly for charitable rather than trading purposes are held by the charity, not the trading subsidiary. Any trading activities of the company can be licensed by the charity to take place within its premises, provided that they are small in relation to the other activities.

Law: The Local Government Finance Act 1988, as amended; the Abolition of Domestic Rates etc. (Scotland) Act 1987

Council tax

Council tax is a tax on private dwellings payable by the owner or occupier. There is no general exemption for charities, but there are specific reliefs.

To calculate the amount of council tax payable, three factors must first be considered:

- the valuation of the property concerned;
- whether the occupants qualify for a reduction or discount; and
- whether the property is exempt.

Charities are responsible for the payment of any council tax as owners of residential property used for any of the following purposes:

- residential care home, nursing or mental home or hostel;
- convent, monastery, vicarage or rectory;
- staff flats in charity property; and
- houses in multiple occupation.

The liability may be reduced by a claim for a discount or an exemption.

Exempt properties include:

- properties occupied only by students;
- forces barracks and married quarters; and
- properties which are vacant for a variety of reasons, including those waiting to be occupied by a minister of religion, and those left empty by someone who has left to go into care, or to care for another person.

Residential properties owned by a charity which are vacant for up to six months are partially exempt.

There are two other specific reductions of application to charities: a disabled reduction scheme and a 50 per cent reduction which depends on the circumstances of the residents.

The disabled reduction scheme applies where at least one person resident in the property is substantially and permanently disabled and the accommodation has either:

- space for the use of a wheelchair where the disabled person needs to use it indoors; or
- a room (other than a bathroom, kitchen or toilet) which is mainly used by the disabled person and is essential to their needs. Additional, specially adapted bathrooms and kitchens in a property may qualify.

The relief provides for the council tax payable to be based on the valuation band below that in which the property is valued, e.g. the tax for a property in band E would be based on that for band D, with no reduction for band A properties.

The 50 per cent reduction in council tax applies where all adult residents in a property fall within certain categories. If only one person is outside these categories the reduction is 25 per cent, and the reduction is lost where two or more residents are outside the categories. The categories are as follows:

- patients in homes receiving treatment or care in a residential care home, nursing home, mental home or hostel;
- certain types of care worker, namely, someone providing care to another, other than their spouse/civil partner or child, where the person being cared for is in receipt of a specified benefit, and the carer resides in the same accommodation and works at least 35 hours a week; or
- a care worker employed by a charity, local authority or the Crown, or introduced by such a body and employed by a third party to work for at least 24

hours a week. Such a care worker must be resident in premises provided by the employer or the specified body for the better performance of his or her work, but must not be paid more than £30 per week.

Both reliefs must be claimed, and if rejected can be appealed to a Valuation Tribunal.

Law: Local Government Finance Act 1988, Sch. 1, para. 7 and 9

Stamp duty and stamp duty land tax

Charitable deeds of covenant are exempt from stamp duty. Any conveyance, transfer or lease to a charity is exempt from stamp duty land tax provided that:

- the purchaser must intend to hold the subject-matter of the transaction for qualifying charitable purposes; and
- the transaction must not have not been entered into for the purpose of avoiding SDLT.

Relief can be lost on the occurrence of a disqualifying event within three years.

Law: FA 2003, Sch. 8

74.4 The tax aspects of giving to charities

74.4.1 Introduction

There is no general exemption or relief granted to a taxpayer who makes a gift to charity. However, the reforms in this area brought about by the Finance Act 2000 and subsequently are intended to encourage charitable giving by making it very much simpler for both individuals and companies to give to charity.

This section will deal with the following.

(1) Gift Aid.
(2) Business gifts.
(3) Gifts of shares.
(4) Gifts of chargeable assets.
(5) Charitable trusts and foundations.
(6) Donated salaries and services.
(7) Interest-free loans.
(8) Capital transfers free of inheritance tax (IHT).
(9) Payroll giving.

74.4.2 Gift Aid post-April 2000

Gift Aid donations by companies

Under the Gift Aid rules, all a company has to do to become entitled to obtain a tax deduction for a payment to a charity is make the payment. There is no requirement to withhold income tax from the payment, and no declaration or certificate need be given. There is no maximum or minimum amount. The new regime applies to all donations, including Deeds of Covenant, whether executed before or after 1 April 2000.

> **Example 74.4**
>
> A company has to pay a covenant instalment in respect of a Deed of Covenant executed in September 1998. The covenant provides for payments of 'such an amount as after deduction of tax equals £2000'.
>
> With basic rate at 22 per cent the company would have paid a net £2,000 under the old rules and paid over £564 income tax to HMRC, making a gross covenant payment deductible for corporation tax of £2,564.
>
> Under the new rules, the payment is merely £2,564.

Where companies are wholly owned by a charity or charities, the payment can be made up to nine months after the end of the accounting period in which the corporation tax deduction is sought but all other companies must take relief in the period of payment. The relief is also extended to non-resident companies liable to corporation tax (e.g. via a branch) but not those liable to income tax.

Gift Aid donations by individuals

Gifts for any amount can now be made under Gift Aid; the previous limit of a minimum donation of £250 to qualify under Gift Aid was abolished.

Generally, the donor makes a donation *net* of basic rate tax. The charity can then reclaim the tax notionally deducted direct from HMRC. If the donor is a higher-rate taxpayer, additional relief can then be obtained through the PAYE coding or via the donor's Self Assessment.

> ⚠ **Warning!**
>
> Consequently, the value of the tax relief to the charity is dependent on the basic rate of income tax in force at the time of the donation. If the basic rate falls, charities will receive less tax in the form of a rebate unless they can persuade their donors to give more in monetary terms. Whilst the latter option should not increase the costs for the individuals concerned, it will not necessarily be so easy to manage in practice.

Planning point

However, the link between the tax relief for the individual donor has been temporarily suspended following the reduction of the basic rate of income tax to 20 per cent from 6 April 2008.

For donations made between 6 April 2008 and 5 April 2011 (inclusive), an additional rebate will be made to the charity. The donor is wholly unaffected by this change and, therefore, donors who have arranged to increase their cash donations (to reflect the fall in the basic rate) will be in the same position as before but the charities will be even better off.

The additional rebate is worth 2 per cent of the gross donation. So, in 2008/09, a charity receiving cash of £780 will be entitled to receive tax of £220 (being the difference between the £780 received and that amount grossed up at the notional rate of 22 per cent). From the perspective of the donor, the gross amount of the donation would be £975 (being £780 grossed up at 20 per cent).

If, in later years, the basic rate of income tax changes from 20 per cent:

- if the basic rate falls, the notional basic rate will be simply 2 per cent plus the reduced basic rate (thus, charities cannot guarantee that donations will always be grossed up at a rate of 22 per cent before 6 April 2011);
- if the basic rate increases again, the notional basic rate will be capped at 22 per cent.

Planning point

Although there is now no minimum donation, it might be administratively simpler for a one-off contribution to be made to a charity account and for individual charitable contributions to be made from this account. This will ensure that the record-keeping for Self Assessment returns is relatively simple. Charities offering account facilities will often charge an administrative fee but this will usually be outweighed by the administrative savings (especially if tax returns are professionally prepared). In any event, the organisations offering charity accounts are themselves charities and the fee will go towards their overheads.

Individuals make Gift Aid donations net of tax but they have to pay tax personally in the year at least equivalent to the tax on the grossed-up Gift Aid payment. If insufficient tax is paid, the individual will be assessed to the difference.

If the individual is a higher rate taxpayer, relief against higher rates is available for the donation.

Planning point

For individuals there is an important difference between the new system of Gift Aid and the old. Under the old system, Gift Aid donations were only deductible from income and only income tax paid by the donor could be used to match the tax reclaimed by the charity. Now Gift Aid donations are allowable against capital gains as well as income, and capital gains tax can be used to match the liability on the Gift Aid donations.

A statutory Gift Aid declaration can refer to a single gift to a charity, a series of gifts, or all gifts from a specified date, depending on the donor's wishes.

Declarations may be written or oral and different procedures must apply depending on the type of declaration. A written declaration must contain the following details for it to be valid in law:

- the donor's name;
- the donor's home address;
- the charity's name;
- a description of the donations covered by the declaration (e.g. whether single or multiple donation); and
- a note explaining the requirement that the donor must pay an amount of income tax and/or capital gains tax equal to the tax deducted from the donations.

There is no statutory requirement that the declaration be signed or dated, although in most cases a date will be needed to identify the donation or series of donations covered by the declaration.

Although HMRC have produced a model Gift Aid declaration there is no requirement that charities must use this format. Providing the statutory requirements are included, charities are free to design their own Gift Aid declaration, for example to be incorporated into a standing order bank mandate. HMRC have also produced guidance and a model Gift Aid form in respect of multiple donations collected by participants in sponsored events.

The procedure regarding oral declarations is different. Until 31 October 2005, when a charity received an oral declaration, for example a credit card donation made by telephone during a television appeal, it was required to send the donor a written record of the declaration showing:

- the date on which the declaration was made to the charity;
- all details of amount, name, address, etc. provided by the donor in his or her declaration;
- the date on which the written record is provided by the charity to the donor;
- a note explaining the requirement of the donor to pay income tax and/or capital gains tax equal to the amount deducted from the donations; and
- a note explaining the donor's entitlement to cancel the declaration

retrospectively within 30 days of the date of the written record provided by the charity.

These requirements were waived by the Government in respect of donations in aid of victims of the tsunami disaster which struck South East Asia in December 2004. With effect 1 November 2005, it is now merely [*sic*] necessary for the charity to retain an auditable record of the declaration but a written notification to the donor may be given instead.

Declarations can be cancelled at any time, subject to any legally-binding commitment entered into by the donor (e.g. a covenant) if the donor has no tax liability for a year. To cancel a donation the donor must notify the charity of the cancellation, which must be from the date of cancellation or such later date as may be specified. If a donor cancels an oral declaration within the 30-day period the donations/declaration will be treated as never having occurred.

Where deposited covenants were made after 6 April 2000, the whole payment paid over was treated as a Gift Aid donation in the first year.

Prior to 6 April 2000, individuals could only make Gift Aid donations if they were UK tax residents. The scheme has now been widened to include two types of non-UK residents:

- Crown servants or members of the armed forces serving overseas; and
- any non-resident individual with sufficient UK income and gains charged to UK tax at least equal to the value of the grossed-up donation.

Law: ITA 2007, Pt. 8, Ch. 2; CTA 2010, Pt. 6, Ch. 2; FA 2008, Sch. 19; Donations To Charity By Individuals (Appropriate Declarations) Regulations 2000 (SI 2000/2074)

Common features

Whilst the tax rules contain a number of differences between the way Gift Aid applies for companies and individuals (e.g. no requirement for companies to pay or withhold tax or provide a declaration), a number of features are common to both types of donor:

- the donation must be a payment of a sum of money; a Gift Aid donation cannot be made by loan waiver or conversion, or in kind. HMRC auditors will expect to find an audit trail showing the movement of money, whether by cheque, direct debit, credit/debit card, telegraphic transfer, etc.;
- foreign currency donations qualify provided that the donation is converted into sterling at the rate on the day the donation is made;
- payments must be gifts and must not be repayable, and they must not be payments for goods or services supplied. They must not be conditional upon the charity acquiring property or services from the donor; and

- any benefits received by a donor or any person connected with the donor must be within certain *de minimis* limits described below.

Benefits

Benefits may be provided by a charity as an appreciation of a donation, or even as a right (for example, where a deed of covenant to a membership charity brings entitlement to publications, etc.). The tax implications can be tricky and may involve some complex valuations and calculations. It is important to understand what is not regarded as a benefit, what the permissible monetary limits are, and how the value of some benefits must be calculated.

A mere acknowledgement of a gift will not amount to a benefit, provided that the acknowledgement does not extend to being an advertisement for a donor's business or products. That said, HMRC now appear to accept that an acknowledgement can include a donor's corporate logo. They also accept that the provision of literature describing the charity's work involves no benefit even if the literature concerned has a cover price.

There is a parallel relief in relation to wildlife or heritage charities. A benefit is disregarded if the donation brings entitlement to free or reduced price admission to view wildlife or heritage property where the charity's main objects are the preservation of the wildlife or property concerned.

Some wildlife and heritage charities have used this legislation effectively to reclassify admission fees as Gift Aid donations. The Budget statement of 16 March 2005 announced proposed revisions to this relief which came into force with effect from 6 April 2006. It was intended to broaden the scope of property to which the benefit of free admission may be extended, but to restrict the provision of the benefit to situations where the benefit gives unrestricted free access to view the property or wildlife for at least a year, or where the amount paid by the donor is at least ten per cent more than the normal daily price of admission.

Subject to this, the value of any benefit provided in return for a donation must not exceed the following limits.

Amount of donation	Value of benefit
Up to £100	25%
£101–£1000	£25
Over £1000	5% or £500 whichever is lower

In addition, the total aggregate benefit received by a donor in respect of donations to the same charity in the same year must not exceed £500. In arriving at the aggregate benefits value, it is the actual value of benefits which has to be taken into account, not the 'annualised' value, as explained below.

⚠ Warning!

Whilst these limits appear relatively simple to operate, special rules apply to 'annualise' the value of benefits and the period over which they are paid, to see if the limits shown above are broken in relation to any donation or series of donations. These rules may be of particular importance to membership subscription charities.

Where a benefit consists of the receipt of benefits at intervals over a period of less than 12 months, relates to a period of less than 12 months or is related to a series of donations for a period of less than 12 months, an annualising calculation must be undertaken to see if the benefit levels are reached.

Example 74.5

Mr A pays a subscription to a charity under a deed of covenant of £120 per annum and receives the monthly charity journal, priced at £2.50, free for the first six months of his membership, following which he has to buy the journal.

The value of the benefit for Gift Aid purposes is calculated as follows:

Value of free journals received: $6 \times £2.50 = £15$

Annualised value: $(12 \text{ months}/6 \text{ months}) \times £15 = £30$

Amount of subscription/donation: £120

Annualised value of benefits: £30

Planning point

If, exceptionally, a charity is going to provide a benefit in excess of the permissible limits, some measure of Gift Aid relief may be available.

Example 74.6

In a special appeal a charity seeks donations of £500 each from its supporters and in return provides a china figurine which normally retails at £50. It is clear that the value limit is exceeded in relation to the donation of £500. However, if the donor and the charity agree either before or at the time of the gift to allocate £50 to the purchase of the figurine and £450 to a Gift Aid donation, Gift Aid relief will be available on £450.

Law: ITA 2007, s. 414–417; CTA 2010, s. 191–202

74.4.3 Business gifts

Donations to charity by a business are not normally deductible for tax purposes unless they can be shown to have been incurred wholly and exclusively for the purposes of the trade. For example, a reasonable gift to a local charity, such as an old people's home, or a donation to a charitable trade association may be said to be of benefit to the trade. The gift must be reasonable and either boost the goodwill of the business or benefit the staff morale.

The costs of business gifts and entertaining are specifically disallowed for tax purposes but gifts to local charities of wine or entertainment are not affected by this additional rule and will therefore qualify for tax relief if they meet the 'wholly and exclusively' requirement.

Sometimes businesses make gifts to charities in the ordinary course of their trade, for example:

- supplying goods and services at reduced rates or free of charge;
- paying for advertising space in charity brochures at prices in excess of their commercial value.

To the extent that such activities can be shown to be in the normal course of business, creating goodwill and advertising, the cost to the business is allowable. Where, however, the goods or services are provided below cost or the amount paid for advertising is unreasonable in relation to the possible business generated therefrom, there may be a disallowance of the amount deemed to be a gift as opposed to the amount deemed to be an expense. This is a question of what is reasonable which has to be determined according to the circumstances.

For the secondment of staff to a charity see **74.4.7** below.

Law: CTA 2009, Pt. 20, Ch. 1 (especially s. 1300); ITTOIA 2005, s. 45

74.4.4 Gifts of shares and securities to charity

Gifts of assets generally, including shares and securities are free of capital gains tax (see **74.4.5** below).

However, where a donor either gives or sells, at an undervalue, certain quoted shares or securities to a charity, a further relief is available. The donor can claim a deduction from income for the net cost of the gift for income tax purposes.

Example 74.7

Mr B gives quoted shares worth £20,000 to his favourite charity. He pays a broker's transaction fee of £100 in connection with the transfer, and receives a gift worth £200 in appreciation from the charity. The amount he can take as a tax allowable deduction against income is calculated as follows:

	£
Value of quoted shares given	20,000
Add broker's fee paid	100
	20,100
Less: benefits received	−200
Deduction against income available	19,900

In ascertaining the value to be used for London Stock Exchange quoted shares, the shares are to be valued at the lower of two bases:

- quarter up from the lower of the two quotes for the day in the Stock Exchange Daily Official List; and
- the mid-point of highest and lowest bargains of the day, ignoring special prices.

In most other cases, it will be sufficient to obtain the quoted price on the date of the gifts. Recognised stock exchanges include the Alternative Investment Market (AIM). Gifts of units in authorised unit trusts also qualify, as do shares in open ended investment companies and certain foreign collective investment schemes.

Law: ITA 2007, s. 431–436; CTA 2010, s. 203–217

74.4.5 Gifts of chargeable assets free of capital gains tax

Planning point

A gift to a charity is exempt from the normal rule whereby the donor is deemed to have disposed of the chargeable asset at its market value at the date of transfer. Instead, it is treated as having been made for such consideration as will secure that neither a gain nor a loss accrues on the disposal.

It must be stressed, however, that this exemption applies only to the gift of a chargeable asset. It will not apply if the donor sells the asset first and gives the proceeds to the charity.

Planning point

Consequently, a donor wishing to give shares or their value to charity should first consider the capital gains position. If assets are showing a loss, the donor should realise them first and give the proceeds to the charity, and if they are

> showing a gain he or she should give the assets themselves to the charity. In this way the donor will receive the benefit of any losses and be relieved of liability on any gains.

If, where the asset is showing a loss or no taxable gain, the donor can sell the asset and give the proceeds using the Gift Aid scheme, the donor will effectively receive the benefit of any capital losses and receive higher rate income tax relief on the same gift, while the charity will receive basic rate tax relief on the net payment made.

> ⚠ **Warning!**
>
> Care must be taken to ensure that the value of any such payment resulting from the sale of an asset does not exceed the donor's taxable income. If the benefits of Gift Aid are to be obtained, the net payment made must be capable of being met out of taxable income.

See also **74.4.4**, for the relief for gifts of quoted shares.

Law: TCGA 1992, s. 257

74.4.6 Charitable trusts and foundations

Charitable foundations are normally created by wealthy individuals or their families to carry out such charitable objects as the founders wish. Typically, they are established by the transfer to the trustees of the foundation of a substantial block of shares in the company controlled by the founder. They may also receive substantial gifts of property or works of art. Such gifts enjoy tax exemption, as described above.

> *Planning point*
>
> There are attractions to the founder of giving his assets away in this manner, as it may enable him to avoid significant amounts of capital gains tax or inheritance tax while still being able effectively to control his company during his lifetime and, to a large extent, enjoy the property and possessions. At the same time, he has the satisfaction of seeing his charitable foundation enjoying all the tax privileges accorded to a charity, thus increasing the level of charitable support that it can give. The founder can add to his charitable foundation payments out of income by Gift Aid.

There are some disadvantages for an individual who wishes to donate to charities by means of deeds of covenant, including the need to execute Gift Aid declarations in respect of each covenant, the administration of numerous standing orders and their cancellation when the covenants expire.

> **Planning point**
>
> The solution for an individual is to create his own charitable trust to which he either transfers a capital amount or to which he gives a substantial annual sum under Gift Aid. Providing the trust has charitable status, income tax can be reclaimed and donations can be made of such gross amounts as the trustees wish; the whole income, including the tax repayment, should be utilised each year (see **74.3.4**). Recipients need not necessarily have charitable status themselves, but any payments must fall within the charitable purposes specified in the trust deed itself.

Similar opportunities exist for corporations to make a single annual payment under Gift Aid to a charitable trust under their control and for the trustees to make a series of charitable payments therefrom. The payment to the trustees by the company is deductible for corporation tax purposes.

Alternatively, a Gift Aid donation can be made to one of the organisations offering a charity 'cheque book' which they issue to those wishing to use the facility.

74.4.7 Donated salaries and services

Some individuals, particularly members of religious organisations, such as nuns, donate their services to their charitable trust or order. This may include services for which they receive a salary, e.g. from teaching or nursing. As individuals, they are entitled only to personal tax allowances and gain no tax relief on the gift of the rest of their salary to the charity.

> **Planning point**
>
> However, by covenanting their salary with the appropriate Gift Aid declaration, they effectively convert their own earnings into the income of the charity. In theory, they should deduct income tax at the basic rate when paying the net salary over and issue the appropriate tax certificate to enable the charity to recover the tax. In practice, the PAYE tax office will issue a no-tax coding and the charity will receive the gross salary direct.

> **Planning point**
>
> Alternatively, it sometimes happens that a person who is employed is seconded by his or her employer to work for a charity (whether or not full-time) while the employer remains fully or partly responsible for the person's salary. The gift of

the employee's salary is not a business expense in the normal sense but it is specifically allowed as such.

⚠ Warning!

When employers second staff to a charity, the strict position was that the employment costs are not deductible if the employee is ordinarily employed on capital (or other non-deductible) projects. The HMRC practice was not to take this point but they reserve the right to do so. This practice was codified when the legislation was rewritten in 2005 (income tax) and 2009 (corporation tax).

Law: ITTOIA 2005, s. 70; CTA 2009, s. 70–71

74.4.8 Interest free loans

Planning point

Individuals or companies can benefit charities in a tax-effective manner by making loans to them free of interest. The interest forgone by the depositor is net of tax whereas the interest gained by the charity is gross.

Example 74.8

A lender has a marginal rate of tax of 40 per cent. He deposits £100,000 with a charity for two years free of interest.

Position of the lender:

	£
£100,000 transferred at a loss of gross interest of, say, 5%	5,000
Less: tax @ 40%	2,000
Net cost per annum	3,000
Two years	6,000
Position of the charity:	
£100,000 received free of interest deposited at, say, 5%	5,000
Two years	10,000

By this simple device, the lender has given to the charity, over two years, £10,000 at a net cost to himself of only £6,000.

⚠ Warning!

Technically, the provision of interest free loans in this way can fall within the settlement provisions.

However, it is understood that provided:

- the loan is in cash;
- there are no arrangements either directly or indirectly about the manner in which the loan should be invested or how the income should be applied;
- the loan will be repaid in cash and not by transfer of assets; and
- the loan does not form part of any larger or wider arrangements.

HMRC will not seek to impose any tax liability on the lender.

Law: ITTOIA 2005, Pt. 5, Ch. 5

74.4.9 Donations from settlor interested trusts

In the normal course of events, income arising to a UK trust into which the settlor retains an interest is assessed on the settlor. This rule will not apply insofar as the income is given to charity by the trustees or where the charity has an entitlement to the income.

Law: ITTOIA 2005, s. 628 and 630

74.4.10 Capital transfers free of inheritance tax

All transfers of value to charity, whether made during a person's lifetime or by will, are exempt from inheritance tax (IHT) entirely.

> ⚠ **Warning!**
>
> To be effective, the gift must be absolute. If it takes effect only after the termination of another interest or is dependent upon a condition which is not satisfied within 12 months of the transfer or is defeasible, the exemption will not apply. In particular, the exemption is not available if the donor, his spouse/civil partner or any connected person retains any interest in the property transferred to the charity.

Law: IHTA 1984, s. 23(1)

74.4.11 Payroll giving

> **Planning point**
>
> Any employer may set up a scheme by which the employees can give to charity by direct deduction from their pay. The deductions are made from gross pay before deductions of income tax, but after deduction of National Insurance.

There is no upper limit to the level of deductions that may be made under the scheme. Agency charities (see below) must pay over all donations to the charities concerned within 60 days.

The conditions of a payroll deduction scheme are as follows:

- the deductions must be made in accordance with a scheme which is (or is of a kind) approved by HMRC;
- the amounts deducted must be handed over by the employer to an agency charity approved by HMRC;
- the agent must pay the amounts over to the charity or charities of the employee's choice;
- the sums to be deducted can only be withheld by the employer at the request of the employee; and
- the sums so deducted must constitute gifts by the employee to charity and must not be payments under a deed of covenant.

The salient features of an approved scheme are:

- one or more employees wish their employer to operate a scheme;
- the employer agrees to do so;
- the employer makes the necessary contractual arrangements with an approved agency;
- the employer makes the deductions as requested by the employees and gives the tax relief under a 'net pay' arrangement;
- the employer hands the deductions to the agency; and
- the agency distributes the money to the charities in accordance with the wishes of each employee.

The salient features of an approved agency are:

- it must itself be a charity;
- it must act in accordance with the employee's wishes;
- it must ensure that gifts go only to charities;
- it must ensure that no payments are refunded;
- it must distribute the gifts promptly;
- it must keep records; and
- it must make returns to HMRC.

Practical points for employers and employees to bear in mind include:

- form P60 will be affected. End of year returns will show the net pay, i.e. gross pay less charitable donations in the box for 'pay in this employment';
- form P45 will similarly be affected. The same procedure will apply;
- on leaving, the employee will need a separate note to give to his next employer regarding gifts deducted to date;
- Class 1 NIC will be payable on the gross amount before the gifts are deducted from pay;
- spouses and civil partners can both join a scheme provided that their pay is subject to PAYE; and

- pensioners may be included.

> **Planning point**
>
> Under the Payroll Giving Grants programme, sponsored by the Home Office, the Government will give employers grants of up to £500 (until December 2006) and will match employee donations pound for pound for six months (up to a maximum of £10 per month) until March 2007.

Law: ITEPA 2003, s. 714 and 715; SI 1986/2211

74.5 The beneficiaries of charities

74.5.1 The nature of the grant – capital or revenue

A charity is generally exempt from tax on the income it receives but what is the position of those individuals who are the beneficiaries of the charity? These may include persons who are poor, ill, handicapped, studying or otherwise needing support; they may also include those who are rewarded for their contributions to art, literature, scientific research, etc. through prizes, travelling fellowships and the like.

An isolated payment to an individual for charitable purposes will normally be treated as a payment with no tax consequences. Regular payments will, however, normally be regarded as income payments and taxable in the hands of the recipient. These will include income from investments purchased from an initial capital payment. In many cases it is likely that the personal allowances of the recipient will be more than enough to absorb the income tax liability.

74.5.2 Scholarships

A scholarship gives rise to a series of regular payments which would normally be treated as the income of the recipient. However, in principle, such payments are treated as not being income.

Over the years, a number of companies have established educational trusts to grant scholarships to the children of employees and the question has arisen as to whether the amounts of the award should be assessed upon the parent as a benefit arising by virtue of his or her employment or whether it is exempt under the special provisions. In the case of *Wicks v Firth* [1982] BTC 402, it was decided that the exemption took precedence and that no liability to tax arose. The effect of the decision has, however, been reversed by legislation that taxes such awards as benefits of the employment. The legislation does not, however, affect scholarships awarded otherwise than by virtue of employment, which remain tax free.

> ⚠ **Warning!**
>
> There is no reason why the beneficiary of a scholarship cannot be connected with the sponsoring employer (for example, a parent of the student might be an employee). However, the scholarship would be treated as a taxable benefit in kind if more than 25 per cent of such payments were attributable to an employment.

Law: ITEPA 2003, s. 211–215; ITTOIA 2005, s. 776

74.5.3 Prizes

A prize for an achievement which qualifies as an object of charity is normally a unique event treated as capital in nature and not taxable. If it were given in the form of regular payments, for example as a fellowship for several years' research, it may be treated as taxable income in the hands of the recipient. On the other hand, if the recipient can show that the money has been expended on objects of research, such as travel and research rather than mere subsistence, then such expenditure may rank as an eligible deduction so that there is no actual tax liability.

74.5.4 General benevolence – social welfare

A large amount of charitable giving is channelled through voluntary institutions established to care for people who may be old, infirm, handicapped, or otherwise in need. Grants and donations made to such institutions are exempt from tax because they are charities. The beneficiaries are generally supported in whole or in part by these grants but, because they are not entitled to the payments personally, they are not regarded as being liable to tax thereon.

Recent changes in procedure, whereby such payments may be made to the institution as agent for the individual, complicate the position and it should not be assumed that such income can be ignored when assessing the income tax liability of a person in care who is in receipt of personal income.

74.6 Foreign aspects

74.6.1 UK charities operating overseas

These will include missionary societies, bodies established to provide relief for the poor and hungry, societies for the protection of animals and the environment, and many others.

> ⚠ **Warning!**
>
> In such cases, the charity must be careful to ensure that it applies its income and gains for charitable purposes only (see **74.3.4**). Many such charities can be drawn into the politics of the country in which they operate. Indeed, it is difficult to see how an organisation established to give relief to the poor cannot concern itself with the social and political problems of the country which gave rise to the poverty. Similarly, the question of human rights can quickly lead to the issue of political prisoners.

It is, therefore, important for any charity operating in this field to ensure that it distances itself from political activity. As mentioned at **74.2.1**, Amnesty International has approached the problem from the other end, accepting that it is not itself charitable, having political aims to free prisoners, and establishing a separate charitable fund for the assistance of prisoners and their families who are in need.

74.6.2 Payments made by UK charities to bodies outside the UK

> ⚠ **Warning!**
>
> Where payments are made by a charity to bodies outside the UK, these count as 'qualifying expenditure' only to the extent that the charity concerned has taken such steps as may be reasonable in the circumstances to ensure that the payments will be applied for charitable purposes.

The legislation was primarily designed to counteract tax avoidance schemes which used charitable money for non-charitable purposes by passing it through a foreign 'charity' which, being outside the jurisdiction of the UK, could perhaps use the money more flexibly than a UK-registered charity.

Bona fide charities operating overseas, and their supporters in the UK, will normally have nothing to fear from this provision.

Law: ITA 2007, s. 547; CTA 2010, s. 500

74.6.3 Foreign 'charities' operating overseas or in the UK

Gifts to foreign organisations carrying on activities which are considered to be charitable under UK law will be treated as having been made for charitable purposes.

> ⚠ **Warning!**
>
> However, if the foreign organisation is not registered in the UK as a charity, its UK-resident supporters will receive no tax relief on their donations, and a UK charity making payments to it may need to ensure that its money is spent for charitable purposes, as discussed immediately above.

In all other respects, the effect of the gift is the same as if it had been made to a UK-registered charity.

The position of the foreign 'charity' itself may be different. If it is not registered as a UK charity, it will not be within the various UK tax exemptions and reliefs. Hence, it:

- will not be able to reclaim tax on its income;
- will not be able to take advantage of the Gift Aid system; and
- will pay tax in the UK on income from UK property by deduction at source.

Moreover, if the fund is based in an offshore tax haven which does not enjoy a double taxation agreement with other countries, it will be unable to recover any of the withholding tax levied by the country in which the investment is made. For example, a UK charity receiving dividends from the USA will suffer half of the 30 per cent withholding tax under the double tax treaty and be exempt from the other half. However, a 'charity' based in the Channel Islands would have to suffer the full 30 per cent withholding tax, having no such reciprocal arrangement on double taxation irrespective of its nil tax status in the Channel Islands.

> **Planning point**
>
> It is, therefore, vital for a foreign 'charity' operating in the UK to become a registered charity under UK law.

> ⚠ **Warning!**
>
> Furthermore, many *bona fide* UK charities raise money for overseas causes which do not appear to be obviously charitable in nature. If one examines the application of the funds, it soon becomes clear that they are charitable and that the tax relief follows. However, difficulties can be encountered with HMRC if

Tax Aspects of Charities

one is not precise both when making the gift and when describing the effect of it during a later enquiry.

Example 74.9

Mabel leaves a gift in her will to a UK charity that supports projects in the Sahara. The amount of the gift is for so much money that will purchase 100 trees in the desert.

Because the gift is for an ascertainable amount to a UK charity, there should be no difficulty in relief being given.

However, if the executors receive any queries from HMRC about the estate, it might be suggested that the gift is simply for 100 trees in Africa. In such a case, HMRC might then disallow the gift even though it was perfectly charitable.

74.6.4 UK charities seeking money from abroad

Many UK charities seek to raise funds abroad, particularly from the USA where, in general, gifts to charity are tax-deductible. However, just as the UK tends not to recognise foreign charities unless they register a branch as a UK charity, so the USA expects foreign charities to register as separate US non-profit-making organisations to which US citizens and corporations must make their gifts for these to be deductible for US tax. Similar rules operate in other countries.

Planning point

So, if a UK charity contemplates substantial fundraising in a foreign country, it will normally be beneficial to set up an equivalent organisation in that country to collect the money for onward submission to the UK charity.

75 Tax-Efficient Investments

75.1 Introduction

75.1.1 What is a tax-efficient investment?

Some investments have built-in tax advantages: usually the Government, usually for policy reasons, has provided an exemption from one or more of the taxes. Other investments are attractive because they fall within a category of asset which is favoured by the tax code. This chapter deals with both types of investment. It does not give investment advice.

75.1.2 Investment efficiency

To use this chapter as a means of choosing an investment would be wrong. Every investment produces a return and every investment has a cost. Investment efficiency is to look at the return on the sum expended, after deductions of all costs. Taxation is one such cost, and an important cost for the individual investor. It is, in principle, neither more significant nor less significant than any other cost. It is trite but true that an individual is better advised to deposit his or her cash with a reputable bank and pay a full charge to income tax on the interest generated rather than put his or her wealth into an investment with particular tax advantages if, after deducting all fees, the return the individual enjoys is less than on the bank deposit.

> **Planning point**
>
> What is an efficient investment depends on the particular individual. An exemption from capital gains tax is of no relevance to the individual who can confidently expect to have the full annual exempt amount available each year. Tax relief is of no interest to the non-taxpayer, yet thousands of non-taxpayers hold exempt National Savings products. Every so-called 'tax-efficient investment' must be judged against other action available to the individuals. For many, paying off a mortgage, on which there is no tax relief, produces a higher effective return than an investment in an ISA.

Caution should be employed in advising those who are geographically mobile. There is, in general, no international recognition of the tax-exempt status of investments. An individual who moves abroad and who holds an Individual Savings Account can well find that the foreign jurisdiction provides no exemption for the income and gains within an ISA and there is a charge to tax in the individual's new country of residence. Similarly, an investment purchased abroad

Tax-Efficient Investments

for its tax-exempt status in the country of purchase, is unlikely to avoid a charge to UK tax if the holder moves to become within the charge to UK tax.

75.1.3 Investments providing tax advantages

The various investments discussed in this chapter are only some of the investments that can provide an advantageous tax treatment for the holder. There are many other homes for investment that have particular attractions for particular individuals. For a business person, investment in the business itself may be attractive as this can fund expenditure that attracts a high rate of capital allowance or may be fully deductible as a revenue expenditure and thereby lead to a high return on the capital employed.

> *Planning point*
>
> In addition to the investments discussed elsewhere in this chapter, the following may, depending on the individual's circumstances, provide tax advantages for those seeking to invest:
>
> - an approved pension scheme, whether an employee scheme or a personal pension plan;
> - a funded unapproved retirement benefit scheme (FURBS);
> - unquoted shares providing 100 per cent inheritance tax business property relief;
> - investment in your own business to provide 100 per cent inheritance tax business property relief;
> - investment in a private house to provide a tax free capital gain on sale;
> - subscription by employees for shares under the enterprise management initiatives;
> - purchase of government stock or qualifying corporate bonds, providing the possibility of a capital gain that is exempt from capital gains tax (CGT) at sale;
> - the special deposit for a Lloyds name, which attracts 100 per cent inheritance tax business property relief; or
> - an individual could consider putting funds into a company the individual controls where the company then seeks tax relief under the corporate venturing scheme.

75.2 Enterprise Investment Scheme

75.2.1 Overview

The Enterprise Investment Scheme (EIS) is dealt with in **Chapter 64**. However, for completeness and ease of reference, the main issues are summarised in the following paragraphs.

Enterprise Investment Scheme **75.2.1**

The EIS is a Government initiative to promote the raising of equity finance for new and small companies, which is seen as a major problem for the UK economy. The scheme has its origins in the Business Start-Up Scheme, which provided income tax incentive for investors between 1981 and 1983. The Business Start-Up Scheme was then converted to the Business Expansion Scheme (BES) which ran from 1983 up to December 1993. The BES was criticised for not being targeted carefully, so that substantial tax relief was given under the scheme to investors who put funds into freehold property through BES companies or, in the early years, received loanbacks. This meant that substantial amounts of tax relief were being given to individuals who either had no real cost to their investment or had an investment return that was effectively guaranteed when the investment was made. The BES was replaced by the EIS for investments on or after 1 January 1994.

> **Planning point**
>
> The EIS is a series of potential reliefs for the investor:
>
> - income tax relief at 20 per cent of the amount invested is available up to a maximum of £500,000 per year for 2007–08 onwards (£400,000 prior to this), as long as the investor has less than 30 per cent of the shares of the company and certain other conditions are satisfied (see **75.2.2**);
> - a gain made by the investor prior to investment can be deferred by rolling into the EIS shares for which the investor subscribes. This relief is available even if the investor has more than 30 per cent of the company share capital. It is even possible for the investor to create the company himself;
> - any gain made on the ultimate disposal of EIS shares is exempt from CGT, if income tax relief was given on the subscription for these shares (i.e. the investor owned less than 30 per cent, subscribed less than the annual maximum permitted amount and other relevant conditions were satisfied);
> - even though a gain is exempt, the loss arising on the ultimate disposal of shares can be relieved against any capital gains and an election can be made when the loss is suffered to relieve the loss against income; and
> - if EIS shares that did not qualify for income tax relief are sold, the gain triggered can be rolled into a second EIS investment.

The Government's intention as stated in 1994 was to create legislation that provided relief for investors who provide funds for new business that would otherwise find difficulty in raising finance as there is a real and genuine risk in the investment. In seeking to target the relief correctly, the Government drew up conditions that need to be satisfied, which are detailed, complex and extend to 52 pages of legislation. This led to a Confederation of British Industry (CBI) report stating that business official networks do not recommend EIS investment as they consider the availability of relief to be 'misleading and unsustainable'. Changes introduced by Finance Act 2000 were designed to answer some of this criticism. Further changes were made to the EIS legislation by Finance Act 2004. Despite these changes, it is probably the case that the EIS scheme continues to be of greater attraction for CGT deferral than for the income tax relief. For an individual investor to obtain EIS relief, the investor must accept the risks inherent in holding unquoted shares with the inherent difficulty in disposing of a minority holding in a small company.

> **Planning point**
>
> The EIS scheme provides the facility for sheltering a capital gain as an investor can defer a gain made on any disposal by a subscription for cash in shares that qualify under the EIS rules. The gain thus deferred comes into charge when the shares in the EIS company are ultimately sold, or when there is a clawback as a result of infringement of the conditions for EIS relief. In contrast to the income tax relief, CGT deferral is available for an individual investing in his or her own company, without limit as to the percentage shareholdings.

> **⚠ Warning!**
>
> The capital gains tax rate(s) on a gain subject to deferral relief such as under the EIS are those applicable when the deferral ends and becomes liable to tax. Hence pre-23 June 2010 gains which are deferred until 23 June 2010 or later will be liable to CGT at the 18 per cent or 28 per cent rates.

Law: ITA 2007, s. 158; FA 2008, s. 31

75.2.2 Income tax relief

An individual is eligible for EIS income tax relief for cash subscribed for new shares issued to him or her. The shares must be issued in order to raise money for a business activity that qualifies under the EIS scheme (most grades qualify). The company must use the money raised for the trading activity. The time limit for employing invested money (broadly 80 per cent within 12 months of the share issue or commencement of trading (if later) and the balance within a further 12 months) has been relaxed from 22 April 2009, so that all money raised by the issue of shares must be wholly employed in a qualifying activity within two years of the EIS share issue, or (if later) within two years of the qualifying activity commencing.

> **⚠ Warning!**
>
> The subscription must be entirely for cash. In *Thompson v Hart* [2000] BTC 151, EIS relief was denied as the shares were issued in exchange for the transfer of properties.
>
> This is a strange rule. If a company has previously given cash which is then held on a loan account for the investor, converting that loan account into shares does not attract EIS relief. However, this problem can easily be circumvented by the company repaying the loan to the intending investor, who then pays cash to the

> company for his shares. (If income tax relief is sought, the 'connected persons' provision in **75.2.3** may be more difficult to satisfy.)

Relief is available to an individual for a minimum subscription of £500 and a maximum of £500,000 in a fiscal year (for 2007–08 onwards). These limits are applied separately to husband and wife, or between civil partners, and so can provide a reduction of tax for a married couple, or civil partners of up to £200,000 (2 × 500,000 × 20 per cent). The investment can be direct into a company, or can be through an investment fund approved for EIS purposes.

Prior to 2009–10, where shares were issued before 6 October, the individual could elect that relief was given in the previous fiscal year for a sum specified by the taxpayer that was up to the lower of: (a) one half of the sum subscribed and (b) £50,000 (£25,000 prior to 2006–07). Finance Act 2009 extends the carry-back period so that, for 2009–10 onwards, investors may carry back the full amount subscribed for shares (subject to the EIS qualifying limit). Claims can be made in the self-assessment tax return for the preceding year, or can be independent claims. The facility to relate back a subscription, requires rules for the attribution of relief to shares. Where there is more than one issue, the relief is given in proportion to the amounts subscribed for each issue. A bonus issue of shares leads to the relief being spread over the entire new holding, both the original shares and the new bonus issue.

Unless the subscription is through an approved BES investment fund, it is necessary for the individual obtaining relief to subscribe the shares. There is no requirement under the EIS rules that an investor should be resident in the UK. Thus, a non-resident who, for example, receives rent from land in the UK, could reduce or eliminate the liability to income tax on the rental income by an EIS investment.

Example 75.1

Geoff has taxable income (after personal allowances) of £40,000 in 2010–11. None of it is savings income or dividend income. During the year, he invests £35,000 in shares qualifying for EIS relief. Geoff's income tax liability is:

	£	£
37,400 at 20%		7,480
2,600 at 40%		1,040
40,000		8,520
Less: tax relief for EIS subscription (£35,000 at 20%)		(7,000)
Income tax liability		1,520

Tax-Efficient Investments

> ### Example 75.2
>
> Assume that in the previous example Geoff invests £450,000 in EIS shares. The maximum reduction from his income tax liability in respect of the EIS investment is now the lower of:
>
> (1) 20% of the amount of the subscription £90,000 (£450,000 at 20%); and
> (2) the amount that reduces his tax liability to £Nil – i.e. £8,520.
>
> The relief for the year is thus £8,520.
>
> The excess of £81,480 (£90,000–£8,520) remains unrelieved.

Law: ITA 2007, Pt. 5; FA 2009, s. 27 and Sch. 8

75.2.3 Investor connected with the company

For EIS income tax relief (but not for the CGT deferral relief) the individual must not be connected with the company into which the individual makes the investment at any time during a period that begins two years before the issue of shares and normally ends three years after that issue. Where the company has raised funds through the subscription to carry on a trade which has not yet commenced, the three-year period during which the investor must not be connected with the company starts with the date of commencement of the company's trade.

An individual is connected with a company, for the purpose of EIS relief, in any of the following circumstances:

- the individual controls the company;
- the individual owns shares that give him or her more than 30 per cent of the votes;
- the individual's shares plus his loan capital exceed 30 per cent of the company's share capital (measured at par value) plus its loan capital;
- the individual trades in partnership with the company;
- the individual is an employee of the company;
- the individual is a director of the company, unless exempted by the rule below; or
- the individual subscribes for shares as part of an arrangement under which another individual subscribes for shares in another company to which the first individual is connected.

A director is not treated as connected with the company if he or she is unpaid. 'Unpaid' is given a wide definition as including becoming entitled to any payments either from the company or from a related person at any time during the three-year exclusion period. However, for this purpose, the following payments are ignored:

- reimbursement of expenses wholly, exclusively and necessarily incurred in performance of duties of the director;
- a reasonable return by way of interest on funds lent to the company;

- a 'reasonable' dividend on the investment in the company;
- a market rent on property let to the company; and
- 'reasonable' charges for services provided to the company.

> ⚠ **Warning!**
>
> These exclusions are applied from the period of subscription onwards. The EIS income tax relief is not available where the individual has served as a director of the company before the share subscription; the individual is then treated as connected with the company. Where the target company has taken over a trade from another company, a directorship in the predecessor company would also deny relief.

75.2.4 Capital gains tax exemption

Where shares are issued on which income tax relief has been given, any gain made on the ultimate disposal of those shares by the individual investor is exempt from CGT. In order for this CGT exemption to apply, income tax relief must have been given and not withdrawn, otherwise the exemption is lost. Income tax relief can be withdrawn in two alternative scenarios.

1. There can be a clawback of relief by a failure of the conditions that are necessary for the three years following the subscription. This could be a result of an action by the company (see **75.2.8**) or by the individual becoming connected with the company, such as taking paid employment or directorship (see **75.2.3**).

2. The individual's liability to income tax for the year's subscription could be reduced to nil. This could arise, relief given for trading losses under ITA 2007, s. 72. Hence, any decision as to the way in which trading losses are to be relieved must take account of the possibility of the withdrawal of EIS relief and its effect on a potential exposure to CGT at a later date.

75.2.5 Capital gains tax deferral relief

Unlike EIS income tax relief, CGT deferral relief, when there is investment in shares that fulfil the EIS requirements, can be claimed by trustees as well as individuals.

Where a capital gain arises to an individual or to trustees, deferral relief can be claimed if the taxpayer subscribes for shares that fulfil the EIS requirements at any time during a period that begins 12 months before the disposal that caused the gain and ends 36 months after the date of disposal. Deferral relief operates so that the gain that would have been charged is frozen and brought into charge when there is ultimately a disposal of the 'EIS shares'. If the conditions for EIS relief are contravened at any time during the three years following the investment, such as by value being received from the company, the deferred gain is treated as arising on the date that the contravention occurs.

> ⚠ **Warning!**
>
> It should be noted that the mechanism for the operation of deferral relief is no reduction in the base cost of the shares acquired by subscription; instead, the disposal of those shares causes the original gain to be brought into charge, as well as any gain on the shares themselves.

Unlike the provisions for EIS income tax relief, CGT deferral relief is available to individuals who are 'connected with the company'. This means that a company can be set up to carry on a new trade with the entire shareholding spread around members of the family, whilst still allowing a gain that has accrued to be deferred by reference to the investment made in the company. In contrast to the position for income tax, deferral relief for investment into EIS eligible shares requires the investor to be either resident or ordinarily resident in the UK and not to be exempt from CGT by virtue of a double tax agreement. There is no maximum to the size of the gain that can be deferred. Virtually any gain that arises on an individual or on trustees can be deferred (other than a gain imputed by TCGA 1992, s. 86 or s. 87 on a settlor or a beneficiary of a non-resident settlement or the gain arising under TCGA 1992, s. 161 where a capital asset is appropriated for trading stock).

> *Planning point*
>
> A taxpayer obtains deferral relief by making a claim. The taxpayer is free to claim part of a gain. This means that a gain equal to the annual exempt amount can be left in charge, without any actual tax cost. If the investor has capital losses available, a larger part of the gain can be left in charge to be put against the losses. The use of deferral relief is, thereby, very flexible and it can be a valuable planning device.

75.2.6 Criteria for the company

The restrictions on the relationship between the individual investor and the company apply for a period of three years only. This starts on the date of subscription, unless the company is then not carrying on the trade for which the funds are being raised, in which case the period starts on the later date that trade commences.

The company issuing the shares must, throughout the three-year period, be an unquoted company which exists 'wholly for the purpose of carrying on one or more qualifying trades' (subject to a *de minimis* exemption) or is the parent company of a trading group.

Qualifying trades are all trades other than:

- dealing in land, commodities, shares, etc.;
- dealing in goods other than as a wholesaler or retailer;
- banking, insurance or other financial activities;
- oil extraction;
- leasing;
- providing legal or accountancy services;
- property development;
- farming or market gardening, forestry, etc.;
- managing hotels;
- managing nursing homes, etc.;
- providing services for any of the foregoing trades, where the service providing company and the company to which the services are provided are under common ownership;
- shipbuilding;
- producing coal; and
- producing steel.

The last three items apply from the date of Royal Assent to Finance Act 2008 (21 July 2008).

It is, however, possible for a company to qualify as an EIS company when it has a property managing subsidiary. (This is permitted by Finance Act 2004, which also relaxed some of the more technical restrictions where the company is the parent of a group of companies.)

> ⚠ *Warning!*
>
> Finance Act 2007 introduced a new qualifying company rule for EIS. From the date of Royal Assent to the Act, a company (or group of companies) raising money under EIS must have fewer than 50 full-time employees (or their equivalents) at the date on which the relevant shares or securities are issued.

> ⚠ *Warning!*
>
> A new investment limit applies to a company raising money under the venture capital schemes. For an 'investment' to qualify for relief under the EIS or CVS, or be treated as a qualifying holding of a VCT, the company (or group of companies) must have raised no more than £2m under any or all of the schemes in the 12 months ending on the date of the relevant investment.

Tax-Efficient Investments

> If the limit is exceeded, none of the shares or securities within the issue that causes the condition to be breached will qualify for relief under the EIS or CVS, or rank as a qualifying holding for a VCT.
>
> This measure applies to EIS shares issued after the date of Royal Assent to Finance Act 2007.

The balance sheet total of the company must not exceed £7,000,000 before the issue of eligible shares, nor £8,000,000 after the issue of eligible shares.

The taxpayer must subscribe for 'eligible shares'. These are defined as new ordinary shares which, throughout the period of three years beginning with the date on which they are issued, carry no present or future preferential right to dividends or to a company's assets on its winding up and no present or future right to be redeemed. Ordinary shares are defined as 'shares formerly part of the ordinary share capital of the company'. Shares are treated as never having been eligible if the cash raised by the company on the issues of those shares was used for a purpose other than a qualifying business activity.

Eligible share are treated as ceasing to be eligible if an event occurs after the date of issue which causes the company not to be a qualifying company or, in the case of a group of companies, ceases to be the parent company of a trading group.

> **Planning point**
>
> The current legislation requires that there is a qualifying trade carried on wholly or mainly in the UK. The Finance Bill planned for the autumn of 2010 will contain legislation to the effect that for shares issued on or after the commencement date of the legislation, the requirement will be that the company issuing the shares must simply have a 'permanent establishment in the UK'.

> **Planning point**
>
> The link to other shares of the same class issued at the same time as the qualifying shares has been removed from 22 April 2009, so there is now no restriction on the use of money raised by non-EIS shares. The provisions preventing the capital gains tax share-for-share exchange rules from applying when all deferral relief has been recovered have also been removed.

Law: FA 2009, s. 27 and Sch. 8; FA 2008, s. 32 and Sch. 11; FA 2007, s. 50 and Sch. 16; FA 2006, s. 91 and Sch. 14

75.2.7 Procedure

In order to obtain EIS income tax relief, the company must first apply to HM Revenue & Customs (HMRC) on form EIS 1 for permission to grant certificates to its investors. HMRC then issues the company with form EIS 2, which is authority to send its investors certificates demonstrating that the company fulfils the EIS requirements (form EIS 3). A claim for income tax relief is then made by the investor on receipt of his or her certificate. It is usual for HMRC to ask for certificate EIS 3 also in claims for deferral relief. As certificate EIS 3 can only be issued after following the procedure of application form EIS 1 and authority form EIS 2, the effect of the HMRC approach is to force a company to carry through the EIS application procedure even where deferral relief only is being claimed.

Relief can be claimed at any time up to five years after the 31 January following the year in which the shares were issued.

A company can obtain advance clearance from HMRC that it meets the EIS requirements. Application should be made to:

HM Revenue & Customs
Centre for Research and Intelligence (CRI)
Ty-Glas
Llanishen
Cardiff CF14 5ZG
Tel: 029 2032 7400
Fax: 029 2032 7398
Email: *enterprise.centre@ir.gsi.gov.uk*

This office also provides advance clearance for companies under the venture capital trust (VCT) scheme and monitors the action of companies that have issued shares under EIS or VCT.

Law: ITA 2007, s. 202

75.2.8 Clawback of relief

EIS income tax relief is clawed back and any CGT deferral relief is brought into charge if at any time during the three-year period from the date of the issue of the shares (or, if later, the date of commencement of the trade financed by the issue) any one of the events takes place:

- the shares are sold;
- the company ceases to carry on as a qualifying trade (see **75.2.6**);
- value is received by the investor; or
- the individual becomes 'connected with' the company (income tax relief only).

> ⚠ **Warning!**
>
> If the qualifying trade ceases before the issue of shares or, more likely, never commences or alternatively, if value is treated as being received by the investor before the issue of shares, the shares are treated as having never been eligible. If the failure of the conditions takes place at a later date, the shares are treated as ceasing to be eligible at that time. It should be noted that the shares ceasing to be eligible causes any gain that was deferred to be brought into charge. Hence, if £100,000 of gain has been deferred but later, during the three-year period, there is £1 of value received by the EIS investor, the whole £100,000 gain is thereby brought into charge.

An individual is treated as receiving value from the company if the company:

- repays, redeems or repurchases any of its share capital or securities which belong to the individual or makes any payment to the individual for giving up the individual's right to any of the company's share capital;
- repays any debt owed to the individual (subject to some exemptions) or makes a payment for giving up the individual's right to any debt;
- releases or waives any liability of the individual to a third person;
- makes a loan or advance to the individual;
- provides 'a benefit or facility' to or for the individual;
- transfers an asset to the individual at undervalue; or
- makes 'any other payment' to the individual (unless otherwise exempted).

Payments to an individual investor who is a director are exempted when they are within the categories listed in **75.2.2** above.

A similar list applies for CGT deferral relief.

> *Planning point*
>
> If there is reorganisation of the company or there is a share-for-share exchange whereby a newly created company issues shares in exchange for 'EIS shares' that are held, the shares acquired on the reorganisation are to be treated as if they were the original shares issued. However, it is necessary for an acquiring company to fulfil the EIS provisions in its own right. The takeover of a company by a quoted company will normally cause clawback and crystallisation of any deferred gain.

75.2.9 Permitted payments from the company

Finance Act 2001 introduced complex provisions that omit certain types of payment received from the company without causing clawback of EIS relief.

In summary, the following are possible, but all are subject to carefully defined restrictions:

- if a company has been unsuccessful, reorganisation of the company so that trade can continue under the ownership of a new company normally can be achieved without clawback of the EIS relief;
- payments can be made to an investor who sells goods or services to the company as long as the amount paid does not exceed the market value of the supply;
- interest can be paid to the investor on any sum linked to the company, as long as the rate of interest represents reasonable commercial return;
- the investor can sell an asset to the company for its market value;
- rent can be paid to the investor for the company's occupation of property, as long as the payment does not exceed a commercial rent for that property;
- the company can pay off a trade debt owed to the investor;
- the investor can sell other shares to the company, as long as no more than market value is paid; or
- other payments totalling not more than £1,000 in aggregate can be made to the investor (described in the legislation as 'receipts of insignificant value').

75.3 Venture Capital Trusts

Venture Capital Trusts (VCTs) are dealt with in detail in **Chapter 77**. However, for completeness and ease of reference, the main issues are summarised in the following paragraphs.

The role of a VCT company is to provide a means for the equivalent of EIS relief where either the individual investor has insufficient funds to make a direct investment into an individual company worthwhile or, alternatively, the individual wishes to spread risk by investing in more companies than would be practical if the individual arranged investment directly into the various companies.

A VCT is a quoted investment company. The investor subscribes for shares in a VCT and that company, in turn, uses the subscription monies raised to subscribe for new share capital issued by companies that qualify under the EIS rules.

> ⚠ **Warning!**
> Finance Act 2007 introduced a new investment limit applicable to companies raising money under the venture capital schemes. For an 'investment' to qualify for relief under the EIS or CVS, or be treated as a qualifying holding of a VCT, the company (or group of companies) must have raised no more than £2m under any or all of the schemes in the 12 months ending on the date of the relevant investment.

Tax-Efficient Investments

> If the limit is exceeded, none of the shares or securities within the issue that causes the condition to be breached will qualify for relief under the EIS or CVS, or rank as a qualifying holding for a VCT.
>
> For the purpose of this test an 'investment' will be any investment made by a VCT from funds raised on or after 6 April 2007.

An individual can subscribe up to £200,000 in a tax year and obtain tax relief. For shares issued between 6 April 2004 and 5 April 2005, the rate of tax relief is at 40 per cent. For 2006–07 onwards income tax relief is at 30 per cent.

Unlike an EIS investment, CGT deferral relief is not available to an investor subscribing into a venture capital trust. However, the disposal of the VCT shares, themselves, is exempt from capital gains tax, as long as income tax relief has been given on the subscription and not subsequently been withdrawn.

A VCT is required to meet the following conditions:

- its income must be derived wholly or mainly from shares or securities;
- its ordinary share capital (and the share capital of each class, if it has more than one) must be quoted on a recognised stock market;
- it must not retain, for any accounting period, more than 15 per cent of the income it derives from shares or securities; and
- at least 70 per cent of its investments must be represented throughout its accounting period by 'qualifying holdings' of shares or securities.

Planning point

The current legislation requires shares in a VCT's ordinary share capital to be included in the official UK list throughout the relevant accounting period. This requirement is to be replaced with a requirement that the shares instead be admitted for trading on any EU regulated market. This means that VCTs will be able to be listed on markets throughout the EU/European Economic Area (EEA).

In addition, under current rules at least 30 per cent of the VCT's qualifying holdings must be represented throughout the relevant accounting period by holdings of eligible shares. New legislation will increase the eligible shares holding requirement to 70 per cent and also change the definition of 'eligible shares' to allow VCTs to include shares which may carry certain preferential rights to dividends.

These changes are to be legislated for in the Finance Bill planned for autumn 2010 and will generally take effect from a date to be appointed.

⚠ Warning!

Finance Act 2007 introduced the requirement that, from 6 April 2007, a company (or group of companies) raising money under the VCT scheme must

> have fewer than 50 full-time employees (or their equivalents) at the date on which the relevant shares or securities are issued.

At least 50 per cent by value of those 'qualifying holdings' must be represented by 'eligible shares', that is, ordinary shares carrying no present or future preferential rights to dividends or to assets on a winding up, and no present or future preferential right to be redeemed.

VCTs are required to ensure that at least 10 per cent of the total investment from the VCT in any one company is in ordinary, non-preferential shares. Guaranteed loans and securities do not count towards this fixed proportion of qualifying investments which a VCT must hold.

Example 75.3

A trust company's holding includes the following:

- 200 ordinary shares issued at £20.00 a share partly paid; and
- a bonus issue at 1:2 comprising a further 100 ordinary shares.

A year after the original issue, the trust company pays a further £10 a share in payment of a call on the first 200 shares.

To ascertain whether the eligible holding of ordinary shares amounts to at least 10 per cent of the trust company's total investment, the 200 shares comprised in the original issue should be valued immediately after payment of the £1 call. The bonus shares are not taken into account.

The specification for the 'qualifying holdings' into which a VCT is permitted to invest is complex. The company must not hold shares or securities listed on any stock market, either in the UK or abroad, nor on the unlisted securities market. However, a VCT is permitted to hold shares that are dealt with on the Alternative Investment Market (AIM). There are provisions whereby the VCT can receive quoted shares as a result of its exercise of conversion rights.

To be a 'qualifying holding', the shares must be in a company that has gross assets that do not exceed £7,000,000 before the subscription by the VCT, nor £8,000,000 after that subscription. Each company into which the VCT invests must exist for the purpose of carrying on one or more qualifying trades. The company can be the holding company of a trading group except that investment can be made into a parent company of a trading group even though a subsidiary is a property managing company. An institution wishing to establish a VCT can obtain HMRC clearance that the arrangements it proposes satisfy the VCT requirements by making application to HMRC Small Company Enterprise Centre TIDO, details of which are given in Section **75.2.7** above. This office monitors the operation of a VCT, once it has been established.

A VCT is not prevented from distributing, by way of dividend, surpluses arising on the disposal of investments.

Investors must hold their shares for a minimum of five years to qualify for income tax relief.

> **Planning point**
>
> The current legislation requires that there is a qualifying trade carried on wholly or mainly in the UK. The Finance Bill planned for the autumn of 2010 will contain legislation to the effect that for shares issued on or after the commencement date of the legislation, the requirement will be that the company issuing the shares must simply have a 'permanent establishment in the UK'.

Law: ITA 2007, Pt. 6; FA 2009, s. 27 and Sch. 8; FA 2008, s. 32 and Sch. 11; FA 2007, s. 50 and Sch. 16; FA 2006, s. 91, Sch. 14

75.4 Individual Savings Account

75.4.1 Overview

Introduced with effect from 6 April 1999, the Individual Savings Account (ISA) is the tax-exempt investment that has attracted numerically the largest number of savers. ISAs can hold cash, certain stocks and shares, certain collective investment scheme units, certain life insurance policies, certain stakeholder products and National Savings in a single account.

An ISA fund is exempt from income tax and CGT. But tax credits on dividends cannot be reclaimed.

There is an overall investment limit of £10,200 per tax year from 6 April 2010 (from 6 April 2009, the limit is £7,200). Up to one-half of that allowance can be saved in cash with one provider. The remainder can be invested in stocks and shares with either the same or a different provider. (For investors aged 50 and over, the increase to £10,200 from £7,200 took effect from 6 October 2009.)

There is no 'lifetime' investment limit.

Withdrawals may be made at any time without loss of tax relief, but once a withdrawal is made a further deposit cannot be made to make up for it once deposits have already been made up to the allowed limits.

> **Planning point**
>
> Husbands and wives each have their own subscription limits. Income and gains are exempt from tax.

> **Example 75.4**
>
> Sally invests £5,000 in an ISA on 1 July 2010. In October 2010 she withdraws £500. In December 2010 she wishes to make a further investment. The maximum further investment she can make is £5,200 (£10,200 − £5,000). The amount withdrawn is not taken into account.

Law: Individual Savings Account (Amendment) Regulations 2009 (SI 2009/1550); Individual Savings Account Regulations 1998 (SI 1998/1870)

75.4.2 Eligibility

ISAs are available to individuals over the age of 18 (or over the age of 16 for cash ISAs with effect from 6 April 2001), who are resident and ordinarily resident in the UK for tax purposes.

The detail of the Individual Savings Account system is given by statutory instruments issued by the Treasury. It is a remarkable development in UK fiscal legislation that tax relief is given to a fifth of the UK's population each year and this relief does not require statute but is given by subordinate legislation brought into effect and changed by laying a statutory instrument at the Palace of Westminster. The amassed regulations provide a scheme whereby HMRC authorises institutions to act as ISA account managers. The mechanism for control that is applied by HMRC consists, to a large extent in HMRC officers examining a sample of the returns made by the approved account managers. Thus, the effect is akin to the operation of PAYE, in that commercial organisations administer a tax system for a large percentage of the population.

There is an overall investment limit of £10,200 per tax year from 6 April 2010 (from 6 April 2009, the limit is £7,200). Up to one-half of that allowance can be saved in cash with one provider. The remainder can be invested in stocks and shares with either the same or a different provider. (For investors aged 50 and over, the increase to £10,200 from £7,200 took effect from 6 October 2009.)

A major part of HM Revenue & Customs' routine work in respect of ISAs is to seek to identify those individuals who have opened an account with more than one provider. Where this is identified, the manager of the second ISA account to be opened is required by HMRC to return to the investor the cash sum invested and to repay to HMRC any tax relief given in error. Court proceedings have been taken by

HMRC against certain individuals who have attempted to open a large number of ISA accounts.

75.4.3 Cash component

The cash component can be:

- a bank account;
- a building society account;
- units in authorised unit trust money market funds ('cash funds') and authorised unit trusts which invest in other authorised unit trusts ('funds of funds') investing in money market funds; or
- a National Savings product which is specifically designed for ISAs.

Interest arising on the cash component only is exempt from tax. From time to time, there will be cash in the other two components; interest arising on this cash is subject to tax at basic rate (20 per cent), which is withheld and paid by the ISA account manager. There is never any tax liability on the investor, even if the investor is a higher or additional rate taxpayer.

Law: SI 1998/1870, reg. 23.

75.4.4 Stocks and shares component

The stocks and shares component can include the following:

- shares issued by companies listed on a recognised stock exchange anywhere in the world;
- corporate bonds issued by companies listed on a recognised stock exchange anywhere in the world;
- securities issued by a company that is a 75 per cent subsidiary of a company listed on a recognised stock exchange anywhere in the world;
- UK government stock ('gilts');
- securities equivalent to gilts issued by governments and central banks of all countries in the European Community and other members of the European Economic Area (EEA);
- strips of gilts and of their foreign EEC equivalents;
- units in UK authorised unit trusts which invest in shares and securities (securities funds, warrant funds and 'funds of funds' that invest in them);
- shares in UK open-ended investment companies (OEICs);
- shares and securities in approved investment trusts (other than property trusts);
- units or shares in Undertakings for Collective Investment in Transferable Securities (UCITS) funds based in a member state of the European Community (i.e. the mainland EC equivalent of a UK unit trust or OEIC); and
- Crest depository interests representing shares that would, themselves, qualify under the conditions stated above.

The cash sum paid by the investor into the stocks and shares component (which can be the whole subscription limit invested in the year, if there is neither a cash element to the account, nor a life assurance element) is invested by the account manager who purchases stocks and shares, which are held by the account manager and registered in the account manager's name (not the name of the investor) but held as the individual's ISA fund.

An individual can transfer stocks and shares in his or her personal portfolio into his or her ISA account, but such a transfer must be treated as taking place at the market value of the holding on the day of transfer. Thus, it is a CGT disposal for the individual and potentially creates a liability to pay CGT as the CGT exemption is on gains made by the approved ISA account manager within the ISA account; there is no exemption on disposals made by the individual investor. An employee who has obtained shares under an Employee Share Ownership Plan is entitled to transfer those shares directly into the stocks and shares component of an ISA.

The investments in the stocks and shares component produce cash by means of dividends, interest and other payments. This cash is collected and held by the account manager in the stocks and shares component as a temporary fund. This cash is not added to the cash component. This cash will, itself, produce an interest payment. This 'secondary interest' does not attract the full tax exemption for the component of an ISA. Instead, Individual Savings Account Regulations give a special tax regime, whereby the ISA account manager is required to withhold tax at lower rate (20 per cent) on the 'secondary interest' and the account manager pays the tax withheld to HMRC. No entry is required on the tax return of the investor and there is no tax liability on the investor, even if the investor is a higher rate taxpayer.

75.4.5 Death of an ISA investor

When an investor dies, the ISA is treated as ceasing at the time of the investor's death and all income arising from the fund after the investor's death is subject to tax in the usual way. During the period of administration, this is income of the personal representatives and tax liabilities are assessable on the personal representatives.

75.5 Friendly societies

A registered friendly society acts as a mini tax shelter. Premiums on a ten-year endowment policy can be paid into the friendly society's tax-exempt fund and the total generated by the society's investment of the premiums over the life of the endowment is then paid to the investor, without suffering any charge to tax.

Tax-Efficient Investments

> **Planning point**
>
> The benefit of this tax free investment is restricted by the maximum premiums that can be paid by any one individual into a qualifying exempt friendly society policy being £270 a year in total.
>
> As an alternative to paying a lump sum at the end of an endowment period, the contributions can be used to build up a fund for paying off an annuity. However, in order for the fund to be tax-exempt, the annuity payable to any one individual is limited to £156 per annum.
>
> These limits have not been changed since 1995.
>
> There is no connection between sums paid to a friendly society and sums paid to any other tax-exempt fund. Hence, a premium of up to £270 per annum can be paid to a friendly society on an endowment policy in addition to paying the maximum allowed into an ISA. Similarly, a premium can be paid to a friendly society to fund an annuity without reduction of the sum that can be paid into a personal pension plan.

A registered friendly society is, in effect, a mutual insurance company in relation to its life insurance business. The availability of a tax-exempt fund to this particular type of organisation was justified by the Secretary of State to the Treasury during the debates on Finance Bill 1995, as a recognition that there are fixed costs in administering life policies and this means that a society that has many policies with small premiums suffers administration costs as a higher percentage of the fund created by those policies than is the case for a company with predominantly large premium policies. The tax relief given to the investor is justified as a means of redressing the balance, so that there is a viable option for very small savers.

Law: ICTA 1988, s. 460

75.6 Child trust funds

A child trust fund is available to a child born on or after 1 September 2004. In order to qualify the child must be settled in the United Kingdom and have a right of abode in the UK.

The Child Trust Fund Account is opened by the parent (or guardian), who can choose the commercial provider and can choose the type of account. Grandparents and other family members, friends and the child him- or herself can contribute into the account, but only the parent or guardian can choose the account to be opened.

Types of Child Trust Fund account include:

- a savings account for a cash deposit;
- a shares account; and

- a stakeholder account. This invests in company shares until the child's 13th birthday, when equities are sold and the proceeds are held as cash, or government stock.

Any account can be moved from one category to another. Until the child is aged 16 the transfer is made by the parent. Once the child is aged 16, he or she controls the account but cannot make withdrawals until age 18.

The maximum amount that can be invested in a child's Trust Account is £1,200 each year (excluding the government contribution). For this purpose a year starts as commencing on the child's birthday.

Formerly, the Government contributed £250 for each Child Trust Fund account that was opened (£500 for households on low incomes). A further £250 was contributed when the child reached seven years of age. However, as announced on 24 May 2010, government contributions to child trust funds were reduced to a basic £50 from 1 August 2010 with contributions ceasing completely from 1 January 2011.

The Child Trust Fund is exempt from income tax and capital gains tax.

For further commentary on CTFs, see **Chapter 30**.

75.7 Life assurance (qualifying policies)

75.7.1 Overview

A life assurance company is exempt from tax on both the income arising and the capital gains made in the fund it holds for qualifying life assurance policies. Therefore, for the investor the premium paid on such a policy is invested (after management charges) in a fund that is tax free and the tax exemption will increase the sums that can be paid out to the investor. In practice, investment in a qualifying life policy falls into two categories:

- providing a fund to pay at death, typically either to fund inheritance tax or to take advantage of the facility to write the policy in trust and, thereby, pass the fund free of inheritance tax to the next generation; and
- building up a fund, typically over ten years, after which the policy matures and pays out.

75.7.2 Conditions to satisfy for a qualifying policy

The tax free fund consists of premiums from 'qualifying policies' only. In order to be a 'qualifying policy', it must satisfy the statutory conditions in full. For whole life or endowment assurances the term must be at least ten years. The premiums must be payable at yearly or shorter intervals for at least ten years or until the event specified, whether death or disability. The total premiums payable under the policy in any period of 12 months must not exceed twice the amount payable in any other 12-month period or one-eighth of the total premiums payable if the policy were to run for the specified term.

The policy must guarantee that the sum payable on death will be at least 75 per cent of the total premiums payable if the policy were to run its term, except that a two per cent reduction for every year by which the person exceeds 55 years of age is permitted and when a new policy is issued for an old one the part of the premiums that are is attributable to the old policy are ignored. Where a policy includes one or more options, the policy must be tested on each option and will only 'qualify' if it meets the conditions on every such test. A policy may make provision for total or partial surrender without ceasing to qualify but if an option in a qualifying policy is exercised after 13 March 1984, and either extends the term of the policy or increases the benefits payable under it, the policy ceases to qualify.

A temporary assurance for a period of not more than ten years may be a qualifying policy but only if the surrender value is not to exceed the total premiums previously paid. A term policy of less than 12 months cannot be a qualifying policy. This provision is likely to make a policy issued for less than ten years unattractive.

75.8 Life assurance (single premium bonds)

75.8.1 Overview

Quite apart from life assurance taken out to provide a lump sum on an individual's death, perhaps to pay funeral expenses or an inheritance tax liability, life policies can be used as an investment mechanism. Although usually referred to as either life assurance bonds or investment bonds, these are, technically, single premium whole life insurance policies. Having taken out such a life assurance bond, the investor can withdraw a sum up to five per cent of his or her initial purchase consideration in each fiscal year and the withdrawal is treated as a withdrawal of capital, with no income tax consequences. If less than the five per cent is taken in one year, the surplus is carried forward to the following year.

A withdrawal greater than the five per cent and, indeed, full encashment of the bond, can be made without any charge to tax by a basic rate taxpayer, as long as the 'chargeable event' that arises, when added to the taxpayer's other income, does not exceed the basic rate band.

For a higher rate tax payable, or one for whom the 'chargeable event' takes the taxpayer into higher rates, there is a charge to income tax at higher rate only.

75.8.2 Chargeable event

For this purpose, a chargeable event is any one of the following:

- a payment under the policy at death;
- a payment at the maturity of the policy;
- a surrender of the policy rights;
- an assignment of policy rights for money or money's worth; and
- a withdrawal in excess of 5 per cent.

Even if an assignment is taxed as a chargeable event, this does not stop a later assignment giving a second charge to tax by virtue of the second chargeable event. This provision was introduced to cancel the advantages that were enjoyed under the so-called second-hand bond scheme.

75.8.3 Computing the gain

On death, maturity or assignment, the gain is the difference between the amount received from the insurance company and the initial premium paid, less any withdrawals that have been made.

If there is a partial, rather than a complete, encashment of the policy, the gain brought into charge is the sum that is paid out of the policy, less five per cent of the initial subscription for each year during the life of the policy, insofar as this has not been taken into account in previous gain computations. The five per cent is calculated by reference to the policy year, not the tax year. A policy year commences on the day the policy is taken out and on each 365-day anniversary thereafter. Many modern policies allow partial surrenders at frequent intervals and such surrenders gave rise to complex calculations. In an attempt to reduce the work involved, both for life offices and HMRC, a different system of determining both whether there has been a gain and its extent applies.

On assignment, the gain is the excess of the consideration received, except when assignment is between connected persons when market value is substituted, plus the amount or value of any relevant capital payments over the total amount of premiums paid with adjustments for the assignment.

Where the chargeable gain arises on death, the chargeable event is the income of the individual who owns the policy and not of his or her personal representatives.

75.8.4 Top-slicing relief

The gain is brought into charge after top-slicing relief. The gain is spread back over a number of years by dividing it by the number of complete years:

- for the first chargeable event – since the start of the policy;

Tax-Efficient Investments

- for any later chargeable event other than final termination – since the previous chargeable event; and
- on final termination – the number of whole years from the start of the policy.

The slice of the gain is then added to the taxpayer's other income to discover the amount of extra tax payable by reason of its addition. If the addition of that sum does not give rise to anything but tax at the basic rate, no tax is payable. If the sum gives a liability at higher rate, the charge is computed as if there were a credit for tax at basic rate.

When there is a chargeable event through death or maturity and there is a loss, an individual may deduct that loss from total income so far as it does not exceed gains taxed in earlier partial surrender or assignments. Thus, the tax on gains made earlier may be recovered. The relief does not apply to losses on assignments.

75.8.5 A policy held by trustees

The chargeable event is assessed on the individual whose life is insured. This formulation means that a policy written in trust, which is commonly the case, gives rise to a tax charge on the individual who created the trust if the individual is alive at some time during the year of assessment in which the chargeable gain arises.

Where a policy has been held by trustees prior to the event causing the chargeable event, the charge to tax falls on the settlor, if the settlor is alive. If the settlor is dead, the charge arises on the trustees.

In general, a gain on a policy that is held by a company is treated as income of the company, subject to corporation tax.

75.9 National Savings

75.9.1 Generally

Certain investment products supplied by National Savings are exempt from income tax and capital gains tax. There are currently four such products.

75.9.2 Fixed-interest saving certificates

These are lump sum investments that earn guaranteed rates of interest over set periods of time, called 'terms'.

Certificates can be held by individuals, as joint holdings, by trustees, by charities and by some clubs.

75.9.3 Index-linked savings certificates

The minimum holding is £100 and the maximum is £15,000.

Certificates can be held by individuals, as joint holdings, by trustees, by charities and by some clubs.

75.9.4 Children's bonus bonds

A five-year bond (issue 34) is currently available. Interest of 2.50 per cent per annum is payable if held to the fifth anniversary. The minimum purchase is £25 and the maximum is £3,000.

The bond must be purchased by an individual aged 16 or over and be provided for the benefit of an individual under 16 (it is not necessary for the child and the adult to be related).

The bond matures on the bond holder's twenty-first birthday but can be cashed in earlier.

The interest is tax free. The tax exemption apples not only to the child's income but also excludes any charge on the parent that may otherwise arise by virtue of the parent having supplied the fund.

75.9.5 Premium bonds

National Savings is keen to promote the holding of premium bonds as a form of investment. Each month there is one prize for every 24,000 £1 bonds in issue. The value of the prizes is such that the overall return is currently 1.50 per cent on the 27 billion Bond numbers in each monthly draw. Prizes range from £25 to £1m. Any one individual can hold up to £30,000 in premium bonds.

75.10 Purchased life annuities

The monthly sum paid from a purchased life annuity is treated as if it were two separate payments, the first being a capital content which does not attract a charge to income tax (nor to CGT) and the second a pure income payment, which attracts a charge to income tax. However, this treatment is only available where the purchase is made by an annuitant.

The apportionment between income and capital is made by dividing the purchase cost into the two elements by reference to government mortality tables. Even where an individual receives special terms from a company as the individual has a lower than average life expectancy, the government tables are automatically applied for tax purposes. The capital element that is computed by reference to the table remains constant, even if the individual lives to such an age that the payments made that have been deemed to be capital exceed, in aggregate, the initial purchase price. In this respect, the treatment is in contrast to that which applies to insurance bonds.

> ⚠ **Warning!**
> A purchased life annuity can be structured so that the monthly payments increase each year in line with inflation. This does not affect the calculation of the division between the deemed capital element and the income element. The calculation of the division is made as at the date of the first payment. The consequence of this treatment is that inflationary increases in the annuity paid are automatically treated as income attracting a charge to income tax.

75.11 Investments with IHT relief

75.11.1 Introduction

It is frequently the case that the amount paid for inheritance tax at a death greatly exceeds any other single tax payment made in respect of that individual. Investing in order to reduce the inheritance tax payment that may ultimately be required is, thus, potentially a highly tax-efficient investment.

The choice of investment for this purpose requires the adviser to look at the personal circumstances of the individual and also the likely destination of the funds left at death. If funds pass to the surviving spouse, the nature of the investments is unlikely to be of direct relevance as no inheritance tax is, in general, payable on an inter-spouse transfer.

In this chapter a note is made of three types of investment that have significant potential for mitigating inheritance tax, plus a fourth category that is of especial importance for those who are likely to be treated as not domiciled in the UK at the time of death.

75.11.2 AIM shares

Relief at 100 per cent is given against an inheritance tax liability on qualifying business property. There are three categories of business property that attract 100 per cent relief:

- an unincorporated business, either owned alone or in partnership;
- unquoted shares in a trading company; and
- quoted shares which give control in a trading company.

A substantial investor may be attracted to purchase an entire business, or alternatively he may find the inheritance tax relief a reason for retaining a partnership interest, even after active work in the partnership has ceased.

For a more modest investor, holding unquoted shares can be attractive. Shares listed on the Alternative Investment Market are treated as unquoted for the purpose of the 100 per cent IHT relief.

Statute does not define 'share' for this purpose. IHT relief is potentially available on voting or non-voting shares, on ordinary or on preference shares.

Excluded from business property relief are shares in companies where the main activity is dealing in securities, in land, in buildings, or the making or holding of investments. All other trades can, potentially, qualify for the investor enjoying 100 per cent inheritance tax relief.

Shares must be held for at least 24 months before the date of death for any IHT relief to be available. (If the consideration is IHT relief on settling shares into trust the period of 24 months is counted up to the date of settlement.)

75.11.3 Nursing home

Like AIM shares, the IHT relief potentially available on a nursing home is merely one example of the operation of 100 per cent business property relief.

Business property relief is available on the value of assets used in a qualifying trade. The trade of running a nursing home can be of interest to an investor as the fund used to finance the business will typically be applied in purchasing a property whose value is likely to move in line with property values generally, irrespective of the fortunes of the trade that is carried on. In other words, a large house used for a nursing home can often be sold as a domestic dwelling house and any increase in house prices generally is likely to be reflected in the value of the building used for the nursing home.

As with IHT business property relief generally, no relief is available until the investor has owned the property for 24 months.

75.11.4 Agricultural land

Inheritance tax relief at 100 per cent is enjoyed by the holder of agricultural property. The relief is, however, 100 per cent of the agricultural value only; that is, if there is any additional value by virtue of the property being used for other purposes, this additional value does not attract APR.

Agricultural property is defined as meaning agricultural land or pasture which includes woodlands (but not timber) and buildings occupied with such agricultural land. Agricultural property extends to fish farming, as well as livestock rearing.

A dwelling-house can attract agricultural property relief if it falls within one of two alternative categories:

- a dwelling-house that is occupied 'with agricultural land or pasture and the occupation is ancillary to that of the agricultural land or pasture', or
- the dwelling house is within the designation of 'cottages, farm buildings and farm houses' together with the land occupied with them, as are 'of a character appropriate to the property'.

The first category is applicable mainly to farm workers, rather than the farmer himself. Not every farm worker's house will qualify under this first category; case law shows that the relief is only available where occupation is necessary, not where the property is provided as a perk of the employment.

Of greater interest to the investor, is the second category. One hundred per cent of the agricultural value of a farm house can be excluded from the inheritance tax charge by virtue of agricultural property relief.

There is substantial case law on the designation of a house as a farm house. In 2002 the Special Commissioners in *Lloyds TSB (personal representatives of Antrobus) v IR Commrs* granted 100 per cent agricultural property relief for a substantial house occupied with 126 acres, even though farming had not been profitable on the land for some years, the house had recorded history dating from 1188 and had been the centre of a farming operation for much of its history. By contrast, also in 2002, the Special Commissioner denied agricultural property relief in *Dixon v IR Commrs* where the house, Nook Cottage, was on a land holding of 0.6 acres on which damson trees were planted.

It is suggested that the guiding principle was neatly stated by Lord Upjohn giving the decision of the House of Lords in *IR Commrs v Korner*.

> 'I would think that to be "the farmhouse" for the purposes of the section, it must be judged in accordance with ordinary ideas of what is appropriate in size, content and layout, taken in conjunction with the farm buildings, and the particular area of farmland being farmed, and not part of a rich man's considerable residence.'

Agricultural property relief is also available against the value of shares of a company owning agricultural land. In order to obtain agricultural property relief, the property must have been owned for two years if the farming has been carried on by the owner, or for seven years if let to another person.

75.12 Woodlands

Prior to 6 April 1988, tax under Schedule B was charged on one-third of the rateable value of the land used for woodlands, with no regard being taken for income tax purposes of any cost or any receipts from the sale of wood. Schedule B was abolished by Finance Act 1988. The result is, that any profits arising from the occupation of commercial woodlands are wholly outside the scope of income or corporation tax. Profits from the occupation of commercial woodlands are specifically exempted from the charge under Schedule A. As the profits from woodlands are exempt, no relief is available for interest paid on a loan to purchase woodlands. Similarly, capital allowances are not available for the cost of construction of machinery buildings, nor for the cost of machinery or plant used for commercial woodlands.

Any capital gain made on the disposal of woodland is exempt insofar as it is attributable to trees growing on the land, saleable underwood or felled timber.

For inheritance tax, agricultural property relief, normally 100 per cent, is put against the value of land used as woodlands, subject to the normal provisions for agricultural property relief.

A special inheritance tax regime applies to any charge to inheritance tax that arises on death in respect of trees or underwood growing on commercial woodlands. Where the deceased has owned a woodland for at least five years, the personal representatives can elect that the value of the trees and underwood is left out of account in charging inheritance tax at death. However, this election is not available in respect of any inheritance tax that arises in respect to a transfer made during lifetime, nor can it be made where the woodland is outside the UK.

Example 75.5

Andrew, who has made lifetime transfers amounting to £80,000, dies on 1 March 2004, leaving a chargeable estate valued at £300,000, plus woodlands which are left out of account. The woodlands are left to Graham and Craig.

In July 2006, Graham fells the trees on his land and sells the timber for £45,000. Allowable expenses amount to £10,000.

In January 2009, Craig makes a gift of his woodlands to David at a time when they are worth £80,000 (including £25,000 attributable to the underlying land). There are no allowable expenses.

Sale by Graham		£
Andrew's cumulative total at death		380,000
Proceeds of sale	45,000	
Less: allowable expenses	(10,000)	
		35,000
		415,000
Tax thereon (2006–07 rates)		52,000
Less: tax on Andrew's cumulative total (2006–07) rates		(38,000)
Tax payable		14,000
Gift by Craig		£

Andrew's cumulative total (including previously chargeable amounts)		415,000
Value at date of disposal	80,000	
Less: value of land (which would not be left out of account on A's death)	(25,000)	
		55,000
		470,000
Tax thereon (2008–09 rates)		63,200
Less: tax on £415,000 (2008–09 rates)		(41,200)
Tax payable		22,000

Where such an election is made, a charge to inheritance tax arises on the subsequent disposal of the timber if the disposal is made by the person who has inherited the woodland, or the person's spouse. In computing the charge on this subsequent event, tax is charged on the proceeds of sale less the costs of felling and selling and after deducting the cost of expenditure on any replanting that takes place within three years after the sale. If the disposal is not for full consideration, the inheritance tax charge is computed on the net value of the timber at the time of disposal, less the deductions for selling and replanting costs. The rate of charge is that which would have applied to the timber at the date of the preceding death, had the election not been made. Thus, the effect is a deferral of payment, rather than exemption. However, if the person who inherits the woodland, and also his or her spouse, dies before there is a disposal of timber, the inheritance tax charge never crystallises.

75.13 Tax-efficient investment checklist

	EIS	VCT	ISA	Friendly Societies	Child Trust Funds	Life Assurance	National Savings	Purchased life annuities	AIM	Nursing Home	Agricultural Land	Excl. property for a non-dom.	Woodlands
Income tax relief for initial investment?	Yes	Yes	No	No	No	No	No	No	No	No	No	No	No
CGT deferred on investment?	Yes	No	No	No	No	No	No	No	No	No	No	No	No
Tax exemption for income arising on investment?	No	No	Yes	Yes	Yes	Yes	Yes	Yes	No	No	No	Yes	Yes
CGT exemption?	Yes	Yes	Yes	No	Yes	No	Yes	No	No	No	No	Yes	Yes
Tax relief on interest paid on loan to acquire investment?	No	No	No	No	No	No	No	No	No	Yes	Yes	No	No
Maximum annual investment?	£500,000	£200,000	£10,200	£270	£1,200	No limit	£15,000 (fixed and indexed linked)	No limit	No limit	No limit	No limit	No limit	No limit
Investment easily cashed in?	No	Possibly	Yes	Yes	Yes (after age 16)	Yes	Yes	No	Yes	No	No	Yes	No
Can you lose money?	Yes	Yes	Yes	No	Yes, if share fund chosen	Unlikely	No	Yes	Yes	Yes	Yes	Yes	Yes

Tax-Efficient Investments

	EIS	VCT	ISA	Friendly Societies	Child Trust Funds	Life Assurance	National Savings	Purchased life annuities	AIM	Nursing Home	Agricultural Land	Excl. property for a non-dom.	Woodlands
Inheritance tax relief?	Yes	No	No	No	No	No	No	No	Yes	Yes	Yes	Yes	Yes

76 Pensions

76.1 Introduction

The Government is consulting on a range of pension changes affecting contribution levels and tax relief, benefit crystallisation ages and income levels, contracting out, annual and lifetime allowance levels, and employer schemes. Many of these have a possible implementation of April 2011. Advisors need to confirm the correct situation from April 2011 before giving advice.

The aim of this chapter is to provide professional advisers, who are not regulated by the Financial Services and Markets Act 2000, with guidance to help them:

- have an overview of the main types of pension;
- understand the tax, and other issues, associated with each type of pension; and
- be aware of some of the major tax planning opportunities.

The subject of pensions is a vast one, and therefore it is impossible to do justice to all pension related issues in just one chapter. Further information or advice is likely to be required before detailed guidance can be provided to clients.

This chapter covers the following.

- Types of pension schemes.
- Pension transfers.
- Pensions Simplification.
- Types of Retirement Income Arrangements.
- Annuities.
- Investment options while drawing income.
- Pension increases.
- Death benefits.
- Inheritance Tax implications.
- State Pension.
- Contracting-out.
- Changes in personal circumstances.
- Tax planning opportunities.

76.2 Types of Pension Schemes

Although there is now one universal tax regime for pensions, some pension arrangements still continue to be affected by older legislation and therefore it is important to have an understanding of these issues and how they affect an individual's retirement planning.

Whilst legislation lays down the legal parameters with which schemes must operate, it is important to remember that particular schemes may apply more restrictive rules to the benefits they provide.

There are two main generic types of pension scheme.

(1) Occupational schemes.

(2) Personal schemes.

76.2.1 Types of Occupational or Company-sponsored Pension Schemes

Final Salary Scheme

These are also known as 'defined benefit' schemes. They are established by companies to provide retirement benefits for their employees based on salary and length of pensionable service. They are normally regarded as the gold standard for pensions, despite the high profile failure of some schemes, since the employee is guaranteed a certain level of retirement income irrespective of investment performance, and this will increase in retirement (see section on pension increases). Although employees may be required to make contributions, the employer is required to underwrite benefits.

Changes in legal solvency criteria and past stock market declines have put financial pressure on many final salary schemes and increased the level of contributions required which, in turn, has led many employers to seek to wind up their final salary schemes and to switch to alternative arrangements. Clients who have the chance to join a final salary scheme should almost certainly do so, although it may be wise to check the solvency position if personal contributions are required. The benefits are based on the length of a member's pensionable service and their final pensionable salary. A common basis is an initial retirement benefit of 1/60th of final pensionable pay for each year of service. Part of this can be commuted for a tax free Pension Commencement Lump Sum. Other rates, such as 1/80th may also be used, in which case the tax-free Pension Commencement Lump Sum may be additional. Schemes may be contributory or non-contributory. If a scheme is contributory, members will be required to pay a percentage of their salary to the scheme.

Career Average Scheme

These schemes are a 'paired-down' final salary scheme and are becoming increasingly popular as employers try to find a middle ground between maintaining the defined benefit scheme whilst controlling the costs of funding it. At the point of retirement, the pay that the individual has earned in each year will take inflation into account, and then be aggregated. The total will then be divided by the number of years service to provide the 'average' pay, on which the pension will then be based.

Money Purchase Scheme

Also known technically as 'defined contribution' schemes, these depend on investment performance and annuity rates at retirement to determine the final pension payable. The employer and, normally, the employee contribute a percentage of salary into a pension fund for the employee, which hopefully accumulates over time. This money purchase scheme can either be trust based with trustees to look after scheme members' interests, or can be a group personal pension or stakeholder arrangement. Once again, clients who are offered the opportunity to join an occupational or company-sponsored arrangement should usually do so, not only to obtain the benefit of any employer contribution, but also because the charges are generally lower than a scheme organised by the individual.

> ### Planning point
>
> There were 3 sets of rules governing the old occupational schemes dependent on when the scheme was established and when the individual joined: pre-1987; 1987–1989; and post 1989. The differences between these rules centre on:
>
> - the length of service required before maximum benefits can be paid;
> - the maximum percentage of income that was pensionable (the earnings cap); and
> - the calculation of the tax-free cash.
>
> Depending on the regime, some individuals were able to accrue very large pension income entitlements, and tax free lumps sums in excess of 25 per cent of the fund value. These entitlements can be protected if they exceed the maximum entitlements under the new pension rules.

Contracted-out Pension Schemes

Occupational schemes can either be contracted in, or out, of the State Second Pension (previously State Earnings Related Pension Scheme). See section on contracting-out.

Additional Voluntary Contribution (AVC) Schemes

Members of occupational schemes who wish to make additional contributions in order to enhance their final retirement benefits would normally have done so into an AVC scheme. Benefits are usually based on a money purchase arrangement, although some public sector schemes may provide additional years of pensionable service.

> **Planning point**
>
> The maximum contribution that members could make prior 6 April 2006 was 15 per cent of total remuneration. So, if the main scheme required contributions of 9 per cent, this only allowed AVC contributions of 6 per cent. This has now changed (see section on maximum contributions) but many individuals may not be aware that they can make increased contributions.

Free Standing Additional Voluntary Contributions (FSAVC) Schemes

Where the individual wished to make private arrangements, for example because the investment options under the AVC were limited, this could be done through FSAVCs. The same contribution limits applied to FSAVCs, except that if the total annual contributions were £2,400 per annum or less, then no formal test for excessive benefits was necessary. In many cases this set the actual amount of the contribution for the sake of simplicity.

> **Planning point**
>
> Before 6 April 2001, it was not possible for a member of an occupational pension scheme to contribute to a personal pension. However, since the introduction of stakeholder pensions from 6 April 2001 a member of an occupational pension scheme who earned less than £30,000 gross per annum could also contribute to a stakeholder pension as long as HMRC contribution limits were not exceeded, and £3,600 in any case. From 6 April 2006, this earnings restriction has been removed (see section on annual allowance). The charges under stakeholder pension plans are likely to be less than those of an FSAVC, and individuals may wish to review this aspect.

Section 32 Policy

This is a policy that can be used to take a transfer from an occupational pension scheme. Although the structural differences between occupational and personal pension regimes have been removed, a Section 32 policy can be appropriate where a transfer from an occupational pension is required while maintaining enhanced benefits.

Executive Pension Schemes

These are plans set up for directors or senior employees. Benefits are provided on a money purchase basis.

Small Self-Administered Pension Schemes (SSAS)

A SSAS is a pooled executive pension plan. For a scheme to qualify as a SSAS it must abide by the following.

(1) Have no more than 11 active members, of whom at least one must:

    (a) be a controlling director; or
    (b) have been a controlling director in the last 10 years; or
    (c) be closely related to:

- Another member of the scheme; or
- A trustee of the scheme; or
- A partner (if the sponsoring company is a partnership); or
- A person who is, or at any time has been in the last 10 years, a controlling director (if the sponsoring employer is a company).

(2) Not have all the assets invested only in insurance policies.

SSAS's were popular because they offered the opportunity of wide investment options and in particular the possibility to purchase property. They have therefore been ideal for directors who wish to purchase the company's premises. However, most of the special features of a SSAS have been removed by the new pension regime.

> **Planning point**
>
> The requirement to appoint a 'pensioneer trustee' to ensure that the scheme did not breach the winding-up rules has been removed with effect from 6 April 2006.

Funded Unapproved Retirement Benefit Schemes (FURBS)

These arrangements were introduced to provide additional retirement benefits for some employees whose earnings were in excess of the pensionable limit. Although their relevance diminished with the introduction in 2006 of the generous annual allowance and the fairly restrictive Lifetime Allowance, were they saw a resurgence following the new anti-forestalling rules from 22nd April 2009. FURBS are an individual trust based arrangement between the employee and the employer with the employer acting as the trustee. The contributions do not benefit from tax relief, but there is no limit to the benefits payable, and if required, the entire fund accumulated prior to 6 April 2006 could be taken on retirement as a tax-free lump sum. HMRC now refers to FURBS as Employer-Financed Retirement Benefits Schemes (EFRBS).

Issues surrounding Employer-Financed Retirement Benefits Schemes (EFRBS)

The term Employer Financed Retirement Benefit Scheme (EFRBS) was introduced by the Finance Act 2004; this amongst other things amended the definition of the previously used terminology: 'non-approved' schemes (outlined in Income Tax Earnings and Pensions Act 2003). Non–approved was the collective pre-A day term used for Funded Unapproved Retirement Benefits (FURBS) and Unfunded Unapproved Retirement Benefits Schemes (UURBS) and all such schemes became EFRBS w.e.f 06/04/2006. HMRC must be notified within 3 months of an EFRBS commencing and by 7th July following the tax year any benefit is provided.

There are special transitional rules for non-approved schemes as the tax position of an EFRBS is markedly different to non-approved schemes.

An EFRBS is an arrangement entered into by an employee and an employer to provide relevant benefits. Relevant benefits are any lump sum, gratuity or other benefit (including non-cash benefits) paid in respect of:

- retirement or death;
- anticipation of retirement;
- after retirement or death in connection with past service;
- anticipation or connection with a change in the nature of the employee's service; or
- a result of a pension sharing order.

Benefits can be constructed either on a money purchase or final salary basis. Regardless of how benefits are accrued under an EFRBS, currently they do not count towards the Annual Allowance, Special Annual Allowance and Lifetime Allowance as EFRBS are not registered pension schemes (this may be subject to legislative change in 2011).

EFRBS can be both funded and unfunded; however, if unfunded there is an obvious lack of security (n.b. any provision of security/insurance on an unfunded arrangement will give rise to a benefit kind charge on the employee equal to the cost of provision). EFRBS are also not subject to the contribution and investment restrictions which apply to registered pension schemes, providing greater flexibility in design.

The Pension Schemes Act 1993, Pensions Act 1995 and 2004 are generally applicable, although they are exempt from a number of provisions, e.g. scheme funding requirements. Preservation and transfer value rights for early leavers apply to funded EFRBS, which places certain administrative responsibilities on the EFRBS provider. Unfunded EFRBS do not have a corresponding legislative requirement; however, the scheme may still apply a similar approach to these rights but this will be down to the scheme documentation to dictate.

EFRBS (funded and unfunded) fall within the accounting requirements/scope of FRS17 and IAS19.

The advantages of an Employer-Financed Retirement Benefits Scheme are:

- it avoids employee NI and employer NI liability if the relevant criterion is met;
- it provides employees with an uncapped pension and lump sum and the employer with a valuable recruitment/retention tool;

- it avoids some issues associated with registered schemes such as the SAA, AA, LTA, unauthorised payments and investment restrictions;
- the possibility of wider investment opportunities;
- it could be used to make loans to either the employer or employee. The facility to utilise loans via registered pension schemes are restricted, i.e. not permitted to connected parties via a SIPP but a loan to the sponsoring employer is possible via an SSAS; and
- it's a way of extracting profit from the business in a similar way to dividend but with the deferral of income tax on the individual until benefits are paid (possibly at a time when the individual is subject to a lower rate of tax).

The disadvantages are:

- corporation tax relief is deferred until the member draws benefits which may be years away (any attempt at accelerated CT deductions are extremely likely to provoke HMRC reaction);
- no tax privileges, which are available in alternatives such a pension, ISA, EIS or VCT;
- investment returns are subject to income and capital gains in a UK based trust;
- trust subject to IHT periodic and exit charges on funds;
- high set up and ongoing administration costs (particularly if run offshore);
- onward portability is limited, i.e. if member leaves employment;
- HMRC is viewing these arrangements with suspicion and further legislation is on the way in 2011; and
- offshore EFRBS expose clients to the potential of changing legislation in overseas jurisdictions.

Unfunded Unapproved Retirement Benefit Schemes (UURBS)

These arrangements are a means that some employers used to enhance a selected individual's occupational pension scheme. As with FURBS, they were an individual trust based arrangement between the employee and the employer with the employer acting as the trustee. They differ in that no contributions were actually made at the time to provide the future retirement benefits, which meant that the employee had no tax liability for any employer contributions. However, there is also no guarantee that a pension will be paid in the future. As with FURBS, the pension promise can be exchanged for a lump sum instead. HMRC now refer to UURBS as an Employer-Financed Retirement Benefits Scheme (EFRBS).

76.2.2 Types of Personal Pension Schemes

Individuals who are either self-employed, not employed, whose employer does not offer occupational pension arrangements, or who simply wish to establish a private pension scheme (which may be additional to an occupational one) will do so through either a personal or a stakeholder pension plan. These are invariably money purchase schemes in which contributions accrue in selected fund(s) and are subsequently converted into retirement benefits in the future. There are three main personal schemes: retirement annuities, personal pensions, and stakeholder pensions.

Retirement Annuities

Also known as s. 226 contracts, these were the precursor to personal pensions, which were introduced in July 1988. Contributions can continue to be made to these policies, but no new plans can be established.

> ⚠ **Warning!**
>
> There are a number of features that can apply to these policies of which professional advisers need to be aware.
>
> (1) Under the original legislation the death benefits of these policies could not be written in trust so that on the member's death in service the lump sum death benefit was payable to the estate and so liable to Inheritance Tax. As from 6 April 1980 the member could assign the death benefits on trust. The consequence is that many of these policies are not written in trust at all. This means that if the policyholder dies before taking benefits then the proceeds fall into his estate. Bearing in mind that these policies have to have been started at least 20 years ago, their value may be substantial. Advisers of individuals with retirement annuities should check that they are written in trust.
>
> (2) Many of the older ones were written with a fixed guaranteed annuity rate. Although the terms of the annuity can be inflexible, the rate is generally very attractive compared with what is currently available.
>
> (3) Some of these old funds also have a guaranteed annual interest rate, which can be beneficial during market downturns.
>
> (4) Many are invested in with-profits policies, which may not now be optimal.
>
> (5) Some of the older policies do not pay a full return of the fund value on the death of the policyholder prior to retirement. Some will only pay a return of contributions, and some will pay a return of contributions with interest. It is important that these plans are identified and that the client understands the risks.
>
> (6) Both the Myners Report in 2001 and the Sandler Report in 2002 highlighted that asset allocation decisions can be critical determinants of investment performance. It is therefore vital that this aspect of a client's pension is properly assessed. Investment management issues are covered later in this chapter.

Personal Pension Plans

These were introduced in July 1988. They are usually offered by life offices, and have a range of charging structures. The investment options are set by the life office although many now have a range of external funds links.

> ⚠ **Warning!**
>
> There are a number of features that can apply to these policies of which professional advisers need to be aware.
>
> (1) Although many of these are written under a master trust with a nomination of beneficiary form, this is not necessarily the most inheritance tax efficient solution. Consideration should be given to using a spousal bypass trust as an alternative to the nomination form.
>
> (2) Many older policies are still invested in with-profits, which may no longer be optimal.
>
> (3) Some early personal pensions were written with a fixed guaranteed annuity rate. Although the terms of the annuity can be inflexible, the rate is generally very attractive compared with what is currently available.
>
> (4) Some of these old funds also have a guaranteed annual interest rate, which can be beneficial during market downturns.
>
> (5) Both the Myners Report in 2001 and the Sandler Report in 2002 highlighted that asset allocation decisions can be critical determinants of investment performance. It is therefore vital that this aspect of a client's pensions is properly assessed. Investment management issues are covered later in this chapter.

Stakeholder Pension Plans

Stakeholder pensions were introduced from 6 April 2001. They were an attempt by the government to introduce low cost, simple pension plans in which the charges that could be levied were controlled. At first, no initial charges could be taken and the maximum annual management charge (AMC) was restricted to 1 per cent. Whilst no initial charge can still be taken, the maximum AMC for individuals who join a stakeholder pension scheme on or after 6 April 2005 is now 1.5 per cent for the first 10 years, reducing to 1 per cent thereafter if the individual remains in the scheme. Other mandatory standards required to qualify as a stakeholder pension are that:

- the scheme cannot charge for transfers into or out; and
- the scheme must accept contributions of as low as £20.

> ⚠ **Warning!**
>
> There are a number of features that can apply to these policies of which professional advisers need to be aware.
>
> (1) The earlier schemes had very limited investment options. There may be an opportunity to improve this choice.
>
> (2) As the funds increase over time, the issue of asset allocation becomes increasingly important and a balance needs to be struck between cost and investment risk.

Group Stakeholder Pension Plans

Since 6 April 2001, all employers have been required to provide access to a workplace stakeholder pension scheme unless they meet one of the following exemptions.

(1) They employ fewer than 5 people. Part-time and non-permanent (i.e. agency) employees have to be included in this total.

(2) All employees are offered access to an occupational scheme that they can join within 12 months of commencing employment.

(3) The company has established a group personal pension scheme that meets the following requirements:

   (a) all relevant employees are eligible to join;
   (b) the company makes employer contributions of a minimum three per cent of basic salary to the personal pension;
   (c) the pension scheme is not permitted to impose penalties on those who cease contributions or who transfer to a different arrangement;
   (d) if requested, the company will deduct employees' contributions at source and pay them direct to the scheme.

(4) The company has a restricted membership occupational scheme, but offers the remainder of the workforce the opportunity of joining a group personal pension scheme, which meets the conditions described above.

National Employment Savings Trust (NEST)

The Government will introduce new responsibilities for both employers and employees from 2012 aimed at encouraging greater private pension saving via the workplace. These changes will include the introduction of a new type of multi-employer national pension scheme. Originally these were referred to as 'Personal Accounts' but have now been renamed 'National Employment Savings Trust' (NEST). They will be available for use by employers who do not have, or choose not to use, any existing pension schemes to meet the new obligations.

A qualifying workplace pension scheme will have to provide benefits which are considered to be at least as generous as NEST and will have to operate auto-enrolment and the associated provisions.

To be exempt from using NEST, an employer's defined contribution pension plan must meet the following conditions:

- eligible employees (i.e. those who would otherwise qualify for NEST) must be automatically enrolled;
- contributions must be at least equal to the minimum being paid into NEST (i.e. a minimum overall contribution total of 8 per cent, of which at least 3 per cent must come from the employer);
- the scheme must offer a default investment option so that members do not have to make an investment choice if they do not wish to do so; and
- employees must not be required to complete any forms in order to join the scheme.

Self Invested Personal Pension (SIPP)

A SIPP is simply a personal pension arrangement that allows investors maximum flexibility in the choice of the underlying investments. It is a registered pension scheme for the purposes of Section 150 of the Finance Act 2004, and it is now a financial product regulated by the Financial Services Authority. The following table shows the permitted range of investments within SIPPs. This is not exhaustive, but includes the most common assets that are held:

Stocks & Shares	Cash Deposits	Discretionary Management
Internal Life Office insured funds	Corporate Bonds	OEICS, Unit Trusts and Investment Trusts
Commercial Property & Land	Fixed Interest/Gilts	Futures and Options

There are now (post 6 April 06) new rules governing the level of borrowing in respect of a SIPP. A member can now borrow up to 50 per cent of the value of the SIPP, with the most popular reason being for commercial property purchase.

76.3 Pension Transfers

There are two main types of pension transfer, which may broadly be described as either from an occupational pension scheme, or from a private arrangement.

Occupational Pension Transfer

The Financial Services Authority's (FSA) definition of an occupational pension transfer is a transaction resulting from a decision made, with or without advice from a firm, by a customer who is an individual, to transfer deferred benefits from:

(a) an occupational pension scheme; or
(b) an individual pension contract providing fixed or guaranteed benefits that replaced similar benefits under a defined benefits pension scheme.

Advisers advising on occupational transfers need to be specifically authorised to do so by the company for which they work, and require their recommendations to be signed-off by a designated pension transfer specialist. This specialist needs separate FSA approval in a controlled function (CF24) for which specific qualifications are necessary. At present, a pension transfer specialist must hold one of the following approved examinations.

(1) Fellow or Associate of the Faculty of Actuaries.

(2) Fellow or Associate of the Institute of Actuaries.

(3) Fellow or Associate (by examination) of the Pensions Management Institute.

(4) Fellow or Associate of the Chartered Insurance Institute (including three pensions-related subjects as confirmed by the examining body).

(5) G60 paper of the Chartered Insurance Institute.

(6) Pensions paper of the Chartered Institute of Bankers Professional Investment Certificate.

Personal Pension Transfer

Personal pension transfers are from an existing personal, including stakeholder, pension scheme to another personal pension scheme (including a Self Invested Personal Pension). These switches do not require the oversight of a pension transfer specialist, but still require detailed justification to avoid the accusation of 'churning' (where the main motivation of the switch is the generation of commission for the adviser).

76.3.1 Reasons for Pension Transfer

A pension transfer must always be appropriate for an individual's personal circumstances. Some common reasons to make the consideration of a transfer appropriate are as follows.

(1) Changing jobs. Where the occupational pension is a final salary benefit, or a trust based money purchase scheme, then the default position would be to leave the deferred benefits with that company pension scheme. However, there are circumstances where a transfer might be appropriate, such as:

   (a) consolidation – it is not uncommon for individuals saving for retirement via personal pensions to accumulate a number of separate policies, often with different providers, and invested in a range of funds. This makes it difficult to apply a coherent asset allocation model, and a consistent investment strategy. There may also be issues concerning ease of administration and investment review. Consolidation of all these disparate policies into one plan, normally a SIPP for the investment freedom this offers, can bring the benefits of a coordinated asset allocation, consistent approach to investment risk, ease of investment monitoring and re-balancing, and broader fund selection;

(b) the new scheme will give equivalent added years of service for the transfer;

(c) the old scheme is being 'wound up';

(d) the employee wants to make a clean break, although if this is not justifiable on financial grounds, any emotional decision needs to be challenged.

(2) Charges. Some long established personal pension schemes have higher charges than newer arrangements, and this may justify a transfer if the costs of the transfer do not outweigh the gains.

(3) Lack of investment options. Some pension schemes have a limited range of investment funds, and these tend to be 'internal' funds (i.e. the pension company's own funds). This can inhibit asset allocation strategies. However, these schemes tend to be the lower cost arrangements, meaning that a transfer to a facility with greater investment options may well result in greater costs. This needs to be justified, and may be inappropriate for low value pension plans.

(4) Contract Terms. Some older pension plans, particularly old retirement annuities, may have disadvantageous death benefits, such as only returning the contributions paid, or returning them with interest, rather than paying out the full fund value. Some companies will remove these terms on request, but others may refuse or may make it conditional on evidence of good health.

76.4 Overview of 'Pension Simplification'

FA 2004, s. 149–284 and Schs. 28–36 laid out the rules for a revamped approach to pensions. These rules have been amended by FA 2005 and successive finance acts. The aim of this new approach is to rationalise the plethora of previous regimes and their associated tax regulations, and to replace them with one single regime. The new rules came into effect on 6 April 2006. There are provisions available to protect individuals whose previous schemes were more advantageous than the new rules permit.

76.4.1 Summary of Pension Simplification

Further details are available from the HMRC website, but in summary.

(1) The previous rules that limited contribution levels by reference to age, salary, or type of regime have all been superseded.

(2) There is now no limit on the level of contributions that can be made to a pension plan, but there is instead a limit on the level of tax relief that can be claimed. This does, in effect, place a de facto limit on the contributions since there would be little merit in contributing to a pension if that contribution did not attract income tax relief.

(3) The new regime allows individuals more flexibility in phasing in retirement, since those in occupational pension schemes can now continue to work while drawing their pension.

(4) It is now possible to draw up to 25 per cent of the total pension fund as a tax free lump payment, even from the protected rights element. This tax-free cash is now called Pension Commencement Lump Sum (PCLS).

The earliest age at which one can start to take pension benefits changed to age 55 from 6 April 2010. There are no changes to the rules on premature retirement due to ill-health. Individuals in professions which had a statutory early retirement age (such as footballers), can protect that right. It is also worth remembering that between 2010 and 2020 the minimum age at which women will be able to claim their State Pension will gradually rise from 60 to 65.

There arose a potential issue in that it appeared that those who commenced an unsecured pension prior to the 6th April 2010, who were under the age of 55 at that time, and who wished to transfer funds from one provider to another and/or to continue to draw an income, would thereby incur an unauthorised payment tax charge.

HMRC have now announced that current legislation will be amended to allow those currently under age 55 and receiving an unsecured pension to transfer their unsecured pension fund and continue to take income payments (within permitted limits) without giving rise to unauthorised tax charges. Draft regulations will follow shortly and the legislation will be backdated to 6th April 2010 to include anyone who may have transferred since the change in minimum retirement age. HMRC have confirmed that transfers that now go ahead can rely on the announcement prior to the regulations being passed.

Scheme Rules

Please note that whilst the new pension regime sets the framework of what is legally permissible, it is open to individual scheme rules to set more restrictive conditions if considered appropriate. It is also the case that not all schemes have updated their rules since 6 April 2006. It is therefore important for advisers to check that the scheme itself is as flexible as the actual legislation.

76.4.2 Contributions and Tax Relief

Personal Contributions

Tax relief is available on contributions of up to 100 per cent of relevant UK earnings, subject to legislation enacted in Finance Act 2009 to restrict the tax relief on pension contributions for high earners. Details of these restrictions are at the end of this section, together with planning points.

Contributions are permissible in excess of these amounts, but will not attract tax relief. For personal and stakeholder pensions, tax relief of the basic rate of tax is reclaimed directly by the pension provider and credited to the plan. Higher rate tax relief is reclaimed through an individual's self assessment tax return. For occupational schemes, the tax relief on personal contributions is usually granted through the 'net pay' arrangement.

Tax relief is available on pension contributions up to £3,600 gross per annum, even if the individual has no earnings at all. This provides the opportunity to contribute for a non-working spouse, or even for children.

Employer Contributions

Employers can make unlimited contributions but tax relief will only be allowed if these are seen to have a wholly and exclusively business purpose. The current HMRC guidance is given below.

The new (2006) pension rules permit annual contributions from all sources up to an Annual Allowance without incurring a tax charge on the beneficiary. If total contributions, both personal and employer contributions combined, exceed the Annual Allowance, the excess will be subject to a personal tax charge on the recipient which, given that the earnings will be subject to higher rate of tax, will be 40 per cent.

The Finance Act 2009 announced that legislation will be enacted so that from 6 April 2011 pensions tax relief will be restricted for 'high income individuals', i.e. those with an annual income ('relevant income') of £150,000 or more. This restriction also applies to employer contributions. If the amount of new or additional pension saving, which is an adjusted pension input amount, exceeds the special annual allowance (£20,000) there will be a special annual allowance charge in respect of the excess amount. The individual scheme member who benefits from the new pension saving is liable to the charge. This includes new or additional pension saving made by the individual, on behalf of the individual (such as by a relative of the member) or in respect of the individual (by the individual's employer).

A late amendment was added before Royal Assent was granted. The amendment applies where the mean average amount of non regular (i.e. not monthly or quarterly) pension contributions in 2006–07, 2007–08 and 2008–09 exceeds £20,000. Under these circumstances, an amount greater than £20,000 can form the protected pension input but is restricted to a maximum of £30,000.

Subsequent to the Finance Act, in the Pre-Budget Statement, the Government announced that the anti-forestalling regime is extended by replacing the current £150,000 relevant income threshold with a £130,000 threshold as from 9 December 2009. The Government also announced that tax relief will not be restricted for those with income (which must include pension contributions made personally and gift aid contributions for these purposes) below £130,000, even if total income when employer pension contributions are included exceeds £150,000. But this means:

- if income including own pension contributions and gift aid contributions exceeds £130,000 then employer contributions must be added to determine if the £150,000 threshold is exceeded; and
- otherwise there is no back tracking on restricting relief if income exceeds £150,000; this will result in the erosion of higher rate relief until it is restricted to the basic rate above £180,000.

Planning points

The Budget changes to income tax where the basic personal allowance is reduced by £1 for every £2 of adjusted net income above £100,000 can present planning opportunities. Making a pension contribution to reduce adjusted net income to below the £100,000 threshold may mean that the income tax personal allowance is preserved. This could provide an effective tax relief rate of up to 60 per cent on the tranche of earnings between £100,000 and £112,950 (assuming current (2009–10) personal allowance).

Many people may benefit from a review of salary exchange opportunities, to reduce National Insurance Contributions and increase tax credits. Putting these arrangements in place now could preserve benefits in the future if changes similar to those announced in FA 2009 for pension contributions by high earners are introduced on a wider scale without warning.

The Finance Act 2009 has build in anti-forestalling measures to prevent individuals from acting to circumvent the rules, for example by sacrificing salary for pension contributions in order to reduce their income below the £130,000 threshold. For this reason, it is important that those with relevant income above £130,000 assess the impact of these changes on their eligibility for higher rate tax relief. They will continue to benefit from 40 per cent tax relief on any protected pension input and on contributions within the special annual allowance in 2010–11. However, it will no longer be appropriate for them to

> make additional pension contributions where their pension savings will be above £20,000 per annum. Where they currently have no 'protected pension input' they should look to fully utilise their £20,000 special annual allowance for 2010–11.
>
> These high earners will need to investigate alternative means of long-term retirement planning. This may involve structures that offer both tax advantages and flexibility for retirement planning and they may also benefit from specialist advice on tax-led investments offering income tax reductions.

The Annual Allowance

The Annual Allowance limits the amount of tax relief available on total pension savings (by both the individual and where applicable by their employer on their behalf) in any particular tax year.

Where the increase in 'pension savings' exceeds the Annual Allowance in relation to a tax year, an Annual Allowance charge will arise.

The Annual Allowance for the current tax year (2010–2011) is £255,000 (frozen for the five following tax years).

For defined contribution schemes, 'pension savings' will be the total contributions paid by the employee and their employer. For defined benefit schemes, there is a more complex calculation where the annual increase in pension entitlement is capitalised using a factor of 10:1.

Care must be taken as total 'pension savings' are calculated by reference to the 'pension input period' (as defined in legislation) which is specific to each pension scheme and may not coincide with the tax year and so professional advice is recommended for those who are likely to be affected.

The Annual Allowance charge is a tax charge on the individual. The amount of the charge is 40 per cent of the amount in excess of the allowance and is declared and paid through the individuals' self assessment tax return.

It is important to note however, that the annual allowance charge does not apply in the year in which all retirement benefits are taken. This is covered later in this chapter.

HMRC Guidance on Interpretation of 'Wholly and Exclusively'

The latest guidance is contained in BIM 47106. It confirms that a pension contribution paid by an employer to a registered pension scheme in respect of any director or employee will be an allowable expense, unless there is a non-trade purpose for the payment, provided it is part of a remuneration package paid 'wholly and exclusively' for the purposes of the trade.

For employer contributions paid for a controlling director or an employee who is a close relative or friend of the director where there is no unconnected employee with a comparable remuneration package, HMRC will consider whether the amount of the overall remuneration package, not just the amount of the pension contribution, was paid 'wholly and exclusively' for the purposes of the employer's trade.

HMRC has stated that local inspectors have been advised that it is unlikely there will be a non-business purpose in respect of controlling directors. There should be no difficulties with other directors, or employees who are close relatives or friends, of the controlling director, provided that the remuneration package is commercial 'and commensurate with the duties undertaken'.

Where a local inspector thinks that a remuneration package is demonstrably in excess of what is commercially reasonable, they may rule that the payment is not 'wholly or exclusively' for the purposes of the trade and, as an ultimate sanction, they might decide that it is in fact part of the director's remuneration and rule that it is taxable as earnings of the director rather than the employee. The text of the guidance is at *www.hmrc.gov.uk/manuals/bimmanual/BIM47106.htm* and states:

> '**BIM47106 – Specific deductions: staffing costs: remuneration payments to friends and relatives: wholly and exclusively**
>
> **Controlling directors**
>
> Controlling directors are often the driving force behind the company. Where the controlling director is also the person whose work generates the company's income then the level of the remuneration package is a commercial decision and it is unlikely that there will be a non-business purpose for the level of the remuneration package. It should be noted that remuneration does not include entitlement to dividends arising in the capacity of shareholder.
>
> **Other employees**
>
> Where the remuneration package paid in respect of other directors (or an employee who is a close relative or friend of the business proprietor or controlling director) is in line with that paid to unconnected employees, you should accept that the package is paid wholly and exclusively for the purposes of the trade.
>
> However, precise comparisons are not always possible. Careful consideration of the facts will be required in worthwhile cases to establish whether the level of the remuneration paid to a friend or relative of the proprietor is commercial and commensurate with the duties undertaken. The chosen comparators need to have similar qualifications, experience and job description.
>
> It may be helpful to consider variations in the level of remuneration over time; however it is important to establish the reasons for such variations, which may include an element of catch up. One element of the remuneration package where this may apply is with regard to employer contributions to the employee's pension (BIM46035).

If the amounts involved indicate that a remuneration package is demonstrably in excess of what is commercially reasonable, then there may be other avenues to consider in addition to the question of whether an element of the payment is wholly or exclusively for the purposes of the trade. In particular it may also be appropriate to consider whether the settlements legislation might apply or if payment is in fact part of the controlling director's remuneration or the proprietor's drawings rather than market rate remuneration of the relative/friend employee.

Whose remuneration package?

If a payment or part of a payment to a relative or close friend of a director appears not to form part of their remuneration, to the extent that it appears to exceed what is reasonably commercial, then it may actually be part of the director's own remuneration. So although the payment may be wholly and exclusively for the purposes of the trade, it will in the following circumstances be taxable in the hands of the director rather than the employee if the spouse or close relative is simply acting as a conduit for the director, then the payment may be taxable as earnings of the director (ITEPA 2003, s. 62), or the payment is made to a relative or a member of the director's family or household (ITEPA 2003, s. 201(2) and s. 721 (5), see EIM 20504) then it may be taxable on the director under the benefits legislation.'

Settlements legislation

Where remuneration that cannot be justified on ordinary commercial grounds is paid to a director/employee who is the husband, wife or minor child of the controlling shareholder(s) or director(s), liability to tax may also arise under the settlements legislation in Pt. XV ICTA 1988, see TSEM 4000 onwards.

High earners

The Finance Act 2009 enacted legislation will be enacted so that from 6 April 2011 pensions tax relief will be restricted for 'high income individuals', i.e. those with an annual income ('relevant income') of £150,000 or more. From that level of income, the value of pensions tax relief will be tapered down until it is 20 per cent for those on incomes over £180,000, making it worth the same for each pound of contribution to pension entitlement as for a basic rate taxpayer. The Government will consult on how these rules should apply to high income individuals who are members of defined benefit pension schemes and on valuing related employer contributions. However, the Coalition Government is reviewing the whole issue of pension contribution levels and tax relief, and this situation may well change.

To forestall planning ahead of the start of this regime, the new rules restrict tax relief to the basic rate on some contributions made on or after 22 April 2009, and 9 December 2010 for the subsequent Pre-Budget statement, or impose a tax charge in some circumstances where changes to existing defined benefit schemes are made on or after that date.

These changes do not apply if:

- 'relevant income' is less than £150,000 in each of the current tax year and the two previous tax years (£130,000 from 9 December 2009);
- normal ongoing pension saving arrangements in place before 22 April 2009 continue unaltered (a 'protected pension input'), even if relevant income is £150,000 or more in any tax year from 2007–08 to 2010–11 (£130,000 from 9 December 2009); or
- overall annual pension savings in 2010–11 is less than the 'special annual allowance'.

Looking now at the new terminology:

Relevant income is not the same as 'adjusted net income'; it is total income (not just salary) chargeable to income tax plus any deductions from employment income for pension contributions made under net pay arrangements and before deductions for personal allowances or other reliefs less total pension contributions for which relief is due but up to a maximum of £20,000 only and less deductions for trading losses and Gift Aid payments. However, any employment income forgone as a result of a salary exchange arrangement made on or after 22 April 2009 where salary is given up in return for pension contributions or benefits must be included in the calculation of 'relevant income' for the purposes of testing it against the £150,000 threshold (£130,000 from 9 December 2009).

Protected pension input can mean one of two things. Firstly a protected pension input can arise from an individual's normal pension savings arrangements in place before 22 April 2009, including salary exchange arrangements, which:

(a) are not changed and; and
(b) involve contributions paid quarterly or more frequently, i.e. annual or single contributions are not protected if in excess of the special annual allowance.

Secondly, a protected pension input can arise in respect of an individual's membership of a pension scheme set up after 22 April 2009 or where an individual joins a new employer with an established pension scheme already in place. The pension scheme concerned must be either an occupational pension scheme or a public service pension scheme or a group personal pension scheme (Group stakeholders and SIPPs are included in this category). The pension scheme must relate to the employment of the individual and there must be at least 20 other arrangements for other members under the same scheme accruing pension on the same basis. Only contractual contributions can count towards the protected pension input and any voluntary contributions or contributions used to secure added years cannot be included.

Special annual allowance is set at £20,000. This is **not** in addition to the protected pension input, i.e. if the protected pension input is less than £20,000, a client can top-up to this amount in 2010–2011 and still get tax relief at up to 40 per cent but if the protected pension input is more than £20,000, any additional pensions saving by someone with relevant income of £150,000 (£130,000 from 9 December 2009) or more will be restricted to 20 per cent tax relief. If the contribution is paid by the employer it will generate a tax charge on the individual.

Subsequent to the budget statement, and not part of original proposals, is an amendment added before Royal Assent was granted. The amendment applies where the mean average amount of non regular (i.e. not monthly or quarterly) pension contributions in 2006–07, 2007–08 and 2008–09 exceeds £20,000. Under these circumstances, an amount greater than £20,000 can form the protected pension input but is restricted to a maximum of £30,000.

The special annual allowance will operate alongside the standard annual allowance (£255,000 for 2010/11). Where an individual's pension savings exceed both allowances, any tax charge will be adjusted to avoid any double recovery of tax relief that might otherwise arise.

> ⚠ **Warning!**
> It is important to note that if those with incomes in excess of £130,000, but with protected pension inputs above the special annual allowance, then transfer their pensions to a new scheme, this will raise a number of issues, as discussed below.

On the 19th March 2010 legislation came into effect that permits an individual to transfer their Protected Pension Input from one pension scheme to another, as long as certain strict conditions are met. The effect is to maintain the Protected Pension Input amount and avoid any special annual allowance of £20,000. This is being challenged with HMRC at the time of writing, but these are the proposals as they stand.tax charge for the 2010–11 tax year. In order to qualify certain conditions must be met, namely:

- some or all of the pension input amount under the old arrangement qualified as a protected pension input, i.e. was in place prior to the 22nd April 2009/9th December 2009 and was paid at least quarterly;
- the individual had been an active member of the old scheme;
- the individual ceased active membership of the scheme for which they have a Protected Pension Input, after the 22nd April 2009;
- the individual starts the new arrangement to which the Protected Pension Input is being transferred no later than 3 months after cessation of the old scheme;
- for money purchase schemes, the Protected Pension Input does not increase (except as contractually agreed) and there has been no failure to pay the contributions on a quarterly or more frequent basis;
- the Protected Pension Input is transferred to 'a new arrangement'; and
- the old arrangement is not reactivated.

Where the individual is a member of an employer-sponsored scheme, the following are the only two circumstances that will allow an individual to transfer their Protected Pension Input from one scheme to another:

(1) where the individual's employer rearranges their pension scheme arrangements; or

(2) where an employer takes over another employer's business and the individual was a member of the 'taken over' employer's pension scheme.

If the employer's existing scheme is a DB scheme, an individual's Protected Pension Input can only be transferred and remain protected if the new scheme is also a DB scheme and the rules of the new scheme are not materially different and the reason for the new scheme is solely due to one of the two reasons above.

Where the current employer's scheme is a money purchase scheme then a Protected Pension Input can be transferred and protected even if it moves between an occupational scheme and personal pension, so long as the reason for the change is as above and the same employer sponsors both schemes and all the other criteria are met. The complexity of these rules is illustrated by HMRC's definition of a 'new arrangement'.

The table below shows the type of arrangement an individual may hold in any existing pension scheme and whether a protected pension input could be successfully redirected.

Type of Arrangement already held in the receiving registered pension scheme	Can PPI be retained if redirected?
a) No existing arrangement, i.e. new scheme	✓
b) Fully Uncrystallised Non-Protected Rights only	X
c) Fully Uncrystallised Protected Right only	✓
d) Partially Uncrystallised and Partially Crystallised Non-Protected Rights only (Pre Age 77)	X
e) Partially Uncrystallised and Partially Crystallised Protected Rights only (Pre Age 77)*	✓
f) Partially Uncrystallised Non-Protected Rights and Uncrystallised Protected Rights (Pre Age 77)	X
g) Partially Uncrystallised Non-Protected Rights and Partially Uncrystallised Protected Rights (Pre Age 77)	X

Type of Arrangement already held in the receiving registered pension scheme	Can PPI be retained if redirected?
h) Fully Crystallised Non-Protected Rights only (Pre Age 77: USP)	✔
i) Fully Crystallised Protected Rights only (Pre Age 77: USP)	✔*
j) Pre A Day Rights only	✔
k) Fully Crystallised Non-Protected Rights and Fully Crystallised Protected Rights (Pre Age 77)*	✔*

* As Non-Protected Rights will be introduced to the registered pension scheme, the proportionality rules will have to be applied.

Please note that it is NOT possible to contribute to a pension plan after age 75, although the requirement to crystallise benefits at age 75 has been pushed back to age 77 pending a wider review by the Government.

Pensions savings means savings in all registered pension schemes including:

- final salary (defined benefit) schemes;
- money purchase (defined contribution) schemes;
- contributions paid by individuals, anyone on their behalf and by their employers; and
- savings in non-UK pension schemes that benefit from UK tax relief.

The implications in summary are that:

- those who have never had relevant income of £150,000 or more are unaffected;
- those who have relevant income in excess of £150,000 but who continue with their regular (at least quarterly) pattern of contributions or with normal benefit accrual are also unaffected; but
- if relevant income in any of the current or previous two tax years is £150,000 or more, then tax relief on any annual, single or additional regular pension savings, will be limited to 20 per cent unless total pension savings are less than £20,000.

Note: that pensions savings made between 6–21 April 2009 reduce the special annual allowance but are eligible for full tax relief. Unlike the standard annual allowance, the special annual allowance applies even where benefits are fully crystallised before the end of the tax year. It also applies where the taxpayer dies (unless a defined benefit scheme with at least 20 members) or takes ill-health early retirement (unless an occupational, public service or GPP scheme).

If tax relief is restricted or additional tax becomes payable because pensions savings exceed the special annual allowance in 2010–11, employers will continue

Pensions

to receive full relief on their contributions into employees' pensions through corporation tax and NICs.

So, if the client falls into the high income bracket, and the pension payments either by him or his employer have been on a single basis, or paid less frequently than quarterly (i.e. annually or six-monthly), then that client is caught.

Refund of contributions

Because the new rules have been brought in with immediate effect, people who are above the income limit for the new charge in the year the contribution was made may find that they have inadvertently exceeded the special annual allowance through making non-regular contributions to personal pension schemes (including retirement annuity contracts) and additional voluntary contributions (AVCs). In such cases, if the scheme rules allow, it may be possible for the pension scheme administrator to refund those contributions to the individual. The legislation refers to a refund of contributions in these circumstances as a 'contributions refund lump sum'.

A lump sum payment can qualify as a 'contributions refund lump sum' only if it is paid after the end of the tax year in which the contributions were made. The first year this applies to are contributions made in 2009–10.

If the scheme does pay a 'contributions refund lump sum':

- the scheme administrator will be liable for a tax charge which is designed to recoup the rate at which tax relief was given on the contributions (40 per cent for refunds made in 2010–11);
- the scheme administrator will pay the tax charge through their Accounting for Tax return for the quarter in which the refund was made; and
- if the individual has already reported the excess over the special annual allowance charge on their self assessment tax return and later receives a refund, they will need to amend their tax return so that the correct amount of tax is collected.

⚠ **Warning!**

In the Emergency Budget of 2010, it was stated that from 6 April 2011 there will still be restrictions on tax reliefs, but the complex rules which the previous Labour government intended will be abandoned. The present coalition government has made clear that it still needs to raise the £3.5 billion of revenue through restricting pensions tax relief as would have been generated by the Labour measures. However, the government will consult with the pensions industry on alternative ways to implement restrictions. Reducing the annual allowance (currently set at £255,000 for the next 5 tax years) is an alternative which will be considered. Provisional Treasury analysis suggests that an annual allowance in the region of £30,000 to £45,000 might deliver the necessary yield. This would also have the added advantage of recreating a level playing field for

> all pension savers and maintaining the principle of tax relief at the highest marginal rate on personal contributions.

76.4.3 Retirement Benefits

Lifetime Allowance

As well as controlling pension contributions through tax reliefs, the total amount that can be accumulated, without penalties, in pension funds is restricted by the 'Lifetime Allowance'. The Lifetime Allowance is £1.8m (2010–11) and is frozen for the next five years. Any amounts in excess of the Lifetime Allowance when benefits are taken will be subject to a tax charge, the amount depending upon how the surplus is taken. If the excess is taken as a lump sum then the charge is 55 per cent on the excess. Where the surplus is used to provide retirement income, then the tax charge on the excess is 25 per cent, but the income itself is also taxed under PAYE and that will, given the limit of the lifetime allowance, be 40 per cent (currently).

Individuals whose pension funds exceeded the Lifetime Allowance on 6 April 2006 should have protected their funds from the Lifetime Allowance Charge by submitting an application to HMRC by 5 April 2009. It is now too late to register if this has not been done.

Primary Protection

Primary protection is a transitional arrangement for members of approved pension arrangements whose total pension benefits as at 5 April 2006 exceeded the Lifetime Allowance for the 2006–07 tax year of £1.5m. The pre-5 April 2006 value will be indexed in parallel with the indexation of the statutory lifetime allowance up to the date that benefits are taken.

Those who have registered will have received a certificate from HMRC with a unique reference number giving details of the enhanced lifetime allowance for that individual.

Enhanced Protection

Enhanced protection was available to anyone who felt that their pension plan may exceed the Lifetime Allowance in the future, regardless of the actual value of their pension on 5 April 2006. To claim enhanced protection, an individual must have personally notified HMRC of his or her intention to rely on this protection, using the 'Protection of Existing Rights' form (available from the HMRC website), which had to reach HMRC on or before 5 April 2009. Those who have registered will have received a certificate from HMRC with a unique reference number giving details of the enhanced lifetime allowance for that individual.

However, it is an absolute requirement that no further contributions be paid after 6 April 2006 or the enhanced protection will be lost. Under enhanced protection the entire value of the fund is protected from the lifetime charge. It should also be noted that if any rights existed at 5 April 2006 that were in excess of those permitted by the maximum benefit limits then in force, those rights must have been surrendered before an application for enhanced protection was made.

Loss of Enhanced Protection

Enhanced protection will be lost in the following circumstances.

(1) A contribution to a money purchase arrangement is made to a pension plan after 5 April 2006 either by an individual or by an employer on an individual's behalf. This means that pension contributions must have ceased by 5 April 2006. Contracted-out rebates and premiums for life assurance cover under existing pension arrangements may continue without affecting enhanced protection.

(2) Accrual of benefits under a final salary pension scheme above the permitted limits.

(3) A transfer out is made that is not a 'permitted transfer'.

(4) A transfer in is received that is not a 'permitted transfer'.

It is therefore important that where clients have protected pension arrangements, specialist advice is taken before any changes are made.

Tax Free Lump Sum

Subject to the scheme rules, it is possible to take 25 per cent tax-free cash (now called Pension Commencement Lump Sum) from all pension arrangements. This lump sum must be taken by age 77, after which time no cash payment of any kind is permitted. In some cases, this 25 per cent is substantially less than what was available under the previous legislation. In these circumstances the higher tax-free lump sum can be preserved.

There are three ways in which the tax-free cash may be protected, depending on the specific pension arrangements and value.

(1) **Primary protection applies and tax-free cash entitlement at A-day exceeds £375,000.** In this case the higher lump sum entitlement as at 5 April 2006 is indexed in parallel with the indexation of the statutory lifetime allowance up to the date that benefits are taken.

(2) **Enhanced protection applies and tax-free cash entitlement at A-day exceeds £375,000.** In this case the higher lump sum entitlement is expressed as a percentage of the fund value at 5 April 2006. This percentage is then used to calculate the tax-free lump sum when benefits are taken.

(3) **Neither enhanced nor primary protection applies and tax-free cash at A-

day is greater than 25 per cent of the fund value. In this case the higher lump sum entitlement as at 5 April 2006 is indexed in parallel with the indexation of the statutory Lifetime Allowance up to the date that benefits are taken plus 25 per cent of the notional post A Day value, if this is a positive value. If it is not a positive value, then just the indexation in line with the increase in the LTA is added. This form of protection only applies in the existing pension arrangement and will be lost if there is a transfer away, unless part of a 'bulk transfer'.

76.5 Types of Retirement Income Arrangements

One of the objectives of 'pension simplification' is to provide more flexibility as to how and when retirement benefits can be taken, subject to the individual pension scheme rules. There are now four broad choices.

(1) Take a scheme pension. This provides a guaranteed income for life paid directly out of the scheme assets.

(2) Buy a lifetime annuity. This can be provided either from an occupational money purchase pension or from a personal pension. This involves exchanging the value in the pension plan for a guaranteed income for life.

(3) Take an 'Unsecured Pension'. This is the new terminology for 'Income Drawdown'. It involves drawing an income directly from an invested pension fund until a maximum age of 77.

(4) For those aged 77+, take an 'Alternatively Secured Pension'. This is similar to Unsecured Pension, but with stricter conditions.

The Emergency Budget 2010 announced some changes to the rules for registered pension schemes, specifically that the requirement to purchase an annuity at age 75 would be abolished from April 2011. In the meantime, the age 75 limit will be replaced for those reaching 75 on or after 22 June 2010, with an age 77 limit, while the Government fine tunes the new rules. The current Government proposals, which are out for consultation, with the intention of enacting changes in the Finance Bill 2011 are:

Basic proposals

- there will be no specific age for compulsory annuitisation;
- the age at which an individual will cease to receive tax relief on contributions will remain at 75;
- tax free pension commencement lump sums can be taken at any age after 55;
- unsecured pensions (USP) can be paid for the whole of an individual's retirement and will continue to have a maximum annual income limit;
- the maximum annual income limit will be reviewed to ensure that it remains appropriate with advancing age;
- unlimited withdrawals in excess of the maximum annual income limit will be

allowed subject to the individual being able to show that they have secured sufficient minimum income to prevent them falling back on the State (see Minimum Income Requirement below);
- alternatively secured pensions (ASP) will cease to exist;
- no change to the current rules requiring pension savings to be tested against the lifetime allowance at age 75; and
- trivial pension payments will be available at any age.

Death benefits

- uncrystallised funds lump sum death benefits accessed prior to age 75 will continue to be paid free of tax;
- uncrystallised funds lump sum death benefits paid out after age 75 will be subject to a tax relief recovery charge;
- the tax relief Recovery charge is expected to be around 55 per cent;
- any lump sum death benefits paid out of crystallised funds will be subject to the tax relief recovery charge;
- the tax relief recovery charge will not apply to funds used to provide income for dependants, although the income will continue to be taxed at the recipient's marginal rate; and
- restrictions on limiting the payment of value protected lump sums on annuities beyond age 75 will be removed although payments will be subject to the tax relief recovery charge as detailed above.

Minimum income requirement

The Minimum Income Limit (MIR) is intended to be a reasonable proxy for an income above which an individual is unlikely to need to fall back on the State should they prematurely exhaust pension savings. It must be in payment, guaranteed for life and take into account reasonable expectations of future living costs.

The proposed requirements for MIR are:

- only pension income will be taken into account. The following will constitute pension income;
    (a) State pensions;
    (b) scheme pensions from occupational schemes that are increased annually by at least the limited price indexation (LPI);
    (c) any guaranteed annuity income increasing by at least LPI (this would include index linked payments and those with fixed increases of at least 2.5% p.a.);
- testing will be at the time the individual wishes to take income in excess of the normal maximum annual income limit;
- the MIR may possibly be higher for younger ages and may be set differently for couples as against single pensioners; and
- it is to be reviewed on a regular basis.

76.5.1 Scheme Pension

A scheme pension is one where the occupational pension scheme trustees make the decision regarding the form of the retirement benefits rather than the member. These benefits can either be paid direct from the existing pension funds, or by the purchase of an annuity, purchased in the name of the trustees using the designated scheme assets.

76.5.2 Pension Annuities

A pension annuity is simply the exchange of a lump sum for a guaranteed income which is payable for the whole of an individual's life. The income that is paid will depend on several factors, some of which the individual can choose, and some which cannot be chosen, such as age, gender and health. The main optional benefits include escalation, guaranteed periods, spouse benefits, and investment type. Some of these will result in a comparatively modest reduction in income, such as a five-year guarantee period, while others will reduce the initial payment by a substantial amount. The following is a description of the major factors impacting on annuity rates:

Age and Gender

The life expectancy of each applicant for an annuity is assessed by reference to mortality tables, and is dependent both on the actual age and the gender of the individual. As a rule, women live longer than men and so a woman of the same age as a man would, all other factors being equal, obtain a lower annual income. However, the total amount paid (the whole of life value) should be the same. The man may obtain a higher initial pension, but would receive it for a shorter period of time if he met the statistical norms.

Health

Because the income from an annuity depends on average mortality tables, individuals with impaired lives (i.e. in poor health) can obtain enhanced rates, which can sometimes be significant. Applicants for such annuities have to be medically underwritten so that an assessment can be made as to the deviation from the actuarial norm. Conditions that generally lead to enhanced rates include smoking, diabetes, heart complaints, cancer, liver and kidney damage, or major surgery. Any individual who has a history of poor medical health should consider the option of an impaired life annuity.

Lifestyle

There is an increasing trend for some annuity companies to weight longevity depending on social factors such as an applicant's previous employment and geographic residence. A labourer from a deprived area of Scotland may qualify for a higher annuity than a clerical worker from the south coast of England with all other factors being the same.

The above factors are, at the point of annuity commencement, immutable. Those that follow are, largely, issues of choice.

Frequency of Payment

Annuity payments can be monthly, quarterly, half yearly, or annually. In addition, the payment can be in advance or in arrears. Those paid in arrears will pay a slightly higher rate. Whilst this may be very modest on a monthly basis, the difference may be significant if paid annually since, in effect, the individual is now one year older on the date of the first payment. The decision as to which is appropriate will depend on the individual's cash flow requirements. Those selecting payments substantially in arrears should consider having the annuity set up 'with proportion'. This means that on death a final payment of the outstanding amount due since last payment would be made. Those with policies 'without proportion' would not receive this payment.

Guaranteed period

An annuity with a guaranteed period provides the reassurance that a benefit will still be available if death occurs within the guaranteed period. The inclusion of a guaranteed period will reduce the initial income. The older the annuitant, or the shorter the assessed longevity, the more expensive the guarantee will be.

Joint Life Pensions

It is often the case that an annuitant wishes to include his/her spouse/partner in the annuity in order to provide for their future financial security. The spouse can either be a named spouse (i.e. the one to whom the individual is married at the time) or any spouse at the time of the annuitant's death. This latter option will be more expensive. It is also possible to include a financial dependant. The extent of the reversionary annuity is decided at the outset, and is usually 50 per cent, 67 per cent or 100 per cent. The amount by which the annuitant's own annuity will reduce in order to pay for this reversionary benefit will depend on the age and health of the spouse/partner, and the residual percentage payable. Where a guaranteed period has also been selected, it should be considered whether or not the spouse/partner annuity is with or without 'overlap'. Most such pensions do not have an overlap, meaning that the reversionary annuity will not start until the end of the guaranteed period.

76.5.3 Conventional Annuities

A conventional annuity is simply the exchange of a lump sum for a guaranteed, defined, regular income for life. Since the only variable between the different providers is the annuity rate (i.e. the amount of income purchased per £1,000 of capital), purchasers should shop around for the best rate. This is known as the 'open market option', and all companies who provide pension arrangements have to offer their investors the option of using it. Some companies do not offer their own annuities, and thus the open market option is the only choice. Others do not wish to take on large amounts of annuity business, and therefore offer unfavourable rates. Some companies specialise in annuities, and offer competitive rates, and these are the companies to identify. Conventional annuities offer a range of options, among which are:

Level Annuities

The level annuity pays a fixed rate of interest, which is established at the start of the contract and is based on the current rates at the time. This rate will then not change. These annuities are appropriate for those who need the certainty of a fixed income for life, or the highest initial income and who are not concerned about income erosion due to inflation.

Escalating Annuities

The solution to the inflation issue is an escalating annuity. This is one where income increases each year in line with a level agreed at the outset. This may be linked to an index, such as the retail price index, or increase by a fixed amount such as three per cent or five per cent. Choosing this option will result in a lower starting income than the equivalent level annuity, with a correlation between the level of the escalation and the amount of the initial income. In considering the benefit of an escalating annuity, age is an important factor since the compounding effect of inflation bites hardest over the longer term. It is also important in order to assess the 'pay-back' period. Since the initial income is reduced, there will be a number of years before the escalating income increases to the same level as that which could have been purchased with a level annuity, and for that period the annuitant is worse off. Once the crossover point has been reached, there will then be another number of years until the increased income compensates for the lost income in the early years. Depending on the age of the annuitant at outset, the break-even point may be longer than the average life expectancy for the individual. The Table below makes this point based on a comparison of a level annuity (with a rate of 7.2 per cent) for a 65-year-old male with a fund of £100,000, and a five per cent escalating annuity starting at about a third less. It can be seen that it will take about 11 years to catch up with the income payable initially from the level annuity, and 20 years to break even.

Comparison of level and escalating annuities

Year	Level annuity	Annuity escalating at 5%	Cumulative additional income from level annuity
1	£7,200	£4,464	£2,736
2	£7,200	£4,687	£5,249

3	£7,200	£4,922	£7,527
4	£7,200	£5,168	£9,560
5	£7,200	£5,426	£11,334
6	£7,200	£5,697	£12,836
7	£7,200	£5,982	£14,054
8	£7,200	£6,281	£14,973
9	£7,200	£6,595	£15,577
10	£7,200	£6,925	£15,852
11	£7,200	£7,271	£15,781
12	£7,200	£7,635	£15,346
13	£7,200	£8,017	£14,529
14	£7,200	£8,418	£13,312
15	£7,200	£8,838	£11,673
16	£7,200	£9,280	£9,593
17	£7,200	£9,744	£7,049
18	£7,200	£10,232	£4,017
19	£7,200	£10,743	£474
20	£7,200	£11,280	−£3,606

The decision will largely depend on when the greater cash flow is needed.

Guaranteed Annuities

Some older retirement annuities and personal pensions have 'guaranteed annuities'. These are normally, but not exclusively, pension plans that are invested in with-profits funds. These contracts guaranteed, at the outset, a set level of income per £1,000 of capital, payable at retirement. Many of these guarantees have rates that are far in excess of what could now be achieved through an open market option. Some have very restrictive terms, such as single life only with no guarantee period, to be taken at a fixed retirement age, but others are more flexible. It is essential that these guarantees are identified, and an assessment made as to their importance in each specific case.

Capital Protected Annuities

Capital protected annuities were introduced under the new pensions regime from 6 April 2006. They will repay, on death before age 77, the balance between the initial amount used to purchase the annuity and any income paid out. This lump sum is taxable at 35 per cent. Just as with Unsecured Pension, there is no mortality cross subsidy, and so the annuity rate from these annuities will be lower than from a non-protected annuity.

76.5.4 Investment Options while drawing income

It is possible to start drawing an income from a pension fund while having that pension fund invested. This can be achieved through Unsecured Pension or Alternatively Secured Pension (covered below) or through an investment-linked annuity. With these annuities, there are options that can be made as to how the annuity is invested, and this will depend on the risk that the annuitant is prepared to take. Whilst there is the potential for a level of income that increases more than that available from a conventional annuity, unlike an escalating annuity these increases are not guaranteed and the income could well drop. The initial amount of the annuity is thus not the most important factor, since issues like investment choice, flexibility, financial strength, past performance, asset allocation, and investment expertise are all significant. The main options follow.

With-profits Annuities

In addition to the individual's age, initial purchase price, and other options, the income that an individual receives from a with-profits annuity will depend on the performance of the company's with-profits fund. This is in turn linked to the asset allocation of the underlying fund.

In order to set the initial year's income, the applicant has to choose an anticipated bonus rate (ABR), which is his guess of how much the return will be in that first year. The guess will be restricted to a range from zero per cent to a maximum, which recently has been less than five per cent. At the end of the year, the pension provider will apply a retrospective bonus rate based on how the fund has actually performed. If this is more than the selected ABR, then the income for the coming year will be increased. The converse is also true. Some individuals play safe by deliberately selecting a zero per cent ABR; whilst this will mean that the first year's income is low, this level is guaranteed not to reduce. On the other hand each year that the provider declares a bonus will see the income increase. Once selected, the ABR cannot be changed in future.

Unit-linked Annuities

Unit-linked annuities work in a similar way to their with-profits cousins, but are aligned to the provider's unit-linked funds. The initial income is set by the selection of an anticipated growth rate (AGR), and the ongoing income will be determined by the extent to which the actual returns exceed or under-perform the anticipated growth. However, unlike the with profits fund, selecting a growth rate of zero per cent will not ensure a guaranteed minimum income since the fund could fall in value.

Some providers permit the funds chosen at the outset to be switched, or even to move to a conventional annuity.

Pensions

Unsecured Pension

Unsecured pension is the new terminology for what used to be known as 'Income Drawdown'. The main feature is that it allows an individual to start to take benefits without committing to buying an annuity. It allows the customer to draw an income from their pension while leaving their fund invested. The features of an Unsecured Pension are as follows.

(1) It is available for individuals between the ages of 50 (55 from 2010) and 77.

(2) The decision to take any Pension Commencement Lump Sum (previously the tax-free lump sum) has to be made at the outset. If PCLS is not taken then, it cannot be taken at a later date.

(3) There is no requirement to draw a minimum level of income.

(4) If an income is required, this can be any amount up to a maximum of 120 per cent of the amount payable on a single life annuity basis, as laid down by the Government Actuary Department tables for an individual of that age.

(5) This income limit is reviewed every five years.

(6) The income amount can be varied at will.

(7) If the Unsecured Pension is being taken by way of a Self Invested Personal Pension, then the full range of investment options are available.

(8) It must be recognised that an Unsecured Pension is a higher risk retirement option than the purchase of an annuity, and advisers who work in this area should have specialist qualifications. Unsecured Pension is not recommended for smaller pension plans, generally under £100,000, and individuals need to have the capacity, as well as the attitude, to tolerate investment risk. The following risks are associated with Unsecured Pensions plans:

  (a) the charges could be high, which would erode the investment return;
  (b) if the fund remains invested in the stock market, it may reduce in value yet still be required to deliver the same income; and
  (c) since Unsecured Pension does not benefit from mortality cross subsidy (the 'topping-up' effect on the plans of others by those individuals who die before their actuarially calculated age whilst taking an annuity), the underlying investments need to out-perform the returns of a conventional annuity in order to maintain the same eventual purchasing power when an annuity is bought.

(9) On death before age 77 whilst in Unsecured Pension, the following options are available:

  (a) a spouse can continue taking Unsecured Pension, based on rates determined by his/her own age, until age 77;
  (b) a spouse can choose to buy an annuity subject to any income not exceeding the maximum amount which would have been payable to the original purchaser of the Unsecured Pension plan; or

(c) a spouse, or any other beneficiary, can opt to take the value of the remaining fund as a cash lump sum, although this will be subject to tax at 35 per cent. This payment should be exempt from inheritance tax unless the plan was taken out in the knowledge of ill health and death occurs within two years, in which case HMRC may challenge the IHT status.

Alternatively Secured Pension (ASP)

Alternatively Secured Pension was introduced to allow those individuals with a 'principled objection' to the purchase of an annuity to continue to draw benefits without having to gamble on human longevity (the basis of an annuity). When first introduced, there was no minimum income requirement, and ASPs allowed individuals to pass any remaining funds on death to the pension funds of other members of the same scheme if there were no surviving dependants, with the result that many advisers saw ASPs as a useful mechanism to pass pensions across the generations – effectively a 'family pension' arrangement.

As a result, the Government has acted to block these planning measures. From 6 April 2007 new rules require that an income must be taken with a range of a minimum of 55 per cent and a maximum of 90 per cent of the Government Actuary's Department annuity tables for a 77 year old (regardless of the individuals actual age) and this limit must be reviewed every year.

Where the member dies in receipt of an Alternatively Secured Pension leaving a dependant, the remaining funds must be used to provide a dependant's pension either by purchasing an annuity or providing an Unsecured Dependant's Pension (where the dependant is under age 77) or a dependant Alternatively Secured Pension (where the dependant is over age 77).

Where there is no surviving dependant the funds can be paid to a charity nominated by the deceased member. Any attempt to pay benefits in any other form (including transfers to other members of the same pension scheme) will be treated as an unauthorised payment and attract a tax charge of up to 70 per cent and possibly inheritance tax as well, depending on the size of the individual's estate.

ASP may therefore only be attractive in limited circumstances, for example where the age of a dependant makes the purchase of a joint life annuity prohibitive.

Alternative to ASP

Instead of taking continuing benefits from ASP, it is possible to consider a Scheme Pension instead. The attractiveness of a Scheme Pension is that, unlike ASP where the income is proscribed by reference to existing annuity rates and Government Actuary Development figures, the Scheme Pension income is based on the individual's personal circumstances. The income calculation is based on the client's own age, own mortality expectation, fund size, and assessment of performance.

This potentially allows a much larger income than could be paid either by an annuity or under ASP. This is particularly the case if the individual is in poor health. Calculations carried out by Hornbuckle Mitchell, a specialist provider of these arrangements, and published in Financial Advisor magazine on 28 February 2008, show the following comparison:

ANNUAL INCOME: SCHEME PENSION V ASP			
Scheme Pension	Health	Male aged 75 (Life expectancy)	Male aged 85 (Life expectancy)
	Good	£53,224 (14.9)	£92,441 (6.7)
	Fair	£56,199 (13.6)	£98,558 (6.2)
	Poor	£60,085 (12.2)	£105,619 (5.7)
	Very Poor	£80,528 (8.1)	£133,808 (4.3)
ASP	Common to all	£49,500	£45,900
(Assuming male with £500,000 and 7.5% annual growth)			

It can clearly be seen that under a Scheme Pension, an individual may obtain an increased income when he reaches 77, since under ASP, the income is always pegged at the income payable to a 77 year old, irrespective of the actual age.

It is also possible to build in a ten year guarantee period to the Scheme Pension, meaning that if the member dies within ten years of starting the Scheme Pension, a spouse or other beneficiary can continue to obtain the income (at the same level) for the balance of the period, subject of course to income tax.

Planning points

There are three advantages to this approach to retirement income:

(1) Unlike ASP, the rules for which have been specifically designed to prevent people from depleting their fund, Scheme Pension allows the value to be reduced to as near nil as possible by the time of death. This maximises the value that the client obtains from his pension. Do not forget that the tax on leaving pension benefits other than to a spouse/dependant or charity is 82 per cent.

(2) The higher income available under Scheme Pension means that there is additional scope to use the 'gifts out of normal income' exemption for inheritance tax purposes.

(3) The availability of a guarantee period means that far more of the pension fund could be extracted subject only to income tax than would be the case under ASP.

Phased retirement/Staggered Vesting

Those individuals who do not wish to commit all of their pension funds to the purchase of an annuity, or for investment in Unsecured Pension, in one go can opt for 'phased retirement', which is also referred to as 'staggered vesting'. This involves holding the existing funds in a personal pension that is sub-divided into (normally) 1,000 separate segments of identical size. Each time the policyholder wishes to vest part of his pension, sufficient segments will be encashed to provide the required income. This will be made up partly of the 25 per cent PCLS (the tax free cash) with the balance being provided by income either from an annuity, or from Unsecured Pension, depending on the factors described above. The fund that is not required for vesting remains in the personal pension plan. The advantage of staggered vesting over Unsecured Pension is that it allows the unvested part to remain under the personal pension regime. This means that should the owner die before vesting the entire fund, the unvested part can pay out the full amount free of inheritance tax and without the 35 per cent tax charge applicable to Unsecured Pension. The main disadvantage of staggered vesting is that it consumes the PCLS as part of the income stream, thus preventing it from being kept as a lump sum.

76.5.5 Pension Increases

The level of pension increase, if any, will depend upon a number of factors, such as:

- whether the pension scheme is occupational or private;
- the dates of membership of the scheme;
- when benefits started to be drawn from the scheme;
- decisions taken by the member at the time of starting retirement benefits; and
- whether the scheme is subject to statutory requirements.

The following paragraphs aim to provide an overview of the main requirements for pension increases. However, this is a complex area with considerable interplay between a number of factors including scheme rules, statutory requirements, and personal choices. It is essential to consult the pension administrators or a pension specialist if detailed analysis is required.

Defined Benefit Occupational Schemes (Final Salary Schemes)

Non contracted-out benefits

There is no legal requirement for benefits earned from contributions paid prior to 6 April 1997 to be increased although some schemes may voluntarily do so. Benefits in payment derived from employer and employee contributions paid between 6 April 1997 and 6 April 2005 are required by Pensions Act 1995 to be increased annually in line with the Retail Price Index (RPI) up to a maximum of five per cent. This is technically known as Limited Price Indexation (LPI). This requirement does not extend to any additional contributions that the employee may have made to an additional voluntary contribution (AVC) adjunct to the main scheme. Benefits in payment earned from employer and employee contributions made after 6 April 2005 only need to be increased annually in line with RPI to a maximum of 2.5 per cent.

Contracted-Out benefits

If the scheme was contracted-out of the State Earnings Related Pension Scheme (SERPS) then it is required to increase the benefits from that element of the scheme known as the Guaranteed Minimum Pension [GMP] by the rate of the annual increase in the RPI subject to a limit of three per cent for benefits accrued between 6 April 1988 and 5 April 1997. There is no requirement for increases of benefits accrued prior to 6 April 1988.

Defined Contribution Occupational Schemes (Money Purchase Schemes)

Non-protected rights

As with defined benefit schemes, there is no legal requirement for benefits earned from contributions paid prior to 6 April 1997 to be increased, although the scheme rules may so require. Benefits in payment derived from employer and employee contributions paid between 6 April 1997 and 6 April 2005 are required by Pensions Act 1995 to be increased annually by LPI. There is no legal requirement to increase benefits in payment earned from employer and employee contributions made after 6 April 2005. It should be noted that the pensioner could always request that escalation be built into the benefits payable, though this will reduce the initial level of benefit.

Protected rights

There is no longer any requirement for an annuity purchased with protected rights funds to have any level of escalation in payment. This change took effect from 6 April 2005.

Personal and Stakeholder Pensions

Non-Protected rights

The decision as to whether to build in escalation for retirement benefits accruing from personal (and employer where appropriate) contributions is entirely up to the individual. Whilst escalation would have the advantage of hedging against inflation in part or in total, it would result in a significant drop in the initial income payable. Depending of the level of escalation chosen, the cross-over point at which the escalating income will catch up with the level annuity otherwise payable could be many years in the future. The break-even point, when the total income paid under the escalating pension matches that drawn from the level annuity, will be even further in the future. The decision will therefore depend on the extent to which a high initial income is required, or whether inflation hedging is needed to meet anticipated longer term needs such as long term care.

Protected Rights

As with defined contribution occupational schemes, there is no longer a requirement for an annuity purchased with protected rights to have any level of escalation in payment.

76.5.6 Death Benefits paid from Pensions

Death benefit options differ depending upon whether the benefit is paid before or after vesting.

The pension options and income tax consequences are known and described below.

Death Benefits before taking Retirement Benefits

The options are:

A Lump Sum

There is no limit where the death benefit is return of fund. The total is tested against the Lifetime Allowance (LTA) or the personal LTA if the deceased registered for protection at that time. If the total amount paid as a lump sum exceeds the LTA a 55 per cent charge is applied to the excess. This charge is effectively apportioned against the recipients.

Dependant's Pension

Dependants are spouses, civil partners, dependent children and financially dependent (e.g. unmarried partner) or dependent because of disability. Pensions paid are not tested against the LTA and can be paid in addition to the lump sum thus avoiding tax on the excess. The upper age for payment to children is age 23 but there is no longer a full time education qualification requirement. The dependant's pension can be paid as the following.

(1) **Secured Pension** through the payment of an annuity or direct from the scheme.

(2) **Unsecured Pension** through Income Drawdown. There is no requirement for a minimum income but the maximum is set at 120 per cent of the Government Actuary Department's published rate for a single life annuity. Short-term 5-year annuities can also be used up to age 77.

(3) **Alternatively Secured Pension** if aged over 77 through income drawdown but with the minimum income requirement set at 55 per cent of the annual amount of a comparable annuity rate for a 77 year old, and the maximum income set at 90 per cent.

Death Benefits after taking Retirement Benefits

These benefits will depend upon how the pension was paid and the age of the member at death. The options are as follows.

Death Before 77
Secured Pension – benefits could be:

- an annuity paid to a dependant for life (23 for a child) but not exceeding the deceased's own pension;
- continuing payments for the remainder of a guaranteed period of no more than ten years from the start of the initial annuity;
- a lump sum (taxed at 35 per cent) based on the difference in the capital value of the scheme pension at commencement (or the annuity purchase price) and the total of all income payments to the date of death.

Unsecured Pension – benefits could be:

- a lump sum can be paid less a 35 per cent tax charge (see Inheritance Tax below);
- dependant(s) annuity(ies);
- an Unsecured Pension for a dependant aged under 77 or part used to purchase a short-term annuity;
- if the dependant is over age 77 the drawdown fund can provide an Alternatively Secured Pension.

Death On or After 77
Secured Pension – benefits are either a dependant's annuity or the balance of any instalments for the rest of a guaranteed period. No lump sums are available.

Alternatively Secured Pension (ASP) – benefits could be as follows.

- The remaining fund can be used to provide an income for dependants through annuity purchase, continued ASP if the dependant is over 77 or Unsecured Pension if aged under 77. (If to a child, when they reach the age of 23).
- Lump sum benefits can be paid to a charity at the discretion of the scheme administrator where there is no member nomination.
- There is no facility to make payments under a guarantee from an ASP fund.
- If there is any attempt to pay benefits in any other form, then there will be an unauthorised payment charge of up to 70 per cent. In addition, there may also be an IHT charge on the funds, which potentially means an 82 per cent tax charge.

76.5.7 Inheritance Tax Treatment (IHT)

Death of Scheme Member before age 77

Currently, by concession, IHT is not charged in respect of death benefits where the beneficiary is a spouse, civil partner or person who is financially dependent on the scheme member. Nor is IHT applied where a scheme member chooses not to exercise a right to retire (this increases the value outside the estate) at a time when the choice does not trigger a charge to inheritance tax i.e. the member is in good health. This treatment applies only where the member does not subsequently vary that choice, even when a reduction in their life expectancy would in strictness trigger an inheritance tax charge.

This gives more certainty to the treatment of death benefits where the member dies before aged 77. It means that, provided the member is in good health, a decision to postpone taking pension benefits will not trigger a charge to IHT. In addition, if death benefits are written in a properly constructed trust they will remain outside the member's estate even if he/she subsequently becomes ill. If they do become ill then they must take care before making any changes to their pension arrangements.

Death on or after age 77

Any attempt to make other lump sum payments, such as where the fund remains within the scheme for the benefit of other members, or is refunded to an employer, or used to provide benefits for a dependant in the same pension scheme who is not a spouse, civil partner or person financially dependent, will be subject to an IHT charge on the death of the member as if the funds were part of the member's own taxable estate. The total tax charge is 82 per cent.

Any funds paid on the death of the scheme member to a charity would be exempt as will funds expended for a scheme member's spouse, civil partner or person who is financially dependent on the scheme member. Any leftover funds, once used by the spouse, civil partner or financially dependent person will be chargeable to IHT on the earlier of the cessation of those benefits or the death of the recipient. These remaining funds will be treated as if they were an addition to the original scheme members' estate. Leftover funds paid to charities will be exempt from IHT.

In certain circumstances an IHT charge will fall on the estate of the dependant rather than the original member. This will apply where a dependant opts for an ASP derived from benefits inherited from a scheme member who died before aged 77. Here, any leftover funds on the dependant's death will be charged to inheritance tax as if they were part of the dependant's estate.

IHT is charged on the value of the fund when the charge arises and calculated by reference to the IHT nil rate band at that time. The pension scheme administrator will be responsible for accounting and paying for IHT on ASP funds. There are two circumstances where the tax charges on ASP funds overlap:

- where the funds are paid to an employer;
- with the death of the dependent, under age 77, and remaining funds paid out as a lump sum (other than to a charity).

Here the IHT charge takes priority over the pension scheme tax charge, which is then applied to the net fund after the deduction of IHT.

76.6 Overview of State Retirement Benefits

76.6.1 Basic State Pension

In 2010–11, the full basic State Pension is £97.65 a week for a single person and £156.15 a week for a couple, although individual circumstances may affect the amount payable. From April 2011 the basic State Pension will be increased every year by whichever is the highest of:

- the growth in average earnings;
- the growth in prices; and
- or 2.5 per cent.

This does not apply to the additions to State Pension. The starting age is 65 years for men and between 60 and 65 years for women, depending on their year of birth. Currently men normally need 44 qualifying years, and women normally need 39 qualifying years, to get the full basic State Pension. However those reaching State Pension age on or after 6 April 2010 will only need 30 qualifying years for a full basic State Pension.

76.6.2 State Second Pension (S2P)

In addition to the basic state pension, employees may be credited with additional benefits that have accrued since 1978. S2P was introduced by the Child Support, Pensions and Social Security Act 2000 and replaced the State Earnings Related Pensions scheme (SERPS) from April 2002.

The introduction of S2P was planned to be in two stages:

(1) The first stage took effect from 6th April 2002. It is an earnings related scheme which provides benefits at least equal to SERPS. Those on moderate to low earnings accrue more pension under S2P than they would have under SERPS.

(2) S2P was originally expected to move to a flat rate contribution in April 2006 or 2007. This has been changed by the Pensions Act 2007 which states that S2P will be a flat rate scheme by 2030.

From April 2002 to April 2010 there were three contribution tiers. For the 2009/10 tax year the Lower Earnings limit (LEL) was £4,940 p.a., the Lower Earnings Threshold (LET) was £13,900, the Middle Earnings Threshold was £31,800 [(3 x LET) – (2 x LEL)] and the upper accrual point (UAP), £40,040. People earning below the LET are treated as if they earned the full LET. Individuals such as carers are also treated as if they have earnings equal to the LET and receive S2P accrual on this basis.

S2P accrual table

Tax year in which state pension falls	Earnings between £4,940–£13,900	Earnings between £13,900–£31,800	Earnings between £31,800–£40,040
2009–10	40% Accrual	10% Accrual	20% Accrual

*Benefits accrue on deemed earnings of £13,900, provided actual earnings are over £4,940 except for full time carers who have no income; these individuals are still deemed to earn £13,900.

From April 2009 the upper accrual point was fixed at £40,040.

From April 2010 the 20 per cent and 10 per cent bands have **merged** to form one 10 per cent band, as shown by the table below.

Tax year in which state pension falls	Earnings between £5,044–£14,200	Earnings between £14,200–£40,040	N/A
2010–11	40% Accrual	10% Accrual	20% Accrual

From April 2012, the 40 per cent band is expected to be replaced with a weekly flat accrual rate. The LET will continue to rise in line with earnings until it reaches the upper accrual point (UAP, £40,040), by which point S2P will become a flat rate system. This is estimated to be around 2031–32. Like SERPS, benefits are calculated each year for an individual and revalued up to the individual's State Pension Age. The effect of these changes is that the amount of S2P accruable will gradually reduce over time and the total pension payable will be less than the SERPS that it replaced.

Advisers might want to discuss with their clients the amount of any state pension that the client could expect to receive. Completion of form BR19 from DWP will give the client the amount of basic state pension and additional state pension they have accrued to date, and an estimate of what they might have accrued at their state pension age if their circumstances do not change.

Please note that state pensions are 'unfunded', meaning that their payment in future years depends on the availability of resources to meet their commitments. For this reason they are, and have been, subject to change, most of which has been disadvantageous. It may therefore be unwise to rely on these benefits being available on current terms at retirement.

76.6.3 Pension Credit

The Government has introduced a Pension Credit to help those aged 60 or over who have little or no savings at retirement. In 2008–09, if a person or their partner is aged 60 or over, Pension Credit guarantees an income of at least £130 a week (single) or £198.45 a week (couple). Whilst, as with all state benefits, it might not be wise to assume that Pension Credit will be available in the future, this does cause a problem in retirement planning since it may not be in a client's best interests for him/her to contribute to a personal pension now only to provide a very small annuity income in the future, but which is sufficient to disallow pension credit. From 2010, the age from which Pension Credit is payable will gradually increase.

76.6.4 Personal accounts

'Personal accounts' have now been renamed 'National Employment Savings Trust' (NEST). They will be available for use by employers who do not have, or choose not to use, any existing pension schemes to meet the new obligations. Details are given at the start of this chapter.

76.7 Contracting-out of S2P

It is possible to opt out (known as 'contracting out') of S2P. This can be done in two ways.

(1) Involuntarily. By contributing to an employer's occupational pension scheme, which is a 'contracted-out' scheme. Individuals have no control over this since the decision is taken by the pension trustees.

(2) Voluntarily. By deciding to opt out personally. If this decision is taken, HMRC will pay a rebate of part of the NICs into a personal or stakeholder pension plan established by the individual. This decision can be reviewed in the future and, if appropriate, a decision taken to contract back into the S2P. There may be some future changes to S2P since the government is considering the removal of the option to contract-out on a money purchase basis.

Any decision to contract out of S2P needs to be based upon proper financial advice. The risk of contracting out is that the future returns are insufficient to match the pension payable in the future under S2P. A study for the Financial Services Authority (FSA) in August 2005 gives the following table indicating the annual returns in excess of earnings growth needed to match the 2004 benefits payable under S2P.

Critical yield required (in excess of earnings growth) to match 2004 S2P benefits on a range of ages, income and for males and females

Age	Male Income			Female Income		
	Low	Average	High	Low	Average	High
18	3.0%	2.9%	2.8%	2.8%	2.7%	2.6%
19	3.0%	2.9%	2.8%	2.8%	2.7%	2.6%
20	3.0%	2.9%	2.8%	2.8%	2.7%	2.7%
21	3.0%	2.9%	2.8%	2.8%	2.7%	2.6%
22	3.0%	3.0%	2.9%	2.8%	2.7%	2.7%
23	3.0%	2.9%	2.9%	2.8%	2.7%	2.7%
24	3.1%	3.0%	2.9%	2.9%	2.8%	2.7%
25	3.1%	3.0%	3.0%	2.9%	2.8%	2.7%
26	3.1%	3.0%	2.9%	2.9%	2.8%	2.7%
27	3.2%	3.1%	3.0%	2.9%	2.8%	2.8%
28	3.2%	3.1%	3.0%	2.9%	2.8%	2.7%
29	3.2%	3.1%	3.0%	3.0%	2.9%	2.8%
30	3.2%	3.1%	3.0%	3.0%	2.9%	2.8%
31	3.3%	3.2%	3.1%	3.0%	2.9%	2.8%
32	3.3%	3.2%	3.1%	3.0%	2.9%	2.8%
33	3.4%	3.3%	3.2%	3.1%	3.0%	2.9%
34	3.4%	3.3%	3.2%	3.1%	3.0%	2.9%
35	3.4%	3.3%	3.2%	3.1%	3.0%	2.9%
36	3.4%	3.3%	3.2%	3.1%	3.0%	2.9%
37	3.5%	3.4%	3.3%	3.2%	3.1%	3.0%
38	3.6%	3.5%	3.4%	3.3%	3.2%	3.0%
39	3.6%	3.5%	3.4%	3.3%	3.2%	3.0%
40	3.7%	3.6%	3.5%	3.4%	3.3%	3.1%
41	3.8%	3.7%	3.5%	3.4%	3.3%	3.1%
42	3.9%	3.8%	3.6%	3.5%	3.4%	3.2%
43	3.9%	3.8%	3.7%	3.5%	3.4%	3.2%
44	4.0%	3.9%	3.7%	3.6%	3.4%	3.3%
45	4.1%	4.0%	3.8%	3.6%	3.5%	3.3%
46	4.3%	4.2%	4.0%	3.8%	3.7%	3.5%
47	4.4%	4.3%	4.1%	3.9%	3.7%	3.6%
48	4.6%	4.4%	4.2%	4.0%	3.9%	3.7%

Pensions

49	4.8%	4.6%	4.4%	4.1%	4.0%	3.8%
50	4.5%	4.4%	4.2%	4.6%	4.4%	4.2%
51	4.2%	4.0%	3.8%	5.0%	4.8%	4.5%
52	3.6%	3.5%	3.2%	5.6%	5.4%	5.1%
53	3.0%	2.8%	2.6%	6.6%	6.4%	6.0%
54	3.2%	3.0%	2.7%	10.4%	10.1%	9.5%
55	3.7%	3.6%	3.3%	14.5%	14.1%	13.3%
56	4.6%	4.4%	4.1%	22.3%	21.7%	20.5%
57	5.6%	5.4%	5.0%	40.6%	39.5%	37.4%
58	7.2%	7.0%	6.5%	100% +	100% +	100% +
59	9.2%	8.9%	8.3%	100% +	100% +	100% +
60	12.8%	12.4%	11.6%	100% +	100% +	100% +

Notes:

- This table shows the yields that rebates, received in respect of the 2004 tax year, need to earn in excess of earnings growth (assumed to be four per cent per annum) up to State Pension Age to match the S2P benefits foregone. Data is provided for males and females on various income levels.
- Age is defined as that on 6 April 2004.
- Policy charges have been assumed to be a flat one per cent annual management charge.
- An annuity expense loading of four per cent has been assumed.

Contracting out through defined contribution schemes (i.e. money purchase, personal pension and stakeholder arrangements) is to be abolished from 6 April 2012. Anyone contracted out of a defined contribution scheme at that time will automatically be contracted back into the State Second Pension.

Contracting-out of S2P

This table compares the main differences between being in and out of the State Second Pension. The table is based on current law and government proposals, which could change.

	Contracting out or staying contracted out of S2P	Contracting in to S2P
How does your pension grow?	The government pays your rebates into a personal or stakeholder pension of your choice. Personal and stakeholder pensions invest in, among other things, the stockmarket. The amount you will get from your contracted-out pension will, in particular, depend on: • the amount of the rebates paid in; • how this money is invested and how the stockmarket changes; • annuity rates at retirement; and • any charges you pay the pension company for running your fund. Investments can go down as well as up, so you may end up with a smaller pension than you would with S2P.	The amount you will get from your S2P will depend on the amount of National Insurance contributions you pay and the government's pension policy. Governments may change pension policy. If that happens, you may end up with more or less S2P than calculations based on current pension policy would suggest.
What happens when you retire?	Most people use their pension fund to buy a lifetime annuity. An annuity is a special type of investment that converts your pension fund into retirement income. The amount of retirement income you get will, in particular, depend on your age, health and personal circumstances. For more information on this and other options, read the **FSA guide to pensions 3: Annuities and other retirement options**. To get a copy, see *Useful contacts* on page 7. The minimum age at which you can take your pension is going up from 50 to 55 by 2010. Pension providers can raise the age at any time between April 2006 and April 2010. Make sure you check this with your pension provider.	The government will pay your S2P at the same time as your basic State Pension. You can currently claim your State Pension at age 65 for men, and 60 for women. By 2020, the pension age for women will be 65, the same as for men. The government has proposed further increases to the pension age, so that by 2046, the pension age for both men and women will be 68.
What happens if you die before you retire?	If you have a spouse or civil partner and die before you retire, your contracted-out fund must be used to provide benefits for them. If you don't have a spouse or civil partner, your contracted-out fund can be left as part of your estate.	If you have a spouse or civil partner and die before you start taking your State Pension, they may be eligible for half the S2P you have earned. If you don't have a spouse or civil partner, your S2P benefits are not payable to your estate. For further information read the Department for Work and Pensions (DWP) leaflet, **Inheritance of SERPS pension**. To get a copy, see *Useful contacts* on page 7.
What happens if you die after you retire?	If you have a spouse or civil partner when you retire, you will have to buy a lifetime annuity that will pay out half the income to your spouse or partner if you die before them.	If you have a spouse or civil partner, they may qualify for a portion of your S2P if you die before them. For further information read the DWP leaflet, **Inheritance of SERPS pension**. To get a copy, see *Useful contacts* on page 7.
Is there a tax-free lump-sum option?	You are able to take up to 25% of your contracted-out fund as a tax-free lump sum when you retire. This will reduce the amount you have left to buy your annuity.	You cannot take a tax-free lump sum. However, you can now defer taking your S2P beyond State Pension age. If you do this, you will have the choice of increasing the amount of your S2P or taking the additional benefits as a taxable lump sum. For further information read the DWP leaflet, **Your guide to State Pension Deferral**. To get a copy, see *Useful contacts* on page 7.

76.8 Changes in Personal Circumstances

76.8.1 Bankruptcy

On bankruptcy, all assets come under the control of the Government's Official Receiver who then passes them to a Trustee in Bankruptcy (TIB) to settle outstanding creditors. Pensions are an asset from which the bankrupted individual can benefit at some time and are therefore property that can be potentially passed over to the TIB. The actual situation depends on:

- the date the bankruptcy was declared;
- whether the bankruptcy has been discharged; and
- whether the pension is an occupational pension or a personal pension.

Registered and approved pension schemes cannot be taken into account as part of the bankrupt's estate for bankruptcies arising after 29 May 2000, by virtue of the Welfare Reform and Pensions Act 1999. This means that the capital in the fund cannot be used to the benefit of creditors.

The issue of pensions in payment is different. The TIB can apply to the Court for an Income Payments Order to control the payments from a pension plan. However, the impact of this Income Payments Order has been lessened by the fact that the Enterprise Act 2002 has reduced the automatic discharge period for bankruptcies occurring after 1 April 2004 to 12 months. There is, however, the possibility of this period being extended in cases of breaches of the bankruptcy order, or if there had been excessive contributions to a pension plan prior to bankruptcy where the motivation was one of removing assets from the estate.

76.8.2 Divorce

Most pension assets are taken into consideration by the Court in the division of property on divorce. Arrangements that are excluded are state benefits, Equivalent Pension Benefits earned between 1961 and 1975, or any pension benefits as a result of being widowed or financially dependant. This is a complex area and whilst the bare bones are provided here to permit a general understanding of the options, this is an area in which specialist advice is essential. The pension options open to a divorcing couple (or separating civil partnership) are as follows.

Pension Offsetting

This is achieved by balancing the value of the pension fund (or the future benefits in a defined benefit scheme) against other assets, such as investments or the matrimonial home. The spouse who owns the pension plan retains its ownership and the other spouse is compensated by an equivalent value of other assets. Issues to consider. Comparing the value of a pension and another asset can be difficult since the current value may not reflect the future investment risks. For very large pension plans, it might also be hard to find another compensating asset.

Pension Earmarking

Pension Earmarking was introduced for petitions filed on or after 1 July 1996 (19 August 1996 in Scotland) by the 1995 Pensions Act. This is achieved by placing an injunction on a pension scheme to ensure that when this pension eventually comes into payment, an agreed amount (payment and/or PCLS) will be paid for the benefit of the other party.

Issues to consider. There are a number of significant drawbacks to this arrangement. It does not achieve a 'clean break' since the ex-spouse has to wait until the pension owning ex-spouse decided to retire before receiving any benefit. If the Earmarking Order is for the payment of a regular income, that income will cease (or not even start!) on the death of the pension-owning ex-spouse. Furthermore, the payments may cease on the remarriage of the ex-spouse to whom the payments are being made.

Pension Sharing

In order to resolve the problems with Pension Earmarking, the Welfare Reform & Pensions Act 1999 gave powers to the Court to split pension rights between spouses on divorce for petitions filed on/after 1 December 2000. This is potentially the cleanest break, since the effect is to divide the value of the scheme in an agreed percentage, which each party will then hold separately in their own names (the ex-spouse receives a pension credit). The value is a fixed percentage of the 'cash equivalent transfer value' of the pension rights the day before the Pension Sharing Order is granted, and this value may fluctuate over time.

Issues to consider. The spouse receiving the pension credit can transfer the value to a different pension scheme of their choosing, subject to the rules of that scheme. The existing scheme from which the credit came has no obligation to accept the ex-spouse as a member and can insist on an external transfer.

Pension Credit Protection

If a pensions credit was received before 6 April 2006 it can be protected, provided that there is no existing primary protection, and the application is made before 5 April 2009. Pension credits received after 5 April 2006 can only be protected if they are derived from a pension which has been tested against the ex spouse's Lifetime Allowance. An application for protection must be made within six years of the Pension Sharing Order.

76.8.3 Maternity Leave – Pension Contributions

Occupational Pension Schemes

All paid maternity leave must be treated as pensionable service based on the salary immediately before the start of the leave.

Employee contributions must be based on the actual pay, whilst employer contributions have to be based on the salary the employee would have received, including any pay rises, had the employee not taken maternity leave.

Unpaid maternity leave (of any type) does not qualify as pensionable service although employment before and after the break must be treated as continuous.

Personal/Stakeholder Pensions (including Group Schemes)

Where an employee is contributing, she will continue to do so during paid maternity leave based on the amount of pay actually received.

Where the employer also contributes to the policy, these contributions must continue during paid maternity leave based on the pay the employee would have received had she not gone on maternity leave.

Where the employer has agreed to match the employee's contribution, the employer's contributions must continue at the level the employee would normally pay and cannot be reduced to what she is actually paying during her maternity leave.

There is no requirement for any contributions during unpaid maternity leave.

76.8.4 Moving Abroad

The transfer of a UK pension scheme to an overseas scheme has become simpler since 6 April 2006. Provided that the overseas scheme is recognised by HMRC as an approved arrangement, technically known as a Qualifying Recognised Overseas Pension Scheme (QROPS), the transfer can be processed in a similar way as a UK transfer. There are a number of regulator requirements to be observed, and the advice of a pension specialist or the scheme trustee/administrator should be obtained.

To qualify as an approved overseas scheme, HMRC has to be satisfied that:

- it is regulated as a retirement benefit arrangement in the country in which it is established; and
- the scheme will notify HMRC if it ceases to meet the criteria to be deemed 'a

recognised overseas pension scheme' and will undertake to provide HMRC with information on certain member payments made.

HMRC publish a list of QROPSs.

The transfer is assessable for the purpose of the member's Lifetime Allowance. If the transfer results in the Lifetime Allowance being exceeded, the rate of tax chargeable is 25 per cent of the excess.

76.9 Tax Planning Opportunities

76.9.1 Doubling the Annual Allowance in Same Tax Year

> ⚠ **Warning!**
> This facility was a neat way to get tax relief in one tax year in respect of contributions allocated to two consecutive tax years. Because of the anti-forestalling measures and restrictions for tax relief for high earners discussed in **76.4.2**, then this tax planning opportunity will become unattractive to those above the earnings limit. It has, however, been an effective tax planning tool for high earning individuals who had sufficient free assets to make large pension contributions and could still be so for those who have had low earnings in the past 3 years, but with the capacity to make large contributions now.

It was and still is possible to make two pension contributions in the same tax year, up to the annual allowance. This might be appropriate for individuals who are:

- ceasing work;
- taking a significant reduction in salary in the next tax year;
- leaving the UK for more than five years and want to boost pension provision; or
- high earners who wish to claim tax relief as early as possible to be invested for as long as possible.

Note: none of the above negate the effect of the special annual allowance.

The ability to pay two contributions in one tax year that exceed the annual allowance for that tax year and not have to pay an annual allowance charge is made possible because since 6 April 2006 contributions to a pension scheme are deemed to fall within a 'pension input period'. A pension input period can be less than one year.

The end date of this pension input period determines the tax year to which the annual allowance applies, i.e. if a contribution was made on 1 March 2010 and the pension input period runs for a year (the maximum), then it will end on 29 February 2011. This is within the 2010–11 tax year. So, the individual could have paid a contribution of £255,000 in the 2009–10 tax year and claim tax relief on it even though this annual allowance does not take effect until the 2010–11 tax year. Full tax relief prior to 22 April 2009 would have been available on the whole contribution, as long as the individual had sufficient earnings to justify the contribution. In the post-2009 budget world, contributions of this magnitude may get caught by the anti-forestalling rules (subject to earnings).

Within the Personal Pension regime, the individual can ask the scheme administrator for any pension input period they want. This is referred to as the 'nominated date'. The administrator does not have to agree to it and it is the individual's responsibility to make such a request and if the request is granted, to monitor the payment of their contributions against their chosen pension input period.

The general principles are as follows.

(1) At a simple level and to demonstrate maximum tax efficiency if two contributions are paid in a given tax year (tax year 1) one of which equals the annual allowance applicable in tax year 1 and the other equals the annual allowance applicable in the following tax year (tax year 2), any further contributions paid in tax year 2 would be subject to the annual allowance charge unless they fulfilled the requirements for exemption (death or fully vested). Contributions can recommence in the annual allowance year following tax year 2.

(2) If only one contribution is paid in a given tax year (tax year 1) and the individual makes no request for a pension input period, the pension input period will last for 12 months from the date on which the contribution is paid. This means the individual can pay a further contribution in the following tax year (tax year 2).

(3) It is not necessary for a given contribution to equal the applicable annual allowance, i.e. a desired contribution of £255,000 in respect of a pension input period running from 6 April 2010 to 31 October 2011 could be paid in two halves provided the total of £255,000 has been paid by 31 October 2010.

(4) Only one pension input period can end in any given tax year and it is the pension input end date that dictates the annual allowance to use and hence the contribution limit which applies.

76.9.2 Salary/Bonus Sacrifice

Salary Sacrifice

A method of achieving a personal pension contribution and also avoiding the payment of NIC is the 'salary sacrifice' arrangement which turns an employee contribution into an employer contribution. This obviously requires the consent of, and participation by, the employer. The process involves the employee asking the employer to make a permanent reduction in salary, and to pay an employer's contribution to the pension scheme of the level of the gross salary reduction. In fact, the astute employee may also persuade the employer to include the proportionate saving in the employer's level of NIC achieved by the reduction in the salary. There are potential disadvantages to this arrangement, since the reduced salary could affect any income protection plans, death in service arrangements based on a multiple of salary, redundancy payments, potential contributions to the state second pension, and any other benefits that are calculated with reference to level of salary. (The pros and cons of such an arrangement are discussed in greater detail at **36.2**).

Bonus Sacrifice

This works in the same way as 'salary sacrifice', but applies to any lump sum bonus payments that are made. The request for bonus sacrifice should be in writing from the employee to the employer, and must be made before the bonus has been awarded.

HMRC Reference

The relevant reference is 'BIM 46020: Specific Deductions: Registered Pension Schemes: Wholly & Exclusively: Employer contributions linked to salary sacrifice arrangements'. This states:

'A salary sacrifice happens when an employee gives up the right to part of the cash remuneration due under their contract of employment. An employee may also sacrifice a one-off item such as a bonus. Usually, the sacrifice is made in return for the employer's agreement to provide the employee with some form of non-cash benefit, such as an increased contribution by the employer to a pension scheme. An increased pension contribution by an employer resulting from a salary sacrifice arrangement of the type set out in the Employment Income Manual at EIM 42750 onwards, will be wholly & exclusively for the purposes of the trade and allowable as a deduction in arriving at the employer's taxable profits.'

76.9.3 Recycling of Tax Free Cash

Since it is now possible to contribute 100 per cent of earnings into a pension plan, and receive full tax relief at the marginal rate of tax, there is a clear opportunity at the point of retirement to draw the maximum tax free lump sum and to re-invest this back into a new pension plan to avail of the tax relief. 25 per cent of this sum would then be available as tax-free cash, and so the process can be repeated, albeit with ever-reducing amounts. In order to forestall this 'abuse', HMRC will target individuals who:

- are identified as having the intention to recycle;
- have received pension tax-free cash lump sums in excess of one per cent of the Lifetime Allowance in the preceding 12 months;

Pensions

- pay a contribution that is 30 per cent greater than average contributions paid in previous years; and
- where the contribution paid is greater than 30 per cent of the total tax-free cash received in the previous 12 months.

Where all these conditions are met, HMRC will assess that the contribution amounts to 'recycling', and treat it as an unauthorised payment, which attracts a tax penalty on the policy holder of 40 per cent of the premium paid. Where this contribution exceeds 25 per cent of the total value of the scheme an additional surcharge of 15 per cent may be applied, bringing the total tax payable to 55 per cent of the contribution.

Consequently, where individuals wish to boost their contributions in their last year of service, care needs to be taken not to breach the recycling rules.

76.9.4 Tax Free Lump Sum – Opportunity Cost in Final Salary Schemes

Much of the appeal of a pension benefit scheme is seen to lie in the tax free Pension Commencement Lump Sum (PCLS) – the 'tax free cash'. However, where this is not actively required as part of the retirement strategy, for example to clear a mortgage, or debts, or to provide an essential emergency fund, and provided that the pensioner is in good health, then the consequences of taking this lump sum need to be explored.

Unless the lump sum is additional to the income (some 1/80th schemes are like this), the provision of the lump sum is achieved by reducing the retirement income by a commutation factor of, normally, 12. This means that £1 of annual pension income is surrendered for every £12 of tax-free cash. To show the implications of this, let us take an example of an individual who:

- retires at age 60;
- with a final salary of £45,000;
- after working for 40 years at the same company;
- belongs to an unaltered 1/60th scheme; and
- qualifies for a retirement income of (initially) £30,000 a year.

Since the scheme rules have not been changed to permit the new 25 per cent level of tax free cash, the cash calculation is based on the old rate of 1.5 times final salary, which is £67,500. Using the 12:1 commutation factor, the reduction in initial pension income is £5,625.

However, an index-linked annuity, with 50 per cent residual spouse benefit, for a 60-year-old male will currently pay about 3.1 per cent of the purchase cost. This means that the lump sum necessary to replace the lost income of £5,625 is £181,451.

The consequence of accepting the tax-free cash is that the individual is accepting £67,500 for a benefit actually worth £181,451. The justification for this needs to be sound, and retiring individuals made fully aware of the implications. This is particularly important where the scheme rules have been altered to permit commutation up to 25 per cent of the pension value. Many schemes have now implemented these changes as it can be seen that there is an advantage to occupational pension schemes for annuitants to withdraw the maximum tax-free cash.

76.9.5 Triviality – Total Funds of Less than one per cent Lifetime Allowance

If the total value of all of an individual's pension arrangements does not exceed one per cent of the Lifetime Allowance, it is possible to convert these plans into cash, and avoid buying an annuity. For the tax year 2010–11, the total value of the pension plans cannot exceed £18,000 if they are to qualify as 'trivial'.

Existing pension rights are valued as follows.

(1) Defined Benefit pension rights that are not yet in payment are valued using a factor of 20:1. Thus a projected pension of £5,000 has a value of £100,000.

(2) Pensions that came into payment before 6 April 2006 are tested using the income as at 5 April 2006 multiplied by a factor of 25:1.

(3) Defined Contribution pension rights that are not yet in payment (this will include retirement annuity, personal and stakeholder plans) are valued by reference to the market value of the plan.

(4) Future pension rights will be valued against the Lifetime Allowance in the year of payment.

The rules for 'triviality' are:

- the option to obtain a cash sum on triviality grounds can only be exercised between the ages of 60 and 77;
- 25 per cent of the total sum is available tax free, with the balance taxed against the individual's marginal rate of income tax;
- if the individual has more than one pension plan, all policies must be encashed within 12 months of encashing the first policy; and
- the encashment of any occupational pension will require the agreement of the trustees of the scheme.

Tax planning opportunities

The opportunity surrounds the availability of tax relief on the contributions and the following scenarios can be envisaged.

(1) A self-employed individual employs his wife in the business. She has no

existing pension. The husband is a higher rate taxpayer and both are in their middle 50s. If the husband were to make an employer's gross contribution of £3,600 p.a., he would obtain 40 per cent tax relief on this (business expense). The triviality level in 2010–11 is £18,000, which represents five years contributions. Clearly this ignores any growth in the fund, which would require monitoring and which may require the last contribution to be withheld. However, there is the potential for £7,200 tax relief, £4,500 tax-free cash, and a lump sum of £10,800 after basic rate of income tax of £2,700 (at 20 per cent – the post 2008 basic rate). Thus, the £18,000 has actually cost £10,800, with £15,300 net being returned to the wife.

(2) Exactly the same scenario can apply to the self-employed individual himself if he has no previous pension history, and will be a basic rate taxpayer in retirement.

(3) The opportunity still exists for individuals who do not qualify for higher rate tax relief, though the benefits are not as great. If a husband were to make a net contribution of £2,880 on behalf of his wife, this would currently be increased by tax relief to £3,600. Thus the total outlay has been £14,400 with £15,300 net being returned to the wife, giving a profit of £900. This may be greater if growth has increased the value of the fund, perhaps dispensing with the need for the last contribution (equally, poor returns may erode the potential gains).

Occupational schemes

The government announced in the Budget that it will introduce legislation in Finance Act 2008 introduced legislation which provided easement to the regulations covering trivial commutation under occupational schemes. This greatly eased the administration of occupational schemes since this legislation allows a member's benefits to be commuted on grounds of triviality where the total value of these benefits under the scheme is less than £2,000. It also clarified the conditions under which 'orphan funds' (small funds which are not large enough to be able to be used to purchase an annuity) can be paid out without breaching the unauthorised payments rules. This easement has now been extended to all schemes, and is in addition to the one per cent triviality rule covered above.

76.9.6 Spouse's Pension

Few people consider the benefits of pensioning their spouse. There are, however, some significant advantages to be had.

(1) Tax relief on the contribution is available at 20 per cent even if the spouse is not in employment and pays no tax. The government permits net contributions of up to £3,600 per annum gross to be made for/by any individual under the age of 77. This includes children, low-earners, and the non/unemployed.

(2) The invested fund benefits from tax efficient roll-up.

(3) 25 per cent of the fund is available tax-free on retirement.

(4) As stated above, income from a pension is taxed at the pensioner's marginal rate. However, if this income is contained within the individual's personal allowance, it will be tax-free. Based on a 6 per cent annuity rate this would allow a fund of £79,000 after 25 per cent tax-free cash (£105,300 before the tax free cash).

(5) If the spouse's total pension funds are less than £18,000 after April 2010, then the triviality rules will apply.

The above scenario is even more tax-efficient for a self-employed husband/wife (40 per cent tax payer) who employs his/her spouse. As long as an income is paid, (s)he can then pay £3,600 per annum gross into a pension plan for the spouse, and claim tax relief on it as a business expense.

76.9.7 Fat Cats – Fat Kittens

All individuals under age 77 can invest a minimum of £3,600 gross per annum into a pension arrangement and benefit from initial tax relief. This provides the opportunity for tax efficient, long term, investments for children. Contributions made during the first 18 years of life could be worth more than the equivalent contributions made during the 42 years from 18–60*.

This table illustrates the potential benefits of starting pension contributions at an early age.

Contributions of £3,600 per annum between ages	Potential fund value at age 60*
0–16 then stopped	£1,230,000
0–18 then stopped	£1,310,000
0–21 then stopped	£1,430,000
From 18–60	£659,000
From 30–60	£298,000
From 40–60	£139,000
From 50–60	£50,100

*These projections are based on a medium growth rate of 7 per cent with an Annual Management Charge of 1 per cent.

Of course, these benefits will not be payable until the child is aged 55 (under current legislation), and will then be payable mainly as income. However, given the current anxieties about under-provision of future retirement income, and doubts about the long-term sustainability of the state pension, this planning may be advantageous to children where it is affordable.

Inheritance Tax Benefits

Where the pension contributions can be paid by a grandparent, then there may also be inheritance tax benefits as well as the immediate tax relief. The reason is that the £2,880 net contribution may either fall within the £3,000 annual gift exemption or else qualify as normal expenditure from income. If the latter applies, then the requirements are that the contributions are funded from taxed income rather than from capital, are set up with the intention of maintaining them as a regular contribution, and that their payment does not adversely affect the donor's standard of living.

By way of illustrating the benefits, if a grandparent pays £240 per month in pension plans for each of four grandchildren out of surplus pension income, the contributions are immediately increased by basic rate tax relief to £300 per month. Five years later the grandparent dies, having reduced the estate by £57,600 in respect of these contributions. The full nil rate band (currently £325,000) is still available, and the grandchildren have £72,000 (ignoring investment issues) between them in their pension plans. The total tax saving is therefore £23,040 (IHT saving at 40 per cent) plus £14,400 (pension tax relief) which totals £37,440.

76.9.8 Unsecured Pension – surplus cash gifted under 'normal expenditure out of income exemption'

One common objection to pensions is that the residual fund cannot, from age 77, pay a lump sum on death. This has come to be seen as poor value. However, where part or all of the income payable from the pension plan is surplus to requirements, this can be reinvested in a number of ways in order to drawdown capital from the pension plan into another plan that can provide a future lump sum for the benefit of others.

(1) Pension contributions. This has been described in the section above.

(2) Into a whole of life policy. Provided that the policy is written in trust, the benefits will be immediately exempt from inheritance tax on death, with the advantage that premature death will result in a much larger payment than the value of the contributions due to the insurance element of the policy. The disadvantage of a whole of life plan is that it does require the commitment, and the affordability, to maintain the contributions throughout life. This option would not be suitable if there was the likelihood that future income requirements from the pension would increase over time.

(3) Into a trust. Where there is insufficient confidence that the contributions will be affordable throughout life, the surplus income can be accumulated into a trust. Since these contributions would be subject to the normal expenditure exemption, a discretionary trust can be used without potentially falling foul of the lifetime transfer limits. The contributions and any growth are immediately exempt from IHT. The disadvantage of this arrangement over the whole of

life is that there is no life cover, and so if death occurs in the short term the amount transferred is likely to be small, though over time the growth may overtake the cover under the whole of life.

76.9.9 Single Premium Investment Bonds – Chargeable Event

Where an individual is a higher rate tax payer and has a single premium investment bond with a significant gain, he can use the opportunity of a large pension contribution to reduce, or even eliminate the tax payable as a result of the chargeable event. The reason is that personal contributions to a pension plan extend the basic rate tax band, which has the benefit of making this extended band allowable against other chargeable events.

The following worked example illustrates how this tax planning can work.

An individual resident in the UK for tax purposes purchased a £200,000 single premium investment bond (onshore) on 6 April 1999, which has now doubled in value to £400,000 and he wishes to encash it. The 'top-sliced' gain is therefore £20,000.

The individual is just at the threshold of higher rate tax, with gross earnings of £43,875.

The tax payable on this encashment without any tax planning is therefore:

£20,000 per year × 20%	£4,000
£4,000 × 10 years	£40,000

However, if they make a payment of £10,000 to a personal pension, the basic rate band will be extended by the grossed up £10,000 (£12,500) to £56,695.

This alters the tax calculation as follows:

0% tax on £12,820 × 0% – basic rate band extended by that amount, and basic rate tax is deemed already paid internal to the investment bond	£0
£7,500 × 20%	£1,5000
£1,436 × 10 years	£15,000

It can be seen that there is a tax saving of £25,000 from a pension contribution of £10,000, as well as tax relief on the pension contribution of £2,500. The total tax relief is therefore £27,500.

77 Venture Capital Trusts

77.1 Introduction and overview

77.1.1 Background

Venture Capital Trusts (VCTs) exist to encourage investment in unquoted trading companies. As such, they form part of a package of measures designed to support young, growing businesses by enabling them to raise money without facing punitive interest charges.

Individual investors will need to weigh up the considerable tax advantages on offer and to decide whether, on balance, these counter the (also considerable) risk of investing in businesses that do not have an established track record.

> ⚠ **Warning!**
> The tax breaks are for individuals only – companies, trusts, etc. are not entitled to any of the forms of tax relief described below.

The VCT itself is a quoted company, similar in concept to an investment trust. It has HMRC approval and subscribes for shares in, or lends money to, small unquoted companies. The theory is that the individual investor can spread his risk as the VCT itself spreads its investments between a range of unquoted businesses.

77.1.2 Forms of tax relief – overview

VCTs offer the potential investor three main types of tax relief:

- income tax relief at 30 per cent on investment of up to £200,000 per tax year;
- unlimited tax relief on dividends received from the VCT shares (but no repayment of the tax credit attaching to such dividends); and
- disposals of VCT shares free from all capital gains tax (CGT).

> ⚠ **Warning!**
> It was previously possible to defer liability to CGT on other gains by reinvesting the proceeds into VCT shares . However, this part of the relief was abolished for VCT shares issued from 6 April 2004.

The conditions attaching to each type of relief are different but overlapping.

The VCT itself is exempt from corporation tax on any chargeable gains it may make.

77.1.3 Recent changes

The VCT rules have been changed in various ways in recent years. The following paragraphs provide a quick summary of the most recent changes.

Finance Act 2006

The size of company able to qualify under the VCT rules was reduced.

Income tax relief fell from 40 to 30 per cent (though the higher rate had been a temporary measure only).

The period for which investors must hold their shares was increased from three to five years.

Income Tax Act 2007

The enactment of ITA 2007 was part of the tax law rewrite process. The intention is not to change the underlying way in which the rules operate but rather the terminology in which those rules are expressed. The VCT rules are now found in Pt. 6 of ITA 2007, starting at s. 258.

Finance Act 2007

This Act, by contrast, introduced some substantive changes. Key changes were as follows.

- A VCT company must now have fewer than the equivalent of 50 full-time employees at the time the relevant shares are issued (ITA 2007, s. 297A).
- The total amount of relevant investments made in the issuing company in the year ending with the date the relevant shares are issued must now not exceed £2m (ITA 2007, s. 292A), though investments made before 6 April 2007 are not counted for this purpose (FA 2007, Sch. 16, Pt. 2, para. 8(2)).
- In a change designed to allow VCTs greater flexibility to dispose of qualifying holdings without breaching their approval conditions, the disposal for money of a qualifying holding and the proceeds arising are disregarded for 6 months for the purposes of determining whether the 70 per cent qualifying holding condition has been met by a VCT.
- Groups of companies have greater flexibility than previously as to which group company carries on the qualifying trade: that trade may now be carried on by the VCT company itself, its direct 90 per cent subsidiary or a 100 per cent subsidiary of that subsidiary. The trade may also be carried on by a 90 per cent subsidiary of the VCT company's direct 100 per cent subsidiary (ITA 2007, s. 190).

Finance Act 2008

The list of excluded activities for EIS purposes has been expanded to include shipbuilding, coal extraction and production, and steel production.

Transitional rules allow VCT relief to be claimed where gains that were deferred before 6 April 2008 because of a VCT investment become chargeable on or after that date. Relief is given if the disposal that gave rise to the deferred gain would have qualified for relief if the rules had been in force at the time of that earlier disposal.

> ⚠ **Warning!**
>
> A claim for relief under these provisions has to be made by the first anniversary of the 31 January following the tax year in which the first chargeable event occurs (FA 2008, Sch. 3, para. 8(4)).

Finance Act 2009

The time limits for the employment of money by companies receiving VCT investments has been replaced with a single requirement that all money raised must be wholly employed within two years, or (if later), within two years of the qualifying activity commencing. This relaxation applies in respect of funds raised by VCTs from 22 April 2009.

Proposed changes to legislation with effect from 6 April 2010

In order to comply with EC rules on State Aid to industry, certain changes in the VCT legislation are required. These are:

- a new requirement is to be introduced that the issuing company is not 'in difficulty'. The European Commission regards a firm as being in difficulty where it is unable, whether through its own resources or with the funds it is able to obtain from its owner/shareholders or creditors, to stem losses which, without outside intervention by the public authorities, will almost certainly condemn it to going out of business in the short or medium term (*Community Guidelines for Rescuing Restructuring Firms in Difficulty*, (2004/C244/02));
- the current requirement that the relevant company's qualifying trade is to be carried on wholly or mainly within the UK is to be replaced with a requirement that the issuing company must have a 'permanent establishment' in the UK. The definition of 'permanent establishment' will be based upon Article 5 of the OECD Model Tax Convention;
- the requirement that a VCT's shares must be included in the Official UK List is replaced with one requiring that the shares must be traded on an EU regulated market; and
- changes in the rules on the amount of a VCT's investment which must be held

as equity. Currently VCTs are required to have 70 per cent of their investments in shares or securities as qualifying holdings and 30 per cent of the qualifying holdings held as equities. The changes will increase that 30 per cent requirement to 70 per cent.

These changes were confirmed in the June 2010 budget, but the relevant legislation will be included in the autumn 2010 Finance Bill, and will generally take effect from a date to be appointed (after the print date of this publication).

77.2 Income tax relief on investment

77.2.1 Overview of income tax relief on investment

> **Planning point**
>
> An investor, aged 18 or over, obtains income tax relief for VCT investments at 30 per cent. Relief, which must be claimed, is given by way of an income tax reduction.

To qualify for relief, the individual must subscribe on his own behalf for new ordinary shares in a VCT. Relief will be given on subscriptions up to the 'permitted maximum' of (currently) £200,000. The shares must carry no present or future preferential rights to dividends or to the VCT's assets on winding up and no rights to be redeemed.

Shares must be held for at least five years to retain the relief. This increase (from three years) applies in relation to shares issued from 6 April 2006. The references in this chapter to a five year period should therefore be read as if they were to a three year period if the shares were issued before that date.

The maximum relief which can be given will be an amount which reduces the individual's liability to nil, and in determining an individual's liability, this relief is given before any reliefs given by way of an income tax reduction. Relief is given before any of the following:

- Enterprise Investment Scheme relief;
- Community Investment Tax Relief;
- income tax reduction in respect of personal reliefs or maintenance payments;
- double taxation relief; or
- basic rate tax to be retained on charges.

Interest on repayments of tax arising from a claim for a VCT investment is calculated according to the normal rules for self assessment repayments.

No relief is given if the circumstances are such that any relief, which might previously have been given, would have had cause to be withdrawn; furthermore, relief is not available unless the shares were both issued and subscribed for bona fide commercial purposes, and not as part of any tax avoidance scheme.

Law: ITA 2007, s. 261ff, s. 266(4)

77.2.2 Loan-linked investments

Individuals are denied income tax relief on subscriptions for shares where those shares are linked to the making of loans (or any equivalent act such as the giving of credit or the assignment of a debt) to the individuals, or their associates, at any time during a specified period. This period begins when the venture capital trust is incorporated, or two years before the shares are issued, whichever is the later, and ends five (or three: see **77.2.1**) years after the shares are issued.

> ⚠ **Warning!**
>
> The purpose of this rule is to restrict VCT relief to those investors who genuinely lay out capital for at least five (or, as the case may be, three) years. Relief is denied where the individual, or an associate of his, receives a loan which would not have been made, or would not have been made on the same terms, had the investor not subscribed, or planned to subscribe, for the shares.

When applying this rule in practice, HMRC are primarily concerned with the motive of the lender in making the loan, rather than the reasons why the borrower applied for it. The crucial test is whether the lender would have made the loan on the same terms had the eligible shares not been involved. In determining whether this is the case, HMRC will have regard to:

- the qualifying conditions which the borrower must satisfy;
- whether any incentives or benefits were offered to the borrower;
- the time allowed for repayment;
- the timing of interest payments;
- the amount of repayment and interest charged; and
- the nature of the security involved.

For example, a loan would be linked with the investment if it was made on a specified security which included eligible shares for which the borrower had subscribed or was intending to subscribe. By contrast, HMRC will not seek to deny relief where the investor, for example, obtains a bank loan for the purpose of buying eligible shares if that loan would have been made on similar terms to another borrower intending to use it for a different purpose.

The approach of HMRC is set out more fully in Statement of Practice SP 6/98.

Law: ITA 2007, s. 264

Other guidance: Statement of Practice SP 6/98

77.2.3 Loss of investment relief

If investment relief has been given to an individual, it will be lost in whole or in part if the individual disposes of the shares in the VCT within the period of five (or three: see **77.2.1**) years beginning with the issue of those shares to that individual. If the original subscriber makes a disposal to his or her spouse or civil partner, then the spouse (or partner) is treated as if he or she was the original subscriber for the shares.

If the disposal within the five- (or three-) year time limit is by way of a bargain not at arm's length, then the relief is withdrawn in full, but if the disposal is at arm's length, then the amount of relief withdrawn is based on the consideration for the disposal.

Where it is necessary to identify which shares have been disposed of, eligible shares acquired on different days will be deemed to be disposed of on a FIFO (first in, first out) basis. Where eligible shares acquired on the same day are disposed of, and only some have qualified for relief under these provisions, then the shares which have not qualified for relief are deemed to be disposed of first.

If a VCT loses its approved status, then any person holding shares in that VCT is deemed to have disposed of them immediately prior to that time, and not at arm's length, with the result that all the relief previously granted will be withdrawn.

If relief, once given, needs to be withdrawn, it will be withdrawn by way of an assessment for the tax year in respect of which the relief to be withdrawn was originally given. No assessment will be made to withdraw or reduce relief as a result of an event occurring after the subscriber's death.

> ⚠ **Warning!**
>
> An individual investor must inform HMRC within 60 days if he becomes aware of an event that would cause his relief to be reduced or withdrawn. Equally, HMRC may require an individual to supply any information (within a period of not less than 60 days) which HMRC believe may be reasonably required regarding an event which may cause relief to be reduced or withdrawn.

Law: ITA 2007, s. 266ff

77.3 Relief for dividends received

Planning point

No tax liability arises on a VCT dividend paid in respect of ordinary shares in the VCT, where the relevant conditions are met.

The recipient, who must be at least 18 years old, must be beneficially entitled to the dividend, whether as the direct holder of the shares or as the person for whom, or for whose benefit, they are held by a nominee.

Relief is due only if the shares are acquired for genuine commercial purposes and not as part of a scheme or arrangement, the main purpose of which is tax avoidance.

Where shares are acquired in excess of the permitted maximum, specific rules apply – broadly – to give relief on the first £200,000 worth acquired in any year. The £200,000 is thus not an overall limit but an annual one.

Planning point

If the investor acquires new shares in a VCT in exchange for shares in another VCT (which were originally acquired in whole or in part within the permitted maximum for the year), then the value of the new shares is ignored in calculating the permitted maximum for the year in which the new shares were acquired. However, the new shares still qualify for dividend relief, with the proviso that if only part of the original shares qualified for such relief, then a similar part of the new shares continues so to qualify.

Law: ITTOIA 2005, s. 709–712

77.4 Tax-free sale of VCT shares

77.4.1 Outline of relief

Planning point

If an individual makes a 'qualifying disposal' of ordinary shares in a company which was a VCT at the time of acquisition of the shares, and is still a VCT at the time of their disposal, then a gain on the disposal is not chargeable for capital gains purposes. Similarly, a loss on such a disposal is not allowable.

A disposal is a qualifying disposal for these purposes if it is made by an individual aged 18 or over and is made of shares which were acquired for bona fide commercial purposes (i.e. not as part of a tax avoidance scheme). Investing in a VCT will be driven mainly by the available tax breaks so it is fortunate that HMRC accept that:

> 'this restriction is only likely to apply in exceptional circumstances. For example, where artificial arrangements are made to convert shares which do not qualify for exemption into shares which do.'

The shares disposed of must not have exceeded the permitted maximum in the tax year in which they were acquired and the principles discussed at **77.3** above apply for this purpose. In this respect, by contrast to the words quoted above, there may well be difficulties, for HMRC comment that 'this is the restriction you are most likely to see broken in practice'.

The annual limit applies to all shares the VCT acquired in any given tax year. The starting point is that shares acquired earlier in the tax year count towards the permitted maximum first. If, however, shares in different VCTs, or in different classes of ordinary share in the same VCT, are acquired on the same day then these are identified on a *pro rata* basis.

> **Planning point**
>
> There is an important distinction between this CGT relief and the income tax relief for investment in a VCT. For the income tax relief, there must be a cash subscription for new shares. By contrast, CGT relief on disposals is available (but subject to the annual maximum) on *any* acquisition of qualifying VCT shares even if, for example, they were bought from a previous holder of the shares.

Other guidance: VCM 66050

77.4.2 Identification of shares

Share identification rules are needed where shares acquired in the year exceed the limit for which tax relief may be due. The ordinary share identification rules do not apply to VCT shares that are exempt from CGT.

It is possible that only some of the ordinary shares the taxpayer owns in a VCT will qualify for capital gains tax relief on the disposal. If a taxpayer disposes of some but not all of the shareholding then it will be necessary to identify whether, or to what extent, the disposal is exempt. The usual share identification rules are disapplied. Instead disposals are identified:

- first, against shares acquired before the company was approved as a VCT; and

- next, against shares acquired after the company was approved as a VCT on a first in, first out basis.

If shares are acquired on the same day, then shares acquired in excess of the permitted maximum are treated as disposed of before other shares acquired on that day.

Law: TCGA 1992, s. 151A; ITTOIA 2005, s. 709

77.4.3 Supplementary provisions

Where shares which enjoy different tax reliefs (specified in TCGA 1992, s. 151B(3)) are involved in a reorganisation under TCGA 1992, s. 126, then the shares are treated (under TCGA 1992, s. 127) as being different holdings according to the different tax reliefs they enjoy. If a reorganisation such as a rights issue affects an existing holding, and results in the individual holding shares in a VCT (as defined), then the reorganisation provisions contained in TCGA 1992, s. 127–130 will not apply to the existing holding.

On a reconstruction, the rules contained in TCGA 1992, s. 135, 136 are disapplied where a VCT acquires another company which is not a VCT, or is acquired by such a company.

Where approval of a VCT is withdrawn, then an individual holding shares in the VCT is deemed to have disposed of those shares and immediately re-acquired them for their market value. The disposal is deemed to take place whilst the VCT is still approved, so that no chargeable gain or allowable loss arises, but the re-acquisition, for the purposes of the share pooling rules, is deemed to take place immediately after the company ceases to be a VCT.

Law: TCGA 1992, s. 151B

77.5 Approval of companies as VCTs

The individual investor will not generally need to be unduly concerned with the mechanics of obtaining approval for the VCT itself.

The HMRC manuals list the following key conditions that will need to be satisfied by the company in relation to its most recently completed accounting period for such approval to be granted:

- its income in that accounting period must have been derived wholly or mainly from shares or securities;
- at least 70 per cent by value of its investments must have been in qualifying holdings of shares or securities throughout that accounting period (the '70 per

Venture Capital Trusts

cent test'). The conditions to be met for the holding to be 'qualifying' broadly cover:

(a) the form of the investment;
(b) the type of company invested in; and
(c) the way in which the money raised is to be used.

See warning point below regarding proposed changes from April 2010.

- at least 30 per cent by value of its qualifying holdings must have been in holdings of eligible shares throughout that accounting period (the '30 per cent test'). Subject to a possible relaxation where provisional approval is given (see below) shares will be 'eligible' if they:

  (a) are comprised in the company's ordinary share capital;
  (b) carry no present or future preferential right to dividends or to the company's assets in a winding up; and
  (c) carry no present or future right to be redeemed.

- no holding in any company may have represented more than 15 per cent by value of the VCT's investments at any time during that accounting period (the '15 per cent value test');
- its ordinary share capital must have been quoted on the London Stock Exchange throughout that accounting period; and
- it must not have retained more than 15 per cent of its income derived in that accounting period from shares and securities (the '15 per cent retention test').

The legislation also lays down conditions relating to the company in the following areas:

- a requirement that the company must be unquoted;
- detailed requirements relating to the company's business;
- a definition (tightened from April 2008) of qualifying trades;
- rules relating to qualifying subsidiaries;
- requirements relating to use of the money raised under the scheme;
- a cap on the amount of qualifying investments in the company;
- a test relating to the maximum assets to be held by the company; and
- a number of further requirements.

⚠ Warning!

The June 2010 budget confirmed proposed changes in the rules on the amount of a VCT's investment which must be held as equity. Currently VCTs are required to have 70 per cent of their investments in shares or securities as qualifying holdings and 30 per cent of the qualifying holdings held as equities. The changes will increase that 30 per cent requirement to 70 per cent. Whilst this change was confirmed in the June 2010 budget, the relevant legislation will be included in the autumn 2010 Finance Bill. The change will take effect from a date to be appointed (after the print date of this publication).

The company must also satisfy HMRC that these conditions will be met in relation to the accounting period which is current when the application for approval is made, though this is relaxed in certain circumstances where the VCT issues further ordinary shares.

Where not all conditions can be met immediately, there is a provision for HMRC to give provisional approval. Where conditions are breached, possibly by reason of circumstances outside the company's control, HMRC has limited powers to allow VCT approval to continue. This might apply, according to HMRC's *Explanatory Notes* to SI 2008/1893, 'provided that either it takes action to rectify the situation, or that it can show that while there is no such action it could reasonably take, the situation will rectify itself within a reasonable length of time'.

Planning point

Finance Act 2009 contained provisions to relax the time limits for the employment of money by companies receiving VCT investments. For investments made on or after 22 April 2009 there is a single requirement that all money raised must be wholly employed within two years, or (if later), within two years of the qualifying activity commencing.

Law: ITA 2007, s. 274ff; FA 2009, s. 27 and Sch. 8; SI 1995/1979 (as amended)

Other guidance: VCM 60110

Case Table

(References are to paragraph numbers)

A

	Paragraph
Alloway v Phillips [1980] 1 WLR 888	57.12.6
American Foreign Insurance Association v Davies (1950) 32 TC 1	57.12.4
Anderson (Exor of Muriel S Anderson) v IR Commrs (1997) Sp C 147	57.4
Anderton v Lamb (1980) 55 TC 1	65.10.2
Atlantic Computer Systems plc, Re [1992] Ch 505	67.5.6
A-G v Antoine (1949) 31 TC 213	55.4.4
A-G v Pratt (1874) LR 9 Ex 140	57.13.4
A-G v Yule & The Mercantile Bank of India [1931] All ER 400	57.5
Auntie's Café Ltd v R & C Commrs (2007) Sp C 588	66.9.6
Ayerst v C & K (Construction) Ltd (1975) 50 TC 651	67.5.2; 67.5.4
Ayrshire Pullman Motors Services v IR Commrs (1929) 14 TC 754	63.1.3

B

Barclays Bank plc v IR Commrs [1994] BTC 236	64.2.5
Barclays Mercantile Business Finance Ltd v Mawson [2004] BTC 414	63.1.3
Bayfine UK v R & C Commrs [2010] BTC 467	58.5
Beaumont, Re [1893] 3 Ch 490	57.10
Begg-McBrearty v Sitwell [1996] BTC 269	61.8.5
Bergner and Engle Brewing Co v Dreyfus 70 American States Reports 251	57.12.2
Billingham v Cooper [2000] BTC 28	60.7.6
Bispham v Eardiston Farming Co (1919) Ltd (1962) 40 TC 322	65.2
Blackburn v R & C Commrs [2008] BTC 158	64.3.9
Boehm v Goodall [1911] 1 Ch 155	67.5.11
Boston Deep Sea Fishing and Ice Co Ltd v Farnham [1957] 1 WLR 1051	57.12.4
Brittain v Gibbs [1986] BTC 348	66.7.2

	Paragraph
Brown v Richardson (1997) Sp C 129	65.3.3
Bruns (t/a TK Fabrications) [2010] TC 00371	62.8
Burt, Boulton & Hayward v Bull [1895] 1 QB 276	67.5.11
Buswell v IR Commrs (1974) 49 TC 334	57.5

C

Cable & Wireless plc v Muscat [2006] EWCA Civ 220	71.2.6
Cairns v MacDiarmid [1983] BTC 188 (CA); [1982] BTC 74	68.9.1; 73.5.5
Cenlon Finance Co Ltd v Ellwood (1962) 40 TC 176	63.3.7
Clark (HMIT) v Oceanic Contractors Ltd [1982] BTC 417	62.5
Clayton's Case [1816] 1 Mer 529	57.14.3
Clore (dec'd), Re [1984] BTC 8,101	57.5
Collector of Stamp Revenue v Arrowtown Assets Ltd [2003] HKCFA 46	63.1.3
Cooke (on the application of) R v R & C Commrs [2007] EWHC 81 (Admin)	66.4.3
Corinthian Securities Ltd v Cato (1969) 46 TC 93	68.9.1
Cottle v Coldicott (1995) Sp C 40	65.10.5
Coy v Kime [1987] BTC 66	66.7.1; 66.7.2
Cruh v Cruh [1945] 2 All ER 545	57.8

D

Davies v Hicks [2005] BTC 331	60.6.1
Davis v Powell (1976) 51 TC 492	65.10.4
Derby (Earl of) v Aylmer (1915) 6 TC 665	65.7
Dickenson v Gross (1927) 11 TC 614	65.9.1
Dixon v IR Commrs (2001) Sp C 297	75.11.4
Donaldson v Donaldson [1949] P 363	57.5
Dronfield Silkstone Coal Co, Re (1880) 17 ChD 76	67.5.4

	Paragraph
Duckworth, Re (1867) 1 Ch App 578	67.5.4

E

Ebsworth [2009] TC 00152	67.5.10
Edwards v Fisher [2000] BTC 28	60.7.5
English, Scottish and Australian Bank Ltd v IR Commrs [1932] AC 238	57.13.8
Entores v Miles Far East Corporation [1955] 2 QB 327	55.6
Erichsen v Last (1881) 8 QBD 414; 4 TC 422	55.6; 57.12.6

F

Faulks v Faulks [1992] 15 EG 15	65.10.5
Figg v Clarke [1997] BTC 157	61.9
Firestone Tyre and Rubber Co Ltd v Lewellin [1957] 1 WLR 464; (1957) 37 TC 111	55.5.2; 55.6; 57.12.6
Food Controller v Cork [1924] AC 647	67.3.2
Forthright (Wales) Ltd v Davies [2004] BTC 298	64.2.5
Fowler v Broad's Patent Night Light Co [1893] 1 Ch 724	67.5.2
Fox v Stirk [1970] 2 QB 463	59.3.1.1
Fuld, In the Estate of (No. 3) [1968] P 675	57.5
Furse v IR Commrs [1980] 3 All ER 838	57.5
Furse (dec'd), Re [1980] 3 All ER 838	57.5

G

Gaines-Cooper v R & C Commrs (2006) Sp C 568	55.2.4; 56.1.2
Gallagher v Jones [1993] BTC 310	68.10
Gasque v IR Commrs [1940] 2 KB 80	57.12.1
Gaughan v R & C Commrs (2006) Sp C 575	66.8.1
Genovese v R & C Commrs (2009) Sp C 741	59.4.1
Getty Oil Co v Steele [1990] BTC 312	58.3
Georgiou (t/a Marios Chippery) v United Kingdom (Application 40042/98)	66.9.6
GHE Realisations Ltd (formerly Gatehouse Estates Ltd), Re [2005] EWHC 2400 (Ch); [2006] 1 WLR 287	67.7

	Paragraph
Gilmour v Coats [1949] AC 426	74.2.1
Glasdir Cooper Mines, Re [1906] 1 Ch 365	67.5.11
Goodwin v Curtis [1998] BTC 176	59.3.1.1
Gordon (James A) & Sons Ltd No. 2790; (1988) 3 BVC 1,383	66.7.4
Gosling v Gaskell [1897] AC 575	67.5.2; 67.5.11
Grainger & Son v Gough [1896] AC 325; 3 TC 462	55.5.2; 55.6; 57.12.6
Greenwood v FL Smidth & Co [1921] 3 KB 583; (1922) 8 Tc 193	55.6; 57.12.6
Gresham Life Assurance Society Ltd v Bishop [1902] AC 287	57.16
Grosvenor [2009] TC 00227	62.8
Gutteridge v R & C Commrs (2006) Sp C 534	71.4.9

H

Haig, Re (1922) 17 ATC 635	57.13.4
Haldane v Eckford (1869) LR 8 Eq 631	57.5
Harmel v Wright (1974) 49 TC 149	57.16
Harris v Drayton (1922) 17 ATC 635	57.13.3
Hawksworth (1988) 2 BVC 1,421	66.7.4
Haworth v IR Commrs (1974) 49 TC 489	61.2
Henderson v Karmel's Exors (1984) 58 TC 201	65.10.4
Hertel v Minister of National Revenue 93 DTC 712 (TCC)	58.3
Holly and Laurel v HM Inspector of Taxes (1999) Sp C 225	66.3.5
Hossain v C & E Commrs [2004] BVC 826	66.7.3
Household Fire & Carriage Accident Insurance Co v Grant (1879) 4 Ex D 216	55.6
HPJ UK Ltd (in admin'), Re [2007] BCC 244 (ChD)	67.7
Hurren (a bankrupt), Re [1982] BTC 373	67.4
Hydrodan (Corby) Ltd (in liq'), Re (1994) BCC 161 ChD	67.5.2

I

IR Commrs v Brebner (1967) 2 AC 18 (HL)	67.5.10
IR Commrs v Brown (1926) 11 TC 289	59.3.1.4

	Paragraph
IR Commrs v Bullock (1976) 51 TC 522	57.2; 57.3; 57.4
IR Commrs v Christian Churches of England and Wales (1926) 10 TC 748	74.2.1
IR Commrs v Combe (1932) 17 TC 405	59.3.1.1
IR Commrs v Duchess of Portland [1982] BTC 65	57.4; 57.7; 57.10
IR Commrs v Duke of Westminster (1935) 19 TC 490	63.1.3
IR Commrs v Gordon (1952) 33 TC 226	57.16
IR Commrs v Helen Slater Charitable Trust Ltd (1981) 55 TC 230	74.3.4
IR Commrs v Herd [1993] BTC 245	55.4.3; 55.4.4
IR Commrs v Joiner (1975) 50 TC 449	67.5.10; 67.9
IR Commrs v Korner (1969) 45 TC 287	75.11.4
IR Commrs v Lawrence [2001] BCC 663; [2001] BCLC 204; [2001] ICR 424	67.7
IR Commrs v Leiner (1964) 41 TC 589	60.12.6
IR Commrs v Olive Mill Ltd (1963) 41 TC 77	67.5.2
IR Commrs v Scottish & Newcastle Breweries Ltd [1982] BTC 187	65.7
IR Commrs v Scottish Provident Institution [2004] BTC 426	63.1.3
IR Commrs v Thompson (1936) 20 TC 422	67.5.11
IR Commrs v Woollen [1992] BTC 633	67.4
IR Commrs v Zorab (1926) 11 TC 289	59.3.1.1; 59.3.1.4
Iveagh v IR Commrs [1930] IR 386	55.2.2

J

Jade Place Ltd v R & C Commrs (2006) Sp C 540	66.9.1
James A Gordon & Sons Ltd No. 2790; (1988) 3 BVC 1,383	66.7.4
Johnathan David Ltd [2009] TC 00233	62.7.5
Jonas v Bamford (1973) 51 TC 1	66.8.1

K

Kahn v IR Commrs [2002] UKHL 6; [2002] BTC 69	67.5.6

	Paragraph
Khan (t/a Greyhound Dry Cleaners) v C & E Commrs [2005] EWHC 635 (Ch); [2005] BVC 518	66.10.3; 66.10.4
Kaytech International plc, Re (1999) BCC 390 CA	67.5.2
King v Walden [2001] BTC 170 (Ch); (1999) Sp C 235	66.9.4; 66.9.6; 66.9.8
Kretztechnik AG v Finanzamt Linz (Case C-465/03) [2006] BVC 66	73.5.1
Kwok v Commr of Estate Duty [1988] BTC 8,073; (1988) 1 CTC 303	57.13.8

L

Laerstate BV [2009] TC 00162	58.3
Langham v Veltema [2004] BTC 156	66.3.8
Lawson v Hosemaster Machine Co Ltd (1966) 43 TC 337	67.5.11
Leeds Lifts Ltd [2009] TC 00231	62.7.5
Levene v IR Commrs (1928) 13 TC 486; [1928] AC 217	55.2.4; 59.2.2; 59.3.1.1
Lloyds TSB (personal representatives of Antrobus) v IR Commrs (2002) Sp C 336	75.11.4
Longworth (A) & Sons Ltd [2009] TC 00230	62.7.3
Lord v Tustain [1993] BTC 447	68.3.1
Lysaght v IR Commrs (1928) 13 TC 511	59.3.1.1; 59.3.1.2; 59.4.1

M

Mackenzie, Re [1941] Ch 69	57.11
Maclaine & Co v Eccott [1926] AC 424; 10 TC 481	55.6; 57.12.4; 57.12.6
Major v Brodies [1998] BTC 141	68.6.2
Marsden (t/a Seddon Investments) v Eadie (1999) Sp C 217	66.5.4
Mawcon Ltd, Re [1969] 1 WLR 78	67.5.2
Megtian (in admin) v R & C Commrs [2010] BVC 314	67.5.10
Minsham Properties Ltd v Price [1990] BTC 528	68.9.1
Moore (dec'd) (Exors of) v IR Commrs (2002) Sp C 335	57.3
Moorhouse v Lord (1863) 10 HL Cas 272	57.5
Morgan Grenfell & Co Ltd, ex parte [2003] 1 AC 563; [2002] BTC 223	63.10; 66.4.3

	Paragraph
Mumford (1987) 3 BVC 1,307	66.7.4
Munby v Furlong (1977) 50 TC 491	65.7
Munns [2009] TC 00234	62.8
Mutch [2009] TC 00232	62.7.3

N

	Paragraph
National Provincial Bank v Evans [1947] Ch 695	57.8
National Westminster Bank v IR Commrs [1994] BTC 236	64.5
New York Life Insurance Co v Public Trustee [1924] 2 Ch 101	57.13.8
Nielsen, Anderson & Co v Collins (1927) 13 TC 91	55.6
Nightingale Ltd v Price (1995) Sp C 66	74.3.2
Nine Miles Down UK Ltd, Re [2009] EWHC 3510 (Ch)	67.5.10
Norris, Re (1888) 4 TLR 452	55.2.5; 59.4.1
Nursing Council for Scotland v IR Commrs (1929) 14 TC 645	74.3.4

O

	Paragraph
OJSC Oil Company Yugraneft (in liq') v Abramovich [2008] EWHC 2613 (Comm)	59.3.1.4
Oriental Inland Steam Co, Re (1874) 9 Ch App 557	67.5.2
Oxford Group v IR Commrs (1949) 31 TC 221	74.2.1

P

	Paragraph
Pegasus Management Holdings SCA v Ernst & Young (a firm) (2008) EWHC 2710 (Ch); (2009) PNLR 11	67.5.10
Pegler v Abell (1972) 48 TC 564	71.9.3
Plummer v IR Commrs [1987] BTC 543	57.3
Pommery & Grena v Apthorpe (1885) 2 TC 182	55.6
Pooley v R & C Commrs (2006) Sp C 525	66.2.5
Prior Roofing Ltd [2009] TC 00246	62.8

Q

	Paragraph
Qureshi v Qureshi [1972] Fam 173	57.6

R

	Paragraph
R v Barnet London Borough Council, ex parte Shah [1983] 2 AC 309	59.4; 59.4.1
R v Gill [2003] BTC 404	66.10.1; 66.10.2; 66.10.3
R v IR Commrs, ex parte Taylor (No. 2) [1990] BTC 281	66.4.2
R v Special Commr, ex parte Morgan Grenfell & Co Ltd [2003] 1 AC 563; [2002] BTC 223	63.10; 66.4.2
R v Williams [1942] AC 541	57.13.6
R (on the application of R & C Commrs) v General Commrs of Income Tax for Berkshire [2007] EWHC 871 (Admin)	66.9.8
Ramsay v Liverpool Royal Infirmary [1930] AC 588	57.4
Ramsay (WT) Ltd v IR Commrs [1982] AC 300	63.1.3
Reed v Clark [1985] BTC 224	56.1.4; 59.3.2.3
Reid v IR Commrs (1926) 10 TC 673	59.3.1.1
R & C Commrs v Grace [2009] BTC 704	59.3.1.1; 59.3.1.4; 59.4.1
R & C Commrs v Holland [2009] EWCA Civ 625	67.5.2
R & C Commrs v Livewire Telecom Ltd [2009] BVC 172	67.5.10
Richart v Lyons & Co Ltd [1989] BTC 337	65.8.3
Rosette Franks (King Street) Ltd v Dick (1955) 36 TC 100	66.5.4

S

	Paragraph
Sainsbury (J) v O'Connor [1991] BTC 181	67.9
Sargent v Eayrs (1972) 48 TC 573	65.1.1
Saywell v Pope (1979) 53 TC 40	65.9.1
Schofield v R & H Hall Ltd (1974) 49 TC 538	65.7
Scorer v Olin Energy Systems Ltd (1985) 58 TC 592	66.3.8
Scott (t/a Farthings Steak House) v McDonald (1996) Sp C 91	66.7.1; 66.9.1
Scottish Mortgage Co of New Mexico v McKelvie (1886) 2 TC 165	57.16

	Paragraph
Sharkey v De Cross (2005) Sp C 460	66.9.6
Shepherd v R & C Commrs (2005) Sp C 484	56.1.2
Shepherd v R & C Commrs [2007] BTC 426	59.3.1.3; 59.3.1.4
Silk v Fletcher (2000) Sp C 262	68.9.3; 73.2.2
Smidth (FL) & Co v Greenwood (1922) 8 TC 193	55.5.2
Special Commrs v Pemsel (1891) 3 TC 53	74.2.1
Squirrell v R & C Commrs (2005) Sp C 493	58.3
Standard Chartered Bank Ltd v IR Commrs [1978] 3 All ER 644	57.13.6
Stanley v IR Commrs [1944] KB 255; 26 TC 12	61.2
Stekel v Ellice [1973] 1 All ER 465	71.9.3
Strongwork Construction Ltd [2009] TC 00236	62.8
Sulley v A-G (1860) 2 TC 149	55.6
Surveyor v IR Commrs (2002) Sp C 339	57.3

T

Thompson v Hart [2000] BTC 151	75.2.2
Thompson v IR Commrs (1936) 20 TC 422	67.5.10
Thomson v Moyse [1961] AC 967	57.16
Three Rivers District Council v Bank of England [2004] UKHL 48	63.10
Threlfell v Jones [1993] BTC 310	68.10
Tischler v Apthorpe (1885) 2 TC 89	55.6
Trinity Mirror plc v C & E Commrs [2003] BVC 572	73.5.1
Tuczka [2010] TC 00366	59.4.1
Turberville [2010] TC 00381	59.4.1

U

Udny v Udny (1869) LR 1 Sc & Div 441	57.2
Union Cold Storage Co Ltd v Adamson (1931) 16 TC 293	65.9.4
Unmarried Settlor v IR Commrs (2003) Sp C 345	60.11.2

V

Vandervell v IR Commrs [1967] 2 AC 291	61.2

W

Waddington v O'Callaghan (1931) 16 TC 187	65.9.1
Wahl v A-G [1932] All ER 922	57.5
Waterhouse v Jamieson (1870) LR 2 HL Sc 29	67.5.4
Werle & Co v Colquhoun (1886) 2 TC 402	55.6
Westmoreland Investments Ltd v MacNiven [2001] BTC 44	63.1.3
Whittaker v R & C Commrs (2006) Sp C 528	71.4.9
Wicks v Firth [1982] BTC 402	74.5.2
Wilcock v Pinto (1925) 10 TC 415	55.6
Wilkie v IR Commrs (1951) 32 TC 495; [1952] Ch 153	55.2.2; 55.2.4
Williams v Grundy Trustees (1933) 18 TC 271	66.3.8
Winans v A-G [1904] AC 287	57.5
Wing Hung Lai v Bale (1999) Sp C 203	66.3.5
Wyndham v Egremont [2009] EWHC 2076 (Ch)	61.3.3

Y

Yarmouth v France (1887) 19 QBD 647	65.7
Yates v GCA International Ltd (formerly Gaffney Cline and Associates Ltd) [1991] BTC 107	58.5
Yip [1993] BVC 1,531	66.7.4
Yoon v R 2005 TCC 366	58.3
Young v Pearce [1996] BTC 322	61.3

Legislation Finding List

(References are to paragraph numbers)

Provision	Paragraph
Abolition of Domestic Rates etc. (Scotland) Act 1987	74.3.6
Adults with Incapacity (Scotland) Act 2000	76.4.5; 76.5.2
Capital Allowances Act 2001	
11	68.10
36	73.3.2
173(2)	63.12.11
221	63.12.11
228F(5)	63.12.11
264	68.2
266	65.2
393A	72.7.5
Capital Gains Tax Act 1979	
126C	60.5.3
Charitable Deductions (Approved Schemes) Regulations 1986 (SI 1986/2211)	74.4.11
Charities Act 1992	
59	74.3.2
Charities Act 1993	
See generally	74.2.1; 74.2.3
2	74.2.6
3	74.2.1
16	74.3.3
21	74.2.6
97(1)	74.2.1
Charities Act 2006	
See generally	74.2.2; 74.2.3
2	74.2.1
6	74.2.4
Child Support, Pensions and Social Security Act 2000	76.6.2
Companies Act 1985	
425	67.6.3
736	67.9
Companies Act 2006	
See generally	67.5.10
170(3), (4)	67.5.10
172(3)	67.5.10
Companies (Northern Ireland) Order 1986	
art. 418	67.6.3
Corporation Tax Act 2009	
3	73.5.1
5(1)	57.12.4
15(2)–(4)	57.12.1
Pt. 3, Ch. 4	73.2.4
54	73.2.1
70–71	74.4.7
105	73.5.4
116	65.5.1
131	68.9.1; 73.5.3
196	67.9
297	73.2.4
299–301	73.2.4
307(3)	73.5.1
322	67.9
344–346	67.9
630–632	67.9
631(2)(a), (b)	67.9
Pt. 20, Ch. 1	74.4.3
1219–1223	58.7.5
1259, 1260	65.9.3
1300	74.4.3
Sch. 1, para. 309	57.12.1
Sch. 2, para. 13–15	57.12.1
Corporation Tax Act 2010	
34	73.3.3
34(1), (2), (6)	68.3.2
37	65.3.3
54	58.4
Pt. 4, Ch. 5	73.4.4
109(1)	57.12.5
158	64.2.4
166	64.2.4
Pt. 6, Ch. 2	74.4.2
191–202	74.4.2
199(3)	63.6.2
203–217	74.4.4
450, 454	60.11.2
Pt. 11	74.3.1; 74.3.2; 74.3.5
478–479	74.3.1
480, 482	74.3.1
483	74.3.1; 74.3.5
500	74.6.2
502–510	74.3.5
Pt. 14, Ch. 2	65.2
748	63.6.2
Pt. 18	74.3.2
1009(3)	63.6.2
1044	63.6.2
1091	63.6.2
1120	63.6.2
1122	63.6.2
1181	58.7.1
Sch. 3	58.7.1

Legislation Finding List

Provision	Paragraph
Customs and Excise Management Act 1979	
167, 167(3)	70.4.2
Data Protection Act 1998	66.4.2
Domicile and Matrimonial Proceedings Act 1973	
1, 1(2)	57.7
3	57.10
Donations to Charity by Individuals (Appropriate Declarataions) Regulations 2000 (SI 2000/2074)	74.4.2
Double Taxation Relief (Taxes on Income) (United States of America) Order 1980 (SI 1980/568)	
art. 4(4)	57.7
EC Directive 90/434	58.4
EC Directive 2003/48	
art. 6	58.10.2
art. 15	58.10.2
Employment Rights Act 1996	71.4.5; 71.4.6
English Trustee Act 2000	61.5.5
Enterprise Act 2002	
See generally	67.5.2; 67.6; 67.7
248	67.5.1
251	67.3.1
Enterprise Act 2002 (Commencement No. 4 and Transitional Provisions and Savings) Order 2003 (SI 2003/2039)	67.3.1
European Convention on Human Rights	
art. 6	66.9.6; 66.9.7
Family Law Reform Act 1969	
1	61.8.2
1(7)	61.8.5
Finance Act 1930	
27	67.9
42, 42(2)	67.9
Finance Act 1976	
131(2)	57.13.6
Finance Act 1981	
79	60.5.2
80	60.1
Finance Act 1986	
79	67.9
Finance Act 1989	
115	58.3
Sch. 6, para. 20	76.5.5
Finance Act 1991	
See generally	60.1; 60.9.1
72	72.9.6
Sch. 17, para. 2	60.9.3
Finance Act 1992	
59	72.10.1
Sch. 10	72.10.1
Sch. 10, para. 6	72.10.3
Finance Act 1993	
171(1), (2)	69.5
172(1)	69.3
172(1)(a)	69.3.4
172(1)(b)	69.5
172(1)(c)	69.3.4
176	69.2.1; 69.5
179	69.4
180	69.3.3
182(1)	69.7.6
184(1)	69.5
Sch. 19	69.7.6
Finance Act 1994	
See generally	69.3
229	58.7.3
Sch. 21, para. 2	69.3
Finance Act 1995	
See generally	62.9.1
Finance Act 1996	
See generally	62.9.1
83(2)(a), (d)	58.7.5
200(1)	57.8
200(2), (3), (4)	57.8; 57.14.1
Sch. 9, para. 5(3)	67.9
Sch. 9, para. 6, 6A	67.5.2
Sch. 9, para. 12A	67.9
Finance (No. 2) Act 1997	
48	67.5.10
Finance Act 1998	
Sch. 18	66.1.2
Sch. 18, para. 7	66.1.3
Sch. 18, para. 8(1)	73.4.4
Sch. 18, para. 17(3)	66.9.6
Sch. 18, para. 20	66.9.3
Sch. 18, para. 21	66.2.4; 66.5.2
Sch. 18, para. 24	66.1.4; 66.2.2; 66.3.1; 66.3.3; 66.3.5; 66.3.6
Sch. 18, para. 24(1)	66.1.3; 66.3.3
Sch. 18, para. 27	66.3.7
Sch. 18, para. 32	66.9.1
Sch. 18, para. 33	66.2.1
Sch. 18, para. 33(1)	66.9.1
Sch. 18, para. 41, 46	66.3.8

Provision	Paragraph
Finance Act 1999	
39	68.8.1
40	68.8.1
82	69.2.6
Finance Act 2000	
46	74.3.2
63	73.4.4
83	68.8.1
Sch. 15	73.4.4
Sch. 16	73.4.4
Sch. 30	58.7.1
Sch. 30, para. 4(14)	58.8.2
Sch. 30, para. 7(4)	58.7.5
Sch. 30, para. 21	58.9.1
Sch. 30, para. 24(4)	58.7.5
Finance Act 2001	
See generally	58.8.3
Sch. 27	58.7.1
Finance Act 2002	
Sch. 11	60.7.2
Sch. 26	63.12.7
Sch. 26, para. 4	63.12.7
Sch. 26, para. 30A, 30A(2)(a)	67.9
Finance Act 2003	
57A	63.12.2
60	63.12.2
61	63.12.2
64	63.12.2
64A	63.12.2
65	63.12.2
66	63.12.2
67	63.12.2
69	63.12.2
71	63.12.2
71A	63.12.2
72	63.12.2
72A	63.12.2
73	63.12.2
74	63.12.2
75	63.12.2
116	63.12.2
118	63.12.2
163(5)	60.10.4
Sch. 6	63.12.2
Sch. 6A	63.12.2
Sch. 7	63.12.2; 67.9
Sch. 7, para. 4	67.9
Sch. 8	63.12.2; 74.3.6
Sch. 9	63.12.2
Sch. 15, para. 1	63.12.2
Sch. 29	60.10.6
Sch. 29, para. 1(2), 7A	60.10.3
Sch. 33	76.9.16
Finance Act 2004	
See generally	76.2.1
19	63.1.4

Provision	Paragraph
30–37	58.5
59	62.4.1
60	62.4.5
70–71	62.7.5
72	62.7.6
74	62.4.4
85	71.3.9
96, 97	66.1.1
108	58.10.2
149–284	76.1
165	76.5.10
166	76.5.1; 76.5.2; 76.7
179	76.9.3
192	76.9.4; 76.9.5
194	76.9.4; 76.9.5
196	76.9.6
206(1)	76.8
207	76.9.12
210	76.4.3
212	76.4.3; 76.5.4
215	76.6.4
216	76.6.2; 76.6.4
218(6)	76.6.1
219	76.5.9; 76.5.10; 76.5.11
227–238	76.9.14
239	76.6.2
241(2)	76.6.2
270	76.3.5
276	76.5.3
277	76.4.3; 76.6.2
277(a)	76.4.3; 76.5.4; 76.6.2
283	76.2.16
306–319	63.1.4
306(1)	63.1.4; 63.2.2
306(1)(a)	63.2.2
306(1)(b)	63.4.1
306(1)(c)	63.5
306(2)	63.3
306A	63.2.4
306A(6)	63.6.2
307(1), (2), (3), (4), (5)	63.6.2
307(1A), (4A), (4C)	63.6.2
308–310	63.1.4
308	63.6.2; 63.8; 63.8.8
308(1)	63.6.2
308(2)	63.1.2
308(4)–(4C)	63.6.2
308A	63.6.2
309	63.6.3; 63.8; 63.12.2
309(1)	63.6.4
310	63.6.3; 63.8; 63.12.2
311	63.7; 63.8.1
311(1), (2)	63.7
311(3)	63.8.1
312	63.8.2
312(1)	63.8.2; 63.8.3
312(2)	63.8.4; 63.8.8
312(6)	63.8.6

Finance Act 2004 – continued

Provision	Paragraph
312A	63.8.6
313	63.9.4; 63.11
313(1)	63.9.1; 63.9.2
313(3)	63.9.3; 63.9.4
313(4), (4)(g)	63.11
313ZA	63.8.8
313A	63.2.3; 63.2.4
313B	63.2.3; 63.2.4
313C	63.2.6
314	63.6.2; 63.10
314A	63.2.5
316	63.1.4; 63.6.2; 63.6.3; 63.6.4; 63.8.5; 63.9.3
316(1)	63.4.2
318(1)	63.2.2
319(3)	63.1.2; 63.6.2
319(3)(b)	63.6.2
319(4)	63.1.2
319(5)	63.1.2; 63.9.4
Sch. 2	63.1.4
Sch. 5	58.5
Sch. 16	71.3.9
Sch. 24	66.1.1
Sch. 28–36	76.1
Sch. 29	76.6.2; 76.6.4; 76.7
Sch. 29, para. 1, 1(1)	76.6.2
Sch. 29, para. 2	76.6.2; 76.6.4
Sch. 29, para. 2(2)	76.6.4
Sch. 29, para. 2(6)	76.6.1
Sch. 29, para. 3	76.6.2; 76.6.4
Sch. 29, para. 3(1)–(3), (5)–(7)	76.6.2
Sch. 29, para. 3A	76.10.3
Sch. 29, para. 14(1), (1)(d), (2)	76.8
Sch. 29, para. 16(2)	76.8
Sch. 29, para. 17(1), (3)	76.8
Sch. 34	76.9.16
Sch. 36	76.2.16; 76.5.1; 76.6.4
Sch. 36, para. 1–6	76.3.1
Sch. 36, para. 1	76.3.2
Sch. 36, para. 1(1)	76.3.2; 76.3.3; 76.3.5; 76.4.3; 76.5.2; 76.5.3; 76.6.1; 76.6.2; 76.6.4; 76.8; 76.9.11
Sch. 36, para. 2	76.3.3
Sch. 36, para. 3	76.3.4
Sch. 36, para. 4	76.3.5
Sch. 36, para. 5	76.3.6
Sch. 36, para. 6	76.3.7
Sch. 36, para. 7	76.4.2; 76.6.2
Sch. 36, para. 7(3)	76.4.6
Sch. 36, para. 8	76.4.2; 76.4.3; 76.4.8; 76.5.2; 76.5.3; 76.5.4; 76.6.2; 76.6.4
Sch. 36, para. 8(5)	76.6.4
Sch. 36, para. 9	76.4.1; 76.4.2; 76.4.8; 76.5.3; 76.5.4; 76.6.2; 76.6.4
Sch. 36, para. 9(1)	76.6.2
Sch. 36, para. 9(3)	76.5.2; 76.6.4
Sch. 36, para. 10	76.4.2; 76.4.10
Sch. 36, para. 10(1)	76.5.4
Sch. 36, para. 10(2)	76.4.10; 76.5.10
Sch. 36, para. 11	76.4.2; 76.4.8
Sch. 36, para. 12	76.5.2; 76.6.2; 76.9.14
Sch. 36, para. 12(1)	76.5.2
Sch. 36, para. 12(3)	76.5.1
Sch. 36, para. 12(5)	76.5.2
Sch. 36, para. 13	76.5.2; 76.5.3; 76.6.4
Sch. 36, para. 14	76.5.2; 76.5.3
Sch. 36, para. 15	76.5.2; 76.5.3; 76.5.4
Sch. 36, para. 16	76.5.3; 76.5.4; 76.5.5
Sch. 36, para. 17	76.5.5; 76.5.6
Sch. 36, para. 17A	76.5.2; 76.5.7
Sch. 36, para. 17A(1), (2), (3)	76.5.2
Sch. 36, para. 18	76.5.8
Sch. 36, para. 19	76.5.9; 76.6.1
Sch. 36, para. 19(3)	76.5.9
Sch. 36, para. 19(4)	76.6.1
Sch. 36, para. 20	76.5.10
Sch. 36, para. 21	76.6.1
Sch. 36, para. 22	76.5.9; 76.6.1
Sch. 36, para. 22(6)	76.6.4
Sch. 36, para. 23	76.5.9; 76.6.1
Sch. 36, para. 23A	76.6.1
Sch. 36, para. 24	76.6.4
Sch. 36, para. 25–30	76.6.2
Sch. 36, para. 25	76.6.2
Sch. 36, para. 25(5)	76.6.4
Sch. 36, para. 26	76.6.2; 76.6.4
Sch. 36, para. 27, 28, 29, 30	76.6.2
Sch. 36, para. 27–29	76.6.2
Sch. 36, para. 31–34	76.6.4
Sch. 36, para. 31–36	76.6.4
Sch. 36, para. 32, 33, 34	76.6.4
Sch. 36, para. 35	76.7
Sch. 36, para. 36	76.8
Sch. 36, para. 37–58	76.9.1
Sch. 36, para. 37	76.9.2
Sch. 36, para. 38	76.9.3
Sch. 36, para. 39	76.9.4
Sch. 36, para. 40	76.9.5
Sch. 36, para. 41	76.9.6
Sch. 36, para. 42	76.9.7
Sch. 36, para. 43	76.9.8
Sch. 36, para. 44	76.9.9
Sch. 36, para. 45	76.9.10
Sch. 36, para. 46	76.9.11
Sch. 36, para. 47	76.9.12
Sch. 36, para. 48	76.9.13
Sch. 36, para. 49	76.9.14
Sch. 36, para. 50	76.9.15
Sch. 36, para. 51	76.9.16
Sch. 36, para. 52–56	76.9.17
Sch. 36, para. 52	76.9.17
Sch. 36, para. 53, 54, 55	76.9.18
Sch. 36, para. 53–55	76.9.18
Sch. 36, para. 56–58	76.9.19
Sch. 36, para. 56, 57, 58	76.9.19

Legislation Finding List

Provision	Paragraph
Finance Act 2004, Section 61(2), (Relevant Percentage) Order 2007 (SI 2007/46)	62.7.3

Finance Act 2005
14	61.7.2
23–45	61.2; 61.5.5
25–29	61.5.6
30–33	61.5.7
31, 32	61.8.2
34	61.5.5
35	61.5.5
37	61.5.5
38	61.5.5
39	61.5.5
40	61.5.8
42	61.5.5
91(4)–(6)	58.8.3
104	58.8.3
Sch. 1	61.5.5; 61.5.7
Sch. 1, para. 4	61.5.7
Sch. 11, Pt. 2(9)	58.8.3

Finance (No. 2) Act 2005
See generally	67.9
Sch. 10	67.9

Finance Act 2006
See generally	74.3.5; 76.10.1; 77.1.3
75	68.6.2
88	61.2
89	61.2
91	75.2.6; 75.3
Sch. 12	61.2
Sch. 13	61.2
Sch. 14	75.2.6; 75.3

Finance Act 2007
See generally	64.1.3; 66.3.2; 77.1.3
18	72.4.12
50	75.2.6; 75.3
82	66.1.1
96	66.1.1; 66.3.1; 66.3.2; 66.3.3; 66.3.5
97	66.1.1; 66.9.5
Sch. 16	75.2.6; 75.3
Sch. 16, para. 8(2)	77.1.3
Sch. 24	66.1.1; 66.9.5

Finance Act 2008
See generally	57.15.1; 60.1; 60.10.1; 63.1.4; 63.6.2; 63.7; 63.12.12; 64.1.3; 66.1.1; 66.1.6; 66.2.4; 66.3.1; 66.3.7; 66.4.2; 66.5.2; 75.2.6; 76.9.5; 77.1.3
24	55.2.1
32	75.2.6; 75.3
31	75.2.1
96	67.9
113	66.1.1; 66.3.1
114	66.1.6; 66.5.5
115	66.1.1

Provision	Paragraph
118	58.7.3; 66.1.1; 66.3.8
119	66.3.8
122, 123	66.1.1
Sch. 3, para. 8	64.3.2
Sch. 3, para. 8(4)	77.1.3
Sch. 7	57.15.2; 57.15.6; 57.15.7; 57.15.8
Sch. 7, para. 86	57.15.8
Sch. 7, para. 116–126	60.7.3
Sch. 7, para. 124	60.4
Sch. 11	75.2.6; 75.3
Sch. 19	74.4.2
Sch. 36	66.1.1; 66.1.2; 66.1.6; 66.3.1; 66.3.7; 66.4.1; 66.4.2; 66.4.3; 66.9.4
Sch. 36, para. 60	66.4.3; 66.5.1
Sch. 37	66.1.1; 66.1.6; 66.5.3
Sch. 39	66.1.1; 66.1.6
Sch. 39, para. 3	66.3.8
Sch. 39, para. 24	58.7.3
Sch. 40, 41	66.1.1

Finance Act 2009
See generally	64.1.3; 76.4.2
23	67.9
27	64.3.8; 75.2.2; 75.2.6; 75.3; 77.5
42	67.9
59	58.6
Sch. 6	67.9
Sch. 8	75.2.2; 75.2.6; 75.3; 77.5
Sch. 14, para. 9	58.9.4
Sch. 36	66.1.6
Sch. 55	62.7.6; 64.2.3; 64.2.5; 64.3.8

Finance Act 2009 Schedule 56 (Appointed Day and Consequential Provisions) Order 2010 (SI 2010/466) 62.7.6

Finance Act 2010
35	66.9.5
Sch. 6, para. 1, 2, 3	74.2.1
Sch. 6, para. 4–5	74.2.1
Sch. 6, para. 4	61.4.1
Sch. 6, para. 6	74.2.1
Sch. 10	66.9.5

Housing Associations Act 1985 .... 62.4.1

Housing (Northern Ireland) Order 1981 (SI 1981/156) 62.4.1

Human Rights Act 1998
See generally	66.9.6; 66.9.7; 66.10.4
art. 8	66.4.2; 66.5.4

Income and Corporation Taxes Act 1970
208	76.4.10

Income and Corporation Taxes Act 1988
8	58.5

Income and Corporation Taxes Act
1988 – continued

Provision	Paragraph
8(2)	67.5.5; 67.5.6; 67.5.7
8(4)	67.5.8; 67.7
12(3)(da), (5B)	67.5.2
12(7)	67.5.2; 67.5.3; 67.5.7
12(7ZA)	67.5.2
15, 18, 19	58.5
22–24, 26	58.5
31, 32, 36	58.5
40, 41	58.5
57	58.5
60, 67	58.5
74(1)(a)	67.5.5
74(2)	67.6.3
75	76.9.6
76	58.7.5
76(7)	76.9.6
81–83, 89	58.5
90–103	58.5
94	67.9
94(1)	67.6.3
103(4)(b)	67.6.3
105	67.9
112	56.1.4
131	58.5
203(1)	67.7
208	76.3.2; 76.6.2
297	64.1.3
342	67.5.8
342(5), (6)	67.5.7
342(7)–(9)	67.7
342A	67.7
343, 343(1)(b), (2), (4), (4A)	67.9
343(8), (10)	67.9
344, 344(5), (6), (8)–(10)	67.9
349	67.6.4
353	73.3.4
359(1)	68.2
361	68.4.1
362	68.6.1; 68.6.2
364	68.7.1
365	68.8.1
370	68.8.1
393(1)	67.9
393A, 393A(2A)	67.9
410	67.8
410(1)(b)(i), (ii)	67.8
417	60.12.6
419(4)	66.9.8
431B(2)	76.3.3
444A	63.6.2
460	75.5
466(2B)	76.3.3
590–612	76.3.2; 76.3.7; 76.4.3; 76.4.10; 76.6.2
590–659E	76.3.4
590C	76.5.5
591	76.5.5
591B	76.4.3; 76.6.2

Provision	Paragraph
591B(1)	76.3.6
591C, 591D	76.3.6
592(6)	76.9.7
595	76.9.17
595(1)	76.9.18
605	76.9.15
611	76.3.2; 76.6.2
611(1)(a)	76.6.2
611A	76.3.2; 76.4.10
611AA	76.3.3; 76.3.5
613(4)(b)–(d)	76.3.2; 76.4.10
615(3)	76.9.19
619(4)	76.9.4
620	76.3.2; 76.4.10; 76.9.2; 76.9.5
620(7)	76.3.6
621	76.3.2; 76.4.10; 76.9.2; 76.9.5
622(3)	76.3.2; 76.4.10; 76.9.2; 76.9.5
630–655	76.3.2; 76.3.7; 76.4.10; 76.9.2
634A	76.4.10; 76.5.10
634A(1)	76.4.3; 76.4.10
634A(4)	76.4.10; 76.5.10
638(1)	76.3.3; 76.3.5
650(1)	76.3.6
650A	76.3.6
651	76.3.6
651A	76.9.15
660A	61.5.6
660G(1), (2)	60.7.1
681(4)	60.7.1
686D	61.7.2
703–709	67.9
703, 704D	67.5.10
709	67.5.10
730A(1)(a)–(c)	63.12.7
762(3)	60.10.4
768–769	67.9
787	68.10.1
795	58.8.3
795(2)(a)	58.10.2
797(1)	58.9.4
799(1)(b)	58.9.4
806A–806K	58.9.4
806A(1)	58.9.3
806A(3), (4)	58.9.4
806B(6), (7)	58.9.4
806C	58.9.3
806D, 806D(4), (5)	58.9.3
806J(7)	58.9.4
824(3)	58.10.2
826	67.7

Income Tax Act 2007

Provision	Paragraph
See generally	64.1.3; 64.1.4; 65.1.1; 77.1.3
9	61.7.2
23	68.1.5
27	68.8.1
28	68.8.1
Pt. 4, Ch. 2	65.3.1
64	69.4

Legislation Finding List

Provision	Paragraph
66	65.3.3
67	65.3.2
71	69.4
72	75.2.4
74	65.3.3
89	69.4
131	64.4.3; 73.4.3
139	64.2.6
145	64.2.4
Pt. 5	75.2.2
158	64.2.1; 75.2.1
159	64.1.4; 64.2.4
159(3)	64.2.5
163, 164, 167, 169	64.2.4
173	64.2.5
173A	64.1.3; 64.2.5
175	64.2.5
177	64.2.4
179	64.2.5
179(2)	64.1.4
Pt. 5, Ch. 4	64.3.6
180	64.2.5
181	64.2.5
184, 186	64.2.5
186A	64.1.3; 64.2.5
189	64.2.5
190	64.1.3; 64.2.5; 77.1.3
201	64.2.3
202	64.2.2; 64.3.3; 75.2.7
205	64.2.2
209	64.2.6
213	64.2.6
231, 232	64.2.6
239(1)	64.2.4
246, 247	64.2.6
250	64.2.4
251(1)(c)	64.1.3
256	64.1.4; 64.2.4
257(1)	64.2.5
Pt. 6	75.3; 77.1.3
258	77.1.3
261	77.2.1
264	77.2.2
266	77.2.3
266(4)	77.2.1
274	77.5
292A	77.1.3
297A	77.1.3
383	68.1.5; 68.8.1; 71.9.3; 73.3.2; 73.3.3
388	68.2; 73.3.2
392	68.3.1; 68.3.2; 73.3.3
393	68.3.2
394	73.3.3
396	68.5.2; 73.3.5
397	68.5.1; 68.5.2
398	68.6.1
399, 399(5)	73.3.6
399(6)	68.6.1

Provision	Paragraph
400	68.6.2
400(3)	68.6.2
401	68.4.1; 68.4.2; 73.3.4
405–430	68.7.1
406(2)	73.3.3
409	73.3.3
409(1)–(2)	68.3.1
410	68.3.1; 73.3.3
410(1), (2)	68.3.2
Pt. 8, Ch. 2	74.4.2
414–417	74.4.1
431–436	74.4.4
491	61.7.2
Pt. 10	74.3.1; 74.3.2; 74.3.5
524–525	74.3.1
526	74.3.1
528	74.3.1; 74.3.2
529	74.3.2
543	74.3.2; 74.3.5
547	74.6.2
549–557	74.3.5
558	74.3.5
Pt. 13, Ch. 1	67.9
701	63.6.2
Pt. 13, Ch. 2	60.6.4; 60.10.2
733	60.10.2
748	60.3
Pt. 13, Ch. 3	74.3.2
Pt. 13, Ch. 7	73.5.5
809B	57.15.2
809C	57.15.1; 57.15.2
809H, 809I	57.15.3
809L–809T	58.10.2
Pt. 14, Ch. A1	58.8.3
Pt. 14, Ch. 2	59.3.2.1
829	59.3.2.3
829(1), (2)	55.2.4
831	55.2.2; 55.2.4; 59.3.2.2
831(2)	59.3.2.2
832	55.2.2; 55.2.4; 59.3.2.2
874	73.2.4
994(1)	68.6.2
1016	74.3.1
Sch. 2, para. 96	68.6.2

Income Tax (Construction Industry Scheme) Regulations 2005 (SI 2005/2045)

reg. 7	62.7.5
reg. 27, 28	62.8

Income Tax (Construction Industry Scheme) (Amendment No. 2) Regulations 2008 (SI 2008/1282) ... 62.8

Income Tax (Earnings and Pensions) Act 2003

See generally	62.9.1; 71.2.3; 76.2.1
4	63.6.2

Income Tax (Earnings and Pensions) Act 2003 – continued

Provision	Paragraph
10(2)	55.1
Pt. 2, Ch. 5	56.1.2
22	57.16
23(2)	55.1
26	57.16
27, 28	55.3.3
Pt. 2, Ch. 7	62.4.2; 62.4.5
211–215	74.5.2
216	74.3.1
333–360	76.9.16
355	76.9.16
370, 371	55.3.4
373, 373(3), (4)	55.3.4
374, 375	55.3.4
376	55.3.5
386–400	76.9.18
386	76.9.17
386(1)	76.9.18
392	76.9.17
393–400	76.9.18
394, 394(2)	76.9.18
395	76.9.18
421J	71.11.7
551	68.3.2
579A–579D	76.9.8; 76.9.9; 76.9.10
590–592	76.9.9
590–594	76.9.10
596	76.9.9; 76.9.10
605–608	76.9.8
612	76.9.11
636B	76.7
683	55.4.4
683(3)	76.9.11
687(4)	55.4.2
689	55.4.2
690	55.4.3; 55.4.4
690(4), (6)	55.4.3
691	55.4.2
702(6)	63.12.11
710	55.4.2

Income Tax (Entertainers and Sportsmen) Regulations 1987 (SI 1987/530)

	Paragraph
	55.5.5

Income Tax (Pay As You Earn) Regulations 2003 (SI 2003/2682)

Provision	Paragraph
reg. 21(1)	55.4.4
Pt. 8	55.4.4

Income Tax (Trading and Other Income) Act 2005

Provision	Paragraph
See generally	62.9.1
3–259	76.9.6
7	55.5.1
9, 10	65.2
13–14	55.5.5
17	55.5.3
29	73.2.1
34(1)	73.2.1
45	74.4.3
52	68.9.1
57	72.2.3
58	68.9.1; 73.5.1
58(2)	73.5.2
59	73.5.1
59(3)	68.10.4
70	74.4.7
92, 93, 94	55.5.4
118(1)–(5)	65.5.1
Pt. 2, Ch. 9	68.6.2
221	65.6.1
222	65.6.3
223	65.6.2; 65.6.3
224, 225	65.6.3
Pt. 3	72.1.1
266(1)	72.6.2
269	55.5.1
271	72.2.6
272	72.2.3
272(1)	72.4.1
Pt. 3, Ch. 4	72.3.8
287	72.3.8
305	72.3.8
312–314	72.4.12
315	72.4.18
323(2)	72.9.2
323(3)	72.9.3
324	72.9.3
326	72.9.4
362(1)–(2)	68.9.1
Pt. 4, Ch. 5	61.9
508	72.3.2
568	61.9
647	60.3
Pt. 5, Ch. 5	74.4.8
620	60.7.1; 61.2
628	74.4.9
630	74.4.9
Pt. 5, Ch. 6	72.9.1
709–712	77.3
709	77.4.2
714, 715	74.4.11
731	63.12.8
776	74.5.2
789(4)	72.10.3
800	72.10.5
811–813	55.6
832	57.7; 58.8.3
834	57.17
858	55.5.3
Pt. 14, Ch. A1	58.8.3

Individual Savings Account Regulations 1998 (SI 1998/1870)

	Paragraph
See generally	75.4.1
reg. 23	75.4.3

Legislation Finding List

Provision	Paragraph
Individual Savings Account (Amendment) Regulations 2009 (SI 2009/1550)	75.4.1
Industrial Common Ownership Act 1976	
2	68.4.1
Inheritance Tax Act 1984	
3(3)	60.6.4
6(1)	57.13.1
8A–8C	61.9
12	76.11.1
23(1)	74.4.10
43	61.2
58–85	76.9.19
58(1)(d)	76.9.19
71, 71(1A), (1B)	61.5.4
74(1), (4)	61.5.5
88, 89	61.5.2
151	76.9.19
151A	76.11.2
151B–151C	76.11.3
200(1A)	76.11.3
210(2)	76.11.3
211	57.13.4
218	60.3
226(2)	68.7.1
267	57.8
267(1)	57.13.1
267(1)(a), (3)	57.8
Insolvency Act 1986	
See generally	67.4; 67.6; 67.6.3; 67.7; 67.8
Pt. I	67.6.2
7(3)(d)	67.1.1
19(5), (6)	67.7
29, 29(2)	67.1.1
37, 37(1)(a), 38, 39	67.1.1
40, 43	67.1.1
44(1)(a), (b), (c)	67.1.1
48	67.1.1
91(2)	67.5.2
103	67.5.2
109(3)	67.1.1
145	67.5.4
165(3)	67.5.5
167(1)(a)	67.5.5
175, 175(2)	67.3.2
176A(2)	67.7
189	67.6.4
212	67.5.2
214	67.5.10
230(2)	67.1.1
233	67.1.1; 67.9
234–237	67.1.1
328(1), (2)	67.2.2
328(4)	67.6.4
386	67.3.2
387	67.3.2

Provision	Paragraph
388(1)(a)	67.1.1
434(b)	67.3.2
Sch. 6	67.3.2
Sch. B1	67.5.2
Sch. B1, para. 65	67.7
Insolvency Act 1986 (Prescribed Part) Order 2003 (SI 2003/2097)	
art. 1	67.7
Insolvency (Northern Ireland) Order 1989 (SI 1989/2405)	
See generally	67.6.3
art. 496	67.5.4
Insurance Companies Act 1982	69.1
Law of Property Act 1925	
109(2)	67.1.1; 67.5.10
164–165	61.3.1; 61.3.3
164(1)	61.3.2
Lloyd's Act 1871	69.1
Lloyd's Act 1981	69.1
Lloyd's Act 1982	69.1
Lloyd's Underwriters (Gilt-edged Securities) (Periodic Accounting for Tax on Interest) Regulations 1995 (SI 1995/3225)	69.7.6
Lloyd's Underwriters (Tax) Regulations 1995 (SI 1995/351)	
reg. 12	69.6
Local Government Finance Act 1988	
See generally	74.3.6
Sch. 1, para. 7, 9	74.3.6
Mental Health Act 1983	61.5.5
Mineral Workings (Offshore Installations) Act 1971	62.4.4
Money Laundering Regulations 2003 (SI 2003/3073)	66.11.1; 66.11.7
Money Laundering Regulations 2007 (SI 2007/2157)	
See generally	70.1; 70.6.1
reg. 26	70.2
National Insurance Contributions Act 2006	
See generally	63.1.1; 71.11.11
7(2)	63.4.3
National Insurance Contributions (Application of Pt. 7 of the Finance Act 2004) Regulations 2007 (SI 2007/785)	63.1.2; 63.12.14

857

Legislation Finding List

Provision	Paragraph
New Towns Act 1981	62.4.1

New Towns Act (Northern Ireland) 1965 .... 62.4.1

New Towns (Scotland) Act 1968 ...... 62.4.1

OECD Model Tax Convention 1992
art. 4(1), (2), (3) 58.3
art. 4(9)–(20) 58.3
art. 7, 15, 15(2)(a), 17, 18 .... 58.3
art. 19, 19(2), 20 .... 58.3

Partnership Act 1890
See generally 68.6.2
4(2) 68.6.2

Pensions Act 1995 .... 76.2.1

Pensions Act 2004 .... 76.2.1

Pensions Act 2007 .... 76.6.2

Pension Schemes Act 1993
See generally 76.2.1
8 .... 76.5.3

Pension Schemes (Enhanced Lifetime Allowance) Regulations 2005
reg. 3 .... 76.4.2
reg. 4 .... 76.5.2

Pension Schemes (Prescribed Schemes and Occupations) Regulations 2005 .... 76.5.9; 76.6.1

Perpetuity and Accumulations Act 1964
See generally 61.3.1; 61.3.3
1, 3(4), 13 .... 61.3.2

Perpetuity and Accumulations Act 2009
See generally 61.3.1; 61.3.3
2, 5, 12, 13, 14, 15 .... 61.3.3

Police and Criminal Evidence Act 1984 .... 66.1.1

Proceeds of Crime Act 2002
See generally 66.11.1; 66.11.6; 66.11.7; 70.1; 70.4.3
Pt. 7 .... 70.7
327, 328, 329 .... 70.4
330 .... 70.5
333 .... 70.4
336 .... 70.6.4
339A 70.4.3
340 .... 70.3; 70.4
340(1), (2) 70.3

Public Trustee Act 1906 .... 74.2.6

Registered Pension Schemes (Provision of Information) Regulations 2005 .... 76.5.2

Provision	Paragraph

Representation of People Act 1983
12(1) 57.8; 57.14.1

Representation of People Act 1985
1 .... 57.8; 57.14.1
3 .... 57.8; 57.14.1

Saving-Energy Items (Deductions for Expenditure etc) Regulations 7304 (SI 2004/2664) 72.4.12

Saving-Energy Items Regulations 2005 (SI 2005/1114) 72.4.12

Saving-Energy Items Regulations 2006 (SI 2006/912) 72.4.12

Saving-Energy Items Regulations 2007 (SI 2007/831) 72.4.12

Serious Organised Crime and Police Act 2005
102–107 .... 70.4.3

Social Security Contributions and Benefits Act 1992
See generally 71.3.1
6 .... 67.7
11(1) 71.7.3
11(4) 71.7.5
15(1) 71.9.1; 71.9.3
15(3A), (4) 71.9.3
16(3) 71.9.3
Sch. 1 .... 67.7
Sch. 1, para. 3A, 3B 71.3.7
Sch. 2, para. 3 .... 71.9.4
Sch. 2, para. 4 .... 71.9.3

Social Security Contributions (Intermediaries) Regulations 2000 (SI 2000/727) 71.2.6

Social Security Contributions (Intermediaries) (Amendment) Regulations 2003 (SI 2003/2079) 71.2.6

Social Security (Contributions) Regulations 2001 (SI 2001/1004)
reg. 2(1) 71.4.6
reg. 43 .... 71.7.4
reg. 44(4)–(6) 71.7.5
reg. 45(2) 71.7.5
reg. 46 .... 71.7.5
reg. 126–139 .... 71.4.9
reg. 127(1)(b) 71.7.6
Sch. 4, para. 23 .... 71.11.7

Stamp Act 1891
57 .... 67.9

Provision	Paragraph
Stamp Duty Land Tax Avoidance Schemes (Prescribed Descriptions of Arrangements) Regulations 2005 (SI 2005/1868)	
See generally	63.4.3
reg. 2(1)–(3), (4)–(6)	63.12.2
Sch.	63.4.3; 63.12.2
Taxation (International and Other Provisions) Act 2010	
See generally	58.7.1; 58.9.4
Pt. 2	58.2; 58.10.1; 58.10.2
2	58.7.1
6	58.3
6(5)	58.10.2
8–17	58.8.1
8	58.7.1
9, 10	58.7.1
18	58.7.1
19	58.7.3
21	58.10.2
21(1)	58.10.2
26, 29	58.7.1
30	58.7.1; 58.8.2
31–32	58.10.2
32	58.8.3; 58.10.2
33	58.7.4
37, 38	58.4
42	58.7.1; 58.7.5
43	58.7.5
52–56	58.7.5
54	58.7.5
63–66	58.8.3
70	58.4
71–77	58.9.2
71	58.9.2
72	58.9.1
73	58.9.2
79, 80	58.7.3
107	58.7.5
112	58.6
122	58.4
129	58.7.1
134	58.7.1
135	58.10.2
136	58.10.2
137–140	58.10.2
137, 137(5)	58.10.2
138(4)	58.10.2
139	58.10.2
140	58.10.2
141	58.10.2
142–143	58.10.2
142, 143, 144	58.10.2
Sch. 6, para. 4	55.6
Sch. 6, para. 25, 26	55.6
Sch. 6, para. 33	55.6
Sch. 7, para. 12, 13, 14	55.4.5

Provision	Paragraph
Taxation of Chargeable Gains Act 1992	
2	56.1.4; 60.7.2
2(1)	61.5.7
2(2)	57.14.2; 58.10.2; 60.8.5; 60.10.4
2(4)	57.14.2
2(5)(a)(i)	60.10.4
2(5)(aa), (aa)(i)	60.10.4
2(5)(b)	60.7.2
3	58.10.2
8(6)	67.5.4
9	59.3.2.1
10A	56.1.4; 60.10.4; 60.12.7
12	57.14.2; 58.10.2
12(2)	57.14.2; 57.14.3
12(3)	57.14.2
16(4)	57.14.1; 57.14.2
16ZD(3)	57.14.2
17(1)(a)	67.5.5
24	67.9
37	58.10.2
60	61.2
62(1)(a)	64.3.7
68	61.2
69(1)	67.5.4
76, 76(1)	60.8.1
77–79	61.5.7
77	60.10.4
80	60.6.1
80(6), (7)	60.6.2
81	60.6.5
82, 82(4)	60.6.4
83(1)(b)	60.6.3
84	60.6.6
85	60.8.2; 60.8.3
85(3)	60.8.3
86	60.7.2; 60.8.3; 60.11.1; 60.12.7; 75.2.5
86(4)	60.10.4
86A–96	60.7.4
86A	60.12.7
86A(1)	60.12.7
86A(1)–(4)	60.12.7
87–89	60.10.3; 60.10.4
87–90	60.3
87	60.1; 60.7.1; 60.7.3; 60.8.5; 60.9.3; 60.10.2; 60.10.3; 60.10.4; 60.12.7; 75.2.5
87(2)	60.9.3
87(4)	60.7.5
87(4)(a)	60.8.5
87A	60.7.3; 60.8.4; 60.10.1; 60.10.4
87B	60.10.4
88	60.8.5
88(4)	60.10.4
89	60.4; 60.10.3; 60.10.4
89(2)	60.8.3
90	60.8.6; 60.10.4
91–94	60.9.1

Taxation of Chargeable Gains Act 1992 – continued

Provision	Paragraph
91	60.10.4
91(3)	60.9.2; 60.10.4
92	60.7.5
92(2)	60.7.5; 60.9.3
93–96	60.10.1
97	60.7.4; 60.7.5; 60.8.4; 60.10.2
97(2), (4)	60.7.5
120(5)	65.10.3
122	67.5.5
126	64.3.8; 77.4.3
126(2)(a)	64.3.8
127–130	77.4.3
127	77.4.3
135, 136	64.3.8; 77.4.3
137	64.4.3
138	63.6.2
138(2)	64.2.6
139	63.6.2
140	58.10.1
140B, 140D	63.6.2
142	61.9
150A	64.4.1; 64.4.3
150B	64.4.2
151A	77.4.2
151B, 151B(3)	77.4.3
152	60.6.2; 60.6.6
161	75.2.5
170	58.10.1; 63.6.2
170(6)–(8)	63.6.2
171A	67.9
179	67.9
179A–179B	67.9
179A	67.9
242	65.10.3
256	74.3.3; 74.3.5
257	74.4.5
260(2)(d)	61.8.2
263B, 263B(1)	63.12.7
277(1B)	58.10.2
283	58.10.2
Sch. 4B	60.8.6; 60.10.3; 60.10.4
Sch. 4B, para. 2(2)	60.10.4
Sch. 4C	60.7.4; 60.8.5; 60.10.3; 60.10.4
Sch. 4C, para. 7	60.10.4
Sch. 4C, para. 7B	60.10.4
Sch. 4C, para. 8	60.8.3; 60.10.4
Sch. 4C, para. 8(3)	60.8.3; 60.10.4
Sch. 4C, para. 8(4)	60.10.4
Sch. 4C, para. 8A(2), (3), (4)	60.10.4
Sch. 4C, para. 8AA	60.10.4
Sch. 4C, para. 9	60.10.4
Sch. 4C, para. 12, 12(1), (4)	60.10.4
Sch. 4C, para. 12A(2)	60.10.4
Sch. 4C, para. 13, 13(4), (5)	60.10.4
Sch. 4C, para. 14(1), (2)(a), (b)	60.10.4
Sch. 5	60.3; 60.11.1; 60.11.2; 60.12.3
Sch. 5, para. 1, 1(1), (2)(a), (b)	60.12.7

Provision	Paragraph
Sch. 5, para. 1(3), (7)	60.12.7
Sch. 5, para. 2–2A	60.12.8
Sch. 5, para. 2	60.11.2
Sch. 5, para. 2(1), (3)	60.12.8
Sch. 5, para. 3–5	60.12.9
Sch. 5, para. 6	60.12.7; 60.12.10
Sch. 5, para. 7	60.7.1; 60.11.2; 60.12.6
Sch. 5, para. 8	60.7.1; 60.12.6
Sch. 5, para. 9(3)	60.12.3
Sch. 5, para. 9(5)	60.12.4
Sch. 5, para. 9(6)–(7)	60.12.5
Sch. 5, para. 9(9)	60.12.1
Sch. 5, para. 10A	60.12.2
Sch. 5A	60.3
Sch. 5A, para. 2	60.3
Sch. 5A, para. 2(1)	60.12.8
Sch. 5A, para. 3, 4, 5	60.3
Sch. 5A, para. 6	60.3
Sch. 5B	64.3.1; 64.3.2; 64.3.8
Sch. 5B, para. 1	64.3.4
Sch. 5B, para. 1(1)(b)	64.3.2
Sch. 5B, para. 2	64.3.2
Sch. 5B, para. 3, 4	64.3.7; 64.3.8
Sch. 5B, para. 5	64.3.7
Sch. 5B, para. 8, 9	64.3.8
Sch. 5B, para. 10, 11, 12, 14, 15, 19	64.3.9
Sch. 5B, para. 19(1)	64.3.5; 64.3.6

Tax Avoidance Schemes (Information) Regulations 2004 (SI 2004/1864)

reg. 1(2)	63.1.2
reg. 2(1)	63.4.3
reg. 3, 3(2)	63.6.2
reg. 3(3)	63.6.2; 63.6.3
reg. 3(4)	63.6.4
reg. 3(5), (10)	63.6.2
reg. 4(1A), (2), (3), (3B)	63.6.2
reg. 4(4)	63.6.2; 63.6.4
reg. 4(5)	63.6.4
reg. 4(5A)	63.10
reg. 4(5ZA)	63.6.4
reg. 4(6)	63.6.2; 63.6.4
reg. 4(7)	63.6.2
reg. 5, 6	63.6.2
reg. 7	60.8.3
reg. 8	63.6.4
reg. 8(1)	63.9.3
reg. 8(1)(a)	63.9.2
reg. 8(2)	63.9.4
reg. 8A(1), (2)	63.2.3
reg. 9	63.11
reg. 10	60.6.4; 63.6.2; 63.6.3; 63.9.3

Tax Avoidance Schemes (Information) (Amendment) Regulations 2005 (SI 2005/1869)

reg. 1(2)	63.1.2

Provision	Paragraph
Tax Avoidance Schemes (Prescribed Descriptions of Arrangements) Regulations 2004 (SI 2004/1863)	
See generally	63.2.2
Sch., para. 2(4)	63.12.5
Sch., para. 8	63.12.5
Tax Avoidance Schemes (Prescribed Descriptions of Arrangements) Regulations 2006 (SI 2006/1543)	
reg. 1(2)	63.1.2; 63.2.2
reg. 3	63.1.2; 63.12.3
reg. 5(3)	63.10
reg. 6	63.12.4
reg. 7	63.12.5
reg. 8	63.12.6
reg. 9	63.12.7
reg. 10, 11	63.12.8
reg. 12	63.12.10
reg. 13–17	63.12.11
reg. 18	63.12.13
Tax Avoidance Schemes (Prescribed Descriptions of Arrangements) (Amendment) Regulations 2009 (SI 2009/2033)	
reg. 3	63.12.13
Tax Avoidance Schemes (Promoters and Prescribed Circumstances) Regulations 2004 (SI 2004/1865)	
reg. 1(3)	63.6.2
reg. 2	63.6.2
reg. 3	63.6.2
reg. 4	63.6.2
reg. 5	63.6.2
Tax Avoidance Schemes (Promoters, Prescribed Circumstances and Information) (Amendment) Regulations 2004 (SI 2004/2613)	
reg. 1(3)	63.1.2; 63.10
Taxes Management Act 1970	
See generally	62.8; 66.4.3
7, 8. 8A	58.10.1
9	58.10.1; 66.1.3
9A	66.1.2; 66.1.3; 66.1.4; 66.2.2; 66.3.1; 66.3.2; 66.3.5; 66.3.6
12AA	66.1.3
12AC	66.1.3; 66.1.4; 66.2.2; 66.3.1; 66.3.2; 66.3.5; 66.3.6
12B	66.2.4; 66.5.2; 66.5.3
17, 18	66.2.6
19A	66.1.1; 66.1.6; 66.3.7; 66.4.1; 66.5.4; 66.9.4; 66.9.6; 66.9.8
20	66.1.1; 66.4.1
20(3)	66.1.1
20A	66.4.4
20BA	66.4.4
20C	66.4.4

Provision	Paragraph
28A	66.2.1; 66.9.1
28A(4)	66.9.1
28B	66.2.1; 66.9.1
28B(5)	66.9.1
29	66.1.4; 66.3.8
29(5), (6)	66.3.8
30B	66.3.8
31	69.7.6
33	66.9.8
34, 36	66.3.8
54	66.1.6
55	69.7.4; 69.7.6; 73.4.4
59A, 59B	58.10.1
82	57.12.4
86, 88	66.9.2
95	66.9.3; 66.9.6
95A	66.9.3
97AA(1)(a), (b)	66.9.6
98	60.3
98A(4)	63.11
98C	63.2.3; 63.11.2
98C(2A)	63.2.4
98C(2B)	63.2.5
98C(3), (4)	63.11.3
99	66.4.4
Sch. 1A, para. 5	66.3.5
Terrorism Act 2000	
See generally	66.11.6; 70.1
18	70.7
21A	70.7
Trustee Act 1925	
See generally	61.8.1
31	61.2; 61.8.2; 61.9.5
31(1)	61.5.2
31(1)(i), (ii)	61.8.2
31(2)	61.2; 61.8.2; 61.8.5
32	61.8.2
33	61.2
69(2)	61.8.2
Trustee Act 2000	
See generally	61.8.1; 61.8.4
8	61.8.4
Trustee Act (Northern Ireland) 1958	61.5.5
Trustee Investment Act 1961	61.8.4; 74.2.7
Trusts of Land and Appointment of Trustees Act 1996	61.8.1; 61.8.3
Value Added Tax Act 1994	
Sch. 9, Grp. 12	74.3.2
Sch. 10, para. 2	63.12.2
Sch. 11A	63.1.4
Value Added Tax Regulations 1995 (SI 1995/2518)	67.9

Provision	Paragraph
Venture Capital Trust Regulations 1995 (SI 1995/1979)	77.5
Venture Capital Trust (Amendment) Regulations 2008 (SI 2008/1893)	77.5

Provision	Paragraph
Welfare Reform Pensions Act 1999	
29(1)	76.5.8

Index to Concessions and Statements

(References are to paragraph numbers)

Provision	Paragraph
Extra-Statutory Concessions	
A11	55.2.4; 55.2.3; 56.1.4
A33	68.6.2; 73.3.6
A43	68.6.2
A78	55.2.2; 55.2.4
B11	65.8.2
B47	72.8.2
C4	74.3.2
D2	56.1.3; 56.1.4; 60.11.1
D22	65.10.2
D26	65.10.2
F7	57.13.4
Statements of Practice	
E8	61.9.5
3/78	68.3.1; 68.3.2; 73.3.3
3/81	55.2.5
5/81	65.8.4
6/88	58.10.1

Provision	Paragraph
2/91	55.2.2; 55.2.4
3/91	68.10
7/91	58.5
8/91	66.3.7
17/91	55.2.5
5/92	60.12.1; 60.12.3
5/92, para. 3	60.6.1
5/92, para. 4–6	60.6.4
5/92, para. 4	60.7.5
5/92, para. 6	60.10.2
5/92, para. 9	60.6.4
5/92, para. 12–15, 16–17, 18	60.12.3
5/92, para. 24, 33	60.12.3
6/98	64.2.4; 77.2.2
3/2000	65.2.5
3/2001	58.8.3
01/06	66.3.8

Index

(References are to paragraph numbers)

A

Accommodation
. agricultural employees 65.8.6
. foreign, overseas employments 55.3.5

Accumulation and maintenance trusts 61.5.4

Administration – see Insolvencies

Advertising
. property rental business, deductions 72.4.8

Agencies
. subcontractors 62.6.3

Agricultural buildings
. capital allowances 72.7.4

Agricultural land
. inheritance tax relief 75.11.3

Agricultural tenancies
. capital gains tax 65.10.5

Agricultural workers
. accommodation 65.8.6

Agriculture – see Farming and market gardening

Air transport
. double taxation relief 58.3

Annuities – see also Pensions; Purchased life annuities
. National Insurance Class 4 contributions 71.9.5

Anti-avoidance
. deduction of interest 73.5.5
. disclosure of direct tax schemes – see Disclosure of tax avoidance schemes
. enterprise investment scheme reinvestment relief 64.3.9
. hive down 67.9
. National Insurance Contributions Act 2006 . . . . 71.11.11
. remittance basis 57.15.5

Appeals
. HMRC enquiry notices 66.3.4
. HMRC's determination, managing agent returns 69.7.4
. records 66.5.3

Artistes – see Entertainers

Avoidance of tax – see Anti-avoidance

B

Bad debts
. property rental business, deductions 72.4.9

Bankruptcy
. pensions 76.8.1

Bare trusts 61.2; 61.5.1; 61.5.2

Bearer securities
. domicile, inheritance tax 57.13.7

Beneficiaries
. charities – see Charities
. offshore trusts – see Beneficiaries of offshore trusts
. vulnerable persons – see Trusts with vulnerable beneficiaries

Beneficiaries of offshore trusts
. attributed gains
. . deduction of personal losses 60.7.2
. . dual resident trusts 60.8.5
. . transfers of value 60.10.3
. . UK trusts exported pre-19 March 1991 . . . . 60.5.4
. capital payments 60.7.1
. . interaction of charge and ICTA 1988, s. 740 charge 60.10.2
. . meaning 60.7.4
. . valuation 60.7.5
. consequences of FA 2008 reforms 60.7.3
. disposal of settled interests 60.8.1
. . disposals of interests after 5 April 2008 . . . . 60.8.4
. . emigration of trust on or after 21 March 2000 . . . . 60.8.3
. . gains of dual resident trusts attributed to beneficiaries 60.8.5
. . migration of trust post-18 March 1991 . . . . 60.8.2
. . transfers between settlements 60.8.6
. exemption 60.7.6
. matching capital payments with gains
. . charge to tax 60.10.4
. . generally 60.10.1
. . interaction of capital payments charge and ICTA 1988, s. 740 charge 60.10.2
. . transfers of value, attribution of gains to beneficiaries 60.10.3
. supplementary charge
. . chargeable period, qualifying amount 60.9.3

Index

Beneficiaries of offshore trusts – continued   Paragraph
.. generally 60.9.1
.. rate 60.9.2
. transfers between settlements
.. disposal of settled interests 60.8.6

Bonus sacrifice
. pension contributions 76.9.2

Branch or agency – see Permanent establishment

Business assets
. domicile, inheritance tax 57.13.5
. gifts – see Gifts of business assets

Business economics exercise – see HM Revenue and Customs enquiries

Business gifts
. charities – see Charities

Business profits
. double taxation relief 58.3

Business rates
. charities, exemption 74.3.6

C

Capital allowances
. farming and market gardening 65.7
.. horses and other animals 65.7
.. machinery and plant 65.7
. property rental business – see Property income

Capital gains tax
. disclosure of avoidance schemes, rules applying since 1 August 2006 ..... 63.12.3
. domicile
.. generally 57.14.1
.. nationality 57.14.4
.. relief for non-domiciliaries 57.14.2
.. remittances 57.14.3
.. double taxation relief 58.10.1
.. special withholding tax 58.10.2
. enterprise investment scheme
.. deferral relief 75.2.5
.. exemption 64.4.1; 75.2.4
.. reinvestment relief – see Enterprise investment scheme (EIS)
. exemption
.. charities 74.3.3
.. enterprise investment scheme 64.4.1; 75.2.4
.. gifts of chargeable assets to charities 74.4.5
. farming
.. hold-over relief 65.10.1
.. milk quotas 65.10.5
.. part-disposals 65.10.3
.. potato quotas 65.10.5

   Paragraph
.. roll-over relief – see Roll-over relief
.. tenancies 65.10.4
. trusts with vulnerable beneficiaries 61.5.7
. working abroad 56.1.3

Chargeable gains
. Lloyd's underwriters 69.5
.. non-syndicate gains and losses, 1992–93 and subsequent tax years 69.5

Charitable trusts 61.2

Charities
. beneficiaries
.. general benevolence, social welfare 74.5.4
.. nature of grant, capital or revenue 74.5.1
.. prizes 74.5.3
.. scholarships 74.5.2
. charitable purpose, definition 74.2.1
. Charity Commission (formerly the Charity Commissioners) 74.2.4
. charity, definition 74.2.1
. exemptions and reliefs
.. abolition of advance corporation tax 74.3.1
.. application for charitable purposes only 74.3.4
.. business rates 74.3.6
.. capital gains tax 74.3.3
.. corporation tax 74.3.1
.. council tax 74.3.6
.. directors 74.3.1
.. income tax 74.3.1
.. inheritance tax 74.3.3
.. restriction 74.3.5
.. stamp duty 74.3.6
.. stamp duty land tax 74.3.6
.. trading activities 74.3.2
. foreign charities operating overseas or in the UK 74.6.3
. forms of constitution 74.2.2
. generally 74.1
. Gift Aid post-April 2000 .... 74.3.2
.. benefits 74.4.2
.. donations by companies 74.4.2
.. donations by individuals 74.4.2
. Gift Aid pre-April 2000 .... 74.3.2
. gifts
.. business gifts 74.4.3
.. capital transfer free of inheritance tax 74.4.10
.. chargeable assets free of capital gains tax 74.4.5
.. charitable trusts and foundations 74.4.6
.. donated salaries and services 74.4.7
.. donations from settlor interested trusts 74.4.9

Index

	Paragraph
.. generally	74.4.1
.. interest-free loans	74.4.8
.. payroll giving	74.4.11
.. shares and securities	74.4.4
. HM Revenue and Customs	74.2.5
. investment management	74.2.7
. Official Custodian	74.2.6
. registration	74.2.3; 74.2.5
. returns	74.2.5
. UK charities	
.. overseas operations	74.6.1
.. payments made to bodies outside the UK	74.6.2
.. raising funds abroad	74.6.4

Children
. domicile 57.10

Child trust funds 75.6

Close companies
. investment loans, interest relief – see Interest relief

Companies
. double taxation relief – see Double taxation relief
. enterprise investment scheme – see Enterprise investment scheme (EIS)
. Gift Aid donations 74.4.2
. HMRC enquiry window 66.3.3
. liquidation, administration or receivership – see Insolvencies
. loan relationships and related transactions, incidental costs 73.5.4
. new penalty regime for returns for periods commencing on or after 1 April 2008 .... 66.9.5
. non-resident – see Non-resident companies
. residence – see Company residence
. venture capital trusts – see Venture capital trusts (VCTs)

Company residence
. carrying on trade in the UK 57.12.6
. change of residence 57.12.3
. dual resident companies 57.12.5
. generally 57.12.1
. permanent establishment 57.12.4
. tax liability 57.12.2

Company-sponsored pension schemes – see Pensions

Connected persons
. qualifying for enterprise investment scheme relief – see Enterprise investment scheme (EIS)

Construction industry scheme
. background 62.2

	Paragraph
. compliance	
.. audits	62.9.2
.. background	62.9.1
. contractors	
.. construction operations	62.4.4
.. construction payments	62.4.5
.. deemed contractors	62.4.3
.. definition	62.4.1
.. IR35	62.4.6
.. mainstream contractors	62.4.2
.. multiple	62.4.7
.. non-resident	62.5
. employment status	62.3
. generally	62.1
. online service	62.1.1
. payments to subcontractors	
.. monthly returns	62.7.5
.. payments under deduction	62.7.4
.. penalties	62.7.6
.. rate of deduction	62.7.3
.. verification	62.7.1
.. verification reference number	62.7.2
. subcontractors	
.. agencies	62.6.3
.. definition	62.6.1
.. gangs	62.6.4
.. labour-only subcontractors	62.6.2
.. non-resident	62.5
.. payments to	62.7.1–62.7.6
.. registration	62.8

Contractors within the construction industry – see Construction industry scheme

Corporate venturing scheme
. conditions 73.4.4
. deferral relief 73.4.4
. generally 73.4.4
. investment relief 73.4.4
.. interaction with enterprise investment scheme income tax relief 64.2.7
. loss relief 73.4.4

Corporation tax
. double taxation relief – see Double taxation relief
. loan relationships 73.2.4
. rates and fractions, companies in liquidation 67.5.8
. relief, charities 74.3.1

Corporation tax self-assessment (CTSA)
. enquiries – see HM Revenue and Customs enquiries

Council tax
. charities, exemption 74.3.6
. deductions 72.4.4

Index

Paragraph

D

Death
- individual savings account investor 75.4.5
- personal representatives, penalty 66.9.7
- trustee, export of trust 60.6.5

Debts
- domicile, inheritance tax 57.13.8

Deductions
- interest and other costs of borrowing
  - . costs of loan finance 68.9.2
  - . generally 68.9.1
  - . interest paid on business loan to fund proprietor's overdraft 68.9.3
- Lloyd's underwriters 69.3.4
- property rental business expenses – see Property income

Deeds of covenant
- charitable, withdrawal of relief 74.3.2

Definitions and meanings
- charities
  - . charitable purpose 74.2.1
  - . charity 74.2.1
- construction industry scheme
  - . contractor 62.4.1
  - . subcontractor 62.6.1
- earnings 71.3.1
- money laundering 66.11.2
- offshore trusts
  - . capital payments 60.7.4
  - . protected settlements 60.12.2
  - . qualifying settlement 60.12.1
  - . residence 55.2.1
  - . ordinary residence 59.4
  - . trust 61.2

Deposits
- tenants, chargeable income 72.3.7

Derivative contracts
- degrouping charge 67.9

Directors
- consequences of liquidation 67.5.10
- National Insurance contributions – see National Insurance contributions (NICs)
- qualifying for enterprise investment scheme relief – see Enterprise investment scheme (EIS)

Disclosure of tax avoidance schemes
- brief history of avoidance 63.1.3
- confidentiality
  - . no promoter involved 63.12.5
  - . promoter involved 63.12.4
- disclosure duties
  - . clients 63.6.3
  - . generally 63.6.1

Paragraph

- . parties where no promoter involved 63.6.4
- . parties where promoter's disclosure restricted by legal professional privilege 63.6.5
- . promoters 63.6.2
- duties with respect to reference numbers
  - . clients 63.8.7
  - . form of notification 63.8.5
  - . generally 63.8.1
  - . information to be provided 63.8.3
  - . providers' duties to provide details to clients 63.8.8
  - . removal of requirement to notify 63.8.6
  - . responsibility for providing information 63.8.2
  - . time-limits 63.8.4
- general hallmarks
  - . confidentiality 63.12.4; 63.12.5
  - . off market terms 63.12.7
  - . premium fees 63.12.6
  - . standardised tax products 63.12.8
- generally 63.1.1
- hallmarks of avoidance 63.12.3
- HMRC's response 63.7
- legal professional privilege 63.10
- legal professional privilege, disclosure by parties 63.1.2
  - . promoter's disclosure restricted 63.6.5
- National Insurance contributions, rules applying since 1 May 2007 ...... 63.12.14
- notifiable arrangements
  - . clients' duty 63.6.3
  - . doubt as to notifiability 63.2.4
  - . generally 63.2.1
  - . information provided to introducers 63.2.6
  - . order that scheme notifiable 63.2.5
  - . parties' duties 63.9.1–63.9.4
  - . pre-disclosure enquiry 63.2.3
  - . promoters 63.6.2
  - . time limits on what needs to be notified 63.2.2
- notifiable proposals 63.3
- overview of rules 63.1.4
- parties, disclosure 63.1.2
  - . duty where no promoter involved 63.6.4
- parties' duties with respect to notifiable arrangements
  - . generally 63.9.1
  - . information to be disclosed 63.9.2
  - . method of disclosure 63.9.3
  - . no reference number given 63.9.4
- penalties
  - . failure to provide details of notifiable proposal or arrangement 63.11.2

Index

	Paragraph
. . failure to provide reference number and timing of tax advantage	63.11.3
. . generally	63.11.1
. prescribed schemes	63.12.1
. . rules applying since 1 August 2006, income/corporation and capital gains tax	63.12.3
. . stamp duty land tax transactions	63.12.2
. promoters	
. . disclosure duties	63.6.2
. . notifiable proposals or arrangements	63.1.2; 63.11.2
. rules applying since 1 August 2006, income/corporation and capital gains tax	63.12.3
. specific types of scheme	
. . leasing arrangements	63.12.11
. . loss creation	63.12.10
. . obtaining additional annual investment allowance	63.12.12
. . pension charge forestalling	63.12.13
. start dates, summary	63.1.2
. tax advantage	
. . generally	63.4.1; 63.4.2
. . main benefit	63.5
. . taxes covered by rules	63.4.3
. . timing, penalties	63.11.3

Discovery assessments 66.3.8

Discretionary trusts 61.2; 61.5.4

Dividends
. double taxation relief 58.3
. . underlying tax 58.8.3
. . unrelieved foreign tax 58.9.4
. venture capital trusts, relief 77.3

Divorce – see Separation and divorce

Domicile – see also Residence; Working abroad
. capital gains tax
. . generally 57.14.1
. . nationality 57.14.4
. . relief for non-domiciliaries 57.14.2
. . remittances 57.14.3
. children 57.10
. choice 57.3
. . abandonment 57.6
. corporations – see Company residence
. dependency 57.9
. determination for tax purposes, overseas electors 57.8
. fiscal 57.8
. inheritance tax
. . bearer securities 57.13.7
. . business assets 57.13.5
. . debts and other legal choses 57.13.8
. . equitable interests 57.13.9
. . generally 57.13.1

	Paragraph
. . interests in land	57.13.3
. . non-UK domiciled persons	57.13.2
. . shares and securities	57.13.6
. . tangible movable property	57.13.4
. intention	57.5
. married women	57.7
. mentally incapacitated persons	57.11
. miscellaneous considerations	57.8
. non-domiciliaries	
. . capital gains tax relief	57.14.2
. . foreign income, remittance basis – see Remittance basis	
. origin	57.2
. relevance	57.1
. residence	57.4
. UK tax position of overseas voters	57.8

Double taxation relief
. calculation of double tax credit relief available 58.5
. capital gains tax 58.10.1
. . special withholding tax 58.10.2
. companies
. . calculation of credit 58.7.5
. . claims and time-limits 58.7.3
. . duty to minimise tax available for claim 58.7.4
. . generally 58.7.1
. . tax credit relief against corporation tax 58.7.2
. effect of exemptions under double tax treaties 58.4
. foreign tax as an expense 58.6
. forms of relief...................... 58.2
. generally 58.1
. model treaty provisions as typically used in the UK 58.3
. non-residents working in the UK 55.3.6
. unilateral relief
. . amount of foreign income assessable in UK – see Foreign income
. . generally 58.8.1
. . UK permanent establishments of non-resident companies 58.8.2
. unrelieved foreign tax companies
. . dividends........................58.9.4
. . generally 58.9.1
. . outline of rules 58.9.2
. . pre-FA 2009 rules 58.9.3

Double tax treaties – see Double taxation relief

Doubtful debts
. property rental business, deductions 72.4.9

Dual resident companies
. residence 57.12.5

Dual resident individuals
. double taxation relief 58.3

Index

Paragraph

E

Emoluments
. non-residents working in the UK 55.3.1

Employee-controlled companies
. investment loans, interest relief – see Interest relief

Employees
. agricultural, accommodation 65.8.6
. loans to purchase plant or
 . machinery........................ 73.3.2
.. interest relief........................ 68.2
. National Insurance contributions – see National Insurance contributions (NICs)
. non-residents working in the UK – see Residence

Employee share schemes
. National Insurance contributions
.. convertible shares 71.3.9
.. share options 71.3.7; 71.11.7
.. shares subject to forfeiture 71.3.8

Employers
. National Insurance contributions – see National Insurance contributions (NICs)

Employment status
. decisions, National Insurance contributions liability............... 71.2.7

Employment tribunal awards
. National Insurance contributions 71.3.10

Energy saving items
. property rental business, deductions 72.4.12

Enquiries – see HM Revenue and Customs enquiries

Enterprise investment scheme (EIS)
. capital gains tax
.. deferral relief 75.2.5
.. exemption 75.2.4
. criteria for company 75.2.6
. generally 75.2.1
. income tax relief..................... 75.2.2
.. claims 64.2.2
.. clawback 75.2.8
.. conditions 64.2.3
.. conditions to be satisfied by company......................... 64.2.5
.. generally 64.2.1
.. interaction with corporate venturing scheme 64.2.7
.. investor connected with company 75.2.3
.. permitted payments from company......................... 75.2.9
.. procedure...................... 75.2.7

Paragraph

.. qualifying individuals............... 64.2.4
.. withdrawal................ 64.2.6; 64.4.2
. legislative changes 64.1.3
. periods A, B and C 64.1.4
. reinvestment relief
.. anti-avoidance..................... 64.3.9
.. chargeable events 64.3.7
.. claims 64.3.3
.. eligible shares 64.3.5
.. generally 64.3.1
.. manner and amount of 64.3.2
.. qualifying companies 64.3.6
.. qualifying investments 64.3.4
.. reorganisations and reconstructions 64.3.8
. relief available under scheme 64.1.1
.. background and history 64.1.2
. tax-free sale of shares
.. allowable losses 64.4.3
.. exemption from capital gains tax 64.4.1
.. withdrawal of income tax relief 64.4.2

Entertainers
. double taxation relief 58.3
. non-resident
.. charge on income 55.5.5
.. payment of tax 55.5.5

Equitable interests
. domicile, inheritance tax 57.13.9

Exemptions
. beneficiaries of offshore trusts......... 60.7.6
. capital gains tax – see Capital gains tax
. charities – see Charities
. inheritance tax – see Inheritance tax

Expenses
. deductible, property rental businesses – see Property income
. raising finance
.. anti-avoidance.................... 73.5.5
.. companies 73.5.4
.. generally 73.5.1
.. life insurance premiums 73.5.2
.. permanent interest bearing shares 73.5.3

F

Farming and market gardening
. averaging of fluctuating profits
.. calculation of relief 65.6.2
.. claims 65.6.3
.. generally 65.6.1
.. tax and financial planning 65.6.4
. capital allowances................... 65.7
.. horses and other animals 65.7
.. machinery and plant 65.7
. capital gains tax
.. hold-over relief................... 65.10.1
.. milk quotas 65.10.5

Paragraph

.. part-disposals 65.10.3
.. potato quotas 65.10.5
.. roll-over relief – see Roll-over relief
.. tenancies 65.10.4
. herd basis
.. generally 65.5.1
.. partnership changes 65.5.2
. losses
.. farming not conducted on commercial
    basis 65.3.3
.. generally 65.3.1
.. hobby farming 65.3.2
. one trade treatment 65.2
. partnerships and joint ventures
.. joint ventures 65.9.2
.. partnerships 65.9.1
.. pension funds 65.9.4
.. share farming 65.9.3
. revenue receipts and payments
.. compulsory slaughter 65.8.2
.. drainage 65.8.4
.. employee accommodation 65.8.6
.. other receipts and expenses 65.8.5
.. set-aside 65.8.3
. stocks 65.4
. taxation
.. other considerations 65.1.2
.. trading income 65.1.1

Finance
. raising
.. expenses – see Expenses
.. generally 73.1
.. loans – see Loans
.. share issues – see Share issues

Finance lease rental payments 68.10

Flat conversion allowances 72.7.5

Foreign emoluments
. non-residents working in the
    UK 55.3.1; 55.3.3

Foreign income – see also Residence
. amount assessable in UK 58.8.3
. remittance basis – see Remittance basis
. underlying tax
.. calculation 58.8.3
.. dividends 58.8.3
.. relief 58.8.3
.. treaty relief, required level of
    control 58.8.3
.. UK tax 58.8.3

Foreign nationals – see Non-residents

Foreign tax
. double taxation relief – see Double
    taxation relief

Friendly societies 75.5

Paragraph

Furnished holiday lettings
. advantages of furnished holiday lettings
    treatment 72.9.5
. application of property income
    rules 72.9.1
. application of rules to properties
    elsewhere in UK 72.9.7
. commercial letting of furnished holiday
    accommodation 72.9.2
. furnished holiday accommodation 72.9.3
. multiple units and averaging 72.9.4
. proposed changes to tax rules 72.9.8
. separate calculation of profits and
    losses 72.9.6

Furnished lettings
. fixtures integral to business 72.8.5
. renewals basis 72.8.3
. treatment of furnished residential
    lettings 72.8.1
. wear and tear allowance 72.8.2
. wear and tear allowance v renewals
    basis 72.8.5

G

Gift aid – see Charities

Gifts
. charities – see Charities

Gifts of business assets
. emigration of controlling trustees 60.5.3
. emigration of recipient trust 60.5.2

Government salaries and pensions
. double taxation relief 58.3

Grandchildren
. inheritance tax benefit of grandparent
    paying pension contributions 76.9.7
. settlements, charge on settlors 60.12.8

Ground annuals
. chargeable income 72.3.3

Group relief
. administration 67.8
. liquidation 67.5.9

Groups of companies
. degrouping charge 67.9

H

**Herd basis – see Farming and market
gardening**

Hive down
. anti-avoidance 67.9
. capital assets 67.9
. degrouping charges 67.9

Index

Hive down – continued	Paragraph
. details	67.9
. generally	67.9
. intangible assets	67.9
. loan relationships and derivative contracts	67.9
. loss relief in corporate insolvency	67.9
. method	67.9
. preservation of losses	67.9
. pricing structure	67.9
. sale by way of	67.9
. stamp taxes	67.9
. . stamp duty	67.9
. . stamp duty land tax	67.9
. value added tax	67.9
. . transfers of a going concern	67.9
. . VAT groups	67.9

HM Revenue and Customs (HMRC)
- . charities
- . . publications 74.2.5
- . . registration 74.2.5
- . . returns 74.2.5
- . enquiries – see HM Revenue and Customs enquiries
- . response to disclosure of avoidance schemes 63.7

HM Revenue and Customs enquiries
- . business economics exercise
- . . construction 66.7.2
- . . gathering information 66.7.3
- . . generally 66.7.1
- . . practitioner's approach 66.7.3
- . . review 66.7.4
- . completion
- . . certificate of disclosure 66.9.8
- . . closure notices 66.9.1
- . . deceased persons 66.9.7
- . . interest 66.9.2
- . . mitigation of penalty for periods commencing before 1 April 2008 .... 66.9.4
- . . new penalty regime for returns for periods commencing on or after 1 April 2008 .... 66.9.5
- . . penalties and the Human Rights Act 66.9.6
- . . penalties for incorrect returns for periods commencing before 1 April 2008 .... 66.9.3
- . . re-opening a settlement 66.9.8
- . . statement of assets and liabilities 66.9.8
- . compliance checks 66.1.6; 66.4.3
- . covert observation 66.7.3
- . demand for information 66.1.5
- . enquiry window
- . . companies 66.3.3
- . . individuals, partnerships and trustees 66.3.2

	Paragraph
. information and inspection powers – see Information and inspection powers	
. interviews	
. . agenda	66.6.2
. . no legal right	66.6.1
. . notes of meeting	66.6.3
. money laundering – see Money laundering	
. no reason to be given	66.1.4
. opening enquiry	
. . appeals	66.3.4
. . discovery	66.3.8
. . enquiry window for companies	66.3.3
. . enquiry window for individuals, partnerships and trustees	66.3.2
. . generally	66.3.1
. . only one enquiry per return	66.3.6
. . opening letter	66.3.7
. . validity of enquiry notice	66.3.5
. powers	66.1.1
. process now, check later regime	66.1.3
. records	
. . additional FA 2008 requirements	66.5.3
. . computerised	66.5.5
. . enquiries into accounting matters	66.5.5
. . generally	66.5.1
. . HMRC approach to examination	66.5.4
. . obligation to keep pre-FA 2008	66.5.2
. re-opening earlier years	
. . additional reliefs	66.8.3
. . legal basis	66.8.1
. . negotiation	66.8.2
. . value added tax	66.8.4
. selection	
. . by risk assessment	66.2.3
. . critical review	66.2.5
. . generally	66.2.1
. . interventions to assure compliance	66.2.7
. . random	66.2.2
. . risk assessment	66.2.4
. . small business letters	66.2.6
. serious fraud investigations – see Serious fraud investigations	
. stages of enquiry	66.1.7
. statutory framework for investigations	66.1.2

Hobby farming
. losses 65.3.2

Hold-over relief – see also Gifts of business assets
. agricultural land 65.10.1

Holiday lettings – see Furnished holiday lettings

Holiday pay
. National Insurance contributions 71.3.11

Hotels
. capital allowances 72.7.4

Husband and wife
. benefits of pensioning spouse 76.9.6
. married women
. . domicile 57.7
. . National Insurance Class 1
    contributions, reduced rate
    elections 71.4.9
. . National Insurance Class 2
    contributions 71.7.6

I

Implied trusts 61.2

Income tax
. disclosure of avoidance schemes, rules
    applying since 1 August 2006 . . . . . 63.12.3
. relief
. . charities 74.3.1
. . enterprise investment scheme – see
    Enterprise investment scheme (EIS)
. . interest payments – see Interest relief
. . venture capital trusts – see Venture
    capital trusts (VCTs)
. trusts with vulnerable beneficiaries 61.5.6
. working abroad 56.1.2

Individual savings accounts (ISAs)
. cash component 75.4.3
. death of investor 75.4.5
. eligibility 75.4.2
. generally 75.4.1
. stocks and shares component 75.4.4

Individuals
. dual resident, double taxation relief 58.3
. Gift Aid donations 74.4.2
. HMRC enquiry window 66.3.2
. insolvency – see Insolvencies
. loans for business-related purposes
    – see Loans
. qualifying for enterprise investment
    scheme relief – see Enterprise
    investment scheme (EIS)
. residence and residence status – see
    Residence

Industrial buildings
. capital allowances 72.7.4

Information and inspection powers
. generally 66.1.6; 66.4.1
. information powers 66.4.2
. . less commonly used powers 66.4.4
. . offshore trusts 60.3
. . private records 66.4.2
. . taxpayer notices 66.4.2
. inspection powers 66.4.3
. . visits 66.4.3

Inheritance tax
. domicile – see Domicile; Working
    abroad
. exemption
. . capital transfers to charity 74.4.10
. . charities 74.3.3
. investments, relief
. . agricultural land 75.11.4
. . AIM shares 75.11.2
. . generally 75.11.1
. . nursing home 75.11.3
. loan to pay, interest relief 68.7.1
. pensions
. . benefit of grandparent paying
    contributions 76.9.7
. . death benefits, treatment 76.5.7

Inland waterways
. double taxation relief 58.3

Insolvencies
. administration under post-14 September
    2003 Insolvency Act 1986
    procedures 67.7
. companies in liquidation/administration/
    receivership
. . administration 67.5.2
. . basis and periods of assessment 67.5.7
. . consequences of liquidation for
    directors personally 67.5.10
. . consequences of liquidation for group
    relief 67.5.9
. . date of commencement of
    winding up 67.5.3
. . generally 67.5.1
. . loan relationships 67.5.2
. . position of liquidator and vesting of
    assets 67.5.4
. . rates and fractions for
    corporation tax 67.5.8
. . receiverships 67.5.11
. . trading by liquidator 67.5.6
. . transactions by liquidator involving
    company assets 67.5.5
. . winding up 67.5.2
. consequences for group relief
. . administration 67.8
. . liquidation 67.5.9
. Crown's priority
. . proceedings commenced pre-15
    September 2003 . . . . 67.3.2
. . withdrawal of Crown preference 67.3.1
. generally 67.1
. hive down – see Hive down
. Insolvency Act 1986 pre-15 September
    2003 and related problems
. . administration orders 67.6.2
. . debts released on voluntary
    arrangements 67.6.3

Index

Insolvencies – continued   **Paragraph**
- . generally 67.6.1
- . interest payments 67.6.4
- . measures to help businesses meet liabilities 67.2
- . penalties 67.4
- . types of insolvency 67.1.1

Insurance premiums
- . property rental business, deductions 72.4.6

Interest
- . annual 68.9.1
- . double taxation relief 58.3
- . payable – see Interest payable; Interest on overdue tax
- . relief – see Interest relief

Interest in possession trusts 61.2

Interest in settled property – see Beneficiaries of offshore trusts

Interest on overdue tax
- . changes to way in which interest charged 66.9.2
- . National Insurance contributions 71.11.10

Interest payable
- . business loan to fund proprietor's overdraft 68.9.3; 73.2.2
- . generally 68.9.1
- . income tax relief – see Interest relief
- . Insolvency Act 1986 .... 67.6.4
- . loan finance 68.9.2
- . National Insurance Class 4 contributions 71.9.5
- . non-residents, to 68.9.2

Interest relief
- . claims 68.1.5
- . close company, loan to invest in
- .. acquisition of interest in close company 68.3.2; 73.3.3
- .. generally 68.3.1
- . co-operative, loan to invest in
- .. acquisition of interest in co-operative 73.3.4
- .. generally 68.4.1
- . employee-controlled company, loan to invest in
- .. application of proceeds of loan 68.5.2
- .. generally 68.5.1; 73.3.5
- . form of relief 68.1.3
- . generally 68.1.1
- . indirect recoveries of capital 68.1.4
- . inheritance tax, loan to pay 68.7.1
- . life annuity, loan to purchase 68.8.1
- . machinery or plant, loan to purchase 68.2
- . partnership, loan to invest in
- .. acquisition of interest in partnership 73.3.6

     Paragraph
- .. generally 68.6.1
- .. partners eligibility 68.6.2
- . property rental business
- .. deposit provided by remortgage of own home 72.5.4
- .. general rule 72.5.1
- .. interest paid abroad 72.5.2
- .. release of equity 72.5.3
- . qualifying loans, categories 68.1.2

Interests in land
- . domicile, inheritance tax 57.13.3

Intermediaries – see Personal service companies

Interviews
- . HMRC – see HM Revenue and Customs enquiries

Investments
- . tax efficient
- .. checklist 75.13
- .. child trust funds 75.6
- .. enterprise investment scheme – see Enterprise investment scheme (EIS)
- .. friendly societies 75.5
- .. generally 75.1.1
- .. individual savings accounts – see Individual savings accounts (ISAs)
- .. inheritance tax relief – see Inheritance tax
- .. investment efficiency 75.1.2
- .. investments providing tax advantages 75.1.3
- .. life assurance, qualifying policies – see Life assurance policies
- .. life assurance, single premium bonds – see Life assurance policies
- .. National Savings – see National Savings
- .. purchased life annuities 75.10
- .. venture capital trusts – see Venture capital trusts (VCTs)
- .. woodlands 75.12

Investment trusts
- . qualifying for enterprise investment scheme relief – see Enterprise investment scheme (EIS)

IR35 – see Personal service companies

J

Joint ventures
- . farming – see Farming and market gardening

Index

L

Land
. development, charities 74.3.2
. interests in, domicile and inheritance tax 57.13.3

Legal fees
. property rental business, deductions 72.4.7

Legal professional privilege – see also Disclosure of tax avoidance schemes
. HMRC's power to call for documents 66.4.2
. money laundering 66.11.6

Life annuity
. loan to purchase, interest relief 68.8.1

Life assurance policies
. qualifying
.. generally 75.7.1
.. satisfying conditions 75.7.2
. single premium bonds
.. chargeable event 75.8.2
.. gain, computation 75.8.3
.. generally 75.8.1
.. policy held by trustees 75.8.5
.. top-slicing relief 75.8.4

Life insurance premiums
. loan finance 73.5.2

Liquidation – see Insolvencies

Lloyd's underwriters
. annual subscription 69.2.7
. chargeable gains 69.5
.. non-syndicate gains and losses, 1992–93 and subsequent tax years 69.5
. funds at Lloyd's 69.2.3
. generally 69.1
. Lloyd's deposit 69.2.4
. Lloyd's estates 69.6
. losses, treatment 69.4
. members' agents pooling arrangement 69.2.6
. membership 69.2.2
.. first three years and after 69.2.8
. overall premium limit............... 69.2.5
. payment of tax
.. apportionments of profits 69.7.5
.. generally 69.7.1
.. HMRC's determination, appeals 69.7.4
.. managing agents returns............ 69.7.2
.. managing agents returns, HMRC's determination 69.7.3
.. variation of determination 69.7.6
. syndicate accounts 69.2.1
. syndicate gains and losses, 1994 and subsequent accounts 69.5.1

. taxation
.. allowable deductions 69.3.4
.. generally 69.3.1
.. trading income 69.3.3
.. underwriting income and gains 69.3.2

Loan relationships
. companies
.. incidental costs 73.5.4
.. liquidation or administration 67.5.2
. corporation tax 73.2.4
. degrouping charge 67.9
. double taxation relief 58.7.5

Loans
. generally 73.2.1
. incidental costs 68.9.1
. individuals for business-related purposes
.. generally 73.3.1
.. purchase of plant and machinery...... 73.3.2
. interest – see Interest; Interest payable; Interest relief
. interest free, charities 74.4.8
. property rental business, deductions 72.4.11
. separate loan for specific assets or purpose........................ 73.2.3

Local authority grants
. chargeable income 72.3.6

Losses
. farming and marking gardening – see Farming and market gardening
. Lloyd's underwriters 69.4

Loss relief
. corporate insolvency................. 67.9
. corporate venturing scheme 73.4.4
. enterprise investment scheme 64.4.3
. National Insurance Class 4 contributions 71.9.4
. unquoted shares 73.4.3

M

Machinery – see Plant and machinery

Market gardening – see Farming and market gardening

Married persons – see Husband and wife

Maternity leave
. pension contributions
.. occupational pension schemes 76.8.3
.. personal/stakeholder pensions (including group schemes) 76.8.3

Meanings – see Definitions and meanings

Index

Paragraph

Mentally incapacitated persons
. domicile 57.11

Mitigation of penalties
. periods commencing before 1 April
  2008 .... 66.9.4

Money laundering
. compliance with regulations, steps
  required 66.11.7
. definition 66.11.2
. generally 66.11.1; 70.1
. internal reporting procedures
. . commonly used techniques 70.6.6
. . crime, identifying 70.6.3
. . facilitating money laundering 70.6.5
. . generally 70.6.1
. . proceeds of crime 70.6.4
. . process of money laundering 70.6.5
. . when to report 70.6.2
. key concepts 70.3
. legal professional privilege 66.11.6
. offences
. . failure to disclose 70.5
. . generally 70.4.1
. . overseas offences 66.11.5
. . Serious Organised Crime and Police
    Act 2005 .... 70.4.3
. . tax related 70.4.2
. reporting
. . requirements 70.2
. . when to make report 66.11.3
. tipping off 66.11.4
. training requirement 70.7

Mortgages
. overseas, remittance basis 57.15.8

N

National Insurance contributions (NICs)
. administration
. . Class 1 returns 71.11.1
. . Class 1A information
    requirements 71.11.2
. . Class 1B information
    requirements 71.11.3
. . Class 2 information requirements 71.11.4
. . Class 3 .... 71.11.5
. . Class 4 information requirements 71.11.6
. . enforcement 71.11.8
. . interest on underpaid/overdue
    contributions 71.11.10
. . payment and collection of
    contributions 71.11.7
. . penalties 71.11.9
. avoidance and the 2006 Act 71.11.11
. Class 1 contributions
. . aggregation of earnings 71.4.7
. . calculation methods 71.4.8

Paragraph

. . charge 71.4.1
. . contracting out 71.4.4
. . deferment 71.10.3
. . directors 71.4.6
. . earnings period 71.4.5
. . married women, reduced rate
    elections 71.4.9
. . payment and collection 71.11.7
. . primary contributions 71.4.2
. . returns 71.11.1
. . secondary contributions 71.4.3
. Class 1A contributions
. . calculation of charge 71.5.3
. . charge 71.5.1
. . information requirements 71.11.2
. . liability 71.5.2
. . payment and collection 71.11.7
. Class 1B contributions
. . calculation of charge 71.6.2
. . charge 71.6.1
. . information requirements 71.11.3
. Class 2 contributions
. . calculation of charge 71.7.2
. . charge 71.7.1
. . incapacity exemption 71.7.4
. . information requirements 71.11.4
. . married women and widows 71.7.6
. . payment and collection 71.11.7
. . residence 71.7.3
. . small earnings exception 71.7.5
. Class 3 contributions
. . administration 71.11.5
. . charge 71.8.1
. . eligibility 71.8.2
. . payment and collection 71.11.7
. Class 4 contributions
. . calculation of charge 71.9.6
. . charge 71.9.1
. . earnings 71.9.3
. . exceptions 71.9.2
. . information requirements 71.11.6
. . interest and annuity payments 71.9.5
. . loss relief 71.9.4
. . payment and collection 71.11.7
. disclosure of avoidance schemes, rules
    applying since 1 May 2007 ...... 63.12.14
. earnings
. . calculation 71.3.2
. . convertible shares 71.3.9
. . definition 71.3.1
. . directors 71.3.4
. . employment tribunal awards 71.3.10
. . holiday pay 71.3.11
. . non-cash vouchers 71.3.12
. . pay in lieu of notice 71.3.20
. . personal incidental expenses 71.3.14
. . prize incentive schemes 71.3.15
. . readily convertible assets 71.3.6
. . redundancy payments 71.3.16

Index

	Paragraph
. . relocation expenses	71.3.17
. . retirement benefit schemes	71.3.13
. . round sum allowances	71.3.18
. . settling pecuniary liability	71.3.5
. . share options	71.3.7
. . shares subject to forfeiture	71.3.8
. . timing of payment	71.3.3
. . travel and subsistence	71.3.19
. generally	71.1
. interaction of classes and annual maxima	
. . annual maximum amounts	71.10.2
. . Class 1 deferment	71.10.3
. . need for interaction rules	71.10.1
. . repayment	71.10.4
. liability	
. . charge	71.2.1
. . classes of contributions	71.2.2
. . deemed non-employment	71.2.5
. . employed earners	71.2.3
. . employment status, decisions	71.2.7
. . personal service companies	71.2.6
. . self-employed earners	71.2.4

National Savings
. children's bonus bonds 75.9.3
. fixed-interest saving certificates 75.9.1
. index-linked savings certificates 75.9.2
. premium bonds 75.9.4

Non-cash vouchers
. National Insurance contributions 71.3.12

Non-domiciliaries
. capital gains tax relief 57.14.2
. foreign income, remittance basis – see Remittance basis

Non-resident companies
. trading through UK permanent establishment 57.12.4
. . unilateral relief 58.8.2

Non-resident landlords' scheme 72.11.2

Non-residents
. contractors and subcontractors 62.5
. working in the UK – see Residence

Non-resident trusts – see Offshore trusts

Nursing homes
. inheritance tax relief 75.11.3

O

Occupational pension schemes – see Pensions

Offences
. money laundering 70.4.1
. . failure to disclose 70.5

	Paragraph
. . Serious Organised Crime and Police Act 2005	70.4.3
. . tax related	70.4.2
. penalties – see Penalties	

Offshore trusts
. beneficiaries – see Beneficiaries of offshore trusts
. creation 60.2
. export of UK trusts
. . attribution of trust gains to beneficiaries 60.5.4
. . gift hold-over relief, emigration of recipient trust 60.5.2
. . gift of business asset to company, emigration of controlling trustee 60.5.3
. . March 1991 watershed 60.5.1
. export of UK trusts on/after March 1991
. . acquisitions by dual resident trustees 60.6.6
. . assets subject to roll-over relief 60.6.2
. . death of trustee 60.6.5
. . exit charge 60.6.1
. . liability of former trustees 60.6.4
. . trustees ceasing to be liable to UK tax 60.6.3
. history of taxation 60.1
. HMRC information powers 60.3
. migrant settlements 60.4
. qualifying settlements
. . charge on settlor 60.12.7
. . charge on settlors of settlements for grandchildren 60.12.8
. . exceptions to settlor charge 60.12.9
. . meaning 60.12.1
. . property/income provided for purposes of settlement exported pre-19 March 1991 .... 60.12.3
. . protected settlements 60.12.2
. . settlor defined for purposes of attributing gains of non-resident settlements 60.12.6
. . settlor, right to recover tax paid 60.12.10
. . ultra vires payments in connection with settlements exported pre-March 1991 .... 60.12.5
. . variation in terms of settlement exported pre-March 1991 .... 60.12.4
. settlors, liability
. . circumstances in which settlor has an interest 60.11.2
. . generally 60.11.1

Overdrafts
. interest – see Interest payable

Overseas mortgages
. remittance basis 57.15.8

Index

	Paragraph
Overseas property	72.11.1

Overseas trusts – see Offshore trusts

P

Partnerships
. farming – see Farming and market gardening
. HMRC enquiry window 66.3.2
. insolvency – see Insolvencies
. interest relief on loans – see Interest relief
. joint tax and National Insurance assessments 71.11.7
. loans to purchase plant or machinery 73.3.2
.. interest relief 68.2

PAYE
. non-resident employers and employees – see Residence

Pay in lieu of notice (PILON)
. National Insurance contributions 71.3.20

Payment of tax
. foreign entertainers and sportsmen 55.5.5
. Lloyd's underwriters
.. apportionments of profits 69.7.5
.. generally 69.7.1
.. HMRC's determination, appeals 69.7.4
.. managing agents returns 69.7.2
.. managing agents returns, HMRC's determination 69.7.3
.. variation of determination 69.7.6
. property income 72.12.2

Payroll deduction schemes 74.4.11

Penalties
. Human Rights Act 66.9.6
. insolvencies 67.4
. mitigation for periods commencing before 1 April 2008 .... 66.9.4
. records 66.5.3
. returns
.. contractors failure to submit 62.7.6
.. failure to keep records 66.5.2
.. incorrect, periods commencing before 1 April 2008 .... 66.9.3
.. new regime for periods commencing on or after 1 April 2008 .... 66.9.5
. unpaid National Insurance contributions 71.11.9

Pension funds
. agricultural land 65.9.4

Pensions
. additional voluntary contribution (AVC) scheme 76.2.1
. bankruptcy 76.8.1

	Paragraph
. benefits of making contributions at early age	76.9.7
. bonus sacrifice	76.9.2
. career average scheme	76.2.1
. contracted-out pension schemes	76.2.1
. contracting-out of S2P	76.7
. divorce	76.8.2
. doubling annual allowance in same tax year	76.9.1
. employer-financed retirement benefits schemes (EFRBS)	76.2.1
. executive pension schemes	76.2.1
. final salary scheme	76.2.1
. free standing additional voluntary contributions (FSAVC) schemes	76.2.1
. funded unapproved retirement benefit schemes (FURBS)	76.2.1
. generally	76.1
. government, double taxation relief	58.3
. grandparent paying contributions, inheritance tax benefits	76.9.7
. maternity leave – pension contributions	76.8.3
. money-purchase scheme	76.2.1
. moving abroad	76.8.4
. non-government, double taxation relief	58.3
. personal pension schemes	
.. generally	76.2.2
.. group stakeholder pension plans	76.2.2
.. national employment savings trust (NEST)	76.2.2
.. personal pension plans	76.2.2
.. retirement annuities	76.2.2
.. self invested personal pension (SIPP)	76.2.2
.. stakeholder pension plans	76.2.2
. recycling of tax free cash	76.9.3
. retirement income arrangements	
.. conventional annuities	76.5.3
.. death benefits paid from pensions	76.5.6
.. generally	76.5
.. inheritance tax treatment	76.5.7
.. investment options while drawing income	76.5.4
.. pension annuities	76.5.2
.. pension increases	76.5.5
.. scheme pension	76.5.1
. salary sacrifice	76.9.2
. Section 32 policy	76.2.1
. simplification – see Pension simplification	
. single premium investment bonds – chargeable event	76.9.9
. small self-administered pension schemes (SSAS)	76.2.1
. spouse's pension	76.9.6

	Paragraph
. state retirement benefits	
.. basic state pension	76.6.1
.. pension credit	76.6.3
.. personal accounts	76.6.4
.. state second pension (S2P)	76.6.2
. tax free lump sum	
.. opportunity cost in final salary schemes	76.9.4
.. recycling of tax free cash	76.9.3
.. retirement benefits	76.4.3
. total funds of less than one per cent lifetime allowance	76.9.5
. transfers	
.. moving abroad	76.8.4
.. occupational pension transfer	76.3
.. personal pension transfer	76.3
.. reasons for	76.3.1
. unfunded unapproved retirement benefit schemes (UURBS)	76.2.1
. unsecured – surplus cash gifted under 'normal expenditure out of income exemption'	76.9.8

Pension simplification
. contributions and tax relief
.. annual allowance 76.4.2
.. employer contributions 76.4.2
.. high earners 76.4.2
.. HMRC guidance on interpretation of 'wholly and exclusively' 76.4.2
.. personal contributions 76.4.2
. generally 76.4
. retirement benefits
.. lifetime allowance 76.4.3
.. loss of enhanced protection 76.4.3
.. tax free lump sum 76.4.3
. summary 76.4.1

Permanent establishment
. non-resident companies – see Non-resident companies
. non-residents trading through 55.6

Permanent interest bearing shares (PIBs)
. incidental costs of issuing 73.5.3

Personal allowances and reliefs
. double taxation relief 58.3
. remittance basis 57.15.2

Personal incidental expenses
. National Insurance contributions 71.3.14

Personal pension schemes – see Pensions

Personal service companies
. construction industry 62.4.6
. National Insurance contributions – see National Insurance contributions (NICs)

	Paragraph
Plant and machinery	
. additional annual investment allowance, obtaining	63.12.12
. capital allowances	72.7.2
.. farming and market gardening	65.7
. loans to purchase	73.3.2
.. interest relief	68.2
Premium bonds	75.9.4
Premiums	
. chargeable income	72.3.8
Prize incentive schemes	
. National Insurance contributions	71.3.15
Prizes	
. beneficiaries of charities	74.5.3
Professional fees	
. HMRC enquiries	66.8.3
. property rental business, deductions	72.4.7
Professional services	
. double taxation relief	58.3
Property income	
. basis period	72.2.3
. capital allowances	
.. agricultural buildings	72.7.4
.. flats above shops	72.7.5
.. hotels	72.7.4
.. industrial buildings	72.7.4
.. no deduction for capital expenditure	72.7.1
.. plant and machinery	72.7.2
.. restriction in respect of properties not let commercially	72.7.3
. chargeable income	
.. rental business	72.3.1
.. separate sums for use of furniture	72.3.2
. deductible expenses	
.. additional services	72.4.14
.. advertising	72.4.8
.. bad and doubtful debts	72.4.9
.. energy saving items	72.4.12
.. expenditure on common parts	72.4.10
.. fees for loan finance	72.4.11
.. general rule	72.4.1
.. insurance premiums	72.4.6
.. legal and professional fees	72.4.7
.. owner occupied property	72.4.13
.. rates and council tax	72.4.4
.. rent collection	72.4.15
.. rent paid out	72.4.5
.. repairs	72.4.3
.. sea walls	72.4.18
.. travelling expenses	72.4.17
.. wages and salaries	72.4.16
.. wholly and exclusively rule	72.4.2
. furnished holiday lettings – see Furnished holiday lettings	

Index

Property income – continued
Paragraph
- furnished lettings – see Furnished lettings
- HMRC guidance 72.1.2
- interest, deductibility
  - deposit provided by remortgage of own home 72.5.4
  - general rule 72.5.1
  - interest paid abroad 72.5.2
  - release of equity 72.5.3
- local authority grants 72.3.6
- non-resident landlords' scheme 72.11.2
- overseas property 72.11.1
- payment of tax 72.12.2
- properties not let at a commercial rent
  - deduction for expenses, properties let at less than commercial rent 72.6.1
  - periods of commercial and uncommercial lettings 72.6.3
  - properties let rent-free 72.6.2
- property rental business
  - application of trading rules 72.2.5
  - cessation 72.2.4
  - chargeable income 72.3.1
  - chargeable persons 72.2.6
  - commencement 72.2.3
  - concept 72.2.1
  - deposits from tenants 72.3.7
  - jointly-owned properties 72.2.6
  - premiums 72.3.8
  - separate sums for use of furniture 72.3.2
- rent-a-room relief – see Rent-a-room relief
- rent-charges, ground annuals or feu duties 72.3.3
- self-assessment 72.12.1
- single rental business, concept 72.2.2
- sources 72.1.1
- sporting rights 72.3.4
- waste disposal rights 72.3.5

Protective trusts 61.2

Purchased life annuities 75.10

Q

Quotas
- milk and potatoes, roll-over relief 65.10.5

R

Rates
- deductions 72.4.4

Receivership – see Insolvencies

Reconstructions
- enterprise investment scheme reinvestment relief 64.3.8

Paragraph

Records
- examination – see HM Revenue and Customs enquiries

Recovery of tax
- settlors, tax charged on gains made by non-resident trustees 60.12.10

Redundancy payments
- National Insurance contributions 71.3.16

Reliefs
- charities – see Charities
- income tax – see Income tax

Relocation
- employees, National Insurance contributions 71.3.17
- moving abroad, transfer of pensions 76.8.4

Remittance basis
- anti-avoidance 57.15.5
- cash only 57.15.7
- ceased sources 57.15.6
- generally 57.15.1
- location of source of income or asset 57.15.9
- overseas mortgages 57.15.8
- personal allowances 57.15.2
- £2,000 de-minimis rule 57.15.4
- £30,000 annual charge 57.15.3

Remittance of money
- non-domiciled individuals 57.16
- individuals ordinarily resident 57.16
- remittance of money 57.16

Rent – see Property income

Rent-a-room relief
- conditions 72.10.2
- exempt amount 72.10.3
- expenses, no relief 72.10.4
- generally 72.10.1
- rent-a-room v normal basis of assessment 72.10.5

Reorganisations
- enterprise investment scheme reinvestment relief 64.3.8
- interest relief 68.3.2

Repairs
- deductions, property rental business 72.4.3

Replacement of business assets – see Roll-over relief

Residence – see also Domicile; Working abroad
- employees
  - double tax treaties 55.3.6

	Paragraph
. . emoluments	55.3.1
. . foreign accommodation and subsistence costs and expenses (overseas employments)	55.3.5
. . procedures	55.3.2
. . tax treatment	55.3.3
. . travel costs and expenses, non-domiciled employee, duties performed in UK	55.3.4
. foreign entertainers and sportsmen	
. . charge on income	55.5.5
. . payment of tax	55.5.5
. foreign income from trade, profession or vocation	
. . charge to tax	55.5.1
. . expenses connected with foreign trades	55.5.4
. . non-resident entertainers and sportsmen	55.5.5
. . trading in the UK	55.5.2
. . UK resident trading wholly abroad	55.5.3
. individuals	
. . establishing ordinary residence	55.2.5
. . generally	55.2.1
. . physical presence in UK, six-month rule	55.2.2
. . 'split-year' concession	55.2.3
. . status	59.1–59.4
. . UK visits and temporary residence	55.2.4
. National Insurance Class 2 contributions	71.7.3
. non-residents trading through branch or agency	55.6
. PAYE	55.4.1
. . intermediate employers, etc.	55.4.2
. . payments to non-resident employees	55.4.3
. . relevant payments	55.4.4
. . returns for foreign secondees	55.4.5
. status, individuals	
. . generally	59.1
. . ordinary residence, meaning	59.4
. . residence, common law meaning	59.3.1.1–59.3.1.4
. . sources of definitions	59.2.1
. . statutory provisions	59.3.2.1–59.3.2.3
. . types of residence	59.2.2

Retirement annuities – see Pensions

Retirement benefit schemes – see also Pensions
. National Insurance contributions 71.3.13

Returns
. charities 74.2.5
. foreign secondees 55.4.5

	Paragraph
. managing agents, Lloyd's underwriters	69.7.2
. . HMRC's determination	69.7.3
. penalties	
. . incorrect returns for periods commencing before 1 April 2008	66.9.3
. . new regime for periods commencing on or after 1 April 2008	66.9.5
. share options	71.11.7
. subcontractors within construction industry scheme	
. . payments made to	62.7.5
. . penalty for failure to submit monthly return	62.7.6

Roll-over relief
. acquisitions by dual resident trustees 60.6.6
. export of trusts 60.6.2
. farming
. . cottages 65.10.2
. . improvements 65.10.2
. . joint ownership 65.10.2
. . land overseas 65.10.2

Royalties
. double taxation relief 58.3

S

Salaries – see also Wages
. donated to charity 74.4.6
. double taxation relief 58.3
. property rental business, deductions 72.4.16
. sacrifice, pension contributions 76.9.2

Savings certificates – see National Savings

Scholarships
. beneficiaries of charities 74.5.2

Scotland
. feu duties, chargeable income 72.3.3
. interest relief, partners eligibility 68.6.2

Sea walls
. property rental business, deductions 72.4.18

Self-assessment
. enquiries – see HM Revenue and Customs enquiries
. property rental business 72.12.1

Self-employment
. National Insurance contributions – see National Insurance contributions (NICs)

Index

	Paragraph
Separation and divorce	
. pension earmarking	76.8.2
. pension offsetting	76.8.2
. pension sharing	76.8.2
Serious fraud investigations	
. civil investigation of fraud procedure	66.10.2
. generally	66.10.1
. major changes	66.10.3
. new Code of Practice	66.10.4

Settled property
. interest in – see Beneficiaries of offshore trusts

Settlements
. offshore trusts – see Offshore trusts

Settlors
. offshore trusts – see Offshore trusts

Share issues
. corporate venturing scheme – see Corporate venturing scheme
. generally 73.4.1
. losses on unquoted shares 73.4.3
. tax considerations 73.4.2

Shares and securities
. domicile, inheritance tax 57.13.6
. employee shares schemes – see Employee share schemes
. enterprise investment scheme – see Enterprise investment scheme (EIS)
. gifts to charities 74.4.4
. venture capital trusts – see Venture capital trusts (VCTs)

Shipping
. double taxation relief 58.3

Short rotation coppice – see Farming and market gardening

Sponsorship
. charities 74.3.2

Sporting rights
. chargeable income 72.3.4

Sportspersons
. double taxation relief 58.3
. non-resident
. . charge on income 55.5.5
. . payments of tax 55.5.5

Spouses – see Husband and wife

Stamp duty
. charities, exemption 74.3.6
. hive down 67.9

Stamp duty land tax (SDLT)
. charities, exemption 74.3.6

	Paragraph
. disclosure of avoidance schemes	63.12.2
. hive down	67.9

State pension – see Pensions

Students
. double taxation relief 58.3

Subcontractors in the construction industry – see Construction industry scheme

Subsistence costs and expenses
. overseas employments 55.3.5

T

Tangible movable property
. domicile, inheritance tax 57.13.4

Teachers
. double taxation relief 58.3

Time-limits
. claims for double taxation relief, companies 58.7.3
. discovery assessments 66.3.8

Trade or business
. farming and market gardening – see Farming and market gardening

Trading income
. farming and market gardening, taxation 65.1.1
. Lloyd's underwriters 69.3.3

Trading losses – see Losses

Travel
. costs and expenses
. . non-domiciled employees, duties performed in UK 55.3.4
. . property rental business, deductions 72.4.17
. travel and subsistence allowances, National Insurance contributions 71.3.19

Trustees – see also Enterprise investment scheme (EIS); Offshore trusts; Trusts
. HMRC enquiry window 66.3.2

Trusts
. accumulation and maintenance trusts 61.5.4
. bare trusts 61.2; 61.5.1; 61.5.2
. charitable trusts 61.2
. checklist of considerations when using 61.10
. definition 61.2
. discretionary trusts 61.2; 61.5.1; 61.5.4
. generally 61.1; 61.2

	Paragraph
. implied trusts	61.2
. interest in possession trusts	61.2
. legal considerations	
. . age of majority	61.985
. . generally	61.8.1
. . Trustee Act 1925	61.8.2
. . Trustee Act 2000	61.8.4
. . Trusts of Land and Appointment of Trustees Act 1996	61.8.3
. life interest trusts	61.5.1; 61.5.2
. management	
. . trustees	61.4.1
. . trust protector	61.4.2
. offshore – see Offshore trusts	
. protective trusts	61.2
. reversionary interests	61.5.3
. rules against perpetuities and restriction of accumulation periods	61.3.1
. . Perpetuities and Accumulations Act 2009	61.3.2
. . rules prior to 6 April 2010	61.3.3
. settlor interested, donations to charities	74.4.9
. tax aspects	
. . benefits	61.7.1
. . lower rates band	61.7.2
. tax planning opportunities	61.9
. trusts with interests in possession	61.5.2
. trusts without interests in possession	61.5.4
. types	61.5.1
. uses	
. . discretionary settlements	61.6.2
. . life interest settlements	61.6.1
. vested and contingent interests	61.2

Trusts with vulnerable beneficiaries
. administration and information 61.5.8
. generally 61.2; 61.5.5
. special capital gains tax treatment 61.5.7
. special income tax treatment 61.5.6

U

Underlying tax – see Foreign income

Unilateral relief – see Double taxation relief

V

Value added tax (VAT)
. HMRC enquiries, re-opening earlier years 66.8.4
. transfer of assets – see Hive down

Venture capital trusts (VCTs)
. approval of companies 77.5
. dividends received, relief 77.3
. forms of tax relief 77.1.2
. generally 75.3; 77.1.1
. income tax relief on investment
. . generally 77.2.1
. . loan-linked investments 77.2.2
. . loss of relief 77.2.3
. legislative changes 77.1.3
. tax-free sale of shares
. . identification of shares 77.4.2
. . outline of relief 77.4.1
. . supplementary provisions 77.4.3

Vouchers – see Non-cash vouchers

W

Wages – see also Salaries
. double taxation relief 58.3
. property rental business, deductions 72.4.16

Waste disposal rights
. chargeable income 72.3.5

Wear and tear allowance
. furnished lettings 72.8.2; 72.8.4

Wholly and exclusively rule
. deductions, property rental business 72.4.2

Widows
. National Insurance Class 2 contributions 71.7.6

Winding up – see Insolvencies

Woodlands 75.12

Working abroad
. capital gains tax 56.1.3
. generally 56.1.1
. income tax 56.1.2
. inheritance tax 56.1.4

Working in the UK
. non-residents – see Residence